The Abdominal and Pelvic Brain

THE
Abdominal and Pelvic Brain

With Automatic Visceral Ganglia

BY

BYRON ROBINSON, B. S., M. D.

CHICAGO, ILLINOIS

Author of "Practical Intestinal Surgery," "Landmarks in Gynecology," "Life-size Chart of the Sympathetic Nerve," "The Peritoneum, its Histology and Physiology," "Colpoperineorrhaphy and the Structures Involved," "The Mesogastrium;" Splanchnoptosia, Professor of Gynecology and Abdominal Surgery in the Illinois Medical College; Consulting Surgeon to the Mary Thompson Hospital for Women and Children, and the Woman's Hospital of Chicago.

FRANK S. BETZ
HAMMOND, IND.

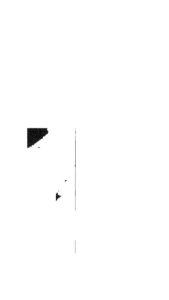

THE

Abdominal and Pelvic Brain

With Automatic Visceral Ganglia

BYRON R

Copyright, 1907,
BY
BYRON ROBINSON

THIS BOOK IS DEDICATED TO THE MEMORY
OF MY FATHER
WILLIAM ROBINSON
WHOSE LIFE-LONG PRECEPTS WERE INDUSTRY
AND HONESTY

PREFACE.

Where a truth is made out by one demonstration, there needs no further inquiry; but in all probability where there wants demonstration to establish the truth beyond doubt, then it is not enough to trace one argument to its source and observe its strength and weakness, but all the arguments, after having been so examined on both sides, must be laid in the balance, one against another; and upon the whole the understanding determines its assent.—John Locke on the Conduct of the Understanding.

The present volume contains views concerning the anatomy, physiology and pathology of the abdominal and pelvic brain. The abdominal brain is the solar or epigastric plexus. The pelvic brain is the cervico-uterine ganglion located on each side of the uterus.

A brain is an apparatus capable of reception, reorganization and emission of nerve forces. It may be composed of one or more nerve or ganglion cells. The book is partly based on the so-called "reflexes," as they are observed in both health and disease. We understand by "reflexes" disturbances which are produced in parts more or less remote from points of local irritation. The reflex is the "referred disturbance" of modern writers. I have attempted to show the extensive utility and dominating influence of the abdominal sympathetic nerves upon the animal economy. The reflexes and rhythm concerning organs under various conditions are discussed. The automatic menstrual ganglia are presented as the peripheral ganglia of the uterus and oviducts. No attempt has been made to divorce the cerebro-spinal and sympathetic nervous systems from their exquisite mutual dependency. Yet, notwithstanding this latter, the abdominal sympathetic nerve, under observed conditions of defect of the cord and cerebrum, acts with a certain degree of independence. I do not claim that deep-seated, grave diseases are caused by reflex irritation, nor that these diseases are dispersed by removal of the reflex or peripheral irritation. However, it may be stated that the chief suffering is not due to deep-seated disease, but to superficial, reflex irritation, which brings in its train innumerable disturbances capable of unbalancing the complex abdominal visceral system.

The course of reflex irritation may be observed clinically as: (1), Peripheral (reflex, infective) irritation; (2), indigestion; (3), malnutrition; (4), anemia; (5), neurosis. The final stage is the irritation of the innumerable abdominal sympathetic ganglia by waste-laden blood, which produces the hysteria and neurasthenia.

This book is practically a treatise on the abdominal sympathetic nerves (nervus vasomotorius abdominalis), a resumé of views which I have discussed in current medical literature for a decade and a half.

The subject of gastro-duodenal dilatation, on which I have studied and practiced since 1893, will be found discussed in detail.

Splanchnoptosia is presented from a practical viewpoint. Its physiology, anatomy, pathology, as well as its treatment—medical, mechanical and surgical—are exposed for general practice. The views noted in this book on splanchnoptosia are the result of observation in seven hundred personal autopsic abdominal inspections and fifteen years devoted to special labors in gynecologic and abdominal surgery. The comparison of the living clinical features of splanchnoptosia and those observed in the dead is not omitted. I have endeavored to present a practical view on the diagnosis and treatment of constipation and sudden abdominal pain, which will be suggestive to the general practitioner. Throughout the book will be observed the dominating influence of the genital viscera over all other viscera, explained by the magnitude of their nerve supply (pelvic brain). For ten years I have attempted to emphasize and teach the importance of knowledge of pathologic physiology. A short pioneer chapter on pathologic physiology of abdominal viscera is introduced to emphasize its signification and practical value to general physicians. This subject I have attempted to teach by word and pen for a decade. The essay on diagnosis and treatment of reflex neurosis from disturbed pelvic mechanism will suggest to the general practitioner rational views of handling such cases.

In this book I wish to recommend vigorously, especially to the younger members of the profession, what I term "*visceral drainage.*" By its systematic, persistent employment the physician can accomplish vast benefit for the patient and successfully establish a permanently increasing clientele on rational treatment.

The chapter on shock has been ably and practically presented by Dr. Lucy Waite, Head Surgeon of Mary Thompson Hospital of Chicago. Neither time nor expense has been spared to produce accurate and original illustrations of practical worth. A definition of a structure is of value, but a picture does it a thousand times as well. I am aware that the present volume does not belong to the stereotyped, systematized text-books; yet I am confident that the thinking reader will find in its pages ample reward for its perusal. It is also hoped that since it is chiefly the fruit of original labor it will prove of interest alike to general practitioner and specialist.

A portion of this book, entitled "Abdominal Brain and Automatic Visceral Ganglia," was published in 1899 by the Clinic Publishing Company, the copies of which were exhausted in 1904. Numerous repetitions occur in the book, arising from the fact that each chapter was written independent of the others and is practically complete in itself. Fragments of this book were published in medical journals such as the *Medical Review of Reviews, Medical Age, Medical Brief, Milwaukee Medical Journal, Medical Fortnightly, Medical Review, Medical Record, Medical Standard, Physician and Surgeon, New York Medical Journal, Alabama Medical Journal, Medical Times, Columbus Medical Journal, American Medical Compend, St. Paul Medical Journal, Central States Medical Monitor* and *Mobile Medical and Surgical Journal.* Zan D. Klopper is the artist. BYRON ROBINSON.

CHICAGO, ILL., October, 1906.

CONTENTS.

CHAPTER		PAGE
I.	A Historical Sketch of the Developmental Knowledge of the Sympathetic Nerves	11
II.	Classification of Diseases Which May Belong in the Domain of the Sympathetic Nerve	28
III.	Applied Anatomy and Physiology of the Abdominal Vasomotor Nerve (Nervus Vasomotorius)	33
IV.	The Trunk of the Sympathetic Nerves (Nervus Truncus Sympathicus)	39
V.	Plexus Aorticus Abdominalis. (A), Anatomy; (B), Physiology	46
VI.	The Vasomotor Iliac Plexus. Plexus Interiliacus Vasomotorius (Sympathicus)	52
VII.	The Nerves of the Tractus Intestinalis. Nervi Tractus Intestinalis. (A), Anatomy; (B), Physiology	62
VIII.	The Nerves of the Tractus Urinarius. Nervi Tractus Urinarius	76
IX.	The Nerves of the Genital Tract. Nervi Tractus Genitalis. (A), Anatomy; (B), Physiology	87
X.	Nerves of the Blood-vessels. Nervi Tractus Vascularis. (A), Anatomy; (B), Physiology	103
XI.	Nervus Tractus Lymphaticus	111
XII.	Abdominal Brain (Cerebrum Abdominale)	112
XIII.	Pelvic Brain (Cerebrum Pelvicum)	131
XIV.	General Considerations	162
XV.	Independence of the Sympathetic Nerve	187
XVI.	Anatomic and Physiologic Considerations	193
XVII.	Physiology of the Abdominal and Pelvic Brain with Automatic Visceral Ganglia	204
XVIII.	Considerations of the Removal of Abdominal and Pelvic Tumors	208
XIX.	The Abdominal and Pelvic Brain with Automatic Visceral Ganglia in Regard to the Sexual Organs	227
XX.	The Automatic Menstrual Ganglia	240
XXI.	Menopause	253
XXII.	General Visceral Neurosis	267
XXIII.	Relation between Visceral (Sympathetic) and Cerebro-spinal Nerves. The Nerve Mechanism of Pelvic and Associated Regions	278
XXIV.	Hyperesthesia of the Sympathetic	302
XXV.	Motor Neurosis	318
XXVI.	Gastro-Intestinal Secretion	329
XXVII.	Secretion. Neurosis of the Colon	334
XXVIII.	Reflex Neurosis from Disturbed Pelvic Mechanism	340
XXIX.	Constipation—Its Pathologic Physiology and Its Treatment by Exercise, Diet and "Visceral Drainage"	351
XXX.	Shock	382
XXXI.	Sudden Abdominal Pain—Its Significance	398
XXXII.	General Pathologic Physiology	432
XXXIII.	Pathologic Physiology of the Tractus Intestinalis	448
XXXIV.	Pathologic Physiology of the Tractus Genitalis	460
XXXV.	Pathologic Physiology of the Tractus Urinarius	479
XXXVI.	Pathologic Physiology of the Tractus Nervosus (Abdominalis)	495
XXXVII.	Pathologic Physiology of the Tractus Vascularis	502
XXXVIII.	Pathologic Physiology of the Tractus Lympathicus	514
XXXIX.	Splanchnoptosia	546
XL.	Sympathetic Relation of the Genitalia to the Olfactory Organs	654

THE
ABDOMINAL AND PELVIC BRAIN
WITH
AUTOMATIC VISCERAL GANGLIA.

PHYSIOLOGIC AND ANATOMIC CONSIDERATIONS.

CHAPTER I.

A HISTORICAL SKETCH OF THE DEVELOPMENTAL KNOWLEDGE OF THE SYMPATHETIC NERVES.

The sympathetic nerve presides over rhythm, circulation, sensation, absorption, secretion and respiration—nutrition.

"The cloud-capped towers, the gorgeous palaces, the solemn temples, the great globe itself, yea all which it inherits shall dissolve and, like the baseless fabric of a vision, leave not a wreck behind."—William Shakespeare's epitaph, written by his own hand, placed on his statue in Westminster Abbey.

The sympathetic system of nerves was discovered by Claudius Galen, who was born 131 and died in 201 to 210 A. D. He lived first at Pergamos, and finally at Rome. Galen considered that the sympathetic nerves acted as buttresses to strengthen themselves as they proceeded from their origin. He studied them in animals and evidently did not know that the sympathetic nerves were a part of the cerebro-spinal system. It appears that before his time the sympathetic ganglionic system of nerves was entirely unknown as to their function or nature. Yet doubtless Aristotle viewed them many times in his dissections, and wondered what such white cords and nodules signified. It appears that the Arabians had some ideas concerning the sympathetic system.

Galen was the author of the dogma that the brain was the place of origin of the nerves of sensation, and the spinal cord of those of motion. In general medical literature he has the credit of discovering the sympathetic nerve, and as Galen was a practical anatomist (learning his anatomy, however, almost exclusively from animals) he perhaps gave a quite accurate account of the sympathetic, and this became quoted, until he was finally announced to be its father and discoverer. Galen gave correct views of the omentum and peritoneum. He seems to have been quite well acquainted with the ganglia of the abdominal nerves.

It is claimed that the sympathetic was known to the Hippocratic school. Hippocrates (460—370 B. C.), who practiced medicine at Athens, Greece, doubtless saw the sympathetic many times, at least in animals, but did not interpret its functions. Yet he was one of the first to cast aside tradition, which, by the way, still lingers, and to practice medicine on a basis of inductive reasoning, just as a carpenter takes careful measurements before building a house, or as a physicist studies astronomy.

Erasistratus (340—280 B. C.) believed that all nerves arise from the brain and cord, but doubtless did not recognize the sympathetic nerves as such. It appears, however, that he separated nerves into those of motion and sensation. He studied particularly the shape and structure of the brain.

Herophilus (300 B. C.), it appears, dissected more than all his predecessors, both in man and animals. He was the first to distinguish nerves from tendons, which Aristotle confounded. Herophilus gave the duodenum its name because it is twelve inches or finger breadths in length. He, like Erasistratus, distinguished nerves of motion from those of sensation, and added a careful study of the brain. We all remember his "Torcular Herophili," or wine-press.

Aristotle (384 B. C.), who widely dissected animals while instructing Alexander, the son of King Philip, no doubt saw the sympathetic system frequently, yet did not interpret its significance, for he confounded tendons and nerves.

B. Eustachius, an Italian anatomist, who died in 1574, considered that the sympathetic nerves originated from the abducens or sixth cranial nerve. It was not until the name of Thomas Willis (1622-1675), an English physician, appeared in anatomical records that the proper significance of the sympathetic nerves was recognized. Willis looked on the sympathetic system of nerves as an appendage of the cerebrospinal system and represented them as growing from the cerebrospinal nerves. Many neurologists hold the same opinion today as did the able Willis two hundred and fifty years ago. He looked upon the sympathetic nerves as a kind of diverticula for the animal spirits received from the brain. In 1660, while Sedleian professor of philosophy at Oxford, he described the chief ganglia.

René Descartes (1569-1650) was one of the first to describe reflex movements from ganglia.

R. Vieussens (1641-1716), a French anatomist, wrote a work entitled

Fig. 1. It presents a general view. 1 and 2, abdominal brain. B represents the pelvic brain or ganglion cervicale. Observe the profound and intimate connection between the abdominal brain (1 and 2) and the pelvic brain (B) by means of the plexus aorticus (10 and 12) and plexus hypogastricus (H). Note the lateral chain of the sympathetic ganglia from the cervical ganglia (1) to the last sacral ganglion (S G). 1 and 2, abdominal brain, is the major assembling point of the plexuses of the abdomen. Observe the plexus aorticus with its multiple ganglia and two lateral cords extending from the abdominal brain (1 and 2) to the bifurcation of the aorta. Next note the hypogastric plexus, beginning at the aortic bifurcation and ending practically in the pelvic brain (B). H, the hypogastric ganglion is a coalesced, unpaired organ. The major sympathetic ganglia are located at the origin of arteries, hence every abdominal visceral artery has at its origin a definite ganglion. In drawing the pelvic brain suggestions of Frankenhauser were employed. The dissection was performed under alcohol.

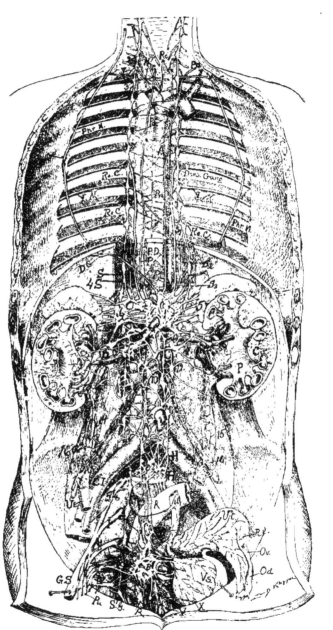

"Neurograph" in 1684, in which he adopted the views of Willis, that the ganglionic nerves were appendages of the cerebrospinal system.

Vieussens wrote of the ganglia of the solar plexus.

Prochaska described the reflex channels.

Duverney (1648-1730) discovered the ciliary ganglia.

J. M. Lancisus (1654-1720), an Italian anatomist, wrote a monograph on the sympathetic nerves, agreeing with the keen Willis as regards structure. His monograph was entitled "Opera Omnia." Lancisus looked upon the sympathetic nerves as a kind of forcing pump adapted to propel the animal spirits along the nerves.

The senior Johann Friedrich Meckel (1714-1774), in his "Memories de Berlin," 1745, held views on the subject of the sympathetic nerves similar to those of Willis, as did also Johann Gotfried Zinn (1727-1759) in a publication in 1753.

J. B. Winslow (1669-1760), a Dane, professor of anatomy in Paris, insisted in his writings on the independence of the sympathetic nerves. Since that time writers have wavered between the opinions of Winslow (independence) and Willis (dependence) in regard to the sympathetic nervous system. Yet up to one hundred years ago actual physiologic and experimental data were quite limited. Bichat, who widely influenced the anatomic world, vigorously proclaimed the independence of the sympathetic ganglia.

Hoare wrote a publication in 1772 on the sympathetic system entitled "De Ganglia Nervorum."

Antoine Scarpa (1752-1832), the Italian anatomist of "Scarpa's Triangle" fame, wrote an essay on the sympathetic system entitled "De Nerv. Gangl." in 1779. This work of course contained the views of previous writers.

Alexander Monro (Monro secundus, 1733-1817), a Scotch anatomist of Edinburgh University, published an essay "On the Structure and Function of the Nervous Ganglia," in 1783. The later writers analyzed more in detail and generalized in a manner superior to that of previous writers, yet all agreed or disagreed with Willis or Winslow.

Johann Friedrich Blumenbach (1752-1840), a German anatomist, in "Institutes of Physiology," published views on the sympathetic nerves in 1786.

François Chaussier (1746-1828), a French surgeon and anatomist, wrote an "Exposition" of the sympathetic nerves in 1807.

In 1812 Le Gallois wrote "Sur le Principe de la Vie," containing views on the sympathetic nerve.

In 1823 views of the sympathetic nerve appeared in Beclard's "El. d'Anat. Gen."

Georges Cuvier (1769-1832), a famous French naturalist, espoused the doctrine of the independence of the sympathetic nervous system as published in his "Lecons d'Anat. Comp.," 1799.

Xavier Bichat (1771-1802), the master intellect of his day in Paris, professor of anatomy and physiology, the associate and rival of the priestly physician, Pinel, may be heard insisting with his accustomed eloquence upon the independence of the sympathetic nervous system, as noted in his "Sur la Vie et la Mort.," 1802. Bichat represented all the ganglia of this system as the particular centers of organic life, that not only were all the ganglia collectively independent, but that each ganglion was independent of every other ganglion, that each nerve proceeding from such a ganglion was in a great measure independent from that ganglion, and even that each point of such a nerve was independent of all the rest and consisted of a distinct focus of nervous influence. Bichat's influence is distinctly traceable through subsequent writings on the sympathetic system.

Wilson Philip wrote "On the Vital Functions," in 1817, analogous to the grand center of animal life. He also held views referring to the sympathetic system.

In Mason Good's work "On the Study of Medicine," 1825, views are expressed in regard to the sympathetic nervous system.

Writers on the sympathetic system became more numerous in the period subsequent to 1800.

Richerand (Phys. 1804), and Gall (Anat. et Phys. du Syst. Nerv., 1810), adopted tenets concerning the sympathetic nervous system similar to those of Bichat.

Wurtzer in 1817 (De Corp. Hum. Gang.) further inculcated Bichat's, Winslow's and Cuvier's views.

Broussais, whose name is indelibly connected with inflammation of the peritoneum as Bichat's is with establishing the independence of the sympathetic, describes a peculiar kind of sensibility or irritability belonging to the sympathetic nerves with which it immediately endows all organs destined for nutrition, secretion and the other organic functions, and, by means of its repeated connections with the cerebrospinal system, all organs of the body.

Brachet, in his "Sur les Fonctions du Syst. Nerv. Gang.," 1823, in an especial manner, distinctly represents the ganglionic system of nerves as the seat of "imperceptible sensation" and as presiding in an especial manner over the several viscera of the body. The author, though not acquainted with Richerand's and Bichat's views, worked out the same views from original studies and experiments, but added the idea that the abdominal brain (solar plexus) is the chief organizing center of the abdominal sympathetic.

The preceding views are simply some of the chief landmarks in the progress of the evolutionary development of the knowledge of the sympathetic nerves, in the direction of their function and signification.

The most significant names among the brilliant galaxy of students of the sympathetic nerves are Willis, Bichat, Cuvier, Winslow and Brechet.

In 1835 articles on the sympathetic nerves began to appear from the pen of James George Davy, of London, England, which study and writing on the sympathetic he continued for about thirty years. In 1858 the same author published a book "On the Ganglionic Nervous System." The work is composed of 109 pages, is interestingly written and contains about all the real knowledge of the subject up to that date (1858). Davy claimed that much of his book was original, and doubtless this industrious worker produced many new views in thirty years of labor. Yet Davy, as we view him forty years past, appears very honest in that he credits the gifted Bichat with so many original views and vast conceptions. The writer can only hope that readers forty years hence will view this present little volume with similar candor and charity.

Bichat's genius established in medical literature the sympathetic nerves under the names "organic and vegetative" system, because he saw analogies between the nerves which preside over viscera (and hence nutrition) and the life of plants. He considered that the sympathetic nerves induce an animal to live, assimilate and nourish, induce circulation and excretion—in short to have an habitual succession of assimilation and excretion sufficient to preserve life's integrity by a vital inherent process. No effort was required of the animal—all was done in the so-called sub-conscious region, by what we might call today unconscious or imperceptible sensation. It is especially the sub-conscious, the imperceptible traumatic insults of pathologic processes among viscera, which the writer will attempt to elucidate.

Bichat paved the way for a more ready appreciation of the physiology of the sympathetic system. Dr. Grant, a writer of some sixty years ago, said that "the sympathetic nerves, appropriated to the more slow and regular movements of organic life, form a more isolated system" (than the cerebrospinal). It appears that Dr. John Fletcher wrote learnedly on the sympathetic system in his "Rudiments of Physiology," published in 1837, for in May, 1853, Dr. Davy read an essay "On the Physiologic Uses of the Ganglionic Nervous System" before the London Medical Society, whereupon M. Walford, of Reading, addressed a curt note to Dr. Davy informing him, politely, that it was Dr. Fletcher who deserved the credit of "establishing on an immutable basis the function of the great sympathetic nerves." Davy very honestly relates how he sent a paper on the sympathetic nerve to the *Lancet*, but the editor not only rejected it, but did not return the manuscript. This was in 1836. The strife concerning priority in regard to views upon the divisions of the nervous system was very active some sixty years ago. Among the participants might be named Marshall Hall, Robert Reid, Davy, Gall, Brechet, Blane, Mayo and others. However, one and all bowed before the magnificent intellect of Bichat. Bichat located the passions in the "epigastric center," and believed that they belong to the sympathetic nerves. Bichat's opinion dominated medical ideas for three-quarters of a century after his death. Buffon, Cabanis, Reil and Broussais, contemporaries of Bichat, located the passions in "the Viscera of the Chest and Belly," or represented them as belonging to the ganglionic system of nerves.

The labors of Morgagni and Petit (1827) should be mentioned, as well as those of Bergen (1731), Walter (1783), Huber (1774), Gerald (1754), Weber (1831), Rudolphi (1818), Lobstein (1823) (nerve tables), Manee (1828), Radcliff (1846), Hall (1847), Moses Gunn, inaugural thesis (1846), Robin (1847), Wagner (1847), and Axmann (1847). Valentin, Kraus (1857), Bourgery (1845), Arnold (1826), Andersch, Haller, Wrisberg, Sommering, Remak,

Muller, Lee (Frankenhauser, 1867), and Baker are but some of the many workers in the field of the sympathetic.

Todd and Bowman named the solar plexus 'the abdominal sympathetic system" (1847). Solly called the solar plexus "the center of the cycloganglionic system" (1848). There is little doubt that to Bichat is due the credit of originating the doctrine of the entirety and independence of the sympathetic nervous system. Later writers, as Cuvier, Richerand, Gall, Wurtzer, Broussais, Brechet, Solly and Fletcher, have taught similar views. Many older neurologists divided the nervous system into three distinct divisions, viz.: (a) cerebral, (b) spinal and (c) sympathetic.

Le Gallois, a noted neurologist, taught that the spinal cord was the source of a part of the ganglionic nervous system, but Davy strenuously denies Le Gallois' assertion and remarks that the medical profession never acknowledged it. About 1840 no less distinguished a person than Marshall Hall asserted that in the removal of the frog's viscera "every portion of the ganglionic system" would also be removed. This showed lack of anatomical knowledge. But by 1840 such writers as Cuvier, Solly, Bichat, Richerand, Wurtzer, Gall and Broussais claimed that every ganglion of the sympathetic was independent of the remainder and that each ganglion is a distinct focus of nervous influence. It was Broussais (the founder of the idea of independent peritoneal inflammation) who claimed that the ganglia presided over the viscera and their functions.

Prochaska and John Hunter asserted that the ganglia of the sympathetic nervous system generate and control nervous power. Any one can witness this fact by separating a frog from its heart. The heart will beat for hours alone. The cerebrospinal nerves together perform the animal functions which prove us to be feeling and thinking and willing beings.

The ganglionic system of nerves, with the abdominal brain as their central organ, performs the vital functions, which are independent of mind and present to us the idea of life. The sympathetic system of nerves presides over the viscera—over secretion, nutrition, gestation, expulsion, respiration and circulation; over sub-conscious phenomena.

Muller, Bayly, Rolando, Akermann, Blumenbach and Gall agreed to the following views (by 1840), viz.: The sympathetic system of nerves of the chest and abdomen are fully formed while the brain is yet a pulpy mass. Now, these ganglia of the sympathetic would hardly be formed before the brain and cord if it were not for the sake of the organs which they supply and rule. Besides, it may be added that the sympathetic controls the viscera, which are as perfect at birth as in the adult. But the mind and brain are very slowly perfected. The priority of the sympathetic nerves over the cerebrospinal is evident and signifies their import in the continuance of the vital forces of life. Babies are born alive with no brains. Dr. Ball, of Ohio, writes me that he found one baby fully formed without even a medulla oblongata. Marshall Hall records that a fetus was born "without either a brain or spinal marrow, without a particle of either of those organs, yet perfectly developed." Blumenbach furnishes an equal example, when he says, "In fetuses without brain or spinal marrow the circulation, nutrition. secretion, etc., proceed equally as in others, who, besides spinal marrow, nerves and ganglionic nervous system, possess a brain."

Children are born quite well developed without the vestige of a cerebrospinal system,—only possessing a sympathetic system. It might be argued that often these children originally possessed a cerebrospinal system, but that through pressure, as hydrocephalic conditions, the fluid had pressed the nerve-cells out of existence. Yet this does not explain all the cases.

In 1872 there appeared one of the best and most reliable books on the sympathetic system of nerves up to that date. The authors are Guttmann and Eulenberg. It was translated from the German into the English in 1878 by Dr. C. Napier. This work was based on physiologic and pathologic labors. It was for this essay of Eulenberg and Guttmann that the Astley Cooper Prize for 1877 was originally awarded—a decision which was subsequently overthrown, however, on the technical ground that the essay was the work of two authors and not one only, as the terms of Sir Astley Cooper would seem to require.

In 1802 William Hunter presented the nerves of the uterus. The Osianders, father and son, also did similar work in 1808-1818. Tiedemann (1822) made valuable observations on uterine nerves. Lobstein, in 1823, produced excellent views on the sympathetic. He carefully described the various plexuses by the names we now give them.

In 1889 Robert Lee gave some good descriptions of the sympathetic uterine nerves, as also Snow Beck (1845) with Clay, Goetz, Schlem, Swan 1846), Killian (1834) and Lambell (1841).

In 1867 a most excellent work was published by Dr. F. Frankenhauser, entitled: "The Nerves of the Uterus." It contains finely executed tables of the sympathetic nerves of the abdomen.

The sympathetic nervous system is shown to be supremely evident when we note the body nourished, the viscera perfected and the bony structures finished, without a brain or cord, and still more evident when we observe the finely balanced circulation, delicate absorption and secretion, in full and perfect operation for nearly a year without a cord or brain—only a sympathetic nervous system to rule. Should the main-spring of life, the abdominal brain, solar ganglion, cease its activity, then life itself disappears. The sympathetic nerves carry on life's functions during sleep, like the additional spring to a watch which enables it to go while being wound.

By 1850 the physician had not lost sight of the fact that the sympathetic nerve, being so intimately associated with the vital action of every viscus, could become involved in disease. For the past fifty years the pathology of the sympathetic has been studied. In the work of Davy may be found numerous diseases attributed to the sympathetic. Dr. Marshall Hall stated that: "The ganglionic system is that power under which all formation, all nutrition, all absorption and all secretions are performed; therefore, that being affected may affect different acts."

The opinions of men famous, though dead, still prevail. Bidder produced a celebrated article, in Müller's Archives for Physiology, in 1844, entitled: "Experience over the Functional Independence of the Sympathetic as the Center of Motion and Sensation for all the Vegetative Organs." Volkmann assumed the same views as Bidder in his well-known article: "The Independence of the Sympathetic Nervous System Demonstrated through Anatomical Investigations" (1842). Prof. Albert V. Kölliker, of Wurtzburg, who is now celebrating his fifty-year jubilee as a medical teacher, assumed an intermediate ground between Bidder and Volkmann, when in 1845 he wrote his article entitled, "The Independence and Dependence of the Sympathetic Nervous System Demonstrated by Anatomical Observation." Budge in 1864 gave some reliable data in regard to the nerves of the bladder, in Henle's and Pfeufer's "Landschrift für rational Medicin," as did also Gianozzi in 1863.

The history of the developmental knowledge of the sympathetic is not complete without the names of Schiff, Henle, Ludwig, Heffer and especially the often-quoted experiments of Nasse found in his article: "Lecture on the Physiology of Bowel Motion," Leipsic, 1866. Henle stated, in 1840, that the peristalsis of the intestines was due to ganglia scattered among the intestinal nerves. Brown-Sequard, Pickford, Remak (1864), Jastrowitz (1857,) Rochefontaine, Tarchanoff, Pflueger, Bernard, Golz and Knoll aided in the building of the present knowledge of the sympathetic.

In 1860 DuBois-Reymond inferred that migraine was due to the influence of the cervical part of the sympathetic, i. e., it produced a kind of tetanic contraction of the vessels, showing the influence of the sympathetic over vessels. He styled it *Hemicrania sympathetica atonica*. Cruveilhier and Aran are credited with discovering muscular atrophy, but Charles Bell (1832) gives several cases. Bell places muscular atrophy under the domain of the sympathetic. Parry (1825) discovered a group of symptoms which we now call exophthalmic goiter (Graves' or Basedow's disease) which many place in the field of the sympathetic nerve. The three great symptoms are (a) cardiac palpitation, (b) goiter and (c) finally exophthalmos. Basedow (1840) claimed to have first described the disease, but the priority of Graves is now universally known.

Angina Pectoris, described by Heberden in 1768, is considered by many as caused by the sympathetic nerves, especially the three cervical ganglia and the cardiac plexuses. Addison's disease is placed by some in the field of the sympathetic.

In 1783 Walter presented the best tables of the sympathetic nerves up to his day. It appears that Walter was the first who represented in his cuts the cervico-uterine ganglia, i. e., lateral ganglia of the uterus.

The above authors discuss in a very instructive method the various diseases of the sympathetic and attempt to establish, as far as possible, the physiologic, anatomic and pathologic limits of the domain of the sympathetic nerves. Especially interesting and valuable, though unfortunately limited, are the discussions upon the abdominal parts of the sympathetic.

Eulenberg and Guttmann discuss as belonging to the domain of the sympathetic system, the following diseases:

1. Functional disturbances, especially those due to irritation and paralysis.
2. Unilateral Hyperidrosis (perspiration).
3. Hemicrania (neuralgia).
4. Glaucoma (Neuro-retinitis, ophthalmia, neuro-paralytica).
5. Progressive Facial Hemiatrophy.
6. Progressive Muscular Atrophy.
7. Exophthalmic Goiter (Basedow's or Graves' disease).
8. Angina Pectoris (steno-cardia).
9. Addison's disease (bronzed skin).
10. Diabetes Mellitus.
11. Hyperesthesias of the sympathetic system:
    (a) Enteralgia, enterodynia, colic.
    (b) Neuralgia celiaca.
    (c) Neuralgia hypergastrica.
    (d) Neuralgia spermatica (ovarica).
12. Anesthesias of the sympathetic system (not well established).
13. Sympathetic paralysis and spasmodic affections of voluntary muscles. Reflex paralysis, diphtheritic paralysis, tabes dorsalis (locomotor ataxia, progressive).

The above thirteen classes of disease discussed as belonging to the domain of the sympathetic nerves have remained a more or less constant quantity with writers on the sympathetic nerve. However, some writers add, others subtract, while still others change the names of the above diseases. The subject is in a state of progress.

In 1867 Griesinger began investigations on the "Pathology of the Sympathetic." Griesinger's enthusiasm stimulated two physicians, Dr. Paul Guttmann and Dr. Albert Eulenberg, to produce one of the best and most reliable books on the pathology of the sympathetic based on physiologic grounds ever published. Griesinger's good work and enthusiasm were productive of practical results; for his remarkable words, that "our positive knowledge of the pathology of the sympathetic should be again collected by skilled hands," induced his scholars, Eulenberg and Guttmann, to study and write their prize book on the sympathetic nerves.

In 1876 a very learned and a very instructive essay appeared from the pen of Dr. Sigmund Mayer, entitled, "Die Peripherische Nerven Zellen und das Sympathetische Nerven System." Dr. Mayer was full five years engaged in the work in his microscopical laboratory and presented many interesting ideas and some of the most suggestive drawings of the nerves and cells. The essay represents many new views and vast labors.

In 1881 there appeared the "Fisk Fund Prize Essay," Rhode Island Medical Society—"The Sympathetic Nerve; its Relation to Diseases," by C. V. Chapin, M. D. This is a valuable essay, as it gives many authorities and references which enable us to enlarge our knowledge of this nerve. Dr. Chapin has sifted out the theoretical and practical knowledge of the nerve quite well. Chapin has but little deviation from the classification of the diseases which belong to the sympathetic of Eulenberg and Guttmann. An epitome of Chapin's book would be, that it is a record of opinions on the sympathetic nerve skilfully collected and arranged in a scholarly manner.

In 1885 Dr. W. H. Gaskell published the results of some excellent labor on the sympathetic system of nerves. One of the best was entitled: "The Structure, Distribution and Function of Nerves which Innervate the Visceral and Vascular Systems." Dr. Gaskell noted some of the following points:

1. The visceral nerves issue from the central nervous system in definite sacral, thoracic and cervico-cranial regions.

2. From the above regions the visceral nerves pass through the ganglia into the visceral system.

3. From the sacral region they pass in a single stream to the ganglia of the collateral chain.

4. From the thoracic region they pass in a double stream, one to the ganglia of the lateral chain, the other to the ganglia of the collateral chain.

5. From the upper cervical region they pass in a single stream to the ganglia on the main stem of the vagus and glosso-pharyngeal nerves.

Gaskell's labors on the sympathetic are of far-reaching value and their utility has been recognized by being copied very generally, and even in detail, in the best modern works on physiology.

Rauber did some excellent work on the sympathetic, and his labor is recognized by Quain's latest edition borrowing one of his cuts.

In 1885 Dr. Edward Long Fox published a well-written and very instructive book on "The Influence of the Sympathetic on Disease." This is the most comprehensive of late books on the sympathetic. He widens the influence of the sympathetic in the domain of disease beyond that laid down by Eulenberg and Guttmann. He includes insomnia, neurasthenia, pigmentation, myxedema and neuroses of the extremities—symmetrical gangrene. The writer can highly recommend Dr. Fox's book as instructive and valuable. Articles of merit and value on the sympathetic nerves have appeared with increasing frequency during the past ten years.

In 1877 Gubler described a morbid symptom of the peritoneum related to the sympathetic system. He called it peritonismus. He included pain, meteorismus in various degrees, hiccough, vomiting, rapid pulse, cyanosis, lowering of the temperature, cerebral symptoms of great activity, depression of mental powers and decrease of amount of urine. The nerves of the heart are affected. This aggregate of symptoms Gubler designated by the word peritonismus. The abdominal surgeon only too frequently sees this clinical picture, but it is doubtful how much is gained by designating it as peritonismus.

THE PELVIC BRAIN.

(A.) Macroscopic.

From the stately rhythm and periodic peristalsis of the uterus in labor, the early observer must have been impressed with the nerves governing the genitals. However, from the unfortunate dogma of the church, the light of knowledge of anatomy and physiology was denied mankind by prohibiting human dissection. So far as I have been able to note almost all observations on the nerves of the genitals (uterus), previous to the fifteenth century, were almost valueless.

Among the first names I find in literature referring to the nerves of the uterus is that of A. Vesallus, a Belgian by birth, professor of anatomy at the famous school of Padua, Italy. He was born in 1514 and died in 1564. Vesalius made the general statement (partly false and partly true) that the cervix was supplied by the sacral nerves (spinal) while the fundus was supplied by the sympathetic.

This view of Vesalius generally prevailed for two centuries and was practically confirmed by the following famed eponymic names on anatomy: Eustachius (died 1574), Reignier de Graaf (1641-1673), Thomas Willis (1622-1675), Albert Haller (1708-1777), Johann G. Walter (1734-1818). With investigation (anatomic and physiologic), and lapse of time, views changed, especially among the French, English and Germans. Definite records of dissection and observation on the nerves of the tractus genitalis (uterus) begin to accumulate in literature.

Eustachius, an Italian anatomist of Eustachian tube fame, published at Amsterdam in 1722 *Tabulæ Anatomicæ*. Eustachius described the nerves connecting the lumbar ganglia with the hypogastric plexus, which in union with branches from the sacral nerves arrived at the side of the uterus.

Reignier de Graaf, a Dutch anatomist of Graffian follicle fame, published at Amsterdam in 1705 "*Opera Omnia.*" He dissected and pursued the nerves to the uterus, ovary, oviduct and ligamentum latum. The presentations are schematic and description crude.

Thomas Willis, an English anatomist and philosopher of Circle of Willis fame, published at Geneva in 1680 "*Cerebri Nervorumque Descriptio.*" Willis first described the course of the ovarian nerves, though defectively. He styled the solar plexus, *cerebrum abdominale*.

Albert Haller, a Swiss anatomist of multiple eponymic fame, published at Lausanne in 1778 Elementa Physiologiæ. He limited the origin of the ovarian nerves to the plexus renales and lateral sympathetic chain only. This error was repeated by Tiedemann in his 1822 publication. He left no illustration.

R. Vieussens (1641-1716), a French anatomist of multiple eponymic fame (the ganglion of Vieussens—solar plexus), left a rough presentation of the sympathetic.

Johann Gottlieb Walter, a German anatomist of "coccygeal ganglion" fame, published at Berlin in 1783 *tabulæ nerv. Thoracis et Abdominis*. He presents several excellent copper-plate tables of the thoracic and abdominal nerves, which have become famous for accurateness and careful preparation. To 1875 Walter's tables were the best presentation of the sympathetic, especially the best and most accurate in their presentation of the sympathetic nerves supplying the female tractus genitalis. Walter's tables are not schematic but naturally correct, excelling the later much-lauded tables of

Tiedemann (1822). It is the first presentation of the tractus genitalis in its natural position and in connection with the pelvic and abdominal viscera. Unfortunately the plexus aorticus and especially the plexus hypogastricus is incompletely presented. Also the course of the nerves in the uterus and ovary is not indicated. Walter was the first who presented a ganglion on the lateral borders of the cervix uteri. Hence these nerve masses or nodes should be known by the eponym "Walter's cervico-uterine ganglion." Walter's plates of the sympathetic are superior to those of Tiedemann but are not so well known. It is a rare book.

William Hunter (1718-1788), the celebrated English obstetrician, published an atlas on the nerves of the pregnant human uterus which is a noteworthy work. I could find no presentation of the uterine nerves originating from the sacral nerves in the atlas. Hunter asserted that the uterine nerves all rise from the intercostal, that they assume the same course as the bloodvessels and that therefore on each side will occur a plexus spermaticus and plexus hypogastricus. A plexus springs from the ganglion semilunare and while it passes to uterus is strengthened by branches from the intercostals. The plexus aorticus emits nerves to the plexus renalis, which gives origin to the plexus spermaticus. The plexus aorticus divides into two nervi hypogastrici, distal to the aortic bifurcation. Each hypogastric nerve divides into a dorsal branch supplying the rectum and a ventral branch which follows the arteria uterina to supply the uterus. The greatest number of nerve branches tend toward the cervix uteri, according to Hunter. He believed that the uterine nerves increased in dimension during gestation, furnishing no proof by specimen however.

John Hunter (1728-1793), the famous brother of William Hunter, asserted that its nerves did not increase in dimension during gestation, also adding no proof by specimen. William Hunter shows sympathetic nerves supplying the cervix, corpus and fundus uteri. Previously and subsequently to Hunter's time it was a widespread dogma that the sympathetic nerve supplied corpus and fundus uteri only—not the cervix uteri.

Johann Friedrich Osiander (son, 1787-1855), obstetrician at Göttingen, published a prize essay in 1808 on Nerves of the Uterus, noting that he believed that nerves were present in the uterus but could not detect them.

Friedrich Benjamin Osiander (father, 1759-1822), obstetrician at Göttingen, inventor of uterine traction forceps, asserted in his Handbook of Obstetrics, 1818, that he doubted if any man had seen nerves in the uterus.

Friedricus Tiedemann (1781-1861), German professor of anatomy in Heidelberg from 1816 to 1844, published in Heidelberg in 1822 Tabulæ Nervorum Uteri, which has become extensively and favorably known, *many times* copied, and prized as the best presentation of the nerves of the uterus in connection and with the natural position of the viscera. Tiedemann's plates are schematic, defective and inferior to those of Walter—his predecessor by thirty-seven years. Tiedemann's plates, like Walter's and Hunter's, are the most imperfect in presenting the relations of the sacral nerves to the hypogastric plexus and uterus. Tiedemann advocated that the nerves of the uterus were enlarged during gestation and atrophied during senescence.

J. G. C. F. M. Lobstein (1777-1815), a French anatomist and obstetrician at Strassburg published at Paris in 1823 *nervi sympathetici Humani Fabrici, etc.* Lobstein accentuated the plexus mesentericus superior and inferior. He practically denied the existence of the plexus spermaticus.

My observation of Lobstein's book on the sympathetic induces me to think that he obscured and retarded its knowledge rather than advanced it. For fifty years, to 1875, no special work appeared on the nerves of the tractus of the female. The general assertion for half a century, on whose authority I know not, was that the sacral nerves supplied the cervix and the sympathetic the body and fundus. In 1839, in an atlas to the book of Frances Joseph Moreau (1789-1862) entitled *Traite pratique des accouchemans,* appeared a new illustration of the nerves of the pregnant uterus after J. M. Jacquemier (1806-1879). It is schematic, defective, imitates Tiedemann's plates and their errors and adds practically nothing new.

From 1838 to 1846 occurred the fierce polemic on the nerves of the uterus between Robert Lee and Snow Beck, chiefly found in the Philosophical Transactions. Robert Lee (1793-1877), an English obstetrician, physician to the British Lying-In Hospital, published several papers on the nerves of the uterus from 1838 to 1846. Lee claimed to find under the perimetrium several nerve plexuses which were connected with the ovarian and hypogastric plexuses as well as the sacral nerves. Since Lee produced no convincing evidence, no microscopic demonstration as regards the cellular structure of the claimed nervous ganglia, suspicion arose among his colleagues (especially Snow Beck) that he had mistaken elastic fibres, connective or muscular tissue of the uterus for nerve plexuses. Lee was an Englishman of typical vigor, possessing the spirit of progress and was not easily turned aside by adverse criticism of opposing colleagues. He said the processes which he had held for nerves branched with the arteries of the uterus, a fact which, according to Lee, occurred nowhere with elastic or muscular tissue. By an industrious prosecution of his dissecting labors he rediscovered in 1841, Walter's cervico-uterine ganglion (of 1783) and proved it a constant structure.

Lee's Monograph, the anatomy of the nerves of the uterus, 1841, lies before me. It is an excellent labor by an earnest investigator. It contains two plates some 10x10 inches illustrating the dissected nerves and ganglia of two pregnant uteri, one in the sixth and the other in the ninth months of gestation. Lee said, in short, that his dissections prove that the uterus possesses a great system of nerves, that they enlarge with gestation and return to the original condition subsequent to parturition.

Also, if the nerves of the uterus could not be demonstrated to exist, its physiology and pathology would be completely inexplicable. Lee repeatedly demonstrated the cervico-uterine ganglion in the pregnant and non-pregnant uterus. He showed that the plexus hypogastricus ended in the great cervico-uterine ganglion, which he claimed was composed of six or seven smaller united by nerve strands and located on the lateral border of the cervix uteri. He noted that the branches of the second and third sacral nerves entered the cervical ganglion. Lee located a ganglion at the junction of the uterus and the oviduct. He also located a subperitoneal ganglion on the dorsum of the corpus uteri and one on the ventrum of the corpus uteri of the extensive surface dimension. These subperitoneal ganglia, according to Lee's illustrations, extend over large surface areas of the corpus uteri and stand in connection with the hypogastric plexus and cervico-uterine ganglion.

Modern investigations, especially by the aid of the microscope, demonstrate that Lee's extensive subperitoneal ganglion do not exist. Later in Lee's dissecting labors he had Dalrymple make microscopic sections of the nerve plexuses which confirmed their nervous structure, but no mention is made of a microscopic examination to confirm the nervous structure of the uterine ganglia. Robert Lee located three vesical ganglia, viz: (a), external vesical ganglia; (b), middle and (c), external vesical ganglia. Later he described but two internal and external vesical ganglia. Dr. Robert Lee made valuable additions to the literature of the nerves of the uterus. His labors aroused vigorous opponents and valuable polemics by which was instigated extensive additional researches. He rediscovered Walter's cervico-uterine ganglion, hence, the memory of this earnest investigation should be entitled to the eponym, "Lee's cervico-uterine ganglion."

T. Snow Beck, an English anatomist, published in 1846 in the Philosophical Transactions, several investigations concerning the nerves of the uterus, which were almost a complete negation of Lee's views. Snow Beck claimed that Lee's cervico-uterine ganglion was merely a mass of connective tissue containing a few small ganglion cells, that it was due to the union of the branches of the sacral nerves and hypogastric plexus. He similarly disposed of Lee's other uterine ganglia. Snow Beck gave detailed descriptions of the uterine nerves, adding some illustrations which contain numerous errors. He, like Lee, had prepared the specimens on the extirpated genitals—not while they were in situ. This insured confusion in non-accuracy and supposed schematism.

In 1894 I advocated that the ganglionated mass located at the lateral border of the uterus should be termed the pelvic brain (cerebrium pelvicum).

T. Snow Beck introduced the term *pelvic plexus*, which is the result of the union of the branches of the sacral nerves second, third and fourth with the distal end of the hypogastric plexus. Secondary to Snow Beck the second sacral nerve sends one branch to the pelvic plexus, the third sends 12 or 13, the fourth, 5 or 6. Small ganglia are distributed over the pelvic plexus, which sends nerves to the bladder, vagina (10 to 12) and rectum but not to the uterus. T. Snow Beck indicates that many of the uterine nerves are very fine, threadlike and without plexiform character. T. Snow Beck's illustrations are obscure, the descriptions contradictory, and doubtless prepared after being extirpated from the body, which increased the errors. He denied the claim of Robert Lee that the uterine nerves enlarged in dimensions during gestation. T. Snow Beck's iconoclastic negation of Lee's conclusions in regard to the nerves and ganglia of the female genitals served rather as a sample of medical polemic of those times than to enhance knowledge. The work of Clay, 1845, and that of Swann, 1846, The Physiology of the Nerves of the Uterus, were not to me accessible, but since I find nowhere citations from them perhaps they contain nothing new.

Antoine Joseph Jobert (de Lamballe) (1799-1867), a French anatomist and surgeon, published in 1841 in *Comptes Rendus de Science de l' Academie*, T XII, No. 20, his *Researches sur la Disposition des Nerfs de l' uteres*. His illustrations are faulty and his work adds little new data. Jobert announces that no nerves penetrate the portia vaginalis uteri.

Ludwig Moritz Hirschfield (1804-1876), professor of anatomy at Paris and Warsaw, and Jean Baptiste Françoise, Leville (1769-1829), French anatomist, published in 1858 *Neurologic des Cript et Icongraphie du System Nerveaux*. The same illustrations are employed in the Atlas of Savage, 1863. The illustrations are not clear and visceral positions with nerve relations are incorrect.

Ferdinand Frankenhauser (died 1894), a German obstetrician, published at Jena in 1867 *Die nerven der Gebaermutter*. This book is excellent, accurate, comprehensive, unique and instructive. Though a book of 82 pages only, it is a monument of industry for all time. His descriptions are accurate, his illustrations are according to Nature. I am indebted to Dr. Frankenhauser for his labors in the sympathetic nerves, especially those of the tractus genitalis. His honor is admirable in crediting justly to every author his share in the developmental knowledge of the sympathetic nerves. Other authors have labored in the microscopical field of the sympathetic nerve but space forbids further mention.

(B.) Microscopic.

Reliable microscopical examinations of the nerves of the tractus genitalis are limited in number and separated by long intervals. Microscopic anatomy began about 1850. W. M. Hunter (1805), Robert Lee (1846) and Fr. Tiedemann (1822) claimed that the uterine nerves increased in dimension during gestation. John Hunter, the brother of William Hunter, denied that the nerves enlarge during gestation, that the thickening was due to multiplication of the connective tissue.

Herman Friedrich Kilian (1800-1863), a German obstetrician, published in 1851 in the *Zeitschrift fur rationelle medicin*, a work *Die Nerven des Uterus*, which founded for all time the microscopic structure of the uterine nerves. Kilian attempted to determine which part of the uterus was supplied by sympathetic and which by spinal nerves by the aid of the microscope. He claimed that both sympathetic and spinal nerves supplied all parts of the uterus, but sympathetic nerves only were found in ovarian plexuses. He claimed that the cervix is richer in nerves than the body. Ganglion cells lie nowhere in the uterus. Kilian announced an age relation of uterine nerves. During pueritas the nerves were limited in number and dimension. During adolescence the number increased. During gestation the number and dimension were marked. During senescence the nerves became lessened in number and dimension. Kilian concerned himself with: (a) the origin of the uterine nerves; (b) the changes experienced by a nerve passing through the uterus; (c) the age relations. Frankenhauser of Jena in 1864, Koerner of Breslau in 1864, Kehrer of Giessen in 1864, Polle of Göttingen in 1865, Frey, 1867, and Kolliker (1817—living) and Koch (1843—living,) in 1865 published accounts of ganglia on the uterine nerves (in addition to the cervico-uterine ganglion). To 1867 little was added to the great work of Kilian except ganglia on the uterine nerves and special nerve ending in the uterus.

We have thus finished a very limited and meager sketch of the sympathetic nerve. Vast numbers of worthy names and workers have not been mentioned for want of space. However, a few of the landmarks in the development of the knowledge of the sympathetic nerves have been noted, from Galen, its discoverer, to the present time. The sympathetic nerve has long been an unknown field as to facts. Our knowledge of the nerve is still incomplete and will be for some time to come.

To the scholar and investigator the steps by which knowledge is gained are not only interesting but of value for further progress.

CHAPTER II.

A CLASSIFICATION OF DISEASES WHICH MAY BELONG IN THE DOMAIN OF THE SYMPATHETIC NERVES.

The sympathetic nerve concerns itself with the life of the viscera. It presides over the visceral economy.

"A man's power is hedged in by necessity, which, by many experiments, he touches on every side, until he learns its art."
—Ralph Waldo Emerson.

We here present the classification of diseases considered to belong to the domain of the sympathetic nerve by various writers. The classification has no hard or fast lines, but we present it for the purpose of securing a general or bird's-eye view of the field of the sympathetic. The field of definite action, physiologic, anatomic or pathologic, of the cerebrospinal and sympathetic nerves, is not yet settled. The pathology of the sympathetic must rest on its physiologic paths. Physiology, with our present limited anatomical means of tracing nerve fibers, is surer than anatomy. It is difficult to make a satisfactory classification of diseases of the sympathetic, for a multitude of symptoms, which may reasonably be supposed to depend upon the sympathetic nerves, are encountered without our being able, by minute examination, to recognize the morbid process upon which they depend. Their chief manifestation is through reflex action, referred disturbance.

Again, many sympathetic nerves, and especially ganglia, are found at the autopsy sclerosed, pigmented or possessed of increased connective tissue, yet the patient left no records of physical complaints during life. Hence, it is difficult to retrace, in such cases, the interpretations of Nature's physiologic experiment. Also, one is not always able to decide whether the pathologic findings at the autopsy are not secondary. No doubt there is a special pathology of the sympathetic nerve, or rather ganglia; but it may not be a recognized pathology. In normal and pathological states the sympathetic nerve is constantly affected by reflex irritations. The pathology of the sympathetic is chiefly observed in the cervical and abdominal ganglia, and is characterized by vascularity, deposit of excessive connective tissue, pigmentation, atrophy, hypertrophy, sclerosis, fatty infiltration, accumulation of microbes and leucocytes in the ganglia, amyloid or fatty degeneration. Sometimes the blood-vessels of the ganglia are found dilated and engorged with white blood corpuscles.

Classification of diseases which are certainly, or probably, connected with the sympathetic nervous system:

1. Functional disturbances:
    (a) Irritation (hyperesthesia).
    (b) Paralysis (anesthesia).

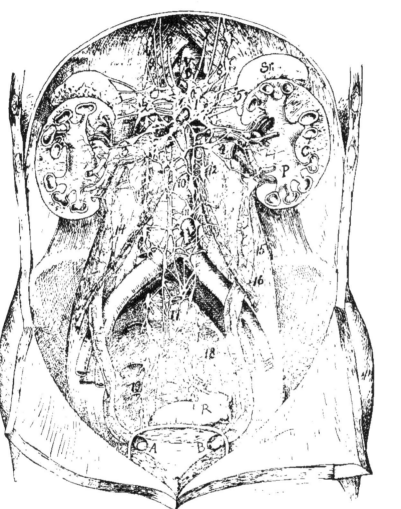

AN ILLUSTRATION OF THE ABDOMINAL SYMPATHETIC NERVE OF THE MALE

Fig. 2. It is accompanied by ureteral dilatation.

Drawn from a specimen under alcohol which I secured at an autopsy through the courtesy of Dr. W. A. Evans and Dr. C. O'Byrne. 1 and 2, abdominal brain; 10 and 12 represent the spermatic ganglia emitting their plexuses along the spermatic artery; H represents the coalesced hypogastric ganglia. 11, inferior mesenteric ganglia. Note the network of nerves ensheathing the ureters and also the anastomosis of the plexus spermaticus with the plexus ureteris, hence, the testicular pain is explained in ureteral calculus. Observe the numerous and marked dimensions of the ganglia renalia.

2. Hyperesthesia of the sympathetic (reflex irritation):
    (a) The abdominal brain (neuralgia celiaca).
    (b) The mesenteric plexus (enteralgia, enterodynia, colic).
    (c) Hypogastric plexus (neuralgia hypogastrica).
    (d) Gastric plexus (gastralgia, gastrodynia).
    (e) Spermatic or ovarian plexus (ovarian neuralgia).
    (f) Splenic plexus (splenic neuralgia).
    (g) Hepatic plexus (hepatic neuralgia).
    (h) Renal plexus (nephralgia).
    (i) Pelvic brain or cervico-uterine ganglia (irritable uterus, uterine neuralgia).
    (j) Aortic plexus.
    (k) Diaphragmatic plexus.
    (l) The cervical ganglia.
    (m) The cardiac ganglia (cardialgia, angina pectoris).
    (n) Trigeminus (facial neuralgia).
3. Anesthesia of the sympathetic.
4. Paralysis or spasmodic affections of voluntary muscles:
    (a) Locomotor ataxia.
    (b) Epilepsy.
    (c) Diphtheritic paralysis.
5. Progressive muscular atrophy:
    (a) Pseudo-muscular atrophy.
    (b) Progressive facial hemiatrophy.
6. Visceral neuroses:
    (a) Hysteria.
    (b) Gastralgia.
    (c) Gastrodynia.
    (d) Insomnia.
    (e) Pleurodynia.
    (f) Peritonismus.
    (g) Mastodynia.
7. Neurasthenia.
8. Pigmentation:
    (a) Spleen.
    (b) Liver.
    (c) Uterus.
    (d) Adrenals.
9. Addison's disease (bronzed skin).
10. Hemicrania (headache).
11. Trigeminal neuralgia (facial neuralgia).
12. Exophthalmic goiter, Pavy's (1825), Graves' (1835), or Basedow's (1840) disease.
13. Angina pectoris or stenocardia (Heberden's disease (1768).
14. Diabetes mellitus (hepatic neuralgia).
15. Diabetes insipidus (renal neuralgia).

16. Unilateral hyperidrosis (sweating).
17. Edema.
18. Diarrhea.
19. Glaucoma.
20. Myxedema (sterodema).
21. Symmetrical gangrene of the extremities.
22. Pathologic changes in the sympathetic in other diseases:
    (a) In syphilis.
    (b) In old age.
    (c) Leukemia.
    (d) Sunstroke.
    (e) Infectious diseases.
    (f) Cardiac diseases.
    (g) Malignant diseases.
    (h) Pigmentation.
23. Splanchnoptosia.

The above table records diseases which are certainly or probably connected with the sympathetic nervous system. However, some of them are much more doubtfully connected than others.

We will here consider briefly the hyperesthesias (neuralgias) of the abdominal brain and its closely related plexuses of nerves. In regard to the functional disturbances, or reflex irritation, we have hyperesthesia or exalted irritability of the sensory nerves. The hyperesthetic nerve manifests itself first by pain, secondly by a reflex act on a motor apparatus. Hyperesthesia, or exalted irritability of the sympathetic nerves, is liable to manifest pain irregularity, periodically, paroxysmally, and yet retain some irritability during the intervals. The symptoms of hyperesthesia are generally uniform and persistent throughout the duration of the disease. Early life is very free from hyperesthesia of nerves and it does not endanger life. Anatomically, we know little of the characteristic changes in structure in hyperesthesia. The etiology of hyperesthesia is obscure; however, malnutrition is perhaps a bottom factor. The presence of certain substances, such as lead, will induce hyperesthesia or lead colic (neuralgia saturnina). Climate, sex and age play a role, as does anemia or plethora. Checking of secretions induces hyperesthesia, as does rheumatism or congestion. Hyperesthesia generally runs a chronic course, is periodic, is seldom completely recovered from, is often a forerunner of organic disease, is very persistent individually, and is doubtless accompanied by tonic spasm of vessels.

Hyperesthesia of the nerves of special sense is manifested by phantasms. One of the objects of this little volume is to attempt to show anatomically and physiologically how reflex irritation in one diseased viscus will unbalance the rest. For example, what gynecologist has not personally observed that a tender, irritable uterus will unbalance the other viscera (abdominal and thoracic) year after year. From some form of malnutrition or other morbid process the uterus has become chronically hyperesthetic, and the result is that the secretions and excretions, visceral rhythm and circulation, are disturbed, while malnutrition results with an accompanying neurosis, which is due to the nerve apparatus being bathed in waste-laden blood.

It is not easy, practical or even useful to discriminate between hyperesthesia and a visceral neurosis, as one may blend into and become identical with the other. The active hyperesthesias of the great ganglia of the sympathetic system are characterized by an overpowering sense of prostration, a sense of impending dissolution, as if the center of life itself would be destroyed. This is the essential and common story of neurotic women. A blow on the pit of the stomach makes one stand with overwhelming awe of a coming danger, a sense of death-like anxiety and annihilation. These profound impressive sensations are characteristic of the sympathetic nerve. He who has once fainted need not be told of profound sensations. It may be stated here that the indefiniteness of the symptoms and findings in the sympathetic tracts have induced theoretical writers to offer placebos to the profession in the form of a profusion of terms, such as gastralgia, gastrodynia, gastric neuroses, and gastric neuralgia, terms some of which mean nothing to the diagnostician, and are confusing to physicians.

From a careful study of visceral neuralgia it is evident that it is a secondary disease. It consists of a peculiar malnutrition of a sensitive nerve apparatus. The treatment of visceral neuralgia consists in improving nutrition, relieving present distress by harmless means and removing all depressing causes. The cause producing the reflex irritation of different viscera must be discovered and the appropriate remedial agent employed.

CHAPTER III.

APPLIED ANATOMY AND PHYSIOLOGY OF THE ABDOMINAL VASOMOTOR NERVE (NERVUS VASOMOTORIUS).

A complete nervous apparatus consists of nerve or ganglion cell (e. g. cerebrum), a conducting cord (e. g. spinal cord, peripheral nerve), a periphery (e. g. Touch corpuscle).

"Defeated o'er and o'er but ne'er disgraces."—From the London Times and placed on a monument to Lord Beaconsfield.

The sympathetic system of nerves (nervus vasomotorius) has experienced a variety of names. *Synonyms*: The vasomotor nerve (nervus vasomotorius) (Benedict Stilling, 1840—German anatomist and surgeon, 1810-1879). The sympathetic nervous system (systema nervorum sympathicum). The vegetative nervous system (systema nervorum vegetatorum). The ganglionic nervous system (systema nervorum ganglionicum). The nervous system of organic life (systema nervorum vitæ organicæ.) The nerve system of nutritive life (systema nervorum vitæ nutritiæ). The great sympathetic nerve (nervus sympathicus magnus). The intercostal nerves (nervus intercostalis, Thomas Willis, 1622-1674, English anatomist). The great intercostal nerve (nervus intercostalis magnus). The trisplanchnic nerve (nervus trisplanchnicus, François Chaussier, 1746-1828, French anatomist). The ganglionic nerves (nervus gangliosus). The visceral nervous system (systema nervorum visceralis). The trunk nervous system (systema nervorum trunci) (Rumpf nerven system, K. F. Burdach, German anatomist, 1776-1847). Grand sympathetic. Since this system of nerves rules the motion of the heart and blood-vessels I shall assume with Stilling that the most appropriate term is the vasomotor nerve (nervus vasomotorius). The term "sympathetic" nerve is without signification and hence should be discarded for a term significant of function; therefore, nervus vasomotorius, since the blood carries nutrition to all organs, the term "nerves of nutritive life" is included in the term nervus vasomotorius.

The Vasomotor Nerve

(nervus vasomotorius) or unfortunately the meaningless term sympathetic nerve consists of: I, nerve ganglia, II, nerve cords, III, nerve plexuses.

I. The *nerve ganglia*, for practical purposes, present three grand divisions, viz.: (1) the bilateral chain of trunk ganglia (trunci nervi sympathici) extending from the base of the skull (ganglion of François Ribes, 1800-1864—French professor of hygiene in Mont Pieler) to the distal end of the coccyx or coccygeal ganglion. (2) Three great *ganglionated plexuses* or aggregations of ganglia known as (*prevertebral plexuses*) the prevertebral plexuses of the thorax, abdomen and pelvis. (3) *Automatic visceral ganglia*

THE ABDOMINAL AND PELVIC BRAIN

or peripheral ganglia located in relation with the thoracic, abdominal and pelvic viscera. The ganglia composed of nerve cells receive, reorganize and emit nerve forces. II. (*Afferent and efferent apparatus.*) The nerve cords composed of nerve fibers consist of conducting, communicating or distributing apparatus. III. The vasomotor nerve possesses peculiar ganglionated plexuses and nonganglionated plexuses. The vasomotor nerve is connected to the spinal cord through the (a) rami communicantes; (b) nervi sacralia and (c) to the cerebrum by the vagi.

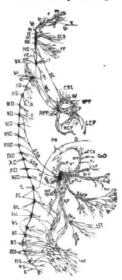

Fig. 3. A diagram of the nervus vasomotorius (sympathetic) from the proximal end (ganglion of Ribes) to the distal end (coccygeal ganglion of Luschka) presenting a lateral view of the truncus vasomotorius (lateral chain) and the three prevertebral ganglia (cardiac, coeliac and pelvic plexuses). Observe the exit of the three cardiac nerves, the three abdominal splanchnics and the 3 (or more) pelvic splanchnics (after Flower).

GENERAL VIEW OF THE VASOMOTOR SYSTEM.

The vasomotor nerves or nervus vasomotorius originate in the cerebrospinal. The bilateral halves of the vasomotor nerves (sympathetic) anastomose at the proximal and distal ends in the medium plexuses, especially through the cardiac plexus, the abdominal brain and pelvic brain, thus solidly and compactly anastomosing, connecting all viscera into a balanced system. The vasomotor or sympathetic nerves are practically the visceral branches of the spinal nerves. At the origin of the visceral vessels from the aorta, vasomotor ganglia as a rule exist according in size with that of the vessel, e. g., at the origin of the aorta from the heart is located the cardiac ganglia or plexus of Wrisberg (German anatomist [1739-1808], professor at Göttingen). At the origin of the cœliac axis is located the abdominal brain. At the origin of the common iliacs originally existed the pelvic brain. As a rule large vasomotor or sympathetic ganglia are located at the origin of large visceral vessels from the aorta.

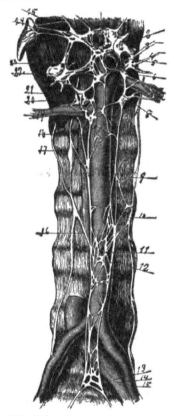

Fig. 4 (Jacob Henle, 1809—1885). Represents the abdominal brain, the lumbar lateral chain, the inferior mesenteric ganglion and the hypogastric plexus; 2, abdominal brain; 3 great splanchnic; 4, small splanchnic; 5, superior mesenteric artery; 6, renal ganglion; 7, renal artery with its ganglionic plexus surrounding it; 8, superior mesenteric ganglion; 9, ramus communicans; 10, lumbar lateral chain; 11, inferior mesenteric artery surrounded by its plexus; 12, 13, sacro-iliac point; 14, innominate vein; 15, innominate artery; 16, ramus communicans to inferior mesenteric ganglion; 17, ramus communicans; 18, lateral chain; 19, right renal artery; 20, splanchnic minor; 21, renal ganglion; 22, splanchnic ganglion; 23, splanchnic major; 24 ad-renal; 25, ganglion phrenicum.

The chief manifestation of the vasomotor nerve is that it is endowed with a peculiar rhythmical phenomenon. The ganglia of the nervus vasomotorius alone possess rhythm. (Some advocate that muscle possesses inherent power of rhythm, however, so far it is found in muscle supplied by the sympathetic nerve, e. g., muscles of the various visceral tracts.)

The vasomotor nerve is particularly connected to the cerebrum through the vagi (proximal end) and to the spinal cord by the sacral nerves (distal end).

The vasomotor nerves may pass directly from the bilateral chain of ganglia to the viscera without passing through intervening ganglia or plexuses, viz.: (a) pharyngeal plexuses located at the bifurcation of the carotids; (b) the cardiac plexus—located at the origin of the aorta from the heart; (c) the cœliac plexus (abdominal brain) located at the origin of the cœliac axis from the aorta; (d) the pelvic plexus (pelvic brain) located originally at the bifurcation of the aorta. These four great ganglionated nerve plexuses are located intermediary between the bilateral vasomotor ganglionic chain and the automatic visceral ganglion located in relation with the organs. The vasomotor ganglia are originating centers for nerve fibers, hence there is no relation between the number of nerve fibers which enter (afferent) and the number of nerves which depart (efferent) from a ganglion. The ganglia of the vasomotor nerve (composed of ganglion cells) may be viewed as nervous centers, i. e., receive, reorganize and emit nerve forces—to which all the physiologic and pathologic phenomena of the viscera may be referred. The three prominent systems or series of ganglia constituting the vasomotor nerve, for convenience of description and practical purposes, may be termed: (a) *primary* ganglia (the vasomotor bilateral chain). They appear assomatic or segmental in location on the lateral borders of the vertebra; (b) *secondary* ganglia (the four great prevertebral plexuses). They appear to be located in relation to major blood-vessels, ventral to the vertebra; (c) *tertiary* ganglia (automatic visceral ganglia). They appear to be located in relation to viscera; in or on visceral wall. The vasomotor visceral plexuses differ as much in arrangement from the vasomotor bilateral chain as the latter does from the spinal cord.

The prevertebral plexuses form a kind of fusion between the cerebrospinal and vasomotor nervous systems; also they solidly and compactly anastomose, unite the bilateral ganglionic vasomotor chain and the automatic visceral ganglia as well as fuse the lateral halves of the nervus vasomotorius. The signification of the vagi nerves may be observed when it was noted that they assist in the formation of three of the four great prevertebral vasomotor plexuses (see a, b, c, above).

There is a peculiar balanced relation between the vagi and vasomotor nerves. In animals especially, but also in man, there is a tendency to fusion of the vagi and vasomotor nerves. They act vicariously for each other. The greater the dimensions of the vasomotor nerves the less the dimensions of the vagi and vice versa. The vagi are practically visceral nerves supplying, viz.: larynx, lung, heart, gastrium, liver, pancrea. The vasomotor plexuses differ essentially from nerve plexuses formed by the cerebrospinal nerves. In cerebrospinal nerve plexuses the afferent and efferent nerves are identical, however the afferent and efferent cords may be differently combined previous to entrance and subsequent to the formation of the plexus.

The efferent branches departing from the plexus are precisely the same as the afferent branches that entered it. On the contrary, in the vasomotor

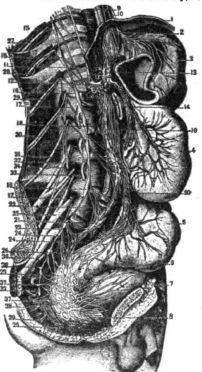

LUMBAR AND SACRAL PORTIONS OF THE SYMPATHETIC

Fig. 5. 1, incised edge of diaphragm; 2, lower end of œsophagus; 3, left half of stomach; 4, small intestine; 5, sigmoid flexure of the colon; 6, rectum; 7, bladder; 8, prostate; 9, lower end of left vagus; 10, lower end of right vagus; 11, solar plexus; 12, lower end of great splanchnic nerve; 13, lower end of lesser splanchnic nerve; 14, 14, two last thoracic ganglia; 15, 15, the four lumbar vertebræ; 16, 16, 17, 17, branches from the lumbar ganglia; 18, superior mesenteric plexus; 19, 21, 22, 23, aortic lumbar plexus; 20, inferior mesenteric plexus; 24, 24, sacral portion of the sympathetic; 25, 25, 26, 26, 27, 27, hypogastric plexus; 28, 29, 30, tenth, eleventh and twelfth dorsal nerves; 31, 32, 33, 34, 35, 36, 37, 38, 39, lumbar and sacral nerves. (Sappey, 1810.)

nerve plexuses there is no relation in dimension, number and structure of the afferent and efferent nerves with each other and the vasomotor nerve plexus itself. The mode of distribution of the cerebrospinal and vasomotor nerves differ.

The cerebrospinal nerves practically follow blood vessels; however, they divide by acute angles and do not form plexiform sheaths around blood vessels.

The vasomotor nerves are generally distributed in the plexiform network ensheathing vessels and entering with them into the parenchyma of viscera. From the reason that the vasomotor nerves are distributed in a plexiform gangliated network intimately ensheathing vessels (especially arteries) continuously to their destination, i. e., to the viscera, it has long originated the idea that the nervus vasomotorius belongs exclusively to the vascular system (blood, lymph vessels). This view was especially promulgated by Claude' Bernard, a French physiologist in 1851 (1813-1878). The vasomotor nerves accompany the arteries not the veins, the trunk of the vena porta forming the exception to the rule. In this chapter of applied anatomy and physiology of the nervus vasomotorius abdominalis I shall mention essential features only for practical reasons. I shall consider in order regardless of any exact system the following subjects: Chapter IV, truncus sympathicus; Chapter V, nervus plexus aorticus abdominalis; Chapter VI, nervus plexus interiliacus; Chapter VII, nervi tractus intestinalis; Chapter VIII, nervi tractus urinarius; Chapter IX, nervi tractus genitalis; Chapter X, nervi tractus vascularius; Chapter XI, nervi tractus lymphaticus; Chapter XII, the abdominal brain (cerebrum abdominale); Chapter XIII, pelvic brain (cerebrum pelvicum).

CHAPTER IV.

THE TRUNK OF THE SYMPATHETIC NERVE—(NERVUS TRUNCUS SYMPATHICUS).

"*One glorious hour of conquering strife is worth an age of quiet peace.*"
—*Shakespeare.*

We do well what we do automatically.

The trunk of the vaso-motor (sympathetic) nerve has experienced a variety of names:

SYNONYMS: The lateral cords of the sympathetic; the principal cords of the sympathetic; the lateral ganglionic chain of the sympathetic; the nodular cords of the sympathetic.

GERMAN: Grenzstrang, Hauptstrang, Knotenstrang.

The nerve strands connecting the ganglia of the sympathetic trunk are termed commissural cords. The trunk of the sympathetic nerve presents the *form* of an elongated elipse enclosing the vertebral column, united at the proximal and distal ends by unpaired ganglia. The trunk consists of a vertical, symmetrical, bilateral ganglionated cord with indefinite union at the proximal end (ganglion of Ribes) and distal ends (Ganglion Coccygeum). The number of ganglia and roots correspond in general to the number of spinal nerves. Exceptions occur in which the ganglia coalesce, as in the reduction of the seven cervical to the usual number of three. The total number of trunk ganglia (3, cervical), (11, dorsal), (4, lumbar) and (4, sacral) vary from 20 to 25. The form of the trunk ganglia varies and may be elongated, olive, spindle, triangle, pyramidal, irregular shaped. The ganglia in general are *located* ventral to the transverse processes and on the lateral surfaces of the vertebræ. However, the relation of the ganglia in each segment to the vertebra varies. The trunk ganglia vary in *dimension* from ¼ of an inch long (inferior cervical ganglion) to less than the size of a grain of wheat. The terminations, both proximally and distally, of the elongated elliptical ganglionated trunk are obscurely united by ganglia or commissura, cords.

A ganglion is composed of a larger or smaller number of multipolar nerve cells enclosed in a capsule of connective tissue.

RAMI COMMUNICANTES.

The bilateral symmetrical vertical ganglionated trunk of the sympathetic is connected to the spinal cord by means of the rami communicantes, which are two bands of nerves extending from the spinal nerves to the ganglia of the trunk of the sympathetic. These central communicating branches are known as gray (sympathetic) and white (visceral) rami communicantes. The ganglionated trunk of the sympathetic nerve emits important visceral branches from its different segments (cervical, dorsal, lumbar and sacral) to the viscera of the thoracic, abdominal and pelvic cavities. The following table will present a bird's-eye view of the segments of the trunk of the sympathetic nerve with their important branches.

SUPERIOR MEDIAN GANGLION (RIBES) (GANGLION SUPERIOR MEDIUS).

I. Trunk of the cervical sympathetic (Truncus Sympathicus Cervicales). Two to three.	1. Superior cervical ganglion (ganglion cervicale superior). 2. Middle cervical ganglion (ganglion cervicale medium). 3. Inferior cervical ganglion (ganglion cervicale inferior).
II. Trunk of the dorsal sympathetic. (Truncus Sympathicus Dorsalis).	Ten to twelve. Emits splanchnic nerves. (Coeliac Plexus).
III. Trunk of the lumbar sympathetic. (Truncus Sympathicus Lumbalis).	Four to five. Emits lumbar branches to plexus aorticus.
IV. Trunk of the pelvic sympathetic. (Truncus Sympathicus Pelvinus).	Four to five. Emits visceral nerves.

INFERIOR MEDIAL GANGLION (GANGLION COCCYGEUM).

I. Branches of the Cervical Trunk of the Sympathetic.

The cervical sympathetic trunk is a projection proximalward (toward the cranium) along the great cervical vessels.

The branches of the three cervical ganglia and commissural cord are distributed to structures of the head, neck and thorax and consist of:

(a) Motor fibres to involuntary muscles (pupil dilators).
(b) Vaso-motor fibres to head, neck and proximal limbs.
(c) Pilo-motor fibres along cervical spinal nerves.
(d) Cardiomotor fibres.
(e) Secretory fibres.

The trunk cervical ganglia are located on the prevertebral muscles dorsal to the carotid artery. It extends from the first rib to the base of the skull.

The cervical sympathetic trunk is characterized by the absence of the white rami communicantes. The cervical ganglia, usually coalesced, from seven to three in number, are important on account of the emitting of the pharyngeal plexus and cardiac nerves.

A. Superior Cervical Ganglion (Ganglion Cervicale Superius).

SYNONYMS: Supreme cervical ganglion (ganglion cervicale supremum);

Fig. 6. The trunk of the vasomotor nerve here presented was dissected under alcohol with care as regards connexions and relations. The ellipse formed by the two lateral trunks is evident. The ellipse extends from the cranium to the coccyx. The two nerve trunks are especially united at the cranium (cervical part) at the cœliac axis (abdominal part) and the distal end (pelvic part). Between the two lateral trunks of the nervus vasomotorius lies the plexus aorticus, thoracicus, cerebrum abdominale, plexus aorticus abdominalis, interiliac nerve disc, plexus interiliacus, cerebrum pelvicum.

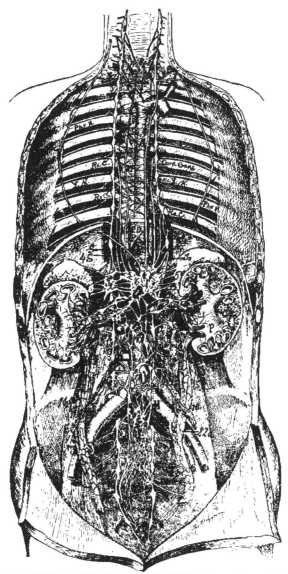

FIG 6. TRUNK OF THE VASOMOTOR NERVE (Truncus Vasomotorius).

the great cervical ganglion (ganglion cervicale magnum); the fusiform cervical ganglion (ganglion cervicale fusiforme); the olive-shaped cervical ganglion (ganglion cervicale olive).

The superior cervical ganglion, ¾ of an inch in length is the largest of the sympathetic trunk ganglia. It is located at the base of the skull between the internal jugular vein and internal carotid artery. It is irregular in form, however, chiefly spindle-shaped. The commissural cord connects it to the middle cervical ganglion.

The main branches of the superior cervical ganglion are:

Central communicating branches
{ 1. Gray rami communicantes (no white).
{ 2. Communicantes with cranial nerves.

Peripheral branches of the distribution.
{ 3. Emits branches to pharynx.
{ 4. Emits superior cervical cardiac nerves.
{ 5. Branches to vessels (controlling lumen).

B. Middle Cervical Ganglion (Ganglion Cervicale Medium).

SYNONYMS: The thyroid ganglia (Ganglion Thyroideum).

The middle cervical ganglion sends branches:

1. (*Central Communicating Branches*) gray rami communicantes (no white).

2. The subclavian loop (Ansa Vieusseni, French anatomist, 1641-1716) enclosing the subclavian artery and joining the middle and inferior cervical ganglia.

3. *Peripheral branches of distribution*, the middle cervical cardiac nerve.

4. Branches to the thyroid body.

C. *Inferior Cervical Ganglion* (Ganglion Cervicale Inferius).

SYNONYMS: The first thoracic ganglion (Ganglion Thoracicum primum); the vertebral ganglion (Ganglion Vertebrale); the stellate ganglion (Ganglion Stellatum).

The inferior cervical ganglion is irregular in dimension, form, location and branches. The inferior cervical nerve emits:

1. (*Central Communicating Branches*) gray rami communicantes (no white).

2. Subclavian loop.

3. Communications with larynx.

4. (Peripheral branches of distribution). The inferior cervical cardiac nerve.

5. Branches to vessels
{ (a) Vertebral plexus.
{ (b) Subclavian plexus.

The bilateral trunks of the cervical sympathetic are not directly united by transverse nerve strands.

II. Branches of the thoracic or dorsal trunk of the Sympathetic.

The dorsal or thoracic ganglia composing the dorsal or thoracic trunk of the sympathetic generally consists of eleven ganglia of varied form and dimension connected by commissural cords of marked dimension. The important feature of the thoracic sympathetic trunk is that the distal five or six ganglia give origin to the three splanchnic or visceral nerves which richly supply the abdominal viscera. The branches forming the ganglionated thoracic cord may be divided into two kinds (a) central branches connecting with other nerves; (b) peripheral branches distributed in a plexiform manner to the thoracic and abdominal viscera. The significant feature of the thoracic trunk of the sympathetic is the presence of the white rami communicantes (visceral nerves). The central communicating branches are (both) the white and gray rami communicantes. The peripheral branches of distribution of the thoracic trunk arise both from the ganglia and the commissural cord. The important distributing branches in the practice of medicine for the abdominal viscera are the three splanchnic nerves; the distal ends of the splanchnic nerves practically form the abdominal brain—the visceral ruler of the peritoneal organs. The splanchnic nerves are the abdominal visceral nerves. The following table presents a bird's eye view of the branches of the thoracic sympathetic trunk:

Branches of the thoracic sympathetic trunk.
1. (*Central communicating branches*) white rami communicantes.
2. Gray rami communicantes.
3. (*Peripheral branches of distribution*). Pulmonary (from II, III and IV ganglia) to form the pulmonary plexus.
4. Aortic (from proximal 5 ganglia) to supply aorta.
5. The three splanchnic nerves (from the distal 7 thoracic ganglia and commissural cords) to supply the abdominal viscera.

A. *The Great Splanchnic Nerve* (Nervus Splanchnicus Major).

arises from the thoracic trunk between the fifth and ninth ganglia. By the coalescence of several irregular strands a nerve of marked dimension is formed which passes distalward in the dorsal mediastinum and perforating the crus of the diaphragm terminates as the principal mass of the abdominal brain (semilunar ganglion). The great splanchnic ganglion (ganglion splanchnicum maxium) is found on the trunk of the great splanchnic nerve within the thoracic cavity.

B. *The Small Splanchnic Nerve* (Nervus Splanchnicus Minor).

The small splanchnic nerve arises from the trunk of the thoracic sympathetic in the region of the ninth and tenth ganglia. It courses adjacent to the bodies of the distal thoracic vertebræ, perforates the crus of the diaphragm adjacent to or with the great splanchnic and terminates irregularly in the abdominal brain, (and occasionally in the so-called aortic-renal ganglion).

C. *The Least Splanchnic Nerve* (Nervus Splanchnicus Minimus (inferior or tertius).

The least splanchnic nerve arises from the last thoracic ganglion in the sympathetic trunk (or from the small splanchnic). It perforates the diaphragm and terminates in the plexus renalis. The bilateral thoracic trunks of the sympathetic are not directly united by the transverse nerve strands similar to the lumbar and sacral trunks.

III. Branches of the Lumbar Sympathetic Trunk.

The lumbar trunk of the sympathetic consists usually of four ganglia joined by commissural cords. It is continuous proximally with the thoracic and distally with the sacral trunk of the sympathetic. The lumbar trunk is located on the bodies of the lumbar vertebræ internal to the origin of the psoas muscle and ventral to the lumbar vessels. The lumbar ganglia are not always bilaterally symmetrical in dimension, location, distance from each other and form. The ganglia are larger than those of the dorsal or sacral trunk. The commissural cords of the lumbar sympathetic trunk are longer, stronger and more irregular in number than the dorsal or sacral. The branches from the lumbar gangliated trunk consist of two sets, viz.:

A. *Central Communicating Branches.*

1. The first two or three lumbar spinal nerves possess visceral branches which form *white rami commnnicantes* joining the proximal lumbar ganglia or commissural cord.

These white rami communicantes comprise vaso-motor fibres for the tractus genitalis and motor fibres for the uterus and bladder.

2. Gray Rami Communicantes which pass to the ventral primary divisions of the lumbar nerves. The rami communicantes (white and gray) are irregular in length, dimension and location.

B. *Peripheral Branches of Distribution* from the lumbar ganglia and commissural cord arises and pass to the plexus aorticus and aorta. The lumbar sympathetic trunk sends branches to the plexus ureteris. The branches are irregular in length, dimension, number and location. The bilateral sympathetic trunk is directly united by several transverse nerve strands, chiefly extending from ganglion on one side to that on the other.

IV. Branches of the Sacral Sympathetic Trunk.

The sacral trunk of the sympathetic is a continuation of the lumbar trunk. It terminates in a plexiform coalescence over the coccyx with the trunk of the opposite side. The distal termination of the sacral sympathetic trunks are known as the ganglion impar or coccygeal ganglion. There are usually four ganglia which united by a commissural cord decrease in dimension from sacral promontory to coccyx. The ganglia are generally not bilaterally symmetrical in location, dimension or equidistant from each other. The usual location is on the ventral surfcae of the sacrum on the internal border of the sacral foramina. The ganglia scralia vary in number, dimension, location and form. The bilateral sacral sympathetic trunks are united directly by numerous transverse nerve cords which are arranged in a plexiform manner (which I have termed plexus intertrunci sacralis). The middle sacral trunk of the sympathetics, like that of the cervical and distal lumbar receives no white rami communicantes from the spinal nerves.

The visceral branches (Pelvic Splanchnic) of the II, III and IV sacral nerves join the pelvic plexus (pelvic brain) without being directly connected with the sacral sympathetic trunk. These nerves, however, are to be considered homologous with the white rami communicantes of the thoracic and lumbar (abdominal splanchnics).

The II, III and IV sacral nerves transmit to the tractus genitalis (uterus) tractus intestinalis (rectum) and tractus urinarius (bladder) motor and inhibitory nerves, and also vaso-dilator fibres for the tractus genitalis.

The branches of the sacral sympathetic trunk are of two kinds, viz.:

A. *Central Communicating Branches.*

I. Gray rami communicantes arise from the ganglia and join the ventral primary division of the sacral and coccygeal nerves. There are no white rami communicantes.

B. *Peripheral Branches of Distribution* are:

1. Visceral branches of limited dimension which arise mainly from the proximal ganglia of the trunk and commissural cord and pass medianward to join the interiliac plexus and pelvic brain as well as the three kinds of pelvic viscera and adjacent vessels.

2. Parietal branches limited in dimension which ramify on the ventral surface of the sacrum, especially in relation with the sacral artery, forming what I have termed the plexus intertrunci sacralis.

The four segments of the trunk of the sympathetic nerve, cervical, dorsal, lumbar and sacral, differ according to location and environment.

The white rami communicantes (visceral nerves abdominal splanchnics) stream from the dorsal and proximal lumbar ganglia.

The visceral nerves of the pelvic sympathetic trunk (pelvic splanchnics) do not pass through the sacral ganglia but through the II, III and IV sacral nerves.

The distributing branches of the pelvic sympathetic trunk are the least important of any segmental trunk. The bilateral cervical and dorsal sympathetic trunks are practically not directly united by transverse nerve cords, the bilateral lumbar and pelvic trunks are united by numerous transverse nerve cords (and plexuses).

The bilateral cervical sympathetic trunks are united by two localized prevertebral plexuses, the pharyngeal and cardiac.

The bilateral dorsal sympathetic trunks are united by a single prevertebral colossal pelvus—abdominal brain.

Ganglionic coalescence occurs chiefly in the cervical trunk. The ganglia are the most irregular in the pelvic trunk, the largest in the cervical and lumbar trunks.

The commissural cords are multiple supernumerary in the lumbra and sacral trunks only.

The cervical sympathetic trunk and pelvic brain are the only segments so far subject to surgical intervention (extirpation).

CHAPTER V.

PLEXUS AORTICUS ABDOMINALIS.—(A) ANATOMY, (B) PHYSIOLOGY.

One's rainbow of desires changes color with the passing years.
"Instead of condemning me to death the city (Athens) should grant me a pension." The defense presented by Socrates in his trial.

(A) ANATOMY.

The plexus of the abdominal aorta extends from the coeliac artery to the aortic bifurcation. It extends from the abdominal brain to the hypogastric ganglion or disc. At the proximal end of the aortic plexus is located the abdominal brain, at the distal end is located the hypogastric ganglion or disc. It consists of a wide meshed network of anastomosing nerve bundles and ganglia. The main nerve cords, two in number, course parallel to the lateral borders of the abdominal aorta, constituting the aortic plexus, anastomosing with each other by means of nerve strands coursing obliquely or transversely ventral or dorsal to the aorta, and also with the lateral chain of lumbar ganglia by means of short nerve cords. The plexus aorticus practically ensheaths the aorta, especially ventrally, with a wide meshed network of nerves and ganglia.

(a) *The Ganglia of the Plexus Aorticus.*

The ganglia of the aortic plexus are numerous and important, being located practically at the origin of visceral vessels from the aorta. They consist of multiple bordered, irregularly flattened bodies located mainly on the ventral and lateral borders of the aorta. Originally the aortic plexus consisted of a bilateral gangliated cord located along the lateral aortic border, each ganglion representing the origin and mission of a visceral vessel. By evolutionary processes and change of attitude the ganglia become removed, changed from this original site which was at the origin of the arterial vessels. In general the ganglia of the plexus of the abdominal aorta are *located* at the exit of the visceral vessels from the aorta abdominalis, viz.: (a) *ganglion diaphragamaticum* (paired), located on the proximal border of the abdominal

---

Fig. 7. This illustration is from a dissection made under alcohol. It is a drawing from a subject possessing a typical large abdominal brain with the ureter, bladder and urethra dilated into a single channel without sphincters intact. 1 and 2, abdominal brain; 3 and 4, renal plexuses; 5, plexus adrenalis; 6 and 7, the two vagi; 8 and 9, the three splanchnics on each side; 10, two spermatic ganglia; 11 inferior mesenteric ganglia; 12 and 13 lumbar lateral chain of ganglia; 14 and 15, dilated ureters wrapped by nerve plexuses; 16 arterio-ureteral crossing; 17, hypograstic plexuses; 18, and 19, lateral chain of sacred ganglia; A and B, Patulous ureteral orifices. The Plexus aorticus extends from the abdominal brain (1 and 2) to the aortic bifurcation, whence the Plexus interiliacus (hypogastricus) begins and extends to the Pelvic brain. I consider the Plexus Aorticus in this subject as a typical one.

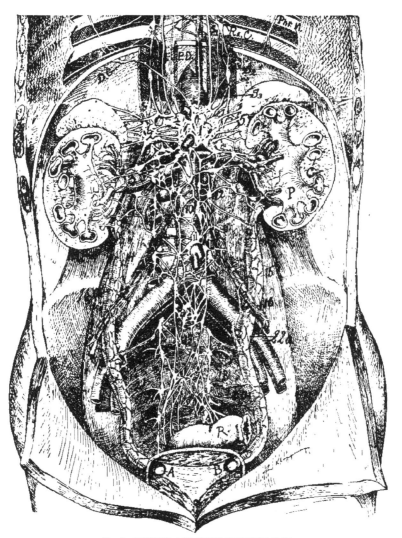

Fig. 7. PLEXUS AORTICUS ABDOMINALIS

brain in the form of a conical projection simulating the olfactory bulbs of the cranial brain; (b) *ganglion coeliacum* (unpaired), located at the origin of the coeliac, superior and inferior mesenteric and renal arteries; (c) Ganglion renalis, located at the origin of the arteria renalia; (d) *ganglion ovaricum* (paired), located at the origin of the arteria ovarica; (e) *ganglion mesentericus inferior* (unpaired), located at the origin of the arteria mesenterica inferior; (f) *ganglion hypogastricum* (unpaired), a coalesced disc located at the origin of the arteria iliacacommunicus at the aortic bifurcation. The hypogastric ganglion, or disc, arises at the bifurcation of the abdominal aorta. Its existence is according to the rule (modified by environments and erect attitude) that a sympathetic ganglion occurs at the exit of the abdominal visceral arteries from the aorta abdominalis.

The position of the ganglia appears to have experienced changes with evolutionary development as they become transported by detachment from the base of the visceral artery toward the corresponding viscus or along bones and muscles. Some visceral arteries, like the renal, possess a wealth of separate ganglia. The ganglia are located in general: (a) at the origin of the visceral artery from the aorta; (b) along the lateral borders; (c) on the ventral surface of the vessel. The ganglia mainly surround the root of the visceral vessel like a collar or fenestrated sheath and encase it towards its viscus with a plexiform network of nerves.

The dimension of the ganglia in the aortic plexus practically correspond with the volume of the corresponding visceral artery. The longest ganglion is that of the arteria coeliaca. The smallest constant ganglion is perhaps that at the base of the arteria diaphragmatic.

The form of the ganglia are oval, triangular or multiple bordered flattened bodies. *The surface* of the ganglia are uneven, with irregular, fenestrated spaces and occasionally perforated by blood vessels.

(b) *The Nerve Trunks and Cords of the Plexus Aorticus.*

The ganglia of the aortic plexus are united or anastomosed into a wide meshed plexus by two general methods: (1) By two trunk cords extending along the lateral borders of the aorta from the ganglion coeliacum to the ganglion hypogastricum or hypogastric discs; (2) by cords of smaller and larger caliber coursing irregularly from ganglion to ganglion, from cord to cord and from one lateral trunk to the other. The plexus aorticus is solidly and compactly united to the bilateral chain of lumbar ganglia by short, strong strands and to all visceral nerve plexuses of the abdomen.

The plexus aorticus practically ensheaths the abdominal aorta (especially lateral, and ventrally) with a plexiform network of nerve cords and ganglia. From the plexus aorticus abdominalis arise: (a) the plexus diaphragmaticus (paired), which accompanies and ensheaths the arteria diaphragmatica (the right possesses a ganglion); (b) plexus coeliacus (unpaired), which accompanies and ensheaths the arteria gastrica (supplying the stomach), hepatica (supplying the liver) and lienalis (supplying the spleen); (c) the plexus mesentericus superior (unpaired), which accompanies and ensheaths the arteria mesenterica superior with a network of nerve cords and ganglia to supply the enteron, right colon and right half of transverse colon; (d) plexus renalis (paired), which accompanies and ensheaths the arteria renalis with a network of nerve cords and wealth of ganglia to supply the kidney and proximal ureter; (e) plexus ovaricus (paired), which accompanies and ensheaths the arteria ovarica with a network of nerve cords and ganglia to supply the ovary, oviduct and ligament a lata; (f) plexus mesentericus inferior (unpaired), which accompanies and ensheaths the arteria mesenterica inferior with a mesh-work of nerves and ganglia to supply the right half of the transverse colon, right colon, sigmoid and rectum; (g) plexus hypogastricus (unpaired coalesced) which originally accompanied and ensheathed the arteria hypogastrica with a network of nerve cords and ganglia to supply tractus genitalis (especially the uterus and vagina) and distal segment of the tractus urinarius (especially the bladder and distal segment of the ureter). The plexus aorticus abdominalis includes the abdominal aorta from the coeliac axis to its bifurcation on the sacral promontory, hence its profound connection to every abdominal visceral tract through the arteries. The vital signification of the plexus aorticus abdominalis is at once evident when it is observed that from it issues practically nine great visceral arteries (the coeliac, two mesenteric, two renals, two ovarian and two iliacs) accompanied by great nerve plexuses and having at least one marked sympathetic ganglion at their origin. Each of the eight nerve plexuses of the plexus aorticus are solidly and compactly anastomosed with every other plexus and connected with all other abdominal plexuses, making a compact network of abdominal sympathetic nerves perfectly planned to report functions to the ruling potentate, the abdominal brain.

(B) PHYSIOLOGY.

The physiology of the plexus aorticus abdominalis comprises the function of the viscera to which it supplies nerves viz.: tractus intestinalis, urinarius, genitalis, vascularis and lymphaticus. The three great common functions of the abdominal viscera are: (a) Peristalsis, absorption, sensation and secretion. To the common functions must be added for the tractus genitalis, (d) ovulation; (e) menstruation; (f) gestation. We unconsciously employ the physiology of the aortic plexus in the practice of obstetrics for uterine hæmorrhage. When, after parturition, there is undue bleeding the physician attempts to check it by compressing the aorta. He is in error for what the practitioner really performs is to irritate the aortic plexus and this results in exciting uterine contraction, the uterine muscular and elastic bundles act like living ligatures which limits the lumen of the vessels. In irritating the aortic plexus no trauma or roughness need be employed. Simple, light stroking of the abdomen or gentle kneading will quickly stimulate the aortic plexus which sends branches to supply the uterus through the pelvic brain, inducing it to contract and check hæmorrhage. The peristalsis of labor may be hastened by administering hot drinks to the patient. The heat in the stomach stimulates the aortic plexus through the gastric plexus and consequently the nerves which supply the uterus inducing more vigorous and frequent uterine rhythm. Friction on the nipple or massage of the breasts will induce more frequent and vigorous uterine rhythm during labor. The stimulation from the mammæ travels to the abdominal brain (and consequently to the aortic plexus and uterus) over the nerve plexus accompanying the mammary, intercostal, inferior epigastric arteries. In abdominal massage we apply practical physiology to the various abdominal visceral tracts. For example in constipation one or all the great visceral functions (peristalsis, absorption, sensation and secretion) are defective. By stimulating the aortic plexus through massage intestinal peristalsis, secretion and absorption are enhanced as the irritation passes over the gastric plexus to the stomach over the superior mesenteric plexus to the enteron and over the inferior

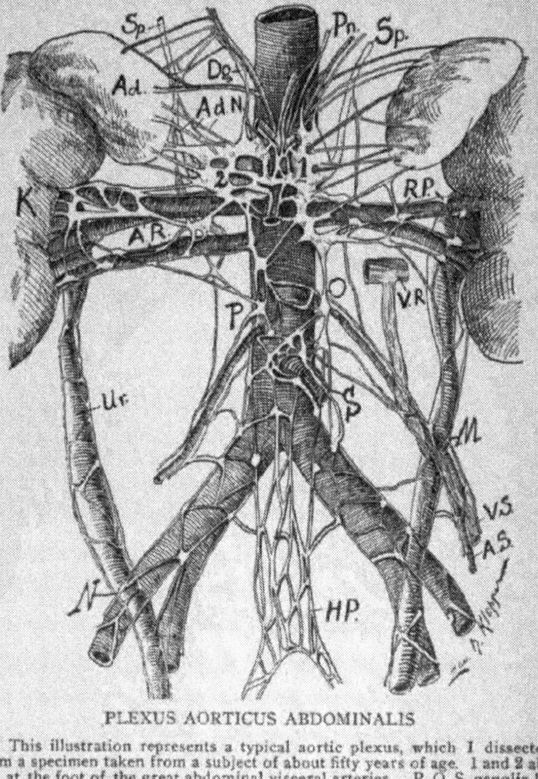

PLEXUS AORTICUS ABDOMINALIS

Fig. 8. This illustration represents a typical aortic plexus, which I dissected under alcohol from a specimen taken from a subject of about fifty years of age. 1 and 2 abdominal brain lying at the foot of the great abdominal visceral arteries. P. O. S. ganglia located at the other visceral arteries. HP. represents the fenestrated interiliac nerve disc.

mesenteric plexus to the colon. Constipation may be cured by massage of the abdomen. Massaging the abdominal brain induces more active renal peristalsis, absorption and secretion. The physiology of the sympathetic presents a vast field for future therapeutics, especially in the direction of visceral massage. The massage of the abdominal sympathetic (plexus aorticus) will assume three directions of physiologic utility, viz.: (a) The great ganglia of the plexus aorticus will be stimulated, that is, the ganglion at the root of each visceral artery will be stimulated, which will excite the pulsating vessel (and the heart), supplying more blood to its corresponding viscus and consequently individual and collective visceral peristalsis, absorption and secretion is enhanced—this is administering a vascular tonic. It also aids visceral drainage which consists in elimination of waste laden blood and lymph products. In short, massage of the plexus aorticus abdominalis enhances visceral function (rhythm) and visceral drainage (elimination); (b) massage of the plexus aorticus enables the operator to manipulate each, individual, viscus which not only excites the capsule or muscularis of the organ to enhance peristalsis, but the parenchyma of each viscus receives a direct stimulus for increased absorption and secretion. This is again administering a natural tonic for the massage of a viscus enhances its function and drainage. Visceral stimulation and visceral drainage must be complements and compensatories of each other; (c) in performing massage of the plexus aorticus abdominalis, the voluntary abdominal muscles are invigorated in function and usefulness. The active contraction and relaxation of the abdominal muscles on the viscera is a necessity for their normal function (rhythm, absorption, secretion) and support, e. g., splanchnoptotics possess relaxed abdominal walls and consequent distalward movements of viscera and elongated mesenteries—resulting in disturbed, compromised, visceral peristalsis, absorption and secretion as constipation, indigestion and neurasthenia. Every organ has its rhythm. In the rhythm or peristalsis of an organ undoubtedly lies the physiologic secret of correlated secretion and absorption. Hence one of the essential duties of a physician is to aid in maintaining a normal visceral rhythm. In conditions of acute inflammation or irritation of viscera, the abnormally active rhythm is best treated by anatomic (quietude of voluntary muscles) and physiologic rest (prohibition or control of fluid and foods). In conditions of defective rhythm of organs as in constipation, splanchmoptosia, the best means to stimulate normal rhythm is systematic abdominal massage and vigorous visceral drainage. A rational method to stimulate visceral rhythm is to administer coarse foods (cereals and vegetables) that leaves a large fecal residue which irritates the intestines into vigorous peristalsis or rhythm.

CHAPTER VI.

THE VASOMOTOR INTERILIAC PLEXUS (PLEXUS INTER-ILIACUS VASOMOTORIUS—SYMPATHICUS).

Immaterial, irrelevant, incompetent.—Attorney's objection to evidence in law trials.
Industry wins living, honesty wins respect.

Extending from the abdominal brain (the coeliac axis) to the pelvic brain (cervico-uterine junction) there exist two rich and mighty nerve plexuses, plexus aorticus and plexus interiliacus.

For convenience of description and significance in practice I will divide this plexus into two grand divisions, viz.:

(a) The plexus aorticus extending from the coeliac axis to the aortic bifurcation; (b) the plexus hypogastricus or more significantly plexus interiliacus, which extends from the bifurcation of the aorta (sacral promontory) to the junction of uterus and vagina. The plexus interiliacus is important because it is the great highway of travel for afferent (initiative or spontaneous) and efferent (reflex peripheral) genital nerve forces. I shall view the plexus interiliacus as originally belonging and accompanying the common iliac vessels. However, by erect attitude, distalward movements of the tractus genitalis and increasing dimensions (especially lateralward) to the pelvis, coalescence of the proximal extremities of the two branches of the plexus interiliacus arose. That is, the original nerve plexuses accompanying the common iliac arteries gradually moved medianward from them. Hence the term plexus interiliacus is particularly appropriate. The plexus interiliacus has experienced a variety of names during the past two centuries.

Synonyms: Superior hypogastric plexus (plexus hypogastricus superior, Tiedemann, 1822). Medial hypogastric plexus (plexus hypogastricus medius). Impar (odd, single, impaired) hypogastric plexus (plexus hypogastric impar). Interiliacal plexus (plexus interiliacus, Waldeyer, living). The great uterine plexus (plexus uterinus magnus, Tiedemann, 1822). Pelvic plexus (plexus pelvicus, Thomas Snow Beck, 1845, 1814, 1847). The hypogastric ganglion, i. e., layer (lamina gangliosa hypogastrica, Gabriel Gustave Valentine, German anatomist, 1810-1883). The common uterine plexus (plexus uterinus communis, Tiedemann, 1822). Iliac plexus (plexus iliacus—anatomica nomina, Basel). Distal part of the aortic plexus (plexus aorticus distal, Henle—Fred Gustav Jacob Henle, German anatomist, 1809-1885).

The plexus interiliacus I shall consider under three distinct headlines, viz.: (a) interiliacal nerve disc (proximal end); (b) trunk of the plexus interiliacus (central segment); (c) pelvic brain (distal end or ganglion cervicale).

THE VASOMOTOR INTERILIAC PLEXUS

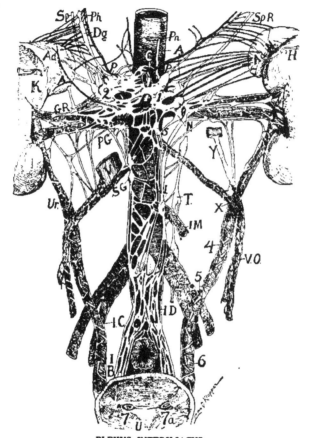

PLEXUS INTERILIACUS

Fig. 9 This illustration presents the sympathetic nerves following the arteries. I dissected this specimen (man 40) with care, and the artist, Mr. Klopper, sketched exactly from the model. 1 and 2, abdominal brain. Pn, Pneumogastric nerve; sp. Nervus Splanchnicus major. Ad, adrenal; Dg, ganglion diaphragmaticum; Adn, 10 adrenal nerves (right), (left), 7. G. R. arteria renalis (right and left partially duplicate). N. Ganglia renalia (left). Ur, ureteral nerves. S. G. and 5 upper ganglia spermatica. I, ganglion mesentericum inferior; X, ganglionic coalescence of nerves at the vasa spermatica and ureteral crossing. 5 ganglionic coalescence of the nerves at the crossing of the ureter and vasa iliaca communis. IB, Plexus interiliacus (hypogastricus) surrounding the rectum. ID is the fenestrated nerve disc of the sacral promontory. V, Vena cava emitting the vena ovarica on which is ensheathed the plexus ovaricus.

(a) INTERILIAC NERVE DISC.

The proximal end of the plexus interiliacus, which I shall term the interiliacal nerve disc of the sacral promontory, is practically a plexus of nerve cords compressed or flattened dorso-ventrally. The interiliacal disc is the result of coalescence of the distal end of the plexus aorticus, located at the aortic bifurcation, practically on the sacral promontory and the distalward movements of the tractus genitalis producing traction and extension on the nerve disc of the sacral promontory. The interiliac nerve disc is practically a plexiform nerve mass located at the proximal end of the plexus interiliacus. The *arrangement* of the interiliacal disc consists in the coalescence on the same promontory of the afferent nerve—plexus aorticus and branches from the distal bilateral lumbar ganglia—and the emission of efferent nerves: (a) two bilateral large plexuses to the pelvic brain; (b) branches to the tractus intestinalis (rectum hæmorrhoidal); (c) branches to the tractus genitalis (uterus, vagina, oviduct); (d) branches to the tractus urinarius (ureter, bladder).

POSITION.

I. Holotopy (relation to general body). The interiliac nerve disc is located on the median line in the space between the major bifurcation and the distal end of the abdominal end cavity immediately proximal to the lesser pelvis. It is a coalesced unpaired organ situated extraperitoneally on the sacral promontory, dorsal to the peritoneum. It is strongly ensconced in connective tissue at the most accessible portion of the abdomen for palpation.

II. Skeletopy (relation to osseous system). The interiliac nerve disc lies on the ventral surface of the distal lumbar and proximal sacral vertebræ. It lies practically on the brain of the inner osseous pelvis.

III. Syntopy (relation to adjacent viscera). The interiliac nerve disc, coalesced (unpaired), is located centrally in the space between the major aortic bifurcations which practically includes the ventral surface of the two distal lumbar and two proximal sacral vertebræ. It is securely ensconced in strong dorsal subperitoneal connective tissue. It is situated between the peritoneum and pelvic fascia. The interiliac nerve disc is limited to the space between the coalescence of the plexus aorticus (aortic bifurcation) and the emission or divergence of the plexus interiliacus (second sacral vertebræ). The interiliac nerve disc lies dorsal to certain changeable mobile loops of the enteron and mesenteron and possess variable relations to the sigmoid and mesosigmoid. In peritonotomy, in spare subjects, the interiliac nerve disc may be observed shimmering whitish through the dorsal peritoneum.

IV. Idiotopy (relation of the component segments). The interiliac nerve disc consists of a nerve plexus compressed, flattened, dorso-ventrally, and interspersed with fenestra of varying number and dimension. The fenestra increase in number and dimension from proximal to distal borders. *Dimensions.* The interiliacal disc is some two inches in length and three-

THE VASOMOTOR INTERILIAC PLEXUS

fourths of an inch in width. *Form.* The form is that of truncated cone. The lateral borders are bounded by nerve cords. The proximal border fuses with the plexus aorticus. The distal border coalesces with the emerging efferent lateral interiliacal plexuses.

GENERAL REMARKS IN REGARD TO THE INTERILIAC NERVE DISC.

It consists of a flattened, band-like nerve plexus in a sheath of firm, dense, connective tissue, located in the interval between the two common iliac arteries. It is formed by a continuation of the plexus aorticus plus prolongations from the ganglia lumbales. It is a flat plexiform nerve mass

FIG. 6.—PELVIC BRAIN.

PLEXUS INTERILIACUS OF ADULT

Fig. 10. This specimen I dissected with care under alcohol. The plexus interiliacus extends from the discus interiliacus (D) to the pelvic brain (A). Observe: (1) Two nerve strands are emitted from the interiliac plexus to the uterus previous to passing through the pelvic brain (A). (2) Note the contribution of the lateral sacral chain of ganglia and II and III sacral nerves to the plexus interiliacus. (3) Bear in mind the intimate relation of the plexus interiliacus to the rectum proximalward and distalward.

at the junction of the distal lumbar and proximal sacral vertebræ. I have termed it the interiliac nerve disc, as it contains no constant distinct ganglia. Some authors claim it contains no ganglia, while others claim it contains some ganglia, the latter being the more probable. The interiliac disc is significant as it emits (efferent nerves) from its distal border, the two nerve plexuses which rule the pelvic viscera. The interiliac nerve disc is an example of the principle elsewhere noted that at every emission of a major (visceral) artery from the abdominal aorta there exists a ganglion (or nerve disc). Practically there should be two ganglia at the aortic bifurcation. However, coalescence occurred and one ganglion or disc resulted—the interiliac nerve disc (or ganglion). Efferent nerve branches from the interiliac disc not only accompany the two common iliac, ovarian, superior hæmmorhoidal and sacral arteries but emit the two great interiliac plexuses (for the pelvic viscera) as well as branches to the ureters, left colon and sigmoid. The interiliac nerve disc is important in practice because it is practically accessible to manipulation, massage. By gentle irritation or massage of the interiliac disc in post partum hæmorrhage the plexus interiliacus will be stimulated, which, supplying the uterus, will induce the elastic and muscular bundles of the myometrium to act like living ligatures, limiting the uterine vessels, and checking hæmorrhage. It is not the supposed constriction of the aorta that checks the hæmorrhage.

(b) TRUNCUS PLEXUS INTERILIACUS SYMPATHICUS.

The trunk or central segment of the interiliac plexus (paired) extends from the interiliac nerve disc to the pelvic brain. The plexus interiliacus consists not merely of nerve strands, for it is composed of nerve plexuses the commissures and cords of which are band or ribbon-like in character surrounding apertures or fenestra of various dimensions which increase in area toward the distal end. The plexus interiliacus increases in breadth from proximal to distal end, i. e., from interiliac nerve disc to pelvic brain. The proximal end is relatively small and composed of a few nerve cords, the distal end is broad and divides into numerous branches. The course of the interiliac plexus is proximally along the internal side of the pelvic vessels while distally it courses along the dorsal and rectal wall with which it is intimately connected by connective tissue and, when it again resumes intimate association with the pelvic vessels the length of the trunk of the plexus interiliacus averages some 3½ inches. Numerous nerve branches from the V lumbar ganglion and from the I, II, III and IV sacral ganglia join the external border of the plexus interiliacus. From the internal border of the plexus interiliacus numerous branches pass to the rectum, ureter, uterus, vagina, bladder. From the plexus pass numerous nerves to the pelvic vessels. The trunk of the plexus interiliacus is profoundly associated with the rectal wall, sharing in its movements or contraction of and dilatation. The intimate and profound connections of the trunk of the plexus interiliacus with the rectal wall explains the favorable therapeutic value of the rectal enema due to stimulation of the plexus. The rectum is practically surrounded, ensheathed by two great bilateral interiliac plexuses, i. e., the rectum lies in the boot-jack angle produced by the divergence of the plexuses. The plexus interiliacus possesses a remarkable anatomic feature, which is that it sends some two strong nerves directly to the uterus without first passing through the pelvic brain (demonstrated with very extraordinary facility in infant cadavers).

THE VASOMOTOR INTERILIAC PLEXUS

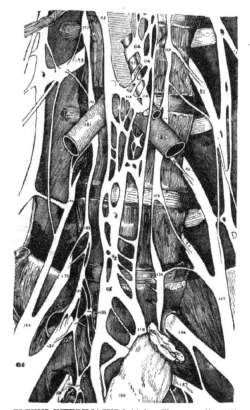

PLEXUS INTERILIACUS (with interiliac nerve disc, 115).

Fig. 11. I dissected this specimen in 1894 from a spare subject having enormously large vasomotor nerves' The aorta divided into the iliacs at the junction of the III and IV lumbar vertebræ. 112, genital ganglion; 173, third lumbar ganglion (R); 114, genito-rectal ganglion; 103, lumbar lateral chain of ganglia; 173, third lumbar nerve (R); 90, lumbar nerve; 91, lumbar nerve; 179, fourth lumbar ganglion (R); 104, lateral chain of ganglia; 181, com. iliac artery arising in this case at third lumbar vertebra; 188, inferior renal ganglia; 174, fourth lumbar nerve (R); 189, fifth lumbar ganglion (R); 93, lumbar nerves; 114, genital ganglion; 115, hypogastric plexus; 134, first sacral ganglion (L); 179, fourth lumbar ganglion (R); 116 hypogastric plexus; 125, lumbo-sacral cord; 135, first sacral ganglion (R); 136, genital ganglion; 118, hypogastric plexus; 126, first sacral nerve (L); 170, lumbar sacral cord; 130, first sacral nerve (R); 158, right sacral plexus; 137, second sacral ganglion; 117, hypogastric plexus; 156, rectum; 127, second sacral nerve (L). From author's life-size chart on the sympathetic nerve.

(c) DISTAL END OF THE PLEXUS INTERILIACUS OR PELVIC BRAIN.

The broad distal end of the plexus interiliacus, a plexiform fenestrated nerve mass, unites with the branches of the II, III and IV sacral nerves to form the pelvic brain (ganglion cervicale). The resulting union of the distal end of the plexus interiliacus and sacral nerves—a plexiform ganglionated mass, the pelvic brain—rules the physiology of the pelvic viscera, especially the vascularity of the genitals. The pelvic brain is elsewhere described in detail.

GENERAL REMARKS ON THE PLEXUS INTERILIACUS.

The plexus interiliacus, like the plexus aorticus, is one of the great and important nerve plexuses of the abdomen. It practically supplies the tractus genitalis; distal end of tractus intestinalis (rectal, sigmoid); and distal end of tractus urinarius (ureter, bladder). The plexus interiliacus is double, bilateral, presenting practically no anastomosis. It is accessible to manipulation through the abdominal wall as well as per rectum and per vaginam. Dilatation of the rectum produces its favorable therapeutic effects through the plexus interiliacus by flushing the capillaries and stimulating visceral function, especially respiration. The plexus interiliacus is the dominating plexus of the pelvis. It is the great assembling nerve center of the pelvic organs and is solidly and compactly bound and anastomosed to all other pelvic sympathetic nerves as well as the I, II, III and IV sacral spinal nerves. The following table presents an idea of the vast extent and richness of distribution of the branches of the plexus interiliacus. It should be remembered that the vast majority of the branches of the plexus interiliacus first pass through the pelvic brain before supplying the pelvic viscera (especially those to the tractus genitalis).

1. Tractus Intestinalis
   - (Hæmorrhoidal)
     - a, colon (left)
     - b, sigmoid
     - c, rectum

2. Tractus Genitalis
   - ovary
   - oviduct
   - ligamentum latum
   - uterus
   - vagina
   - pelvic subserosium

3. Tractus Urinarius
   - ureter
   - bladder
   - urethra

4. Tractus Vascularis
   - arterial plexuses accompanying all pelvic arteries

5. Tractus lymphaticus (all pelvic lymphatic glands are richly supplied).

A peculiar character of the plexus interiliacus is that it is considerably disassociated from arterial vessels—unlike the plexus aorticus. The pelvic visceral plexus or branches of the plexus interiliacus possess similar features. On the contrary, the visceral plexuses or branches of the abdominal brain notably accompanying the visceral arteries.

THE VASOMOTOR INTERILIAC PLEXUS

AGE RELATION OF THE PLEXUS INTERILIACUS.

The plexus interiliacus experiences an age relation according to the sexual phases as presented by the utero-ovarian artery in: (a) *pueritas*, (childhood), a quiescent, undeveloped state with limited blood, ganglion cells and neurilemma; (b) *pubertas*, a developmental state (of congestion) of multiplication of ganglion cells and increased neurilemma; (c) menstrual phase, a functional state of engorgement (of the vaso uterina), which

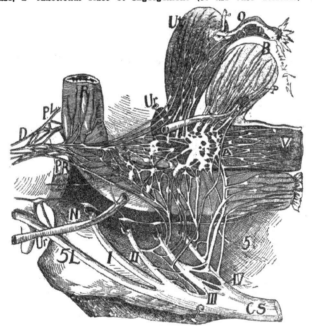

FIG. 3.—PELVIC BRAIN OF ADULT.

PLEXUS INTERILIACUS OF ADULT

Fig. 12. This specimen I dissected under alcohol. D, interiliac nerve disc. Interiliac plexus extending from the interiliac nerve disc (D) to the pelvic brain (A). Observe: (1) That two large nerve strands are emitted from the interiliac plexus to the uterus without first passing through the pelvic brain. (2) The plexus interiliacus is intimately associated with the rectum. (3) The lateral sacral chain of ganglia and sacral nerves contributes branches to the interiliac plexus.

The II, III, IV, and V sacral nerves contribute to form the pelvic brain, while in some specimens the I sacral nerve contributes a branch or branches.

further increases the neurilemma if not the ganglion cells; (c) *gestation*, a state of complete development of the tractus genitalis (continuous maximum engorgement of the utero-ovarian artery) with the multiplication of ganglion cells and periganglionic tissue with neurilemma; (d) *puerperium*. The elastic and muscular bundle of the myometrium having contracted like living ligatures, the enormous volume of blood passing through the utero-ovarian artery is checked, maximum engorgement suddenly ceases, the ganglion cells perhaps remain the same in number, however, decreasing in dimension; while the periganglionic tissue, the neurilemma and associated connective tissue decrease, degenerate; (e) *climacterium*. This phase of sexual life represents beginning atrophy from lessening of blood volume in the utero-ovarian artery. The ganglion cells diminish in size and number as well as the periganglionic tissue, while the associated connective tissue multiply; (f), *senescence*. This is the atrophic sexual phase—death of parenchymatous and increase of connective tissue framework of viscera. The muscularis and elastic fibres of the myometrium and oviduct decrease while the connective tissue increases. The wall of the utero-ovarian artery increases in thickness while the lumen decreases in dimension. The ganglion cells of the plexus interiliacus decrease in number and dimension while the ganglion cell, nucleus and body cell outlines become less distinct.

The periganglionic connective tissue and neurilemma decrease while the associated connective multiplies. In senescence the plexus interiliacus, which was originally destined for the tractus genitalis, gradually fades from its maximum dignity of structure and function. Senescence has returned the plexus interiliacus to its primitive phase of pueritas or quiescent existence.

UTILITY OF THE PLEXUS INTERILIACUS IN PRACTICE.

It is accessible to manipulation from proximal to distal end through the abdomen, per rectum or per vaginam. Massaging or stimulating the plexus interiliacus induces the muscular and elastic bundles of the organ which it supplies to contract by controlling the blood volume. The most typical example for the employment of therapeutics on the plexus interiliacus is during post-partum hæmorrhage. It is the irritation, massage of the plexus interiliacus, that induces muscular and elastic bundles of the myometrium to contract and consequently control the hæmorrhages. It is not the obstruction produced in the aorta by the pressure, the technique of which is almost impossible, for the two ovarian arteries would still continue to force large volumes of blood to the uterus. Light abdominal stroking, digital manipulation of the uterus in post-partum hæmorrhage irritates, massages the plexus interiliacus and its branches, which induce the elastic and muscular bundles of the uterus to contract like living ligatures on the blood vessels, checking hæmorrhage. The so-called uterine inertia of long, tedious labor may be due to paresis of the plexus interiliacus from trauma by the child's head. Sudden cessation of parturient peristalsis—arrest of labor—is doubtless due to trauma by the child's head on the plexus interiliacus, a sudden paresis. Vaginal or rectal injections (hot or medicated) stimulate the plexus interiliacus, hastening labor. Electricity will accomplish similar effects. The flat, band-like form of the plexus interiliacus protects it from trauma during parturition. Massage of the plexus interiliacus will end all alleviating constipation by stimulating active peristalsis and secretion of the left colon, sigmoid and rectum. The plexus interiliacus may be stimulated by means of hot fluid or food taken, in the stomach. The irritation passes from the stomach over the plexus gastricus to the abdominal brain, whence it is reorganized and emitted over the plexus interiliacus, inducing more vigorous uterine contractions. By appropriate systematic massage of the plexus interiliacus stimulation of the pelvic viscera may be effected, resulting in a vigorous circulation.

CHAPTER VII.

THE NERVES OF THE TRACTUS INTESTINALIS (NERVI TRACTUS INTESTINALIS).—(A) ANATOMY, (B) PHYSIOLOGY.

"To be or not to be, that is the question."—Shakespeare.
"I came, I saw, I conquered."—Cæsar's report to the Roman senate.

(A.) ANATOMY.

The abdominal sympathetic emits the great nerve plexuses to the tractus intestinalis (accompanying corresponding named arteries), viz.: (1) **plexus coeliacus** (unpaired) consisting of: (a) plexus gastricus; (b) plexus hepaticus; (c) plexus lienalis. (2) Plexus mesentericus superior (unpaired); (3) **plexus mesentericus inferior** (unpaired); (4) plexus hæmorrhoidalis medius et superior (paired). The above five nerve plexuses are not only solidly and compactly anastomosed, united with each other but are anastomosed, connected with all other abdominal plexuses. The nerves of the tractus intestinalis are *motor* (rhythm, peristalsis—Auerbach's plexuses), *secretory* (tubular visceral glands Meissner's plexus and glandular appendages) and *sensory* (peripheral reporters to the abdominal brain). The nerves of the tractus intestinalis are preponderatingly sympathetic, however, the cranial (vagi) share in supplying the proximal segment.

The spinal (second, third and fourth sacral) share in supplying the distal segment.

While the rami communicantes (spinal) share in supplying the medial segment, the abdominal brain was doubtless a primitive brain for the tractus vascularis and secondarily for the tractus intestinalis.

(1) *Plexus Coeliacus (Unpaired).*

The coeliac plexus arising from the abdominal brain is about one-half inch in length, encases the coeliac artery in a dense plexi-form network of nerves, cords, commissures and ganglia. It is the largest and most luxuriant sympathetic plexus surrounding the arteria coeliaca with a rich, closely fenestrated nerve sheath, solidly united by connective tissue. The origin of the coeliac plexus is the ganglion coeliacum located in the region of the emission of the great visceral arteries including three sources of nerves, viz.: (a) vagus, right (cranial); (b) splanchnic, the most important (spinal cord, rami communicantes); (c) sympathetic. The plexus coeliacus is one of the great assembling plexuses of the abdomen. It divides into three branches of vast importance in medical practice, viz.: (a) plexus gastricus; (b) plexus hepaticus; (c) plexus lienalis.

(a) *Plexus Gastricus (Unpaired).*

THE NERVES OF THE TRACTUS INTESTINALIS 63

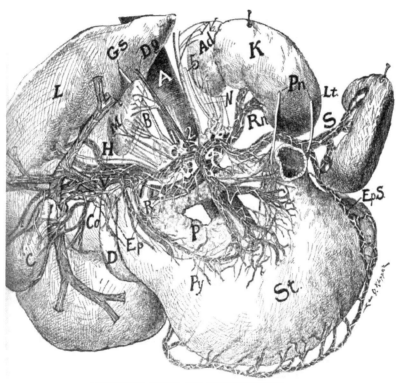

ABDOMINAL BRAIN AND CŒLIAC PLEXUS

Fig. 13. This figure presents the nerves of the proximal part of the tractus intestinalis that is, the nerve plexuses accompanying the branches of arteria cœliaca. 1 and 2 abdominal brain surrounding the cœliac axis drawn from dissected specimen. H. Hepatic plexus on hepatic artery. S. Splenic plexus on splenic artery. Gt. Gastric plexus on gastric artery. Rn. Renal artery (left). R. Right renal artery in the dissection was rich in ganglia. Dg. diaphragmatic artery with its ganglion. G. S. Great splanchnic nerve. Ad. Adrenal. K. Kidney. Pn. Pneumogastric (Lt. left). Ep. right and Eps. left epiploica artery. St. Stomach Py, Pyloric artery. C. cholecyst. Co. chole-dochus, N, adrenal nerves (right, 10, left 10). The arterial branches and loops of the cœliac tripod (as well as that of the renals) with their corresponding nerve plexuses demonstrate how solidly and compactly the viscera of the proximal abdomen are anastomosed, connected into single delicately poised system with the abdominal brain as a center. Hence local reflexes, as hepatic or renal calculus, disturb the accurate physiologic balance in stomach, kidney, spleen, liver and pancreas.

I. *Plexus Gastricus Superior.*—It is recognized as the plexus coronarius ventriculis superior. The accompanying table illustrates a scheme of gastric nerve supply.

1. Plexus gastricus superior (sympathetic) (plexus coronarius ventriculi superior).
  (a) Plexus ramus dexter.
  (b) Plexus ramus sinister.
(2) Plexus gastricus inferior (sympathetic) (plexus coronarius ventriculi inferior).
  (a) Plexus ramus dexter (arteria hepatica).
  (b) Plexus ramus sinister from (arteria lienalis).
3. Vagi plexuses (cranial).
Dorsal, ventral (cranial).

The gastric or superior coronary plexus consists of a fine plexiform network which ensheathes and accompanies the curved gastric artery along the lesser gastric curvature. It lies between (however, proximalward) to the two gastric plexuses of the vagi (cranial) dorsal and ventral anastomosing with both, hence solidly and compactly connecting, uniting the gastric plexuses (cranial) with the gastric plexuses (sympathetic).

II. *Plexus Gastricus Inferior.* (Unpaired). This is recognized as plexus coronarius ventriculi inferior. (The inferior gastric or coronary plexus supplying the greater curvature is mainly from the hepatic and splenic plexuses accompanying the arteria gastro-epiploica dextra et sinistra). The stomach is supplied by the cranial (vagus), right phrenic (spinal) and the sympathetic nerves from the plexus coeliacus. However, since the sympathetic nerves dominate in supply to the stomach it possesses a rhythm or peristalsis. The nerves of the sympathetic plexuses at first course beneath the peritoneum and finally penetrate the gastric muscularis, becoming Auerbach's plexus, destined to rule the gastric rhythm. The ultimate termination of the gastric sympathetic nerves becomes the Meissner-Bilroth plexus destined to rule the gastric secretion and absorption. The gastric rhythm is modified by the vagi (cranial) and spinal (ramus communicantes and phrenic). The location of the gastric nerves is important by reason of the diagnosis of gastric disease from pain and reflexes.

(b) *Plexus Hepaticus (Unpaired).*

The hepatic plexus (sympathetic) arises from the coeliac plexus and joining with the hepatic plexus (cranial) from the right (and left) vagus accompanies the arteria hepatica as a coarse plexiform sheathed network of nerves and ganglion (ganglia hepatica).

The hepatic plexus consists of strong flattened nerves arranged in the form of a closely fenestrated meshwork, surrounding the hepatic artery on its journey through the liver. A peculiarity of the hepatic plexus is that it emits plexuses to ramify on the vena porta and its branches in their course through the liver. The hepatic plexus is the largest and coarsest of the three branches of the coeliac plexus. The sympathetic nerves preponderate in the liver, hence it possesses a rhythm (through its elastic capsule, parenchymatous cells, vessels, biliary ducts).

The following plexuses, important in modern practice, are branches of the hepatic plexus:

PLEXUS HEPATICUS.

1. Plexus arteriæ hepaticæ.
    (a) Plexus ramus communis.
    (b) Plexus ramus dexter.
    (c) Plexus ramus sinister.
    (d) Plexus arteriæ pylori.
    (e) Plexus arteriæ gastricæ epiploicæ dextra.
2. Plexus ductus bilis.
    (f) Plexus ductus choledochi.
    (g) Plexus ductus cystici.
    (h) Plexus cholecysticus.
    (i) Plexus ductus hepatici.
3. Plexus venæ portæ.
    (j) Plexus ramus communis.
    (k) Plexus ramus dexter.
    (l) Plexus ramus sinister.

The hepatic nerve plexus accompanies the three important apparatus of the liver, viz.: (a) artery; (b) biliary channels; (c) portal vein; (d) the liver is supplied by nerves directly and indirectly from the abdominal brain.

(a) *Plexus arteriæ hepaticæ* consists of numerous strong gray nerve fibres arranged in a plexiform network ensheathing the hepatic artery. At the points of nerve crossing or anastomosis occur flat enlargements—ganglia hepatica. The plexiform network is a closely fenestrated sheath.

The branches of the hepatic plexus accompanies richly the branches of the hepatic artery through the five liver lobes; they accompany the pyloric artery to the lesser gastric curvature; they ensheath the arteria gastro epiploica dextra to the greater gastric curvature; they supply the duodenum and caput pancreatica and encase the two arteries which supply the lateral borders of the cholecyst. In short, the nerve plexuses accompany the hepatic artery and all its branches.

(b) *Plexus ductus bilis.* Nerves of the biliary channels consist of a rich plexiform network which accompanies and ensheaths each segment of the biliary passages, viz.: (1) ductus choledochus communis; (2) ductus cysticus; (3) cholecyst; (4) ductus hepaticus. Each of the segments of the biliary channels possess a fine meshed, grayish red, nongangliated nerve plexus. The localization of the nerve plexuses of the biliary passages, the direction of their reflexes with the position of reorganized focal symptoms are extremely important in the modern practice of cholelithiasis and inflammatory processes in the segments of the ductus bilis. In dissecting with a magnifying lens it is evident that the ductus bilis is rich in nerve plexuses. The nerve plexuses of the biliary channels are chiefly derived from the plexus arteriæ hepaticæ; however, large numbers of nerves pass to the biliary channels independent from the abdominal brain. Especially rich and abundant nerve plexuses are found accompanying the ductus choledochus communis, ductus cysticus and cholecyst, which explains the severity of the pain from infection of any of its segments inducing disordered, wild, violent peristalsis of the bile channels. Recent advances in surgery of the biliary passages have directed attention to the nerve supply of the bile channels. Dissection demonstrates that they are richly supplied with numerous nerve strands and ganglia which accounts for the terrible pain in cholecystitis calculosa. The different segments of the biliary passages are so abundantly supplied with nerves that they have assumed the name plexuses. The significance of the nerves of the biliary channels is evident in pain during the passage of a calculus or in pain from localized infection of any segment of the bile channels.

(c) *Plexus venæ portæ* consists of a strong plexiform network of nerves surrounding and accompanying the portal vein and its branches through the liver parenchyma. The portal vein is a voluminous tube with extensive ramifications in the liver and hence possesses an enormous nerve supply. The sympathetic nerve is destined for the arteries; however, the portal vein is a marked exception, as it receives an abundant sympathetic nerve supply. (I have traced large sympathetic nerve supplies to the vena cava distal).

The liver is supplied directly from the abdominal brain (sympathetic): (a) by nerves accompanying the arteria hepatica; (b) by nerves originating from the abdominal brain and passing directly to the liver; (c) by nerves originating in the abdominal brain and accompanying the venæ portæ; (d) (cranial) vagi, right (and left); (e) (spinal) right phrenic.

(c) *Plexus Lienalis (Unpaired).*

Plexus lienalis, a branch of the coeliac plexus, a fine and wide-meshed network of nerves accompanying the spiral splenic artery as a sheath to the spleen. The accompanying table presents the nerve supply of the spleen:

PLEXUS LIENALIS.

(a) Plexus arteriæ lienalis.
(b) Plexus ramus gastricus.
(c) Plexus ramus pancreaticus.

The plexus lienalis is less in dimension than the plexus hepaticus. The splenci plexus is joined by branches from the right vagus, which modifies the splenic rhythm. It furnishes a branch plexus to the arteria gastrica epiploica sinistra which courses along the major curvature of the stomach to meet the right artery of corresponding name. It emits branch plexuses to the pancreas. The splenic plexus emits branches from the omentum majus. The splenic plexus anastomoses with the plexus suprarenalis. Practically the splenic plexus supplies the left half of the stomach, the spleen, and the pancreas.

The main nerves of the plexus lienalis, much diminished from omission

THE NERVES OF THE TRACTUS INTESTINALIS

of branches, enters the hilum of the spleen with the sheath of the splenic artery to be distributed to the splenic parenchyma to the Malpigian bodies.

(2.) *Plexus Mesentericus Superior (Unpaired).*

The superior or proximal mesenteric plexus consists of large, coarse, dense, whitish gray nerve fibres which arise in the abdominal brain at the

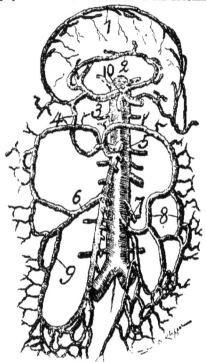

THE SOLID AND COMPACTLY ANASTOMOSING ARTERIES OF THE TRACTUS INTESTINALIS

Fig. 14. This illustration demonstrates that the arteries of the tractus intestinalis are solidly and compactly anastomosed by vascular circles, arcs and arcades. To recall the plexus vasomotorius abdominalis one need to remember the arteriæ abdominalis only. The circles, arcs and arcades of the abdominal arteries are richly ensheathed with a nodular plexus of nerves. 10 arteria cœliaca emitting the arterial tripod (tripus Halleri), hepatic, splenic and gastric, presenting circles, arcs and arcades. 5 arteria mesenterica superior with its circles, arcs and arcades. 7, arteria mesenterica inferior with its circles, arcs and arcades. 2-10, gastro-hepatic vascular circle (of author) anastomosed to the circles, arcs and arcades of the superior mesenteric arteries with their circles, arcs and arcades by means of the arteria pancreati co-duodenalis superior (a branch of the hepatic) and arteria duodenalis inferior (a branch of the superior mesenteric artery).

root of the arteria mesenterica superior, which it accompanies as a plexiform network of nerves and ganglia. Branches of right vagus joins the plexus. The superior mesenteric plexus is composed of thick, flat, ganglionated masses (ganglia mesenterica superior) of oval, crescentic or stellate form, which, woven into thick sheath, surrounds the superior mesenteric artery and accompanies it to the enteron (with the exception of the duodenum) and colon (with the exception of the left colon, sigmoid and rectum). The plexus mesentericus superior not only arises from the entire abdominal brain but from the plexus renalis, bilateral. It also arises by several cords from the plexus aorticus abdominalis.

The plexus mesentericus superior contains ganglia relatively less in number and dimension than the plexus coeliacus.

A smaller portion of the plexus mesentericus superior accompanies the arteria pancreatico-duodenalis inferior proximalward to the duodenum and caput pancreatica (rami pancreatici duodenales).

The greater portion courses on the arteria mesenterica superior distalward in the form of a long white closely fenestrated plexiform sheath to the enteron, coecum, right and transverse colon (rami enteron and rami colici).

The nerves course between the blades of the mesenteron and mesocolon partly closely adjacent to the artery and partly at a distance from the same. The nerves anastomose here and there more irregularly than the arteries as curved arches. The termination of the plexus mesentericus superior is: (a) between the longitudinal and circular muscles of the enteron and colon—ruling rhythm—(plexus myentericus externus—Auerbach's, Leopold Auerbach, German Anatomist Prof. at Breslau, 1823-1897); (b) in the intestinal submucosa—ruling secretion—(plexus myentericus internus—Meissner-Bilroth, George Meissner, 1829-1905, German Anatomist Prof. in Goettongen. Theodor Bilroth, German—Prof. surgery in Vienna, 1829-1894, German Surgeon Prof. in Vienna). The meshwork of the plexus myentericus internus is not so regular nor the ganglia so large or numerous as that of the plexus myentericus externus. On the nerve plexuses which accompany the vasa intestini tennis and on the nerve plexuses more distantly removed from the vessels, may be found diminutive plexuses and ganglia. The nerves end in the wall of the tractus intestinalis as automatic visceral ganglia. Ganglia exist at the origin of the arteria mesenterica superior which endow the enteron with several, three or four rhythms, daily (three meals). There may be more or less. The superior mesenteric plexus is fan-formed, is the largest plexus in the abdomen. It accompanies the mesenteric artery coursing dorsal to the pancreas. The mesenteric nerves are remarkable for strength, number, length and thickness of their neuri lemma. They are placed in contact with the vessels and also at variable distances from the same. They course toward the intestine in straight lines without emitting branches. At a limited distance from the concave intestinal border they pass directly toward the enteron and colon, or they anastomose with an adjacent nerve at an angle or in an arch. From the convexity of the anastomotic arches the branches pass directly to supply the enteron and part of the colon. There is only one series, row, of nerve arches in the plexus mesentericus superior regardless of the number of series, rows, of arterial arches (in the vasa intestini tennis). The simple nerve arch corresponds to the vascular arch, the most adjacent to the intestine. The superior mesenteric plexus anastomoses with the renal ganglia, plexus mesentericus inferior and ovarica. Practically it is a continuation of the plexus coeliacus and aorticus abdominis.

(3) *Plexus Mesentericus Inferior (Unpaired.)*

The inferior mesenteric plexus consists of a rich plexiform network of nerves and ganglia ensheathing and accompanying the inferior mesenteric artery to the left colon, sigmoid and rectum (as nervi colici sinistri et

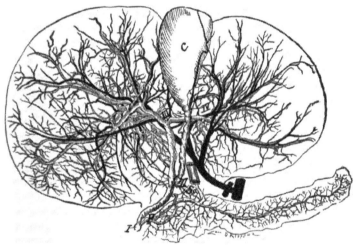

NERVES OF THE HEPATIC ARTERY AND BILIARY DUCT

Fig. 15. Presents the copy of an X-ray of the hepatic artery, biliary and pancreatic ducts which are each richly ensheathed by a nodular, plexiform web of nerves. The quantity of nerves may be estimated by the number of arteries and ducts in the liver and pancreas. I, Vater's papilla at duodenal end of ductus chcledochus communis. II, junction of ductus hepaticus (III) and ductus cysticus (IV). C, cholcyst, P, ductus pancreaticus, Sa, ductus pancreaticus accessorius. The black conduit coursing parallel to the biliary ducts is the hepatic artery.

hæmorrhoidales superiores). It arises from the aortic plexus and especially from the ganglion located at the origin of the arteria mesenterica inferior (ganglion mesenteric inferior) as well as from the lumbar lateral ganglionic chain (plexus lumbales aorticus). The fenestra or meshwork of the inferior mesenteric plexus are not so compact or close as that of the superior mesenteric plexus. The nerves of this plexus form in its course subordinate plexuses, accompanying or lying between the arterial branches, and produce curved, arc anastomoses. They terminate the colonic muscularis as Auerbach's plexus (rhythm) and the colonic submucosa as Meissner-Bilroth plexus (secretion and absorption).

The plexus mesentericus inferior arises from: (a) abdominal brain (plexus mesentericus superior); (b) plexus aorticus; (c) ganglion mesentericum inferior.

The plexus mesentericus inferior is not only solidly and compactly anastomosed in all its branches, but solidly and compactly with all other abdominal sympathetic plexuses. There exist nerve nodes—ganglia mesenterica inferior—along the course of the plexus. At the origin of the arteria mesenterica inferior there is located a mass of nerve tissue—ganglion mesentericum inferior—which doubtless endows the fæcal reservoir (left colon, sigmoid and rectum) with a daily rhythm for fæcal evacuation. The inferior mesenteric plexus anastomoses or is connected with: (a) second lumbar ganglion in the lateral chain; (b) plexus aorticus abdominalis; (c) plexus mesentericus superior; (d) plexus ovaricus; (e) plexus hypogastricus; (f) plexus hæmorrhoidalis (medius and inferior) from the arteria pudendalis. The plexus mesentericus inferior ends in the colonic wall as automatic visceral ganglia, Auerbach's (plexus myenteric externus) and Bilroth-Meissner's (plexus myentericus internus). The nerves of the inferior mesenteric plexus are remarkable for their tennity, length and general non-branching state. The nerves of the inferior mesenteric plexus are not the most numerous in the mesosigmoid. The plexus mesentericus inferior terminates, like the inferior mesenteric artery, by bifurcating the two divisions of this bifurcation are called the hæmorrhoidal plexus superior. They course bilaterally distalward on the rectal wall accompanying two lateral superior hæmorrhoidal, terminating partly in the rectum and partly in the plexus hypogastricus.

(4) *Plexus Hæmorrhoidalis Medius et Inferior (Paired).*

The sources of the median and inferior hæmorrhoidal plexuses are: (1) from the dorsal part of the plexus hypogastricus; (2) the nerves accompanying the middle (vaginal) and inferior hæmorrhoidal artery; (3) from the pelvic brain (ganglion cervicale). The numerous nerves course bilaterally through the mesorectum to the rectum. The proximal portion of the two hæmorrhoidal plexuses curve proximalward to anastomose with the plexus hæmorrhoidalis superior. The distal portion passes distalward to supply the rectum and vagina. Small swellings may occur at the nerve crossings or anastomoses, however, ganglia hæmorrhoidalia are doubtful nervus hæmorrhoidalis medius and inferior are branches of the plexus pudendus. The nerves of the tractus intestinalis are not an independent system as it is solidly and compactly anastomosed with all other abnormal systems. However the hæmorrhoidal nerves are a spur which complicates the distal end of the intestinal tract and separates the great partially independent nerves of the tractus intestinalis for the rectum. The change is due to the distalward movement of parts of the tractus genitalis and tractus urinarius

THE NERVES OF THE TRACTUS INTESTINALIS 71

and their function with the rectum. In general I think the older anatomists with the exception especially of Henle represented the nerves and ganglia supplying the tractus intestinalis rather too rich, too abundant. Tedious dissection will lessen the number of nerve strands by eliminating white fibrous connective tissue.

(b) *Physiology of the Nerves of the Tractus Intestinalis.*

The physiology of the nerve plexus supplying the tractus intestinalis is important both theoretic and practical. The sympathetic nerves dominate,

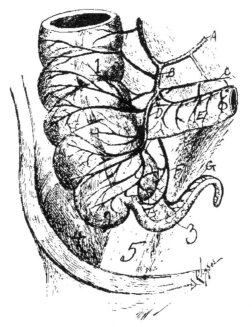

ARTERIES OF CÆCUM AND APPENDIX

Fig. 16. The nerves in the important appendiculo-cæcal region may be estimated by observing an illustration of the arteries of this segment of the tractus intestinalis. The nervus vasomotorius richly ensheaths the artery in a plexiform network.

rule, the intestinal tract, hence it possesses a rhythm, peristalsis—only sympathetic ganglia possess the power of rhythm. In the physiology of organs the course of nerves must be considered. First, the vagus (as cranial nerve) supplies the proximal end of the tractus intestinalis as well as its appendage; especially the liver with numerous fibres. The vagus aids to check rhythm, especially of the stomach. Second, the spinal nerves at the distal end of the tractus intestinalis particularly the middle and inferior hæmorrhoidal nerves supplying the rectum and interfering with its rhythm or peristalsis. The spinal nerve attending the rectum places it partially under the will in controlling to some extent the evacuation of fæces or gas. Third, there is the great splanchnic nerves, chief delegates in the function, rhythm or peristalsis of the tractus intestinalis (median) especially in the enteron or business segment. The splanchnic nerves though preponderatingly sympathetic possess a rich source in the spinal cord. Therefore though the tractus intestinalis is preponderatingly supplied with sympathetic nerves (hence rhythmic) it is supplied at its proximal end by cranial nerves (vagi) and at its distal end by spinal nerves (hæmorrhoidal). The general function of the tractus intestinalis under the sympathetic nerve is: (a) peristalsis (rhythm); (b) absorption; (c) secretion. Its object is digestion. The business of a physician is chiefly to aid in maintaining normal functions, i. e., peristalsis, absorption and secretion in the intestinal tract. In the general application of the physiology of the nerves of the tractus intestinalis for practical purposes there should be considered: (a) those of the proximal end, stomach and appendages; (b) the nerves supplying the medial region (enteron) and (c) the nerves supplying the distal end (colon). The great sympathetic nerve plexuses accompany the arteries.

(a) *The Physiology of the Nerves of the Proximal End of the Tractus Intestinalis (Stomach, Liver, Spleen and Pancreas).*

Since the arterial branches of the coeliac axis (hepatic, gastric and splentic) are solidly and compactly anastomosed at their peripheries by means of circles and arcs the three branches of the coeliac plexus which accompany the hepatic, gastric and splenic arteries are solidly and compactly anastomosed on the arterial circles and arcs. This anatomic fact solidly and compactly anastomoses the nerve plexuses of the liver, stomach, pancreas and spleen as well as that of the duodenum and pancreas forming a single apparatus thus inducing the nerve arrangement of the liver, stomach, duodenum, pancreas and spleen to act as a unit or single apparatus with the abdominal brain as a reflex, focal or reorganizing center. In practice this is found true, e. g., the irritation of a calculus in a segment of the biliary passages from inflammation or irritation will be transmitted to the abdominal brain as a focal center, become reorganized and emitted over the gastric plexus, inducing nausea or vomiting, thus disordering the gastric rhythm. Irritating food or liquid (alcohol) in the stomach quickly disorders the hepatic rhythm and if gall stone be present hepatic colic is liable to arise. Again, the introduction of food and fluid into the stomach incites the rhythm, peristalsis and secretion of the stomach, liver, duodenum and pancreas, demonstrating the anatomic and consequently the physiologic connection and anastomoses of the nerve plexus apparatus of the stomach, liver, duodenum, pancreas (and spleen). The nerve apparatus of the viscera in the proximal abdomen is a finely balanced structure with the abdominal brain as a reorganizing, focal, center. Subjects with hepatic calculus are ample evidence of the solid and compact anastomoses of the nerves of the stomach and liver, for they avoid many kinds of food, as their experience has taught that stimulating foods in the stomach will excite hepatic colic. The rhythm of the proximal end of the tractus intestinalis (stomach) being supplied by two powerful cranial nerves (vagi) is the most irregular of any segment of the intestinal tract.

(b) *Physiology of the Nerves Supplying the Middle Region of the Tractus Intestinalis (Enteron).*

The superior mesenteric plexus is the largest and richest sympathetic plexus in the body. It has an extensive and an enormous surface area (a

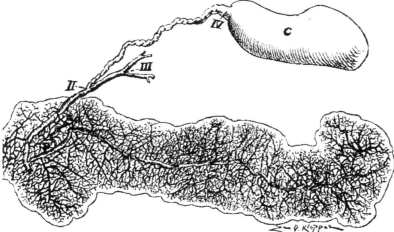

AN X-RAY OF THE DUCTUS PANCREATICUS AND PART OF THE DUCTUS BILIS

Fig. 17. This illustration represents the ductus pancreaticus with its lateral ducts, all of which are richly ensheathed in a plexiform, nodular meshwork of nerves. It is an X-ray of part of the ductus bilis and ductus pancreaticus of a girl of 11 years old. I to II, ductus choledochus communis. II to III, ductus hepaticus. II to IV, ductus cysticus. C, cholecyst. It is easy to observe the segments of the pancreas, viz.:—caput, collum, corpus, cauda. In fact, this beautiful accurate illustration establishes final anatomy. Sa, ductus Santorini functionated as the celloidin projected from its exit duct during the injecting of it. The proper eponym for the pancreatic secretory channel is the Hofman-Wirsung duct. The liver of this patient was advanced in sarcomatous disease but the pancreas appeared healthy. P, ductus pancreaticus.

truncate cone, the base of which is twenty-one feet; apex six inches; height six inches—covering an area of many square feet). The superior mesenteric plexus consists of a closely fenestrated meshwork of powerful nerves and ganglia ensheathing in a plexiform manner the superior mesenteric artery which practically supplies the digestive portion of the tractus intestinalis.

The first factor in the physiology of the superior mesenteric plexus is that it controls the volume of blood-supply of the enteron. It is nervus vasomotorius of the enteron. Stimulation of the splanchnics (which constitutes the major portion of the superior mesenteric plexus) produces hyperæmia of the enteron. The function of the enteron depends on its blood supply. The stimulus which induces necessary blood supply to the enteron for digestion is the irritation that the food produces on its mucosa. A full enteron is hyperæmic, active one. An empty, evacuated enteron is an anaemic, quiet one. The three great manifest functions of the superior mesenteric plexus is to produce in the enteron rhythm, peristalsis, secretion and absorption. There can be little doubt that included in the rhythm of the enteron (dependent on hyperæmia) is the factors of secretion and absorption. So long as enteronic rhythm is not interfered or especially the enteronic (fœcal) current is not obstructed the enteron performs its function (rhymth, secretion and absorption.) However, as soon as mechanical obstruction to the enteronic (food) current occurs (as flexion, volvulus stricture) the nondrainage induces residual deposits resulting in accumulation of bacteria and consequent infection. The enteron possesses a periodioc rhythm about every six hours (ingested meals and fluids) which enables absorption and secretion to complete itself and the rhythm to transport the residual *debris to the colon.*

(c) *The Physiology of the Nerves at the Distal End of the Tractus Intestinalis.*

The physiology of the sympathetic nerve at the distal end of the tractus intestinalis is interfered, complicated by the addition of the spinal nerves (as the proximal end is complicated by the addition of the cranial nerves—vagi). The physiology of the distal end of the tractus intestinalis (left colon, sigmoid and rectum) is chiefly included in the so-called hæmorrhoidal nerves—a developmental addition, an imposition on the original markedly independent sympathetic nervous system of the intestinal tract, through the coalesce of the tractus intestinalis, tractus genitalis and tractus urinarius—the coloaca has disappeared and its place is supplied by a rectal, vaginal and urethral sphincter. The hæmorrhoidal nerves are a spur which complicates anatomically and physiologically the distal end of the intestinal tract and separates the great practically independent nerves (plexus mesentericus inferior) of the tractus intestinalis from the rectum. The hæmorrhoidal nerves can not manifest definite action on the tractus intestinalis (left colon, sigmoid and rectum) which I shall term the fæcal reservoir, which has a daily rhythm. It is practically, for local purpose, under the rule of the inferior mesenteric ganglion. Numerous phenomena of the rectum in disease, in pain, do not belong to the sympathetic nerve but to the spinal nerves accompanying it, as the sharp pains in the anal fissure.

The expiratory moan resembling the bray of an ass in rectal dilatation is explained by the irritation being transmitted over the hæmorrhoidal plexuses (inferior medius and superior) to the abdominal brain, whence it may pass: first, over the diaphragmatic plexus (right side) to the right phrenic nerve (contracting the diaphragm); second, over the splanchnics to the inferior cervical ganglion, which is connected to the phrenic by a nerve cord, whence the route is direct to the diaphragm (inducing the diaphragm to contract); third, the irritation from the rectal dilatation may pass over the third and fourth sacral nerves, proximalward of the spinal cord to the cranial cerebrum where reorganization and emission occurs over the cord and phrenic nerve to the diaphragm, inducing contraction and an expiratory moan or bray. The disordered functions of the digestive canal are chiefly excessive (diarrhœa, colic),'deficient (constipation), or disproportionate (fermentation). In the excessive rhythm (colic) or secretion of the tractus intestinalis, we possess effective remedies, as anatomic and physiologic rest; with the holding of food and fluids and the administration of anodynes (opiates). The treatment consists in securing normal rhythm, peristalsis, absorption and secretion. In deficient rhythm (constipation) and secretion in the tractus intestinalis we possess effective remedies in the restoration of the normal rhythm and secretion as diet. Coarse food, as cereals and vegetables, leave ample fæcal residue to stimulate the colon, intestine to vigorous peristalsis; the evacuation of the colon at regular intervals; exercise and massage of the abdomen; electricity. It is a known physiologic principle that regular habits of bowel evacuation daily will maintain the rhythm normal, but that neglect of regular evacuation will destroy the rhythm; in fact, induce constipation. The normal rhythm of bowel evacuation is a delicate matter and mental disturbance, change of habits, different environments, may viciate the rhythm of the fæcal reservoir (left colon, sigmoid and rectum). In disproportionate peristalsis (colic) and secretion (fermentation), the effective remedy is to regulate the diet and fluid to restore normal rhythm and secretion; to introduce disinfectants to check fermentation, as sulphocarbolates. It will be observed that the sympathetic system of the entire tractus intestinalis, consisting of six great plexuses (nerve cords and ganglia), viz.: (a) gastric; (b) hepatic; (c) splenic; (d) superior mesenteric; (e) inferior mesenteric; (f) hæmorrhoidal, is not only profoundly connected with the coeliac plexus or abdominal brain, but the five plexuses are all solidly and compactly anastomosed, bound together and also anastomosed (connected) with all other plexuses of the abdominal visceral tracts, in order that the chief potentate—the abdominal brain—may rule as a single unit of power. No conflict of power arises, as all ganglia of the tractus intestinalis are subordinate to the abdominal brain—however, local rulers, as the ganglion mesentericum inferior, are allowed to rule, to dominate, with a daily rhythm, the fæcal reservoir (left colon, sigmoid and rectum). The nerve plexuses of the various abdominal visceral tracts are anastomosed, connected, solidly and compactly, in order to maintain a balanced system and for local and general physiologic reports to the abdominal brain.

CHAPTER VIII.

NERVES OF THE TRACTUS URINARIUS (NERVI TRACTUS URINARIUS).—(A) ANATOMY, (B) PHYSIOLOGY.

These are times which try men's souls.—Thomas Paine.
The object of research is not to know the truth merely but to discover something that will benefit some one—relieve suffering and prolong life.

(A) ANATOMY.

To the urinary tract pass nerves from: (1) plexus suprarenalis, (2) plexus renalis, (3) plexus ureteris, (4) plexus ovaricus, (5) ganglia lumbales, (6) plexus communis arteriæ iliacus, (7) ganglia sacrales, (8) plexus hypogastricus (9) plexus vesicalis, (10) plexus urethralis, (11) plexus mesentericus superior, (12) plexus mesentericus inferior, (13) plexus arteriæ uterinæ, (14) plexus sacralis (spinal). The above nerve plexuses solidly and compactly anastomose with each other and with all abdominal sympathetic plexuses, thus connecting the tractus urinarius intimately and profoundly through the nerve plexuses with all other abdominal viscera.

(1) *The Plexus Suprarenalis (Paired).*

Bilaterally from the external border and proximal angle of the abdominal brain depart from five to eight coarser and finer nerves to supply the adrenals. These nerves are remarkably developed in infancy. The strands of the suprarenal plexus possess many small ganglionic masses in their course, and at the points of division. For the small adrenal the nerve supply is enormous. In the plexus suprarenalis may be found the ganglion suprarenale or nervus splanchnicus minores. The plexus suprarenalis sends branches to the plexus renalis and on the right side also branches to the plexus diaphragmaticus.

(2) *Plexus Renalis (Paired).*

Bilaterally from the external border and distal lateral angle of the abdominal brain departs a wide meshed plexus of nerves along the renal arteries to the kidneys. The renal plexus is composed of larger and smaller ganglia with larger and smaller strands and it is extensively fenestrated. Nerve branches from the renal ganglia course distalward on the ureter and obliquely medianward to join the plexus aorticus. The renal plexus is one of the richest in ganglia and strands. In fact, the renal plexus frequently appears as a continuation of the cœliac ganglion. There is a profound and solid connection between kidney and abdominal brain. The renal plexus ensheathes the renal artery with a network of ganglia and cords arriving at the kidney through the hilum. The plexus renalis receives strands from the second and third ganglia of the lumbar lateral chain. The renal plexus is connected with the plexus mesentericus superior and inferior. The renal plexus arises from: (a), the major splanchnic; (b), the minor splanchnic; (c),

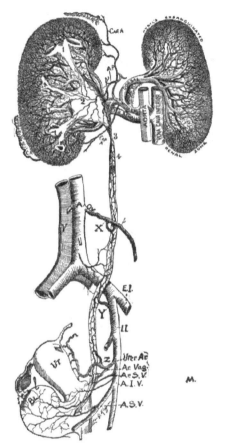

ARTERIAL SUPPLY OF THE TRACTUS URINARIUS

Fig. 18. The proximal part of the figure is from corrosion anatomy. The nerve supply to the tractus urinarius is perhaps best remembered by recalling its blood supply, for the sympathetic nerves accompany the vessels, especially the arteries. The arteries to the tractus urinarius are: (a) the arteria adrenalis; arteria renalis; arteria ovarica (spermatica), (x) arteria media ureteris, (y) arteria uterina, (z) the three vesical arteries, observe each of which is accompanied by its plexus of nerves. The tractus urinarius is richly beset with vasomotor nerves. This anatomic fact is evident from the violent symptoms induced by an ureteral calculus. See also Fig. 8, for rich ganglia renalia.

the first lumbar ganglion; (d), the cœliac ganglion; (e), plexus mesentericus superior; (f) plexus aorticus—six sources. Each renal plexus contains four to six ganglia. A profound connection, anastomosis, exists between the renal plexus and plexus aorticus, hypogastricus and ovaricus—*i. e.*, the kidney and genitals are profoundly and solidly connected or anastomosed, by nerve cords and ganglia.

The renal plexus is practically all sympathetic. Certain nerve nodes—ganglia renalia—remarkable for number and dimension—are distributed in the plexus renalis. The largest renal ganglia lie on the ventral surface of the renal artery, while several smaller ones lie in the bifurcations of the arteria renalis and on the distal and proximal border of the renal artery.

The plexus renalis receives some branches from the plexus adrenalis and the plexus mesentericus superior. The nervus splanchnicus minor supplies a branch to the plexus renalis which is frequently strengthened by branches from the two proximal ganglia of the lateral lumbar chain.

(3) *Plexus Ureteris (Paired)*.

The ureter is supplied by a rich plexus of nerves from many sources, as may be observed from its vigorous and brusque rhythm, resembling cardiac contraction. The ureter consists of calcyces, pelvis and ureter proper, and each segment is supplied in a degree from different areas of the abdominal sympathetic, and lumbar and sacral chain of ganglia, however, united into one unit of power in order that the ureteral rhythm may be periodic and orderly from proximal to distal end. The ureter is supplied by:—(a), plexus renalis; (b), plexus aorticus; (c), plexus ovaricus (spermaticus); (d), lumbar lateral chain; (e), sacral lateral chain; (f), plexus hypogastricus; (g), plexus arteriæ; (h), plexus mesentericus superior; (i), plexus mesentericus inferior; (j), sacral nerves—ten sources. By the silver method on fresh ureters of animals we could demonstrate rich plexuses or networks of nerves on the walls of the ureter, with ganglia at the union of junction of the anastomosing nerves. Three strong and important points of rich anastomoses of the plexus ovaricus and plexus uterinus with the plexus ureteris occurs at (a), where the ureteris is crossed ventrally by the vasa ovarica (spermatica) which solidly unites the ureteral and ovarian (spermatic) nerve plexuses. This explains the reflex pain of ureteral irritation (*e. g.* calculus) on the ovary or testicle—(retraction). (b), Where the ureter crosses dorsally to the arteria uterina a strong and solid anastomosis occurs between the plexus ureteris and plexus arteriæ uterinæ. Ureteral irritation (*e. g.* calculus) may be transmitted to the uterus (genitals) and bladder. (c), The plexus ureteris and plexus communis arteriæiliacus solidly anastomose at the point where the ureter crosses ventrally to the iliac arteries. This explains the reflex pain in the thigh during ureteral irritation, *e. g.*, ureteral calculus.

(4) *Plexus Ovaricus (Spermaticus—Paired)*.

The ovarian plexus arises from the plexus aorticus, extending from the ganglion cœliacum, located at the arteria cœliaca, to the ganglion hypogastricum, located on the promontorium. Its chief origin is from the ganglion ovaricum. Immediately subsequent to its origin from the plexus aorticus it presents about a dozen nerve strands which gradually coalesce and converge into three main nerves trunks, studded with ganglia, and accompany the vasa ovarica to the ovary. At the point where the vasa ovarica crosses ventral to the ureter the accompanying plexus ovaricus forms a rich anastamosis with the plexus ureteris. This anastamosis of the plexus ovaricus with the plexus ureteris explains the reflex pains of the irritated ureter (ureteritis, calculus) in

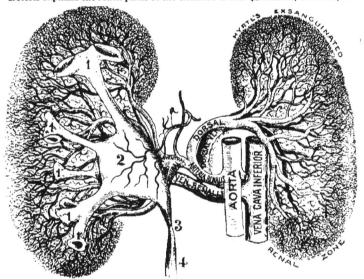

NERVES OF THE TRACTUS URINARIUS—CORROSION ANATOMY

Fig. 19. This specimen presents quite faithfully the circulation, the kidney, calyces and pelvis. The two renal vascular blades I present opened like a book. The corrosion was on the left kidney and the larger vascular blade is the ventral one. The vasomotor nerves accompanying the urinary tract may be estimated by the fact that a rich plexiform network of nerves ensheath the arteries, the calyces, pelvis and ureter proper. When the renal vascular blades are shut like a book their thin edges come in contact, but do not anastomose. The edges of the vascular blades are what I term the exsanguinated renal zone of Hyrtl, who discovered it in 1868, and we, at present, employ it for incising the kidney to gain entrance to the interior of the calyces and pelvis with minimum hæmorrhage.

the ovary and uterus (testicle retraction). The anastomosis of the plexus ovaricus with the plexus ureteris solidly and compactly connects the ureter with the entire length of the plexus aorticus.

(5) *Ganglia Lumbales* (*Paired*).

The two proximal lumbar ganglia send branches to the proximal plexus ureteris, as well as branches to the plexus renalis and plexus ovaricus, thus supplying the proximal end of the ureter.

(6) *Plexus Iliacus Communis Arteriæ (Paired).*

A small artery springs from the common iliac and supplies the lumbar spindle of the ureter. This solidly connects the plexus ureteris with the plexus of nerves that accompanies the iliac and femoral vessels, accounting for the pain in the thigh during attacks from ureteral calculus and ureteritis.

(7) *Ganglia Sacrales (Paired).*

The proximal sacral ganglia send branches to and anastomose with the plexus ureteris, thus intimately connecting the pelvic ureter with all other sympathetic pelvic plexuses.

(8) *Plexus Hypogastricus (Paired).*

This powerful plexus sends several branches to the pelvic ureter, solidly anastomosing the ureter with the genital tract.

(9) *Plexus Vesicalis (Paired).*

The vesical plexus consists of a wide meshed network of nerves supplying the bladder with greater and smaller ganglia studding the plexus at the junction of the anastomosing nerves. The vesical plexus arises from: (a), plexus hypogastricus; (b), ganglion cervicis uteri; (c), nervi sacrales; (d), lateral sacral chain; (e), nerve plexuses following the course of the three vesical arteries (superior, middle and inferior) derived from the hypogastric plexus, (a large spinal nerve supplies the bladder from the third sacral, thus making a mixed nerve supply to the bladder). The rhythm of the bladder (systole and diastole) is not so apparent as that of some other organs, as the ureter, heart, uterus or enteron, being modified by the interference of the spinal nerves.

The vesical plexus is a leash of nerves which supplies the distal ureter and bladder. So far as I can learn from dissection, it originates in the pelvic brain (ganglion cervicale). The plexus vesicalis solidly anastomoses with all other sympathetic plexuses in the pelvis.

(10) *Plexus Mesentericus Superior (Unpaired).*

Sends some branches to the proximal end of the ureter.

(11) *Plexus Mesentericus Inferior (Unpaired).*

Sends several branches to the ureter. Nos. 10 and 11 anastomose the ureter with the tractus intestinalis, and hence when ureteral pain arises it will be diffused through the intestines, and will confuse ureteral and intestinal colic.

(12) *Plexus Arteriæ Uterinæ (Paired).*

The uterine artery is accompanied by a strong nerve plexus ensheathing it. At the point where the uterine artery crosses ventrally to the uterer the nerve plexuses of the artery and ureter anastomose with each other. This explains the uterine reflex pain during attacks of ureteral calculus and ureteritis.

NERVES OF THE TRACTUS URINARIUS

(13) *Plexus Urethralis (Paired)*.

The urethral plexus is a continuation of the vesical plexus accompanied by the sympathetic nerves which arrive at the urethra on the supplying blood vessels.

The above thirteen plexuses are sympathetic, hence it is evident that the tractus urinarius is dominated by the sympathetic nerve in its function (rhythm).

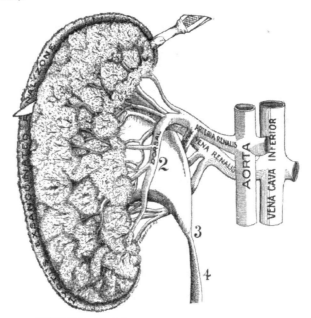

CORROSION ANATOMY (Hyrtl's exsanguinated renal zone)

Fig. 20. In this specimen of corrosion anatomy the renal vascular blades (ventral and dorsal) are closed like a book. It presents (left kidney) on the margin of the dorsal lateral surface the exsanguinated zone of Hyrtl—the line of minimal hæmorrhage for cortical renal incision. A rational method to estimate the quantity of nerves of the tractus urinarius is to expose the number and dimension of the arteries and other tubular ducts which are ensheathed in a plexiform network—a fenestrated, nodular, neural vagina of nerves.

(14) *Plexus Sacralis (Spinal)*.

The sacral spinal plexus sends nerves to the bladder, and hence gives rise to a mixed nerve supply. However, the sympathetic dominates, as it compels the bladder to assume rhythm (diastole and systole). The chief spinal nerve to the bladder arises from the III sacral, and supplies the body of the bladder.

(B) PHYSIOLOGY.

The establishment of the nerve supply to the tractus urinarius serves as a foundation to an understanding of its physiology. A complete nervous system comprises (a) a peripheral apparatus, (b) a conducting cord, and (c) a ganglion cell. The object of the nervous system is that the peripheral apparatus shall collect data (sensation), the conducting cord shall transport it, and the nerve ganglion shall reorganize and utilize the nerve forces.

The collection, transportation, and utilization of nerve forces from and to the tractus urinarius is a matter of vast importance in diagnosis and practice.

The function of the tractus urinarius is practically comprised in four acts, viz.:—peristalsis (rhythm) secretion, sensation and absorption. All visceral muscles, being under the sympathetic nerves, must execute rhythm, contract and relax, or atrophy. The object of the kidney is to secrete fluid while the object of the urinary tract (ureter, bladder and urethra) is to conduct a stream of fluid to the external body by means of periodic rhythmical movements. From ureteral sensibility, $i. e.$, from urine flowing on the sensitive ureteral mucosa, every three to five minutes a brusque, peristaltic wave passes from the proximal to the distal end of the ureter. The vesical and urethral waves are more irregular, as the bladder is practically a reservoir. The periodic ureteral peristalsis is due to the sympathetic ganglia located within the ureteral wall. So long as the ureteral peristalisis is not interfered and especially the ureteral stream is not obstructed, the ureters perform their periodic rhythm. However, as soon as mechanical obstruction to the ureteral stream arises (as from flexion, calculus, ureteritis or stricture) the non-drainage induces residual deposits with resulting accumulations of bacteria, whence the vicious circle occurs in the tractus urinarius exactly similar to the vicious circles arising from obstruction in the pylorus or the biliary ducts. The urinary ducts are independent organs conducting the urine to the external body by means of rhythmic, periodic waves, regardless of the bodily attitude or force of gravity. The kidney is a composite organ, consisting of numerous secretory organs—malpigian corpuscles and tubuli uriniferi—and no doubt these secrete rhythmically, periodically, though the urine exists constantly in the ureteral calcyces and pelvis—that being the accumulative results of secretion. The sympathetic nerve, however, is a silent, ceaseless, painless agent, unconsciously increasing its function—rhythm, secretion and absorption—as food and fluid are offered.

It should be remembered that nerve forces travel in the direction of least resistance, $i. e.$, a nerve plexus containing the greatest number of nerve strands. It is not multiplication of ganglion cells that increases intelligence, it is multiplication of nerve connecting cords that facilitates transmission. Hence in diseases of the channels of the tractus urinarius, as calculus, stricture, ureteral flexion, or ureteritis, the organs connected with the tractus urinarius by the greatest number of nerve strands will suffer the most trauma. For example, in ureteral calculus the pathologic irritation from

NERVES OF THE TRACTUS URINARIUS

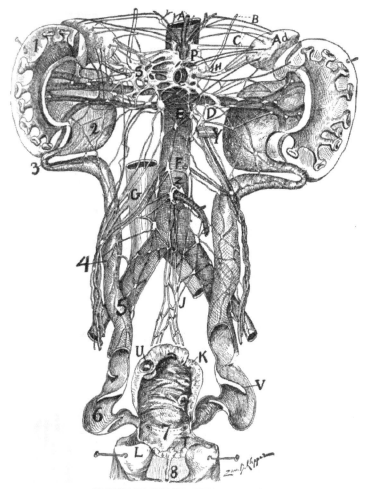

NERVES OF THE TRACTUS URINARIUS

Fig. 21. The nerves of the urinary tract were dissected in this specimen under alcohol. The ureters, which I term swan-shaped, were irregularly dilated and contained valves (V), SP, abdominal brain, D, ganglia renalis distributed over the dilated ureteral pelvis. C. plexus adrenalis. The plexus ureteris is rich in plexiform network. B, great splanchnic, Observe that the proximal ureteral isthmus (neck) lying in a groove in the renal pole is not dilated.

the ureter passes over the giant renal plexus to the abdominal brain, whence reorganization and emission occurs on the plexus gastricus to the stomach, inducing nausea or vomiting. Again, the plexus ureteris is profoundly connected or anastomosed with the plexus ovaricus (spermaticus); hence during attacks of calculus the testicle suffers pain and is retracted, also the ovary suffers pain. In short, an irritation in the tractus urinarius will induce the most pain in the viscera possessing the plexuses with the greatest number of nerve strands.

The influence of the plexus ureteris is patent when micturition is so urgent and irregular in the presence of calculus or ureteritis. The plexus

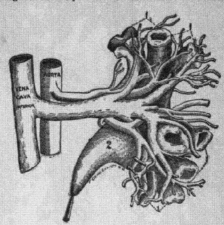

CORROSION ANATOMY

Fig. 22. This specimen of corrosion anatomy presents the ureteral calyces, ureteral pelvis, and proximal end of ureter proper together with the arteria and vena renalis. All segments except the vein are ensheathed in a rich plexiform network of the nerves governing peristalsis, absorption, secretion, sensation. When a ureteral calculus becomes mobile in the ureter, peristalsis (violent) and sensation (pain) become evident.

vesicalis is influential in indicating the line of pain in calculus, and the plexus urethralis is a continuation of it, localizing the pain in the glans penis (male) and the pudendum and clitoris (female). Hence, as regards pain in the tractus urinarius, it aids in diagnosis by manifesting the most prominent symptoms along the nerve plexus containing the greatest number of nerve strands, such as the plexis renalis (stomach—vomiting), plexus ovaricus or spermaticus (retraction of the testicle).

Since the nerve plexuses of the tractus urinarius are solidly and compactly anastomosed with all the other nerve plexuses of the abdominal sympathetic, the pain from ureteral disturbances is rather diffuse. However, since the nerve plexuses of the tractus urinarius are extensively and profoundly connected with the plexuses of the tractus genitalis, ureteral disturbances are more intensely reflected over the plexuses of the tractus genitalis, *e. g.*, in the nerve plexus of the ovary, pudendum, clitoris (female), and of the testicle, perineum, penis (male).

As regards lithiasis, the chief manifestation from the tractus urinarius is pathologic physiology, that is, disordered function, rhythm, absorption,

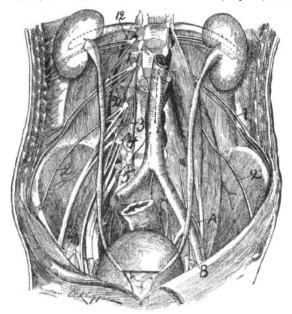

RELATION OF SPINAL NERVES TO TRACTUS URINARIUS

Fig. 23. Illustrates the relation of the spinal nerves to the ureter, especially its plexus lumbalis. The ureter is intimately connected with the genito-crural nerve (A), hence the pain reflected in the thigh and scrotum in ureteral colic and other ureteral diseases. (2) Ileo-inguinal nerve. For illustration of ureteral nerves and legend of same, See fig. 24.

or secretion. Hence the clue to the local disorder must be sought in the nerve plexuses suffering most intensely, associated with the tractus urinarius. For example, in calculus there may be the reno-uterine reflex, the reno-testicular reflex, all indicating intense pain along the above-indicated nerve plexuses.

The stamping pain of Clement Lucas is where one afflicted with a ureteral calculus stands on one foot and stamps, which places the psoas muscle on a violent tension, and traumatizes, massages the ureter, which, if it possesses a calculus, will induce vigorous ureteral peristalsis and consequent ureteral pain, colic. Jordan Lloyd's method of inducing pain in the ureter with calculus, by a blow on the erector spinæ muscles, is simply another process by which the lumbar muscles (especially the psoas) massages the ureter, exciting vigorous ureteral peristalsis and consequent pain and colic.

The explanation of pain intensified in different regions of the body during attacks of calculus or other diseases of the tractus urinarius must be sought in the line of the nerve plexuses and their anastomoses with other nerve plexuses. For example, ureteral calculus produces pain in the plexus spermaticus (pain and retraction of the testicle) because the plexus ureteris anastomoses with the plexus spermaticus where the ureter is crossed ventrally by it (vasa spermatica). A useful suggestion for remembering the nerve plexus of the tractus urinarius is to recall the arterial supply, as the ureteral nerve plexuses accompany the arteries of the tractus urinarius.

The function of the tractus urinarius is rhythm (peristalsis), absorption, sensation, and secretion. The rhythm keeps its tract always full. It is a perfect system of waterworks whose stop-cocks or sphincters are always in order and on guard.

CHAPTER IX.

THE NERVES OF THE GENITAL TRACT (NERVI TRACTUS GENITALIS)—(A) ANATOMY, (B) PHYSIOLOGY.

The American government is not in any sense founded upon the Christian religion.—Treaty with Tripoli signed by President George Washington.

The appointive power of a political party vitalizes its energy and locates its responsibility.

(A) ANATOMY.

The origin of genital nerves are: I, nervus vasomotorius (sympathetic—abdominal brain); II, spinal cord (medulla spinalis), through rami communicantes and rami nervorum sacralium (II, III, IV), cerebrum (vagi).

The three major nerve streams to the tractus genitalis are (a) the plexus interiliacus (which is a continuation of the plexus aorticus) originating in the abdominal brain; (b) the plexus ovaricus originating from the whole plexus aorticus; (c) plexus sacralis spinalis (rami nervorum sacralium—II, III, IV). The minor nerve streams to the tractus genitalis are: (d) lateral lumbar ganglia (truncus nervus lumbales vasomotorius); (e) lateral pelvic ganglia (truncus nervus pelvis vasomotorius); (f) nerves of the uterine artery (nervi arteriæ uterinæ); (g) nerves of the hypogastric artery (nervi arteriæ hypogastricæ) richly demonstrated in infant cadavers. Also nerves of the round ligament and hemorrhoidal arteries.

Practically the nerves supplying the tractus genitalis are solidly and compactly anastomosed connected with the whole abdominal vasomotor nerves (sympathetic), especially with the giant ganglion cœliacum—the abdominal brain—the great assembling center of the vasomotorius abdominale or sympathetic nerve plexus. The anastomosis or connection of the genital nerves to the nervus vasomotorius (sympathetic) and cerebro-spinal is vast and profound. The order of solidarity or compactness of anastomosis or profundity of connection of the vasomotor nerves (sympathetic) to the abdominal viscera is the following, viz.: (A) nervus vasomotorius to the tractus vascularis (blood and lymph vessels); (B) nervus vasomotorius to tractus intestinalis; (C) nervus vasomotorius to tractus genitalis; (D) nervus vasomotorius to tractus urinarius. However, all the abdominal viscera are solidly and compactly anastomosed, connected to the central abdominal sympathetic or vasomotor nerve that no one visceral system can become disturbed, deranged, without affecting profoundly all other visceral systems. The derangement arising in the several abdominal visceral systems caused by irritation or disease in any one abdominal visceral system is produced by reflexes, resulting in the disturbed common visceral function—peristalsis, secretion, absorption, sensation. So far as I am able to observe, the reflexes, or irritation in the tractus genitalis produces the most profound and vast derangement of function in other abdominal viscera of any single visceral system, *e.g.*, irritation, disease in the tractus genitalis, passes to the abdominal brain (over the plexus interiliacus and plexus aorticus) where it is reorganized and emitted to the tractus intestinalis or tractus urinarius, deranging the common function of peristalsis (rhythm), secretion, sensation and absorption—causing deficient, excessive or disproportionate peristalsis, secretion or absorption. The older anatomists, like the philosophic Willis (1622-1675), who was the Sedlian professor in Cambridge, claimed that the nerves supplying the tractus genitalis arose from the intercostal nerves, that is, by means of the rami communicantes, truncus vasomotorius—lateral ganglionic chain and nervi splanchnici. This is as true today as in the days of the ever-memorable Willis; however, we ascribe today more to independent, more differentiation to the vasomotor nerves (sympathetic) than did Willis. These so-called intercostal nerves (rami communicantes) form a nervous center— the abdominal brain—secondary to the cranial brain, which has differentiated functions of the first magnitude as regards existence of life itself. Hence, today we are inclined to believe from experimentation and clinical data that the chief origin of the nerves of the tractus genitalis is the abdominal brain —cerebrum abdominale, and since this giant ganglion controls the vascular supply of the abdominal viscera it should be termed cerebrum vasculare abdominale. In the consideration of the nerve supply of the tractus genitalis it is favorable for convenience of description and practical purposes to present a major and minor nerve stream. The following table presents in a bird's-eye view the major and minor nerve supply to the genital tract:

Major Nerve Supply.

A. Plexus interiliacus (sympathicus).
B. Plexus ovaricus.
C. Plexus sacralis spinalis (rami nervorum sacralium).

Minor Nerve Supply.

D. Lateral lumbar ganglia (truncus nervus sympathicus lumbales).
E. Lateral pelvic ganglia (truncus sympathicus sacrales).
F. Nerves of the uterine artery (nervi arteriæ uterinæ).
G. Nerves of the hypogastric artery (nervi arteriæ hypogastricæ).
H. Nerves of the round ligament artery (nervi arteriæ ligamenti rotundi).

Fig. 24. An illustration of the pelvic brain (B) and the nerve supply in the pelvis, uterus and bladder and rectum. Ut, uterus (with its plexus uterinus); Vs, bladder (with its plexus vesicalis); Ov, ovary (with its plexus ovarica); Od, oviduct (with its plexus oviductus); R, rectum (with its plexus rectalis); GS, great sciatic nerve; 5L, last lumbar nerve; I, II, III, IV, sacral nerves. The nerves supplying the ureter are from (a) the I sacral ganglia (see u on ureter); (b), hypogastric plexus (at P); (c) the III sacral nerve (at X); (d), pelvic brain (at B). The pelvic brain (B) originates the plexus uterinus, plexus vaginalis, plexus rectalis. Suggestions for this drawing were employed from Frankenhauser. H, interiliac nerve disc (the original visceral ganglion located at the aortic bifurcation—at present a dorsoventrally flattened nerve disc with limited number of ganglion cells). S. G., the five sacral ganglia. 16 (a), right ureter at junction with vasa ovarica. Note anastomosis of plexus ureteris and plexus ovarica explaining pain of ureteral calculus in testicle and in ovary. 16, some relations on left side. For illustrations of the nerves of the tractus genitalis see previous figures.

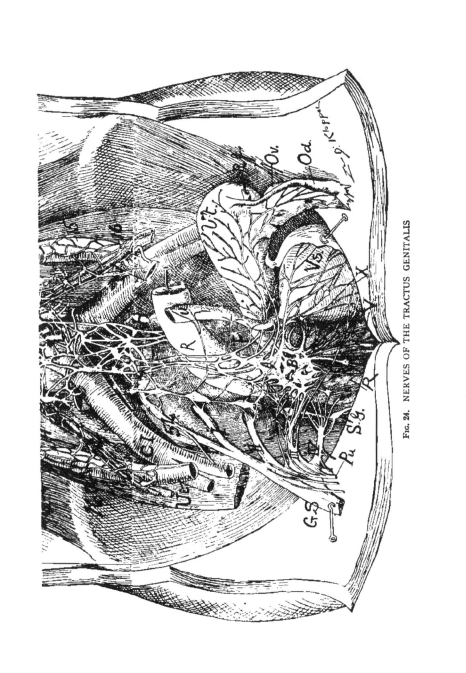

FIG. 24. NERVES OF THE TRACTUS GENITALIS

I. Nerves of the hemorrhoidal artery superior et medius (nervi arteriæ hemorrhoidalis superior et medius).

The major nerve supply consists of (A) plexus ovaricus; (B) plexus interiliacus (vasomotorius); (C) plexus sacralis spinalis rami nervorum sacralium (II, III, IV).

(A) Plexus Ovaricus.

Origin. -According to my dissection the main origin of the ovarian nerves is from the ganglion ovaricum proximal, a definite ganglion of irregular form and dimension located at the origin of the arteria ovarica on the aorta. However, the plexus ovaricus arises also from the adjacent regions in the plexus aorticus both proximal and distal to the ovarian ganglion, especially it may be noted that the renal ganglia contribute ovarian nerves. Frankenhauser (1867) in one of his tables marks the origin of the ovarian nerves extending from the root of the arteria renalis to the interiliac nerve disc located on the sacral promontory. He notes the ovarian nerve composed at the origin of some twelve separate strands, and as they pass distalward on the vasa ovarica coalesce into three main trunks, studded with ganglia. In dissecting it will be observed that the ganglia renalia and ganglia ovarica are closely associated in a solidly fenestrated network indicating identical origin from the Wolffian body. I could not discover such an abundant ovarian nerve supply neither from such an extensive area of the plexus aorticus, as reported by Frankenhauser. However, the explanation may lie in the fact that Frankenhauser dissections were from non-pregnant and infant genitals. The sections disclosed large numbers of nerve fibres originating in various regions from the plexus aorticus, especially the ganglia renalia and ganglia ovarica proximal and directing themselves toward the vasa ovarica coalesce into some three nerve trunks. The ovarian nerves coerce with the ovarian vessels, forming an elongated wide network studded with nerve ganglia limited in number and dimension and located at the crossing, junction of the nerve strands.

The ovarian nerves arise from the ganglion ovaricum proximal in the form of a plexus or a leash which accompanies and ensheaths the arteria ovarica to the union with the vena, ovarica, where both the vein and artery share more equally the attention of the ovarian nerves. The plexus ovaricus in general arises from the following ganglia, viz.: (a) ganglion ovaricum (proximal); (b) ganglia renalia; (c) ganglion mesentericum inferior; (d) ganglia lumbalis. The above ganglia are solidly and compactly connected with the ganglion cœliacum.

(*Note.*—It should be remembered that the numerous pains of which woman complains as being in the ovaries are not located in the ovaries, but reside in the cutaneous distribution of the ileo inguinal and ileo hypogastric nerves. It is hyperesthesia of the skin).

The plexus ovaricus arises from the following plexuses: (a) plexus aorticus; (b) plexus renalis; (c) plexus mesentericus superior; (d) plexus mesentericus inferior; (e) plexus ureteris (where the vasa ovarica cross

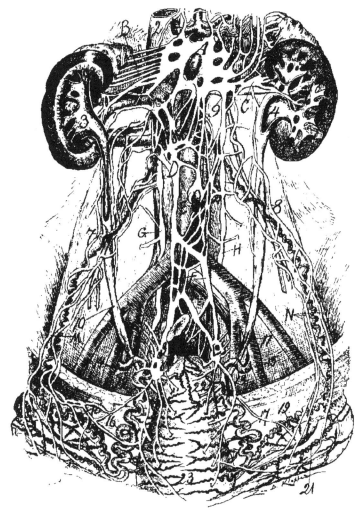

NERVES OF TRACTUS GENITALIS PREGNANT ABOUT THREE MONTHS

Fig. 25. This illustration presents the nerves on its genital vascular circle at about three months gestation. The fundus of the uterus is drawn distalward, exposing its dorsal surface. A, abdominal brain. The pelvic brain is faintly represented. The plexus ovaricus is carefully presented.

ventral to the ureter the plexus ovaricus becomes anastomosed with the plexus ureteris, further solidly anastomosing the plexus ovaricus with the plexus renalis); (f) plexus interiliacus; (g) the plexus ovaricus receives branches from the genito-crural nerve, again solidly anastomosing the plexus lumbalis (spinal) with the plexus ovaricus (sympathetic).

Course.—The plexus ovaricus accompanies the vasa ovarica in their extended journey to the pelvis in erect animals in the form of sheathed network of nerves with extremely elongated fenestra. The plexus ovaricus in its course is studded with spare ganglia of various size. The nerves of the plexus, like many other sympathetic plexuses, are cylindrical—not flat like those of the plexus uterinus—and retain their caliber throughout their course. Toward the distal end of the vasa ovarica the vein and artery become more branched, occupying more space, whence the plexus ovaricus divides its branches to accompany the additional vessels. The distal end of the plexus ovaricus divides and supplies: (a) the ovary; (b) the oviduct; (c) ligamentum latum; (d) the lateral border of the uterus; (e) it anastomoses with branches of the plexus interiliacus.

(*B*) *Plexus Interiliacus (Vasomotorius).*

The interiliac plexus extends from the interialic nerve disc to its union with the sacral nerves of the cervico-vaginal junction. It is the major nerve-supply of the genitals. It is elsewhere described in detail.

(*C*) *Plexus Sacralis Spinalis (Rami Nervorum Sacralium).*

The second, third and fourth sacral, spinal nerves emit branches (pelvic splanchnics) which join, coalesce, with the distal branches of the interiliac plexus to form the pelvic brain (ganglion cervicale—which issues the white rami communicantes) practically the plexus uterinus, plexus vesicalis, plexus rectalis, plexus vaginalis, plexus clitoridis, plexus pudendalis. The spinal sacral nerves passing to the pelvic brain gave rise to the idea that they supplied the cervix uteri, and that they are sensory nerves of the uterus. So far as I have been able to observe, all branches of the sacral spinal nerves first enter the pelvic brain before passing to the uterus and vagina. One nerve from the second sacral passes directly to the bladder without first passing through the pelvic brain. The branches of the sacral nerve passing to the pelvic brain vary in number, origin, arrangement, length, and dimension. They are the most accurately demonstrated in infant cadavers preserved in alcohol. The blending or coalescence of the branches of the sacral nerves (pelvic splanchnics) (I to IV) with the distal branches of the plexus interiliacus (vasomotorius) results in the pelvic brain—a plexiform, multiple, nodular ganglionic nerve mass located where the rectum joins the cervico-vaginal junction, and being of irregular form, dimension, weight. The pelvic brain is practically the source of the genital nerves. The minor nerve supply of the tractus genitalis consists of D, E, F, G, H, I.

(D). The lateral lumbar trunk ganglia send nerves to the plexus aorticus and plexus interiliacus.

(E). The lateral pelvic trunk ganglia send nerves to the genitals by way of the pelvic brain. It sends nerves to the distal ureter.

(F). The nerves accompanying the internal iliac artery continue their course over the arteria uterina as the nervi arteriæ uterinæ.

(G). The nerves of the hypogastric artery (nervi arteriæ hypogastricæ) carries larger numbers of nerves to the genitals in the infant. It also emits branches to the ureter and bladder. With atrophy of the hypogastric artery many nerves fade with the artery.

(H). Nerves of the round ligament artery (nervi arteriæ ligamenti

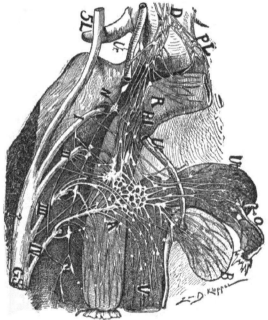

FIG. I.—PELVIC BRAIN OF AN INFANT.

GENITAL NERVES OF INFANT

Fig. 26. The plexus interiliacus in this infant extends from the discus interiliacus (D) to the pelvic brain. (A) A segment of the ureter (Ur) is removed in order to expose the interiliac plexus as it is in relation with the rectum (R). Observe first that the interiliac plexus receives contributing nerves from the I, II and III sacral nerves. Second observe that the interiliac plexus emits three nerve strands to the uterus (Ut), which do not first pass through the pelvic brain. (A) Third, note the large nerve supply that the rectum receives from the plexus interiliacus. This illustration I dissected under alcohol and it was drawn by the aid of a highly magnifying lens. A non-developed pelvic brain. The plexuses of the pelvic brain—uterine, vaginal, vesical and rectal—are distinct.

rotundi) pass from the external common iliac artery to join with the plexus ovaricus and plexus uterinus.

(I). Nerves of the hemorrhoidal artery superior and medial (nervi arteriæ hemorrhoidalis superior et medius) emit nerves to the genitals. It will be observed that the major and minor nerve supply of the genitals is so extensive, so solidly and compactly anastomosed that severing the genital nerves for experimentation is incompatible with life, and consequently reports of such experiments are of limited value only.

The Plexuses of the Pelvic Brain.

The pelvic brain practically emits the nerves to the pelvic viscera, but especially the plexuses of the genital tract. The table represents the scheme:

Plexuses of the Pelvic Brain.—1. Plexus uterinus. 2. Plexus vaginalis. 3. Plexus vesicalis. 4. Plexus rectalis.

1. *Plexus uterinus* is emitted to the uterus from the pelvic brain. In infant cadavers I have counted as many as eight different strands of nerves passing from the pelvic brain to the uterus. In the infant cadavers one can observe several nerves passing from the pelvic brain over the external border of the ureter to penetrate finally the myometrium. The first proposition to assert is that the uterus is practically supplied by two plexuses, viz.: (a) the plexus interiliacus (hypogastricus) sends one (two or three) branches directly to the uterus without first entering the pelvic brain; (b) the plexus uterinus, which passes directly from the pelvic brain to the uterus, where it anastomoses with the branches of the plexus interiliacus. Hence the uterus is supplied by branches of the plexus interiliacus directly from the abdominal brain and the plexus uterinus directly from the pelvic brain—leaving the abdominal brain as the chief ruling potentate of the abdominal viscera, while the pelvic brain is a subordinate, local, ruler of the pelvic viscera. The plexus uterinus accompanies the uterine vessels in general only—not in particular like the intimate relation of the plexuses of the abdominal brain to its visceral vessels. The plexus uterinus presents large, strong branches to the cervix uteri, which is unusually rich in nerve supply. The order of richness of nerve supply to the uterus is (a) cervix, luxuriant; (b) corpus, rich; (c) fundus uteri, abundant. The form of the nerve supply to the uterus imitates it, viz.: fan-shaped. In the illustrations of the nerves of the uterus what is presented is the main superficial branches of the plexus interiliacus and plexus uterinus which accompany the major uterine arteries the most intimately along the lateral uterine borders (see figure 3).

The branches from the plexus interiliacus (one to three) are distributed on the dorsal wall of the cervix, becoming distributed on the dorso-lateral border of the fundus uteri, where they anastomose with the branches of the plexus ovaricus at the junction of the uterus and oviduct, where is located (especially marked in infants) a ganglion. The dorsal surface of the fundus also receives numerous branches from the branches of the plexus interiliacus. Finally the branches directly from the plexus interiliacus (which is directly from the abdominal brain through the plexus aorticus) supply strong, large

THE NERVES OF THE GENITAL TRACT

nerves which are richly distributed to the cervix, corpus, fundus, and oviduct. They anastomose solidly and compactly with the plexus ovaricus and plexus uterinus from the pelvic brain. The plexus uterinus—major nerve supply to the uterus—originates in the pelvic brain. The plexus uterinus, like the plexus interiliacus, approaches the uterus from the neck and lateral border. This leash of ganglionated uterine nerves from the cervico-uterine ganglion in contradistinction to the branches of the plexus interiliacus, supplies the

GENITAL NERVES OF ADULT

Fig. 27. This specimen I dissected with care under alcohol. The plexus interiliacus extends from the discus interiliacus (1) to the pelvic brain (A). Observe: (1) Three nerve strands are emitted from the interiliac plexus to the uterus previous to passing through the pelvic brain (A). (2) Note the contribution of the lateral sacral chain of ganglia and II, III and IV sacral nerves to the plexus interiliacus. (3) Bear in mind the intimate relation of the plexus interiliacus to the rectum proximalward and distalward. Observe the ganglionated plexuses from the pelvic brain—uterine, vaginal, vesical, rectal.

ventro-lateral border of the uterus, and courses more intimately in relation with the uterine segment of the utero-ovarian artery. Many of the large nerves of this plexus are superficial, simulating the superficial position of the artery. As the branches of the plexus interiliacus (direct from the abdominal brain) richly supply the dorsal surface of the corpus and fundus uteri so that the plexus uterinus (directly from the pelvic brain) luxuriantly supplies the ventral surface of the cervix, corpus and fundus uteri. Branches from the vesical ganglia pass to the plexus uterinus, thus aiding to make the uterus and bladder act clinically as one organ. The solidly anastomosed plexuses of the uterine nerves continually increasing their area of distribution and their number of multiplying peripheral branches as they proceed toward the fundus, finally sends branches to anastomose with the plexus ovaricus, especially at the oviductal junction, where lies a marked ganglion. This utero-oviductal ganglion appears to be the nerve center from which radiate nerves to the fundus uteri and distal oviduct as well as to the muscular plates lying in the ligamentum latum. The entire uterus is surrounded and traversed by a closely woven network of ganglionated nerve plexuses. The microscopic ganglia are most numerous in the region of the cervix, especially adjacent to the pelvic brain. The uterus is abundantly and luxuriantly supplied by vasomotor sympathetic nerves from which, could we dissolve the substance of the uterus, leaving the network, they would appear like a spider's web. It must be remembered that the uterus is a coalesced organ, and hence the adult nerve supply is a complex affair resembling the adult circulation, which is most extraordinarily demonstrated by corrosion anatomy.

2. *Plexus vaginalis* is emitted from the pelvic brain to the vagina. The vaginal plexus is a rich leash or ganglionated plexus of nerves which surround the vagina like a network of cords surrounding a rubber ball. The vaginal nerve plexus and vaginal vein plexus, both rich, complicated and abundant, intertwine and interweave with each other. The rich vaginal plexus is bedecked with numerous ganglia at the points of nerve convergence. The meshes of the vaginal plexus, being occupied by fatty tissue, connective tissue, lymph and blood vessels, its dissection is accompanied with difficulty. Infant cadavers should be chosen to facilitate correct exposure of the finer constituents of the vaginal plexus. As the bladder is supplied by a large branch from the third sacral nerve, so the vagina is supplied from a large branch of the fourth sacral nerve. The ganglionated nerve cords from the pelvic brain surround the vagina like a mighty network, ventrally and dorsally. The vaginal plexus also emits many large nerves to the rectum and bladder. The ventral vaginal nerve leashes course proximalward and distalward. The larger ganglia of the vaginal leash or plexus occur at the proximal ventral vaginal fornix, while on the distal ventral end of the vagina the ganglia are numerous, but more limited in dimensions. The ganglia of the dorsal vaginal wall is limited in number. The entire vagina is completely surrounded by a closely woven ganglionated nerve network. These perivaginal and paravaginal plexuses stand in intimate relation with the pelvic brain.

Toward the central longitudinal axis of the uterus and vagina the genital plexuses diminish, simulating exactly the genital blood and lymph supply.

8. *Plexus vesicalis* is emitted from the pelvic brain to the bladder. The vesical plexus is of the powerful, rich, ganglionated plexuses or leashes of the pelvic brain. It is solidly and compactly anastomosed to the plexus rectalis, but especially to the plexus uterinus, inducing the rectum, uterus

THE NERVES OF THE GENITAL TRACT

and bladder to act clinically or symptomatically as one apparatus. For description see nerves of tractus urinarius.

4. *Plexus rectalis* is emitted from the pelvic brain to the rectum as rich network of nerves bedecked with ganglia limited in number and dimension. The rectal plexus emitted by the pelvic brain is a fine plexiform leash of nerves which passes distalward on the lateral borders of the rectum, intimately blending with the tissues of the rectal wall. The rectum has not only a rich and complicated nerve supply, but it has a mixed nerve supply. The following table presents a general view of a rectal nerve supply:

Rectal Nerve Supply.

1. Plexus hemorrhoidalis superior (from the arteria mesenterica superior).

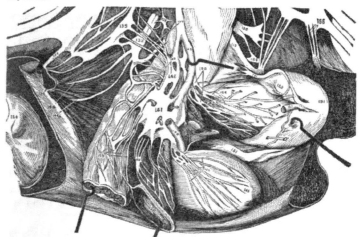

THE NERVES OF THE TRACTUS GENITALIS

Fig. 28. This illustration is a dissection I made ten years ago from a spare subject. The trunk of the cadaver I preserved in alcohol for six months. The vesical, rectal, uterine and vaginal plexuses are evident as they issue from the pelvic brain, which is an elongated ganglionic mass.

2. Plexus interiliacus (from the abdominal brain).

3. Plexus hemorrhoidalis medius (accompanying the arteria hemorrhoidalis media).

4. Plexus hemorrhoidalis inferior (from the arteria hemorrhoidalis inferior and plexus pudendalis sacralis—mixed vasomotor and spinal nerves).

5. Plexus rectalis (from pelvic brain—a powerful, rich nerve plexus solidly anastomosed to the plexus uterinus and vesicalis).

6. Plexus sacralis spinalis (branches from the second, third and fourth sacral nerves).

7. Truncus pelvis sympathicus (lateral sacral ganglia).

The three great hemorrhoidal plexuses arriving at the rectum via the three hemorrhoidal arteries invest it with a network of rich nerve plexuses. A rich leash of nerves passes to the rectum from the plexus interiliacus. Part of the branches of the plexus pass proximalward on the rectum to anastomose with the plexus hemorrhoidalis inferior (from the inferior mesenteric plexus) while part passes distalward on the rectum, penetrating its coats. Some of the branches of the hemorrhoidal plexus supply the bladder and genitals. From this anatomic distribution of the hemorrhoidal plexus—to genitals, rectum and bladder—it is obvious that the genitals, rectum and bladder are solidly and compactly anastomosed. Clinical work demonstrates this balanced union of organs in the pelvis through nerve connection, as rectal or genital operations will induce inability to micturate. The plexus heemorrhoidalis medius (and inferior) corresponds to the plexus pudendalis on the arteria pudenda. For further description of the rectal nerve supply, see tractus intestinalis. The nervous apparatus ventral, lateral and dorsal to the vagina, that supplying the ureter, that coursing through the parametrium and perimetrium, that supplying the bladder, rectum and ureter, are solidly and compactly anastomosed. They form an inseparable nerve plexus bedecked with ganglia of greater and lesser dimensions surrounding the cervico-vaginal junction. The vast plexuses of the pelvic brain, rich in ganglia, extend from the cervico-vaginal junction distalward to the pelvic floor surrounding with a luxuriant closely woven network, uterus and vagina (tractus genitalis), the rectum (distal tractus. intestinalis), the bladder and ureter (distal tractus urinarius).

(B) PHYSIOLOGY.

The physiology of the nerves of the tractus genitalis comprises the function of the genital organs, which are in order of origin: 1, ovulation; 2, absorption; 3, secretion; 4, peristalsis (rhythm); 5, menstruation; 6, gestation; 7, sensation.

First it should be observed that the abdominal brain originates the plexus aorticus, and the plexus aorticus gives origin to two great nerve plexuses, viz., plexus interiliacus and plexus ovaricus. The plexus interiliacus, so far as the genital tract is concerned, divides into two, *i.e.*, one, the larger branch, terminates in the pelvic brain, while the smaller branch terminates directly in the uterus without first passing through the pelvic brain. The plexus ovaricus arises from the plexus aorticus and terminates practically at the ovary; this plexus, however, proceeds to anastomose with the plexus uterinus in the ligamentum latum. Hence, a larger portion of the nerves which supply the genital tract arise in the abdominal brain and pass to it directly through the plexus interiliacus and plexus ovaricus. On the other hand, a massive plexus (the uterine modified by the sacral spinal nerves) passes through the pelvic brain before it arrives at the genital

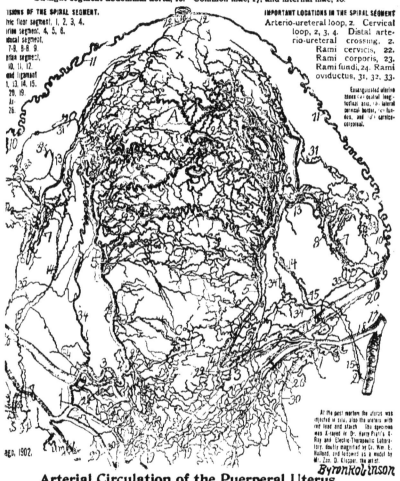

Arterial Circulation of the Puerperal Uterus.
Four Hours Post Partum.—Life Size.
Illustrating the Utero-Ovarian Vascular Circle (the Circle of Byron Robinson)

CIRCULATION OF THE PUERPERAL UTERUS

Fig 29. A reasonable estimate of the richness of the vasomotor nerves (sympathetic) to an organ is made through the number and dimensions of the arteries which are ensheathed by a plexiform, nodular, nervous web. The quantity of nerve supply to the uterus is vast

tract. These anatomical facts demonstrate how solidly and compactly the tractus genitalis is anastomosed to the whole abdominal sympathetic. Besides this must be held in view the modifying influence on the genital tract of the sacral (spinal) nerves through their coalescence with the distal end of the plexus interiliacus, *i. e.*, through the pelvic brain.

Peristalsis—Rhythm of the Tractus Genitalis.

Peristalsis, or rhythm, of the genitals, though one of the common functions of all abdominal viscera (under control of the abdominal brain), is particularly specialized in the tractus genitalis—uterus and oviducts—to a degree of popular demonstration. Rhythm of the uterus to the ordinary observer is its chief characteristic phenomenon. The rhythm, or peristalsis, of the uterus under the direct command of the sympathetic nerve, differs not, except in degree, from the rhythm of other viscera under direct command of the sympathetic, such as the enteron, colon, ureter, spleen, liver, pancreas. Such organs as the lungs, heart, stomach, and bladder, though dominated by the sympathetic, yet are so powerfully supplied by the cranial nerves (vagi) and the spinal nerves (sacral) that their rhythm is modified. The periodic rhythm and stately peristalsis of the uterus has induced observers of all time to enquire and wonder as to its cause. That irritation of the plexus interiliacus and of the plexus uterinus is followed by the rhythmical movements of the uterus, is the main testimony of a vast majority of investigators. The myometrium, the complicated muscle of the uterus in general, is maintained and completely developed by menstruation and gestation, otherwise it would atrophy. In the uterus are located nerve ganglia, little brains, smaller ganglia—extended or transported from the pelvic brain to the uterus, which I termed fifteen years ago automatic menstrual ganglia. They are local rulers of muscle or myometrial rhythm. When the automatic menstrual ganglia are periodically bathed in extra blood (which is a stimulant or excitant) they explode rhythmically, the uterine muscle or myometrium assumes an active, vermicular movement; thus the myometrium or uterine muscle is preserved from atrophic death. Extra absorption of the uterine glandular apparatus is due to the extra trauma of the muscular bundles on the utricular glands. The myometrium thrashes, massages, and whips the glands to extra secretory labors. Myometrial activity and glandular activity are concomitant—cause and effect. The chain of events is: extra blood to the automatic menstrual ganglia induces extra myometrial rhythm. Extra uterine peristalsis induces extra massage, excitation, to the uterine glands, which results in extra secretion. Therefore, be it observed the dominating nerve of the uterus—the sympathetic—functionates as a unit—no conflict, in rhythm which develops the myometrium. During gestation the automatic menstrual ganglia become bathed with continual extra blood. Profound congestion, progressive exalted engorgement, produce extra nourishment and multiply elements until the gestating uterus is perhaps fifty times the dimension of the resting uterus. The gestating uterus is always in motion—rhythm. One curious feature I have noted in the arteries of gestating uteri of animals and man, and that is, that the uterine artery was enlarged, hypertrophied, exactly from its origin in the internal iliac. No part of the iliac was enlarged. Hence gestation belongs entirely to the tractus genitalis, to the utero-ovarian artery. The function is distinct, does not glide into any other visceral tract. The sympathetic nerve has through æons of ages become differentiated to perform separately and distinctly the important functions of the tractus genitalis. The sympathetic nerve, nervus vasomotorius, originally belonged to the arterial system. It is differentiated at present to control some veins and also the gradually added tractus lymphaticus. Great importance lies in the tractus vascularis and its ruler, nervus vasomotorius. The future problems, especially as regards shock, must be solved in the wide field of the sympathetic nerve and circulatory system.

Besides rhythm or peristalsis the nerves of the uterus preside over the functions of absorption, secretion, menstruation, gestation, and sensation of the uterus, a description of the physiology of which space forbids. The physiology of the oviduct is under the control of the sympathetic nerve and we may note the following points in its functional activity:

The object of the oviduct is transportation—export and import service —of spermatozoa proximalward and of ova distalward, forcing the impregnated ovum distalward to the uterine cavity. The following are the main physiologic factors in oviductal transportation:

1. The periodic congestion of the genitals, stimulation of the automatic menstrual ganglia by extra blood.

2. The cilia of the oviductal mucosa whip continually toward the uterus distalward, not only forcing the ova distalward, but also creating a fluid current.

3. The congestion induces the endosalpinx to secrete a fluid which makes the oviduct a canal to float the ovum distalward:

4. Congestion induces continual oviductal peristalsis, which forces the ova distalward.

5. The contraction of the muscular processes in the ligamentum latum enhances the peristalsis.

6. The shortening of the fimbria ovarica which induces the infundibulum to apply its mucous surface to the ovary, capturing the ovum.

7. The congestion induces the secretion of mucus and glues the infundibulum on the surface of the ovary.

8. Intra-abdominal pressure aids the distal progress of the ova.

9. The enlarging of the ovum approaching the infundibulum aids.

10. Secretion of the endosalpinx produces a fluid medium adjacent to the proximal oviductal end and the cilia of the fimbriæ induce a current toward the abdominal ostium.

11. The oviduct has an import (spermatozoa) and an export (ova) service. It is analogous to the vas deferens in the male. The spermatozoa pass through the oviduct proximalward, while the ova pass through it distalward.

12. The oviduct is a temporary (or pathologic permanent) depot for conception. The oviduct (ampulla) is a physiologic sporting ground for ova and spermatozoa. It has three general physiologic offices to fulfill, viz.: (a) to secure and transport the ovum (distalward) to the cavity of the uterus; (b) to conduct spermatozoa proximalward; (c) to serve as physiologic temporary (or pathologic permanent) depot of conception. All the physiologic statements in regard to the ovary will be, that the rich plexus ovaricus rules ovulation, but also, perhaps, some form of internal ovarian secretion is necessary for the best normal corporeal existence. The physiology of the tractus genitalis is vigorous, as it is supplied by a luxuriant system of sympathetic nerves. With the higher forms of differentiated animals the magnitude and influence of the genitalis increases. The higher the animal the more thought is applied to the genitals, the more periodic congestion and permaent increase of nerve and blood supply. The intense attention paid to sex in higher animals, such as monkey and man, is a remarkable phenomenon, and attention induces blood flow, congestion. At the bottom of the sex lie ambition, hope, and much of the pride of life. Man's life and thoughts are arranged around sex as a center. Hence the genital nerve and blood supply and consequent genital physiology will remain an increasing maximum. For the detailed physiology noted in the subjects "Abdominal Brain" and "Pelvic Brain" the reader is referred to the *Medical Age* for July, 1905, and the *Medical Review of Reviews* for November, 1905.

CHAPTER X.

NERVES OF THE BLOOD VESSELS (NERVI TRACTUS VASCU-LARIS).—(A) ANATOMY, (B) PHYSIOLOGY.

Our most cherished hopes are frequently maintained in silence.
The curfew tolls the knell of parting day—Thomas Gray (1716-1771), professor of modern history in the University of Cambridge, England.

(A) ANATOMY.

The proper nomenclature to apply to the sympathetic nerves is the nervus vasomotorius. Practically it is a nerve belonging to the arteries. In the anatomy of the nerves of the blood vessels two factors should be considered, viz.: (a) that nerves tend to course with blood vessels as the intercostals, nerves in the extremities, nerve coursing with the aorta and its branches. However, cerebro-spinal nerves course mainly parallel with the vessels and divide mainly as acute angles, while vasomotor (sympathetic) nerves form a plexiform network, a neural meshwork, on the walls of the blood vessel, and are not confined to acute-angled dichotomy but divide and anastomose by angles of all dimensions; (b) the cerebro-spinal nerves in general do not form ganglia in their course along blood vessels. The vasomotor nerve (sympathetic) forms ganglia, plexiform nodular meshwork on the walls of the arterial vessels especially at the bifurcation or point of exit of the arterial divisions. The nervus vasomotorius courses along with the blood vessel as a nodular plexus, a leash woven like a web on the vessel wall. The coarser or finer web-like anastomotic meshwork of nerves surrounding a vessel is characteristic of the nervus vasomotorius (sympathetic). With the development and differentiation of the animal life the nervus vasomotorius becomes distributed in its relation to blood vessels, dislocated, removed, transported along projecting lateral vessels from its direct contact with the original trunk vessel. Excellent examples of removal—dislocation of the vasomotor nerve from contact with its original vessel—may be observed in the plexus aorticus, and especially in the instance of the plexus interiliacus where it is dislocated toward the median line from arteria iliacus communis. The second significant characteristic of the nervus vasomotorius is its numerous nerve ganglia found attached to the vessel wall and the location of marked ganglia at the bifurcation of trunk arteries as at the aortic bifurcations. Ganglia of dimension also exist at the origin or exit of visceral arteries from the great arterial trunk as ganglion cœliacum (abdominal brain) ganglion spermaticum, ganglion renalis, ganglion arteriæ phrenicæ, ganglion mesentericum superior et inferior, ganglion cervicale (pelvic brain). These significant ganglia located on the aorta at the origin or exit of visceral vessels, I shall term the aortic viscerel ganglia—ganglia aorticæ viscerales. The visceral aortic ganglion may have become dislocated from its vascular course during development, the most typical example of which is the ganglion cervicale, which was dislocated, transported medianward from the arteria iliaca communis to the lateral border of the uterus. In the region of the origin of the cœliac axis, the arterial tripod, the ganglia have become dislocated, fragmented and removed, transported along adjacently developed arteries as the renal, mesenteric superior and inferior. From fragmentation and transportation along arteries the renal arteries possess multiple ganglia. In localities of the tractus vascularis where the vascular parietes are of maximum thickness, as the myocardium the ganglion cells collect in masses, known as cardiac ganglia. We thus have the well-known cardiac ganglia of Ludwig (1816-1895), Bidder (1810-1892), Schmidt (1831-1894), Remak (1815-1865). The nervus vasomotorius is an automatic nerve. Ganglia located at the anastomosing points of nerves accompany its network of conducting coils throughout the entire course of the artery, thus automatically controlling each arterial segment. The intimate relations of the nervus vasomotorius with the great arterial vessels may be sufficiently observed in the plexus aorticus thoracicus, plexus cœliacus (abdominal brain) plexus aorticus abdominalis, plexus interiliacus, plexus pelvicus (pelvic brain). Ganglia of maximum dimension are located in intimate relation with the entire course of the aorta. The nervus vasomotorius was originally essentially a vascular nerve, hence its name, nervus vasomotorius. The nervus vasomotorius, vascular nerve plexuses, begin in ganglia (aortic visceral ganglion—ganglion cœliacum, spermaticum, mesentericum, renalis, cervicale), accompanies the arterial vessels as a plexiform nodular meshwork, a neural anastomosed vascular sheath, and ends in automatic visceral ganglia (Auerbach's, Meissner's, automatic menstrual, renal ureteral, vesical, etc., etc.), located in the parenchyma of organs.

In general the dimensions of the ganglia on the arterial plexuses correspond with the dimensions of the vascular channel. However, the renal arterial plexus is supplied with numerous ganglia of maximum dimension, relatively greater in proportion than that of the segments of the arterial channels as the myocardium. The ganglia located on the arteries of the tractus genitalis are relatively numerous and of large dimension. The original great abdominal vascular ganglion is that of the cœliac axis, from which doubtless many adjacent vascular ganglia have become fragmented, and transported on the vessels toward the viscera. Perhaps the most typical example of this transportation of ganglia is the renal artery, on which is distributed relatively numerous small and large ganglia throughout its entire course. A peculiar degenerative developmental process has occurred at the bifurcation of the aorta near the sacral promontory. According to the general rule there should be a ganglion of large dimension located at the bifurcation of the aorta. However, the nervous ganglion located in this region (which I term the interiliac nerve disc) has not only few ganglion cells (some deny the existence of any ganglion cell) but is dislocated distalward from the aortic bifurcation to the promontory of the sacrum. It is mainly a dorso-ventrally flattened nerve disc with disappearing ganglion cells.

NERVES OF THE BLOOD VESSELS

The vascular nerve plexuses vary in dimension and fenestration. The meshwork of nerves may be coarse or fine, wide or narrow. The plexus aorticus abdominalis possesses ganglia, cords and fenestra of maximum dimensions. The fenestra are extensive, elongated, formed by nerve cords of maximum dimension, on the anastomosing points of which are distributed ganglia of maximum dimension. The plexus rénalis is a wide-meshed network richly beset by large ganglia. It is a plexus nervus vasomotorius possessing ganglia, cords and fenestra of maximum dimension. The plexus mesentericus superior possesses numerous fine white cords with relatively large fenestra and ganglia limited in number and dimension. This plexus possesses the peculiarity of the meshes or fenestra deviating considerably from the course of the artery. The plexus hepaticus, composed of branches from the nervus vagus dexter and plexus cœliacus, surrounds the hepatic artery with strong, flat cords in the form of a narrow-meshed network. The

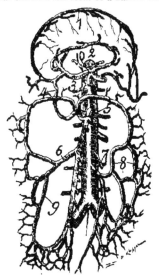

CIRCLES, ARCS AND ARCADES OF THE ABDOMINAL ARTERIES

Fig. 30. This illustration presents two views, viz.: (a) The arterial trunks, arcs, arcades and circles of the tractus intestinalis are solidly and compactly anastomosed, connected through blood currents and channels. (b) The sympathetic nerve (nervus vasomotorius) accompanies the arteries as a plexiform network, as a nerve vascular sheath. This cut demonstrates that the nerves of the tractus intestinalis are solidly and compactly anastomosed; hence irritation on any sympathetic plexus of the tractus intestinalis will effect, reflexly, all others. 10, arcs and arcades of the cœliac axis. 6, 7, 8 arcs and arcades of the superior and inferior mesenteric arteries, all of which are anastomosed united by (4), the pancreatico-duodenalis superior and inferior. The arterial arcs, arcades and circles of the hand and utero-ovarian artery resemble those of the tractus intestinalis. The number and dimensions of the arteries furnish a clue to the quantity of nerve supply.

plexus lienalis ensheath the arteria renalis and is bedecked with numerous ganglia of varied dimension. Microscopic and macroscopic ganglia occur in the vascular plexuses. Some macroscopic ones are constant, as the ganglion located on the external carotid artery. Wrisberg's ganglion is situated in the cardiac plexus, notably the renal ganglia (macroscopic) are found on the plexus renalis. In general the vasomotor nerves, sympathetic, form a plexiform nodular sheath around the blood vessels and enter with it into the substance of parenchyma of the organs. This arrangement of the nervus vasomotorius induces many physicians to adopt the idea that the nervus vasomotorius originally and essentially belonged to the vascular system, and is lost on the coats of the arteries. The nervus vasomotorius invariably accompanies the arteries—not the veins—the trunk of the vena portæ being the only exception. The ganglia of the nervus vasomotorius (sympathetic) are connected with the anterior primary divisions of the spinal by short nerve cords known as rami communicantes, which are gray and white in color.

The gray rami communicantes arise in the ganglia of the nervus vasomotorius (sympathetic) and pass to the spinal cord.

The white rami communicantes arise in the spinal cord and pass to the cords and ganglia of the nervus vasomotorius (sympathetic). Hence the cerebro-spinal nerves and nervus vasomotorius (sympathetic) are distinctly and firmly anastomosed; however, like the federal, state, county and city government, possess many independent functions.

(B) PHYSIOLOGY.

The nervus vasomotorius consists of— (a) the lateral chain and its ganglia; (b) the nerve plexuses and their ganglia accompanying the blood vessels from the aortic ganglia to the viscera; (c) the automatic visceral ganglia. Hence the nervus vasomotorius of the abdomen consists of ganglion cells and nerve cords. It must be remembered that it is not the number of ganglion cells that designates the power of a nervous system to accomplish maximum labor, but it is particularly the number of conducting cords associating and connecting the ganglion cells which decides the superiority of nervous executive ability. The nervus vasomotorius is peculiarly rich in conducting cords, establishing rapid and frequent communication between its ganglion cells—governing every particular segment of the arterial channel. The ganglion cells of the nervus vasomotorius are well informed from the rich association of connecting fiber transmitting news over many lines. To illustrate the eternal vigilance of the nervus vasomotorius it need only to indicate the fact that the artery is always on tension, that the nerve is always on guard—awake or asleep. A ganglion cell at each end of a conducting cord can accomplish more work than the single cord can transmit. A depot at each end of a railroad line can handle more freight than a single road can transmit. Increased number of conducting cords transmit increased information to the ganglion cells. The nervus vasomotorius is partially independent, automatic in action. If a frog's brain and cord be removed or destroyed the visceral functions will proceed for a time. Circulation, respiration,

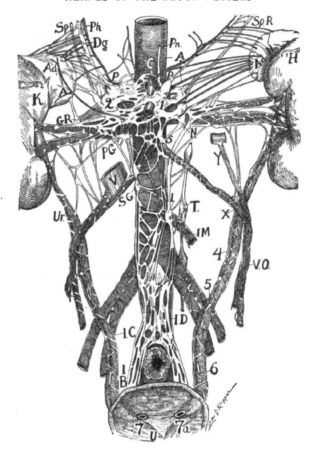

NERVES ACCOMPANY THE ARTERIES

Fig. 31. This illustration presents the sympathetic nerves following the arteries. I dissected this specimen (man 40) with care, and the artist, Mr. Klopper, sketched exactly from the model. 1 and 2, abdominal brain. Pn, Pneumogastric nerve; sp. Nervus Splanchnicus major. Ad, adrenal; Dg, ganglion diaphragmaticum; Adn, 10 adrenal nerves, (right), (left), 7. G. R. arteria renalis (right and left partially duplicate). R. G. Ganglia renalia (left). Ur ureteral nerves. S. G. and 5 upper ganglia spermatica. I, ganglion mesentericum inferior; X, ganglionic coalescence of nerves at the vasa spermatica and ureteral crossing. 5 (Lower) ganglionic coalescence of the nerves at the crossing of the ureter and vasa iliaca communis. ID, Plexus interiliacus (hypogastricus). ID, is the nerve disc of the sacral promontory. The arteries are accompanied by a plexiform nodular neural sheath encasing the vessel.

digestion, which indicates that absorption, secretion and peristalsis, sensation remain intact. The functions manifested by the blood vessels are: (a) peristalsis (rhythm); (b) absorption; (c) secretion; (d) sensation. The plexiform nodular anastomosing neural network ensheathing the artery controls the above four functions. The tractus vascularis contracts and relaxes with clock-like regularity. Sensation is important from the fact that fluid in the vascular channel is required to produce normal vascular peristalsis. Hence the rational idea in "visceral drainage" is to maintain sufficient volume of fluid in the vascular channel to stimulate and insure contraction. It is the functions of the vascular plexiform neural sheath that is of peculiar interest to us. From the fact that the heart will continue its peristalsis some time after removal indicates that the intramural cardiac ganglia are automatic.

That the ganglia are located in the myocardium would indicate that the nervus vasomotorius terminates in the arterial parietes, and hence the contraction and dilatation of the heart are analogous to the contractions and dilatations of the arteries, being due to ganglia located in the vascular wall. There is an intimate relation of the blood vessels within the substance of organs and the automatic visceral ganglia. In general the origin of the nervus vasomotorius is the spinal cord—as there lies the vasomotor center, yet ganglia located on the aorta (*e. g.*, abdominal brain) possess controlling influence.

Aortic Visceral Ganglia—Ganglia Aorticæ Viscerales.

I wish to call attention in the function of the nervus vasomotorius to the ganglia located on the aorta at the exit of the visceral vessels. I have termed them aortic visceral ganglia—ganglia aorticæ viscerales—because they appear not only to influence visceral vessels, but the function of viscera, and to become, with differentiation and developmental processes, definitely associated with distinct individual visceral function, *e. g.*, if one examines systematically in man and animals the arteria uterina ovarica during gestation, and in the resting state, a peculiar phenomenon will be observed. The uterine artery will be enlarged, hypertrophied, exactly from its origin in the internal iliac, and the ovarian will be enlarged, hypertrophied exactly from its origin in the aorta, *i. e.*, both uterine and ovarian arteries are enlarged, hypertrophied, from their exact origin in the arterial trunk. Now the arteria uterina ovarica possesses distinct ganglia belonging to itself and the genitals. In this case it consists of ganglion cervicale, or cervical ganglion (pelvic brain) dislocated from its original position located at the origin of the uterine artery. In other words, through eons of ages the ganglia at the origin of the arteria uterina ovarica have become differentiated, developed into the power of endowing the artery supplying the genitals with function—gestation and menstruation—which requires a certain amount of blood. Again, at the origin of the arteria mesenterica inferior is located a ganglion which irritates peristalsis in the left half of the colon—the fæcal reservoir (left half of the transverse colon, left colon, sigmoid, and rectum) —peristalsis sufficient for a daily evacuation.

NERVES OF THE BLOOD VESSELS

In the tractus nervosus accompanying the tractus vascularis there are differentiations of nerve functions as, *e.g.*, vasomotor dilator nerves and vasomotor constrictor nerves. If vasomotor dilator nerves be stimulated relaxation and rest of the vessels of occur. Hence these nerves have been termed vaso-inhibatory nerves, *e.g.*, stimulation of the nervi eregentes pro-

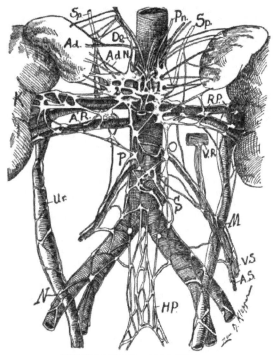

NERVES OF THE BLOOD VESSELS

Fig. 32 represents typical Vascular Plexuses, which I dissected from a specimen taken from a subject of about fifty years of age. 1 and 2 abdominal brain lying at the foot of the great abdominal visceral arteries. P. O. S. ganglia located at the other visceral arteries. The nervus vasomotorius (sympathetic) accompanies the arteries in the form of a plexiform, fenestrated, neural sheath.

ceeding from the plexus sacralis (due to accidental trauma of the spinal cord) will induce dilatation of the arteries of the penis with congestion of the corpora cavernosa and consequent partial erection. Stimulation of the spinal cord induces priapism, *i.e.*, pathologic conditions of the spinal cord may produce erection from stimulation. The vasomotor constrictor nerves are in evidence when the surface of the body from fright or other cause become blanched, pale.

Anatomically the cerebro-spinal nerves and nervus vasomotorius is distinctly and firmly anastomosed, connected, by the rami communicantes, however, like the federal, state, county and city government, the two systems of nerves perform many independent local functions. Long ages of habitat established this function.

CHAPTER XI.

NERVES OF THE LYMPHATIC TRACT (NERVI TRACTUS LYMPHATICUS).

Since the lymphatic vascular apparatus is an appendage of the blood vascular apparatus it will be supplied and governed by the nervus vasomotorius similarly to that of the blood vascular system, hence its discussion will be omitted. See Chapter XXXVIII, Pathologic Physiology of the Tractus Lymphaticus.

CHAPTER XII.

ABDOMINAL BRAIN—CEREBRUM ABDOMINALE—(A) ANATOMY; (B) PHYSIOLOGY.

O, gentle sleep, Nature's soft nurse.
—*Shakespeare (1564-1616).*

Embrouded was he, as it were a mede,
All full of freshe floures white and rede;
Singing he was, or floyting all the day;
He was as freshe as is the moneth of May.
—*Description of the Squire in Geoffrey Chaucer (1340-1400).*

(A) ANATOMY.

The abdominal brain or ganglion cœliacum has experienced multiple names during the past three centuries.

Synonyms.—Celiac ganglion (ganglion cœliacum); solar plexus (plexus solaris, Todd and Bowman, 1847); semilunar ganglion (ganglion semilunare); the great abdominal ganglion (ganglion abdominale maximum); abdominal brain (cerebrum abdominale, Wrisberg, 1780 [1739-1808]); the nervous center of Willis (centrum nervosum Willisii, 1622-1675); epigastric nervous center (centrum nervosum epigastricum); splanchnic ganglion (ganglion splanchnicum); vascular abdominal brain (cerebrum abdominale vasculare); epigastric plexus (plexus epigastricus); celiac plexus (plexus cœliacum).

Some authors have viewed the abdominal brain or celiac ganglion as composed of two parts, right and left, bilateral and paired. I shall consider it as practically one sympathetic ganglion or plexus anatomically and physiologically, and term it the abdominal brain—the celiac ganglion, a coalesced, vascular, visceral brain, unpaired, existing at the origin of the celiac, superior mesenteric, and renal arteries (major visceral arteries).

The *arrangement* of the abdominal brain consists of: (a) afferent or centripetal nerves (entering or contributing nerves from the cerebrum, spinal cord, or sympathetic); (b) efferent or centrifugal nerves (distributing or visceral). The afferent nerves enter chiefly on the proximal and lateral borders, while the efferent nerves radiate from all regions of the abdominal brain—hence solar plexus. There is no relation between the number and dimension of afferent and efferent nerves of the abdominal brain.

Fig. 33. An illustration of the sympathetic nerve with abdominal brain. In this specimen the ureters (calyces, pelvis, and ureter proper) were dilated to the dimensions of an index-finger, the channel of the tractus urinarius presenting no sphincters intact. This subject possessed a typical abdominal brain (1 and 2) as well as a well-marked pelvic brain (B). The ganglion hypogastricum (H) is well marked. This illustration presents fairly well the abdominal sympathetic with their varied anastomoses. The great ganglionic masses of the abdomen (1 and 2) and pelvis (B) are evident. It presents a general outline of its nervous vasomotorius. I secured this specimen from an autopsy through the courtesy of Drs. W. A. Evans and O'Byrne.

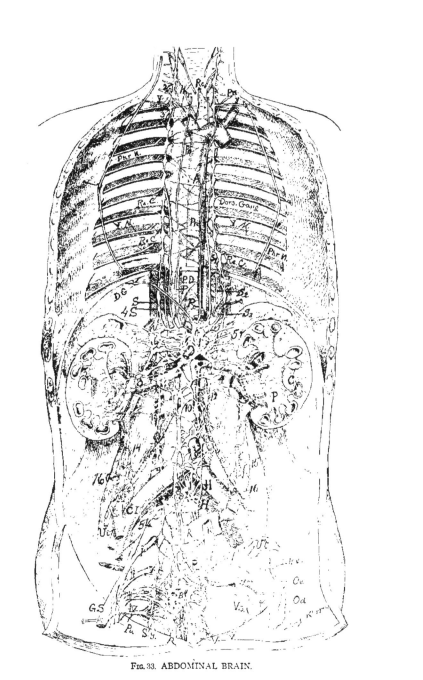

FIG. 33. ABDOMINAL BRAIN.

(a) *Afferent nerves.* The afferent or contributing nerves composing the abdominal brain are: (sympathetic), (1) plexus aorticus thoracicus (unpaired); (2) nervus splanchnicus (paired), constituting the most essential portion of the abdominal brain; (3) branches from the two proximal lumbar ganglia (paired): (cerebrospinal) I, nervus vagus (paired), especially the right; II, nervus phrenicus (paired), especially the right. The abdominal brain consists of the coalesced termination of the above (1, 2, 3, I, II) five nerve apparatus. The abdominal brain is the major assembling center of the abdominal sympathetic.

(b) *The efferent nerves.* The efferent, visceral, or distributing nerves of the abdominal brain of various caliber radiate in a plexiform arterial sheath to every abdominal viscus, viz., to the *tractus intestinalis* and its appendages: plexus hepaticus, lienalis, gastricus, mesentericus superior, mesentericus inferior, hæmorrhoidalis; to the *tractus urinarius:* plexus suprarenalis, renalis, ureteris, vesicalis, urethralis; to the *tractus genitalis:* plexus ovaricus, hypogastricus (pelvic brain), plexus uterinus pudendalis vaginalis; to the *tractus vascularis* and *tractus lymphaticus.* The abdominal brain emits plexiform nerves and ganglia fixed in connective tissue sheaths which intimately encase the vascular tubes. The nerves emitted from the abdominal brain are gray or white in color, limited in diameter, plexiform in arrangement, resist tension on account of the thick fibrous neurilemma, and ganglia are liable to occur at their points of crossing or anastomosis. The radiating, efferent nerves of the abdominal brain accompany the arteries arranged in a plexiform sheath or network. They do not accompany the veins—the trunk of the vena portæ being the only exception.

I. Position: Holotopy (relation to general body).

The abdominal brain is located at the proximal end of the abdominal cavity immediately distal to the diaphragm. It is situated medially, extraperitoneally, and is practically bilaterally symmetrical.

II. Skeletopy (relation to osseous skeleton).

The abdominal brain corresponds to the level of the first lumbar vertebra, on its ventral surface.

III. Syntopy (relation to adjacent organs).

The syntopic relations of the abdominal brain are intimate and profound connections with vascular and visceral organs. It surrounds the roots of the celiac, superior mesenteric, and renal arteries like a collar or fenestrated sheath. It is located extraperitoneally, on the ventral surface of the aorta and crura of the diaphragm. It is situated immediately distal to the hiatus aorticus of the diaphragm. It lies between the diaphragmatic and renal arteries. Right and left it projects against the capsules of the adrenals. It is located between the proximal renal poles. It lies partly dorsal to the corpus pancreaticus and stomach. Its right half lies between the right crus of the diaphragm and the vena cava. Practically the abdominal brain is lodged in the space bounded bilaterally by the adrenals and proximal renal poles; proximally by a line drawn transversely from the proximal point of one adrenal to that of the other; distally by the renal arteries. The situation of the abdominal brain is included within the space of origin of the celiac and renal arteries—some two inches.

IV. Idiotopy (relation of component segments).

The component parts of the abdominal brain are from proximal to distal end in order, viz.: (a) The projecting ganglia of the origin of the diaphragmatic nerves located on the proximal border—conical elevations or bulb of the brain itself; (b) the semilunar ganglia, the essential material in form and dimension of the abdominal brain, constituting its major central segment; (c) the renal ganglia, located generally at the origin of the renal arteries, are practically constant, however varying in location, form, and dimension. The segments proximodistally are compactly and solidly united by ganglionic masses, flattened commissures, and nerve cords along the lateral borders of the aorta. The segments laterally, *i.e.*, the right half and left half, are united transversely around the roots of the celiac, superior mesenteric, and renal arteries by ganglionic arches, flattened commissures, and nerve cords extending transversely from the right to left half of the brain.

Dimensions.—The abdominal brain or celiac ganglion is the largest and richest ganglion of the sympathetic nerve. Hence from a preponderating aggregation of nerve cells it becomes the ruling potentate of the viscera. The left half is more compact, greater in dorsoventral diameter, thicker, less fenestrated, and possesses more definite regular borders than the right; however, the right half is greater in surface area. Its diameters are: (a) transverse about $1\frac{1}{2}$ inches; (b) proximodistal $1\frac{1}{4}$ inches; (c) dorsoventral about $\frac{1}{4}$ inch. The dimensions of the abdominal brain practically correspond with the space bounded bilaterally by the two adrenals and the two proximal renal poles; distally by the two renal arteries; proximally by the diaphragmatic arteries, or a line drawn transversely from the proximal end of one adrenal to that of the other. Its surface dimensions vary extremely on account of the indefinite coalescence, interpolation, distribution, dislocation of ganglion or by transportation along visceral vessels.

The Form.—The form of the abdominal brain is variable; however, in general it is quadrilateral. It may present a half-moon or horseshoe shape, or a ring surrounding the celiac axis and superior mesenteric artery. It may also be represented by a single broad fenestrated ganglionated plate which covers the ventral surface of the aorta adjacent to the celiac axis, and occupies the space between the adrenals and proximal renal poles. The left half may resemble a bean, a retort in compact form, while the right half is more quadrilateral, flattened (from compression of the vena cava), and irregular in contour. The form has changed by development from coalescence, interpolation, isolation, and transportation of ganglia along visceral vessels, the vertebral column and ribs.

The Borders.—The borders of the abdominal brain (margo cerebri abdominalis) are four, viz.: proximal, distal, and two lateral. (a) The proximal border presents three factors of interest. The first is the concave horseshoe-like depression made in it by the celiac axis and the surrounding of the vessel like a collar by nerve cords and ganglia in a connective tissue sheath. The other two factors are the cone-like projections of a portion of the brain which emits bilaterally the nervus (plexus) diaphragmaticus. The proximal border receives the continuation of the nerves of plexus aorticus thoracalis as well as the termination of the right vagus (cranial), and also communication may occur with the right nervus phrenicus. The proximal border is generally blunt and rounded. Practically the plexus gastricus is emitted from its proximal border. (b) The lateral border (left) presents quite an uneven line, with irregular projections for efferent nerves, chiefly destined to the adrenals and kidneys, and for afferent nerves, especially the major splanchnic. The main projections along its border are those produced by the ganglion splanchnicum and ganglia renalia. (c) (right). The lateral border is generally an irregular line caused by the irregular size and location of the ganglion splanchnicum and ganglion adrenalis. The lateral borders receive (afferent) nerves (splanchnic major) and emit (efferent) nerves (plexus adrenalis and plexus renalis). (d) The *distal* border is bounded by the arteria renalia—practically an even line. It emits or distributes efferent nerves of various caliber to the abdominal visceral tracts.

Fenestræ.—The compact left half of the abdominal brain may be limitedly perforated, while the widely meshed right half is considerably fenestrated with larger and smaller, irregular-shaped apertures adding unevenness to the surface. The fenestræ possess sloping, smooth, irregular contoured edges and are occupied with connective tissue, blood and lymph vessels, glands, and areolar tissue. The chief central fenestræ are produced by the celiac axis and superior mesenteric artery. The left half of the brain generally has one major fenestra due to a blood-vessel springing from the aorta. The right half of the brain possesses some three definite apertures, or fenestræ, and several irregular large ones. In general the right half possesses two kinds of fenestræ, viz.: (smaller) those in the more solid median division of the brain, and (larger) those in the lateral, more widely meshed portion. The splanchnic ganglia, located at the termination of the splanchnic nerves, are situated in the middle of the celiac plexus and represent the major ganglionic masses.

The Surfaces.—The surfaces of the abdominal brain (facies cerebri abdominis) consist of two, viz.: (a) the ventral, (b) the dorsal. The ventral surface is uneven, from coalescence of smaller and larger ganglia, irregular coalescence, compression of adjacent viscera (as the inferior vena cava), or dislocation of ganglia by transportation along vessels. The ventral surface is convex from the dorsal compression of the aorta and crura diaphragmatica. The ventral surface receives (afferent) and emits (efferent) nerves; also may be observed nerve loops which originate and insert themselves on the ventral surface. From the ventral surface pass the nerves to the adrenal, pancreas, and plexus renalis—in fact, the nerve plexuses accompanying the branches of the celiac axis and many of the plexus mesentericus superior from the ventral surface. The surface is solidly bound by connective tissue to adjacent structures. The ventral surface of the left half of the abdominal brain is concave from the contact pressure of the cylindrical aorta and crura diaphragmatica.

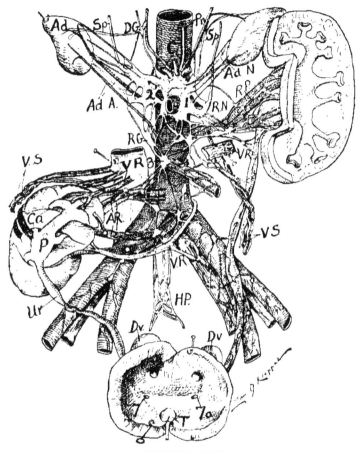

ABDOMINAL BRAIN.

Fig. 34. This illustration is drawn from a specimen I secured at an autopsy through the courtesy of Drs. Evans and O'Byrne. The right kidney was dislocated, resting on the right common iliac artery, with its pelvis (P) and hilum facing ventralward. The adrenal (Ad.) remained *in situ*. It was a congenital renal dislocation, and was accompanied with congenital malformations in the sympathetic nerve, or nervus vasomotorius. 1 and 2 is the abdominal brain. It sends five branches to the adrenal from the right half (2). Though the sympathetic system is malformed, yet the principal rules as regards the sympathetic ganglia still prevail, viz., ganglia exist at the origin of abdominal visceral vessels, *e.g.*, 3, at the origin of the inferior mesenteric artery; at the root of the renal vessels, HP is no doubt the ganglion originally at the root of the common iliacs (coalesced). In this specimen the right ureter was 5 inches in length, while the left was 11½. This specimen demonstrates that the abdominal brain is located at the origin of the renal, celiac, and superior mesenteric vessels—*i.e.*, it is a vascular brain (*cerebrum vasomotorius*).

The fenestræ or perforations of the dorsal surface correspond with those of the ventral. Strong, fine white strands of connective tissue, blood, nerves, and lymph vessels bind the dorsal surface of the abdominal brain solidly to the crura diaphragmatica, but especially strong to the aortic. Nerves originate and depart from the dorsal surface. From the dorsal surface nerves depart to the aorta and diaphragm and the splanchnicus major, bilaterally, arrives on the dorsal surface.

Ganglia.—There are usually six constant ganglia in the abdominal brain, viz.: (a) Ganglia diaphragmatic (paired); (b) ganglia splanchnica (paired); (c) ganglia renalia (paired). They are solidly and compactly united into one anatomic and physiologic nerve center—a brain. In general the ganglia do not agree in form or dimension bilaterally. Practically the ganglia agree in position bilaterally. However, the left semilunar ganglion is nearer the median line than the right, and the left mainly lies on the aorta, while the right chiefly rests on the crus of the diaphragm. The ganglia may rest in an even transverse plane, or lie in superimposed layers in a dorsoventral plane. The ganglia constituting the abdominal brain are as irregular and variable as the plexus in which they are located. The ganglia consist of large, swollen cords, or ganglionic arches or circles arranged in a network. The dimension, form, and number of the ganglia may vary from coalescence, isolation, interpolation, or transportation of ganglia along vessels, bones, and muscles. The coalescence of the ganglia may proceed to such an extent that the abdominal brain will present the appearance of several nodes, or the two semilunar ganglia may coalesce and lie between the celiac and superior mesenteric arteries.

The ganglia may coalesce proximally and distally in the form of a ganglionic ring surrounding the origin of the celiac and mesenteric arteries. The ganglia of the abdominal brain may be flat or elevated, single or multiple, united by gangliated commissures or flattened nerve strands. The nervus splanchnicus major, the essential segment, terminates bilaterally in the abdominal brain in a large semilunar or quadrilateral-shaped nodule—ganglion splanchnicum (paired). The splanchnic ganglia may assume the shape of the letter C. I have seen two splanchnic ganglia on each side of almost equal dimensions formed by the splanchnic major and minor nerves.

1. The *left* semilunar ganglion has a more definite border, is nearer to the median line, greater in dorsoventral diameter, more compact, yet smaller and less fenestrated than the right. It lies transversely on the side of the aorta between the renal and diaphragmatic arteries. Its average diameters are: proximodistal, ½ inch; transverse, 1 inch; dorsoventral, ¼ inch. Its thickest border is the left, its thinnest is the right. Its ventral surface is uneven, convex; the dorsal, concave. It is flask or quadrilateral in form. The right proximal angle is elongated into a horn-like process to join its opposite fellow. Afferent nerves arrive and efferent nerves depart from all surfaces and borders except part of the left. *Proximally* it is connected with the diaphragmatic ganglion—externally with the splanchnic nerve, medially with the opposite fellow (right half of brain).

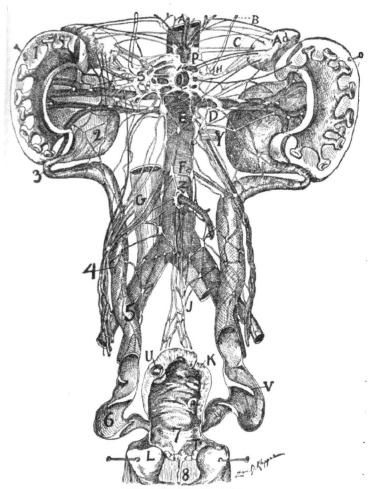

ABDOMINAL BRAIN (S. P.).

Fig. 35. This illustration was drawn from a specimen I secured at autopsy through the courtesy of Dr. W. A. Evans. It is not a typical abdominal brain, on account of the peculiar method of emission of the adrenal nerves (C), 10 on the left side and 14 on the right side. The right side presents duplicate renal and spermatic arteries. This is a typical subject to demonstrate the abdominal brain as a vascular brain (cerebrum vasculare or cerebrum vasomotorius), as it is located at the origin of the abdominal visceral vessels, viz., renal, celiac, and superior mesenteric arteries. B, splanchnic major; H, splanchnic minor; D, renal ganglia. This specimen presents what I term the swan's-neck-shaped ureters (2). Note ureteral valves (5 and 6) and dilated ureters. The bladder and prostate are hypertrophied. The ureters present a network of nerves surrounding them. Observe the large renal ganglion on the ventral surface of the renal artery at D.

2. The *right* semilunar ganglion is more flattened, greater in surface area, more extensively fenestrated, and less in dorsoventral diameter than the left. It lies between the vena cava (ventral) and right crus of the draphragm (dorsal), and between the renal and diaphragmatic arteries. Afferent nerves arrive and efferent nerves depart from its surfaces and borders. The left, proximal, angle is prolonged into a horn-like process to join its opposite fellow. Proximally it is connected with the diaphragmatic ganglion; distally with the renal ganglion; externally with the splanchnic nerve; and medially with the opposite fellow (left half of the brain).

Ganglion of the Phrenic Artery (Ganglion Arteriæ Phrenicæ).—In this brief note I wish to present a sympathetic ganglion (bilateral) which I have not found described in literature.

This ganglion consists of a constant pyramidal, or cone-shaped projection on the proximal border of the abdominal brain in the course of the phrenic artery.

In Fig. 1 on the right side it is located by a hook at the figure 2 in the abdominal brain. On the left side it is located between the splenic and phrenic artery.

The phrenic ganglion projects bulb-like from the proximal border of the cerebrum abdominale similar to that of the olfactory nerve from the cranial cerebrum. It is a part and parcel of it. By a general observation in dissecting the sympathetic nerve (nervus vasomotorius) it will be evident that sympathetic ganglia are located at the origin of the vessels from the aorta, as at the foot of the celiac axis (ganglion semilunare) at the origin of the renal artery (ganglion renale) at the origin of the arteria mesenterica inferior (ganglion mesentericum inferius) at the origin of the two common iliacs from the aorta (the interiliac nerve disc), and so forth. Hence it is in accordance with this rule that the ganglion arteriæ phrenicæ is found in the course of the phrenic artery (bilateral). If the phrenic artery has an anomalous origin and course the phrenic ganglion tends to follow its origin and course, and it was this anatomic relation that called my attention to this heretofore undescribed constant ganglion. I do not refer to the diaphragmatic ganglion (ganglion diaphragmaticum) located on the diaphragm on the right side (only) about two inches from the abdominal brain. The abdominal brain consists practically of three ganglia (bilateral). They are: 1. Ganglion semilunare (bilateral), located on the middle part of the lateral border of the abdominal brain at the termination of the major splanchnic nerve (Sp. in figures). This ganglion is related to the origin of the celiac artery. 2. Ganglion renale (bilateral), located at the distal lateral border of the abdominal brain, and belongs to the origin of the arteria renalis. 3. Ganglion arteriæ phrenicæ (bilateral), located at the proximal border of the abdominal brain in the course of the phrenic artery.

In certain subjects the ganglion of the phrenic artery is located exactly at the origin of the phrenic artery from the aorta. However, the origin of the phrenic artery varies considerably, and this alters to some extent the relations of the phrenic ganglion from physical facts.

The phrenic ganglia are constant structures, constantly located in relation to the course of the phrenic arteries so far as I can determine by dissection. The importance of the abdominal brain, with its ganglia, will sooner or later be realized by the general profession.

The *diaphragmatic* ganglia are practically bilaterally symmetrical in location, form, and dimension. They project as pyramids or cones from the proximal border of the semilunar ganglia, at the origin of the diaphragmatic arteries, giving origin in the diaphragmatic nerve. They project from the

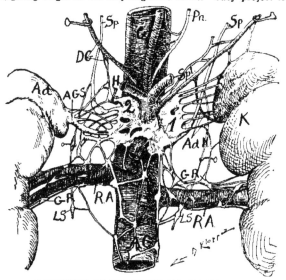

ABDOMINAL BRAIN—CEREBRUM ABDOMINALE.

Fig. 36. This illustration was drawn from a carefully dissected abdominal brain. 1 dissected the tissue under alcohol. The relations and proportions are those of life, being drawn by accurate measurements. 1 and 2, abdominal brain. Observe the nerves which the adrenals receive: Sp, splanchnic major; DG, ganglion diaphragmaticum; GR, renal ganglia; Ad, adrenals; LS, lesser splanchnics; RA, arteria renalis; H, hepatic; G, gastric; and Sp, splenic artery. The hook fixes the ganglion of the phrenic artery which I term ganglion arteriæ phrenicæ.

abdominal brain as the olfactory projects from the cranial brain—being a part of it. The diaphragmatic nerve possesses a small ganglion some 2½ inches from its origin, and it anastomoses with the right phrenic.

5 and 6. The *primary renal* ganglia are practically bilaterally symmetrical in form, location, and dimension. Their location is generally at the origin of the renal arteries.

I. The ganglia of uncertain dimension, location, and form associated with the abdominal brain are: (a) The nervus splanchnicus minor terminates bilaterally more distalward generally on the renal arteries; (b) the ganglion suprarenale supernum, which I have occasionally found chiefly on the right suprarenal nerves. The *color* of the abdominal brain is grayish-red; the *consistence* is moderately dense, due to the presence of abundant connective tissue; the *composition* consists of an aggregation of nerve ganglia, ensconced in dense connective tissue, varying in dimension, number, and form. Each ganglion is composed of oval-shaped nerve cells of various form and dimension.

Relations.—The relations of the abdominal brain well encased in fibrous and connective tissue consist in intimate connection with the abdominal aorta at the origin of the celiac axis, superior mesenteric and renal arteries. It has also intimate but less solid connections with the vena cava and renal veins. It is a vascular brain of the abdomen. The abdominal brain lies in the square formed by the proximal renal poles with adrenals and the renal arteries. It is in relation to the dorsal surface of the body of the pancreas, peritoneum, and stomach. The abdominal brain in general occupies the space including the origin of the major visceral arteries, viz.: (a) arteria cœliaca; (b) arteria mesenterica superior; (c) arteria renalis—three mighty visceral arteries originating from the aorta within the space of an inch and a half. Hence practically the term abdominal brain should include the aggregated or coalesced ganglia located at the origin of the major visceral vessels. With development of viscera and elongation of visceral arteries, the ganglia become isolated from the original abdominal brain and transported along the vessels toward the viscera.

The two best examples are the renal and aortic arteries with their numerous transported large ganglia—ganglia renalia and ganglia aortica. Development has sometimes separated the cord and ganglion of the nervus splanchnicus minor from the abdominal brain by placing it more distalward and lateralward toward the region of the origin of the arteria renalis, thus altering the form and contour of the abdominal brain. The nerve plexuses and ganglia of the abdominal brain, firmly bound in sheaths by strong white connective and elastic tissue, encase the visceral vessels and accompany them to the viscera. The abdominal brain is solidly and compactly anastomosed, connected by nerves of various caliber with all the abdominal viscera, viz., tractus intestinalis, urinarius, genitalis, vascularis, lymphaticus. It is evident from its location at the origin of the celiac axis and superior mesenteric arteries that the abdominal brain in its origin was a primitive brain for the tractus vascularis. With development of viscera and elongation of visceral arteries, dislocation, multiplication, distribution, coalescence or transportation of ganglia, other viscera have acquired local ganglionic rulers, *e.g.*, the pelvic brain—ganglion cervicale. However, present conditions allow the origin of the abdominal brain to remain at the exit of the major visceral vessel. It should be denominated a vascular brain.

From the abdominal brain radiate plexuses of various caliber, chiefly in vessels, to all the abdominal viscera, viz., tractus intestinalis, genitalis, urinarius, vascularis, and lymphaticus. The abdominal brain emits more nerves than it receives, and hence is a creating, producing center, a source for new and increased nerves. Nerve reception occurs chiefly at the proximal (plexus aorticus thoracalis, vagi) and lateral borders (splanchnics, major, medius, minor). Nerve emission occurs mainly at the distal (plexus aorticus abdominalis) and lateral borders (plexus renalis, adrenalis). From the dorsal and ventral surface, from the bilateral proximal and distal borders of the abdominal brain, nerves arrive and depart. Bilaterally radiate the renal and adrenal nerves, and arrive the splanchnicus; proximally radiate a few to the aorta, and arrives the plexus aorticus thoracalis and vagi; dorsally many nerves pass to the aorta and diaphragm, and arrive the branches from the splanchnics; ventrally a number of nerves radiate to the adrenals and pancreas; distally are emitted nerve plexuses of vast importance on visceral arteries of corresponding names, viz.:

I. *Tractus intestinalis*: (1) Plexus cœliacus, emitting (a) plexus gastriticus accompanying the arteria gastrica; (b) plexus hepaticus accompanying the arteria hepatica; (c) plexus lienalis accompanying the arteria lienalis. (2) Plexus mesentericus superior accompanying the arteria mesenterica superior (to the enteron—except the duodenum, and colon, except the cæcum, right colon and right half of transverse colon). (3) Plexus mesentericus inferior accompanying the arteria mesenterica inferior (to the left half of the transverse colon, left colon, sigmoid flexure, and rectum).

II. *Tractus urinarius:* (1) Plexus adrenalis accompanying the arteria adrenalis. (2) Plexus renalis accompanying the arteria renalis. (3) Plexus ureteris accompanying: (a) rami arteriæ renales; (b) arteria ovarica; (c) arteria ureteris media (from common iliac); (d) arteria uterina. (4) Plexus hæmorrhoidalis accompanying the arteria hæmorrhoidalia. (5) Plexus hypogastricus accompanying the arteria hypogastrica. (6) Pelvic brain (ganglion cervicale) emits nerves which pass directly to the ureter without accompanying blood-vessels as well as the plexus vesicalis. (7) Plexus vesicalis accompanying the arteria vesicalis superior, media, and inferior (hemorrhoidal). (8) Plexus urethralis (a continuation of the plexus vesicalis) accompanying arteria pudenda.

III. *Tractus genitalis:* (1) Plexus aorticus accompanying the arteria aortica abdominis. (2) Plexus hypogastricus (a continuation of the plexus aorticus) accompanying the arteria iliaca communis and arteria hypogastrica. (3) Plexus ovaricus accompanying the arteria ovarica. (4) Plexus arteriæ uterinæ accompanying the arteria uterina. (5) Cerebrum pelvicum (pelvic brain), which emits the plexus uterinus without accompanying vessels as well as the plexus vaginalis. The sympathetic nerve cords and ganglia accompanying vessels (blood, particularly arteries and lymph) arranged as a network in a connective tissue sheath which encases the vessel.

(B) PHYSIOLOGY OF THE ABDOMINAL BRAIN.

In mammals there exist two brains of almost equal importance to the individual and race. One is the cranial brain, the instrument of volitions of mental progress and physical protection. The other is the abdominal brain, the instrument of vascular and visceral function. It is the automatic, vegetative, the subconscious brain of physical existence. In the cranial brain resides the consciousness of right and wrong. Here is the seat of all progress, mental and moral, and in it lies the instinct to protect life and the fear of death. However, in the abdomen there exists a brain of wonderful power maintaining eternal, restless viligance over its viscera. It presides over organic life. It dominates the rhythmical function of viscera. It is an automatic nerve center, a physiologic and an anatomic brain. Being located at the origin of the celiac, superior mesenteric, and renal arteries—the major abdominal visceral arteries—it is a primary vascular brain of the abdomen and a secondary brain for visceral rhythm. The abdominal brain presides as the central potentate, over the physiology of the abdominal viscera. The common functions of these viscera are rhythm, secretion, and absorption, and to preside over this triple office is the chief duty of the abdominal brain. To the common functions of the abdominal viscera must be added the special functions of the tractus genitalis—ovulation, menstruation, gestation; however, many of the functions of the visceral tract are delegated to the subordinate local ruler—the pelvic brain. The abdominal brain is a receiver, a reorganizer, an emitter of nerve forces. It has the powers of a brain. It is a reflex center in health and disease. The sympathetic abdominal nerve alone possesses the power of rhythm. Every organ possesses rhythm. In this rhythm of involuntary visceral muscles is doubtless included the factors of initiation, maintenance, and conclusion of visceral absorption and secretion. The rhythmic, peristaltic muscles massage the glands, inciting their function of secretion and absorption.

The individual functions of the abdominal brain are numerous and important, viz.: (1) It is the source of new nerves, as it possesses more efferent than afferent nerves. (2) it demedullates nerves; nerves enter sheathed and depart unsheathed. (3) It presides over the rhythm, peristalsis, of visceral muscles. (4) It presides over the absorption and secretion of visceral glands—*e. g.*, the glands lining tubula rviscera and those denominated glandular appendages. (5) The abdominal brain is a giant vasomotor center, controlling the caliber of the abdominal vessels (blood and lymph); it should be termed *nervus vasomotorius*. (6) It possesses nutritive powers over the nerves passing from it to the periphery. (7) It is the major abdominal reflex center.

The abdominal brain is not a mere agent of the brain and cord; it receives and generates nerve forces itself; it presides over nutrition. It is the center of life itself. In it are repeated all the physiologic and pathologic manifestations of visceral function (rhythm, absorption, secretion, and nutrition). The abdominal brain can live without the cranial brain, which is demonstrated by living children being born without cerebrospinal axis. On the contrary the cranial brain can not live without the abdominal brain. The central idea founded in the abdominal brain should entitle it, in my opinion, to the name vascular or vasomotor brain of the abdomen (cerebrum vasculare abdominale). It initiates, sustains, and concludes visceral rhythm (the peristalsis of involuntary, visceral muscles)—*e.g.*, in the tractus vascularis, intestinalis, genitalis, and urinarius. It presides over the absorption and secretion of the viscera—*e. g.*, the mucous glands of the tubular viscera and visceral glandular appendages. It is evident from the great volume of blood occasionally found in the vastly distended abdominal veins at autopsy that a subject could bleed to death in his own abdominal vessels. The abdominal brain, the vascular cerebrum, is responsible for this condition,

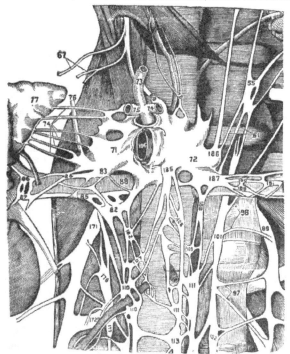

ABDOMINAL BRAIN.

Fig. 37. This illustration drawn from a cadaver, illustrates the location, relation, and radiating plexuses of the solar plexus, or abdominal brain (71 and 72), which is built around the major visceral arteries, the celiac (73, 74, 75), superior mesenteric (106), and renal (88) arteries; hence it dominates the visceral function as to vascularity (blood and lymph), peristalsis, absorption, and secretion. The clinical manifestations of the abdominal brain are coextensive with that of the abdominal viscera. This ganglion of the first magnitude presents radiating plexuses to all the abdominal viscera, presenting an exquisitely balanced and poised nervous mechanism, controlling vascularity (blood and lymph), peristalsis, absorption, and secretion. 76 and 185, splanchnic major; 110, 111, ganglia ovarica. The body from which this dissection was drawn possessed wide, flat nerves, as is noted by the majestic ganglion—the abdominal brain or cerebrum vasomotorius; 69 is the left vagus.

having forgotten, from paralysis, to control the lumen of the vessels. From the anatomic vascular connection it is impossible to extirpate the abdominal brain from living animals, hence the reports of experimentation accompanied with its extirpation are unreliable. The abdominal brain is the nervous executive of the abdominal vessels and viscera, the duties of which are to see that the functions of the viscera (rhythm, secretion, and absorption) are faithfully executed. The abdominal brain assumes practically an independent existence; however, the cerebrospinal axis asserts a controlling influence over it. For example, in children whose cerebrospinal axis is not completely developed, and at death of adults, when the cerebrospinal axis has lost its complete control, the intestines will mutiny, assuming a wild, disordered, violent peristalsis, resulting in intestinal invagination.

The utility of the abdominal brain in practice is important—for example, in postpartum hemorrhage the older practitioners taught that by compression of the aorta the hemorrhage was checked. This, of course, is an error, as the technique, if it were possible to execute, would not materially affect the bleeding, as ovarian blood-supply would continue. The physiologic explanation of checking postpartum hemorrhage by pressure over the abdominal aorta is that the manipulation stimulates the plexus aorticus and plexus hypogastricus, which is transmitted to the pelvic brain, where it is reorganized and transmitted over the plexus uterinus to the myometrium, the elastic and muscular bundles of which being excited, contract like living ligatures, checking the postpartum hemorrhage by diminishing the lumen of the vessels. The irritation, pressure, or trauma of the head of the child on the expanding cervix uteri during the last month of gestation precipitates labor by its effect on the pelvic brain (and consequently on the abdominal brain), by inducing vigorous, persistent uterine contractions. In feeble labor pains, during uterine inertia, vigorous uterine contractions may be excited by the finger per rectum or per vaginam, irritating or massaging the pelvic brain. The pelvic brain is palpated with facility, as it is located on the lateral vaginal fornix. Again, the pelvic brain is subordinate to the abdominal brain; however, the pelvic brain must be intact to allow physiologic orders to pass from the abdominal brain through the pelvic brain to the uterus. For example, during labor sudden cessation of uterine peristalsis may occur—uterine inertia. The probable explanation is that as the head passes through the pelvis it traumatizes the pelvic brain, producing temporary paresis from pressure, and partially checks the uterine rhythm. With the progress of labor the pelvic brain recovers and its dynamics resume.

The temporary paresis of the pelvic brain does not produce complete paralysis, because a few of the nerves of the plexus hypogastricus (directly from the abdominal brain) pass to the uterus without first entering the pelvic brain. The abdominal brain rules the physiology of the abdominal visceral tracts. The methods to utilize the physiology of the abdominal brain in practice are varied. For example, the mammary gland is connected to the abdominal brain by at least three distinct routes, viz.: (a) via the nerve plexuses accompanying the arteria mammaria and arteria subclavia, whence the route is direct to the abdominal brain; (b) via the nerve plexuses accompanying the arteriæ intercostales to the aorta and its plexus, whence the route is direct to the abdominal brain; (c) via the nerve plexuses accompanying the arteria epigastrica superior and inferior to the common iliac, whence the route (plexus) continues on the artery of the round ligament to the plexus uterina, whence the route is direct to the pelvic brain or abdominal brain. Therefore, by stimulating or irritating the nipple with light friction or massaging the mammary gland, the abdominal brain is reached by the above three routes, and consequently the uterus is induced to contract more frequently, and if the experiments be not repeated too rapidly, the uterine contraction will be more vigorous. Again, the uterus may be incited to more frequent and vigorous contractions by administering a tablespoonful of hot

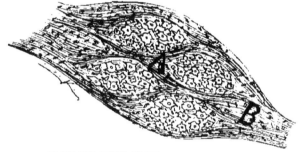

GANGLION CELLS IN THE ABDOMINAL BRAIN.

Fig. 38. Drawn from a microscopic section of the abdominal brain. Observe that the cells lie in connective tissue nests, i. e., the ganglion cells are ensconced in separate chambers of connective tissue. The prolongations of the cells, i. e., the conducting cords, pass hither and yon, forming a network.

fluid, which first emits the stimulation over the plexus gastricus to the abdominal brain, where it is reorganized and sent directly to the plexus uterinus, which incites the uterus to increased peristalsis. The reverse physiology of the influence of visceral tumors or pregnant genitals stimulating the mammary gland (over the above three routes) is evident. The tumor or fetus in the genitals rapidly induces the mammary gland to manifest objective disturbances of dimension, circulation, color, palpation, as well as sensory disturbances.

Practically the uterine nerves originate in the abdominal brain and possess a relative independent existence. Children are born, expelled, from the uterus after the death of the mother. Hyrtl, the celebrated Viennese anatomist, reports that during a war with Spain some bandits hanged a pregnant woman. After she had hung on the gallows for four hours, and consequently was long dead, she gave birth to a living child. I have observed the giant uterus of slaughtered pregnant cows executing with wondrous precision its rhythm hours subsequent to death and evacuation of uterine contents. If one will extirpate an oviduct from a human and place it in warm normal salt solution, oviductal rhythm may be maintained by physical stimulus—*e.g.*, tapping with the scalpel—for some three-quarters of an hour. If one will chloroform a dog to death and incise the abdominal wall, exposing the intestines, in a room of 70°, the intestines will perform their rhythm, on being tapped with the scalpel, for an hour and a half. The large urinary vesical apparatus of steers will perform rhythmical movements for half a dozen hours after death in summer temperature.

The anatomic location and the physiologic function of the abdominal brain dignify it into a basic factor in diagnosis from pain. For example, practically all acute inflammatory pain (localized peritonitis, visceral perforation) or violent visceral irritation (calculus, volvulus, invagination, acute strangulation, obstruction) is first experienced in the epigastric region—*i.e.*, reorganization occurs in the abdominal brain. This means that all visceral pain, irritation, is first transmitted to the abdominal brain, where it is reorganized and emitted to the abdominal viscera, diffusing the wild, disordered, violent peristalsis (colic) universally in the abdomen, which prevents the localizing of the pain by the diagnostician. With the progress of the disease the abdominal brain and associated nerve apparatus become accustomed to the new experience and the pain becomes intensified, localized on definite nerve plexuses, whence the pain, tenderness, can be diagnosed by distinct circumscribed localization. The best example of this view is appendicitis.

The abdominal brain is the seat of shock. A blow over the epigastrium, violent trauma to the abdominal brain, may cause immediate shock, collapse, or death. I performed an autopsy on a subject where invagination of the uterus had killed the patient in two and a half hours. Death was due to shock in the abdominal brain, transmitted to it over the hypogastric plexus from the traumatized (invaginated) uterus.

CONCLUSIONS AS REGARDS THE ABDOMINAL BRAIN.

The abdominal brain is a nervous center—*i.e.*, it receives, reorganizes, and emits nerve forces.

The abdominal brain is the nervous executive for the common functions of the abdominal viscera, as rhythm, absorption, and secretion.

The abdominal brain was originally in function and location a vascular brain—cerebrum vasculare. Though complicated functions have been added, yet it is still a primary vasomotor center controlling the caliber of the blood-vessels and consequently the volume of blood to viscera, which determines visceral function.

The abdominal brain is a reflex center in health and disease.

It is the major assembling center of the abdominal sympathetic.

The abdominal brain is the seat of shock. A blow or trauma on it may cause shock, collapse, or death.

It is the automatic, vegetative, the subconscious brain of physical existence. It is the center of life itself.

In the abdominal brain are repeated all the physiologic and pathologic manifestations of visceral function—rhythm, absorption, secretion, menstruation, gestation, ovulation.

The abdominal brain can live without the cranial brain (and spinal cord), for children have been born alive with no cerebrospinal axis. Children have been born alive hours after the mother was dead.

The abdominal brain may be the agent of valuable therapeutics—*e.g.*, in postpartum hemorrhage massage of the aortic plexus will stimulate the abdominal brain to control the blood-vessels of the uterus. Massage of the aortic plexus will stimulate the abdominal brain to send blood to the viscera, enhancing rhythm, secretion, and absorption, improving constipation and increasing visceral drainage.

The abdominal brain is the primary agent of rhythmic visceral motion. A wide office of the physician is to maintain regular visceral rhythm by means of rational therapeutics, as regular habits and exercise, wholesome coarse food, ample fluids, and proper rest.

CHAPTER XIII.

THE PELVIC BRAIN (CEREBRUM PELVICUM).

We do automatically what we do well.

"La Duma est morte! vive la Duma!"—("The Russian parliament is dead! Long live the Russian parliament!")—Remark of Sir Henry Campbell-Bannerman, Prime Minister of England during the Inter-Parliamentary Congress Session at London, July 24, 1906.

(A) ANATOMY, (B) PHYSIOLOGY, (C) PATHOLOGY.

Prologue.—With the term cervical ganglion the names of Johann Gotlieb Walther (1784-1818), Robert Lee (1793-1877) and Ferdinand Frankenhauser (died in 1894) will be forever connected. Thomas Snow Beck (1814-1847) will be remembered, in the brilliant polemics only, from 1840 to 1846, with Robert Lee. Walter's book appeared in 1783. Lee's in 1841 and Frankenhauser's in 1867—all with illustrations of the cervical ganglion. The first two books are pioneer works executed in the premicroscopical days; the last work, that of Frankenhauser, is a work of scientific merit, and will stand the test of time. I have designated the plexiform ganglionic mass, located on the lateral border of the cervix and vagina, as the *pelvic brain*. The ganglionated mass located at the cervico-vaginal function has experienced a variety of terms during the past two centuries.

Synonyms.—The pelvic sympathetic plexus (plexus sympathicus); Cervio-cuterine ganglion (ganglion cervicis uterinum—Walther, 1783). Hypogastric plexus (plexus hypogastricus—Walter, 1783). The lateral hypogastric plexus (plexus hypogastricus lateralis—Friedrich Tiedemann, 1822) (1781-1861). The ganglionated plexus (plexus gangliosus—Tiedemann, 1822). The inferior uterine plexus (plexus uterinus inferior—Tiedemann, 1822). The hypogastric ganglion (ganglion hypogastrium—Lee, 1841). The uterocervical ganglion (ganglion uterium cervicale—Lee, 1841). The vesicorectal plexus (plexus vesicis rectalis—J. M. Bourgery, 1840) (1797-1845), and Claude Bernard (1813-1878). The ganglion of the cervix (ganglion cervicis—Lee, 1841). The pelvic plexus (plexus pelvicus—Thomas Snow Beck, 1845) (1814-1847). The cervical ganglion (ganglion cervicale—Frankenhauser, 1867). The fundamental nerve plexuses of the uterus (plexus nervosus fundamentalis uteri—G. Rein, 1892), Pelvic brain (cerebrum pelvicum—Byron Robinson, 1894). The lateral cervical plexus (plexus lateralis cervicis). The utero-vaginal plexus (plexus uterinus vaginalis).

Practically three views have been entertained in regard to the nature and character of the pelvic brain; viz.:

(a) It is a more or less solid, composite, ganglionic mass—Walter (1783), Lee (1841), Frankenhauser (1867), Freund (1885), Byron Robinson (1894), Knupffer (1892).

(b) It is a ganglionated plexus or group of connected ganglia—Tiedemann

(1822), Moreau (1789-1862), Jastreboff (1881), Rein (1902), Sabura Hashimoto (1892), Pessimski (1892), Jung (1905).

(c) Jobert (de Lomalle) (1799-1867), 1841, and Thomas Snow Beck, 1845 (1814-1877), are the only authors known to me who have viewed the pelvic brain as a nongangliated nerve plexus.

(A) Anatomy and Topography of the Pelvic Brain.

Position.—I. Holotopy (relation to general body). The pelvic brain is located in the distal end of the abdominal cavity. It is a bilaterally located organ (paired) residing in the lesser pelvic between the cervic uteri and pelvic wall. It is situated extraperitoneally at the base of the ligamentum latum, proximal to the pelvic floor, ensconced in the pelvic subserous connective tissue. The pelvic brain is completely accessible to digital palpation.

II. Skeletopy (relation to the osseous system). The pelvic brain lies in the lesser bony pelvis, located bilaterally closely adjacent to the ischial spine in the planum interspinosum. It lies on a level with the II sacral vertebra and the proximal border of the symphysis pubis. By distention and contraction of rectum, bladder, vagina and uterus the skeletopic relation of the pelvic brain becomes altered. The pelvic brain lies practically midway between the inlet and outlet of the minor osseous pelvis. The skeletopic relation of the pelvic brain has been modified by erect attitude.

III. Syntopy (relation to adjacent organs). The pelvic brain (paired) is located bilaterally to the cervix uteri and vaginal fornix. It is situated in the connective tissue of the parametrium, on a level with the middle of the cervix uteri and about one inch lateralward from the cervix uteri. The pelvic brain is located in the base of the ligamentum latum at the distal end of the plexus interiliacus (hypogastricus). Practically the pelvic brain is located at the crossing of the ureter and pelvic floor segment of the vasa uterina. It lies on the internal border of the ureter midway between the dorsal and ventral blades of the ligamentum latum in the loose connective tissue. It is situated at the junction of the plexus interiliacus, hypogastricus, with the branches of the II, III, and IV sacral nerves (spinal). It is lodged practically at the junction of the cervix uteri with the vaginal fornix. A major portion of it may lodge in the groove or fossa, between the rectum and vagina. It is surrounded and interwoven with dense, subperitoneal, pelvic connective tissue, presenting difficulties in exposition by dissection because of its simulation to adjacent tissue. The pelvic brain has profound and extensive connection with the uterus, vagina, and rectum, ureter and bladder. In the majority of subjects the chief segment of the pelvic brain lies adjacent to the lateral vagina fornix. From erect attitude the pelvic brain has changed its position, having approached more adjacent to the cervico-vaginal junction in the center of the pelvis. From the distalward and ventralward movements of the genitals (in higher forms of life and erect attitude) the plexus interilicus (hypogastricus) has been dragged, forced medianward, isolating it from the arteria iliaca communis and arteria

132   THE ABDOMINAL AND PELVIC BRAIN

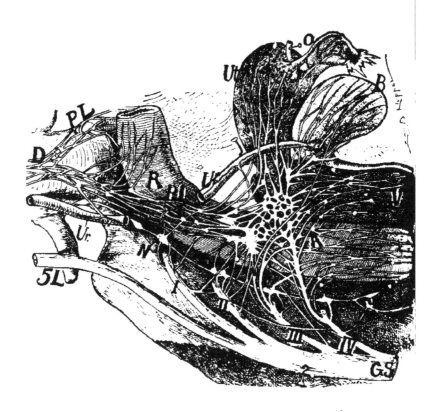

PELVIC BRAIN OF AN INFANT

Fig. 39. A, pelvic brain; B, plexus vesicalis; V, plexus vaginalis; I, II, III, IV, V, sacral nerves with the sacral ganglia (N), plexus (hypogastricus), P, L, Ur, ureter, Ut, uterus, B, bladder; v, vagina; R, rectum; O, oviduct. 5 L V, lumbar nerve; D interiliac nerve disc.

The pelvic brain in this infant, viewed with a lens, presents the *afferent* nerves arriving from the plexus interiliacus (P, L), nervi sacrales, ganglia sacralia, mainly as single nerve cords, at most slightly plexiform at the distal end of the plexus interiliacus. With a magnifying lens the *efferent* nerves of this pelvic brain (plexus rectalis, vaginalis, vesicalis, uterinus) resemble luxuriant leashes (cat o' nine tails) or richly ganglionated plexuses. The pelvic brain in this subject has the following efferent leashes. (a) the plexus rectalis presents some seven emissions of large nerves, coursing distalward on the rectal wall, richly supplying the rectum. It has the most limited number of nerve trunks and ganglia of any of the efferent leashes of the pelvic brain. (b) plexus vaginalis presents some eight emissions hypogastrica, and the sacral nerve branches which unite with the distal end of the plexus interiliacus (to form the pelvic brain) have become elongated, hence the pelvic brain is not intimately and profoundly associated with its original great blood-vessels, resembling the profound connection of the abdominal brain with its blood-vessels. Yet the pelvic brain is still a vascular brain (cerebrum vasculare) associated with blood-vessels or a vasomotor brain (cerebrum vasomotorius), for, by controlling the blood supply of the uterus, it controls its rhythm and secretion. The ganglia of the pelvic brain are interspersed with fenestra, interwoven with rich connective tissue, intertwined with many arteries and numerous veins. The pelvic brain is a ganglionated plexiform apparatus intimately associated with the uterus. Distention and contraction of pelvic organs, with consequent change of visceral location, alters to a relative degree the syntopic relations of the pelvic brain.

IV. Idiotopy (relation of component segments). The pelvic brain is practically a triangle, frequently a quadrangle in form with its apex proximalward. Its base is essentially on a level with the IV sacral nerve. At its proximal end and lateral border it receives (afferent) nerves in the form of cords slightly plexiform. At its distal end (base) and medial border it emits (efferent) nerves in the form of leashes and complicated plexuses. Practically its medial border is divided by two septa; viz., (a) the septum rectale and (b) septum vaginale, which divide the ventral and dorsal nerve branches and leashes supplying the dorsal and ventral surfaces of the respective organs. There is no segmental or other practical division of the component segment of the pelvic brain; it is a single, composite, ganglionated mass—a unit. As to function, the ganglia of the pelvic brain are not differentiated in function similar to those of the ganglia of the cranial brain.

Dimension.—The average dimensions of the adult pelvic brain in the resting uterus are: Length (proximo-distal), three-quarters of an inch; width, one-half inch, and thickness, one-sixth inch. Practically the average

---

of large, strong nerves for the vagina. The nerve supply to the vagina (plexus vaginalis), a richly ganglionated plexus appears more luxuriant, enormous, profound, than that of the uterus, because it is more on the surface, more apparent to the lens and unaided eye. The ganglionated plexus vaginalis surrounds the vagina from the proximal to the distal end with a mighty network, which in its richness resembles the network of cords surrounding a rubber ball. The proximal end and ventral vaginal wall are the most richly supplied; (c) the plexus vesicalis presents some six emissions of large strong nerves for the bladder (besides a large strong nerve which arises from the II sacral and passes directly to the bladder. The bladder is richly supplied by an extensive ganglionated plexus; (d) the plexus uterinus presents some twelve emissions of large nerves passing from the pelvic brain to the uterus. With a lens one can count five of the trunks of the plexus uterinus coursing to the uterus external to the ureter, and about seven trunks pass to the uterus median to the ureter. Also one large or two small strands of nerves pass directly from the plexus interiliacus (hypogastricus) to the uterus without first entering the pelvic brain.

The nerve supply (in this subject) to the uterus (plexus uterinus), a richly ganglionated plexus, is luxuriant, enormous, profound. This infant's uterus and vagina demonstrate that they are profoundly supplied by a richly ganglionated fine nerve plexus which is intimately woven on their surfaces and richly distributed through their parenchyma. The uterus, like the heart, appears to possess single ganglia to rule its functions should the local ruler, the pelvic brain, become incompetent.

dimensions of the pelvic brain remain permanent, though the diameters vary. If the major diameter decreases the minor diameter increases, and *vice-versa*. Solid coalescence or plexiform distribution of the ganglia perhaps alters inappreciably the general number of ganglion cells. The thinnest or most membranous portion is its proximal segment. The thickest or most ganglionic portion of the abdominal brain lies on the lateral vaginal fornix. The pelvic brain (paired), next to the abdominal brain, is the largest and richest ganglion of the sympathetic and combined; the two are almost equal in dimension and number of ganglion cells to the abdominal brain (unpaired). The longest diameter of the pelvic brain courses parallel to the rectum and vagina. Proximalward its dimensions decrease, and when it meets the entering efferent nerves from the hypogastric plexus it is membranous. The largest ganglia are located in the central portion and diminishes from center to circumference. The diameter of the nerves and nerve commissures also decrease from centre to borders. Its plexiform network increases in the dimensions of its fenestra from centre to circumference. Ganglia of various dimensions and form, macroscopic and microscopic, are located adjacent to the abdominal brain. Seldom does one meet in dissection a pelvic brain of the extensive dimensions, definite contour, solidarity and compactness of Frankenhauser's illustration (1867). I think Lee's illustration (1841) is more natural in dimension and form. The macroscopic dimensions of the pelvic brain depends, doubtless, much on the dissector—deficient or excessive removal of connective tissue are frequent errors. The microscope demonstrates enormous numbers of ganglion cells in the pelvic brain, which, combined with periganglionic and connective tissue, produces an organ of significant and marked dimension. Does the pelvic brain increase in dimension during pregnancy? Whether its ganglion cells increase in number, multiply, I am unable to answer. Perhaps, however, I have satisfied myself by careful dissection that the pelvic brain during gestation macroscopically increases its dimension, whether it be from hypertrophy, or hyperplasia increase in vessels, connective tissue, neurilemma or muscle. In the gestating uterus the pelvic brain measures 1½ inches in length, in width 1 inch, thickness ½.

Form.—The pelvic brain is in general triangular, trowel-shaped, frequently quadrangular in outline. It is a more or less solid, compact, composite or compound ganglion, and not merely a nerve-meshed network. If the surface dimension, contour, increases, the thickness decreases, and *vice-versa*, presenting a widely varied form, resembling in this respect the abdominal brain. With more recent repeated dissection of the pelvic brain, especially on infant cadavers, I am inclined to believe the ganglionated plexiform arrangement, the composite, compound ganglion within its usual signification, prevails in the majority of subjects, explaining the numerous irregular and individual forms. The form is modified by coalescence or separation of ganglia by the dimension of the fenestra and diameter of the nerve cords and commissures.

The borders (margo cerebri pelvis).—The countour or borders of the pelvic brain are not well defined and irregular.· They possess projecting lobes for (afferent) nerve reception and serrated processes for (efferent) nerve emission. The thinnest borders are the proximal and lateral, the thickest are distal and medial; the vast majority of nerves arrive and depart from its borders. Some arise and depart from its surface. Nerve loops may arise and insert themselves in the same surface as the abdominal brain. The nerves are chiefly received (afferent) on the proximal and lateral borders and depart (efferent) from the median and distal borders. Practically, however, afferent and efferent nerves arrive and depart from both surfaces and borders of the pelvic brain. For convenience, the pelvic brain may be described with four borders; viz., proximal, distal, median and external. The proximal (afferent) border is of interest as receiving the plexus interiliacus (hypogastricus). The external border is important as it receives (afferent) the sacral (spinal) nerve. The median border is notable for its emission (efferent) of the significant plexus uterinus, plexus vaginalis and plexus vesicalis. The distal border deserves consideration from its emission (efferent) of the plexus rectalis. The afferent nerves arrive generally in the form of single cords slightly plexiform or ganglionated, but especially the efferent nerves depart from the borders of the pelvic brain in the form of leashes or closely meshed ganglionated plexuses.

The *arrangement* of the pelvic brain consists of (a) afferent or centripetal nerves (entering or contributing nerves) from the plexus interiliacus (sympathicus), from the ganglia sacralia, from the sacral (spinal) nerves (uterine, ovarian and round ligament arteries); (b) efferent or centrifugal (distributing or visceral nerves), known as plexuses. The afferent nerves enter chiefly on the proximal and external borders as single, slightly plexiform, cords, while the efferent nerves radiate mainly from the distal and median border of the pelvic brain as luxuriant leashes or richly ganglionated plexuses. There is no relation between number and dimension of the afferent and efferent nerves of the pelvic brain. It is a creating nerve center; however, vastly greater numbers of nerves are efferent (exit) than afferent (arrivals). The afferent nerves are mostly extended, slightly plexiform or ganglionated. The efferent nerves are in the form of leashes, highly plexiform and rich in ganglia. Although the pelvic brain is the major assembling centre for the pelvic vasomotor (sympathetic) nerves—practically the source of the genital nerves—however, nerves (one or more) pass directly from the plexus interiliacus (hypogastricus) to the uterus. This is demonstrated with facility in infant cadavers. Hence, all the nerves supplying the uterus do not first pass through the pelvic brain. The pelvic brain consists of the coalesced termination of the vast majority of (a) plexus interiliacus (hypogastricus); (b) nerves from the ganglia sacralia; (c) nerves from the ii., iii., iv. nervi sacralia; (d) plexus arteriæ uterinæ; (e) plexus arteriæ ovaricæ; (f) plexus arteriæ ligamenti rotundi. The efferent nerves consist of nerve plexuses and leashes emitted to each pelvic viscus. The following table represents the arrangement of afferent and efferent nerves of the pelvic brain.

Afferent Nerves.

1. Plexus interiliacus (hypogastricus).
2. Rami ganglionum sacralium.
3. Rami nervorum sacralium.
4. Plexus arteriæ ovaricæ.
5. Plexus arteriæ uterinæ.
6. Plexus arteriæ ligamenti rotundi.

Efferent Nerves.

1. Plexus uterinus.
2. Plexus ureteris.
3. Plexus vesicalis.
4. Plexus urethralis.
5. Plexus clitoridis.
6. Plexus vaginalis.
7. Plexus rectalis.

The plexuses of the pelvic brain radiate to the tractus genitalis (ovary, oviduct, uterus, vagina, clitoris); to the tractus urinarius (bladder, urethra); to the tractus intestinalis (rectum). The efferent ganglionated plexuses and leashes of the pelvic brain, of varied caliber, ensheathe and accompany arteries as the nerve emissions from the abdominal brain, but pass to the pelvic viscera and weave through and around them a luxuriant, profound, ganglionated, plexiform network, the major part of which is destined for the tractus genitalis (uterus and vagina). The nerves emitted by the pelvic brain are white in color, limited in diameter, plexiform in arrangement, resist tension on account of the powerful fibrous neurilemma and are richly bedecked with ganglia at the points of nerve crossing or anastomosis. The arrangement of the pelvic brain produces a structure consisting of composite or an aggregation of ganglia with nerve commissures or cords.

The Surface.—The surface of the pelvic brain is more smooth even than that of the abdominal brain, as the ganglia and fenestra are less in dimension. One may observe on its surface numerous depressions, fenestra of irregular form and dimension occupied by strong connective tissue, blood and lymph vessels. Some vessels centrally located may present, emerging through perforation of the ganglion. The blood-vessels fix and bind it to vagina. Thin strands or loops of nerves may be observed arising and inserting themselves on the same surface of the pelvic brain, resembling the chordæ tendinæ of the heart. Some smaller nerve strands arrive (afferent) and depart (efferent) from the surface.

Fenestra.—The fenestra of the pelvic brain, irregular in dimension and contour, depend for number and dimension on the coalescence or separation of the ganglia.

The dimensions of the fenestra increase from center to periphery. The fenestra are occupied by connective tissue vessels—arteries, veins and lymph. Lymph glands may also be found in them.

ANATOMY

The *color* is whitish-gray, brown; a liberal admixture of white conectiven tissue.

The *consistence* is moderately dense from association of abundant connective tissue.

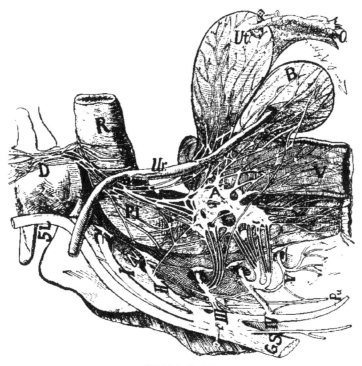

PELVIC BRAIN

Fig. 40. An illustration of the pelvic brain, drawn from my own dissection. The plexus interiliacus (hypogastricus) is distinct, presenting two terminations—*viz*.: (*a*) one part (P) terminates in the uterus without first passing through the pelvic brain (B). The other portion of the plexus interiliacus terminates in the pelvic brain (B). The source of the nerves which compose the pelvic are (*a*) interiliac plexus; (*b*) the sacra' plexus; (*c*) the sacral ganglia. It may be observed that there are small ganglia on the rectum, bladder and vagina and uterus. The pelvic brain rules the physiology of the tractus genitalis; it is a brain, it is a receiver, a reorganizer and an emitter of nerve force. The pelvic brain includes in its dynamics the initiation, maintenance and conclusion of labor. G. S., great sciatic. Pu., pudic nerve. S. G., sacral ganglia. R., rectum. V., vagina. X represents the nerve which arises from the III sacral and ends in the bladder. H., interiliac disc. U., ureter. C. I., common iliac artery. 16, vasa, ovarica crossing the ureter. Ov., ovary. O. D., oviduct. Observe the solid ganglionic mass (A) as a pelvic brain. Note the peculiar origin from the sacral nerves and the tailed division. The pelvic brain is but slightly fenestrated.

The Ganglia.—The ganglia of the pelvic brain vary in location, number, dimension, coalescence, separation and form. Each ganglion is composed of oval or spherical-shaped ganglionic nerve cells, ensconced in abundant and fine strand white connective tissue. Does the pelvic brain, the cervical ganglion, exist as a constant structure in every subject? The answer is a positive affirmative. However, the pelvic brain does not exist with such definitely located and constantly formed ganglia as that of the abdominal brain. The ganglion at the distal end of the major splanchnic nerve cannot be confused in constant dimension and location. It is a constant, permanent ganglionated apparatus, demonstrable in every subject. The macroscopic ganglia are especially numerous adjacent to the cervix uteri. In the pelvic brain the dissector does not find a single definitely located constant ganglion with exact dimensions. What is found in most subjects is an apparatus consisting of composite ganglia and nerve commissures and ganglionated plexus of irregular form and uncertain dimension, but practically constant in location. The ganglia and their commissures vary in dimension, form, location and number. It is a difficult task and time-robbing process to dissect and expose accurately the ganglia and commissures of the pelvic brain. The pelvic brain (the pelvic nerve apparatus), like the plexus interiliacus (hypogastricus) and ganglion interiliacum or interiliac nerve disc, has become dislocated from the vascular route (arteria hypogastrica), due to erect attitude and distalward movements of the tractus genitalis. A nerve ganglion may consist of (a) a single ganglionated nerve cell, surrounded by periganglionic connective tissue; (b) a group of ganglion cells, compound or composite, surrounded by periganglionic connective tissue; (c) it may consist of a plexiform ganglionic mass surrounded by periganglionic tissue. Whether the nerve ganglion (apparatus) be of a single ganglionic cell, composite ganglionic cells or a plexiform ganglionic mass matters not; its function is identical in the histologic sense (viz., reception, reorganization and emission of nerve force). In the composite ganglionic mass of the pelvic brain the function of the ganglia are not differentiated like the composite ganglia of the cranial brain. The pelvic brain is a composite ganglion. It consists of central ganglia of larger dimension surrounded by numerous adjacent ganglia of lesser dimension. The smaller ganglia may possess single afferent and efferent nerves. The pelvic brain, an aggregation of ganglia, is surrounded with periganglionic tissue only, and connective tissue enters with the nerve tissue. The ganglia of the pelvic brain coalesce to a central more or less solid mass and gradually decrease in dimension toward the periphery, while the dimension of the fenestrated network increase and the nerve commissures become elongated and more limited in diameter.

The Ganglionic Cells.—The ganglionic cells lie in oval or spherical spaces of periganglionic tissue. The nerve trunk of a ganglion will divide and reunite between the ganglion cells. The connective tissue, septa, divide the ganglion in departments of oval or spherical form which contain units or groups of ganglion cells. The cell body is generally granular and has a well-defined central nucleus. The nucleus seldom is located against the cell wall

—extra central. The dimensions of the ganglion cells vary. The number of ganglion cells in the pelvic brain is enormous.

GENERAL REMARKS ON THE PELVIC BRAIN.

The relations of the pelvic brain is that it was primarily an executive ganglionic nerve apparatus for the vascularity of the tractus genitalis; secondarily, for the distal end of the tractus urinarius (ureter, bladder, urethra); thirdly, for the distal end of the tractus intestinalis (rectum). At present in man it is a local executive ganglionic nerve apparatus for the general pelvic viscera. Cloacal differentiation has resulted in the more intimate relations of the distal end of the tractus genitalis, intestinalis and urinarius, with consequent solid and compact nerve anastomosis.

The relations of the pelvic brain well ensconced in connective tissue are in intimate connection with the cervix uteri, lateral vaginal fornix, lateral borders of rectum, distal ureter, vasa uterina, plexus sacralis spinalis, plexus interiliacus (hypogastricus) bladder. The pelvic brain is located at the distal end of the plexus interiliacus. It lies ensconced in the dense parametrial tissue perforated and benetted by blood-vessels and offers difficulties for complete exposures by dissection. Nerves arrive (afferent) in the pelvic brain as a rule at the proximal and lateral borders as simple cords chiefly and depart (efferent) mainly from the distal and medial borders as leashes and plexuses. More nerves depart than are received by the ganglion cervicale; hence, it is an originating, a creating center, a source of new nerve strands. The pelvic brain is a constant structure. It is always a multiple or composite ganglionic apparatus. It receives both spinal and sympathetic nerves. The *origin* of the nerves contributed to the pelvic brain; the afferent are: (1) plexus interiliacus (hypogastricus); (2) ganglia lumbalis; (3) plexus hemorrhoidalis; (4) ganglia sacralia; (5) i, ii, iii, iv nervi sacralis spinales. The converging nerves which coalesce to form the pelvic brain, a composite ganglion, are both sympathetic (dominating) and spinal (subordinate). All efferent nerves of the pelvic brain are vasomotor (sympathetic). The cervical ganglion demedullates the spinal nerves, hence all exit efferent nerves are sympathetic. The vast majority of the nerves enter the borders of the ganglion cervicale; some enter its surface. The efferent nerves of the pelvic brain compose (1) plexus uterinus, the main rich ganglionated nerve supply of the uterus—the plexus interiliacus (hypogastricus) sends some nerves to the uterus which do not first pass through the pelvic brain (see Fig. 1); (2) plexus vesicalis, a rich plexiform network studded with ganglia (the iii spinal sacral nerve emits a large branch which courses on the lateral border of the rectum and vagina to supply the bladder; thus, the vesical nerve supply is a mixed spinal and sympathetic, hence obscuring the vesical peristalsis); (3) plexus vaginalis, supplying the vagina with an abundant, mighty, woven nervous network studded with ganglia; (4) plexus rectalis, a network of nerves vastly less rich than either the plexus vesicalis or plexus vaginalis with ganglionated masses at the points of nerve strand coalescence; (5) plexus clitoridis, a rich and luxuriant ganglionated plexus supplying the clitoris with an enormous quantity of nerves. The additional discoveries of increased numbers of microscopic nerve in the uterus (Jung, Koch, Kerner) only further established the principle which I advocated fifteen years ago—viz., that "automatic visceral ganglia exist in every organ—*e.g.*, I advocated a decade and a half past this principle and introduced the terms automatic menstrual ganglia, automatic vesical ganglia, automatic renal, splenic and hepatic ganglia. The composite compound ganglia of the pelvic brain are all identical in function (rhythm)—unlike the differentiated function of the composite ganglia of the cranial brain. No parts of the pelvic cellular tissue remains free from traversing nerves and ganglia. It is not only the subserosium paracervicale and paravaginale immediately adjacent to the uterus and vagina that is richly traversed with gangliated nerves, but also the distant lateral subserous pelvic cellular tissue is abundantly supplied with the same nerve apparatus, however attenuated. The central pelvic visceral apparatus (tractus genitalis) ovary, uterus, oviducts and vagina, is richly and luxuriantly surrounded with a ganglionate nerve plexus resembling the network enclosing a rubber bulb. This wonderful wealth of ganglionated genital sympathetic nerves I have so far been enabled to observe on infant cadavers only and by the aid of a magnifying lens. Gross dissection of adults baffles observation. My dissections have convinced me that the pelvic brain in general subjects is not so compact a ganglion nor so pronounced in contour as claimed by Frankenhauser in his illustration of 1867, which I think is exaggerated in dimension, compactness or solidity and in its definiteness of contour or borders. The pelvic brain is difficult of preparation because of its resemblance to adjacent connective tissue in structure and color. It is whiter than the abdominal brain. To observe correct relations the pelvic brain must be dissected in situ. The most complete observations of the pelvic brain is obtained from infant cadavers preserved in alcohol, in which little dissecting preparation is required and the cellular tissue is transparent whence the nerves, together with their branches and ganglia, the pelvic brain, are distinctly visible and extraordinarily instructive. This method avoids the errors arising during gross dissection of the pelvic brain in adults. The pelvic brain (ganglion cervicale) is a constant ganglionated anatomic structure. It is practically complete in the infant as to form and location, however; its ganglia and periganglionic tissue develops with the development of the arteria uterina and genital functions (menstruation and gestation). Its dimensions and form varies within wide limits. The pelvic brain represents the major ganglionic assembling center of the pelvic (genital) nerves. It is particularly the coalescing termination of the nerves of the tractus genitalis. Investigators agree as to the pelvic brain being a ganglion in animals, but opinions diverge as to whether it is a ganglion or plexus in man. Remak demonstrated in the pig (1841) the presence of ganglia on the nerve trunks which course to either side of the uterus. I have found it a slight task to dissect and definitely expose the pelvic brain in animals in which it is more distinctly an isolated single ganglion. The relations of the pelvic brain to the abdominal brain is subordinate in function

ANATOMY

and location, similar to the relations of the cerebellum to the cranial cerebrum; hence, it might be termed the cerebellum sympathicum. The pelvic brain is the nerve executive apparatus of the pelvic organs—especially the tractus genitalis. The pelvic brain is always a ganglionate plexus. The degree of ganglionic coalescence or isolation decides its unity or multiplicity —its ganglionic or plexiform state. Through the pelvic brain the nerves of the distal end of the tractus urinarius, genitalis, intestinalis are solidly and compactly anastomosed, connected. Hence, irritation of one of the three tracts will irritate, induce reflexes in the other two (as in operation). The pelvic brain is the ganglionic automatic nerve apparatus of the uterus. Together with the ganglia located in the uterus it is the automatic nerve center of the uterus. It is a composite ganglionic apparatus interpolated between the cerebrospinal center and the myometrium—the uterus. About the year 1863 microscopic ganglia were discovered in the walls of the uterus and vagina by Keher, Koerner and Frankenhauser—which I termed automatic visceral ganglia fifteen years ago. The ganglionic theory of an automatic nerve center in the uterus, similar to that of the heart, intestine, bladder, ureter, has a rational anatomic base. Experiments first demonstrated that the muscle of the uterus (myometrium) was irritable—would contract and relax, was rhythmic—after death. Observation demonstrated that children were born, expelled, after the death of the cerebrospinal axis. In short, the uterus is subject to rhythmic movements a certain length of time subsequent to death or extirpation precisely similar to that of the other visceral tracts; viz., tractus intestinalis (gastrium, enteron colon); tractus urinarius (ureter, bladder); tractus vascularis (heart, aorta); tractus genitalis (oviduct, uterus). It is well known that segments of the involuntary muscles of the visceral tracts dominated by the sympathetic may persist in rhythmic movements, accompanied or not by artificial stimulation. It is, doubtless, due to a localized peripheral nerve apparatus—automatic visceral ganglia—located in the parenchyma of the organs possessing a partially independent and more persistent life than that of the cerebrospinal apparatus. The pelvic brain is the ganglionic automatic nerve apparatus for the uterus, subordinate in number of ganglion cells to the abdominal brain, and consequently subordinate in power. There is a genital center in the lumbar cord which, being irritated, induces uterine contraction. This center is of limited importance and subordinate to the sympathetic peripheral center. The lumbar center is not absolutely necessary for conception, gestation and parturition, as these processes will occur when the sacral nerves which supply the uterus are severed. To say that the pelvic brain is the automatic nerve center for the uterine vessels simply is to beg the question, for it is the blood that stimulates the myometrium (or any other organ) to contraction. The peripheral ganglionic nerve apparatus of the uterus (including the pelvic brain), macroscopic and microscopic, is the principal nerve center for its innervation. The pelvic brain (paired) located bilaterally at the cervico-vaginal junction is solidly and compactly anatomosed, connected, by a profoundly rich ganglionated network of nerve plexuses. The pelvic brain is the localized, subconscious, vegetative, sympathetic, automatic nerve apparatus for the organic life of the pelvic viscera, particularly of the tractus genitalis.

The pelvic brain is located closely adjacent to the point of crossing of the ureter by the pelvic floor segment of the utero-ovarian artery, hence in hysterectomy the cervical ganglion is extensively traumatized and damaged.

A curious feature in regard to the pelvic brain is that, however, originally it was a vascular brain, located intimately with the common iliac arteries, at present in man from erect attitude and distalward movements of the tractus genitalis, it is practically removed from great arteries and lies ensconced in a woven web of rich veins. The largest ganglia of the pelvic brain lie in the center, while extending to widely adjacent distances on the viscera are located smaller ganglia, separated by gradually increasing fenestrated areas.

The nerve plexuses and accompanying ganglia of the pelvic brain firmly bound in connective and elastic tissue richly surround the tractus genitalis like a net on a rubber ball and traverse its parenchyma like a spider's web.

In the rich ganglionated plexuses issuing from the pelvic brain to the tractus genitalis, *i.e.* the periuterine and parauterine plexuses, as well as the perivaginal and paravaginal plexuses, the nerves assume an arrangement similar to the arterial blood-vessels, *i.e.* they decrease in dimension in the median plane. The entire uterus is luxuriantly surrounded and its parenchyma richly traversed by abundantly gangliated nerve networks.

The vagina from proximal to distal ends is interwoven with a fine network of nerve fibers interspersed with ganglia to a remarkable degree. (Best observed with a magnifying lens in infant cadavers.)

The pelvic brain receives, reorganizes and emits nerve forces and hence is not a mere agent of the spinal cord. In it are repeated physiologic and pathologic manifestations of general visceral functions (rhythm, absorption and secretion) and special visceral function of the tractus genitalis (ovulation, menstruation and gestation).

The pelvic brain is subordinate in function to the abdominal brain because of less number of cells only, while it is superior in specialized function (as ovulation, menstruation and gestation). The subordination of the pelvic brain to the abdominal brain is evident from the fact that animals and men can live well with the pelvic brain extirpated (*i.e.* with absent genital function or genitals) while life will not continue, or at least under disturbance and for short duration, with the abdominal brain extirpated. (The extirpation of the abdominal brain is practically an anatomic inaccessibility during life.)

It must be admitted from anatomic facts that the abdominal brain partly rules the physiology of the tractus genitalis, one (or several) strong nerves from the plexus interiliacus (directly from the abdominal brain) passes directly to the uterus without first passing through the pelvic brain. However, the plexus uterinus, the major nerve supply of the uterus—passes directly from the pelvic brain to the uterus. It is a large, powerful ganglionated nerve plexus and no doubt accounts chiefly for the wonderful

ANATOMY 143

periodic rhythm, the stately peristalsis of the uterus. In short, the individual functions of the pelvic brain are:

(1) It demedullates nerves; nerves enter it (afferent) sheathed and depart (efferent) unsheathed.

(2) It is a source of new nerves; it has more efferent than afferent nerves.

(3) The pelvic brain is a giant vasomotor center for the pelvic viscera—especially the tractus genitalis.

(4) It shares in executing the six functions of the tractus genitalis—ovulation, secretion, absorption, peristalsis, menstruation and gestation.

(5) It is the major pelvic reflex center.

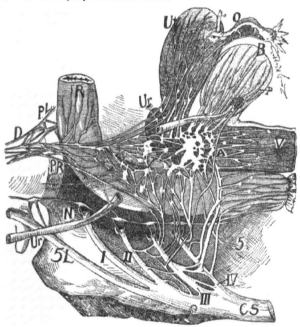

PELVIC BRAIN OF AN ADULT

Fig. 41. Drawn from my own dissection. A., pelvic brain. In this case it is a ganglionated plexus possessing a wide meshwork. Also the pelvic brain is located well on the vagina, and the visceral sacral nerves (pelvic splanchnics) are markedly elongated. V., vagina. B., bladder. O., oviduct. Ut., uterus. Ur., ureter. R., rectum. P. L., plexus interiliacus (left). P. R., plexus interiliacus (right). N., sacral ganglia. Ur., ureter severed to expose the pelvic brain. 5 L, last lumbar nerve. I, II, III, IV, sacral nerves. 5, coccygeal nerve. Observe that the great vesical nerve (P) arises from a loop between the II and III sacral nerves. G. S., great sciatic nerve.

(6) It possesses nutritive powers over its peripheral nerves. It presides, though subordinately, over the rhythm, peristalsis, of involuntary, visceral muscles of the pelvis. It controls secretion and absorption of the glands in tubular viscera (pelvic). The parametrium and entire pelvic subperitoneal tissue is richly traversed by nerves radiating to and from the pelvic brain. An accurate and comprehensive knowledge of the anatomy of the nerve supply of the tractus genitalis (especially the pelvic brain) will enable the gynæcologist to interpret symptoms of disease and to form a correct diagnosis which is the basis of rational treatment. It will aid to extend so-called medical gynæcology which is constructive, and limit so-called surgical gynæcology frequently destructive.

A general view of the pelvic brain is that it is an intermediary agent to receive and modify the spinal and sympathetic nerve forces for utilization in the tractus genitalis. It is a plenary envoy, an ambassador plenipotentiary to reconcile the spinal and sympathetic forces for appropriate use in the genital tract and associated viscera.

(B) *Physiology of the Pelvic Brain.*

The function of the ganglion cervicale—pelvic brain—is practically (a) to rule the physiology of the tractus genitalis (uterus, oviduct, ovary, vagina); (b) part of the tractus urinarius (bladder, distal ureter); (c) part of the tractus intestinalis (rectum). The pelvic brain, subordinate to the abdominal brain, dominates the function of the tractus genitalis, which is under the command of the sympathetic. The dynamics of the pelvic brain comprise the physiology of the tractus genitalis, which is:—(a) ovulation; (b) secretion; (c) absorption; (d) peristalsis; (e) menstruation; (f) gestation (post-natal). It is claimed that the pelvic brain demedullates, unsheaths, the spinal nerves and that all efferent or exit nerves of the ganglion cervicale are sympathetic. The pelvic brain dominates the pelvic viscera as the abdominal brain dominates the abdominal viscera. It assumes the dignity of a brain from its power of reception, reorganization and emission of nerve force. The dynamics of the pelvic brain includes the initiation, maintenance and conclusion of rhythm (peristalsis, labor) in the tractus genitalis as well as the domination of secretion and absorption. The pelvic brain presides over the monthly explosions, monthly rhythm of menstruation, controlling or modifying the automatic menstrual ganglia. The pelvic brain is a giant vasomotor center (cerebrum vasculare) for the tractus genitalis ruling the vast and varying phases of circulation (congestion and anæmia during sexual life, as pueritas, pubertas, menstruation, gestation, puerperium, climacterium and senescence). It presides over the lymphatic circulation and nourishment of the genital tract. The pelvic brain rules the manifest stately, periodic rhythm of the uterus during labor. It is the rhythmic center for the tractus genitalis. The pelvic brain dominates the bladder sufficiently to impose on it a rhythm (diastole and systole), however, powerful spinal nerves are amply present to modify the vesical rhythm. The plexus rectalis emitted from the pelvic brain to the rectum to a limited degree influences the rhythm, secretion and absorption of the rectum. Cerebrum pelvicum—the ganglion cervicale —is an automatic nerve center, a brain, as it has the power of reception, reorganization and emission of nerve force.

The pelvic brain is the local central potentate of visceral rule in the lesser pelvis.

The initiation, maintenance and conclusion of parturition should be referred to the pelvic brain. The stately rhythm and measured peristalsis of the uterus in the evacuation of its contents has excited the wonder and stirred the profound amazement of all observers in all time. The rhythm of the uterus is its protest against all occupants. The gestating uterus is always in a state of rhythm—the most active when most distended. The uterus (corpus and fundus) is always ready for an abortion. Were it not for the guarding, resting cervix, the sentinel of the uterine portals, the continuous myometrial rhythm would expel all uterine contents without regard to time. In the resting uterus the cervical ganglion or pelvic brain is free from pressure, not subject to trauma. In the gestating uterus, since the cervix is not practically involved in the enlargement, distention, the cervical ganglion is free from pressure or trauma because the gestating corpus and fundus pass proximalward in the abdomen in the direction of the least resistance, for ample space, leaving the lesser pelvis free from compromising pressure or trauma as in the resting uterus. During the last month of gestation the fetus (especially the head or perhaps the pelvis) passes distalward into the lesser pelvis and gradually the cervix becomes distended, obliterated from pressure, allowing the fetal parts (head or pelvis) to press, traumatize, mechanically irritate the pelvic brain with gradually increasing intensity, which initiates labor (uterine rhythm).

Pressure or trauma of the cervical ganglion incites the vigor and frequency of the uterine rhythm which is practically painless, however, the traumatism or stretching of the spinal nerves supplying the cervix, vagina and pudendum makes labor painful. Practically the vast majority of the plexus uterinus or uterine nerves originate in the pelvic brain; hence, for the control of uterine hæmorrhage the cervical ganglion must be consulted. In certain cases of postpartum hæmorrhage the older obstetricians claimed that by compressing the aorta the hæmorrhage was checked. This, of course, was an error, as its effective technical execution is practically impossible. The vasa ovarica are not affected by the method. The manipulation on the walls of the abdomen stimulated the plexus aorticus and plexus hypogastricus which transmitted the stimulus to the pelvic brain where it was reorganized and emitted over the plexus uterinus to the myometrium—the elastic and muscular bundles of which under its control act like living ligatures—checking the bleeding. Again, certain cases of post-partum hæmorrhage are fatal. The explanation may be that the trauma of labor, especially the child's head, may have partially paralyzed the pelvic brain (and interiliac plexus), whence the control of the muscular and elastic bundles in the myometrium is lost—they become relaxed and fail to contract the vascular lumen. In post-partum hæmorrhage four procedures are indicated:—First, rapid, light stroking of the abdomen parallel to the plexus aorticus and plexus interiliacus, the effect of which is to stimulate both abdominal and pelvic brain. Second, seize the uterine fundus through the abdominal wall and massage it, whence irritation of the myometrium induces its peripheral ganglia (automatic menstrual ganglia located in the myometrium and the pelvic brain located at the cervico-vaginal junction) to contract the vascular walls, lessening the blood currents. Third, introduce the finger into the vagina at the lateral fornix and excite the pelvic brain, which will emit a stimulus over the plexus uterinus to the myometrium resulting in the contraction of its elastic and muscular bundles. Fourth, intra-uterine digital irritation stimulates the pelvic brain through the peripheral ganglionated nerve plexuses which limits the vascular lumen.

The pelvic brain initiates, sustains and concludes parturition (peristalsis, labor). Alexander Keilmann's theory of the introduction of labor (1881) through mechanical irritation, pressure, or trauma of the pelvic brain is the most rational as it is supported by anatomic and physiologic data. The more mechanical irritation by the fetal pressure the greater the number of ganglia of the pelvic brain are excited, traumatized; hence, with distalward movement of the child the labor is intensified in a geometrical ratio.

The more distalward the child passes the more nerve elements are traumatized. When the head of the child rests on the pelvic floor, it practically presses, traumatizes or mechanically irritates all the pelvic nerve elements (ganglia), hence parturient peristaltic pains are vigorous.

The finger introduced in the rectum can irritate the pelvic brain with facility, which jeopardizes the patient less as regards infection. Hot vaginal douches stimulate uterine peristalsis in labor. The uterus itself may be considered a center with an automatic nerve apparatus (as I advocated in 1890, automatic menstrual ganglia). This idea of partial automatic nerve apparatus being located in the uterus itself is heightened by observation that the uterus is the most vigorously rhythmic in the beginning and ending of gestation. Goltz claims that a genital center is located in the lumbar cord, which has practically demontsrated itself as true on humans from injuries to the spinal cord. Goltz severed the spinal cord at the level of the tenth and eleventh dorsal vertebra on a dog and witnessed normal conception and parturition, hence he concluded that a genital center is located in the lumbar cord. The confusion would here lie in the influencing connection of the vagi with the abdominal brain. Does Goltz's genital center in the lumbar cord explain the common pain in the back in disease of the female genitals? Rein severed the sympathetic system and sacral nerves supplying the uterus, but subsequently normal conception and paturition occurred in the dog. Finally Rein claimed that he severed all the sympathetic nerves to the uterus as well as the sacral nerves and extirpated the pelvic brain (bilaterally) and still a normal parturition occurred in a dog four days post operation. Hence he concluded the uterus possessed a central nerve apparatus which controls its own function (especially peristalsis). This experiment is defective and the consequent conclusion erroneous for one can neither sever all the sympathetic nerves to the uterus nor extirpate all the pelvic brain in the living as the ganglionated plexiform network is too extensive. It is an anatomic impossibility. Besides Rein denies the existence of a ganglion cervicale, placing in its stead plexus nervosus fundamentalis uteri. Also Rein overlooked the extensive ganglionated nerve connection—plexus ovaricus—through the ligamentum latum from the ganglion ovaricum. He who has once observed with a magnifying lens the wealthy labyrinth of luxuriant ganglionated nerve plexuses supplying the tractus genitalis (in the infant) knows how futile it would be to attempt to sever all the nerves of the uterus. Many authors (Ellinger, Rein, Dembo, Cohnstein, Byron Robinson) have assumed a central nerve apparatus located in the pelvic brain or in the uterus. (Similar to the automatic visceral ganglia located in the tractus intestinalis, urinarius, heart, etc., etc.) The extirpated uterus placed in warm normal salt solution will perform its rhythm for some time similar to the extirpated oviduct, ureter, heart, intestine—each has a partial independent nerve center—automatic visceral ganglia. The so-called uterine inertia, or sudden cessation of uterine peristalsis during a long, slow journey of the head through the pelvis may be caused by a partial paralysis of the myometrium due to the temporary impinging of the head on the plexus interiliacus (hypogastricus) or pelvic brain. I observed once during the reduction of an invaginated puerperal uterus of twenty hours' duration that immediately after reduction the blood oozed abundantly from the uterine mucosa although I held my hand within the uterine cavity. Gradually as I irritated the endometrium the hæmorrhage lessened and finally in fifteen minutes ceased. The explanation was the trauma or constriction at the neck of the uterus had partially paralyzed the pelvic brain and its plexuses, and it required some time to recover their power over the elastic and muscular bundles of the myometrium. In slow labors accompanied by uterine inertia the pelvic brain could be stimulated digitally per rectum or by rectal clysters or electricity, inducing more frequent and vigorous contractions of the myometrium. The same physiologic principle is involved in the observation that violent diarrhœa is frequently followed by premature parturition or abortion. Drastic cathartics will produce violent uterine peristalsis sufficient to cause premature parturition or abortion—the pelvic brain is irritated per rectum. This clinical fact demonstrated that the nerves of the tractus genitalis and intestinalis are solidly and compactly anastomosed. The methods to utilize the physiology of the pelvic brain in practice are varied. For example, the mammary gland is connected to the pelvic brain by at least three distinct routes, viz.: (1) via the nerve plexuses accompanying the arteria mammaria and arteria subclavia, whence the route is direct along the aorta and its plexuses to the pelvic brain; (2) via the nerve plexuses accompanying the arteriæ intercostales to the aorta, whence the route is direct over the aorta and its nerve plexuses to the pelvic brain; (8) via the nerve plexuses accompanying the arteria epigastrica superior and inferior to the common iliac artery, whence the route continues on the plexuses accompanying the arteria rotundi ligamenti to the plexus uterinus (and to the pelvic brain). Therefore, by stimulating or irritating the nipple with light friction or massaging the mammary gland (especially the nipple), the uterus can be reached by the above routes and induced to contract more frequently and if the experiment be not too rapidly repeated the uterine contractions become more vigorous. I have experimented on this physiologic phenomenon during labor so frequent with such constant results that no doubt exists as to its correctness. The reverse physiology of the stimulation of the genitals influencing the mammæ through the sympathetic routes from the genitals to the mammæ are still more evident and frequent. If the tractus genitalis be stimulated by pregnancy, uterine myoma or other genital irritation, the mammary glands rapidly manifest disturbance in dimension, circulation, color, sensation, palpation. The sensations in the tractus genitalis have been reorganized in the pelvic brain and emitted over the several nerve routes to the mammary glands. Again the uterus may be incited to more vigorous and frequent contraction during labor by the administration of a tablespoonful of hot water which first emits the stimulation over the plexus gastricus to the abdominal brain, where it is reorganized and transmitted over the plexus aorticus and plexus interiliacus (hypogastricus) to the pelvic brain, whence reorganization and emission over the plexus uterinus occurs with consequent contraction of the myometrium. The pelvic brain must explain the normal and abnormal pains of the uterus as its dominating nerve center. A knowledge of the pelvic brain with its multiple radiating nerve leashes and plexuses is not only valuable for the science alone of obstetrics and gynæcology, but it is important for successful practice. The independence of the pelvic brain is evident when children are born, expelled, from the uterus after the death of the mother. Joseph Hyrtl, the celebrated Viennese anatomist, reports that during a war in Spain some bandits hanged a pregnant woman. After she had hung on the gallows for four hours, and consequently was long dead, she gave birth to a living child. I have observed the giant uterus of slaughtered pregnant cows executing with wondrous precision its stately rhythm and measured peristalsis hours subsequent to death and evacuation of the uterine contents. If one extirpate an oviduct from a human patient and place it in warm normal salt solution oviductal rhythm may be maintained by physical stimulus for some three-quarters of an hour. Labor should be painless, as normal visceral rhythm is painless. Scanzoni reports a woman paralyzed from the dorsal vertebra distalward as having had a painless labor—the spinal nerve of the tractus genitalis was paralyzed—hence, painless dilatation of the cervix occurred, with expulsion of uterine contents. The signification of the cervical ganglion in practice is evident when observed that trauma or shock on the pelvic brain will kill in a few hours. For example, I performed an autopsy on the body of a woman after her first child who had ventral hysteropexy performed on her four years previously and in whom, immediately subsequent to labor, the uterus invaginated, killing her in about two and a half hours. She died from shock, which went swiftly onward and swiftly downward. The pelvic

PHYSIOLOGY

brain dominates the rhythm of the corpus and fundus (uterus). That the uterus is supplied by sympathetic nerves and cervix by spinal is significant in practice. For example, the uterus (corpus and fundus) is always ready for an abortion, because it is always in rhythm. The cervix is never ready for an abortion, because it is not in rhythm, being dominated by sacral spinal nerve. The pelvic brain is intimately and profoundly connected to the abdominal brain by a direct nerve route of vast nerve plexuses and ganglia—viz., by the plexus interiliacus (hypogastricus) and plexus aorticus. Any disturbance in the pelvic brain is flashed with telegraphic rapidity to the abdominal brain, and most of the consequent pathologic physiology is manifest from the stomach by disordered rhythm (vomiting or nausea), absorption and secretion.

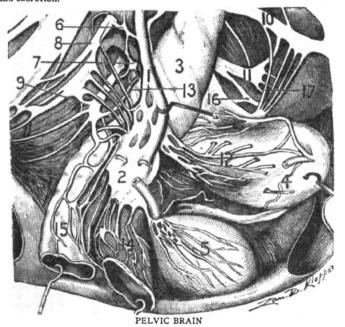

PELVIC BRAIN

Fig. 42. Drawn from my own dissection. Woman about thirty years of age. In this subject the dissection was rather deficient than excessive, hence, the pelvic brain presents more of a solid ganglion than a fenestrated ganglion, or ganglionated plexus. 1 and 2, pelvic ganglion. 3, rectum. 4, uterus. 5, bladder. 6 and 7, sacral ganglia. 8, last lumbar nerve. 9, IV sacral nerve. In this subject the pelvic brain results from the union of the plexus interiliacus (1) and branches from II, III and IV sacral nerves.

The detailed dissection was not continued sufficiently to demonstrate that the plexus interiliacus emitted separate strands directly to the uterus without first entering the pelvic brain. In this subject the pelvic brain was one inch in length. one-half inch in width, and one-fifth inch in thickness. Such a majestic ganglion must be endowed with giant power.

Age Relations.—In contra-distinction to the abdominal brain, a life-long functionating organ, the pelvic brain possesses age relations concomitant with the age relations of the tractus genitalis. The age relations of the pelvic brain, similar to those of the tractus genitalis, depend upon the volume of blood irrigating it at the different phases of sexual life, as pueritas, pubertas, menstruation, gestation, puerperium, climacterium, senescence. The pelvic brain, present at birth, experiences multiplication of its ganglion cells, maximum completion and minimum atrophy during postnatal life. Its function rises and falls with that of the genitalis.

I. *Pueritas.*—In childhood the pelvic brain is present; however, the ganglion cells are few and small. The cell body is small, slightly granular. Cell nucleus is distinct. Cell nucleolus, small and indistinct. The ganglion cells grow, increase gradually with the years. At six years of age the cell nucleus is marked and the nucleolus is distinct.

II. *Pubertas.*—At puberty the ganglion cells are completely developed (simulating the arteria uterina).

III. *Menstruation.*—At the menstrual period the hyperæmia, congestion, may aid in increasing the connective tissue cells.

IV. *Gestation.*—During pregnancy the profound and continuous hyperæmia, the permanent, exalted engorgement, produces an increase, a multiplication of interganglionic cellular nerve and connective tissue, which force the ganglion cells asunder. This lends to the pelvic brain an evident increase in its gross dimension (not positively a multiplication of ganglion cells). The vast majority of investigators admit that the pelvic brain hypertrophies in its nerve and connective tissue department during gestation (not in ganglion cells). However, it is a very difficult problem to solve, as we are not familiar with the number of ganglion cells present at any one epoch of sexual life. Besides, inflammatory processes in the tractus genitalis modify or destroy the ganglion cells. Also individual variations confuse. Connective tissue develops in the pelvic brain during the active function of the genitals, in maximum sexual life (menstruation and gestation). S. Pessimski, in his able production (1908), asserts that the character of the plexus (pelvic brain) and the dimensions of the ganglia are identically the same in gravid and non-gravid subjects.

V. *Puerperium.*—In the devascularization of the puerperal stage cellular elements will perhaps degenerate, atrophy, disappear.

VI. *Climacterium.*—In the climacteric stage the blood supply begins to diminish, increasing the interganglionic cellular elements, which forces the ganglion cells asunder, and the parenchyma (ganglion cells) begins its final long night of atrophy and disappearance.

VII. *Senescence.*—In senescence the arteria uterina loses its spirality, becoming extended, its lumen becomes diminished, its walls become hypertrophied and the volume of blood supplying the pelvic brain (and genitals) gradually decreases with consequent atrophy. The interganglionic connective and nerve tissue increases, multiplies, while the parenchyma (ganglion cells) becomes atrophied, compressed to death by cicatrization and lack of blood. By progressive interganglionic nerve and connective tissue multiplication the ganglion cells are separated and compressed, gradually losing their nucleolus, and later their nucleus, and finally the granulation of the ganglion cell body disappears and the ganglion cells become reduced to a homogeneous mass—atrophic death. They have ceased to command the rhythmic uterus. The senescent decadent process of the pelvic brain is identical with that of the tractus genitalis (*i. e.*, for the segment supplied by the arteria uterina).

(C) Remarks on the Pathology of the Pelvic Brain.

The pelvic brain is subject to disease similar to other abdominal viscera.

Are diseases of the pelvic brain accompanied by a range of recognizable symptoms? In some 700 personal autopsic inspections of the abdominal viscera I observed that in 80 per cent. of female subjects the tractus genitalis presented disease—inflammation. The majority of these inflammatory processes are practically peritoneal only, and would hence not materially interfere with the pelvic brain in structure or function. However, there are two other classes of subjects in which peritoneal inflammatory processes traumatize the structure and compromise the function of the pelvic brain, viz.: (a) Peritonitis, with extensive adhesions, contracting in subjects where the peritoneal adhesions by contraction dislocate the viscera, compromising the circulation (blood and lymph) and function while the traumatism of the peritoneal contractions on the pelvic brain compromises its circulation, function, structure and nourishment. (b) In subjects where the inflammatory process penetrates to various degrees in the pelvic subserosum with resulting round-cell infiltration and subsequent contraction of cellular tissue. In cellulitis the cicatricial contraction is more profound on the pelvic brain, with consequently more profound impression in compromising its circulation (blood and lymph) and traumatizing its ganglion cells, nerve cords and commissures ending in degeneration. Pelvic peritoneal adhesions and pelvic cellulitis are the chief diseases which attack the integrity of structure and function of the pelvic brain. The advance of malignant disease in the organs adjacent to the pelvic brain is so profound in its traumatism and compromisation of structure and function that practically paresis, paralysis or death of its structure and function rapidly ensues.

W. A. Freund's essay on parametritis chronica atrophicans is well known. Inflammation frequently attacks the pelvic brain, and the resulting hypertrophy and atrophy will inevitably damage its delicate structure and function. No abdominal organs present more palpable macroscopic deviation from inflammatory consequences than the tractus genitalis. The inflammations in the uterus (myometritis) and ligamentum latum, with resulting hypertrophy and atrophy, are common observations. These inflammatory processes are accompanied by atrophy and compromisation of blood and lymph vessels. Reflexes of various kinds and degrees follow in the inflamed genitals—from both acute and chronic states. Cicatrization, sclerosis, contracting peritoneal adhesions in the pelvis compromise the function of the pelvic brain and traumatize its structure. The observing gynæcologist notes far more reflexes, hysteria, neuroses from atrophic (genitals) chronic myometritis than from hypertrophic (genitals) myometritis. The rational explanation is that atrophic states in the uterus and parauterine peritoneal and cellular tissue (consequent on inflammation) are accompanied by profound compromisation of function and traumatization of structure in the pelvic brain and its adjacent delicate nerve fibres. As common proof one can cite the neurotic hysterical patient with atrophic pelvic organs.

The pelvic brain will present anatomico-pathologic reactions from toxic agents similar to other viscera-degeneration. The more rapid or intense the toxic agent the more profound the reaction. The toxic infectious changes in the pelvic brain may be parenchymatous and degenerative in the acute forms, nodular in the less acute and sclerotic in the chronic forms. The toxic infections may leave sequels in the pelvic brain as in other viscera.

Laignel Lavastine has made a study of the abdominal sympathetic, and has attempted to demonstrate that some of the neuroses subsequent to infectious disease, as typhoid, scarlet fever, diphtheria, etc., may be due to the changes effected in the sympathetic ganglia.

Some of the numerous neuroses accompanying genital disease may have an anatomic substratum in the pelvic brain. We have noted that the rational explanation of the sudden cessation of labor for a time is doubtless due to trauma, shock on the plexus interiliacus or pelvic brain, which has become paretic by the impinging of the harder parts of the child on the interiliac plexus as it journeys through the pelvis. Though the stately rhythm and measured peristalsis of the uterus during labor presents a wonderfully established phenomenon, yet by trauma of the child's head on the pelvic brain it is quickly deranged. The gynæcologist may claim that, from the frequency with which neuroses, hysteria, visceral reflexes follow pelvic inflammations, with consequent sclerosis atrophy in the tractus genitalis (especially myometritis and inflammations of the ligamentum latum), the neuroses hysteria reflexes are symptoms of diseases in the pelvic brain.

CONCLUSIONS AS REGARDS THE PELVIC BRAIN.

(A) *Anatomy.*—The pelvic brain, a constant structure, is practically formed by the union of the visceral branches (pelvic splanchnics II, III and IV) of the sacral plexus with the interiliac (hypogastric) plexus. It is a composite or compound ganglion, paired and practically symmetrical in dimension, form, position and weight. The pelvic brain is located bilaterally at the cervico-vaginal junction, where the latter is in contact with the rectum. It is situated extraperitoneally in the parametrium at the base of the ligamentum latum, on a level with internal os uteri well concealed in connective tissue. Practically the position of the pelvic brain is at the point of crossing of the ureter with the uterine artery. It is the major assembling center for the pelvic sympathetic. It is surrounded and interwoven with dense subperitoneal pelvic connective tissue, presenting difficulties of exposition by dissection on account of its simulation to adjacent tissue. The pelvic brain has extensive and profound connection with the uterus, vagina, ureter, bladder and rectum. The composite, compound ganglia of the pelvic brain are composed of multipolar ganglionic nerve cells ensconced in periganglionic tissue. From erect attitude the pelvic brain has

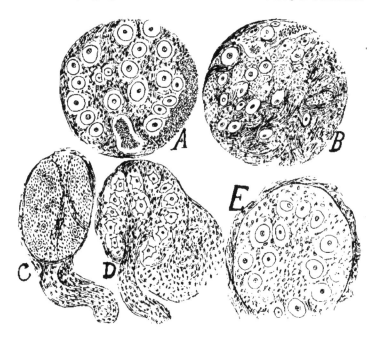

Fig. 43. (A) Drawn from the pelvic brain of a girl seventeen years of age. The ganglion cells are completely developed. (B) Drawn from the pelvic brain of a three months' normal gestation. The ganglion cells are completely developed. Observe the enormous mass of connective tissue present. (C) Child 1½ years old. A nerve process courses within the ganglion. Few and small ganglion cells incompletely developed. (D) Girl 1½ years old. A nerve process branches and reunites itself with the intercellular substance. (E) Girl 6 years old. The ganglion cells are presenting development. (Redrawn after Dr. Saburo Hashimoto.)

changed position, moving more distalward into the lesser pelvis and approaching more the median plane. The average dimensions of the adult pelvic brain, with resting uterus, are: Length (proximadistal), one inch; width, three-quarters of an inch; thickness, one-sixth of an inch. In the gestating uterus the average dimensions of the pelvic brain are: Length, one and one-half inches; width, one inch, and thickness, one-fifth of an inch. The form is triangular, quadrangular. The borders, or contour, are irregular and not well defined. The arrangement of the pelvic brain consists of (a) afferent or centripetal nerves (entering or contributing nerves) from the plexus interiliacus (sympathetic) and plexus sacralis (spinal); (b) efferent or centrifugal nerves (distributing or visceral nerves).

The afferent nerves enter the pelvic brain mainly on the proximal and external borders as single, slightly plexiform cords.

The efferent nerves radiate mainly from the median and distal borders as luxuriant leashes or richly ganglionated plexuses.

There is no relation in number or dimension between the afferent and efferent nerves. The pelvic brain is a fenestrated ganglionic mass. Its consistence is moderately dense from association of abundant periganglionic tissue. The ganglia of the pelvic brain vary in dimension, location, form, coalescence, separat'on.

To expose the pelvic brain by dissection the most perfectly, the cadavers of infants preserved in alcohol are absolutely necessary—superior to that of adults.

The pelvic brain resembles the abdominal brain in that it receives the visceral nerves (pelvic splanchnics) from the II, III, IV, sacral nerves, while the abdominal brain receives the visceral nerves (abdominal splanchnics) from the VII dorsal to the II lumbar (thoracico-lumbar). The pelvic brain is accessible to palpation per vaginam and per rectum.

Practically, the genitals are supplied from two sources, viz.: (a) directly from the plexuses of the pelvic brain; (b) from one (to several) strands issuing directly from the plexus interiliacus (which does not first pass through the pelvic brain).

The plexuses of the pelvic brain (uterine, ureteral, vaginal, vesical and rectal) anastomose, connect, solidly and compactly, the tractus genitalis, part of the tractus urinarius (ureter, bladder), part of the tractus intestinalis (rectum), which induces them to act clinically as a joint organ—injury or disease in any one tract produces reflex effects in the other two, and *vice versa*.

(*B*) *Physiology.*—The function of the pelvic brain is practically to rule the physiology of (a) the TRACTUS GENITALIS; (b) part of the *tractus urinarius* (ureter, bladder); (c) part of the tractus intestinalis (rectum).

The physiology of the tractus genitalis is (a) ovulation; (b) secretion; (c) absorption; (d) peristalsis (prenatal and common with functions of the abdominal brain); (e) menstruation; (f) gestation (special functions of the pelvic brain), and (g) sensation.

The pelvic brain is a nervous center—*i.e.*, it receives, reorganizes and emits nerve forces. The pelvic brain is a local nervous executive for the common functions of the pelvic viscera (peristalsis, absorption and secretion) and for the special function of the tractus genitalis (ovulation, menstruation and gestation.) The pelvic brain was originally in function and location a vascular brain—cerebrum pelvicum vasculare.

The dynamics of the pelvic brain include the initiation, maintenance and conclusion of parturient peristalsis (labor).

The ganglion cervicale assumes the dignity of a brain from its power of reception, reorganization and emission of nerve impulses.

Parturient peristalsis (labor) is initiated by the distalward movement of the child and the consequent mechanical irritation, pressure, excitement on the pelvic brain. The greater the distalward movement of the child in the pelvis the more mechanical irritation from the fœtal head occurs on the pelvic brain, and consequently the greater number of nerve elements (ganglia) are excited.

The pelvic brain functionates as a unit, possessing no segmental ganglionic differentiation as in the cranial brain. It is a source of new nerves, a creating center, as it possesses more efferent than afferent nerves. The pelvic brain is subordinate to the abdominal brain in total number of ganglion cells—not in specific functions (as ovulation, menstruation, gestation). It demedullates nerves—*i.e.*, medullated nerves enter (afferent) sheathed and depart (efferent) demedullated, unsheathed. The pelvic brain is a giant vasomotor center for the pelvic viscera, especially for the tractus genitalis. It shares in the execution of the six functions of the genital tract—viz., ovulation, secretion, absorption, peristalsis, menstruation, gestation. The pelvic brain is the major pelvic reflex center. It is the minor abdominal reflex center, the abdominal brain being the major reflex center. It possesses nutritive power over its peripheral nerves. The pelvic brain arrives at its adult maximum dimensions and functionating power after a complete gestation. The pelvic brain is an intermediary agent to receive and modify the spinal and sympathetic nerve forces for utilization in the tractus genitalis.

The pelvic brain experiences an *age relation* concomitant with that of the tractus genitalis—*i.e.*, with the utero-ovarian artery. The age relations of the pelvic brain depend on the volume of blood irrigating it at different phases of sexual life.

(a) In pueritas the ganglion cells are few and small.

(b) In pubertas the ganglion cells are completely developed.

(c) In menstruation the hyperæmia, congestion, increases the connective tissue.

(d) In gestation the profound and constant hyperæmia, exalted engorgement, produces a multiplication of ganglion cells and an increase of connective tissue.

(e) In puerperium the devascularization of the ganglionic cell elements may produce degeneration, atrophy.

(f) In climacterium the blood supply decreases, the ganglionic cells atrophy and the connective tissue increases.

(g) In senescence the ganglion cells atrophy and disappear, while the connective tissue multiplies, increases. The pelvic brain begins its long night of atrophic death.

(C) *Pathology.*—The pelvic brain is subject to disease similar to other abdominal viscera. As the tractus genitalis is frequently subject to infection and, consequently, inflammatory processes during its maximum activity, the pelvic brain, no doubt, becomes diseased and manifests symptoms. Peritonitis, cellulitis and infectious processes will affect the pelvic brain and induce a series of neurotic symptoms. Atrophic genitals following inflammatory processes are frequently accompanied by neuroses. The most typical disease is that known from W. A. Freund as

Parametritis Chronica Atrophicans.—The anatomic substratum of reflex neuroses, hysteria, may be found in disease of the pelvic brain; cicatricial contraction traumatizes the pelvic brain. The pelvic brain may be the agent of valuable therapeutics—*e.g.*, in post-partum hæmorrhage massage of the pelvic brain may be accomplished per rectum, per vaginam, manipulation of the uterus or light stroking of the plexus interiliacus inducing the elastic and muscular bundles of the myometrium to contract like living ligatures, controlling vessel lumen.

BIBLIOGRAPHY OF THE PELVIC BRAIN (GANGLION CERVICALE).

Eustachius, B. (died 1574). Tabulæ Anatomicæ, Amsterdam, 1722.

de Graaf, Regner (1641-1673). Opera omnia, Amsterdam, 1705.

Willis, Thomas (1622-1675). Cerebri nervorumque descriptio, Geneva, 1680.

Haller, Albertus (1708-1777). Elementa physiologiæ. Laus, 1778.

Vieussens, R. (1641-1716).

Walter, J. G. (1734-1818). Tabulæ nerv. thoracis et abdominis. Berolini, 1783.

Hunter, William (1718-1783). Anatomic description of the pregnant uterus. 1802.

Osiander, F. B. (father) (1757-1822). Handbuch der Entbindungskunst, 1818.

Osiander, J. F. (son) (1787-1855). Literario a mediocrum ordine præmio Commentatio-physiologica quæ disserata uterum nervos habere in certamine. Literario a mediocrum ordine præmiornat. Goettingen, 1808.

Bourgery, J. M. (1797-1845), 1840, and Claude Bernard (1813-1778), 1840.

Tiedemann, Friedricus (1781-1861). Tabulæ nervorum uteri. Heidelberg, 1822.

Lobstein, J. G. C. F. (1777-1815). De nervi sympathici humani fabrica, etc. Paribsii, 1823.

Kilian, F. (1800-1864). Die Nerven des Uterus. Zeitschrift f rationelle Med. 1851. Burns' Handbuch der Geburtshuelfe, herausgegeben von Kilian. Bonn, 1834.

Boivin. Handbuch der Geburtshuelfe, uebersetzt von Robert Kassel. 1829.

Lee, Robert (1798-1878). Philosophical transactions. 1842. Also the anatomy of the nerves of the uterus. 1841.

Beck, Thomas Snow (1814-1847). Philosophical transactions, 1846.

Clay. Nerves of the uterus. 1845.

Swan. The physiology of the nerves of the uterus. 1846.

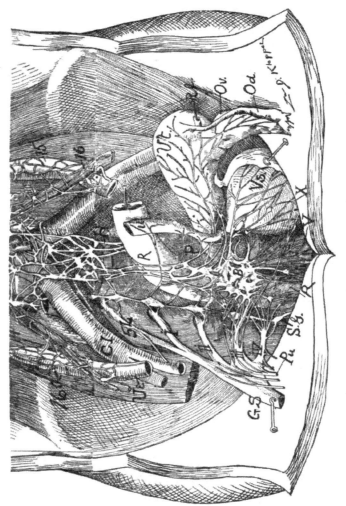

PELVIC BRAIN OF ADULT

Fig. 44. B represents the pelvic brain. The plexus aorticus extends from the abdominal brain to the aortic bifurcation or interiliac disc (H). The plexus interiliacus (hypogastricus) extends from the interiliac disc (H) to the pelvic brain (B). It is evident that the pelvic brain is the result of the coalescence of the plexus interiliacus and sacral nerves II, III and IV. Note that part of the plexus interiliacus sends nerve cords directly to the uterus. 16a and 16 is the arterio-ureteral crossing. The ureters were dilated. Note the great vesical nerve extending from III to X. In this drawing suggestions from Frankenhauser were employed.

Jobert de Lamballe (1779-1867). Comptes des science de L'Académie, T. XII., No. 20, Mai 17. Recherches sur la disposition des nerfs de l'uterus, etc.

Langenbeck's Atlas. Tafel 11 and 12. Fasc. iii. Neurologie.

Louget. Anatomie und Physiologie des Nerven-System. Bonn, 1849.

Hirschfeld and Laville. Neurologie descript. et iconographie du système nerveux. Paris, 1853.

Frankenhauser, Ferdinand (died 1894). Die Nerven de Gebaermutter. Jena, 1867.

Koerner, Thomas. De nervi uteri. 1865.

Polle. Preisschrift (Thesis). Goettingen, 1875.

Koch, Robert. Ganglia of the uterus. 1865.

Keilman, Alexander, Dorpat. Zeitschrift f. Geb. und Gyn. Bd. 22. Ursache des Geburtseintritts. 1881.

Goltz. Pflueger's Arch. Bd. 9.

Rohrig. Virch. Arch. Bd. 76. 1879.

Jostreboff. Thèse St. Petersburg, 1881. Anatomie normal et pathologique du ganglion cervicale de l'uterus.

Freund, W. H. Verh. der Nat. Vers. Strassburg, 1885.

Cohnstein. Arch. f. Gyn. Bd. 18. 1881.

Historical study of the methods of experiments to determine the nerves of the uterus.

Robinson, Byron. 1894 to 1899. A series of articles on the sympathetic nervous system (abdominal and pelvic brain) published in a number of journals. Book on "Abdominal Brain and Automatic Visceral Ganglia," published in 1899.

Mayer, R. Virch. Arch. Bd. 85.

Franz. Centralblatt f.Gynecol., No. 24. 1904.

Freund, W. A. Festschrift für Chrobak. 1903.

von Herff, München. Medicin. Wochensch., No. 4. 1892.

Gawronsky. Arch. f. Gyn. Bd. 47. 1894. Nerve endings in the uterus.

Knupffer. Wegen der Ursache des Geburtseintritts. Inaugural dessertation. Dorpat, 1892.

Waldeyer, Wm. Das Becken. Bonn, 1899.

Pissemski, S. Monatsschrift f. Geburtshülfe und Gynäkologie, Bd. 17. 1903. Zur Anatomie des Plexus fundamentalis uteri beim Weibe und gewissen Thieren.

Ph. Jung. Untersuchung ueber die Innervation der weiblichen Genital-Organe. Monatsschrift für Geburtshülfe und Gynäkologie, Bd. 21. Heft I, Jan., 1905.

Hashimoto, Sabura. Beiträge zur Geburt und Gynäkol. Bd. 8. Heft I, 1894. (Anatomy and histology of the cervical ganglion).

Freund, W. A. Verhand. d. 76. Nat. Vers. Breslau, 1904.

CHAPTER XIV.

GENERAL CONSIDERATIONS.

Every thoracic and abdominal organ has its own rhythm (peristalsis).
A little knowledge is a dangerous thing.—Lord Bacon.

The original investigations of the sympathetic nervous system, in both humans and animals, upon which this work is founded, were begun in 1887, and have been carried on quite steadily since. The works of Fox, Chapin, Gaskell, Eulenberg and Guttmann, Patterson, Robert Lee, Lobstein, Snow-Beck, Rauber and Frankenhauser have been carefully studied. A number of physiologies, as well as some fifty anatomies, were searched. One hundred human cadavers have been dissected with reference to the sympathetic system and also among the lower animals, those of the rodents and solipeds—cow, calf, pig, dog, fish, bird, frog, rabbit, rat and sheep. The dissections have comprised in addition a considerable number of embryos, human and animal. The results of this work demonstrate that the ganglia of the sympathetic nerve are much larger in the lower animals than in man. That is, as the scale of animal life ascends, the sympathetic system proportionately decreases, while the cerebro-spinal system proportionately enlarges. In short the higher the life the more dominant the cerebro-spinal system, and the lower the life the more dominant the sympathetic system.

In mammals there exist two brains of almost equal importance to the individual and also to the race: One is *the cranial brain*, the instrument of mental progress and physical protection; the other is *the abdominal brain*, the instrument of nutrition and visceral rhythm. To the casual observer the cranial cerebrum seems to overshadow all other nervous centers. The anterior brain of mammals, situated in the skull, is so manifest to the practitioner that it seems to do all the business of the nervous system. It is true that the knot of life is situated at the base of the cranial brain, and by one prick of a bodkin in the medulla, life may be quickly extinguished. Yet a derangement of the abdominal brain destroys life as effectually, though not so quickly. A study of the abdominal brain brings to light views which are both important and practical. In the cranial brain resides the consciousness of right and wrong. Here is the seat of all progress, mental or moral, and in it lies the instinct to protect life and the fear of death. But in the abdomen there exists a brain of wonderful powers. It presides over organic life. Its great functions are two—nutrition and visceral rhythm. In this abdominal brain are repeated all the physiological and pathological manifestations of nutrition and rhythm of viscera. It controls nourishment and secretion. It initiates, sustains and prohibits rhythm. It receives sensations and transmits motion. It is an automatic nervous center. It is a physiological and anatomical brain. In short, it is a nervous ganglion; only a ganglion possesses rhythmical power.

The abdominal brain is situated around the root of the celiac axis and superior mesenteric artery. It lies just behind the stomach, consists of a blended meshwork of nervous ganglia, and is made up of the union of the splanchnics, the two pneumogastrics and the right phrenic.

There is a difference between the right and left abdominal brain. The left is more closely packed together; it is retort-shaped, chiefly consists of a large, solid ganglion and is apparently an expansion of the lower end of the left splanchnic nerve and is larger than the right. The right half of the abdominal brain is more of a meshwork than the left; it is perforated with numerous apertures, in short, is flatter and wider than its fellow. I am convinced that its flatness is due to the pressure of the inferior vena cava.

The abdominal brain really consists of two ganglia. These two ganglia are sometimes called semilunar, but I never saw one of such shape. The two ganglia are united by cords at the foot of the celiac axis and are known as the solar or epigastric plexus. This abdominal brain lying along the aorta just behind the stomach is a silent power in assimilation and rhythmical movements, unless some organ is deranged. Observations of the disturbance of visceral functions in women who were the subjects of pelvic disease led me to follow the work.

Disease of the viscera is likely to disturb the two great functions of the abdominal brain: nutrition and rhythm. The abdominal brain distributes its branches to all the vascular system—artery, vein and lymphatic. The branches of nerves will sometimes surround the artery like a sheath or pass along its parallel strands. In short, the branches of the sympathetic nerves are carried to all parts of the economy on the walls of the blood-vessels. The caliber of the blood-vessels, especially the smaller ones, is controlled by these fine strands of nerves. They may produce by their action the scarlet flush (capillary dilatation) of the cheek, or the marble paleness (capillary contraction) of fright. Several years ago, from experiments on the pregnant uterus of slaughtered cows, I became thoroughly convinced that the sympathetic nerve is the cause of rhythm, while the cerebro-spinal nerves prohibit rhythm. It is evident that the rhythmical waves in the fundus and body of the uterus are entirely due to the sympathetic, which almost alone supplies it. The sober stillness and non-rhythmical motion of the uterine neck is due to the excessive supply of spinal nerves. The order from the cranial brain for motion is active, direct and reflex, subsiding after action. But the order from the abdominal brain is rhythmical, and the rhythmical movements play on all vessels and hollow organs, on the circulatory apparatus and the viscera.

The abdominal brain presides likewise over the glandular system. Here it holds the balance of power between normal blood-tissues and substances to be excreted. The abdominal brain controls secretion. The orders which it sends out to each gland, however, must be reorganized in each separate viscus, *i. e.*, in the periphery of the nerves. The orders to the liver are manifest in the products of bile, glycogen and urea. The forces sent to the digestive tract from the abdominal brain are obvious from the secretion of the digestive fluids, from the mouth to the rectum. The sympathetic system holds the glandular system as a unit, *e. g.*, when the ovarian gland is injured or removed, inflammation may arise in the parotid gland. And mumps and parotitis may be accompanied by orchitis. The rhythm of glands, such as the liver and spleen, is possible from their elastic capsules. The orders from the abdominal brain to the digestive glands may become so violent that Auerbach's plexus throws the muscle of the intestine into rigid contraction, and Meissner's plexus may secrete so rapidly that an active diarrhea may arise in a few minutes. It has been observed that herds of cattle on a ship have been attacked with diarrhea five minutes after the boat was put in motion. The abdominal brain was suddenly disturbed. The sweat-glands may be irritated so violently that the entire body becomes suddenly bathed in perspiration. Much execution may be done by inhibiting the sweat-centers.

Excessive or deficient gland secretion, then, depends on the abdominal brain and its principal machines. The gynecologist sees wonderful rhythmical movement in the generative apparatus, and he must refer this to the orders of the abdominal brain. The oviducts and ovaries pass through rhythmical circles due to nervous bulbs situated in their walls. I named and wrote of these as "automatic menstrual ganglia," several years ago. The ganglia of the oviduct and uterus which cause the monthly rhythm are entitled to due respect, as well as the peripheral digestive and cardiac ganglia. Again, there is a mechanism called the vasomotor center, which distributes itself in the medulla and along the spinal cord. If the abdominal brain is disturbed the vasomotor center becomes deranged and the skin will be waxy pale or scarlet red. Under this category come the cold, white hands and feet of women, and the flushes and flashes at the menopause. In some patients I have seen the neck and face show variations of color like that in a revolving electric light. The wave of redness will gradually pass over one side of the face and neck, and as it slowly disappears (two to four minutes), the paleness which follows is of a marble whiteness. Then the other side of the face shows that its capillaries go through a slow rhythm of dilatation and contraction. In ten minutes all the rhythm is over and the nervous, pale face again appears.

Uterine hemorrhage from a myoma is reflex and accomplished by the sympathetic system. The bleeding is due to loss of tone in the vessels of the endometrium. The irritation starts in the mucous membrane of the uterus and passes up to the abdominal brain, where the force is reorganized and sent to the vasomotor centers of the medulla and cord. Now, a continuous irritation soon disarranges a center and the vasomotors sooner or later lose the power to control the blood vessels of the endometrium and become deficient in tone. It may be frequently observed that in a myomatous condition the tone of the vessels in the endometrium is restored and the bleeding ceases for a time, only to be renewed on exhausting irritation.

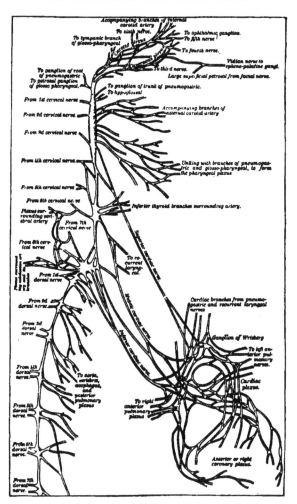

CARDIAC NERVES

Fig. 45 represents the vaso-motor nerves supplying the heart. The heart is the typical organ of popular demonstration of rhythm or peristalsis in the body. It is enormously supplied with nervus vaso-motorius besides by the ganglia of Bidder, Schmidt, Remak, Ludwig, Wrisburg, all but one located in the cardiæ parietes.

Hence, we consider hemorrhage from a myomatous uterus as reflex. It consists in irritation followed, through reflex action, by vasomotor paralysis, which harbors congestion. We note, then, that the abdominal brain presides over significant organs in man. It controls the forces which hold man's body intact. It has a very subtle way of enforcing chemistry to subserve its ends.

A general summary of the abdominal brain is that (a) it presides over nutrition; (b) it controls circulation; (c) it controls gland secretion; (d) it presides over the organs of generation; (e) it influences in a dominant, though not an absolute, control its peripheral visceral automatic ganglia.

Each of the above will again be discussed.

The ideal nervous system is: (1) a ganglion cell; (2) a conducting cord; (3) a periphery. The sympathetic nervous system possesses all three in an eminent degree. The abdominal brain represents the central ganglion cell. Its thousands of distributing and communicating fibers represent the conducting cord. The various ganglionic machines located in each viscus represent the periphery.

In regard to the independence of the sympathetic nerve we wish to say that it is not entirely independent in action, but it may be insisted that it has certain amount of independence which is very manifest in rhythmical motion. The dependence and independence of the (a) cerebro-spinal axis; (b) the abdominal brain and (c) the automatic visceral ganglia may be illustrated by (1) the federal government; (2) the state government and (3) the city or county government.

The cerebro-spinal axis typifies the federal government, and is endowed with the chief rule of the animal. It is the central power and all others must submit to it. It is, moreover, to a large extent, under the will as far as motion is concerned.

The abdominal brain is the state government. In fact, it exercises many functions almost entirely independent. The abdominal brain sends its physiologic orders to all the visceral ganglia. If healthy, all obey, but disturbing pathologic changes cause some to stop, or act irregularly.

The automatic visceral ganglia situated in each organ represent the county or city government. The city, or county, government, is free from neither state nor federal government, but still it has normal independence which it freely exercises. The same views may be illustrated by society and labor in general where division of labor exists, and where certain sections exercise almost independent rights. Thus the sympathetic nervous system may be considered to be independent to a certain degree.

After a large number of dissections on man and animals I find that the ganglionic system of the female is larger and more marked than that of the male. Females seem to have more distinct ganglia and more marked conducting cords. I have not investigated the peripheral nerve supply sufficiently, so far, to render any opinion. I have found the abdominal brain and ganglia relatively larger in animals than in man. The abdominal brain is very large in the dog, in proportion to his cranial brain. Man's cranial brain has grown relatively faster than his abdominal brain, and I think man suffers more from malnutrition than do the animals, so that he pays dearly for his superior cranial brain power. Besides, it appears that man's abdominal brain (and superior cervical ganglion) is very liable to deteriorate with age. Disease is very apt to arise in the above ganglia after forty years of age. Perhaps no animal suffers so much from indigestion as man and so far as I know he has not only the smallest abdominal brain, but it is attacked the most severely with disease. The latest researches seem to show that the sympathetic nervous system originates by sprouting from the ganglia on the posterior roots of the spinal nerves. Some believe that the sympathetic nerve originated from the adrenal. Some points relative to the sympathetic nerve and the suprarenal capsules are quite obscure.

The distribution of the sympathetic nerve is peculiar. It consists of three great parts:

1. There exists a double lateral chain of ganglia lying on each side of the vertebral column and extending from the skull to the coccyx. The ganglia correspond generally in number to the vertebræ, except in the neck, where the seven are blended into three. The ganglia, no doubt, represent the original segmentation of the body. Now, the lateral chain of sympathetic ganglia is connected with the cranial nerves, and with the spinal nerves. It is strongly connected with the cranial nerves, and also very intimately connected to each side of the vertebral columns, out of the way of pressure. A notable feature in regard to the lateral chain of the sympathetic is that it is very intimately connected with the cranial nerves, and also very intimately connected with the sacral nerves. In other words, it blends at the ends very closely with spinal and cranial nerves, but is less intimately associated in the middle with the spinal nerves. The best way to demonstrate the sympathetic system in the human is to place an embryo or fetus in alcohol and then open the thoracic and abdominal cavities, when the chain can be easily observed through the pleura and peritoneum. The sympathetic nervous system is relatively much larger in the fetus than in the adult. In a dog just killed one can see the sympathetic nerves through the pleura very easily and they can be observed also through the peritoneum.

2. The second part of the sympathetic consists of four great plexuses of nerves, situated anterior to the vertebræ, called prevertebral plexuses. One of the pharyngeal, situated around the larynx. Another is the cardiac and pulmonary plexus. A third is the solar or epigastric plexus, situated around the cœliac axis and superior mesenteric artery. The ganglia in the solar plexus are what I am calling the abdominal brain. A fourth plexus lies in the pelvis, and is distributed to the generative and urinary organs and rectum.

3. The third part of the sympathetic consists of the peculiar mechanism at the ends of the nerves situated in each viscus. It is termed the peripheral apparatus. In a diagnostic sense the peripheral apparatus is the most important to the physician, as he can often only make his diagnosis by the manifestation of the disturbances of the periphery of a nerve in a viscus:

e. g., in dyspepsia, Auerbach's and Meissner's plexus may be wrong; in jaundice the automatic hepatic plexus may be wrong, and bile, glycogen and urea fail in proper quantity. It is well to remember that there are three more or less distinct splanchnics distributed in the viscera.

The splanchnics are the inhibitory nerves of the viscera, *e.g.*, of sensation, motion and vasomotor action. We note the following distribution:

1. There are the cervical splanchnics, which arise in the cord from the first cervical to the fourth dorsal. These splanchnic nerves mainly reach the viscera (heart, stomach, etc.) by traveling up the cervical portion of the spinal accessory and then passing down the vagus (especially the right).

2. The second splanchnics arise in the cord from the second dorsal to the second lumbar and pass through the rami communicantes to the three or four abdominal splanchnics, whence they pass to the abdominal brain. These govern the vascular area of the intestines, etc.

3. There is also a third set of these nerves, called the pelvic splanchnics. They pass from the cord by way of the second and third sacral nerves and do not enter the lateral chain, but pass to the hypogastric and thus supply the genitals.

From the origin of these three great splanchnics (cervical, abdominal and pelvic), it is clear why irritation or a blister on the lower part of the back of the neck is so effective in dispelling visceral disturbances The blister inhibits the vasomotor centers and thus soon rights the vascular disturbances in the viscera.

The three splanchnics control the vasomotor region of the viscera. It may be considered that the sympathetic nerve is endowed with sensation and motion. But the sensation is dull in the sympathetic, and its motion is rhythmical. But the utility of the sympathetic in the animal economy is not fully settled. The reason is, that experiments on this nerve are not perfectly decisive, and also because it is so intimately blended with the cerebrospinal nerves. But some study has convinced me that it plays a large role in chronic or remote uterine disease, and that is what has called out this paper. The sympathetic nerve produces involuntary movements. It is called the ganglionic nerve, from the tendency to the formation of ganglia, or knots along its course. In using the term, "abdominal brain," I mean to convey the idea that it is endowed with the high powers and phenomena of a great nervous center; that it can organize, multiply and diminish forces. The views which I wish to bring forward concern the periphery of the abdominal brain, or the mechanism found in each viscus. I mean by viscera those organs contained in the chest and abdomen.

During the investigation of the sympathetic I selected a spare female cadaver, that of a woman about thirty years of age, amputated the thighs close to the body, and then placed it in full strength alcohol. For nearly two years I dissected on this cadaver, as I found time, and finally, after tedious labor, dissected out all the visible sympathetic nerves which lay on the dorsal region, in both chest and abdomen, returning the cadaver to the alcohol when not using it. I then secured a skilled artist, who worked on the drawing of the sympathetic nerve about five weeks, sketching it as nearly according to nature as it was possible, and exactly life size. The most important portions of the nerve are represented in the cuts accompanying this work.

Before discussing other subjects I wish to make a few remarks on three exaggerated ganglia of the sympathetic nerve, viz.: the cervical, the abdomi-

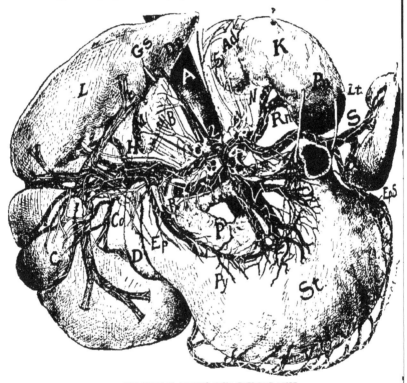

ABDOMINAL BRAIN AND CŒLIAC AXIS

Fig. 46. This cut represents the vaso-motor nerve supply to: (a) liver; (b) spleen; (c) stomach; (d) kidney.

nal and the pelvic. It is easy to dissect out the cervical, and especially the large upper cervical, which is about one and one-half inches long. It is very variable and appears to shrink a little with age, after forty. The middle cervical is often so small that it is difficult to expose. The lower cervical is often difficult to dissect and isolate on account of complicated relations, and also because it is so widely spread out, so fenestrated and because its parts vary so much. The abdominal brain is quite easy to isolate, especially in a fresh cadaver. The best way to dissect and expose it well, without mutilating the body badly, is to tear through the ligamentum gastrocœlicum and pass to the cœliac axis. Then, with a forceps, clear away the tissue just above the middle of the upper border of the pancreas, *i.e.*, at the right and left of the cœliac axis.

In *searching for the abdominal brain* it is best to strike for the entering great splanchnic nerve and then follow it to the side of each ganglion. On the left will be found a large retort-shaped solid ganglion of a pinkish gray color. On the right of the cœliac axis is found a wide, flattened, much fenestrated ganglion. Both are well supplied with blood The most difficult great ganglion to isolate and expose in a natural condition is the uterine ganglion or pelvic brain. It is very large, much fenestrated, quite flattened and richly attached to the second and third sacral (spinal) nerves. It is situated close to the neck of the uterus and sends numerous nerves to this organ and the bladder. It requires much uninterrupted leisure to isolate the pelvic brain and such efforts are almost always a failure in fat subjects. The cause of this difficulty in isolating the pelvic brain lies in the fact that it is whiter than the other great ganglia and more like the surrounding connective tissue, with which it is intimately blended and in which it is imbedded; also because it is so much flattened out. Probably more disputes have arisen over the cervico-uterine ganglion than any other in the body. However, the cut of the pelvic brain, here presented, the author considers quite close to nature.

In each of the viscera are found small nervous ganglia scattered through the organ, or the nervous bulbs are gathered in distinct localities of the viscus, as in the heart or digestive tract. Now it may be understood that these little ganglia found in the organs have the power to maintain movements to some extent. These peripheral ganglia may be looked upon as little brains which are capable of developing nerve force and communicating it to the organs without the aid of the cerebro-spinal axis. They can multiply or diminish nerve force, which is sent to a viscus where they exist. Diseases of any viscus or disturbance of its rhythm must be due to them or to abnormal forces passing through them, arising from the abdominal brain. Again, the rhythm and function of a viscus are involuntary, *i.e.*, beyond control of the will. They are automatic nerve centers placed in the viscus in order to isolate it from the control of man's mind. These little brains induce the viscera to perform their functions independent of the state of mind. They exclude the mind from speculating on the viscus so far as regards function. The will cannot induce the ganglia to do two years' work in one, or one year's work in two. The peripheral ganglia of every viscus assumes its own time of rhythm. The ganglia of each viscus rise to a maximum and sink to a minimum according to their own law of existence. They go through a rhythmical movement, a peculiar cycle. There are explosions of nervous energy from the ganglia during regular periods of time. For example, the heart ganglia thus explode a little oftener than once a second, while those of the oviducts and uterus explode once a month. They are automatic visceral ganglia.

We will consider *the peripheral apparatus* of the heart, lungs, uterus and oviducts, liver, spleen, kidneys, bladder and digestive tract. A study of the ganglia in each organ will enable one to diagnose disease in the said viscus.

1. The peripheral ganglia have been well studied and some of the more important ganglia of *the heart substance* have received definite names. The little brains in the heart are called automatic cardiac ganglia. They are named the automatic centers of Remak, Bidder, Ludwig and Schmidt. These are simply some of the more important automatic motor centers of the heart. In many experiments on dogs I have repeatedly satisfied myself that the automatic cardiac ganglia are mainly aggregated in the auricles and auricular-ventricular septum. Wherever the automatic motor centers are located in the heart anyone can satisfy himself that these ganglia excite and maintain the rhythm of the heart. The frog's heart can be kept in rhythmical motion by stimulation in warm salt water for hours after it has been removed from the body. A few experiments on animals will soon convince one that the peripheral ganglia of the sympathetic nerve located in the heart are a very significant apparatus as regards the cardiac functions. The disturbance of the heart's rhythm by uterine disease is what we shall attempt to demonstrate in its appropriate place. The most striking peripheral apparatus of the sympathetic nerve is found in the heart. Its rhythm is so perfect, its cycle is so apparent and its explosion so manifest, that men sought its origin outside the cerebrum. The dominating influences of the automatic motor-centers on the heart are shown by the idea that in the living fetus, without brain or spinal cord, the heart keeps up its rhythmic beat. In such fetuses the heart ganglia are well developed. One-half of the spinal cord has been removed in pigeons without disturbing the cardiac beat. Besides, the inferior cervical ganglion has very intimate connections with the great ganglion of Wrisberg.

2. The peripheral apparatus of the sympathetic nerve is very prominent in *the digestive tract*. The digestive tract consists of a muscular and a glandular apparatus. The muscular apparatus of the digestive tract consists of a longitudinal and a circular layer, and between these two muscular layers lies a system of nervous ganglia known as Auerbach's plexus. Auerbach's plexus is the peripheral apparatus that induces muscular movements in the gastrointestinal passage. These little brains lying between the muscular layers are the cause of intestinal peristalsis or vermicular movements of the bowels. Undue stimulation of Auerbach's plexus causes colic, and insufficient stimulation is followed by constipation—a muscular paresis. An insufficient activity in Auerbach's plexus induces a kind of ileus paralyticus.

Just under the mucous membrane of the digestive tract there lies a still more delicate system of nerve ganglia called Meissner's plexus. Dr. D. D.

Bishop, late histologist to Rush Medical College, has prepared for me very beautiful specimens of Auerbach's and Meissner's plexus from dogs, by the gold-staining method. These plexuses preside over the production of the secretions of the gastro-intestinal passage. The office of these little brains is really to control glandular secretion. They induce the secretion of digestive fluids. They assume the office of regulating the proper amount of fluids to digest the various foods, which office requires a nice balance. Hence, Auerbach's and Meissner's plexuses are the distinct and marked peripheral apparatuses of the digestive tract. Now these little brains, situated in the intestinal wall, have an action quite independent of the cerebro-spinal axis. I have often chloroformed a dog and then watched the intestines perform their peristalsis after being tapped with a scalpel. If the dog is kept in a warm room, the intestine will go through its peristaltic motion for an hour and a half after death. The peristalsis will be strong and very marked. Half an hour after death, it will be so strong that the circular muscles of the intestine will contract so as to look like pale white cords, or bands, around the intestine. Auerbach's and Meissner's plexuses are what induce rhythm in the bowel. The presence of food, of course, gives the occasion for rhythm. Hence, we must look to the peripheral nervous apparatus of the digestive tract when colic, indigestion, diarrhea and constipation arise, for these little brains induce motion and secretion in the bowel. Of course they are under the physiological and anatomical orders of the abdominal brain—a higher central organism. The pathology of Meissner's plexus is shown in (a) deficient secretion, (b) excessive secretion and (c) disproportionate secretion; that of Auerbach's, in paralysis or contraction (colic).

8. The peripheral nervous apparatus of *the generative* organs is located along the oviducts and uterus. I named these fifteen years ago, "automatic menstrual ganglia." These ganglia can easily be demonstrated by taking a fresh oviduct from the abdomen and putting it in warm salt water. If the oviduct is teased and stimulated it will go through a peristaltic motion for half an hour. It is easy to observe the longitudinal muscles of the oviduct elongate and contract, still easier to watch the circular muscles of the oviduct contract and dilate. I have made this experiment often enough in men and animals to be thoroughly satisfied of the existence of the peripheral ganglia in the oviducts and uterus.

The automatic menstrual ganglia have a monthly rhythm. They rise to the maximum and sink to the minimum every four weeks. The ganglia exist in the uterus, and I have found the proof of this to be most easily demonstrated in the pregnant uterus of slaughtered cows, where my attention was first directed to the matter. Anyone can witness it in a slaughter-house. When a well-advanced pregnant uterus of a cow is cut off between the body and the internal os, a most wonderful rhythmic phenomenon is observed. The cow may have been dead half an hour, yet the two muscular layers of the uterus can be seen to act separately and vigorously. At one time the circular muscles will contract vigorously, and then the longitudinal muscular

170   THE ABDOMINAL AND PELVIC BRAIN

fibers will contract with equal vigor. Then, again, both the layers will work harmoniously together. The irregular action of the muscular layer is due to the irregular traumatic stimulus applied to the uterus. The rhythmical motion applies only to the oviducts and uterus. The neck of the uterus

PELVIC BRAIN

Fig. 47. This cut represents the vaso-motor nerve (sympathetic) supply to the tractus genitalis.

does not go through rhythmical motion, because it is highly supplied by sacral spinal nerves. The spinal nerves prohibit rhythm.

The sympathetic nerves which supply the neck do try to make rhythm, but the spinal nerves to the neck predominate and sober down all rhythm. Hence, the predominating spinal nerve-supply holds the neck in sober, quiet subjection and allows no such wavy rhythm as goes on continually in the pregnant uterus. In this idea lies a great principle in gynecology. The neck of the uterus acts as its guard when pregnant. The waves of its rhythm may dash and sport as they choose, yet the neck stands on sober guard and permits no expulsion of the contents. The neck is never prepared for an abortion, but stands like an unmoved sentinel, so that no storm-waves of the uterus can drive out its contents or allow foreign invasion. The offices of neck and uterus are quite different. The neck has a different blood supply, a different nerve supply, a different muscular supply, and a distinct mucous membrane. It keeps out foreigners and prevents desertion. The nerve supply of the ovary is mainly from the ovarian sympathetic, but as I have so far been unable to determine the rhythm of ovulation, I will investigate that later. Suffice it to say that menstruation and ovulation, so far as I have studied, are different processes, and hence have a different rhythm. The menstrual rhythm is a matter belonging entirely to the monthly movements of the oviducts and uterus. Menstruation might be called oviductal motion or the rhythmic effect of the action of the automatic menstrual ganglia. The menstrual rhythm is an occasional process of the uterus and oviducts, but ovulation is a constant process of the ovaries, whose distinct rhythm is yet to be determined. So far I have been utterly unable to determine the age and duration of the life of a Graafian follicle, for I have seen ovulation in unborn babes and in women of seventy. I have examined pigs, cows and sheep and found that all ovulated before birth. Ovulation continues from before birth until the ovarian tissue is worn out.

I assume, then, that the peripheral nerve apparatus in the organs of generation is a distinct affair, which I designated fifteen years ago as the "automatic menstrual ganglia." Its mechanism is such as to subserve the function of reproduction through a peculiar rhythm. The monthly rhythm in pregnancy is held in abeyance on account of the direction of energy to fetal nutrition. The derangement of the function of the automatic menstrual ganglia will engage our attention later. Any disturbance in these ganglia gives us a clue to the diagnosis of the disease.

We will term the small nerve bulbs situated in the walls of *the bladder* the automatic vesicular ganglia. The peripheral nervous apparatus located in the bladder is markedly sympathetic, and hence will, like other viscera, have its rhythm. The rhythm of the bladder is its contraction and dilatation. It has a diastole and systole. Its rhythm is, to some extent, lost sight of, because the diastole is so much longer than the systole. It requires hours for the diastole to complete itself, while the systole may be completed in a few minutes or less. But the rhythm of other viscera, as the heart, is not dissimilar. The heart has a diastole and a systole, and the diastole of the ventricle is two-tenths of a second longer than the systole. The diastolic wave of the heart is the time when the heart gets its rest—physiologically and anatomically. The bladder has just as much rhythm as the heart, only it is not so strikingly manifested. The bladder gets an effectual rest during its long diastole. By careful dissection of a goodly number of bodies it can be clearly seen that the third sacral nerve of each side sends quite large branches to the bladder. The fourth sacral nerve also sends branches to the bladder. Under such circumstances the bladder is highly supplied with spinal sacral nerves, which would sober down the rhythm and prevent it as much as possible. The sacral spinal nerves distributed to the bladder go mainly to the neck, while the sympathetic mainly supply the fundus—the rhythmical portion.

This rhythm is easily demonstrated by taking the bladder from an ox and filling it with fluid. The contraction of its muscular wall will soon change the shape and gradually expel its contents. The neck of the bladder is more supplied with sacral spinal nerves than the body. In short, the great nerve center of the bladder is in the trigone. Hence, in pregnancy the disturbance in the bladder is due to the uterus dragging on the neck of the bladder where its sensitive (spinal) nerves exist. The female bladder is capable of retaining urine longer than the male bladder, as the neck of the former is not so fixed and hence is not dragged on as much when filling. The neck of the male bladder is fixed with the prostatic capsule, and when filled drags more or less on a fixed neck and so irritates the attending nerves. The peripheral ganglia of the bladder are mainly distributed to the fundus and body. The diastole of the bladder during sleep is prolonged on account of the quietude of the sympathetic. The peripheral ganglia in the bladder, the automatic vesical ganglia, have not received much study so far.

4. The peripheral *nervous apparatus of the lung* I have not especially investigated. That the lungs have an established rhythm is plain, which no doubt is maintained by the ganglia situated in their substance. The peripheral ganglia should be called the automatic pulmonary ganglia. No doubt there also exists a conjoined cerebro-spinal center.

5. The peripheral *nervous apparatus of the liver* may not at first sight seem manifest. But the liver is enormously supplied by the sympathetic, the nerve of rhythm. The liver is a gland, and one who has made a study of the peripheral ends of the sympathetic will have noticed that where it ends in muscular organs the ganglia are large and manifest. But when it ends in glands it forms a fine and delicate plexus of nerves. In the liver, the ganglia are less apparent than the plexus which follows the fine vessels all through the liver. The caliber of these small vessels is subject to dilatation and contraction—rhythm. Every visceral organ during activity is in a state of vascular congestion—a condition of turgescence or enlargement. The surrounding of each viscus in the abdomen is such that it can be rapidly enlarged during its functional activity, and it returns to normal without loss of integrity. Now, the rhythm of the liver consists of its enlargement during functional activity and its return to normal during rest. The rhythm of the liver is made possible by (a) the elasticity of the peritoneum which surrounds it; (b) by its surrounding elastic capsule; (c) by the elastic tissue in Glisson's capsule which surrounds the vessels throughout the liver, and (d) by the dilatability of the blood vessels.

Hence, the liver gland is capable of enlargement and contraction—

GENERAL CONSIDERATIONS

rhythm—from the possession of elastic tissue, and by engorgement. When the liver is functionally active it becomes turgescent, or engorged, and its envelopes or capsules expand from elastic properties. When the liver goes through its active rhythm its vascular excitement attracts large quantities of fluid, from which it makes bile, glycogen and urea; it then returns to its normal condition because the elastic capsule forces the newly-formed products through the tubules to be employed in digestion. The liver in its quiet, reduced form gets self-repair. Thus the liver goes through its rhythm of enlargement (functional activity) and of contraction (self-repair, rest). The occasion of a rhythm of a liver is food in the digestive tract. It is the derangement of the rhythm of the liver by uterine disease which we will call attention to later. The derangement of the liver rhythm will change the three great functions of the gland, which are to make bile, glycogen and urea. The derangement is brought about by disturbing the equilibrium of the abdominal brain. We will term the peripheral nerve apparatus in the liver the automatic hepatic ganglia. The derangement of these is manifested by (a) a deficient secretion (bile, glycogen and urea); (b) excessive secretion, and (c) by disproportionate secretion, especially the last.

6. *The spleen* has a peripheral nervous apparatus which enables it to do its duty in a rhythmic wave. In the case of the spleen the elastic capsule, to which is added involuntary muscular fibers, enables the organ to enlarge during functional activity and then to be reduced by elastic pressure to its normal size. Engorgement and elasticity are the two elements which aid to complete the rhythm of the spleen.

Vascular excitement, with dilatations and turgescence, characterizes the functional activity and enlargement of the spleen. Its capsule expands. Contraction of the elastic capsule and muscle fiber in it characterizes the reduction of the spleen. Its rhythm is made up of its active enlargement and its passive reduction. In the maximum stage of the rhythm, the spleen performs its functions, and in the minimum stage it gets its rest and self-repair. A curious feature is added to the spleen in the form of a tortuous artery. The object of this spiral artery must be to withstand sudden motion or enlargement, for when the spleen is large the artery is just as spiral as it is in the enlarged uterus. But it may be that the tortuous artery allows a greater flow of blood. Hence, the spleen performs its rhythm from the peripheral nervous apparatus situated in its substance. The occasion of its rhythm must be the same as that of the stomach and liver—fresh food. We will term this nervous apparatus the automatic splenic ganglia.

7. The same reasoning applies to the rhythmic functions of *the pancreas and kidney*, and also, probably, to the ovary. They come under the law of vascular engorgement and elastic capsule, which enable the automatic peripheral ganglia to produce and sustain a rhythm. We thus have the automatic renal, and also the automatic pancreatic, ganglia.

(1) We have tried to establish the view that the abdominal brain is the great nerve center of the abdominal viscera and perhaps of the thoracic viscera; (2) that it is the cause of visceral rhythm; (3) that each viscus has

174 THE ABDOMINAL AND PELVIC BRAIN

its own automatic peripheral ganglia or plexuses in the organ; (4) that the duration of the rhythm of each viscus is determined by the mechanism of the automatic ganglia situated in the organ.

The rock and base view maintained in this book is, that the abdominal

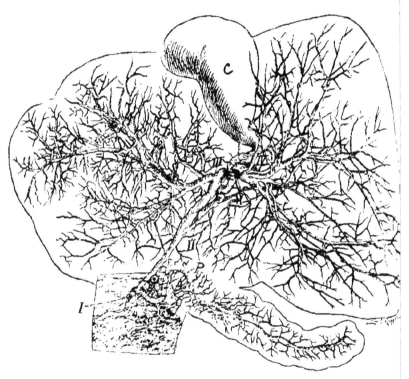

DUCTUS BILIS AND DUCTUS PANCREATICUS

Fig. 48. This cut represents an X-ray of the ducts of the liver and pancreas. Each duct is ensheathed by an anastomosed, nodular, fenestrated meshwork of nerves which demonstrates the enormous nerve supply. This is in addition to the nerve supply ensheathing the arteria hepatica.

brain is a reorganizing nerve center—a brain, a cerebrum. The abdominal brain is capable of reception, reorganization and emission of nerve forces involving the life of viscera (which consists of rhythm, absorption and secretion). The emission of nerve forces will travel as a maximum to organs possessing the greatest number of nerve strands, $e.g.$, the genitals, kidney, heart and stomach, and as a minimum to organs possessing the least number of nerve strands.

Having planted our orchard we will examine its fruits. We now come to the application of these views to the subject of disease. Disease of any of the viscera will very often be preceded by some derangement of their rhythm, absorption or secretion. The common functions of viscera are peristalsis (rhythm), absorption and secretion—all dominated by the sympathetic nerve, *i.e.*, the abdominal brain. To the common functions of viscera (peristalsis, absorption and secretion) must be added, in the genital tract, ovulation, gestation and menstruation.

The two great factors in visceral diseases, so far as regards the sympathetic nerve, are (1) impaired nutrition, and (2) reflex action, referred pain or disturbance. An important central point around which much of the abdominal sympathetic turns is the female generative organs. They are the one cog in the wheel which makes the watch keep defective time.

The pathology of the sympathic nerve is not so distinctly settled as that of the cerebro-spinal. (1) The most significant pathology of the sympathetic is reflex irritation, referred disturbance. (2) Pigmentation and sclerosis. The origin of the pigmentation is primarily in the spleen and liver. Pregnancies, menstruation (periodic congestion), fever (malarial), etc., etc., are accompanied by pigmentation. This may be due to a diseased state of the blood. It is more frequently due to reflex irritation from the distant organs. Some consider violent emotion as a cause of pigmentation, but it is likely that it refers to some unrecognized lesion. (3) The third kind of pathology of the sympathetic would be lesions secondary to those of the cerebro-spinal system. (4) The fourth would be recognized and non-recognized lesions of the sympathetic. I have not space here to discuss these interesting and wide pathological fields, but simply mention them.

Disturbances in the Digestive Tract from Uterine Changes.—In this case we have immediate and remote troubles as regards time. The chronic uterine disease will produce remote malnutrition and remote reflex changes. In these cases I mean diseases of the entire, or part of the generative apparatus—Pudenda, vagina, especially the uterus, oviducts and ovaries. Take, for example, a case where the digestive tract is deranged on account of pregnancy. In the first place the vomiting arises from trauma, stretching on the uterine nerves by an expanding foreign body (contents) and the dragging of the neck of the uterus on the neck of the bladder. This dragging or pressure on the neck of the bladder disturbs the spinal and sympathetic nerves massed there. The irritation is carried up the hypogastric plexus to the abdominal brain. When the irritation arrives at the abdominal brain the forces are reorganized and sent out on the various nerve plexuses which radiate from this nerve center. If the force is emitted along the gastric plexus, which is liable to happen on account of its large size, the stomach receiving sympathetic nerves from the three branches of the celiac axis, the stomach will suffer and vomiting is likely to occur. Now, in the troubles of the stomach resulting from reflex disturbances from the uterus by way of the hypogastric plexus, it may be considered that the stomach is affected in two distinct parts; (a) its muscular wall (Auerbach's plexus), (b) its glandular or secretory apparatus (Meissner's plexus). When the irritation from the generative organs travels up the hypogastric and ovarian plexuses to the abdominal brain it is then reorganized and emitted along the gastric plexus to the automatic gastric ganglia, known as Auerbach's plexus. It affects Auerbach's plexus first because it first meets it in the muscles. The result of irritation of Auerbach's plexus is irregular action of the muscles of the stomach—nausea or vomiting. When the irritation goes farther along the gastric plexus it meets Meissner's plexus, which lies just beneath the mucous membrane, and controls gastric secretion. If Meissner's plexus is considerably irritated it may cause excessive or deficient secretion of the fluids, or the fluids may be secreted in disproportionate quantities. The result will be indigestion and fermentation, causing the development of gases.

The reflex irritation from the uterus may be of such a nature that Auerbach's plexus may be insufficiently stimulated, causing paresis of stomach wall, or that Meissner's plexus is so little stimulated that it will not secrete sufficient gastric fluids. But the track of the nervous irritation is definite from the generative organs, through the hypogastric plexus, to the abdominal brain, where it is reorganized and emitted to the various viscera. This is the interpretation of the old story that uterine disease creates stomach trouble, and *vice versa*. By reference to a cut showing the pelvic brain, or cervico-uterine ganglion, one can see at once the extensive nerve supply which attends the uterus. It may be observed in cases of violent vomiting that digestion and nourishment are quite good. The reason must be that Auerbach's plexus is the main one affected (muscular), while Meissner's (glandular), the one which really digests the food, is not much affected. In the case of chronic uterine disease the whole subject is plain and practical. Such patients have malnutrition for several years. In short, it is noticeable that a woman will apply for treatment of uterine disease some four years after the cervix has been lacerated. The illness was increasing all the time, the last part being more apparent. In stomach troubles from chronic disease of the generative organs, it appears that Meissner's plexus is affected the most, as such patients seldom vomit; but they do not digest their food, which is performed by the gastric fluid secreted by the influence of Meissner's plexus on the cardiac and pyloric glands.

But I wish rather to note the effect of chronic disease of the generative organs on the enteron intestines, which is the location of real digestion. The business part of the digestive tract is the enteron, the small intestines—the jejunum and ileum. The enteron is supplied by the superior mesenteric artery, and along this artery goes the great superior mesenteric plexus of nerves. What we will observe is the mechanism at the end of this superior mesenteric nerve, viz., Auerbach's plexus. This produces bowel peristalsis, rhythm.

Take, for instance, a case of chronic endometritis, salpingitis or ovaritis of several years' duration. Disease of the female organs is a slow, continuous, progressive process. It is a kind of evolutionary process and generally should be read endometritis, plus myometritis, plus endosalpingitis, plus ovaritis, plus as much peritonitis as the infection produces at the ends of the oviducts. Because of this slow, evolutionary progress of female disease the effect through this sympathetic nerve is of slow progress and gradual. The irritation from the generative organs will travel to the abdominal brain by way of the ovarian and hypogastric plexuses. It is a common observation that gases may develop in a few minutes so that fermentation is not the explanation of their origin. Some attempt to explain the origin of this intestinal gas by noting that it collects because the bowel muscle has lost its power to contract; but the gas develops too suddenly for this theory to fit. If the irritation from the uterine disease causes Meissner's plexus to secrete deficient fluids, indigestion and constipation arise. So reflex irritation from the generative organs, by way of the abdominal brain to the small intestine or enteron can act in two ways: (1) It may so stimulate Auerbach's plexus in the intestinal wall as to produce colic, and (2) so stimulate Meissner's plexus as to induce excessive secretion, deficient secretion or disproportionate secretion. The result here will be development of gases and diarrhea.

The abnormal stimulation of Auerbach's and Meissner's plexuses may result in deficient bowel peristalsis and secretion which ends in constipation. The final result of these is indigestion or malnutrition. Hence, chronic uterine disease creates its disasters on the system really by malnutrition. It disturbs the normal visceral rhythm. Malnutrition is manifest in pregnancy, in perceptible disease of the generative organs, and at the menopause. The explanation lies in the abnormal irritation of the nerves in the generative organs, which is reflected through the abdominal brain to the digestive tract. I have never heard or read of the method herein used to explain the action of the abdominal brain on the digestive tract, but I think it is a practical explanation. These views explain why animals or man lose control of the bowels under fright. The violent forces emitted from the abdominal brain induce excessive activity of Auerbach's plexus (colic) and Meissner's plexus (secretion) and a sudden diarrhea results in the animal. In other words, under high emotional influences the animal's rectal sphincters are unable to resist the violent bowel peristalsis. Peristalsis is stronger than the orificial sphincters. Involuntary defecation is common among children and animals from fright. In older animals the cranial brain assumes more influence over the abdominal brain, i. e., it sobers down its violent and irregular rhythm. Chronic disease of the generative organs creates malnutrition in the digestive tract by disturbing its normal functional rhythm and by reflecting irregular rhythms into the digestive tract during its times of rest and repose. It does not matter what the disease of the generative organs is, so that irritation arises and is reflected to the abdominal brain. Inflammation, tumors or the local manifestations of the menopause, will act similarly, according to the degree of irritation. The subject may be considered in the following short summary:

The reflex irritation of the abdominal brain will cause Meissner's plexus

THE ABDOMINAL AND PELVIC BRAIN

to secrete (a) too much secretion (diarrhea), (b) too litte secretion (constipation) or (c) disproportionate secretion (fermentation). The same thing will occur in any secondary organ, i. e., too much, too little or disproportionate secretion. Now, I will point out a matter which long puzzled me, viz., a woman who has a lacerated cervix will go through various pathological stages for some five years and end as a confirmed neurotic. I have observed it for years, and the order of occurrences is as follows:

1. The first stage is irritation. The irritation does not arise so much from the lacerated cervix as from the endometrium (infection atrium). The irritation keeps up for years, endometritis, myometritis, endosalpingitis.

2. The second stage is indigestion. The long-continued irritation arising from the genitals and passing up to the abdominal brain, and being

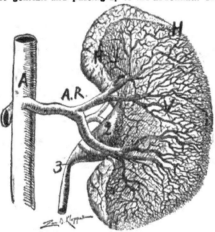

CORROSION ANATOMY OF THE KIDNEY

Fig. 49. This cut represents the rich renal arterial supply. Each arterial branch is ensheathed by an anastomosed, nodular meshwork of nerves which indicates the quantity of vaso-motor nerves attending the renal organ and its duct (ureter).

there recognized and sent out on the plexuses of Meissner and Auerbach of the digestive tract, soon causes too much secretion, too little secretion or disproportionate secretion, which results in indigestion.

3. The third stage is malnutrition. Long-continued indigestion simply results in malnutrition. The reflex irritation goes on continually.

4. The fourth stage is anemia, resulting from the indigestion and malnutrition.

5. The fifth and last stage is neurosis, which is due to the nervous system having been bathed in waste-laden blood for years, neurosis, psychosis.

Hence, a patient with laceration of the cervix passes through five stages:

(1) irritation (infection); (2) indigestion; (3) malnutrition; (4) anemia; (5) neurosis, psychosis.

We will now consider *the liver as disturbed by disease* of the generative organs, whether it be acute or chronic. We noted that the liver was highly supplied with sympathetic nerves; that it had a peripheral plexus in its substance. This we will style the automatic hepatic plexus. We noticed that the liver was induced to perform a rhythm by its automatic plexus, and that its rhythm was made possible by the elasticity of its capsules, the tissue which governs its expansion and contraction (rhythm) being elastic and contractile. Rhythm of the liver is made up of two distinct stages, a time of activity (parenchymal secretion) and a time of repose. Its stage of functional activity is when its capsules are expanding under the vascular excitement of turgescence, the products of cell-work, bile, glycogen and urea being secreted. Its stage of repose and self-repair is when its capsules are contracting, and the blood-vessels are being depleted, the contracting capsule having partly forced the cell products (bile, glycogen and urea) into other regions and organs to accomplish their final object. By means of this rhythm the liver secures a stage of activity and a stage of rest.

It is plain why the liver suffers so badly among liquor drinkers. The drinker has no regard for the time of rest of his liver, so he takes his stimulant especially at times when the liver is at rest. The irritating fluids pass by way of the gastric portal veins into the quiet, resting liver and of course excite it to go through a rhythm at any time. Thus the drinker deprives his liver of the needed rest. The rhythm of the liver is irregularly disturbed and that calls up disease. It is precisely the same in diseases of the generative organs. Irritation starts from a diseased pelvis and travels up the ovarian and hypogastric plexuses to the abdominal brain. Hence, the irritation is reorganized in the abdominal brain and emitted along the hepatic plexus. The automatic hepatic plexus is unduly and irregularly stimulated at times of activity and rest. The result is that the rhythmical function of the liver is deranged. The nice balance of its formation of bile, glycogen and urea is destroyed.

The diseased pelvic organs have no respect for liver rest and they send their uncertain reflexes to the liver at unseemly times. Chronic disease of the pelvic organs will excite impulses which travel to the abdominal brain, which resends them to the liver at such uncertain times that the liver never performs its activity or rest, without more or less attempt to induce irregular rhythms. The final result is that the rhythm of the liver is disturbed and that the cell-products of the liver are formed irregularly. Bile, glycogen and urea are formed excessively, deficiently or disproportionately, and it ends in malnutrition. The skin is yellow and' sallow, the urinary products are abnormal. Diseases of the liver are manifest during pregnancy in demonstrable pelvic diseases, and especially is this true at the menopause. The anatomical nerve track followed by irritation from the generative organs to the abdominal brain, and thence to the liver, is plain, and the physiological results show the theory to be reasonable. Right here we may say that liver disease and disease of the digestive tract are quite common at the menopause. The explanation of this is not difficult. During the thirty years of seed time and harvest of woman the abdominal brain emits its physiological orders to the automatic menstrual ganglia, situated in the uterus and oviducts, to perform their rhythm of menstruation. Thirty years of rhythm in any organ will surely form a habit which it will require force to break. When the menopause arrives, which occurs suddenly, the old beaten paths of the hypogastric plexus, along which the menstrual orders for thirty years had been sent, are suddenly cut off. This sudden cutting off of old channels, by which forces were formerly emitted, is bound to make the latter accumulate in the central organ or abdominal brain. Now, these accumulated, unused energies must have some outlet and they will go in the direction of least resistance. The great channels of easy outlet of pent-up forces in the abdominal brain appear to be the gastric and superior mesenteric plexuses, which supply the digestive tract, and the hepatic plexus. Hence, in the menopause the accumulated force in the abdominal brain is mainly spent on the digestive tract and liver. The accumulated energies go to these in an irregular manner and thus aid in disturbing their rhythm. The result is abnormal products in the liver (bile, glycogen and urea), and for the digestive tract, indigestion (constipation or diarrhea).

The heart of woman does not escape the influence of the chief wheel of her existence. It has very manifest peripheral sympathetic ganglia and is largely under the control of the sympathetic nerve, as may be seen from its nice rhythm. Now, from each of the three cervical sympathetic ganglia on each side of the neck there goes a nerve to the heart (the heart also receives three nerves on each side from the pneumogastrics). When the pelvis contains diseased generative organs, the irritation arising there travels up the ovarian and hypogastric nerves to the abdominal brain.

From the abdominal brain two roads lead to the heart. One road is through the great splanchnics to the cervical ganglia, and as these ganglia act as little brains, the force is here reorganized and sent directly to the heart. Of course all irritation comes irregularly and so aids in disturbing the heart's rhythm. But spinal or cranial nerves prohibit rhythm, so I think the main forces from the abdominal brain travel up the pneumogastrics to the fourth ventricle) and the irritation is then reflected directly to the heart. Irritation, especially that coming along a cranial nerve, quickly affects the rhythm in any viscus. In like manner irritation from diseased generative organs may reach the heart by first going to the abdominal brain and then through the splanchnics to the pneumogastrics and to the heart.

The result is that the heart is disturbed in its rhythm. It palpitates, it beats irregularly. Who has not seen this in female diseases? I think palpitation is most manifest at the menopause. In pregnancy the heart prepares for the emergency by thickening its walls and is generally no worse for undergoing the extra work incident to gestation. But let the heart meet a myoma, which is continually emitting irregular reflections to it, and disturbing its rhythm, and sooner or later it is weakened and degenerated. The heart rests and repairs itself duing part of the rhythm, but irregular reflections from pelvic diseases do not allow it sufficient rest. Fatty degeneration or malnutrition results.

The heart palpitates at the menopause because the accumulated energies of the abdominal brain find an easy outlet through the splanchnics and pneumogastrics. The menopause often requires several years for its completion, so the abdominal brain can get accustomed to controlling and distributing the accumulated energies which were once expended in the menstrual rhythm. The trouble is that its accumulated but irregular energies are apt to dash pell mell over some single plexus to some single viscus and then disaster is sure to follow from inability to resist. If the accumulated energies were evenly distributed, but little visceral rhythm would be disturbed.

I know of no organ so manifestly affected in the menopause as the heart; perhaps for the very reason that the sympathetic nerves chiefly accompany the blood-vessels. Hence, when some portion of the sympathetic system is disturbed, it is apt to affect the nearest structures, which are those of the vascular apparatus, the chief portion of which is the heart.

The same kind of reasoning is applicable to *the spleen*. Diseased generative organs reflect their irritation to the abdominal brain and then to the spleen. Irritation always proceeds irregularly, and so it would disturb the rhythm of the spleen, and thus create malnutrition. The spleen goes through a rhythm just as do other viscera. The spleen is no doubt the chief organ concerned in pigmentation. Jastrowitz, of Russia, first taught that the spleen was concerned in deposit of pigment; for he found that by severing the nerves which pass to the spleen on its vessels, in dogs, irregular pigmentation followed. Every gynecologist knows that pigmentation of the skin is common at the menopause, in pregnancy and at puberty, i. e., when the sympathetic nerves are more or less disturbed. Of course little doubt exists that the liver has something to do with the deposit of pigment, as may be noted in malaria, which exercises its brunt on the liver. Hence, the disturbed rhythm of the spleen in uterine disturbances manifests itself by pigmentary deposit.

In disease of the uterus it is quite easy to note that *the rhythm of the bladder is disturbed*. It is not because the fundus of the uterus rests on the fundus of the bladder, but because the automatic vesical plexus is irritated. The neck is dragged or pressed and the nervous mechanism suffers.

Similar explanations might be made relative to the lungs, kidneys, pancreas and ovaries; but I think sufficient has been said to show that each viscus has its automatic peripheral ganglia, that each viscus executes a rhythm, and that the diseased generative organs may disturb the rhythm of any viscus by reflex irritation through the abdominal brain.

The peripheral nerve supply to the genitals is vast, and no organ can raise such nerve storms as the generative. They are intimately and intensely connected with all nerve centers, but especially those of the sympathetic. How often does one see strong men faint from the simple introduction of the sound into the urethra? The vast peripheral nervous apparatus ending

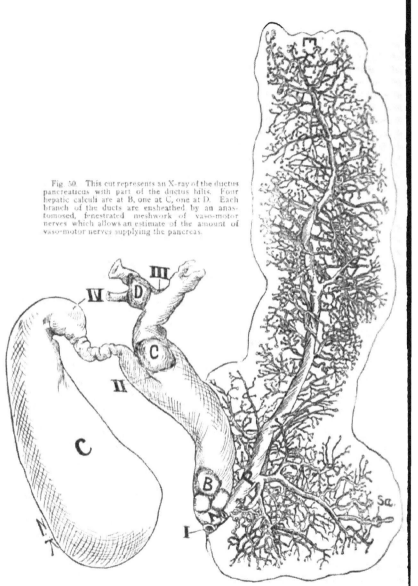

Fig. 50. This cut represents an X-ray of the ductus pancreaticus with part of the ductus bilis. Four hepatic calculi are at B, one at C, one at D. Each branch of the ducts are ensheathed by an anastomosed, fenestrated meshwork of vaso-motor nerves which allows an estimate of the amount of vaso-motor nerves supplying the pancreas.

FIG. 50. DUCTUS PANCREATICUS WITH PART OF THE DUCTUS BILIS

GENERAL CONSIDERATIONS

in the urethra is disturbed, and this nerve storm which sweeps up the hypogastric plexus spends sufficient power on the heart alone to cause faintness. Of course it spends a relatively large amount on every other viscus. Note how pale the man becomes. The storm dwells with equal force on the whole skin surface. Of all viscera the genitals are most intimately and closely connected with the nerve centers, both anatomic and physiologic, for the sexual instinct predominates in all races of mammals. From the very physiologic and anatomic nature of the reproductive organs they demand a close and intimate nervous connection with the great centers, and hence no storms affect adjacent and distant viceras like those arising in the extensive genital nerve periphery.

Cold Hands and Feet in Women.—Every gynecologist has witnessed cold extremities in women with diseased generative organs. In this case we must look to the great dominating vaso-motor center, situated in the medulla oblongata. Secondary vaso-motor centers also appear to exist along the main length of the spinal cord. The vaso-motor centers are reached (a) through the pneumogastrics, especially by irritation coming from the abdominal brain; (b) by the lateral chain of the sympathetic which is prone to emit its irritations along the brachial plexus, or the sacral plexus, or the lumbar plexus. No doubt the irritations are emitted along each intercostal nerve, but vaso-motor contractions are more manifest in the extremities. In vaso-motor contractions the skin is always most blanched at the extremities, as the hands or feet. When the generative organs are diseased, the irritation goes to the vaso-motor centers in the medulla and cord by two routes:

1. It travels over the ovarian and hypogastric plexuses of nerves to the abdominal brain. Then it is reorganized and sent along the pneumogastrics to the dominating vaso-motor center in the medulla, whence it is reflected over the whole body, especially to the small vessels at the extremities, on which it is the most effective in blanching white the skin and cooling the hands and feet.

2. It can also travel on the lateral chain from the coccyx, especially by way of the hypogastric plexus. I found in dissection of cadavers (especially female) that the lumbar lateral chain of ganglia were strongly and liberally connected with the hypogastric plexus by large, thick nerves. Hence, the irritation from the generative organs will go up the hypogastric plexus and be deflected to the lumbar lateral chain and pass both to the spinal cord and medulla. Then the vaso-motor centers in the medulla and cord reflect their irritations to the whole body, but especially to the extremities. So that irritations from the generative organs reach the vaso-motor centers in the medulla and spinal cord by two routes: (a) by the pneumogastrics from the abdominal brain, and (b) by the lateral chain of ganglia. The result after following both routes is similar, viz., paling and cooling of the skin, especially of the extremities. Physiologists have proved that the most powerful vaso-motor constrictions exist in the hands and feet. The conclusions are the same as those discussed in the viscera. The end of the whole matter in malnutrition, for the arterioles and capillaries have been disturbed in

their rhythm. The vascular rhythm exists, but it has not been determined as to time. But when a large area of skin (tissue) is depleted of nourishing blood for a considerable time, malnutrition is sure to result. The cause and effect in the woman are definite. The irritation starts in the generative organs and travels by definite routes to end in influencing the sympathetic nerves to contract the vessels which they surround. I have such women in my practice continually. Vaso-motor effects on the extremities are generally a remote disturbance of chronic pelvic disease. The irritation of almost any viscus which will effectually disturb the abdominal brain is liable to cause vaso-motor constrictions. It is mainly from the generative organs in the female. By carefully studying patients one can see the immediate and remote effects of pelvic disease. The immediate effect may be observed to be from the localized, tangible, gross pathology. It may be pressure troubles, septic troubles or otherwise. But the remote effect is through the sympathetic nerve, or rather through malnutrition. A slight, unnoticed irritable focus begins in the pelvis (it may be endometritis). Months and years go on. Irritations accumulate in the abdominal brain and may radiate on all its various plexuses. Nutrition is insidiously impaired through the months and years, unbalanced reflexes gather in the abdominal brain, which, in turn, disturb the normal functional rhythm of viscera. Accumulated energies, begotten of long continued pelvic disease, are not controlled by the abdominal brain, but irregular, stormy forces are emitted over the plexuses to the viscera, which unbalances their rhythm and ruins their nutrition. The woman with genital disease becomes an object of wretched despair and a miserable invalid. The days of her life are passed between pain and sadness. Our amateur operative gynecologist has forgotten that all her troubles started from a lacerated cervix or endometritis five years ago. He is sure to extirpate her ovaries, if he can, and lo! how disappointed he is if she does not get well in a month! Such a woman will not get well for long periods. The only benefit of extirpating the appendages was that she was compelled to lie still for a month—a dear method of purchasing a few weeks' rest. The proper method to follow in this numerous class of women is to hunt for the old cause and remove it, and then gradually nourish the woman back to normal health. Such women are called hysterical, but there is generally some pelvic pathology that precedes hysteria before the abdominal brain suffers derangement.

Space forbids any discussion as to the dependence or independence of the sympathetic nerve in regard to the cerebrospinal system. Yet we may assert that the sympathetic is independent to a certain degree. Babies have been born at full term with no cerebrospinal axis. The heart will beat some time after death. I have often noted the intestines performing peristalsis more than an hour after death. I have watched the uterus going through its rhythm in slaughtered cows an hour and a half after death. The independence of the sympathetic is seen in vaso-motor neuroses of the extremities. The tone of vessels is maintained by the sympathetic. The sympathetic controls secretion. If the brain and spinal cord of a frog are

GENERAL CONSIDERATIONS

removed, his skin will show pigmentation. The viscera have involuntary movements and are out of will control,—are excluded from the mental sphere. But, like the watch, which requires every cog and wheel to keep time, so the sympathetic needs the cerebrospinal to maintain the balance of life.

A few general ideas of the sympathetic nerve may be of interest. The rhythm of the viscera, due to the abdominal brain, will, no doubt, adequately explain the axial rotation of abdominal tumors. The emptying and filling of hollow viscera in their continual rhythm is apt to rotate adjacent tumors

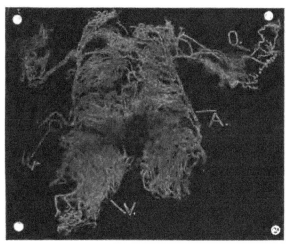

CORROSION ANATOMY

Fig. 51. This specimen of corrosion anatomy of the uterus, oviducts and ovary of a new-born infant represents the blood supply of the genitals in a quiescent state. Each arterial branch is ensheathed by an anastomosed, nodular, fenestrated meshwork of vaso-motor nerves. This method enables one to estimate the quantity of nerve supply to the uterus.

with narrow styles. Narrow pedicles are, of course, more likely to rotate than thick ones. It is a curious fact that when a woman possesses more than one tumor in the abdomen, there is more danger of axial rotation. A pregnant uterus or tumor doubles the danger of the twisting of the tumor on its axis. The axial rotation of a tumor is, no doubt, enhanced by the sudden emptying of the uterus, and its change of location at delivery. But the main point in the matter is visceral rhythm, e. g., of the intestines and bladder. It is estimated that 10 per cent of abdominal tumors rotate on their axes. The reflexes of the abdominal brain and sympathetic ganglia are very numerous.

A blow on the solar plexus causes syncope by reflex action on the heart. The vagus (right) compels the heart to beat soberly, and two-thirds of the right vagus goes also into the abdominal brain. But the cervical sympathetic rules the heart in its rapidity and regularity. The vomiting on the passage of gall-stones, or renal calculi, or that of pregnancy, shows the abdominal brain to be a great reflex center and place of reorganization of forces. Notice the changed pulse in peritonitis, and the tremendous collapse in intestinal perforation, due to disturbed circulation. Watch the shock after colotomy, due to trauma on the peritoneum. The peritoneum is mainly supplied by sympathetic nerves, so it acts through the solar plexus. It is easy to see how nerve storms shock the heart from peritoneal manipulation. I have noted depression of the heart. The peripheral arteries contract and the heart cannot drive the blood home. It is easily seen that in the abdominal brain and cervical sympathetic, the great regions of reflex action play a great role in neuroses and all emotional phenomena. When we feel fear or fright, the effect is noticeable in the solar plexus, which lies behind the stomach. Sorrow and sadness are, frequently, first felt in the abdominal brain. The good-hearted David said that he "yearned for the young man in his bowels." His is only a common experience that the abdominal brain plays a role in emotional and neurotic phenomena because of its capacity for reflex action.

CHAPTER XV.

THE INDEPENDENCE OF THE SYMPATHETIC NERVE.

The function of the tractus intestinalis is sensation, rhythm (persistalsis), secretion and absorption. It has an import and export service.
"A want of individuality is the most dangerous sign in modern civilisation.".—John Stuart Mill.

It may aid in comprehending the structure and function of the sympathetic nerve, and in concluding the discussion in regard to its independence, to arrange in short, concise propositions a number of observations which will show that the sympathetic nerve has a large degree of independence.

1. The independence of the sympathetic system is impressively shown in the distinct rhythmical action of the heart for some time after being removed from the body. This can be best demonstrated in the frog and turtle.

2. The peristaltic and vermicular motions of the intestines after death significantly point to the independence of the sympathetic nervous system. The intestines of a dog will continue in peristalsis for two hours after death if the room temperature be 100 degrees Fahrenheit.

3. The fetus has been born at or about term without a trace of brain or cord. This shows that nutrition, growth, secretion, absorption and circulation were conducted alone by the sympathetic—one of the strongest demonstrations of its independence.

4. Experiment has shown that nutrition (which means life's function) may be carried on after complete destruction of the cerebrospinal centers.

5. Nourishment without the cerebrospinal center would indicate that the arteries (blood-vessels) are under the control of the sympathetic system. Goltz goes so far as to say that the tone of the arteries is maintained by local centers situated in their own immediate vicinity.

6. The manifestations of blushing, local congestions and eruptions would tend to show that the blood acts reflexly on the vessels, affecting the vaso-dilators or the vaso-constrictors. The white line (followed rapidly by a red one) on stroking the skin with the finger, as in scarlet fever, indicates that the vessels possess local nerve centers of control. The trauma produced on the vascular centers by stroking the skin first irritates the vaso-constrictors, and paleness results from constriction of the vessels. The secondary result of the trauma on the vaso-constrictor is that they are paralyzed, and then the vaso-dilators dominate with a resulting red line.

Bernard, in 1851, was the first to show conclusively that the sympathetics controlled the caliber of the blood-vessels. Any one who has long practiced medicine, observing the heart and the aorta, will be able to note that the heart itself, and the aorta, have seasons of dilatation and contraction. For example, in many spare, neurotic women it is common to note that the aorta has periodic times of powerful rhythms or beatings. With the hand on the abdomen the inexperienced announces a growing aneurism of the abdominal aorta. The aorta beats with such tremendous force that the patient will call the physician's attention to the phenomenon. A few hours subsequently its rhythm will be quieted and in a normal state. This phenomenon of the excessive abdominal aortic rhythm, or beat, is perhaps due to the excitation of the local nerve centers which control its caliber; for I could scarcely detect the excessive arterial beat in another portion of the body, as the wrist. At such times the heart acts slightly differently from normal. It is a little more noisy and appears as if it were dilated more than usual. Another phenomenon in regard to nerve centers which control vascular tone (contraction and dilatation) may be observed in the heart. By careful watching of the heart of an individual, one may note that the heart changes at times in both its method of beat and its size. Occasionally the heart will dilate, beat with more noise, continue so for some hours, and then subside to its natural state. This phenomenon, as well as that of aortic dilatation and contraction, is doubtless due to the controlling sympathetic nerve centers localized in the substance or immediate vicinity of the heart and aorta. The heart, like a blood-vessel under the controlling vascular nerve centers of the sympathetic, dilates and contracts and varies its rhythm still more within wide ranges. I have never seen this periodic dilatation noted in any book. Practically nothing is to be found in books concerning this peculiar periodic dilatation and vigorous beating of the abdominal aorta.

7. The abdominal brain (the solar plexus, the semilunar ganglion) may be viewed as a gigantic vaso-motor center for the abdominal viscera. The dilatation and contraction of the heart and aorta, with the periodic varying of the vigor of their rhythm (without recognizable disease), may be referred to this king of vaso-motor centers—the abdominal brain. In the progress of life's vascular phenomena the abdominal brain, as a vaso-motor center, exercises very dominant and quite independent prerogatives.

8. The dependence and independence of the cerebrospinal and sympathetic system of nerves may be compared to the state and federal government, or the municipal and state government. The former run in harmony, when friction does not arise. Yet the state lives quite a distinct individual life, quite independent from the federal government. The life of each is dependent, however, on the other. The internal life of each (as of the sympathetic nerve) maintains itself.

9. The sympathetic system alone would maintain life (sensation, peristalsis, absorption, secretion), especially in each viscus, but the cerebrospinal system coördinates the various viscera as a whole into a definite purpose or plan. The cerebrospinal system is an executive to suggest or organize the efforts of each system, ruled by the sympathetic, to combine for a common object—the continuation of an organized subject. The efforts of the circulatory system would be useless were they not combined with all the efforts of the digestive system, as well as those of the genito-urinary system. The cerebrospinal system simply coördinates the various independent systems (circulatory, digestive and genito-urinary) into a unit of life.

10. The phenomena of vaso-neurosis of the extremities would indicate a great degree of independence of the sympathetic nerve.

11. The ordered richness of the sympathetic nerves in ganglion cells, similar to the cerebrospinal ganglia, would tend to demonstrate its dependence.

12. The accumulation or aggregation of ganglion cells in the sympathetic should be sufficient argument for considering them as small brains, nerve centers of life's action.

13. The independence of the sympathetic nerve may be observed in the fact that as it departs more widely from the cerebrospinal it increases in elements. Increased distribution shows increased aggregation of ganglion cells, e. g., the Meissner-Billroth and Auerbach's plexuses in the small intestines.

14. There is a partial necessity that the sympathetic be relatively independent, at least be out of the control of the cerebral center. The viscera being necessitated to be in constant activity, constant rhythm, should be beyond the control of the will, so that man cannot speculate on his viscera. The intellect cannot disturb the function of the viscera. The actions of the sympathetic ganglion are beyond the power of the will.

15. A stubborn opponent of the independence of the sympathetic nerve (Hermann) freely acknowledged that automatic and reflex coördinate movements and secretions can be the indication of the sympathetic ganglion cells quite independent of the cerebrospinal symptoms.

16. A significant partial independence of the sympathetic may be observed in peritonitis. The reflex irritation induced by the peritonitis causes extreme vaso-motor contraction in the skin. The skin becomes waxy pale, the blood is forced out of the skin by contraction of the vessels and the patient dies gradually from circumference to center. The heart at first attempts to work more vigorously to send the blood to the skin vessels, but the harder the heart works in sending the waste-laden irritating blood to the vessels, the more they contract, and gradually death approaches the heart. The independence of the grip of the sympathetic nerve is seen in the gradual death of the patient, beginning in the skin capillaries and ending at the heart. It is a good illustration of the fact that irritation of the sympathetic nerves may be sufficient to force all blood out of a part even to its death.

17. Vulpian severed the sciatic and brachial plexuses and waited until the pulp of the animal's corresponding paws became pale. Now, by irritating the pulp of the paws a local congestion could be produced. Hence reflex irritation of vaso-motor nerves can be limited to the particular organ or tissue supplied, showing a considerable degree of independence.

18. It has been suggested by Fox that myxedema is associated with the independence of the sympathetic.

19. Compression or macroscopial injuries of the cervical portion of the sympathetic produces such a marked physiologic phenomenon that it demonstrates in itself a considerable degree of independence of the sympathetic. The manifestation of compression or injury of the cervical sympathetic is

that of the irritation or paralysis. Trauma of the cervical sympathetic shows marked independent functional disturbances. Exophthalmic goiter is considered, even by the skeptical Eulenberg and Guttmann, as a paralysis of the cervical sympathetic. If the latter can produce such vast changes, and such a dreadful disease, how great must be the influence of the abdominal brain in its independence. In exophthalmic goiter the independence of the sympathetic seems dominant, for of the great triumvirate in that disease— cardiac palpitation, protrusion of the eyeball and enlargement of the thyroid gland—the cardiac palpitation seldom fails. Few experimenters or observers fail to connect the cardiac disturbance with the cervical sympathetic, showing how dominating it is in this case.

20. The gastro-intestinal secretions appear to be carried on automatically by the Meissner-Billroth (aided by the Auerbach) plexuses of nerves, which are sympathetic ganglia—automatic visceral ganglia. The automatic visceral, hepatic, renal, gastro-intestinal and menstrual ganglia, all show a marked degree of independence. They produce rhythm in the viscera— activity and repose. Undisturbed, they rule secretion harmoniously, but disturbed anatomic visceral ganglia induce (a) excessive secretion, (b) deficient secretion and (c) disproportionate secretion. The last is the most detrimental, for it creates fermentation and unbalances nutrition.

21. The independence of the automatic visceral ganglia of the sympathetic may be noted in the idea that if one viscus becomes diseased it may disturb all the others by reflex action.

22. If one viscus becomes diseased the next to become diseased is the one connected with the diseased viscus by the greatest number of nerve strands. If the uterus becomes diseased the next viscus in order is generally the stomach. However, this is probably due to the fact that the disturbed stomach functions are easily observed.

23. The abdominal brain is a center of organization for impressions received from distal viscera. It is a gigantic vaso-motor center for the abdominal vascular system. The abdominal brain demonstrates its independence by its definite method of reorganizing reflex actions. When an abdominal viscus is mildly ill, the abdominal brain reorganizes the reflex impressions and transmits them mildly to adjacent viscera. But if a viscus is severely and especially chronically ill, the abdominal brain reorganizes the reflexes and transmits them violently to the adjacent viscera, according to the degree of illness. Also the reflexes reorganized in the abdominal brain are transmitted outward to the viscera with greatest force on the lines of least resistance, which means that the nerve forces travel on the plexuses the best where there are the greatest number of nerve strands.

24. The independence of the sympathetic nerve may be observed in the phenomenon of sleep. It never ceases action nor sleeps, while the cerebrospinal is in abeyance for about one-third of our life.

25. E. L. Fox reports two cases of compression myelitis in the cervical portion of the cord unattended by any oculopupillary or vaso-motor paralysis. This would tend to show the independence of the sympathetic, especially the cervical sympathetic.

26. Experimenters report that irritation of some portion of the cervical sympathetic will produce secretions from the parotid and submaxillary glands.

27. Fox asserts that irritation of the peripheral end of the cervical sympathetic will cause protrusion of the eyeball; sedation will cause sinking of the eyeball, and a slight flattening of the cornea. We know that in the lids are sets of smooth, muscular fibers innervated by the sympathetic, and by contraction of these the lids are opened and so the eyeball is uncovered.

28. In general it may be said that the sympathetic presides over involuntary movements, nutrition and secretion, holds an important influence over temperature and vaso-motor action, and is endowed with a dull sensibility.

29. Experiments show that after destruction of the medulla oblongata and brain of the frog irritation will cause congestion of the limbs.

30. The occurrence of pigmentation in the skin of the frog, after destruction of the cerebrospinal axis, shows the independence of the sympathetic.

31. Each histologic unit has its own nervous system, which is sufficient for it within certain limits.

It may be said that the object of the lateral chain of the sympathetic is to make known the great ganglionic system to the cerebrospinal system.

32. The ganglia of the uterus (sympathetic) are independent centers for reflex action. That it can act independently may be shown by the repulsion of a child after the death of the mother. It has a powerful reflex action on the heart. It is a great independent sympathetic ganglion. Associated anatomically with the abdominal brain are the following plexuses: (a) the diaphragmatic; (b) the suprarenal; (c) the renal; (d) the spermatic; (e) the superior mesenteric, which intimately connect it with all the abdominal viscera.

33. The expulsion of feces per rectum after death of the patinet shows that the sympathetic ganglia of the bowels are independent centers for reflex action.

34. Pigmentation of the skin in the frog, after destruction of the cerebrospinal, demonstrates the independence of the sympathetic.

35. The abdominal brain is a great reflex center. Vaso-motor centers are organizing centers, and preside over the coördination of the visceral rhythm. The abdominal brain is a ganglion of far reaching significance. It has many connections with viscera and possesses vast influence over the circulation. It presides closely over the secretion of the abdominal organs.

36. That the sympathetic is the only nervous system belonging to some of the lower animals is open to doubt; for if that were the case, no argument would be required to demonstrate the independence of the sympathetic. The distinction of the cerebrospinal and sympathetic as to sleep or repose, since it cannot be proven, must be dropped. In any argument we must admit the very intimate and mutual dependence of the sympathetic and cerebrospinal nerves on each other.

37. The essential feature of the pathology of the sympathetic, and also

one which tends to show its independence, is that the irritation in one organ may be reflected through a sympathetic ganglion and thus disturb the balance of the viscera. The best, most common and convincing example is irritation of the cervico-uterine ganglia, which is directly reflected to the abdominal brain, where the irritation is reorganized and sent to all the nerve plexuses.

88. The degree of independence of the sympathetic nerve must be worked out on the lines of experiment and observation of the effect of disease on its different parts. To what degree is the abdominal brain a center for the reorganization of forces; how does it modify and transmit receptions? How supreme is it over the visceral ganglia or does it coördinate their action to a definite plan? Does it enhance or prohibit their action? Is the abdominal brain a reflex arc for nerve forces, passing from one organ to another? In other words, will one diseased organ unbalance all other organs by transmitting its irritation by way of the reorganizing abdominal brain?

CHAPTER XVI.

ANATOMIC AND PHYSIOLOGIC CONSIDERATIONS.

The sympathetic rules the rhythm (peristalsis) of vascular canals and glandular ducts of the body.

"The first questions to put to a witness are as to his name and place of residence, and his means of knowledge of the facts concerning which he is expected to testify."—Judge Charles B. Waite.

After considerable microscopical investigation I am convinced that we do not know the whole sympathetic nerve, nor do we fully know its distribution because of its tenuity. This remark is made as evidence gained in long microscopical labors on the peritoneum, in which I have been interested for years. In the peritoneum we cannot tell the function of a nerve from its microscopical appearance. We may assert that the width of the nerve indicates its length, that a wide nerve is a long nerve.

Now a sympathetic nerve is a non-medullated nerve, i. e., the white substance of Schwann is lacking, at least it is not visible by our present optical instruments, or the present known reagents. However, it appears to me to be present in Remak's bands (sympathetic fibers), though in an exceedingly thin layer. Again, many nerves in the peritoneum begin with a medullary sheath and end without one. The nerve is sheathed for part of its course and non-sheathed for another part. But whether we are to call a nerve which is sheathed in its whole course or in a part of its course, a sympathetic or a non-sympathetic, depends upon whether it shows a different function. In ordinary parlance a sympathetic nerve should have no visible sheath of Schwann, i. e., no medullary sheath. A sympathetic nerve is perhaps better known by its function than by its microscopical appearance. In fact no microscopist can decide merely by the appearance whether a nerve be sympathetic or non-sympathetic, unless he claim that all non-sheathed nerves are sympathetic. For one can trace the medulla on a nerve in the peritoneum for a long distance when suddenly it disappears. Should one meet this nerve unsheathed in any portion of the peritoneum, he could not decide upon its function. At present we must discuss the function and not the microscopical structural differences.

One of the best places to study the sympathetic nerves is in the peritoneum of the kitten (when about six weeks old). The reagent best suited for practical microscopical work is as follows: Acetic acid 5 parts, gold chloride 1 part, and water 994 parts. The rabbit's peritoneum is quite good, but not so good as the cisterna lymphatica magna of the frog's peritoneum. Now it is not difficult to trace the gangliated cords lying on each side of the vertebral column. In spare subjects the branches running from the cords and ganglia are plainly visible. By a little care we can trace the branches of

194   THE ABDOMINAL AND PELVIC BRAIN

the ganglia and cords directly to the brain and spinal cord. The sympathetic system lies in front of the cerebrospinal, as a secondary system enclosed in a cavity, the thoraco-abdominal, just as the cerebrospinal is enclosed in the cerebrospinal canal. The sympathetic system is characterized by having non-medullated nerve fibers. It frequently has large round ganglion cells enclosed in thick dense capsules.

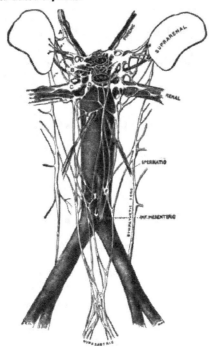

ABDOMINAL BRAIN AND PLEXUS AORTICUS

Fig. 52. This illustration presents a limited amount of sympathetic nerves in outline. (George Dancer Thane).

The ganglion cells lie scattered over considerable areas, and are separated by dense, thick portions of connective tissue. The ganglion cells of the sympathetic do not atrophy in early old age, as claimed by some, for before me lies a beautiful microscopical section of the abdominal brain of a woman who died at about the age of 72, in which the characteristic feature is the numerous large ganglion cells ensheathed in thick connective tissue capsules. It may be that in some cases the superior cervical ganglion does develop an excess of connective tissue which crushes out the delicate ganglion cells, but such cases I have not observed in the abdominal brain, which must serve some great economic plan in the system. The significance of the abdominal brain and sympathetic system must not be forgotten, as children are born without a brain, and some reports note the absence of the medulla also. In such children the heart and viscera have been kept going by the sympathetic system. Dr. W. F. Ball, of Mantua Station, Ohio, reported such a case to me.

The sympathetic nerve is characterized by accumulations of cells at certain points, these being known as ganglia. In the abdomen and chest the ganglia have a regularity of location corresponding to definite segments of the body. There is a long chain of such ganglia situated on each side of the vertebral column, known as the lateral chain of sympathetic ganglia, and extending from the first cervical to the last sacral vertebra. Two fine, small cords connect the spinal cord with each of the ganglia of the lateral chain, making a close and intimate relation of the spinal cord and lateral chain. The spinal cord is doubly connected with the lateral chain. The medullated branch passes from the anterior root to the ganglia. The non-medullated root passes to the blood-vessels of the cord. The lateral chain is well protected by adjacent bony structures from any injury or pressure by viscera.

Ventral to the lateral chain there are located three nerve plexuses: one in the chest, the cardiac; one in the abdomen, the abdominal brain; and one in the pelvis, the utero-cervical, or as I prefer to call it, the pelvic brain. The thoarcic and abdominal plexuses are single, located in the ventral line of the body and possessed of a large amount of nervous ganglia and cells, especially the abdominal brain. The pelvic plexus is double, situated on each side of the cervico-uterine junction, and is quite a massive collection of ganglia and nerve cells. All three central plexuses, the thoracic, abdominal and pelvic, are bound by intimate and very close relations with the lateral chain of sympathetic ganglia. Every viscus is profusely supplied with the sympathetic strands, and the vast number of cords and ganglia, like the equalizers on a horse power, hold in intimate relation all the viscera in a delicate balance. Specialists are beginning to recognize the wonderful sympathetic balance of all the viscera, for when one gets out of order it untunes the chorus of the whole. In fact, if a viscus in an adult is disturbed, it is generally the genitals, and it soon unbalances the remainder. It is easy to note the large cords, the ganglia and the invertebral plexuses of the sympathetic system, to note their distribution and the relations of the ganglia to the viscera in spare subjects hardened by alcohol. It is not difficult to see, even in rough, incomplete experiments, that there is a certain independence of the ganglia distributed to the viscera. Though the latter are seen to be in close relationship with the great structure of the sympathetic, yet they show definite, independent action. An hour after death one can induce the viscera in a dog to act by slight irritation or stimulation. Perhaps little remains to be discovered concerning the arrangement of the automatic ganglia in the viscera, or the structural arrangement of the cere-

196 THE ABDOMINAL AND PELVIC BRAIN

brospinal and sympathetic systems. But much remains to be discovered in regard to the functional relations of the cerebrospinal and sympathetic systems. Each system may contain structures of the other, or not. As a birdseye view of the sympathetic nervous system we may produce the following:

1. A series of distinct ganglia connected by nerve cords, extending from the base of the skull to the coccyx.

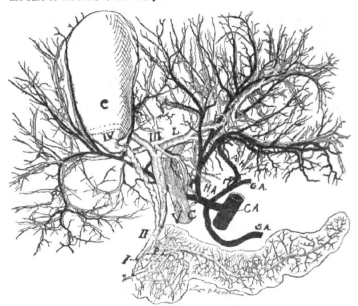

DUCTUS BILIS ET DUCTUS PANCREATIS ET AORTERIA HEPATICA

Fig. 53. This illustration represents the biliary and pancreatic ducts with the hepatic artery, which are each ensheathed with a fenestrated network of sympathetic nerves. A H, hepatic artery; I, vateis diverticulum; II, junction of ductus cysticus and ductus hepaticus; III, ductus hepaticus; IV, cholecyst with its duct.

2. Automatic visceral ganglia.
3. A series of three centrally located prevertebral plexuses, situated in the thorax, abdomen and pelvis.
4. A series of communicating and distributing nerve fibers.

The above propositions may be reduced to three elements, viz., nerve fibers and nerve cells, or ganglia and periphery.

The caudal end of the sympathetic ends in a nerve mass known as the ganglion impar, and the head (frontal) end ceases in the ganglion of Prof.

Francois Ribes of Montpelier, France (1800-1864). I must confess that my searches for Ribes' ganglion have not been fully successful.

We find the sympathetic nervous system very widely distributed and it must not be considered improbable to find sympathetic centers in the cerebrospinal axis. The seat of a ganglion may be anywhere and yet not partake of the adjacent surroundings, i. e., sympathetic ganglia may be situated in the cerebrospinal axis, yet not be an integral part of it, particularly as regards function. Thus we may consider the vaso-motor center, the cardiac, and other centers, located in the medulla and cord, not to be a part of them. This view must hold as a fact, for blood-vessels which necessarily supply all parts of the body, brain or spinal cord, must be supplied with sympathetic nerves to regulate their caliber, but neither the nerves nor the blood-vessels are of the cord or medulla. The sweat, heat (flashes) and vaso-motor (flushes) centers are located in the medulla and segments of the cord. Pathologic states, as at the menopause, make all these centers painfully manifest. Doubtless the genital center lies in the lumbar portion of the cord, though automatic visceral ganglia exist in the genital organs, such as I have formerly designated "automatic menstrual ganglia." Such ganglia require a month to accomplish a rhythmical cycle; they explode monthly. In the spinal cord there exists a linear row of cells known as the columns of the late English investigator, Dr. Clark. Some think that Clark's columns exercise the function of vaso-motor action, i. e., control the caliber of blood-vessels. But as Dr. Fox states, this column of Clark's does not exist throughout the whole length of the cord. Should further investigations demonstrate that Clark's columns have a vaso-motor function it would go a long way in proving considerable independence of the sympathetic nervous system.

This independence, however, does not entirely depend on the supposed vaso-motor column of Clark. Definite, though limited independence can be observed in portions of the sympathetic nerve by any one who will carefully perform experiments on the lower animals. We of course do not overlook the idea that the sympathetic system and cerebrospinal system are so intimately co-related that one so blends with the other that all action seems lost in the cerebrospinal mass.

When the spinal cord and brain have lost control of the intestines they assume a wild and disordered action, as may be seen in a person dying of brain disease. In cases in which at the autopsy we could discover no brain disease I have found from one to four invaginations after death. In such cases, doubtless, after the cessation of the function of the cerebrospinal masses, the sympathetic fell into a wild, confused and disordered action. The muscular wall of the intestine assumed an irregular action producing invagination. This latter is due to irregular action of the muscles in the intestinal wall.

In a certain sense we may look at the nervous system as composed of two parts, viz.: a cerebrospinal part and a sympathetic part, connected by a number of single, fine, short, non-medullated strands. These strands really

198 THE ABDOMINAL AND PELVIC BRAIN

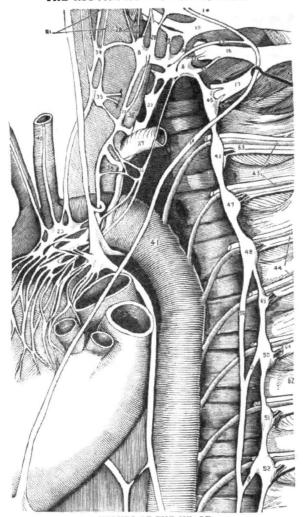

NERVES OF THE HEART

Fig. 54. This figure represents the 3 cardiac sympathetic nerves on the left side to the heart (Nos. 34, 22, 22); 23 is Nrisberg's ganglion; 18 is the phrenic joined to the inferior cervical ganglion at 8 by a branch, 19. This connection explains the braying sound or expiratory moan on sudden rectal dilatation.

connect the ganglia of the sympathetic with the brain and cord. With such a constructed apparatus before us it might be stated that the sympathetic system simply consists of branches of the cerebrospinal system. It may be represented as a branched roadway which distributes forces from the spinal cord to the viscera. It may be considered as overflow paths to carry nervous energy to the periphery. The ganglia of the sympathetic system are entirely outside of man's will-power. He cannot control them to hasten visceral action or retard it. It is plainly of utility to man to place beyond his will-power the action of viscera, as he would doubtless abuse it from selfish and other purposes.

But we must claim that the sympathetic nervous system is more than a mere branched roadway for the mere distribution of nervous energy from the cerebrospinal axis. If nervous energy was merely to flow to the viscera from the cerebrospinal axis, why all this complicated, brain-like apparatus in the various sympathetic ganglia? No, the ganglia of the sympathetic are centers of nervous energy, accumulations of brain cells, of reflex centers, organized receivers of sensation and transmitters of motion. Is the cerebrospinal system closely related to the sympathetic system by mere relations of structure, because the sympathetic ganglia and cells are imbedded in the great centers, or is it because the cerebrospinal system has intrinsic and final control of the sympathetic?

In the dorsal region we find the typical spinal nerve of the morphologist with its three chief divisions, viz.; (a) dorsal; (b) ventral and (c) visceral branch. The visceral and vaso-motor branch is contained in the ramus communicans, which passes from the spinal cord to the lateral chain of the sympathetic or lateral ganglia, the demedullating centers. From this lateral chain of ganglia nerves pass onward to a second chain of ganglia, known as the prevertebral or collateral ganglia, i. e., the cardiac, abdominal brain, inferior mesenteric and pelvic brain. Milne Edwards called the nerves which pass from the lateral sympathetic chain to the collateral (prevertebral) chain, rami efferentes. Again, from the prevertebral (collateral) ganglia or plexus, nerve fibers pass into smaller terminal ganglia in the abdominal organs, or to what we designate the automatic visceral ganglia. We also have, besides the three distinct sets of sympathetic ganglia, connected with the ramus communicans, the posterior ganglia at the roots of the nerves as they issue from the spinal canal. The ramus communicans is then connected with four distinct ganglia:

1. The root ganglia (proximal ganglia), i. e., the ganglia situated on the posterior spinal nerves immediately after issuing from the cord.
2. The lateral chain of sympathetic (proximal sympathetic ganglia).
3. The prevertebral ganglia (distal sympathetic ganglia).
4. The automatic visceral ganglia, or terminal ganglia (distal sympathetic ganglia).

Leaving out the first of the ganglia, we note that the ramus communicans connects the spinal cords with three great systems of sympathetic ganglia, viz.: (a) the lateral chain (b) the prevertebral chain and (c) the automatic

200 THE ABDOMINAL AND PELVIC BRAIN

visceral ganglia, making a complicated and vast system distributed over a wide area. In regard to the relation of this vast sympathetic system to the cerebrospinal axis in general, three views have been held:

1. The first and perhaps the oldest view is that the sympathetic nervous system possesses a very great independence of action. The supporters of this

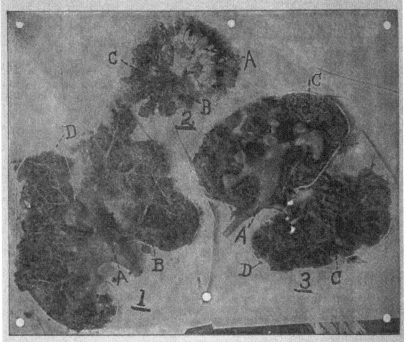

RENAL VASCULAR SUPPLY

Fig. 55. This illustration presents corrosion anatomy of 3 kidneys. The renal vascular blades are opened like a book.
The abundance of sympathetic nerves may be estimated by the fact that each branch of the renal artery is ensheathed by an anastomatic meshwork a fenestrated network of nerves. The renal calyces and pelvis lie within the open book. For nerves of the digestive tract see Fig. 13.

view make the sympathetic system the exclusive center of motion and sensation of the thoracic and abdominal viscera. The chief establishers of this view are Volkmann (1842) and Bidder (1844). Their able defense of the independence of the sympathetic nervous system is still entertained and published in the best anatomies. Bichat (1800) advocates the independence of the sympathetic ganglia, as one of the first and ablest supporters. In fact

Bichat was one of the first to definitely conceive this notion. Before me lies a rare old book which I secured from an old English collection. It is written by James Davey, 1858, on "The Ganglionic Nervous System." Davey gives Bichat credit for knowledge of the sympathetic ganglion. Davey began to advocate the primary and essential independent function of the sympathetic in 1835, as is recorded in the "Lancet." Fletcher wrote (1837) on the independent action of the sympathetic.

2. The second view held was chiefly established by Valentine (1839). This view makes the sympathetic system an offshoot or dependent of the cerebrospinal system. It would contain no fibers except those in the brain and spinal cord.

3. A third view considers the sympathetic to be composed of fibers from the brain and cord, and also of other fibers which arise in the various ganglia. According to this view every sympathetic nerve trunk contains both cerebrospinal and sympathetic fibers. This view should consider all nerves sympathetic which arise in the ganglia and preside over the functions of the organs.

The question might be asked, what are the functions of the sympathetic ganglia? It should be remembered that many different opinions mean unsettled views.

1. We may state that the ganglia demedullate nerves.
2. More nerves pass out of a sympathetic ganglia than enter it; hence the ganglion is likely the originator of nervous fibers.
3. The ganglia possess nutritive powers over the nerves passing from them to the periphery.
4. They are centers of reflex action, i. e., receivers of sensation and transmitters of motion.

We are therefore to consider as the subject of our theme:
1. The rami communicantes.
2. The lateral chain of sympathetic ganglia.
3. The prevertebral plexuses and
4. The automatic visceral ganglia.

There are some differences between the sympathetic system and cerebrospinal axis which may be noted and discussed later.

1. We may claim that the sympathetic nerves are the visceral branches of the spinal nerves and hence have a distinct function, if not structure.
2. The individual fibers of the sympathetic nerves are of smaller caliber than those of the cerebrospinal or somatic nerves.
3. The sympathetic branches preponderate in non-medullated nerves.
4. The fibers of the sympathetic nerves are interrupted by nerve cells or ganglia through which they pass.
5. Nerve cells are liable to accumulate into ganglia along a non-medullated nerve.
6. The sympathetic nerves tend to form closely meshed networks or plexuses, as Auerbach's and Billroth-Meissner's plexuses.
7. The somatic (cerebrospinal) nerves supply the body wall. The sympathetic nerves supply the viscera. In the visceral nerves must be included vascular nerves.

202 THE ABDOMINAL AND PELVIC BRAIN

We might call the various systems of ganglia of the sympathetic by numbers. For example, the lateral chain of sympathetic ganglia may be called primary ganglia. In the primary ganglia the chief nerves of the rami communicantes pass.

Again, we might call the prevertebral plexuses, the secondary ganglia. Many nerves from the rami communicantes enter the secondary ganglia without entering the primary ganglia.

NERVES OF TRACTUS GENITALIS

Fig. 56. This illustration presents the nerves of the genitals according to Frankenhauser.

Finally the automatic visceral ganglia might be called tertiary ganglia. In short we could conveniently speak of the primary, secondary and tertiary system of sympathetic ganglia.

Much interest is attached to the ramus communicans, i. e., the narrow isthmus which joins the cerebro-spinal axis to the sympathetic system It is important to have a clear view of these rami communicantes, for through them pass the rami visceraes and rami vasculares, i. e., the rami communicantes contain and transmit the vascular and visceral nerves, both subjects of profound practical interest in medicine and surgery.

In an anatomical sense writers understand by the term rami communicantes, two short nerves, a double connection between the cerebrospinal axis and the sympathetic system, i. e., with the lateral chain or primary ganglia. One ramus communicans is white, medullated and passes directly out of the anterior root of the spinal cord chiefly to the lateral chain, but some fibers pass directly to the prevertebral plexus. This branch of the communicans contains the visceral and vascular nerves; hence the importance to all practitioners. The other ramus communicans is gray, non-medullated and passes from the lateral chain of ganglia to the spinal cord. It is a vasomotor nerve, the purpose of which is to regulate the vessels of the cord and its meninges. It is well to remember that the term ramus communicans is a general term including all the kinds of nerves which supply the viscera and blood-vessels.

I propose here to consider at some length the ramus communicans which supplies the abdominal viscera and blood-vessels. In the first place, there are certain fine, white, medullated nerves, as Gaskell has pointed out, which pass from the spinal cord, in the white ramus communicans between the second dorsal and second lumbar nerves inclusive, to supply the viscera and blood-vessels. These nerves should be named as Gaskell suggests, splanchnics. Hence we will have: (1) the thoracic splanchnics; (2) the abdominal splanchnics and (3) the pelvic splanchnics: A peculiar feature of these white rami communicantes is that they are only found in a limited region of the spinal column. They begin, as Gaskell notes, at the second dorsal and end in the second lumbar. They have a very fine caliber and pass into the lateral chain, where they become demedullated, and second into the prevertebral plexuses where the remainder become non-medullated. Hence, all the white rami communicantes which pass through sympathetic ganglia leave the ganglia as non-medullated or as sympathetic nerves to attend to viscera and blood-vessels. Above the second dorsal vertebra the rami communicantes consist of the gray variety, i. e., they are peripheral nerves of the lateral ganglia. Below the second lumbar vertebra they are also of the gray peripheral variety.

CHAPTER XVII

THE PHYSIOLOGY OF THE ABDOMINAL AND PELVIC BRAIN WITH AUTOMATIC VISCERAL GANGLIA.

The sympathetic nerve which rules visceral rhythm never sleeps. Visceral rhythm (peristalsis) and life are beyond the control of the will.

'Precedent is the terror of second rate men."—Dr. Joseph Parker.

The physiology of the abdominal and pelvic brain with automatic visceral ganglia comprehends the real physiology of the sympathetic, as the chief portion of the former is included or counted in the latter. It may be asked, "What is understood by the physiology of the sympathetic nerve?" We understand by the physiology of any organ the use it yields to the economy, or the purpose it subserves to the animal. It may be stated in the beginning that it is difficult to definitely and exactly define the physiology of the sympathetic nerves, as they are often largely mingled with those of the cerebrospinal system. The cerebrospinal and sympathetic systems of nerves have a certain initial dependence on each other, like the individuals of well-ordered society. Yet certain limited liberties are assumed by both systems. The Federal government presides as a central power over the various states, but the latter assume many independent liberties of action. The states act and execute independently of the central government. So it is in the human body, an exquisitely perfect product of millions of ages; the sympathetic nerve, though dependent for much of its power on the cerebrospinal axis, has in its influence over circulation and the abdominal viscera a certain independence of function.

The sympathetic is not merely an agent of the brain and cord. It generates action itself. It is, in general, a nerve center characterized by the power to receive sensation and send out motion. It has all the elements of any nervous system, viz.: a ganglion cell, a conducting cord and and a periphery. It is not attempted here to argue that either the cerebrospinal axis or the sympathetic nerve is absolutely independent of the other. The fact is that each nerve system has its own special duties. Both systems must be associated in order to carry on life's functions and purposes. It may be said that man and woman are independent of each other; but their association is required for the perfection of reproduction. In another place I have arranged quite a number of propositions to show that the sympathetic nerve enjoys a large degree of independence. In the discussion of its physiology certain topics must be discussed, in order to better comprehend the limits and factors of the field.

1. The abdominal pelvic brain, i. e., reorganizing centers.
2. A very important factor will be the vaso-motor nerves (i. e., vaso-constrictors and vaso-dilators).

ANATOMY AND PHYSIOLOGY

3. The automatic visceral ganglia.
4. Glandular secretions (bile, urine, gastro-intestinal juices, milk, ova and semen).
5. Temperature.
6. Trophic nerves.
7. Pigmentation.
8. Reflex fibers.
9. Sleep.

The above nine divisions mark out a field for consideration. It may be broadly stated that all healthy movements initiated and sustained by the sympathetic nerves are involuntary movements.

The vaso-motor nerves. They are divided into vaso-constrictors and vaso-dilators, and to Claude Bernard belongs the credit of first conclusively showing (in 1851) that they exerted an influence over the caliber of the vessels. Authors agree, in general, that here are vaso-motor centers located in the spinal cord which control the caliber of vessels. Some place the vaso-motor centers in the vascular columns of Clark. Still another set of authors of great respectability claim that vaso-motor centers are located along the peripheral nerve branches. Doubtless there are in the walls of vessels nerve cells which are in connection with the vaso-motor nerves. These vascular ganglia, or nerve cells, send fibers to the muscularis of the vessel, dilating or contracting it according to the nature of the despatched stimulus.

It is not yet definitely settled whether the vaso-motor nerves are constrictors or dilators, or whether there are distinct constrictors and dilators. Some assert that there is a constrictor nerve only and that dilation of the vessel is paresis of the constrictor. Later authority seems to point to a vaso-dilator and vaso-constrictor, and the fact that there are vaso-motor centers located on the vessel or adjacent to it. It is evident to observers and clinicians that local variation of circulation occurs in the genital or digestive tracts from reflex irritation. By slight irritation one can produce a white line (vaso-constriction) and by more severe irritation one can produce a red line (vaso-dilation). Cold first constricts the vessels, but it is rapidly followed by vaso-dilation, a redness. Now, this local variation of circulation occurs doubtless with more distinctness in the visceral organs which are so highly supplied with vaso-motor nerves, and so closely situated to the gigantic vaso-motor center, the abdominal brain. The significance of vaso-constricting nerves becomes very evident when it is recognized that they are so powerful that they can drive or squeeze all the blood out of a part.

In death from peritonitis the vaso-constrictors drive first all the blood out of the skin or periphery. The blood is forced into the large arteries and veins by the effect of the vaso-constrictors on the peripheral and smaller vessels. The vaso-dilators may be so effectively exercised that the blood escapes through the wall of the blood-vessels as in hemorrhagic peritonitis.

The vaso-motor nerves are of the sympathetic and exercise control over the caliber of vessels. The controlling of the lumen of vessels constitutes a vast field of physiology, in the domain of the sympathetic. It constitutes vascular tone. Section of the sympathetic dilates the vessels beyond the normal. One of the chief offices of the sympathetic nerve is to preserve the tone of vessels. The nerves that insure tone in vessels issue from the sympathetic. They are always active and never in repose,—a characteristic of the sympathetic nerve. They pass to the muscular coat of the vessels and act as their permanent guardian, in preserving permanent vascular tone. Variation in this tone constitutes incipient disease. Doubtless the vascular tone is the result of a reflex matter, and the factor in the reflection is the blood-wave, i. e., the trauma or irritation of the blood-wave on the endothelial membrane of the vessel induces the vaso-constrictors to act permanently in preserving vascular tone. Congestion is only the abolition of vascular tone. Goltz's percussion experiment demonstrates the reflex nature of the action of vaso-motor nerves, as by tapping on the exposed viscera he could produce dilatation of their vessels. Hence in this case the centers for reflex action must lie in the walls of the vessels themselves.

For a reflex act in the vaso-motor field, there must exist several factors, as (a) muscular walls or contractile tissue; (b) centripetal fibers; (c) a center of reflection; (d) centrifugal fibers.

All these factors exist on and adjacent to vessels.

For the reflex centers of vaso-motor movements we may look to the cardiac ganglia, the abdominal brain or, especially, to the ganglia around the vessels or in their walls. Finally, we may claim that the vaso-motor nerves control the caliber of vessels, that they belong to the sympathetic and that those of the abdominal viscera are chiefly under the control of the gigantic vaso-motor center—the abdmoinal brain.

First, we must consider the abdominal brain, the semilunar ganglia or solar plexus, in the physiology of the smypathetic. This large ganglion receives sensation and sends out motion. It is situated at the root of the great visceral artery i. e., at the foot of the celiac axis. It lies behind the stomach and entwines itself about the aorta and root of the celiac axis and superior mesenteric artery. In short, it is located at the roots of the celiac, renal and superior mesenteric arteries. It supplies all the abdominal viscera. It is a gigantic vaso-motor center for the viscera, as is shown by its location at the roots of the celiac, renal and superior mesenteric arteries—the great abdominal visceral blood way. It is connected with almost every organ in the body, with a supremacy over visceral circulation, with a control over visceral secretion and nutrition, with a reflex influence over the heart that often leads to fainting and may even lead to fatality. It rules visceral rhythm. No wonder that we may consider the abdominal brain the center of life itself, as the cranial brain is the center of mental and psychical forces!

The abdominal brain, or solar plexus, is composed of the aggregation of coalescence of a large number of ganglia. On the two sides of the abdominal brain are situated the semilunar ganglia—compact masses of nerve cells, nerve cords and connective tissue. During many dissections I have noted that the right semilunar ganglion is the smaller, doubtless because it lies behind the inferior vena cava, and hence has suffered from pressure atrophy.

Each of the semilunar ganglia receives the great splanchnic nerve of the corresponding side. The other splanchnics may enter it, but it is more to enter the abdominal brain. It may be here stated that although the semilunar ganglia are located on the sides, they are practically so intimately associated with the solar plexus that we insist in combining all the names into one, viz.: that of Abdominal Brain.

All plexuses or strands of nerves are secondary. The significance of the abdominal brain in the visceral physiology, i. e., in life, may be compared to that of the sun over the planets. The influence of the sun rules the planets, though they are influenced by other suns and planets (e. g., the cerebrospinal). The abdominal brain has ganglion cells (brain centers), nerve strands (nerve conductors) and a peripheral nerve apparatus, just as the cranial brain possesses a central, conducting and peripheral apparatus. The abdominal brain can live without the cranial (shown by living fetuses with no trace of cerebrospinal axis), while the cranial brain and the cord cannot live without the abdominal brain.

The great sympathetic ganglia, of which the abdominal brain is the ruling potentate, is the center of life itself. So long as the forces of life, assimilation, circulation, respiration and secretion proceed undisturbed, as in health, the abdominal brain remains a silent, steady, but ceaseless worker; but being unbalanced by peripheral or central irritation, it quickly manifests or resents the insult. From the abdominal brain large plexuses with numerous nerve strands pass to every abdominal viscus, connecting the viscera into a delicately balanced, nicely ordered, exquisitely, arranged apparatus for the object of maintaining life. The nerve plexuses or strands are arranged along the highways of nourishment—blood and lymph vessels, and vary in size according to the importance of the viscus supplied.

Laignel and Lasvastine, in their experiments upon dogs, have found that ablation of the solar plexus is a serious operation; though traumatism of the plexus even may cause death. They have called the *solar syndrome of paralysis* the sum of symptoms produced by ablation of the plexus; it may be superacute, acute, subacute, or chronic. The first form they have found to be present in peritonitis, clinically, the second in lead colic; the others in mucomembranous colitis. Certain affections, therefore, may be attributed solely to disturbance of the solar plexus, and not to general systemic derangement.

CHAPTER XVIII.

CONSIDERATIONS FOR THE REMOVAL OF PELVIC AND ABDOMINAL TUMORS.

The sympathetic is the silent companion of the cerebralspinal. The sympathetic nerve is the nerve of subconscious life.

"But he did not lose sight of the present in these glowing visions of a future."—Mrs. Catharine V. Waite, "The Mormon Prophet and His Harem."

Having devoted some twenty years to the study of pelvic and abdominal visceral disease, I have frequently desired to record some observations on the effect of tumors in the pelvis and abdomen upon the sympathetic system. Many dissections have convinced me that the vast ganglionic system, distributed to the viscera bordering upon the peritoneal cavity, together with other glandular organs of the body, plays a significant role. Besides, when it is noted that the heart and the unstriped muscles of the body, are supplied by the sympathetic system, there becomes at once apparent its extensive as well as intimate connection with the whole body.

Special study in the physiology and pathology of the viscera develops reasons for the removal of abdominal and pelvic tumors not apparent from superficial observations. It is well known that shortly after the appearance of a tumor in the abdomen the health of the patient becomes more or less impaired. The functions of the organs become deranged; the heart suffers from abnormal action and structural change; the digestion becomes more or less deranged. As the tumor increases in size, kidney diseases generally develop. The liver, forming bile, glycogen and urea, sooner or later becomes impaired in its rhythm. The lungs lose their rhythm and become spasmodic, while the spleen shows its disturbance by pigmentary deposits in various portions of the body. An attempt will here be made to explain the pathological result of abdominal tumors on physiological and anatomical grounds.

The basis of the explanation will be by reflex action on the sympathetic nerve. It may be curtly observed that pathological results due to the sympathetic nerve are based upon reflex action. We shall assume that the ganglia which are found in it, especially the abdominal brain and the three cervical ganglia, are points where forces are reorganized and distributed to the viscera. The first essential feature to observe in the diseased viscera is the disturbance in rhythm. Though any abdominal tumor may produce the same results, we shall choose a uterine myoma to illustrate our views. It is a principle in physiology that when a peripheral irritation is sent to the abdominal brain the reorganized forces will be emitted along the lines of least resistance, so that the organ which is supplied with the greatest number of nerve strands will suffer the most. Practically this principle holds true in every viscus.

REFLEX ACTION

The great ganglia and cords, filled with nerve cells and nerve strands, labor in the subconscious region, the vast laboratory of life and assimilation. The cerebrospinal axis receives sensations and emits impulses which express themselves in motion, performing labors which minister to the mind and protect the body in avoiding destruction, or contribute to its nutrition.

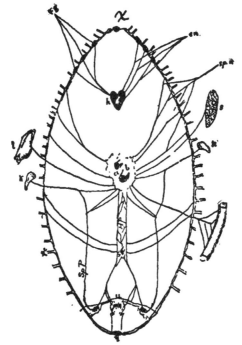

SCHEMATIC DRAWING OF THE SYMPATHETIC NERVE

Fig. 57. X, ganglion of Ribes; y, coccygeal ganglion; h, heart; k, kidney; s, spleen; a b, abdominal brain; s p, spermatic (ovarian plexus); i, intestine; h p, hypogastric plexus; c g, the three cervical nerves.
The sides of the ellipse represent the lateral chain of the sympathetic. All the nerve strands report to the abdominal brain.

The effects of the tumor on the heart may first be considered. An abdominal tumor induces fatty degeneration of the heart. When the uterine tumor irritates the peripheral ends of the hypogastric plexus, the irritation is transmitted to the abdominal brain and there reorganized and emitted along the splanchnic to the cervical ganglia, where, again, a reorganization occurs and the force then passes down to the heart by way of the three cardiac nerves. The irritation could pass directly from the uterine myoma up to the lateral chain of sympathetics to the three cervical ganglia where it becomes reorganized.

It no doubt transmits part of the irritation by way of the abdominal brain and part by way of the lateral chain. So far as the heart is concerned, the result is nearly the same, for the irritation is reorganized in each case in the three cervical ganglia and transmitted to the heart. It is of course necessary to consider that the irritation may be sent to the spinal cord by way of the vagus and there reorganized. In such case it is sent directly to the heart by the vagus.

It should be remembered that the sympathetic ganglia in the walls of the heart (Ludwig's, Bidder's, Schmidt's and Remak's) are numerous and large. Also that the network of cords with their ganglia, situated close to its surface, constitute an extensive nerve system. It consists of the great or deep cardiac plexus, otherwise known as the plexus magnus profundus of Scarpa, besides the superficial cardiac plexus, with the cardiac ganglia of Wrisberg, which is occasionally large from the coalescence of several ganglia, and may be represented by a meshwork. In tumors of the pelvis we are dealing with the effect on the vast cardiac sympathetic nervous system. The first manifest objective heart symptom is irregularity.

The irritation from the uterine myoma reaches the heart in two ways:

1. The irritation passes up the hypogastric plexus to the abdominal brain, where it is reorganized and emitted to all the viscera over their respective sympathetic plexuses. In the case of the heart it passes up the abdominal splanchnics to the three cervical ganglia of the sympathetic, where it is reorganized and sent directly to the heart.

2. Some of the irritation is transmitted by way of the vagi to the medulla, where it is reorganized and sent directly to the heart by the cardiac nerves which supply the heart from the vagus. This is more especially the case in the right vagus, as that is the cranial nerve which largely rules and supplies the heart and abdominal brain. Now, this irritation from the myoma goes on day and night. It gives the heart no rest. It flows to the heart in the midst of a diastole, or a systole. The first great characteristic of the heart (rhythm) is lost. Having lost its rhythm, the heart proceeds irregularly. Irregular action means a changed nourishment; continued irritation with disturbed rhythm induces the heart to overfeed itself, the result being hypertrophy.

It may be noted that this hypertrophy is not brought about in precisely the same way as is hypertrophy from valvulitis or aortic insufficiency; but vaso-motor dilation must play a role in over-nourishing the cardiac muscles. It resembles more nearly the cardiac hypertrophy existing in goiter. That from the reflex irritation in myoma is also a moderate hypertrophy, so far as the writer has observed, and it is a very slow process. In the first stage the heart becomes irregular, in the second hypertrophied, in the third it takes on fatty degeneration. This is no doubt a preservative process, so that a large, vigorously beating heart will not rupture an artery in a degenerated state (atheromatous or fatty). It appears certain that many old cases of large uterine myoma are lost after skillful operations simply from fatty degeneration of the heart. It is common to observe palpitation in patients having uterine myoma, and palpitation is the characteristic symptom of a weak heart.

The automatic cardiac ganglia are disturbed by reflex irritation and take on an excessive nourishment. The irritation, sent to the heart over the hypogastric plexus, is in one sense an increased demand for action. The irritation, passing to the heart day and night, winter and summer, according to a physiological law, provokes hypertrophy, if the nutritive powers are good. If they are not good, the complement of hypertrophy—dilation—results.

A fatty degenerated or weak heart induces low blood-pressure, which is the bottom factor in waste-laden blood and deficient elimination. It allows local congestions and consequent impaired nourishment. The local force of such circumstances teaches to remove uterine and other abdominal tumors as early as possible, so that the patient will not be left with partially or completely damaged viscera.

Reflexes arising from the irritation of the sympathetic in the peritoneal membrane are profound in results. Irregularity, hypertrophy, and degeneration of the heart are the effects of a reflex act, accomplished mainly through the sympathetic system and due to irritation at the periphery of the hypogastric plexus. It is transmitted to the abdominal brain, to the three cervical ganglia, and some to the spinal cord, whence the reorganization of the forces occurs.

The organized nervous impressions then pass to the heart over the six cardiac (vagi) nerves. This abnormal force deranges the fine balance of the heart's rhythm. The automatic cardiac ganglia become discolored, and in time vaso-motor action and consequently nourishment are disturbed.

It may be remembered that the untoward influence on the heart, disturbing its rhythm and consequently its nourishment, is also aided and abetted by disturbing the caliber of distal blood-vessels which are controlled by the sympathetic system.

The liver does not escape the evil influence of the tumor. Abdominal tumors induce fatty degeneration of the liver. It may be asserted that an influence on the hepatic plexus of nerves alone could stop all scretion in the liver. If such a proposition be true, it need not be wondered that lesser irritations of the hepatic nerve plexus could so alter the secretion of the liver that it would degenerate the organ. The characteristic disturbance which arises from the uterine myoma is a derangement of rhythm. The liver has a rhythm due to (a) an elastic peritoneum inclosing it, (b) an elastic capsule (Glisson's) surrounding it, and (c) to the capacity of its cells to enlarge.

The occasion of the liver rhythm is food carried to it by way of the portal vein. When the peritoneal and Glisson's capsules and the cells are expanded to a maximum, the liver rhythm is at its climax. Now, the products of the liver (bile, glycogen and urea) are sent to their respective homes by contraction of the elastic peritoneum and capsule of Glisson. The liver then gets its rest and repair.

The irritation from the periphery of the hypogastric plexus passes up to the abdominal brain, where it is reorganized and emitted to the liver. It goes to the liver from the tumor at all hours and deranges its rhythm. The irritation may attempt to induce a rhythm without food, or it may flash on to the liver at any stage in its rhythm. The liver rhythm is induced by the automatic hepatic plexus. So it may be asserted that the irritation of the uterine myoma deranges the rhythm of the liver.

The second point to consider is the altered secretion in the liver, due to the reflex irritation from the uterine myoma by way of the abdominal brain. The continued irritation increases the derangement and soon changes and impairs the liver nourishment. The complete process from food to end products becomes imperfect and a lower grade of tissue is formed, known as fat. The constantly irritated liver soon becomes able to form but little products beyond fat, and degeneration follows.

It is well known that women at the menopause frequently acquire liver disease. This is owing to the reflex irritation through the abdominal brain. The degeneration of the hypogastric plexus will not allow it to transmit sufficient physiological orders to induce a monthly rhythm, so the accumulated energies flash to the other organs, and the derangement of the liver is especially manifest, because its derangement is often followed by pigmentation (yellow or brown or black) of the skin. The uterine myoma, then, by reflex action, disturbs rhythm and secretion in the liver, and so its nutrition. This ends in fatty degeneration.

For years I have observed that women with pelvic disorders have *disturbed kidney action*. In general this kidney disturbance is renal insufficiency, and it may after long irritation become organic disease. It may be well to give a general hint here as to why the kidneys suffer so much when either irritating tumors or inflammatory processes exist in the pelvic organs.

The kidneys, uterus, ovaries and oviducts develop from two very small points in the embryo called the Wolffian bodies. These develop from the mesoblast, as do the muscles, blood and lymph vessels, and from the genitourinary organs. Arising from the same source and supplied by the same nerves and blood-vessels, the Wolffian bodies, the kidneys and genitals have an intimate and close connection. The abdominal brain sends out a vast chain of nerves to the kidney on each side, and the same brain sends out a vast chain on each side of the genitals. These and the kidneys are only different spokes in the same wheel, the hub of which is the abdominal brain. Diseases in the genitals, whether tumors or inflammatory processes, produce in the urine not only diminished solids but also diminished fluids.

Again on the other hand diminished kidney excretion (renal insufficiency) produces diseased or, at least, disturbed genitals. Any gynecologist of some years' experience has doubtless frequently observed that in women with diseased genitals and deficient renal secretion, by giving diuretics—fluids in small and oft-repeated doses, the diseased genitals will often improve in direct proportion to the increase of renal secretion. Deficiency of renal secretion irritates the genitals by non-removal of urinary solids. Diseased genitals irritate the kidneys by reflex action. This is all accomplished through the abdominal brain as a center. The genitals, kidneys and abdominal brain constitute a very vital triangle. In the middle of its base lies the significant abdominal brain and at the apex the important genitals, while the other two angles are occupied by the kidneys. The uterus and kidneys have the highest nerve and blood supply of all viscera, hence they experience more profoundly than other viscera the forces which are organized and reorganized in the abdominal brain. In the sympathetic nervous system the kidneys play a vast and immeasurable role. If by some irritation in the pelvis or abdomen the kidney begins to secrete insufficiently, the whole organism, together with the ganglionic nervous system, or the cyclo-ganglionic system, as Solly termed it half a century ago, will become poisoned from non-elimination. From this peculiar reflex action, of which the abdominal brain is capable, we may yet learn that disease of the pelvic organs of woman may be cured by diuretics, cathartics or diaphoretics. In other words drain the skin, drain the kidneys and drain the bowels. The intimate and close relations of the genitals and kidneys is plain anatomically and physiologically, as large bundles of nerves from the abdominal brain supply both. Clinically, then, these closer relations have been demonstrated of late years, as gynecology has progressed. The cyclo-ganglionic system is recognized as a finely balanced mechanism capable of prompt response when once its manifestations are understood.

For example, no one understands so well as the gynecologist the vital relation which exists between deficient kidney secretion and diseased pelvic organs. Effective diuretics relieve many pelvic pains. Baths and diaphoretics subdue innumerable neuralgias, and cathartics disperse dragging pains. A woman may have a sound kidney (so far as chemical examination of the urine may indicate) and yet reflex action from the genitals may induce it to secrete deficient or excessive fluids or solids, which not only further disturbs the genitals with waste-laden blood but disarranges the fine balance in other viscera with the same. Wherever this waste-laden blood advances it produces new points for reflex irritation, unbalancing the whole system. It seems to me there is no better point to work from in this consideration than the relation of the genito-urinary system to the abdominal brain. Clinical features are more manifest here than elsewhere. Gynecologists may even cure women of innumerable ailments by simply inducing them to drink water. I have accomplished much for women during the past fifteen years by inducing them to drink a full glass of water, six times daily, containing a pinch of Epsom salt in solution. The late Dr. J. H. Etheridge wrote instructively on renal secretion in gynecologic patients.

During menstruation girls show distinct clinical symptoms of pain in the region of the kidneys, and of variation in urinary secretion, showing the close relation between this and pelvic disturbances. It is clear that this pain in the kidney region is due to reflexes from the menstrual organs, i. e., the uterus and oviducts.

The kidney, in proportion to its size, has the highest nerve and blood supply of any viscus, except the uterus. According to the recent investigations at Johns Hopkins University, the kidney is supplied only by sympathetic nerves. It is a common observation that abdominal tumors are followed by kidney disturbances. Even the gravid uterus does not allow the kidney to escape irritation. This kidney disease brought about by abdominal tumors is reflex. It is a physiological principle that an influence acting through the nerves alone can arrest all secretion. Minor degrees of irritation will suffice to increase, diminish or change the kidney secretions. Irritation of an organ continued indefinitely, and modifying its action, may be sufficient to induce disease. Kidney disease resulting from abdominal tumors is chiefly chronic from the very nature of the case.

The first point to consider, as the initial step in chronic renal disease from abdominal tumors, is partial or complete obstruction to the flow of urine.

The second point to consider in chronic renal disease due to abdominal tumors is reflex irritation from distant viscera.

The third point of consideration is infection.

As regards the first point, *obstruction*, the location and size of the tumor may be noted. A partially occluded ureter, through long-continued pressure, will cause renal disease. Under this head would be classed mechanical impediments to the flow of urine. If the obstruction is sufficient it will create hydroureter. If the hydroureter is long enough maintained the kidney will secrete until blood pressure is impaired, and then in a few months atrophy will follow. The writer has proved by experiments on the dog that when the ureter is completely ligated, the kidney will shrink to about one-fifth its original size, in five months.

The pressure of the tumor on the ureter is a silent process not often recognized by the attendant. The obstruction of the ureter is like the quietly growing intestinal stricture, which is rarely recognized until some terrible disaster reveals a long series of old pathological conditions. The main idea in the obstruction, however, is that it is partial, and by raising the difficulty of urine flow, renal elminiation becomes deficient. The blood then becomes waste-laden. If the obstruction is sufficient, the result will be hydroureter, which being long continued (without infection) results in renal atrophy, as the writer proved by tying the dog's ureter.

The second point, *reflex irritation*, is more significant, because it means that irritation from any viscus can be reflected to the kidney, over the renal plexus. The abdominal tumor irritates some contiguous viscus; this irritation quickly passes to the abdominal brain, by way of the sympathetic plexus of said viscus, where the forces are reorganized and transmitted to the kidney. There is little doubt that the rise of temperature from passing a sound into a man's bladder is due to reflex irritation transmitted from an oversensitive urethra. It is probable that the so-called urinary fever is reflex. It modifies circulation by inducing local anemia and local hyperemia. In this way nutrition quickly changes. Examples may be seen in strictures of the intestine or ureter where the walls above the stricture are greatly thickened.

The chief point in regard to secretions in patients with abdominal tumors is a decreased or disproportionate secretion. It is common to observe a patient with a tumor secreting a small quantity of urine heavily laden with salts. The amount of urine voided at times appears as an alarmingly small quantity. Natural reasoning from clinical and physiological bases attributes the decreased quantity of urine to the irritation from the tumor transmitted over the renal plexus. Autopsies on women who die of tumors prove it beyond the shadow of a doubt.

Disproportionate renal secretion from the irritation of abdominal tumors is also common. Albumen is the chief element found. But phosphates, urates or sugar make up the varying scales of salts. Even the amount of water will vary within wide limits.

The tumor of pregnancy is a common example of disturbed renal secretion due to reflex action. Thus deranged renal secretion is frequently due to reflex irritation, depending on the presence of an abdominal tumor. The change in the secretion consists in increase, decrease or disproportionate quantities. As each organ has its own distinct nerve plexus, so it should be understood that reflex action is carried along distinct anatomical lines.

As regards the third point, *infection*, in chronic renal diease from the presence of abdominal tumors a serious condition appears.

The genito-urinary tract can be infected at any point from the kidney cortex to the urethral end. If the tumor presses severely enough on the urinary tract, a perforation will occur, and from this perforation infection will travel in either direction—toward the urethra or toward the kidney.

The result of perforation of the urinal tract will be nephritis and cystitis. The perforation is most likely to occur in the bladder, from which the infection ascends the ureters to the kidney. It is not necessary to have a large tumor to perforate the urinal tract; simply a suppurating focus is sufficient. It is not necessary to have a complete perforation of the urinary tract to allow infection to gain an entrance, for the germs, or their products (ptomaines), may penetrate a thin pathological wall. The final result of an infected urinary tract is ureteritis, with parenchymatous or interstitial nephritis. The writer has observed some disastrous results from pyosalpinx perforating the bladder and intestines. It may here be noted that Doran, a most excellent observer, made post-mortem examinations of forty women who had died of ovarian tumors, and thirty-two had severe kidney disease. This means that 80 per cent. of those who died from ovarian tumors had kidney disease. No doubt the kidneys were diseased from the presence of tumors. Obstruction, reflex action or infection was the causative factor of renal disease, resulting from pressure of tumors.

A good sample of obstruction, reflex irritation and infection of the urinal tract is seen in cases of *gonorrhea* in men which end in stricture and "catheter life." The stricture generally arises in the urethra and marks the onset of obstruction to the urinary flow. This increasing obstruction induces constant reflex irritation, and yet the man is not subjectively or objectively sick. But now he begins "catheter life," which means infection. It means self-destruction by his own hands. Thus to obstruction and reflex irritation of the urethra he has added the fatal infection carried on his catheter, which too frequently makes the fatal march swiftly onward and swiftly downward.

The kidney suffers similarly from any abdominal tumor, and chiefly by reflex irritation, which passes from the abdominal brain by way of the contiguous plexus, where it is reorganized and emitted on the large renal plexus to the kidney. The writer notes that those women who come to him for the purpose of having tumors removed have a very variable quantity of urea in the urine. At the Woman's Hosipal the writer has the urea tested in every case of laparotomy, and the amount varies from five to eleven grains to the ounce. The tumors appear to play a significant role in the production of varying quantities of urea.

What has been said in regard to kidney disease by reflex irritation is equally prominent in floating or excessively movable kidney. The dragging of the kidney on the abdominal brain, through the renal plexus, unbalances the viscera very distinctly. The patient suffers from nausea, from constipation, from disturbed secretion and circulation and from dull dragging pains. The patient may sometimes suffer similarly from an artificially fixed kidney, as I have observed often after a nephropexy of my own, when viscera, which are normally excessively mobile or fixed, are dislocated, they lose a part of their physiology, which is motion.

Calculus in the ureter is a typical sample of disturbance in the sympathetic nerves. One of my patients was idle ten months before I removed a ureteral calculus, and she suffered from an unbalanced sympathetic nervous system just as a woman would from diseased genitals.

Abdominal and pelvic tumors produce disease in the digestive tract. Object lessons are not only impressive to children, but to adults. The wonder is how the visceral organs can adapt themselves to growing and movable tumors. To-day we removed an ovarian tumor the size of a child's head with a narrow pedicle of seven inches. The tumor could be pushed into almost any position of the abdomen. Yet this tumor, which the patient has had for about ten months, appears to have told on her health. To be sure it glided where it would without any apparent trouble, but doubtless the continued, repeated and accumulated traumas on the other viscera maintained a constant story of visceral insult. Every step she took induced the tumor to jog and roll around in the abdomen. Occasionally it would become partially wedged in the pelvis, producing congestion and disturbed circulation and insults to the delicate nerves of the peritoneum. This solid tumor was not like the yielding, soft viscera; but wherever it would lie it pressed and disturbed circulation. It is probably true that smaller tumors of the pelvis and abdomen produce much more traumatic visceral insult than larger ones which move but little. The real wonder was that such a tumor as the above could glide about among the mobile viscera so long and not become rotated on its axis.

REFLEXES ALTER GLAND SECRETIONS

It is probable that secreting or glandular organs suffer the most from abdominal tumors, because the main damage is through reflex action, and the glands are the most highly supplied with sympathetic nerves. The digestive tract should be studied by means of (a) sensation, (b) motion, (c) secretion, (d) absorption. The slow, continuous pressure of abdominal tumors produces but little recognizable sensation in the digestive tract. Another point is that from inexperience the patient cannot localize the pain in the digestive tract, but refers it mostly to the abdominal brain; so that the subjective sensation in the digestive tract, due to tumors, is of small value. As regards motion in the digestive tract, in cases of abdominal tumors, one can say that in the great majority of fair or large-sized tumors motion is diminished and constipation is the rule. But the main study of damage of abdominal tumors in the digestive tract will be through the secretions. Secretions are altered in three ways: (a) they may be excessive, (b) decreased, or (c) disproportionate.

The final result is indigestion. The irritation from the tumor is carried on the plexus of any contiguous viscus to the abdominal brain, where it is reorganized and emitted to the digestive tract over the gastric plexus, the superior mesenteric plexus and the inferior mesenteric plexus. In any case the brunt of the forces ends in the ganglia which lie just below the mucous membrane; the ganglia constitute what is known as Meissner's plexus, which rules secretion.

If the irritation be of such a nature as to produce excessive secretion, diarrhea may result. The excessive secretions will decompose, ferment, and induce malnutrition. It is common to observe in women with tumors, spells of indigestion, and especially in times of excessive irritability. No doubt at such times the irritation assumes a prominence not experienced on other occasions. If the irritation is of such a nature as to diminish secretion, constipation will likely result. An inactive digestive tract is the forerunner of non-elimination and a waste-laden blood. It is common to observe anorexia for weeks at a time, accompanied by constipation, in women who have tumors. No doubt the main chapter in altered secretion consists in what may be termed disproportionate secretion. The elements which make up the digestive fluid are not secreted in normal quantities; one element is deficient and the other is excessive. The normal relations of acidity and alkalinity are changed so that constant fermentation arises. Again, from the irritation of an abdominal tumor, individual organs do not secrete their normal quantity or quality.

The liver may secrete excessively or deficiently. The pancreas may do too much or too little. The irritation may cause segments of the alimentary canal to secrete excessively or deficiently and thus destroy the finely balanced secretion of the canal as a whole. The stomach enteron, small intestines, may, by the irregular irritation, do too much or too little, or act irregularly. This produces decomposition in the fluid and fermentation results. Such women are continually troubled with "wind on the stomach." Diarrhea and constipation quickly alternate and the result is frequent attacks of acute indigestion.

Disproportionate secretion is the most frequent and disastrous, because the irritation from the tumor is irregular. It storms one day and sleeps the next. But the nature of irritation is to be inconstant and to rush pell mell over the nerve plexuses, or to assume a profound quietude. Irritation scampering over the plexuses month after month is sure to be followed by indigestion, malnutrition, anemia; and the final ending of the poor patient is neurosis.

The subject of pressure of abdominal tumors on the digestive tract may here be considered. The effect of pressure acts in two directions: (a) on the alimentary canal and (b) on the tumor itself. The effect on the canal may be (a) to derange the secretion and motion of the segment pressed on; (b) to perforate the canal; (c) to obstruct the canal. The more serious effect of the tumor pressure on the digestive tract arises from the changes which result in the tumor itself. The changes arising in the tumor from the alimentary canal are: (a) inflammation, (b) adhesion, (c) suppuration and (d) rupture. The main idea is that infection or its product (ptomaines) enters the tumor through the gut wall.

It frequently happens in laparotomy that some part of the digestive tract is firmly adherent to the tumor. The cause of this adhesion is the formation of exudates into organized tissue which binds the intestinal wall and tumor together. The irritation from the contact of the intestinal wall and tumor induces the passage of germs or their products (ptomaines) through the wall of the intestine, which gives rise to an exudate. The writer has fully satisfied himself that considerable inflammation, adhesion and suppuration, which are found to exist in tumors, are due to the passage of the morbid matter through the intestinal canal. It is not uncommon for one to find from an inch to a foot of intestine firmly attached to a tumor, when the great gateway of infection, the oviducts, show no traces either ancient or recent. The vermiform appendix is a certain source of infection, not only in abdominal tumors, but also of the genital organs.

Considerable inflammation and adhesion of intestines (and occasionally of other organs) when abdominal tumors exist is accounted for by infection passing through the intestinal wall into the tumor. As regards suppuration in abdominal tumors, due to infection arising from the alimentary canal, it may be said that it is only a stage in advance of inflammation, and that inflammation is only a degree short of suppuration. So that in one sense they are the same process. In the case of inflammation, the white blood-corpuscles have conquered the invaders and resisted further progress; while in suppuration the invading infection destroys whole fields of vital tissue, leaving focuses of local death—necrosis. The pus formed by these infections through the intestinal wall may be safely evacuated by way of the alimentary canal. But frequently fatal issues follow either rapidly or through long exhausting processes.

The sympathetic pathological course which abdominal tumors induce in women are: (1) irritation, (2) indigestion, (3) malnutrition, (4) anemia, and (5) neurosis. The irritation passes by reflex action to the digestive tract (including the liver and pancreas). The irritation destroys in the digestive tract (a) the rhythm of the liver, pancreas and alimentary canal by emitting irregular forces over the plexuses at irregular periods (the reflex action has no regard for rhythm); (b) the irritation produced by the tumor on the canal destroys its motion; (c) it destroys its sensation; (d) it destroys its normal secretion; (e) it destroys absorption.

Indigestion is a natural result of imperfect rhythm, motion, sensation, absorption and secretion of the alimentary canal. Long continued indigestion results in malnutrition; which finally ends in anemia. In anemia the fluid tissue known as blood is proportionately deficient in its constituents, and the innumerable nerve ganglia being bathed in waste-laden and impoverished blood, the woman is finally reduced to an irritable condition, or neurosis.

One of the strange features of abdominal tumors with long pedicles is that so few rotate on their axes. In autopsies I have noted the spleen resting on the pelvic floor with a long, narrow pedicle, but no symptoms of rotation. Dr. Lucy Waite and I have removed tumors with astonishingly long and thin pedicles with no symptoms of present or past axial rotation. Dr. Orville MacKellar and I removed an ovarian tumor about the size of a year-old child's head with a thin pedicle about eight inches long, with no symptoms of past or present rotation. We could push the tumor all over the abdomen from the pelvic floor to the diaphragm. We observed the long-pedicled tumor roll about among the loose intestines after opening the abdomen, and wondered why its pedicle did not twist.

However, I have removed tumors which had no pedicle. They had been twisted off their pedicles by axial rotation and had assumed new beds, which were nourished by the newly formed vessels from adjacent viscera and tissue, especially the omentum. It is a significant fact, noted by all practical gynecologists, that when a woman acquires a tumor, it may only be recognized, she will frequently fret and chafe under it until she becomes nervous and irritable and her coolness and quiet serenity leave her. She also tires easily and does not sleep well.

Such a case came to me a few days ago, from whom Dr. Lucy Waite and I removed an orange-sized ovarian tumor per vaginam. This lady I treated seventeen years ago, when she was a blooming, vivacious girl. Some ten months ago she began to complain of ill-defined symptoms. A general practitioner treated her a year ago and examined the pelvic organs, but failed to find the tumor. Finally, she and her husband decided to consult a gynecologist, and came to me. In eight to ten months, from the rotation of the tumor, her nervous system had lost its fine, even balance of former years. She slept poorly, was irritable, appetite was poor, and she was easily tired out and had lost all her old vivacity. It was all due to reflex action from a large orange-sized pelvic tumor. The disturbance will disappear with the tumor.

Abdominal tumors should be removed on account of danger of axial rotation. The literature which takes note of a tumor rotating on its axis covers only about thirty years. Rokitansky, of Vienna, was among the first to call attention to the subject. The writer estimates from literature and observation that about 8 per cent. of ovarian and parovarian tumors rotate on their axes. In 1891 Mr. Tait told the writer that he had, up to date, sixty-two cases of rotated tumors. While a pupil of Mr. Tait, for six months, the writer saw four tumors rotated on their axes. Almost any abdominal or pelvic tumor may rotate on its axis. The writer has observed in an autopsy, rotation of the cecum and ileum on each other three-quarters of a turn, but insufficient to obstruct the cecal current. Volvulus is only axial rotation of the sigmoid on the mesosigmoid. In the intestinal tract volvulus occurs in the sigmoid flexure in 60 per cent. of cases; in 30 per cent. at the cecum, and in 10 per cent. in the small intestine. Axial rotation of the digestive tract constitutes about 4 per cent. of all intestinal obstructions. It is no doubt due to a fatless, elongated mesentery (enteroptosis) and previous constipation. As regards the causes of axial rotation of abdominal tumors, the writer is convinced that it is due to visceral rhythm.

The first rotated ovarian tumor I observed was in Prof. Czerny's clinic in 1884. The tumor was removed with fatal issue.

Any viscus which possesses an elongated attachment may rotate more or less on its axis. The uterus has been found rotated so as to demand operation. My assistant, Dr. A. Zetlitz, operated on a patient in whom the uterus was found with almost a full rotation, due to a contracting cicatrix from an old inflammatory attack. The kidney can, and does, rotate on its axis, resulting in partial or complete obstruction—the obstruction of its ureter causing hydroureter and the obstruction of the renal vein due to twisting, interfering with circulation and nourishment. It is possible for the spleen, in certain abnormal conditions, to rotate on its axis. In one autopsy I found the spleen on the pelvic floor with a thin, partially rotated pedicle.

Axial rotation of abdominal tumors may be partial or complete, acute or chronic. An acute case generally acts in the following manner: A woman has an abdominal tumor. She has a sudden onset of pain; she will perhaps vomit. In twenty-four to forty-eight hours the abdomen will gradually enlarge. If it enlarges very extensively, the patient becomes pale and faint. The enlargement is the result of (a) the obstruction of the return venous flow from the tightness of the twist in the pedicle; (b) the dilatation of the veins in the tumor, and (c) the rupture of a vein in the tumor.

The rigid-walled artery is difficult to occlude, and so keeps pumping its stream of blood into the tumor. The soft-walled, easily compressible vein is quickly occluded by the twist in the pedicle, and so all or nearly all the blood pumped in by the artery is retained in the tumor. The consequence is a sudden abdominal enlargement. Of course a woman may bleed to death into her own tumor, and such cases are on record, confirmed by autopsy. The tumor may twist so much on its pedicle that it may occlude both vein and artery. I had such a case in a girl twenty years old. When the abdomen was opened the tumor was gangrenous. It may rotate so vigorously that it will be entirely twisted off or severed from its connections. In such cases the tumor acquires nourishment from the surrounding viscera. The trauma resulting from the axial rotation induces sufficient irritation to produce an exudate on the surface of the tumor. This exudate undergoes organization, acquiring blood-vessels, nerves and lymphatics sufficient to nourish the tumor without its old pedicle. The writer saw, with Mr. Tait, one tumor sufficiently rotated on its pedicle to occlude the vein and artery, which was nourished by innumerable delicate, newly organized processes of visceral tissue.

In my own practice, while performing laparotomy, I have been surprised to find a dermoid ovarian tumor the size of a cocoanut entirely without a pedicle. It was wholly nourished by omental adhesions. The patient gave me a history of a severe attack four years previous, from which time pain and tenderness continuously clung to her. My attention was first called to axial rotation of tumors in 1884, at Heidelberg, in the clinic of Professor Czerny. One day a middle-aged lady suddenly appeared in the clinic who had come from her home in the country very sick. The professor put her on the table and examined her carefully. She had a high pulse and temperature and a dusky countenance. She appeared very ill. Professor Czerny said: "Gentlemen, I cannot make the diagnosis. I will examine her again and perhaps operate tomorrow." The writer anxiously waited until the next day, when, sure enough, the woman was put to sleep on the operating table. On opening the abdomen, a tumor the size of a melon appeared in the wound. It was dark red in color, and Professor Czerny pronounced it gangrenous. It was easily removed and its pedicle ligated. That was a cyst rotated on its axis; and, besides, it was not gangrenous, as such tumors rarely become gangrenous in the abdomen, and, if washed well, will show the color of normal tissue. Gangrene generally comes from tapping such cysts, or the digestive tract may infect them. Cases have been frequently recorded where death followed tapping. Intestinal contents entered the cyst and infection resulted.

Axial rotation of abdominal and pelvic tumors may pursue a chronic or slow course. In such a tumor diagnosis is very difficult. The pain in such cases will be almost wholly carried by the sympathetic nerve, and pain due to irritation of the sympathetic is generally a dull, heavy ache. It is a dragging pain. Cerebro-spinal nerves induce sharp, lancinating pain. So that slow axial rotation of the abdominal tumors will be accompanied by dull, heavy, dragging pain. It may be noted that whenever there is more than one tumor in the abdomen the chances are very much increased for axial rotation. Pregnancy enhances axial rotation much more than the presence of a double tumor, because the uterus empties itself suddenly, and just after labor the tumor is apt to rotate. The writer has seen Mr. Tait operate on a woman six weeks after delivery for an abdominal tumor which rotated about three times and a half on its pedicle. She was quite ill from delivery until after the operation, when she rapidly recovered.

In my practice I have observed axial rotation of ovarian tumors, ileocecal apparatus, sigmoid flexure, ovario—oviductal apparatus in a young girl, with rotation of uterus.

The strikingly easy manner in which operators speak of gangrenous tumors in the abdomen, with recovery, calls for objections. Recovery after gangrene or local death in the abdomen is extremely rare. What is usually called gangrene is simply tissue filled with venous blood.

Now, if this dark tissue is removed and well washed, the gangrenous idea will be dispelled by the frequent appearance of normal white tissue. Air must in some way get to a tumor to admit of gangrene, and air enters by (a) tapping, (b) digestive tract, (c) genito-urinary tract. If a cyst has rotated sufficiently to twist off its pedicle and become nourished by adhesions to adjacent viscera it is more dangerous than the original tumor on account of its fixation and adhesions. It is generally more liable to infection from the natural channels, from its more extensive vascular connection. A tumor should be removed from its liability to axial rotation. A tumor rotated on its axis is dangerous to a patient from (a) hemorrhage into the cyst, (b) gangrene, (c) because it may unduly enlarge from filling the veins of the tumor, (d) it may become fixed by adhesions and thus endanger the viscera, a fixed tumor being more dangerous than a movable one, (e) it may become infected and suppurate, (f) chronic axial rotation may exhaust a patient by pain, (g) it may result in trauma to viscera or perforation of viscera by pressure.

Abdominal tumors should be removed on account of the danger of rupture. It is a fact, which the writer has definitely observed, that tumors (ovarian and parovarian) will repeatedly rupture and fill in the living woman. In one case under my care the parovarian cyst repeatedly ruptured and filled during a year's personal observation. At the time of rupture the young woman of twenty-four would experience a sense of relief. The abdomen would become flattened and during a few succeeding days she would urinate frequently and profusely. Years previously the writer had demonstrated that if a dog's peritoneal cavity was filled with water he would urinate profusely for two or three days. In removing ovarian tumors the writer has found old scars where such cysts had ruptured and refilled. The rupture may be due to violence or the continued pressure on some point of the tumor, thinning its walls so that leakage occurs.

A rupture of non-infected cyst does no harm to a woman, but when a cyst containing infected material ruptures in the abdominal cavity death is almost inevitable. Hence, such tumors which menace life should be removed on discovery. Cystic abdominal tumors are apt to rupture from increase of abdominal pressure, which, being sustained for a long time on single points of the cyst, either thin its walls so that they will leak, or rupture them by any violence. In one case the writer removed an ovarian tumor which gave a distinct history of rupture one year previous. A distinct scar about the size of a fifty-cent piece was found on the cyst to tell the story of rupture. Abdominal tumors may endanger life by rupturing into hollow viscera as intestine, bladder, or vagina. From such rupture infection is almost sure to follow. The worst infection follows rupture into the digestive tract, and second into the bladder. The writer has removed ovarian tumors with success which had ruptured into the digestive tract and almost destroyed the patient by chronic suppuration and exhaustion. About the worst of such tumors are ovarian dermoids, which rupture into the sigmoid or rectum, for they make such dangerous adhesions. The two cysts may press so hard and long against each other that the walls in contact will fuse and the rupture will occur in the fused septum, which complicates by more adhesions and size of tumor.

The pressure occasioned by abdominal tumors demands their removal. A tumor pressing for a long time against a gut wall may thin it so that germs or their products may pass into the tumor and infect it. Inflammation follows and may be accompanied by suppuration. But pressure must be observed to take place in two directions, viz., toward the tumor and toward the viscus. The damage from pressure in the abdominal tumors is threefold: (a) the effect of pressure on viscera; (b) the effect of pressure on the tumor, and (c) the effect of the pressure on the function of viscera, both remote and distant. This last idea was discussed under reflex action. It was shown how abdominal tumors induced hydroureter by partial or complete occlusion of the ureters. Tumor pressure will even induce interstitial and parenchymatous nephritis. Three-fourths of women long possessing abdominal tumors have kidney disease. The tumor may press on some segment of the digestive tract and induce obstruction of the fecal current, either mechanically or by reflex paralysis. The main point of pressure is on some fixed portion of the intestine, the rectum, sigmoid or colon.

The canals, ureter or intestine, curiously maintain their patency for a long time on account of their continual dilatation and contraction. The writer has seen these canals entirely surrounded by dense tissues of tumors, but a distinct tunnel still existed through the tumor, considerably larger than the empty collapsed canal. The abdominal tumors, in a word, by pressure, induce obstruction, mechanically or by reflex irritation (spasm or paralysis), and should be removed. The continued pressure gives rise to (a) inflammation, by allowing infection to travel; (b) the inflammation may go on to suppuration and end in perforation, internally or externally.

The effect of pressure on the circulation (vascularity) is very apparent It acts mainly, or the effect is more evident, on the great venous plexuses. The hemorrhoidal from the inferior mesenteric suffers the most, as many of such patients have hemorrhoids. The effect of the pressure on the plexus pampiniformis is also plain, as also on the vaginal plexus and the venous bulb of the pudendum. Areas of tissue become œdematous. The limbs swell. The pelvic organs suffer the main brunt from mechanical pressure, while distant organs evidently suffer most from reflex action. The effect of mechanical pressure on circulation is (a) congestion, (b) œdema, (c) dilation of veins (hemorrhoids). It must not be forgotten that since the sympathetic is mainly distributed to blood-vessels the reflexes from pressure on the vessels are effective and profound, local and general.

The writer has noted the effect of tumors on the color of the skin for a long time. It has been recognized that pigmentation arises mainly from the spleen. Jastrowitz started the view that the spleen was the source of pigmentation, by dividing the sympathetic plexus going to the spleen on the spiral splenic artery. This experiment enhanced pigmentation. No doubt the liver is a second source of pigment, from the fact that it buries red corpuscles, and pigmentation is very noticeable in malaria which profoundly affects the liver (and spleen also). But still the spleen may be credited with the main origin of pigmentation. The writer has noted nearly all colors of pigmentation (brown, black and yellow) in such women, especially in a woman who has had a tumor a long time. The author saw a woman last month who had had a tumor for sixteen years. Her color was a deep brown and yellow, with patches of atrophied, glistening skin interspersed. The tumor disturbs the rhythm of the spleen. The spleen is capable of a rhythm by (a) its elastic covering of peritoneum, (b) its elastic capsule, (c) by the power of its cells to enlarge on receiving excessive blood. When the tumor irritates the splenic plexus it destroys its rhythm, and hence its nourishment. The nourishment being disturbed, the distribution of its products—pigment— will be disturbed. Irritation induces the spleen to produce excess of pigment. The parts of the body most intensely pigmented are those exposed to air. Yet the pigmentation is general. The simplest example of pigmentation is observed in pregnancy, which is generally localized in the genitals, breasts and linea alba.

But abdominal tumors create more definite and general pigmentation. The pigmentation is effected by the irritation passing to the abdominal brain, where it is reorganized and emitted to the spleen.

The irregular forces coming at irregular intervals to the spleen derange its rhythm, and consequently its nourishment. Pigmentation is the result of a silent process accomplished by reflex irritation, and shows general derangement of the visceral economy. It is merely the outward manifestation of profound processes, indicating removal of the offending invader. It is difficult to convince physicians that a laparotomy is really demanded to remove adhesions. Adhesive bands have blood-vessels, lymphatics and nerves.

A tumor should be removed because of its danger to create adhesions, but after they have formed they often require removal. They should be removed when they give rise to pain, when they distort and unbalance the viscera. They may occasion obstruction to any hollow viscus. They may strangulate some viscus.

Even the lungs do not escape the evil influence of the presence of the abdominal tumor. The disturbance in the lung is mainly due to reflex irritation which disturbs the rhythm of the lungs.

Abdominal tumors should be removed, from their liability to become infected.

The question may be asked, How does an abdominal tumor become infected or inflamed? Tumors frequently become infected, as is easily attested at the operation, by observing adhesions—the result of infection.

The great highway by which abdominal tumors become infected is through the oviducts. Any laparotomist can easily see that inflammatory exudates arise at the fimbriated ends of the oviducts, and from there spread. The infection travels by natural routes, especially along mucous channels. It travels particularly through the left oviduct, because, as the writer has demonstrated, the lumen of the left tube is larger than that of the right.

The second great highway of infection of abdominal tumors is through the digestive tract. Germs or their products pass through the intestinal wall at pressure points and infect the tumor.

The third channel of infection is through the genito-urinary tract. A fourth is by tapping, allowing air to enter. The table presented with this article will show at a glance the reasons for removing abdominal tumors:

EFFECTS AND CONSIDERATIONS FOR THE REMOVAL OF ABDOMINAL PELVIC TUMORS.

Heart—
  1. Irregularity.
  2. Hypertrophy.
  3. Fatty degeneration.
Lungs—
  1. Disturbed rhythm—asthma.
  2. Catarrh—anemic, hyperemic.
Liver—
  1. Disturbed rhythm.
  2. Disturbed secretion.
  3. Pigmentation.
  4. Nerve influence can check all secretion.
(a) Excessive secretion.
(b) Deficient secretion.
(c) Disproportionate secretion.
Kidney—
  1. Nerve impression can check all secretion.
(a) Excessive secretion.
(b) Deficient secretion.
(c) Disproportionate secretion.
  2. Reflex irritation.
  3. Obstruction (hydronephrosis).
  4. Infection.   (a) Parenchymatous inflammation.
                 (b) Interstitial inflammation.
Digestive Tract—
  1. Sensation.
  2. Motion.
  3. Secretion.
  4. Pressure.
  5. Absorption.
(a) Excessive secretion.
(b) Deficient secretion.
(c) Disproportionate secretion.
(a) Inflammation.
(b) Suppuration.
(c) Perforation.
(d) Adhesions.

Spleen—
  1. Disturbed rhythm.
  2. Pigmentation.
Bladder—
  1. Pressure.
  2. Perforation.
  3. Cystitis.
Inflammation—
  1. Through oviducts.
  2. Digestive tract.
  3. Genito-urinary tract.
  4. By tapping.
Circulation—
  1. Congestion.
  2. Œdema.
  3. Hemorrhoids
Suppuration—
  1. Infection.
  2. Fistula.
  3. Adhesions peritoneal.

SYMPTOMS.

Axial Rotation—
  1. Due to visceral rhythm.
  2. Ten per cent. of ovarian and parovarian tumors rotate.
  3. Pregnancy and other tumors enhance axial rotation.
  4. Diagnosticated by sudden pain and increase in size of abdomen.
Rupture—
  1. Sudden changes in form of abdomen.
  2. Diuresis.
  3. Diarrhea.
  4. Cystitis.
Pressure—
  1. Inflammation.
  2. Infection.
  3. Perforation.
  4. Hydroureter.
  5. Obstruction.
  6. Œdema.
Adhesions—
  1. Induce pain.
  2. Check peristalsis.
  3. Cause reflex rhythm.
  4. Disturb secretion.

CHAPTER XIX.

THE ABDOMINAL AND PELVIC BRAIN WITH AUTOMATIC VISCERAL GANGLIA WITH REFERENCE TO SEXUAL ORGANS.

"Instinct is a propensity prior to experience and independent of instruction."—Paley.

"Probability is the rule of life."—Butler.

At this point I desire to call attention to the following points:
1. The intimate and profound connection of the genito-urinary organs with the sympathetic (and cerebro-spinal) nervous system.
2. Its connection with the rectum and relation to coition.
3. The relation of the pelvic organs to the larynx (voice); the fifth (ganglionic) cranial nerve, stomach and eyes.
4. Automatic menstrual ganglia.
5. The menopause.

Every observing physician sees a close connection between the genital organs and the nervous system. This is not strange when one considers existing conditions and the long-continued effect of evolutionary forces. Of all the instincts in the animal race, the sexual instinct is dominant. This instinct has an all-pervading influence in every species of animal. It governs their actions. It forms habits in their lives. It induces new phases of existence. All through the stages of animal evolution, every other instinct must bend to the sexual. Physical and mental forces wonderfully combine to make this instinct the most effectual in its consummation. The sexual instinct dominates most powerfully the males, and hence the physical and mental vigor of the best animals in the race survive. The cow in rut is served, from sheer physical and mental vigor, by the most powerful bull. In herds of animals the sexual instinct dominates most vigorously in the finest males, and the weak males are cast aside that the strong ones may become the parents.

The main study of zoology is reproduction. The weapons of offense and defense possessed by males are primarily to cultivate and defend the sexual instinct. The horns of bulls, the powerful heels of stallions, the eagle's talons, and the claws of powerful feet are the weapons to defend and to carefully cultivate this dominant instinct of animal life. When we pass to man, the sexual instinct is rather heightened than diminished. But in man it is more subtle; secretly in the depths of man's mental forces lies his sexual instinct. As he has gained the ascendency in animal life by his mental activities, in this light alone can be studied his sexual instincts. Thus in the lowest form of physical existence sexual instincts dominate, yet in the higher forms of mental existence these instincts are still more powerful.

From such premises, patent to all observers, it is quite obvious that evolutionary forces have through long ages established a very close connection between the nervous system and the genitals—the organs which gratify the sexual instinct. Forces (mental or physical) acting through eons of ages establish definite results. The increase of man's intelligence is not in proportion to the increase of ganglion cells, but by the increase of conducting cords. Chicago and New York may each represent a ganglion cell, and a single railroad may represent the conducting cord. Now, when there was but one railroad between New York and Chicago, little business could be done on account of the limited amount of commerce which the single road would accommodate. Chicago and New York, as the ganglia cells, could dispose of far more business than the single road would transmit. But when the railroads multiplied between the two centers, the business increased just in proportion to the number of roads or conducting lines. Now, ages of natural forces have established numerous lines, and vigorous lines, of connection between the genitals and the nervous system. The facts which dissection show are positive in demonstrating the widespread and intimate connection of the genitals with the cerebro-spinal and sympathetic system.

The ganglion cells can receive and dispose of far more mental work than a few conducting cords can transmit; so that the progress and advance toward a higher nervous system and a higher intelligence is an increase in the conducting cords or lines to transmit intelligence or ideas. Also a well developed periphery is an absolute necessity for the purpose of collecting ideas for transmission. An increasing sensitive periphery is required to perceive the forces and comprehend ideas so that they can be sent to the central ganglion. Now, the number of conducting cords which attach the genitals to the nervous centers is simply enormous. Besides, the nerve periphery, situated in the external genitals, is highly sensitive and highly developed, so that it quickly perceives and quickly transmits the slightest sensation, and evolutionary forces through the ages seem to increase the sexual instinct with the progress of intelligence and mental growth.

I base these remarks on years of careful dissection of cadavers and of animals. If one carefully dissects a male body he will note the extensive cerebro-spinal nerves supplying the genitals, especially the penis. Of the spinal nerves supplying the genitals, the main one is the pudic. But the pudic nerve is composed of nearly all the third sacral, and branches from the second and fourth sacral. As one examines this nerve he is forced to the conclusion that it is an enormous supply for a small organ.

The periphery of the pudic nerve spreads itself like a fan over the genitals. The branches of this fan-like nerve-apparatus supply also the bladder and rectum—organs which must act and work in harmony. Hence the great disturbance which arises in the pelvis (bladder, rectum or genitals) when any one organ is damaged—e. g., a rectal fissure, a urethritis, or penile irritation quickly disturbs the whole system. The connection of the pudic nerve with the external genitals (where sensation is experienced) is vast. Not less remarkable is the wonderfully harmonious action of the bladder, rectum and genitals through large branches of the same pudic.

Another peculiar spinal-nerve connection of the external genitals is the supply of the pudendal nerve to the lateral walls of the penis. I have time and again called the attention of medical men to the peculiar connection between the gluteus maximus muscle and the external genitals by means of the pudendal nerve or branch of the lesser sciatic. The gluteus maximus is the real muscle that holds man upright (physically), but it is also the main muscle of coition. The lesser sciatic nerve supplies only one muscle, and that is the gluteus maximus, and then sends off the large pudendal branch to the sides of the penis, and hence the friction of coition induces active contractions of the gluteus maximus. The spinal-nerve supply to the external genitals is mainly the large pudic and pudendal nerves. In woman the pudic nerve is equally large; but the pudendal nerve is much smaller in woman than in man, according to my dissections. The lesser size of the pudendal nerve in woman is in direct accord with the methods of cohabitation. The vigorous and aggressive activity of man in coition, and the quiet passive receptivity of woman, explains the larger pudendal nerve in man. But the reverse nerve supply arises in regard to the glans elitoridis and the glans penis. I have dissected many a clitoris, and its nerve supply is three or four times as large as that of the penis in proportion to its size. The clitoris is a veritable electrical bell, which, when irritated, rings up the whole nervous system. There is no doubt that adhesions of the prepuce to the clitoris have led to masturbation in girls. Every gynecologist should examine the clitoris, and, if preputial adhesions exist, simply break them up, for the vast nerve supply of the clitoris gives great chances for profound irritation. The poor girl, neglected by the mother and possibly by the doctor, is soon induced to become a masturbator.

But the extensive spinal-nerve supply to the external genitals, though vast and intimate, is but a small matter relative to the supply to the internal genitals. The spinal-nerve supply to the external genitals is mainly sensitive, so that the sexual instinct may be gratified by the organs. What I wish mainly is to call attention to the profound connection of the internal genitals with the nervous system by means of the sympathetic system. It is in this field that the gynecologist and the genito-urinary surgeon find full play for lucrative operations—for so-called aggressive surgery. In manipulations and instrumental examinations of the genitals one sees the nerve storms flash over the system. These nerve storms radiate over distant nerve plexuses like electricity over a system of wires. Take, for example, the uterus. Its sympathetic nerve supply is enormous. The cervix only, so far as I can see, has spinal nerves, while the body and fundus are supplied by the sympathetic. One can count some twenty or thirty strands of nerves in the hypogastric plexus which originate in the abdominal brain and terminate in the uterus, and the nerves are very large. The ovarian plexus—a very large plexus—goes from the abdominal brain, and many of the nerves of this plexus terminate on the oviducts and fundus of the uterus so that the sympathetic nerve supply of the uterus is enormous. A large nerve supply to any organ subjects it to the danger of sad complications and stubborn pathology. I have seen a patient in the gynecological chair make active efforts to vomit in less than fifteen seconds after careful introduction of the sound. In those few seconds a complicated nervous phenomenon had occurred. The irritation of the endometrium had been flashed up the hypogastric plexus to the abdominal brain, and there it was reorganized and dashed over the various plexuses to other viscera.

The irritation, no doubt, went to every viscus similarly, but the stomach manifested itself in motion (vomiting). The heart, lungs, liver, spleen and digestive organs no doubt suffered similarly, but they were better able to resist the irritation. A study of the hypogastric plexus and its action on the uterus convinces me that pressure on the aorta for post-partum hemorrhage is generally explained wrongly. It is said the pressure obstructs the blood, but in reality the pressure on the hypogastric plexus irritates the peripheral ends in the uterus, and induces it to contract.

This is more reasonable. The dominating influence of uterine disease is due to the vast and intimate connection of the uterus (oviducts and ovary) with the sympathetic nervous system. Besides, a great and complicated network of nerves is easily deranged. The importance of the uterus demands a vast and complicated nerve supply. It may be laid down as a general proposition that the viscera have their normal function in rhythm, and the disturbance of the rhythm induces disease. The main pathology of the sympathetic is reflex action from some distant viscus.

The ganglia controlling the viscera are entirely out of the control of the will. If the visceral movement was not involuntary or out of the mental sphere men would speculate and experiment on their viscera. This fact no doubt explains the curious action of neurotic women. The nerve storms which emanate from a pathological uterus flash over the whole system by distinct nerve plexuses, and, as the will does not control any of such reflexes, the patient acts on the induced feelings. The close nervous connection of the uterus with the nervous system is at once seen in the great changes which uterine disease induces in both the mental and physical life of a woman. But anatomical facts, physiological experiment, and clinical study all show that the genitals and nervous system are more highly and intimately connected than any other system. No organ influences a woman mentally or physically to such a degree as the uterus—the autocrat of menstrual life— even in its normal physiological and anatomical condition, while its pathological condition is still more manifest. It is owing to the very distinct connection of the genitals with the cerebro-spinal and sympathetic system. Let a woman's genitals become pathological and she acquires liver disease and indigestion and becomes anemic and neurotic. Uterine disease also induces eye disease and heart trouble, and the joints and muscles do not escape. Pelvic diseases are often accompanied with hip, knee or ankle trouble. This is no doubt due to the intimate connection of the uterus with these joints through the sacral plexus; e. g., the sacro-iliac joint, the hip joint, and the knee joint are all supplied by three distinct nerves—the great sciatic, the anterior crural, and the obturator. Now, these three nerves are really the sacral plexus. A cold contracted at the monthly period from wet feet is explained no doubt by close connection of the uterus with the sacral plexus, for the lower end of the sacral (the sciatic nerve) supplies the feet. The disturbed circulation in women afflicted with uterine disease is owing to the powerful reflexes sent over the great hypogastric plexus, and the normal rhythmical contractions of the heart and its blood-vessels are broken by reflex due to uterine disease.

But it is not the woman only who is afflicted with reflexes from the genitals. The genito-urinary surgeon who deals with men afflicted with urethral disease knows the effect often of the mere introduction of a sound into the bladder. A healthy man will frequently faint from the introduction of a sound, and if the urethra or genitals are long diseased he will be profoundly shocked. This means that the urethra is extraordinarily supplied with nerves. I do not see, so far, any better explanation of so-called urinary fever after the introduction of a catheter than that it is "reflex." The urethral irritation may travel in two ways and act in two ways: (1) It may travel up the spinal cord, to the heat center either by the sacral plexus through the cord or by the splanchnics through the cord and thus disturb the heat center. (2) But more probably the urethral irritation is transmitted up the hypogastric plexus to the abdominal brain and is reorganized and emitted on the various plexuses.

It travels on the renal plexus more vigorously, owing to the more intimate connection existing between the kidney and the genitals—e. g., the ureter has a plexus, the testicle has a plexus, and, also, a part of the hypogastric plexus forms part of the renal plexus; furthermore the kidney and genitals originally arose from the same body—the Wolffian.

Now, the reflex irritation induced by the catheter on the urethra then flashes up the hypogastric plexus, and the reorganized forces are sent to the kidney and the irritation acts on the kidney to change its circulation; it is congested and urinary fever follows. The fainting of patients on the introduction of a catheter is explained on the same principle. The high nerve supply to the urethra being disturbed, the irritation is transmitted to the abdominal brain, where it is reorganized. The reorganized forces are then radiated on the various sympathetic splanchnics to the three cervical ganglia and are then transmitted by their three nerves to the heart, which is induced to move in a riotous manner. The heart is weakened and the patient faints. The irritation of the genitals being sent to the abdominal brain, it induces dilatation of the abdominal visceral circulation, and this probably explains the rise of temperature. Occasionally the introduction of a sound kills a patient, but that may be due to the weakness of the patient after a long-continued exhausting disease. Thus the nerve storms arising from the genitals are entirely due to the abundant and exhausting nerve supply. The irregular nerve storms arising in genitals highly supplied by nerves are profound in their invasion of the whole system. They pervade all active organs and disturb rhythm and induce further reflexes. Reflex action from the sympathetic explains much—e. g., when a man begins the "catheter life" he rings his own death knell; by the use of the catheter he induces reflexes which will remorselessly follow him until death. Besides, he introduces infection into the urethra and kidneys by the dirty catheter.

Thus the man goes through three stages on his road to the grave: (1) He has acquired some form of obstruction to the outflow of urine from kidney to penis; (2) he introduces the catheter, which calls up the wide domain of reflexes; (3) he introduces infection, and death follows. If the genitals were not so highly supplied by nerves, the terrible reflexes would not arise. As an application of the extensive supply of sympathetic nerves to the genitals and its wonderful reflexes, examine for a moment the result of coition.

The role played by the vaso-motor centers should not be lost sight of. I have found, time after time, that the ganglia of the lateral chain of the sympathetic, situated at the root of the pudic (third sacral), were very large, and this will aid in transmission of irritation.

Conclusions. 1. The sexual instinct is the most dominant instinct of animals.

2. Evolutionary forces have linked the abdominal sympathetic nervous system and the genitals by numerous and intimate bands which increase with the progress of higher development—i. e., sexual instincts dominate and influence man, as well as the monkey and the ape, far more than the lower grades of animals.

3. By reason of the growing and increasing intimate relations between the genitals and the nervous system, mental forces play a greater role in the production of disease.

4. I have observed that the monkey is an inveterate masturbator in confinement, and his persistent attention to the genitals shows that the sexual instincts keep pace with mental progress.

5. The severe shock arising from hysterocotomy shows that the uterus has an extensive nervous connection with the abdominal brain. In this operation one severs the great hypogastric plexus, and I have seen an alarming rise of temperature (103° F.), disturbed respiration and circulation, all from cutting the hypogastric plexus. The disturbance was not due to infecttion, as almost all of it arose a few hours after the operations. Occasionally removing the appendages shocks, but, as the ovarian plexus is small, the shock is limited.

6. The genital and the urinary organs both arise from the Wolffian body, so they are anatomically and physiologically connected, and both have an enormous nerve supply, so that damage to one often injures the other by reflex—e. g., hysterectomy has caused death by inducing nephritis a few days succeeding the operation, the test-tube revealing three-quarters albumin under the heat test.

7. The close connection between the genitals and nerve system is clearly seen from the terrible nerve storms which flash over the system from irritation (manual, instrumental or pathological) of the genitals—e. g., irritation of the clitoris quickly disturbs the whole nerve balance.

8. The great nerve connection of genitals and centers indicates that all

irritation should be at once removed. All preputial adhesions on the clitoris should be broken up, and the same with those of the prepuce. In short, all pathological conditions of the genitals should be at once righted, so that the nerve balance may be maintained.

The reports of fainting and vomiting and even death during coition have a scientific interest in view of the present subject. The celebrated Russian general, Skobeleff, died while cohabiting with a woman of ill-fame. Attila, king of the Huns, died while holding sexual relations with his young wife. In a small town in Ohio, a man nearly 70 years of age was reported to have died during coition. Stock men have made interesting reports in regard to animals. A mare put to a stallion fell dead at the end of coition. Young male animals have often fainted when first allowed to serve the female. The dog coition is prolonged, which limits shock. A dog has no semen sacs. The boar has an intensely violent coition, with consequent effect on his viscera, as in respiration and circulation. Young stallions are the most liable to faint of any of the domestic animals. Young bulls become weak, exhausted and tremble at first coition. A medical acquaintance related to me a death in a middle-aged man about an hour after coition.

Dr. Miller related two instances which interested him very much because he did not understand the explanation. A man about 60 years of age, while walking to the door a few minutes after cohabiting with a strange woman, fell and died immediately. In another case, at the first coition the young husband fainted, and the sphincters relaxed, defecation and urination resulting. One can easily observe in domestic animals that, especially in the male, the respiratory rhythm is disturbed—slowed for a while and then quickened. The heart will also be disturbed in its rhythm—slowed for a time and then quickened. The explanation of these phenomena lies in the sympathetic ganglionic system. The vesiculæ seminales are very highly supplied by the hypogastric plexus of nerves. As soon as the irritation is produced on the nerves of the semen sacs, it is carried to the abdominal brain. Then the irregular, stormy irritation accumulated in the abdominal brain is radiated on the various plexuses of nerves, especially in the direction of least resistance. The disturbance of rhythm will be most manifest in that organ which is weakened or most sensitive.

We will consider first the sudden deaths which are due to rupture of blood-vessels in the brain. Such sudden deaths are apt to occur in elderly men who have weak arteries, and also death is more liable to occur when the man is cohabiting with a strange woman for the first time, when he will be the most excited. Such deaths seldom occur with men who repeatedly cohabit with the same woman, when excitement is but ordinary. The explanation is, that the irritation goes from the semen sacs, during the spasm of expulsion, to the abdominal brain. Here the irritation is reorganized and radiated to the vaso-motor center. The irritation may also go up the spinal cord to this center. The disturbance in the vaso-motor center produces narrowing of the caliber of the peripheral blood-vessels and thus the blood-pressure is suddenly raised. At the same time the heart is slowed and hence the force is increased. It pumps the blood vigorously into the arteries and the weak wall gives way under the sudden pressure. The weak cerebral artery yields to the excessive blood-pressure, and death follows immediately from blood extravasation. It will be noted that all such deaths have occurred with elderly men who generally have weak, atheromatous arteries, with degenerated walls.

In cases of vomiting and fainting, the law is just the same. The irritation due to the emptying of the semen sacs is conveyed to the abdominal brain or up to the spinal cord. The disturbed energies are reflected to the heart and stomach, and fainting and vomiting are apt to arise. It comes under the same law as vomiting in pregnancy. In domestic animals, fainting, vomiting or death is liable to occur in those animals which have a short, intense orgasm, as the horse or pig. The orgasm is much more intense in males, and hence they are nearly always the subjects of disturbances during cohabitation. Females suffer very rarely. All this profound impression in the coition of animals is due to the irritation being sent to the abdominal brain, where it is reorganized and radiated out on the plexuses of the various viscera. The sudden, short irritation deranges the normal rhythm, and hence the pathology of fainting and vomiting. The disturbance of rhythm will be the most manifest in that organ most sensitive or most essential to normal life. The same rules apply precisely to man.

Men during coition occasionally faint, vomit, defecate, urinate, or die. I know of a noted judge who died shortly after connection with a girl in a brothel. In Chicago, a short time ago, at one of the principal hotels, a man of probably forty-eight was found dying after cohabiting with a strange woman. All such deaths that I know or have read of have occurred in elderly men. The smaller manifestations, such as fainting, vomiting, urination, and defecation, have all occurred in quite young men—mainly at the first coition. The elderly men scarcely ever die while cohabiting with their wives, as they are familiar with them, and the excitement of the orgasm is not so violent or intense. It generally occurs with old men (in age, if not in years) in first coition with a strange woman. Death may occur with an old man who has not had connection with his wife for a long period, especially if the orgasm is intense. I do not include in such a subject rupture of some pelvic tumor, due to coition. The explanation of the matter lies in the sympathetic nerve and its reflexes. The irritation of the penis is due to friction, and of the semen sacs to spasm and evacuation, which is transmitted to the abdominal brain and there reorganized.

The accumulated irritation in the abdominal brain is radiated rapidly and on the various directions of least resistance. It rapidly ascends the splanchnics and is reorganized in the cervical ganglia and sent to the heart. The irritation sent so suddenly to the heart at first violently stimulates it to a vigorous action, so that the blood-pressure is raised to a high tension in the brain, especially in the left cerebral artery. Old men often have friable, degenerated arteries, and this sudden rise of blood-pressure induces the middle left cerebral artery to rupture, and thus arises the death from coition.

The primary cause is the reflexes arising from the semen sacs and genitals. During the dissection of quite a number of cadavers, I have noticed that the connections of the lateral chain of sympathetic ganglia are very large at the root of the third sacral nerve. It must be remembered that the third sacral makes up nearly all of the pudic nerve; also that all the external genitals are supplied by the pudic nerve.

Hence, we find that the pudic nerve connects itself with one of the largest ganglia in the lateral chain of the pelvic sympathetic. Irritation of the external genitals is quickly carried to the vaso-motor center by the close and extensive connection of the cerebrospinal sympathetic.

The *rectum* and anus have a close connection with the sympathetic nerve.

The anus is guarded by two kinds of sphincters: (a) One, the internal sphincter, ruled by the sympathetic, and this accounts for the fact that rectal disease (fissure, ulcer) creates such intense disorder and neuroses among the viscera through violent reflexes. (b) The other anal sphincter, the external, is dominated by the spinal nerves and does not create such wild disorder among the viscera by reflexes.

I have often noticed that in dilating the rectum under an anesthetic, the patient would utter a kind of hoarse bray or expiratory moan, similar to the braying of an ass or mule.

The reason for this violent braying or expiratory moan in rectal dilatation is, that there is a distinct nerve strand arising from the inferior cervical ganglion and passing directly to the phrenic, which controls the diaphragm, e. g., rectal dilatation induces the irritation to pass to the abdominal brain over the hypogastric plexus, whence it is reorganized and emitted to the inferior cervical ganglion to the phrenic, which transmits it to the diaphragm, which rapidly forces the air over the vocal cords.

The mare in heat will often utter a similar sound. If the mare is watched, she will be seen to be disturbed occasionally, every five to eight minutes. When a "spell" or disturbance arrives, she will first raise the tail, and then begin to straddle and utter a kind of bray, then the pudenda is spasmodically everted, followed by the emission of fluids from the pudendo-vaginal gland. The explanation of this phenomenon must be made through the pudic and sympathetic nerves of the rectum and genitals on the one hand, and the recurrent laryngeal and sympathetic on the other. In short, there is a distinct relation between the voice and the rectum. This connection must lie in the sympathetic nerve. If one dilates the rectum suddenly the patient's skin capillaries become flushed with blood and sweating is induced.

One of the most prominent features of patients suffering from rectal disease is their manifest nervousness. Rectal patients become irritable and neurotic. The profoundly rich supply of the hypogastric to the rectum explains why disease of the rectum makes neurotic subjects.

There is also an evident connection between pelvic disease and the voice. Menstruating women are likely to have tonsillitis congestion, more than non-menstruating women. Chronic irritation in the pelvic organs will induce chronic disease in the tonsils and throat. In some women the voice changes at menstruation or during aggravation of pelvic disease. Not uncommonly young women have difficulty in swallowing at menstrual times, and their hearing may be a little disturbed, because of the congestion, and the chronic inflammation travels up the Eustachian tube. The distant relation and connection between the ovary and parotid gland is well known, as in mumps and operations on the ovary. Few writers have called attention to the relation of pelvic disease to pharyngeal disturbances, which exist by means of the connection with the sympathetic. The relation of the tripod in exophthalmic goiter—heart, thyroid gland and eyeball—will be more readily understood through the study of the sympathetic nerve. The enlargement of the thyroid in the menstrual life of women rests on the sympathetic nerve. The sexual life of woman is her chief life, from a physical standpoint, and as she has a larger ganglionic system than man, she demands special study; for from this chief function of her life will arise new structures and diseases.

The anus is the last to become insensible under chloroform. One can arouse a patient who is supposed to be dying from chloroform anesthesia, by suddenly dilating the rectum; the peripheral capillaries will also dilate and the cardiac and respiratory action will again resume. It is possible that the same safety arises in dilating the cervix and vagina in labor, as then we may give chloroform with impunity. The heart center lies in the medulla, and one often observes how dilating the rectal sphincter makes the capillaries flush and the skin sweat. Now, the very opposite often happens, for very often when a sphincter is dilated, as in labor, urinating or rectal dilation, the subject has a distinct chill. This is due to the disturbance carried to the heat center in the medulla. The kind of irritation which produces chill and the kind which produces heat are not yet determined, but both arise by means of the sympathetic nerve.

Reflexes from the rectum, e. g., fissure, produce just the same disturbance upon the system as do reflexes from the vagina or uterus. Both arise by means of the sympathetic, and both result, if persistent, in malnutrition. The reflexes seem to alter (stimulate, depress or produce irregularity) the circulation in adjacent or remote organs.

It is well known that young girls who have a uterus badly developed and anteflexed, suffer from constipation and rectal troubles. It is likely that the constipation and rectal trouble is mainly due to reflex action by means of the abdominal brain. It is known that long continued irritation of a voluntary muscle causes fibrous degeneration and finally cicatricial contraction. Now it is also well known that women possessed of rectal trouble soon acquire uterine trouble. It is due to reflex action, the rectal irritation is sent up the abdominal brain and reorganized and then transmitted to the uterus, inducing circulatory and nutritive disturbance.

The sympathetic nerve, as its name implies, is liable to be brought in unison with surroundings. For example, when the young pregnant wife begins to vomit, the young husband may vomit also, a purely mental impression through the sympathetic nerve. The effect of the sympathetic on the glands of woman is important. The main glands are (a) mammary; (b) the sebaceous on the face and (c) those of the pudendum. As soon as menstruation begins (or a little later) the girl begins to have facial acne. The sebaceous glands of the face inflame, enlarge and have a severe exacerbation at each monthly. Some women look almost as if they were chronic drinkers at the time of menstruation. A monthly rhythm excites and exacerbates the facial sebaceous glands into a chronic inflamed condition. (These glands may be trying to imitate the glands in the boy in enlarging a growing beard.) The trouble is due to the sympathetic and is especially active in the face by reason of the presence of the ophthalmic ganglia, Meckel's ganglia, otic ganglia and sub-maxillary ganglia—all sympathetic ganglia situated on the fifth cranial nerve. This facial acne, highest at the maximum of the rhythm of the automatic menstrual ganglia, is very annoying to many women. At the climax of the menstrual rhythm, there may be noticed on some women, dark discolorations, or pigmentation, just below the eyes. This pigmentation of the eyelids is what is so frequently mentioned as the dark rings about the eyes. It is due to deposit of pigment induced by venous congestion. The congestion is brought about by the rhythmic irritation of the ophthalmic ganglia (sympathetic) on the supraorbital branch of the trigeminus. The congestion and pigmentation of the eyelids in menstruation must also be connected with the presence of large glands known as the Meibomian glands. The sympathetic nerve has a predilection and a dominating influence over glands; so that the eyelid congestion and consequent pigment deposit during menstruation must be associated with the ciliary ganglia of the Meibomian glands.

In the pelvic diseases of young girls, I have found quite frequently an association of weak eyes. This is especially the case with endometritis, deficiently developed uterus and dysmenorrhea. They can use their eyes to read but a few minutes at a time, without pain or the letters blurring. I could find no reference to the subject in gynecological text-books. Since writing the above I have learned from Dr. B. Bettman that Dr. Fritsch and others have investigated the connection between pelvic and eye diseases. It must be that there is some prominent connection between certain cases of female generative disease and eye trouble. I have noted so many cases that I cannot consider it an accident and believe there must be some physiological connection. The eyes are worse at the maximum of the menstrual rhythm. The explanation of this association must lie in the sympathetic nerve.

I suggested the subject to Dr. Frances Dickinson, Professor of Ophthalmology in the Chicago Post-Graduate School, who has carefully followed some of the cases. So far, the doctor has reported that the eye trouble seems to be in the general circulation of the eye, the visual apparatus (the cornea, lens and retina) being normal. The endurance of the eye for work is lessened, and it appears to me that the chronic defect in the blood canals is accounted for by the disturbance in the rhythm of the diliary ganglia, and the sympathetic nerve supply of the Meibomian glands accounts for the pigmentation of the lids. What role the lachrymal glands play in the matter of eye trouble through the sympathetic, I am unprepared to state.

The associated disturbances of the mammary glands in menstruation and gestation, have attracted the attention of many thinkers. The problem must be solved through the sympathetic nerve. The spinal nerves supplying the mammary glands come from the cervical plexus and the six upper dorsal nerves. The arteries which supply the gland are the long thoracic, internal mammary, the intercostal arteries under the gland, and a few branches from the axillary arteries. Now, on these arteries, the sympathetic nerve goes to the gland. The first stage of milk secretion is a silent process reflected through the cord. The second stage is a gross reflection through the splanchnic from fetal irritation in the uterus; the cerebrospinal nerves elaborate milk, but the sympathetic hastens its secretion.

The original irritation nearly always arises in the pelvic organs. It travels to the mammary gland in three ways: First, by the way of the spinal cord; second, by way of the lateral chain of the sympathetic; third, the main way is through the hypogastric plexus to the abdominal brain and then through the great sensory nerves of the viscera, viz.: the three splanchnics. But we must again consider that the mammary gland has a peripheral nerve apparatus which not only shares in the genital rhythm, but also has the capacity to form milk. The mammary gland must be looked on as simply a modified sebaceous gland and we have noticed above how the sebaceous glands of the face are affected by menstruation and gestation. The spinal nerves do not induce any rhythm in the glands as is shown in girls up to puberty. But the impetus to rhythm must suddenly arise at the peculiar condition known as puberty, or the period of tubal motion.

The sebaceous glands on the pudendum are large and the odor at menstruation is chiefly due to their increased secretion. The pudendal glands are remnants of ancient life when the female, in heat, attracted the male by the increased odor emitted from the active glands. The odor during menstruation is often due to the activity of the Pudendale sebaceous glands and decomposition of their products, not merely to decomposition of menstrual blood. Here, as in other glandular apparatus, the sympathetic nerves play an important part.

The sympathetic nerve seems to play a significant role on the heat centers of the medulla. I have noticed this especially in laparotomy and vaginal hysterectomy. In short, when certain bundles of sympathetic nerves are cut, especially the hypogastric plexus, the temperature will rapidly rise above or fall below normal.

Surgeons are alarmed at these manifestations until experience teaches their real meaning.

The practical application of the sympathetic nerve in gynecological work lies in its control over nutrition. Reflex irritation from a pelvic viscus will remotely, or through several years, impair the whole visceral economy. Remote effects of pelvic disease must be traced through the nervous system (sympathetic) due to circulatory modifications.

The connection of the cerebral cortex (the seat of epilepsy), with ovarian diseases, resulting in so-called hystero-epilepsy, is far from being proven.

The different sizes of the peripheral ganglia in the various viscera is an important element in studying the sympathetic. Some viscus may have abnormally small ganglia and hence its rhythm and nutrition will be defective. Small automatic cardiac or menstrual or gastro-intestinal peripheral ganglia will be unable to do normal, vigorous, nutritive and rhythmic work, thus making the visceral system defective.

Menstruation and the menopause I shall place in the realm of the sympathetic nerve. The peculiar cycles and rhythms throughout the life of woman demands attention. We may call attention to the wide domain of the sympathetic nerve not only in health, but also in disease. Having made considerable investigation in this subject, some of the resulting views may be of interest and may stimulate the study of the sympathetic nerve.

CHAPTER XX.

THE AUTOMATIC MENSTRUAL GANGLIA.

The function of the tractus genitalis is: Sensation, ovulation, secretion, absorption, peristalsis, menstruation, gestation.

"We are shaped and fashioned by what we love."—Goethe.

Menstruation is a regular periodic monthly rhythm of the uterus and oviducts. In general it begins at the age of 15 and ceases at 45, continues four days, the bloody flow amounting to two ounces and should be painless.

Menstruation belongs distinctly to the oviducts and uterus. It is a singular rhythmic action. It is controlled by the automatic menstrual ganglia situated in the walls of the oviducts and uterus. These rhythmic little brains manifest themselves to the observer by circulatory change and increased motion. Menstruation might be named oviductal motion. By direct observation in the human, and also in animals, I have noted the following condition midway between the monthly periods, or at times far remote from œstrus or rutting: The oviducts and uterus are of quite a pale pink color. In short, they are not congested, and are in repose. But at the menstrual period or season of œstrus the oviducts and uterus are congested and in active peristaltic motion. The oviducts are of a dark blue color from their dilated vessels being filled with blood. The congestion of the uterus is intense but not so manifest as the oviducts. The oviducts are swollen, thickened and œdematous. They are soft and pliable.

At this time a slight irritation while removing them soon excites them into active peristaltic motion. After removing such oviducts and placing them in warm (salt) water they will maintain vermicular movements for half an hour by gentle irritation. I have been able to make these observations in women because I operate at any time in laparotomy, after careful preparation, even if it be in the midst of a menstrual period. As regards animals I have examined several hundred genitals of recently butchered sows, and the oviductal congestion at the œstrus is more apparent in them than in the woman. The sow's uterus is also probably more congested. Observations and experiments indicate that menstruation is a regular, periodical rhythm of a blood-wave in the oviducts and uterus induced by the automatic menstrual ganglia. The continually moving wave rises to a maximum and sinks to a minimum. The menstrual wave continues from puberty to the menopause. It is a nervous phenomenon.

Ovulation is a progressive, non-periodical process. It begins before birth and continues until the ovarian tissue is atrophied or worn out. It is liable to occur at menstruation or œstus because of the vast blood-supply at that time which hastens the follicle to ripen and burst. In the lower animals, so far as I can decide, menstruation and ovulation seem to be coincident, i. e., they occur at the same time. I have examined the cow, dog and sheep, but my observation is especially based on the ovular and menstrual process as seen in the sow. By the examination of some two hundred and fifty specimens of sow's genitals in all conditions it seems to me that the œstrus of the animal embraces both menstruation and ovulation in one physiologic process at the same time. But as the scale of animal life ascends, the processes of menstruation and ovulation seem to become more and more divorced. To my mind, the best animal to begin with is the cow. In the cow one can see more and more distinct processes with the ovaries and oviducts. Their separate workings become more apparent. In the calf, before and after birth, ovulation is very manifest. But the oviducts and uterus before birth and for a considerable time after, are manifestly quiet and pale and rudimentary, non-functional. In woman it is my observation that menstruation and ovulation are found distinctly separate from each other. It is true that ovulation and menstruation may occur together, may be coincident, but that is an accident. The processes are physiologically separate. In the woman ovulation has been observed before birth, and I have seen ovulation in a woman of 70, the specimens of which were presented to me by Dr. Burgess of Milwaukee. Now, of these two great physiologic functions, ovulation is a life-long process. It begins before birth and ends with ovarian atrophy. But menstruation is a periodical process beginning with puberty and ending with the menopause. Puberty must be observed as initiating the new exercise of genital ganglia. A viscus assumes a new rhythm which disturbs the entire system.

The views here contained are that menstruation is governed by nervous ganglia situated in the walls of the oviducts and uterus. I have designated these nervous structures as automatic menstrual ganglia. As a deduction of this theory, oviductal motion and oviductal changes will be considered the most marked phenomena of menstruation. The question may be asked: What is a nervous ganglion? A nervous ganglion is a collection of nerve cells. Its constituents are nerve cells and nerve fibers. It is an ideal nervous center having a central, conducting and peripheral apparatus. A ganglion is a little brain, a physiological center. It has the power of receiving sensation and transmitting motion. It is automatic in itself. It possesses the power of nourishment and controls secretion. Reflex action can be demonstrated in it. What are called motor, sensory, and sympathetic nerve fibers are found in its composition. The peculiar feature of a nervous ganglion is rhythm. It performs cyclical movements. It has a periodic function which continually waxes to a maximum or wanes to a minimum. It lives a rhythmic life. Its periods of action vary from a few seconds to a month. It is beyond the control of the will.

1. The proof of the existence of the ganglia in the oviducts and uterus is from analogy. All hollow viscera have ganglia in their walls. Histologists have long known that many viscera possess ganglia which have automatic power. The names of Bidder, Schmidt, Ludwig, Remak Meissner and Auerbach are associated with the discovery and description of these viscera ganglia.

(a) I have satisfied myself many a time, in vivisection on dogs and other animals, that the heart has nervous centers or ganglia, which will continue to act independently of their cerebrospinal connection. It is not only clear that the heart has automatic ganglia, but that nearly all these ganglia are centered in the walls of the auricles. I have often watched the heart's action gradually die out from apex to base. We know by experiment that the heart will perform its cycle of contraction independently of its external connection. These automatic nervous ganglia situated in the wall of the heart keep up its rhythm, its cyclical action, its periodic movements. They explode oftener than once a second. I have severed the heart from its attachments in some animals and watched its beating cease, when, if left alone, it would be still forever; but by applying stimulus to the ganglia the heart would again perform its rhythm. It would beat and explode just the same as when it was connected to the cerebrospinal system. Hence few observers doubt that the ganglia of Remak, Bidder, Ludwig and Schmidt sustain and control the rhythm of the heart. One can prove by experiment that there are several ganglia situated in the auricle by cutting pieces out of its wall. If these pieces are stimulated they will go through a distinct rhythm.

(b) A large number of experiments on the intestines of animals (especially the dog) convinced me distinctly that the intestines are endowed with automatic ganglia in a similar manner to the heart. These ganglia are called the plexus of Auerbach and the plexus of Meissner-Billroth. If a dog is killed and the abdomen is opened in a room of 75° F., the intestines can be induced to perform peristalsis for an hour after death by tapping them occasionally with a scalpel. As soon as the intestines are exposed to the air or tapped with the scalpel, they begin to go through wonderful vermicular movements resembling a moving bundle of angle-worms. I have often demonstrated the peristaltic movement of the intestines more than an hour after death, so that it can be stated that the automatic ganglia of the bowels will perform their rhythm independently of the cerebrospinal center. In autopsies I have found the intestines invaginated, and from the non-congested and non-inflammatory condition of the intestinal wall I had no doubt the invagination occurred entirely after the patient's death. The non-inflammatory telescoping of the intestines in dying subjects is called the "invagination of death." It can be perfectly demonstrated in a dog's intestines fifteen to thirty minutes after he is dead. Hence the nervous bulbs studded over the plexus of Auerbach and the plexus of Meissner-Billroth are the automatic ganglia which induce, sustain, and control the rhythm of the intestines. The vigorous rhythmic exercise or explosion of the intestinal ganglia is what causes colic, and in bowel constriction occurring in patients having thin belly walls I have observed this with perfection. The intestinal rhythm caused by the ganglia can be beautifully seen in the defecating intestine of a patient on whom colotomy has been performed.

I have never seen the causation of the very severe pain in angina pectoris very satisfactorily explained. I would suggest that it is colic of the heart, caused by abnormally vigorous action of the heart's automatic ganglia; that the desperate pain in angina pectoris is due to the excessive exercise or abnormally vigorous, irregular rhythm of the automatic ganglia situated at the base of the heart. Hence, clinically, no doubt, we see the abnormally vigorous rhythm or irregular rhythm of the heart in what is called neuralgia or spasm of the heart, or angina pectoris. The ganglia offer the best expla-

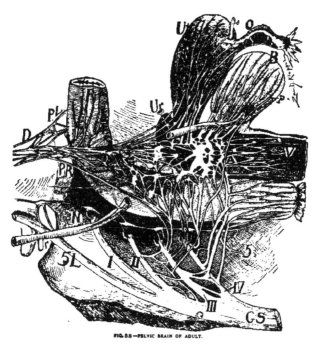

PELVIC BRAIN

Fig. 58. This illustration presents a fragment of the luxuriant nerve supply of the uterus, oviducts and ovaries.

nation. Clinically, we see in the intestines the exercise of Auerbach's and Meissner's ganglia in various diseases.

In colic and also bowel obstruction we see an excessively vigorous, irregular action of the ganglia. We note an excessively irregular action of the ganglia in the desperate, painful colic of children, which I believe amounts in many cases to an invagination with subsequent spontaneous dis-invagination. It may be noted that irregular action of the bowel ganglia occurs in children where the cerebrum is insufficiently developed to force the ganglia of Meissner and Auerbach into subjection and thus secure a regular rhythm of the intestine. We also see irregular ganglionic action in the bowel where the cerebrum is diseased and hence has lost a controlling influence. In chronic constipation, and in the paralysis of the intestine during peritonitis, we see disease of the ganglia producing such loss of power that the ganglia cannot initiate or sustain sufficient peristalsis to expel the bowel contents.

(c) The same statement can be made relative to the bladder. It is supplied with two kinds of nerves. One kind is the cerebrospinal. The other kind is the sympathetic nerves, which especially go to the body and summit of the bladder. These nerves are studded over with ganglia which may be styled automatic vesicular ganglia. These ganglia are closely associated with the blood-vessels and walls of the bladder, and have an influence in controlling the rhythm of this cyst. As an example to demonstrate the action of the automatic ganglia in the bladder, I took from a stag weighing fourteen hundred pounds, the bladder, penis and rectum. Twelve hours after it was contracted quite small. I then dilated it, and thirty-six hours after it had again contracted smaller than ever and would not contain half a pint of fluid. This bladder continued its rhythmic action for more than forty hours. It is not mere elasticity, as one can watch the rhythm of segments. It can be well demonstrated by injecting its blood-vessels with red fluid and then watching it for a day, when the slow, cyclical rhythm can be plainly seen. The sacral spinal nerves preponderate at the neck of the bladder and endow it with sensation. They likely hinder it from rhythm, while the body and summit of the bladder are mainly supplied with sympathetic nerves. They give it blunt sensation and rhythm. But the summit and body of the bladder are the parts endowed with ganglia, and they are also the parts endowed with cyclical rhythm.

If a rubber bag is inserted into the bladder and then filled with fluid, having its external end connected with a mercury gauge, it can be plainly seen that the bladder undergoes intermittent contraction. It will demonstrate its rhythm. Clinically, this rhythm can often be observed in retention of urine. The filling bladder will periodically make vigorous efforts to expel its contents, and the pain felt at those times can be easily mistaken for colic. Hence the bladder is endowed with automatic vesical ganglia, which are mainly situated in the walls of the body and summit, especially localized along its highways of nutrition (blood and lymph tracts). These ganglia preside over the rhythm of the bladder.

(d) The analogies of the heart, intestines and bladder are quite apparent, and can reasonably be carried to the uterus and oviducts. They are all hollow organs. The oviducts and uterus are no exception to the other abdominal viscera. What is said in this paragraph is the result of examination of over seven hundred uteri, oviducts and ovaries, of woman, cow, pig, sheep and dog. Some of the examination was carried on during the life of the animal, and in quite a number of cases I noticed the action of the oviducts in the living woman during operation. Much of the work was done on freshly butchered animals, where the organs were removed before the general muscular twitching had ceased. My first distinct attention was drawn to the idea that the heart, intestines, uterus and oviducts acted similarly, by observation in the slaughter house. Dr. C. S. Miller and myself were watching the slaughter and evisceration of a cow weighing fifteen hundred pounds. The cow was in the eighth month of pregnancy. The butcher amputated the large uterus, containing the calf, a little above the internal os. I noticed that the amputated portion of the uterus containing the calf went through a peculiar series of rhythmic motions. But the interesting scene was the amputated stump left on the body of the cow. The stump was about six inches long and three inches thick. This stump performed its peculiar rhythm long after the cow was dead. It slowly described circles and arcs with diameters varying from an inch to four inches. Each muscular layer of that thick uterus worked in perfect harmony. No uterine layer of muscles interfered with any other. Every part of the uterine stump seemed to work with intelligence or a kind of quasi-judgment during the rhythm. At one time the circular muscular layer would go through a slow but distinct rhythmic circle before any other muscular layer would begin. Then, gradually, the longitudinal muscular layer would begin to act, and the end of the stump would describe a rhythmic cycle, and thus it continued to repeat the rhythmic action until we left, an hour after. During the activity of the stump the most striking example of the action of the two muscular layers of the uterus could be seen, for while one layer worked vigorously the other remained still. Another striking example to show that the hollow uterus has its own automatic ganglia may be observed by removing the uterus from a cow immediately after death. The uterus should be that of a multiparous cow, because such have long, thick, tortuous, helicoid arteries. Now carefully inject the utero-ovarian arteries with red fluid. Observation will easily detect rhythm in the segments of this uterus for some forty hours after death, in a 75° room. The rhythmic waves that pass over the uterus will shift the fluid from one segment to another, so that the quantity of fluid is not uniform in each segment. The rhythm sometimes takes place very slowly. This phenomenon is not elasticity. But, clinically, the rhythm of the pregnant uterus has been known since the art of obstetrics began. My purpose here is simply to draw attention to the independent action of the uterus from a cerebrospinal connection, and to show that the uterus has automatic ganglia like other hollow viscera.

Labor will take place under profound anesthesia. Children have been expelled from the uteri of dead women. All this is due to the nerve apparatus of the uterus. Some Frenchman severed the spinal cord of a pregnant sow below the brain, thus paralyzing all the voluntary muscles which aid in parturition, yet the sow had her pigs. The uterus drove one fetus into the vagina, but as the abdominal muscles were paralyzed this fetus had to be driven out by the second fetus, which was pushed against the first by the contracting uterus.

(c) The oviduct is simply a continuation of the muscular walls of the uterus, but not of the endometrium. The endometrium seems to be a temporary gland, whose duration of active life is the menstrual period. The analogy of the hollow oviduct of the intestine or heart is very close. Nearly all the original work done on this subject was in relation to the oviducts, for I consider them the most important organ in menstruation. The object of menstruation is to transport an egg from the ovary to the interior of the uterus. This can be done by a properly prepared oviduct. It seems to me that menstruation begins and ends in the oviducts, and that the importance of the oviducts overshadows all other organs in menstruation, however, the endometrium is the important prepared nest. When the oviducts begin their rhythm the girl has arrived at puberty. Oviductal motion is a sign of womanhood. When the oviducts begin their cycles it is a heraldic sign that the gland called the endometrium is prepared to nourish an ovum. The endometric gland is no doubt often prepared to nourish an ovum before the oviductal motion or menstruation, and from the examination of nearly eight hundred ovaries I am fully satisfied that ovulation goes on from before birth until the end of life, or till the germinal epithelium is worn out. Actual observation of animals convinced me of this. One can see no changes in the ovary at puberty, except that of increased vascular supply. I never could find any periodicity, nor signs of it, in the ovulation in the human, cow or sheep. The ovules simply ripen progressively and burst when they are mature, whether that be at menstruation or at some other time. I am sure they often burst by mere mechanical accident. Hence, it does seem that menstruation and ovulation are two different processes. Two statements may then be made relative to an egg being carried into the uterus: First, when the oviduct goes through its menstrual rhythm it may secure an agg, if it happens to be ready and bursts. Second, the oviduct may secure an egg, if its fimbriated funnel becomes glued on to the ovary at a point where there is a maturing ovum.

2. *The Proof of the Existence of the Ganglia in the Oviducts from Direct Observation and Experiment.*—If an adult female dog is taken and well anesthetized, and the abdomen opened, the short white oviducts can be found just posterior to the kidney, at the abdominal end of the double uterus. Two important matters will be observed—first, the condition of the oviduct; second, the position of the oviduct. If the animal is not in rut, which is very analogous to menstruation, the oviducts will be very white, small and still. They are very much contracted, and the fimbriated end generally lies as far from the ovary as the fimbria ovarica will permit. In short, in the interœstrual time non-congestion and quiescence mark the oviductal condition. The condition and position of the oviduct at the period of rut are wonderfully changed. The oviduct is very much swollen and elongated; it is dark blue from, especially, venous congestion. The surrounding blood-vessels are enlarged, tortuous and distended. The oviduct shows convolutions and tortuosities plainer now than at other times. The oviduct having become longer and thicker, its entire position is changed. The strip of (muscular) tissue which connects the fimbriated end of the oviduct to the ovary has

shortened, and the funnel mouth of the oviduct is closing on to some portion of the ovary. At the climax of the menstrual rhythm the fimbriated mouth of the oviduct is often glued or cemented on to the ovary by a kind of glairy mucous exudate. The careful examination of nearly eight hundred oviducts satisfactorily demonstrated to me that the oviducts go through a distinct rhythm at menstruation. Menstruation is a periodic cycle of the oviducts. The oviducts go through a peristaltic or vermicular motion exactly analogous to the intestine. Now, there is only one kind of apparatus which produces a rhythm, and that is a ganglion. Hence, as the oviducts go through a rhythm, they must be influenced by a ganglion.

The changes in the oviduct at puberty are as follows: (a) It assumes rhythmic movements; (b) its muscular action increases; (c) its vascularity is much increased; (d) it becomes extended and loses its corkscrew or spiral shape of fetal life; (e) its epithelium becomes ciliated; (f) its gross activity appears mainly at the abdominal end; (g) its lumen becomes filled with fluid. This fluid is to float the egg or ovum into the uterus. The cilia whip the fluid in the oviduct into a current, and this wonderful anatomic and physiological canal floats the ovum to the nourishing gland—the endometrium. The automatic menstrual ganglia during their rhythm produce such changes in the oviduct as will best prepare it to float an egg from the ovary to the uterus. As the rhythmic peristalsis of the oviduct reaches its climax the oviduct becomes thicker, longer and its caliber wider. The fimbria ovarica shorten and draw an oviductal funnel over a part of the ovary. A dry, contracted oviduct with a narrow lumen offers difficulties for the passage of an ovum. If the epithelium of the oviduct is so altered by disease that it does not secrete fluid, the egg may not be able to float through the oviductal canal, but may become arrested in its passage, causing ectopic pregnancy. The reason why an egg does not get into a child's uterus is because its oviduct is deficient in motion; the fluid in its interior and the ciliated epithelium are deficient. The ciliated epithelium whips an egg into the uterus by means of a fluid medium. The rhythm of the oviducts, caused by the ganglia, prepares them for their function. This is done by first drawing the mouth of the oviduct over a part of the ovary; and, second, by flooding the lumen of the oviduct with serous fluid. Of course it will be only accidental that the mouth of the oviduct will cover a matured ovum. The vast majority ovulate into the peritoneal cavity. Ovulation is a life-long process, while menstruation, or rather oviductal rhythm, lasts about thirty years.

The almost entire separation of the oviduct from the ovary is peculiar to the higher animals, and no doubt lessens the chances of excessive reproduction. In the hen the ovary and oviduct are continuous. The active explosion of the automatic menstrual ganglia are the most marked at the abdominal end of the oviduct. By direct experiment it is easy to make the oviducts perform their rhythmic, vermicular movements for half an hour after their removal from the living. The oviducts of a cow, sheep, dog or pig can be kept moving in a warm medium by stimulating or pinching them, just in the same manner as pinching the heart or tapping the intestines will keep up the movements of those organs in vivisection. I have made this experiment many times on the normal oviducts of women where they were removed for various causes. While the operation is progressing one can see the oviducts going through a rhythm from mere manipulation. As soon as an oviduct is removed, if it be normal, a rhythmic action may be produced by pinching it. The two muscular layers of the oviduct will work separately before the eye. The external longitudinal muscular layer shortens the oviduct, while the internal circular muscular layer narrows the oviductal lumen. An oviduct will maintain this rhythmic motion for about half an hour, if pinched or stimulated in a medium (salt water is a very good medium).

The large range of movement of a human oviduct under stimulation is very marked, and the vigorous manner in which the two muscular layers of the oviduct work is very noticeable. If the circular layer is well stimulated, it will contract with such vigor as to resemble a pale, contracted band around the point of irritation. The endometrium may be looked on as a temporary gland, whose duration of life is the child-bearing period. So the automatic menstrual ganglia which govern the rhythm of the oviducts and uterus, and make fecundation possible are only temporary ganglia, at least so far as function goes. The automatic menstrual ganglia begin their functional life in the incipient oviductal motion.

This is not the only organ that acts merely at a definite period of life, though the organs exist anatomically during the whole of life. The thymus gland is largest at birth. The thyroid gland becomes most active in girls at about fifteen. The sebaceous glands of males spring into functional activity at about eighteen. When the menstrual ganglia of woman begin to cease their functions forever, the sebaceous glands of the face assume an active function, and a beard results. The salivary glands do not act for three months after birth. No doubt the facial sebaceous glands existed always, anatomically but not functionally. It has appeared to me for some time that there exists some relation between the testicles and sebaceous glands in the male, as there does between the automatic menstrual ganglia and sebaceous glands in the female.

Whether the rut (œstrus) of animals and the menstruation of woman are the same or different processes we will not discuss now. But the function of the ganglia and their actual rhythmic process would be precisely the same in either case. In mammals an oviductal rhythm with its associated changes is almost a necessity to transport an ovum from ovary to uterus. I could not observe any difference between the state of the oviduct and the relation of its mouth to the ovary in animals in rut and the menstrual process of woman. The gross anatomy of both processes appeared identical.

Premenstrual Pain.—The pain immediately preceding menstruation is generally not well understood. I have observed that many gynecologists of the present day attribute the premenstrual pain to the uterus. They say the pain is due to the mechanical obstruction to the menstrual fluid. These views may apply to certain cases. But I maintain that the premenstrual pain is due to an excessive action of the oviducts or a too vigorous rhythm.

The automatic menstrual ganglia are overexcited and act irregularly. The excessive stimulation arises mainly from the fluid which finds its way into the lumen of the oviduct. The fluid in the lumen of the oviduct, arising out of its congested state, acts like a foreign body and excites oviductal action. The ganglia become immoderately excited in oviducts whose lumen is partially or wholly closed. The vigorous attempts of the oviducts to expel the fluid confined in their lumen produce well-known agonizing pain. I have examined women with distended oviducts who would repeatedly tell me that the pain excited by the examination would last for hours. The oviducts were simply excited into peristalsis by irritation of their ganglia.

Dyspareunia, so frequent in oviductal disease, is not merely a story of pain at the time of connection, but of pain that endures for hours. Part of the pain is due to trauma of irritable nerves, but the worst pain is caused by setting in motion the vermicular action of the diseased oviduct. The confined fluid in the oviducts excites them into peristalsis, just as irritating substances excite the intestine into painful peristalsis. If an intestine, through obstruction, cannot expel its irritating contents, the picture of pain is almost identical with premenstrual pain. In fact, I have often wondered whether I was dealing with intestinal or oviductal colic. It must be remembered that muscle, governed by sympathetic ganglia, acts quite differently from muscle governed by spinal nerves. One is slow and rhythmic, while the other is rapid and more spasmodic.

The pelvic brain (cervico-uterine ganglion) is a large mass of aggregated sympathetic ganglia situated on each side of the pelvis at the junction of the uterus and cervix. It doubtless shares with the abdominal brain in originating, sustaining and inhibiting the menstrual rhythm. The pelvic brain, like the cervical ganglia, or that of Wrisberg, occupies a subordinate position in rgard to the abdominal brain. It is, however, a prevertebral ganglion. It is not easy to dissect and isolate on account of its white color and resemblance to adjacent tissue. It is three-quarters of an inch long and one-half an inch wide in some subjects, and is more like a meshwork than the abdominal brain. Its irregular meshes are pierced by numerous blood and lymph vessels and connective tissue bundles. No doubt the irritable uterus, which Gooch described seventy-five years ago, is caused in a great measure by an irritable pelvic brain. A rhythm produced by a ganglion alone is a very delicate mechanism, and it is no wonder that during the many vicissitudes of menstrual life the rhythm becomes disturbed, irregular and refuses to act. Pressure of the increasing size of the child's head on the cervico-uterine ganglion initiates labor.

Anatomical.—The distribution of the sympathetic nerve supply and the spinal nerve supply to the uterus and oviducts strengthens the theory of automatic menstrual ganglia. Anatomists agree that the uterine sympathetic plexus branches off to supply the uterus and oviducts above the point where the sacral spinal nerves join the sympathetic chain. The sympathetic plexus of nerves with its ganglia supplies the upper portion (body and fundus) of the uterus and the whole of the oviducts, while the sacral spinal nerves mainly go to the cervix. Now, it is very likely that the (sacral) spinal nerves have little to do with any rhythm or cyclical action. It is quite probable that they hinder rhythm.

They would thus influence the cervix to live a steady life. The ganglia on the sympathetic uterine and oviductal plexus, on the other hand, are possessed of a peculiar property called rhythm, so their ganglia would endow the uterus and oviducts with rhythm. This agrees with the observation that the body and fundus of the uterus and the oviducts are the main part of the genital tract involved in menstruation, while the cervix and vagina, mainly supplied with spinal nerves, remain fairly still. The cervix is a mere guard to the uterus, and does not share in menstruation. These ganglia mainly follow the blood-vessels, and the tortuous helicoid arteries supplying the uterus and oviducts, which, being long, give much space for ganglia to exist. The ganglia no doubt control blood-supply by regulating the caliber of the artery and the stay of the blood in the veins.

8. The microscope, or sometimes a strong lens, will demonstrate the existence of the ganglia on the plexus of nerves going to the uterus and the oviducts. The nerves show unevenness. At places they coalesce into masses, and the microscope demonstrates their ganglionic character. I have frequently been able to trace the nerves showing distinct bulbs on the posterior part of the uterus. Histologists have some time ago shown that little ganglia exist in the walls of the uteri of animals. But space forbids further discussion here. Every visceral organ has its own supply of sympathetic ganglia brought to it on the walls of the blood-vessels. Each visceral organ requring it has its own established cycle initiated in primordial life. The rhythm becomes strengthened by differentiation into special organs, and by repetition.

It seems to me that knowledge of the various visceral ganglia will render the function of those organs and their diseases more intelligible. To intelligibly minister to an organ diseased one must know its pathology. The treatment of any disease comprehends part if not all of its pathology. To me the action of the heart under varying states and pressure of the blood is more intelligible with some knowledge of the automatic ganglia which control its rhythm and motion. A knowledge of the functions of the cardiac ganglia clears many an obscure problem and explains the heart's action under varying conditions. The same may be said of the ganglia of Meissner and Auerbach in rendering intestinal peristalsis intelligible. So a study of what may be termed the automatic menstrual ganglia will perhaps throw more light on the action of the oviducts and uterus—organs around which woman is built both mentally and physically. We suggest that the rhythmic function of the endometric gland, its nidation and denidation, should not be neglected as a part of menstruation.

The ganglia in the uterus and oviducts of woman generally induce a cycle once a month during their functional activity. The ganglia explode monthly. In the lower animals the automatic uterine and oviductal ganglia explode in periods which correspond to the cycle of the rut. It is here concluded that whether rut and menstruation be the same or different processes, they are governed in their rhythm by the automatic uterine and oviductal ganglia.

Will these automatic ganglia aid in explaining the function of the uterus, oviducts or ovary after surgical or other destructive procedures on any one of the three? I think they will. That menstruation is closely connected with the nervous system, and that, too, with the sympathetic (as it has rhythm) is a common observation. Nerve disturbances disturb menstruation and its rhythm. A sprain in the wrist has checked menstruation. I knew a patient who, while menstruating, became frightened by a whistle from a train and did not menstruate for a year. Sudden changes in temperature will alter its rhythm. The mere expectation of marriage will occasionally make its rhythm regular. Marriage, by mental and physical stimulation to the genital apparatus, will often induce regular menstruation. When the nervous system is impaired in strength by wasting disease, there may not be enough vital energy to induce and sustain menstrual rhythms. Tubercular girls cease to menstruate. It is a common observation that fleshy persons have weak resisting powers, and fleshy women often menstruate irregularly. In a precocious, abnormally developed girl we may see early menstruation. In pregnancy and nursing, menstruation is arrested because the nervous vitality is expended in nourishment. The miserable and painful failure of an infantile uterus in menstration is rather from a deficient endometrium. If vital energies are directed into different channels, or vitality gets to a low ebb, the remaining powers may be insufficient to initiate and sustain the regular menstrual rhythm. Non-development occurred from insufficient blood.

From the views entertained in this paper, that menstruation and ovulation are separate processes, and that the automatic ganglia are situated along the oviducts and uterus and probably closely related with the ovary, it would not be expected that removal of the ovaries would always cause menstruation to cease suddenly. The automatic ganglia of the oviducts and the uterus are still intact and will execute their rhythm. Many gynecologists testify that this theory agrees with the facts. Ovaries are extirpated and oviductal motion continues. However, the destruction of a part of a connected complex organ soon destroys the nice balance, and nourishment of the ganglia would in time deteriorate, and then insufficient nerve vitality with lack of ganglionic harmony would fail in starting and maintaining a menstrual rhythm. Also, it may be considered that the chief, central, sexual organ of woman is the ovary and the uterus and oviducts are appendages of the ovary. Extirpation of the oviducts would quite effectually aid in arresting menstruation, though not entirely, as many ganglia would remain in the uterine wall. Yet in the very plan of the machinery the oviduct is no doubt designed to execute more motion than the uterus, which could perform its function while remaining quite still. By the German gynecologists, during several years' residence abroad, I was informed that a removal of the oviducts in a vast majority of cases caused a rapid checking of menstruation. Mr. Lawson Tait writes that the total removal of the oviducts arrests menstruation in 90 per cent of cases. Is it not strange that an oviduct cut off two inches from the uterus will maintain the rhythm? Actual cases prove that when only the diseased ovaries are removed from women, with inflammation existing in the oviducts, they are but little helped in their misery. The active organ in menstruation is the oviduct, and it will execute its rhythm unless removed. Ligating the oviducts is not a rational method, as it will not check the rhythm. Nine years ago I began ligating the uterine artery at the neck of the uterus after removing its appendages. This effectually and immediately checked menstruation and rapidly atrophied the organ.

Finally, the oviducts and most of the uterus being removed, menstruation will nearly always stop. The ovary, left without an oviduct, would not sustain menstruation. Cases are reported where the oviducts and ovaries and most of the uterus were removed, but menstruation continued. In such cases, no doubt, a sufficient number of automatic ganglia were left to start and sustain a menstrual rhythm. In such cases I suggest that investigation of total removal of the organs and also of the reality of continued menstruation should be carefully done. Patients often call any bleeding menstruation.

The ovary is the central, essential, sexual organ of woman (requisite not only for ovulation but internal secretion) and should be removed for malignancy and grave disease only.

Other theories have been advanced as to the cause of menstruation. Dr. Christopher Martin claims that the nerve centers are located in the lumbar cord. This is doubtless based on the labors of Budge, who located the center of the bladder in the lumbar cord.

I wish to thank Dr. C. S. Miller, of Toledo, Ohio, who worked long with me on this subject.

CHAPTER XXI.

MENOPAUSE.

"Nature has caprices which art cannot imitate."—Macaulay.

Menstruatio precox is followed by climacterium retardum.

The vagina has two sphincters, viz.: (a) one, the internal, ruled by the sympathetic; (b) the other, the external, dominated by the spinal nerves.

The menopause ends slowly, as puberty begins. It is frequently difficult to decide which produces the most profound impression on the general system. The popular belief is that the period of menopause is a time of danger to woman. It is claimed that she is more liable to malignant growths of the genital organs or the breasts, and the average woman expects disturbances to arise, either bodily or mentally. Popular belief that woman is more liable to disease at the menopause is probably correct.

The symptoms of the menopause are: (a) cessation of the monthly flow, (b) flashes of heat, (c) flashes of circulation, (d) irregular perspiration. The cessation of the flow is a very irregular and indefinite matter, but generally occurs at about 45 years of age. It requires an average of eighteen months for menstruation to become regularly established; besides, the genitals were being prepared for several years. It requires two and one-half years for the monthly flow to cease, on an average. The flow ceases very irregularly, even in normally physiologic cases. The flow may be scant one month, not appear at all the next, and the third or fourth a flooding may occur. Should the flow cease without pathologic manifestations? I would answer "No." Many no doubt will oppose this view and say that it is a purely physiologic process, but it is frequently accompanied by ailments. So is labor a physiologic process, but it is frequently accompanied by pain and other disturbances. The cessation of menstruation means the death of a great function, the atrophy of a dominating organ which has the greatest nerve supply of all the viscera.

The beginning of puberty shows vast changes in the entire vascular system and also much change in the whole sympathetic, besides the field of nutrition. The most manifest change at puberty is shown by a perturbed nervous system.

The nervous apparatus of the visceral organs may well be compared to the equalizers on the horse-power of a threshing machine. When the ten horses pull evenly the gearing works uniformly, but the neglect of one team puts the gearing awry, and though the machine may run, its working is not of such fine balance. The destruction of one function in a well-balanced nervous system is sure to destroy the well-established balance in the others,

254 THE ABDOMINAL AND PELVIC BRAIN

so that in my opinion pathologic disturbances may be looked for at the menopause. In order to make my views clear and reasonable, let us construct a diagram of the sympathetic system. The accompanying cut (fig. 59) represents the sympathetic nerves. It is drawn in the form of an elongated ellipse. At the upper end of the ellipse begins the cerebral communicating artery at the so-called ganglion of Ribes. The lower end of the ellipse ends at the coccyx or ganglion impar. "rc" shows the connection of this ellipse with the cerebro-spinal axis. The interior of this ellipse is of

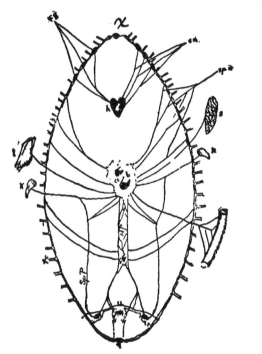

A SCHEMATIC DRAWING OF THE SYMPATHETIC NERVE

Fig. 59. X, ganglion of Ribes. Y, coccygeal ganglion (impar). L., liver. K., kidney. S., spleen. Sp. P., (spermatic) ovarian plexus. I., intestine. A. B., abdominal brain (center of reorganization). Sp. N., splanchnic nerves. C. N., cardiac nerves. H. P., hypogastric (aortic) plexus (coming from three sources). U., uterus, oviducts and ovaries. H., heart. C. G., the three cervical ganglion (secondary center of reorganization).

The sides of the ellipse represent the lateral chain of the sympathetic. One nerve strand goes from the abdominal brain (a. b.) to each viscus to represent its plexus. Observe that the spermatic plexus (sp. p.) arises from the abdominal brain, renal plexus and aortic plexus. Any irritation starting in any viscus will pass to the abdominal brain, where reorganization occurs, and the forces are redistributed over the plexuses to every viscus.

special interest, for here lies the vast and complicated network of this nervous ring. "ab" indicates the abdominal brain, solar plexus or semilunar ganglia—the center or reorganizing locality of the sympathetic system. From this abdominal brain, renal ganglia and the lateral sympathetic chain, passes off a large plexus of nerves, down the aorta to the uterus, oviducts and ovaries. This is known as the hypogastric plexus. The observation which I note in the dissection of quite a number of old women is, that after the menopause the genitals not only atrophy, but the hypogastric plexus also shrinks.

However, the abdominal brain does not atrophy. It retains its function and structure to the end of life. Dr. Adolph Meyer, formerly of Chicago University, now in Worcester, Mass., writes me the following letter, which explains itself:

The Worcester Lunatic Asylum.
Worcester, Mass., Feb. 20, 1896.

My Dear Dr. Robinson:—

Nearly two years ago you asked me to give you some specimens of a sympathetic ganglion, to ascertain that it is not a degenerate organ, but a living organ with numerous ganglion cells. Those of your opponents who would not believe this may see this specimen from a woman of 74, who had been insane thirty years, and died of heart rupture. The ganglion cells of the semilunar ganglion are large, numerous, moderately pigmented (not more than the spinal ganglia and other nerve cells).

Adolph Meyer.

The hypogastric plexus becomes smaller, finer and no doubt some strands disappear at the beginning of the menopause. On this fact must be based the pathologic symptoms accompanying the cessation of the menstrual function. In dissecting infants which have lain in alcohol for some six weeks, the very opposite condition of the hypogastric plexus may be observed, for in the young child the hypogastric (sympathetic) plexus is disproportionately large and can be very plainly dissected out. The explanations of the disturbances of the menopause may be shown as follows: For thirty years monthly rhythmic impulses have passed over the hypogastric plexus to the uterus and oviducts. A fixed habit has been established and the genital organs lie in the sensory and motor grasp of the hypogastric plexus. The importance of the genital organs is shown by the vast nerve supply sent to them and also because the hypogastric originates in great central sources. It arises plainly from the abdominal brain, the renal plexus and sympathetic lateral chain. It is intimately and closely associated with the whole sympathetic ellipse. Now when this great nerve tract, known as the hypogastric plexus, will not transmit the higher physiologic orders, it will unbalance all other parts of the ellipse. If the nervous forces cannot go over an old-established line they will go over the next line of least resistance. The hypogastric plexus cannot carry the orders as it is atrophied and destroyed for the old work. Monthly rhythm of thirty years established in the abdominal brain is not to die without a struggle. This explanation will enable us to understand the many pathologic manifestations of every viscus at the menopause. The irritation which arose by trying to pass more nervous impulses over plexuses than normal, gives origin to what is unfortunately known as "functional disease." It is just as organic as any disease, only we are not able to detect it. Acute atrophy is a pathologic condition and no doubt this is the condition of the hypogastric plexus at the menopause. The sudden assumption of function of the hypogastric plexus at puberty produces similar disturbances, only they do not assume such definite symptoms as at the menopause. The young woman has more depression than the woman in menopause, unless her ovaries be diseased. The advent of menstruation is an important feature in the life of woman.

After the cessation of the flow the most prominent symptom is what is called flushes. Over eighty per cent. of women will experience this peculiar phenomenon at the menopause. Two distinct propositions will explain this subject: Flushes result from a disturbance of the vaso-motor centers, and flashes from irritation of the heat centers. Heat and circulative disturbances are so intimate and go together so frequently that I shall not attempt to describe them separately. The heart and vaso-motor centers are unbalanced by irritation at the menopause. The hot flashes may come on rapidly and irregularly for a short period, and then remain away for days. The patient indicates that the disturbances are first manifest near the stomach, and then rapidly spread over the head and chest. It would seem from carefully watching these manifestations at the menopause that wave after wave succeeds each other. I have watched them under attacks and they seem to be under a desperate struggle to control themselves. The blood-vessels of the head and neck appear most affected, yet the skin of the whole body shares in the disturbance. The nerve impulse, which should be emitted along the hypogastric plexus, is abnormally forced over other plexuses and the vaso-motor becomes irritated, resulting in dilatation and contraction of the peripheral vessels. All molecular action generates heat, and it may be that much of the heat experienced is due to the rapid dilatation of the vast number of vessels and the rapid flow of fresh blood in them. As the cheeks glow the patient experiences sudden heat, the skin grows red with flushing blood. Besides the disturbance of the vaso-motor and the heat center, the sweat center is also irritated, the flushes and flashes followed by various degrees of sweating. This is just as irregular and uncertain. The quantities of sweat vary from a fine moisture to great drops. It is apparent to any ordinary observer that profound disturbances arise at both puberty and menopause and it is not strange that tradition attributes some diseases to the advent of puberty and many grave conditions to the menopause.

The theory of disease at the menopause must rest on the unbalancing of the nervous system by changing the old established nerve channel through which they have carried impulses for a generation. It must rest on actually diseased genitals, or atrophy of the organs on the plexuses which transmit controlling forces to them. Disease at the menopause must rest on some irritating center, which is chiefly the genitals and their nerves. Like many old gynecologists, we need not look for the sole cause in the ovaries, but the trouble is due to reflex irritation. Eighty per cent of such women suffer in general from nervous irritability. Fifty per cent. have disturbance in the heat and circulatory centers. Probably fifty per cent. suffer deranged sensations, hyperesthesia and anesthesia. Perhaps forty per cent. of women at the menopause suffer from the headache, abdominal pain and perspiration. About twenty-five per cent. of women at the menopause suffer from leucorrhea, sudden flooding and sweats. This means that all the secretory apparatus of the skin, mucous membrane and centers are deranged. The first thing to suspect in such patients is deceased genitals. Endometritis is an arch fiend at this period in a woman's menstrual life.

Inflammation of some kind may be found in the uterus, oviducts and ovaries. Acute atrophy—a form of degeneration or malnutrition—must be recorded among the diseases. If no pelvic trouble be found, the whole abdomen and chest must be examined for some disorder. I have found that the glycerin tampon twice weekly, and the hot douche gradually increased to ten quarts twice daily, often cures such patients, at least symptomatically. Curetting may be required in a limited few, however it is not so dangerous in the menopautic as in the young woman on account of atrophy and consequent inability to receive infection. Radical disturbances in the menopause mean disease, and generally it is located in the pelvis. Women are expected to suffer from neuralgia at this time, nerve irritation, but their intellect is also often disturbed, especially in the will power. General treatment especially visceral drainage is right and reasonable, with baths and attention to food and evacuations. The patients fret and worry and do not rest or sleep well. The bromides act well, especially given at night. I make over half the dose sodium bromide, as that does not irritate the skin so much as potassium bromide. The bowels are best regulated by a glass of water each night at bed-time, in which there is from one-half to one dram of epsom salt; with the additional advice to go to stool every morning immediately after breakfast, i. e., after the hot coffee has stimulated peristalsis of the bowel.

It is traditional that women become like men after the menopause and it is common for women to argue against removal of the ovaries, fearing that hair will grow on the face and that they will become mannish. Flesh may increase because of disappearing disturbances. It is common for women to take on fat at the menopause. This is a form of low-grade nutrition. I have examined at least half a dozen patients of this nature who were considered subjects of tumors or pregnancy. But a little experience and patience will prove to the physician that the tumor consists simply in abnormally thick and fleshy belly walls.

No one can number the many and varied pains that attack women in the menopause. Most of the pains arise around the stomach, i. e., in the abdominal brain—the solar plexus. The pains which originate in the epigastric region are innumerable, indefinable and baffle all systematic description. We must, however, have charity sufficient to allow that these numberless disturbances are real to the sufferer. The "something moving in the stomach" may be abnormal peristalsis, induced by a diseased focus, as in the globus hystericus. Whatever opinion is held by the physician, a reasonable treatment should be introduced. Such patients have so little confidences in themselves, their physician and their friends, that they have not the will power to persist a systematic course of treatment. Hence they go around from one physician to another. The duty of the physician is to locate the disease and attempt to restore order in a disordered sympathetic nervous system, which becomes unbalanced by reason of some irritation arising from atrophy, senility and inflammation. A thorough automatic and physiologic knowledge of the sympathetic nervous system is required for intelligent practice in gynecology. The pathologic condition must be found in order to show skill in removing it. It must be remembered that a stormy puberty generally means a stormy menopause. If a girl begins menstruation with pain and disturbance it generally means diseased genitals—oviducts or uterus probably—and the sympathetic system will suffer.

The intimate and wide connection of the nervous system and genitals is phenomenal. The nervous connection of the genitals is profound and any genital trouble deeply impresses the whole system. It would not be strange, also, if one uterus were found with vastly more nervous connections than another, or that is, at least, much more sensitive than others. My experience in the dead-house, as well as observation in the living, is that viscera vary much in size. In some the uterus is small, in others large, without regard to the individual stature.

Menstruation must be looked upon as arising and subsiding in the nervous system, especially in the sympathetic system. I would like to make a plea for more study of the nervous system, and particularly the visceral nervous system. From the lack of this knowledge physicians are constantly mistaking nervous diseases for uterine disease. A great evil is going on today in regard to the misunderstanding, that a little nervousness does not always belong to the ovaries or uterus. The nervous system is a vast, finely-ordered, nicely-balanced machine, which can be easily disordered without the least need of removing the ovary, uterus or oviduct. Some general or local treatment may be amply sufficient. Too many laparotomies are being done today by unskilled men without proper facilities. Sweeping removal of organs is a backward step in surgery, and the general disapprobation of the leading gynecologic surgeons must cry it down. It must be insisted that he who would work in the peritoneal cavity must be trained. Training and skill, coupled with a decent sense of right, will alone stand the test of time in any branch of surgery. The colleges must begin with chairs of anatomy and abdominal experiments for small classes. A large plea should be entered for an attempt to understand the pathology of the sympathetic nervous system, i. e., visceral nervous system.

A pathologic state is one manifesting abnormal conditions, whether they are recognizable changes in structure, or simple deranged functions without perceptible disordered structure. There are reflex neuroses, by which I mean disturbances in distant parts produced by irritation of some sensory or motor-peripheral area. It is easy to note that a woman is irritable or nervous, without in the least being able to locate the pathology from which the disturbance originated. One of the most marked features of the menopause is this kind of nervous irritability. It may be easily observed that women in the menopause do not suffer from tumors and malignant diseases so much as they do from disturbance in the sympathetic system and cerebrospinal axis. Nervous irritability chararcterizes four women out of five during the menopause. How does this come about? Two ideas explain the complicated but slow course of the disease, viz., Reflex irritation and malnutrition. It can be easily seen that the nervous system is out of balance in the menopause. The beginning and end of menstruation is in the sympathetic nerves. Puberty is heralded by ganglionic rhythm and the menopause comes in at the cessation of the rhythm. The entrance and disappearance of menstruation are nervous phenomena. The genitals then become a point of new irritation as puberty begins, and the genitals are again the focus of irritation as the rhythm departs forever. Menstrual starting chafes the system profoundly, but its cessation irritates the system notably with its dying struggles. By the figure it is plain that any genital irritation can be easily carried to the abdominal brain where the reorganization occurs. The newly organized force will go to every viscus in the sympathetic ellipse and damage the rhythm. Now the visceral rhythm is for the purpose of nutrition, and pursues its even tenor in a kind of orderly manner. But irritation from a focus never comes or goes by rule. It goes at all times and any time, while the viscera are performing their nutritive rhythm. The irritation from the diseased focus forces itself up the hypogastric plexus to the organizing center and is emitted to all viscera, in addition to the abdominal nutrition and rhythm and disorders natural to visceral rhythm. Few but the special clinical gynecologist fully recognize that uterine disease is often such a slow process and that it can start a train of evils.

A few weeks or months of pelvic irritation gradually produce deranged visceral rhythm and consequent indigestion. The addition of indigestion to a diseased visceral focus makes a double burden on the whole system. The nerves become more irritable. Indigestion persists and soon brings on distinct malnutrition—another burden to the ganglionic system of nerves. All this continues until anemia arises, the result of waste-laden blood. Now it is apparent to all, when waste-laden blood bathes all the thousands of ganglia and nerve strands in the body, that the patient becomes nervous or irritable. The sympathetic ellipse is unbalanced and its centers are disordered. It is a slow process for a woman to pass from a single focus of visceral disease to a neurotic condition. The whole disturbance becomes intelligible by comprehension of the nervous system and a knowledge of the condition of the diseased genitals. The intelligent practitioner always examines the genitals in a disordered menopause. A stormy menopause means diseased genitals. It means a focus of pathology which is nearly

260   THE ABDOMINAL AND PELVIC BRAIN

always situated in the pelvis. The effects on the individual may be described by noting how the irritation can pass up the hypo-gastric plexus to the abdominal brain and being reorganized be emitted to the digestive tract. The irritation goes on day and night; when it reaches the digestive canal by way of the gastric, superior and inferior mesenteric plexus, it first affects Auerbach's ganglionic plexus of nerves which lie between the muscular layers of the intestinal wall. This simply disturbs peristalsis and induces

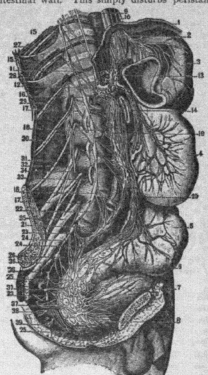

LUMBAR AND SACRAL PORTIONS OF THE SYMPATHETIC (SAPPEY)

Fig. 60. 1, cut edge of diaphragm; 2, lower end of œsophagus; 3, left half of stomach; 4, small intestine; 5, sigmoid flexure of the colon; 6, rectum; 7, bladder; 8, prostate; 9, lower end of left vagus; 10, lower end of right vagus; 11, solar plexus; 12, lower end of great splanchnic nerve; 13, lower end of lesser splanchnic nerve; 14, 14, two last thoracic ganglia; 15, 15, the four lumbar ganglia; 16, 16, 17, 17, branches from the lumbar ganglia; 18, superior mesenteric plexus; 19, 21, 22, 23, aortic lumbar plexus; 20, inferior mesenteric plexus; 24, 24, sacral portion of the sympathetic; 25, 25, 26, 26, 27, 27, hypogastric plexus; 28, 29, 30, tenth, eleventh and twelfth dorsal nerves; 31, 32, 33, 34, 35, 36, 37, 38, 39, lumbar and sacral nerves.

CLIMACTERIUM

perhaps some colic. But as the irritation passes to Meisner's plexus it disorders secretion.

Thus the great assimilating laboratory of life is deranged. Digestive disorders are common in the menopause. Liver disturbances are common. The irritation passes through the abdominal brain to the liver, inducing excessive, deficient or disproportionate bile, glycogen and urea. The rhythm of the liver is deranged. Its rhythmical activity and quiet repose are continually disturbed by reflex irritation. It is easy to observe disease of the liver from the condition of the patient in menopause—skin and bowel abnormalities. The route from the genitals to the heart is made plain by the diagram. The irritation from the diseased genitals passes to the abdominal brain, thence up the splanchnics to the three cervical ganglia, whence the reorganized irritation passes to the heart over the three cardiac nerves. The result is that the heart goes rapidly, irregularly—it palpitates.

After nervous irritability the woman in menopause probably suffers most frequently from flushes and flashes, i. e., irritation of the vaso-motor and heat centers. Her skin glows with fresh red blood or burns with prickling heat. This seems to me to be merely an unbalanced condition of the nervous system due to a disordered focus. The transmission goes in a tumultuous manner, over roads which are not accustomed to so much vigorous commerce and the centers are not able to orderly reorganize it. The circulation floods or depletes the vaso-motor centers.

One may observe that some women enter puberty with many indescribable pains and they continue to complain of peculiar abdominal pains during the reproductive period, and at menopause they simply become chronic grumblers and complain more and more bitterly. What must be said of such women? We must not consider them as fabricating untruths for a whole generation we must attempt to study the ganglionic system of the sympathetic in order to unravel the apparent mystery. We may say that women with these abdominal pains are in a poor state of nourishment. Debility characterizes the ganglionic disease while irritability is the feature of cerebrospinal axis pathology. Women with ganglionic diseases are weak, ill-nourished creatures, often unable to do a little housework. Can we not consider that such patients have hyperesthesia or anesthesia of the visceral ganglia? The ganglia are little brains, for they all have the elements of the cranial cerebrum,—nerve cells and processes. In short every nerve cell is a unit in itself. It is an isolated anatomic unit, a neuron, a brain and a reorganizing center. The essential of the cell is the nucleus because it has the power of nutrition, hence reproduction. Hence each ganglion is a little brain, a reorganizing center.

Now, a brain or ganglion cell receives sensation, emits motion and controls nutrition. It reproduces itself, it controls secretion and lives in balanced relations with its environment. Can we not think that such patients have over-sensitive or irritable abdominal brains? Their visceral nerve apparatus is abnormal, it is out of order. But this center holds in abeyance nerve energy and nerve force. It holds all the assimilating and circulatory laboratory in living tension. Such patients have not a perfect machine with which to work. They are generally congenitally defective, or are made so by the acquisition of some profound function, such as menstruation. The female visceral nerves seem to be peculiarly liable to rapid derangement. Women faint easily and slight occurrences disorder their viscera. The flying of a bird will make the heart palpitate. A sudden noise deranges respiration or circulation. A change of locality either corrects or disorders the nervous system. The female nervous system is much more unstable than the male, and no doubt that is the reason that so many physicians mistake nervous disease for uterine disease. Such physicians are either ignorant of the delicate nerve mechanism or are over-zealous operators.

The pathologic condition of the genital organs in the natural menopause is generally atrophy, absorption of fat and consequent shrinkage, lessened vascular supply and consequent smaller organs. It is a pure senile atrophy. The organs assumed action, served their purpose and subsided forever. Even in a natural menopause the distinct dying struggle may be expected in the hypogastric plexus. Puberty increases the volume of the organs, while menopause lessens it. Puberty is the real birth while menopause is the real death of the female genitals. The appearance of the individual organs at the menopause is peculiar. The pudendum wrinkles and shrivels through the absorption of fat and other tissues. In dissecting senile genitals the pudendal sac of Bichat and Savage become more apparent than ever. One can push the index finger into it and the greater labia will appear and feel very thin, while the sac seems disproportionately large. The fat, rounded form of youth obscures this peculiar pudendal sac, even in dissecting. In old women the sac flattens out and exposes the clitoris and nymphæ. The clitoris becomes smaller and blends with the surrounding parts so much that it is occasionally difficult to find. The vagina becomes smoother in its folds. It contracts in every direction and frequently it may seem to thicken, but that is probably a delusion from blending with other tissue. The cervix gets smaller and may appear entirely absent, from the excessive shrinkage and contracting of the vagina. The uterus becomes smaller and harder. It has a peculiar tough, elastic feeling from the atrophy of muscular tissue. It assumes to some extent the form it had before puberty, except that the neck is more prominent before puberty. It straightens out. Its nerves and vessels shrink. The oviducts are notably thinner and shorter. The circular muscular layers seem to suffer most.

The ovaries atrophy very much and resemble a peach-stone on the surface. In quite a number of old female cadavers I found them the size of beans and in some it required considerable searching to find and recognize them. Then we found in the contracted and atrophic broad ligament the sheaths and nerves themselves atrophied.

In women with a stormy menopause it is not unusual to find subinvolution. While a pupil of Lawson Tait, fifteen years ago, I gained some knowledge in regard to a disease of the pudendum which may not infrequently be seen in women from forty to fifty, or about the menopause. It is a trouble that one would easily pronounce on a glance, eczema of the pudendum. Mr. Tait remarked that it was due to a kind of climacteric diabetes; that is a kind of eczema at the menopause. Dr. Martin, Mr. Tait's assistant, was very kind in displaying to me these unfortunate cases. The labia were swollen and edematous and the red flaming eczema extended far and wide beyond the pudendum. The disease made the patient's life almost intolerable. Mr. Tait's treatment for such cases was a solution of hypophosphite of soda (an ounce to a pint of water). The solution should be applied every two to five hours as required, to destroy the germ which induced the itching. He then gave heavy doses of opium. Mr. Tait claims that there is a kind of diabetes mellitis during the menopause; a limited diabetes, as they all finally recover. The distress of the patient with this climacteric diabetes is due to the sugary urine causing irritation of the pudendum. Peculiar crusts form, due to the multiplication of the vegetable germ known as *Torula cerevisiæ*. The eczema due to this cause will spread over the buttocks, over the abdomen and even to the thighs. In one case I saw the eczema extend so far that the patient could walk only with difficulty. The hyposulphite of sodium arrests the formation of this germ. Mr. Tait would sometimes give as high as one grain of opium three times daily and then two grains at night. After a few months of such treatment the opium was lessened, and in from five to ten months such patients fairly recovered. They are liable to mild relapses.

M. Lécorche, of Paris, has also made researches independently of Mr. Tait and curiously enough they agree in many ways. Mr. Tait carries his views into more definite plans of treatment. This climacteric form of diabetes is then a disease which begins at the menstrual cessation and lasts a few years. Menstruation seems to give immunity from it. Nature appears to finally overcome it. If the hyposulphite of sodium is inefficient to arrest the trouble, on account of the fluid quickly running off the parts, an ointment of sulphur will remain on the pudendum for hours. Any substance which will arrest the fermentation changes in sugar is an effective remedy. I have noted no special form of climacteric vaginitis, but one form is liable to arise which is due to laying bare some peripheral nerves in the vaginal wall. The spots are red and most exquisitely tender; they occur mainly at the pudendal orifice and are very persistent. The treatment consists in applying cocaine and sufficient caustic or Paquelin to entirely destroy the exposed nerves. These neuromatic patches are apt to arise in women at other times also. In severe cases it is best to anesthetize the patient and destroy the exposed nerves widely with the Paquelin.

The special diseases of the uterus which I have observed in menopause are endometritis and myometritis accompanied with leucorrhea. Chronic endometritis with an excoriating discharge is frequently found. The uterus is generally slightly large. The mouth is red, bleeds easily and out of it runs a muco-purulent substance of varied color. The hot douche (15 quarts) twice daily and the additional use of glycerin tampons cure most cases.

Occasionally a curetting is required, followed by the thorough application of 95 per cent. carbolic acid. I apply the 95 per cent. carbolic acid to the endometrium three times, so that it will destroy the old inflamed endometrium, and drain with a little rubber tube or pack in gauze, and remove it in twenty-four to thirty-six hours. Fortunately the senile endometritis is generally cured with one curetting, unlike the stubborn endometritis of youth. Mild forms of endometritis in the menopause I have frequently noted. The subinvolution or suspended involution is a much graver matter. It has had a more evil and wide effect on health and especially on the nervous system. It consists essentially of a myometritis, and so far as I can observe rests on an old endometritis. It is not clear whether Klob or Rokitansky is correct, in regard to the theories of the conditions producing a hypertrophic uterus.

Whether the hypertrophic uterus is due to excess of connective tissue or muscle, or whether it is due to a natural proportionate increase of both is still undecided. In such cases a lax pelvic floor is often observed. So far as my experience goes, the tampons and douche are insufficient and are too slow for satisfactory results. Thorough curetting is the best means at command, with the application of 95 per cent. carbolic acid to the whole endometrium. The cure is slow at best but finally quite satisfactory. The pathology of the climacteric or senile endometritis must not be lost sight of. At first the leucorrhea is more abundant. It may be mucous, muco-purulent and finally purulent. The explanation of the changes of the fluid secreted from the endometrium rests on the endometric glands. At first the glands are able to be increased in their function; with time they atrophy, but the inflammation proceeds and finally only sero-purulent substance or chiefly pus results from the glandular destruction; only now and then a glandular endometritis. The remnants only of the endometrium remain and these are involved in a state of low vitality. Low and mild forms of granulation are visible at the neck and can be scraped out of the uterus. Slow necrosis, local death, gradually proceeds until raw ulcerative surfaces are exposed and only pus will be secreted. The glands have disappeared practically.

We must observe that cervical laceration frequently exists with this trouble. The reason such conditions do not heal well is because the blood supply and nerve supply to the uterus are now being cut off, are imperfect, so that nutrition is very deficient in the uterus. For thirty years the uterus has had high feeding from fresh blood and the fine control of a complicated nerve apparatus, but suddenly the high feeding is curtailed and the delicately balanced nerve apparatus is impaired by the atrophy of the menopause. Hence low granulations, imperfect reproductions of cells, ulcerative surfaces, may be expected. It must be remembered that there are other troubles than cancer in the uterus at the menopause. The essential feature of the climacteric uterine trouble is imperfect nutrition. This will not astonish one so much after he has carefully examined and dissected or post-mortemed a dozen female cadavers above 50 years of age. In them he will note atrophy, shrinkage, contraction and pale white tissue.

The differential diagnosis between cancer and benign uterine disease (endometritis) may be looked for in the case of cancer by infiltration, thickening and peculiar watery, sanious discharges. As regards ovarian tumors at the menopause they grow more rapidly. The vital power of the patient is at a lower ebb, and besides the nutrition of the ovary is degraded by diminshed blood supply and atrophy of its nerve supply.

It would appear that the branches of the hypogastric plexus, which are sent to the bladder and rectum, are not atrophied to the same degree as the branches sent to the genitals (uterus, oviducts and ovaries). Yet in my postmortems and dissections it appears to me that the vesical and rectal branches do atrophy. The present idea of medicine is that there is an automatic structure disordered somewhere to account for disease. A portion only of a man is diseased and pathologic anatomy would always indicate the origin, had we sufficient acumen.

Now in the menopause the cerebrospinal axis is disturbed through the means of the vaso-motor nerves, and the circulation by some form of reflex neurosis. A woman's mind is often disturbed. She has lost her old willpower; her memory is impaired; she cannot concentrate effort. She is liable to do damage from inability to control her own action. The law recognizes any deviation from rectitude during the menopause with leniency. The treatment of women during the menopause must be local, general and moral. The cog in the wheel which disturbs even physical existence must be remedied. General debility and irritability must be allayed by anodynes with both tonics and good nourishment, while the unhinged moral views must be removed by changing the life from the old ruts which caused them. One feature must not be lost sight of. When pelvic disease has started a train of evils and continued for years, we cannot expect very much from mere treatment, but radical removal of diseased organs often alone gives relief.

CONCLUSIONS.

1. The average menopause lasts two and one-half years.
2. It comes on slowly as does puberty.
3. A stormy puberty means a stormy menopause generally.
4. The general rule is that an early puberty means a late menopause. In my opinion it simply means that early puberty and late menopause rest on largely developed abdominal and pelvic brains and hypogastric plexus. Precocious puberty means well developed genitals and ganglionic nerves.
5. The disturbance at the beginning of puberty is profound, but since it is an active (depletive) physiologic process it quickly fits the growing and adaptive nervous system. But the menopause is a destructive process. It breaks up the harmony of the previous processes and unbalances the even distribution of nervous energy and circulation.
6. It is probable that every viscus receives an equal or greater shock at menopause than at puberty.
7. The changes at menopause consist in menstrual cessation, atrophy of the genitals, the hypogastric plexus and pelvic brain.

8. Women do not suffer at the menopause so much from malignant diseases as they do from nervous troubles, neuralgias, mental deviations, disturbed visceral rhythm, disordered circulation, indigestion and above all neuroses.

9. The heat center (flashes), the vaso-motor center (flushes) and the sweat center (perspiration), are the especial centers disturbed. Excessive, deficient or disproportionate blood-supply characterizes the disturbed phenomena of these centers.

10. The etiology and pathology of the menopause lies in the sympathetic or ganglionic nervous system.

11. The sympathetic pathologic stages in menopause are: (a) a focus of disease, or irritation (the genitals), (b) indigestion, (c) malnutrition, (d) anaemia, (e) neurosis. It is a slowly progressive process.

12. Atrophy is a disease just as much as hypertrophy or inflammation. Atrophy traumatises nerves by cicatritial compression.

13. Chief among the actual disease in the menopause is endometritis. This is due to infection from desquation of epithelia. The peculiar floodings doubtless depend on this inflammation.

14. The menopause is characterized by various discharges (mucous membrane), leucorrhea, bronchitis, hemorrhages from the bowels, epistaxis (skin) perspiration.

15. Circulatory, perspiratory and caloric changes are the common heritages of the menopause.

16. A characteristic phenomenon of the menopause is an unbalanced, unstable nervous system; cerebrospinal (irritation), or sympathetic (debility).

17. Debility characterizes the trouble in the ganglionic system, while irritability characterizes the cerebrospinal axis.

18. The explanation of the various phenomena lies in the nervous and circulatory systems.

19. Excessive sexual desire at the menopause is indicative of disease.

20. In the menopause the nutrition is impaired, as is shown by the occurrence of malignant disease in the sexual organs which are in a state of retrogression.

21. A chief characteristic of uterine disease is malnutrition from atrophy, which suddenly limits blood supply. This arises from the sudden degeneration of the genital nerve apparatus, pelvic brain and hypogastric plexus, and consequent impaired control of tissue by defective nourishment. Ulcerative processes, local death and purulent secretions arise from low granular cell-formations.

22. In the menopause a disturbed point has arisen in the harmony of visceral rhythm. This pathologic focus must be looked on as the cause of the innumerable reflex neuroses at this time of life.

23. A reflex neurosis is a disturbance in distant organs caused by the irritation of a peripheral sensory or motor area.

24. The chief manifestations of disturbances during menopause are those of pathologic physiology rather than pathologic anatomy.

CHAPTER XXII.

GENERAL VISCERAL NEUROSES.

The Peritoneum holds in intimate connection the tractus intestinalis, tractus genitalis and tractus urinarius by means of the (a) sympathetic nerve, (b) blood-vessels, (c) lymphatic vessels, and (d) connective tissue.

A pathological focus, a reflex, in any one of the three great abdominal visceral tracts, produces disordered rhythm or wild peristalsis in both of the other tracts.

"The telegraph is the nervous system of the world."—N. Y. Herald.

The subject of visceral neuroses must be considered under three heads, viz.:

1. Sensory Neuroses.—The state of the sensory nerves must be considered. There will be two morbid states of the sensory nerves to consider: (a) pathological lesions of a more or less demonstrable sort, either in actual changes in structure or evident in reflex action, (b) a neuralgic condition, a state in which no pathologic lesion is demonstrable, a kind of morbid or exalted sensibility or over susceptibility are those of the sensory sympathetic nerves. The neuralgias and exalted sensibility will be discussed under the hyperesthesias of the abdominal brain and its radiating plexuses of nerves.

2. Motor neuroses, the second subject, including visceral neurosis, are those of motion, such as visceral rhythm, motus peristaltus.

3. Secretion neuroses, the third subject included in visceral neuroses, will include the phenomena of secretion, such as excessive, deficient or disproportionate secretion.

VISCERAL NEUROSES.

Under this head we will include a series of phenomena of the viscera, partly pathologic and partly reflex, partaking of a disturbance of sensation, motion or secretion. By visceral neurosis we mean an undue irritability or perverted function of one or more of the viscera. The pathologic condition may be demonstrable or not. Frequently it is pathologic physiology.

In the phenomena of visceral neuroses must be included the clinical fact that if one organ is disturbed it will tend to unbalance the remainder, i. e., irritation is reflected by a nerve arc from one viscus to another. A diseased uterus is frequently followed by a disturbed stomach. A checking of normal function not only makes neurosis but indigestion, non-assimilation and anemia. Such a case occurred in the person of a young woman on whom I performed laparotomy. A few months after the operation she began to suffer tenesmus, spasmodic dragging pain in the sacrum at defecation, and colica membranacea arose. She became slowly ill, neurotic and unable to work. Dr. Lucy Waite and I operated on her and all that we found was an organized peritoneal band several inches long stretching from the amputated oviductal stump to the middle of the sigmoid. The peritoneal band checked the normal peristaltic action of the sigmoid, producing pain, non-assimilation, anemia and indigestion. She became well after the operation, gaining some twenty pounds. In over a dozen cases during the past three years Dr. Lucy Waite and I have reoperated for old post-operative peritoneal adhesions. We generally found that some loop of bowel was attached to the amputated end of the oviduct and checked more or less the bowel peristalsis. Hence, partial checking or hindering of bowel peristalsis produces a peculiar kind of neurosis. All one may notice at first in such cases is irritability. Pain may not be spoken of as the chief annoyance. These subjects with peritoneal bands, which more or less interfere with visceral rhythm and peristalsis, suffer in distant organs from reflex irritation radiating to them. It should be remembered that reflex action goes on in health and disease. Nerves like railway cars carry any kind of freight.

The essentials of a nervous system consist of (a) a central nerve cell, (b) a conducting cord, and (c) a peripheral apparatus. However vast the nervous system, the elements are the same. For example, the skin is the peripheral apparatus, the spinal nerves are conducting cords and the spinal cord the central nerve cells. The same form of illustration may be made in regard to the abdominal and pelvic brain as in the central nerve cell. The superior and inferior mesenteric plexuses of nerves are the conducting cords (for the intestines) and the peripheral apparatus is in the mucosa. In visceral neuroses pain is not always the chief symptom. Subconscious irritation plays the chief role; irritation which does not come within the field of recognized pain.

Among visceral neuroses we should include enteroptosia. The *maladie de Glenard* is doubtless a neurotic disease belonging to the domain of the nervous vasomotorius. Recently Dr. Schwerdt has written some interesting and well studied articles on enteroptosia. Visceral neurosis means that the nervous system in the abdomen and the organs are not living in harmony. The gamut of the sympathetic nerve has lost its tone.

Enteroptosia begins in respiration and from a weakness of the abdominal sympathetic, which became tired and slacken in its tone. The sympathetic nerves to the viscera have lost their normal power over circulation, assimilation, secretion and rhythm; but the sympathetic nerves have lost their influence over the viscera very slowly, for the enteroptosia is a very slow disease at first and has a long chronic course from the beginning. It may require years to develop. In a later stage of enteroptosia the disturbance of feeling and motion arises, and the nervous symptoms of disturbed digestion, aortic palpitation and dragging sensation. Later the disturbance of motion occurs. The abdominal walls slacken, lose their tone and atrophy even the extremities losing some of their delicate balance. But with the lowering of the intra-abdominal pressure the real ptosia of the viscera begins and the neurosis rapidly increases. The anatomical visceral pedicles elongate, the organs begin to leave their bed.

GENERAL VISCERAL NEUROSES.

SYMPATHETIC NERVE IN LUMBAR REGION

Fig. 61. 114, ganglia at origin of inferior mesenteric artery; 115, interiliac nerve disc; 112, lateral sympathetic chain; 156, rectum; 181, common iliacs.

The digestive tract being disturbed, the nervous system suffers from auto-intoxication. Assimilation becoming deranged by a continuously disturbed digestive tract, a vicious circle begins its progress. The motor, sensory and secretory nerve apparatus, each and all, become involved. Anatomically, we observe the order of visceral ptosia (I base this on some seven hundred personal autopsies) to be the following: 1, the right kidney; 2, the stomach; 3, the small intestines; 4, the transverse colon; 5, the spleen; 6, the liver, and 7, the genitals. Visceral ptosia belongs in the vast majority of living diagnoses to women, but autopsies show the disease quite common in women and not rare in men.

The slackening and atrophy of the female abdominal wall makes the diagnosis easy, while the retention of tone in the abdominal wall of men not only makes visceral ptosia rare in men but more difficult to diagnose. The typical enteroptosia occurs in old age when the sympathetic has lost its tone and vigor. In a normal condition of the abdominal viscera the several organs hold a harmonious relation to each other, no nerve plexus is stretched or slackened, and function, secretion, assimilation, circulation and rhythm move without friction. Now, with dislocated organs dragging irregularly on the nerve plexuses, deranging secretion and assimilation, the suffering becomes manifest in what we know as visceral neurosis. Some designate it hysteria. The lost tone and vigor of the anterior abdominal wall is unfortunate because its vigorous aid to peristalsis is wanting. The loss of the muscular action of the anterior abdominal wall allows congestion of blood and secretions to arise; and constipation intervenes.

In visceral ptosis the skin presents anesthesia and hyperesthesia, also vicarious actions to elemental products. In enteroptosia we have various functional paralyses. The physical and mental vigor is paretic in enteroptosia. It produces languor. The intestinal tract is sluggish, paretic. The bowel suffers in two ways, first, from auto-intoxication; second, from the irritation of the decomposing material on its mucosa, which reacts on the nervous system. The disturbed skin trouble in enteroptosia points to hydrotherapy as the best way out. Baths open the drains of the skin. Enteroptosia is a functional disease.

In enteroptosia as a visceral neurosis we deal with several stages, each of which presents distinct landmarks.

In the first stage we deal with increasing muscular weakness. The patient complains of manifold sensations on account of disturbances in the sympathetic, anemia, defective assimilation and loss of weight. Physical and mental energy become lowered and intra-abdominal pressure becomes lessened. The disease may not extend further.

In the second stage of enteroptosia the name of the disease is quite apt, for the individual viscera begin to leave their old, natural beds. They become dislocated, and permanently fixed in wrong positions. (However, by force or the patient assuming an unnatural position the dislocated viscera may resume their proper position.) With the dislocated organs begin the visceral neuroses, the indigestion and the auto-intoxication. In this stage the abdominal brain and its radiating plexuses, as well as the vessels surrounded, must become adjusted to the new environments of dragging and pressure; compensations of atrophy and hypertrophy will arise. For example, the power of the muscular wall of the abdomen being lessened, the digestive tract must compensate by increasing its muscular wall in order to drive onward the fecal mass.

The third, and final, stage of enteroptosia may be observed in some old people. It is the stage in which compensatory hypertrophy fails; and the viscera becoming overfilled, depletion is very imperfect. The digestive tract is unable to empty itself from the remnants of its feasts, and excessive venous congestions arise, the bladder is able to expel but a little urine at a time and the digestive tract suffers from the absorption of toxins and the irritation from decomposing material.

In one case of enteroptosia, postmortemed by Dr. Lucy Waite and myself, the greater curve of the stomach rested on the pelvic floor. The subject was an old man. In another case in which I performed the autopsy the spleen was resting on the pelvic floor. It is common in autopsies to find the right kidney movable for two inches proximalward and two inches distalward—a range of four inches. The transverse colon is frequently found in the pelvic cavity.

The treatment of enteroptosia may be summed up in the words, hydrotherapy and abdominal support. The young surgeon who performs nephrorrhaphy for movable kidney will have his hands full, if he has a large practice, for I know from personal experience in autopsy and practice in gynecology and abdominal surgery, that movable kidney is a very frequent occurrence. I should judge that five women out of ten, who come to my office, have a movable right kidney. Movable kidney is a part of enteroptosia—nephroptosia. Now, since patients afflicted with enteroptosia suffer from auto-intoxication, non-elimination, non-drainage and congestion, we must aid Nature by establishing general drainage. Frequent salt baths, persistent massage and abdominal supporters are required in the treatment. Above all, the digestive tract must be frequently evacuated once daily by administering a full glass of water with half a dram of epsom salts and ten drops of tr. nux vomica every night on retiring, and insist on the patient emptying the bowels regularly every morning at the same hour. The abdominal bandage should be of elastic flannel and fit snugly. It may be removed at night. The abdominal binder affords much comfort. In fact, one of the methods of diagnosing enteroptosia is to elevate the viscera and then to note whether the pain ceases.

It may not be forgotten that enteroptosia offers opportunities not only for visceral neuroses, but also for obstinate constipation, which favors the development of visceral neuroses by over-retention of feces, including decomposition of matter, calling up irritation and auto-intoxication. Each factor in enteroptosia induces a vicious circle. The factors in enteroptosia which solicit constipation are:

1. Flexing of the colon by the ligamentum hepato-colicum.

2. Flexing of the colon by the ligamentum phrenico-colicum sinistrum.

3. Flexing of the right colon by the ligamentum phrenico-colicum dextrum. I have seen the right colon in the pelvis hanging by this band.

4. Flexing of the pylorus by the ligamentum hepato-duodenum.

5. Atony of the gastro-intestinal muscularis.

6. A lowering of the intra-abdominal pressure by atony of the anterior abdominal muscles.

7. The excessively mobile viscera with elongated pedicles locally compromise the bowel lumen as well as that of vessels.

In sensory visceral neurosis (or neuralgia) we are doubtless dealing with a peculiar form of malnutrition of the nerves of sensation. Hence in these days of scalpel or no scalpel, of sweeping removal or surgical repair, it behooves us to diagnose with caution the symptoms of disease. In disease we are seldom dealing only with signs, which are distinct clews to disease, but chiefly with symptoms which are only indications of pathology. In visceral (abdominal) neuroses we are dealing with organs which possess (a) motion, (b) sensation and (c) secretion; i. e., such organs have muscles which are set in motion by motor nerves, sensation made manifest by some irritation on the sensory nerve ends, and secretion which proceeds normally in certain quantities, but in disturbed conditions, (a) excessive, (b) deficient, or (c) disproportionate.

In visceral (abdominal and thoracic) neuroses we are chiefly dealing with the vasomotor (sympathetic)—a nerve of rhythmical motion and dull sensation. The term visceral (abdominal and thoracic) neurosis is a mere name of a symptom in the minds of many physicians, as we say the kettle boils when we really mean that the water boils or is raised to such a degree of temperature that the ebullition occurs in the water.

Visceral neurosis indicates that some deep condition, assimilation or vicious process is proceeding somewhere. The observing physician of experience commonly associates in his mind visceral neuroses with (a) some debilitating process in age or sex. We cast about for predisposing causes and examine them as a neurotic temperament, hereditary or acquired. One can acquire a neurotic disposition by dissipation, sexual or with narcotics, by excessive and prolonged labor, the absorption of poisonous substances, as lead, arsenic or phosphorus. Rapid changes of temperature bring on visceral disturbances. (b) We also take into account sex. It is difficult to say which sex suffers the most from visceral (abdominal) neuroses. I should judge women do. But different varieties of visceral neuroses prevail in each sex, and at different periods of life.

(c) The chief age of visceral neuroses is from twenty to sixty. Few cases occur before twenty and rarely after sixty. (d) The sexual life of woman is rich in visceral (abdominal) neuroses at different periods as (1) at puberty, (2) at the menopause, (3) at the menstrual period, (4) during pregnancy, (5) in the puerperium, (6) there are neuroses from excess of abstinence from venery. In the above six factors the circulation plays an important role. In short, the neurosis is secondary to some other process.

(e) Visceral (abdominal) neuroses are commonly associated with genital malnutrition, as in anemia, cachexia from malignant disease, chlorosis, debility, mental or physical, from irritation, reflex action, over-strain. Diabetic, gouty and rheumatic persons suffer from visceral neuroses. In the above factors reflex irritation plays the chief role.

(f) In the etiology of visceral neuroses we must include all kinds of trauma to nerves, contraction of cicatricial tissue, pressure of adjacent organs, tumors and pressure on nerves, adjacent inflammatory tissue, dis-

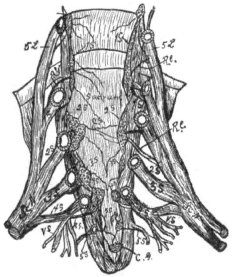

SACRAL SYMPATHETIC AND SACRO-SPINAL NERVES

Fig. 62. This illustration is drawn from a woman about 40 years of age. It represents the sacral sympathetic and sacro-spinal nerves 1s, 2s, 3s, 4s and 5s, sacral ganglia. Sc. N. sciatic nerve. The sacral sympathetic ganglia are connected, anastomosed by transverse strands.

located organs dragging as in visceral ptosia; in short, trauma, pressure and dragging.

(g) Many visceral neuroses rest on infection or intoxication, as malaria, typhoid fever, or poisoning with lead, copper, mercury and other agents.

(h) Catching cold, rapid changes of temperature, cold and wet weather, play a role in the etiology of visceral neuroses.

(i) Visceral neuroses may depend on (1) a small abdominal brain, (2) deficient blood supply, (3) continued disease, (4) premature senility, (5) temporary invagination of the bowels.

(j) A peculiar affection of the rectum of a neuralgic character sometimes arises. It occurs in robust as well as neurotic persons. The patient will go to bed well and wake up at any hour of the night, with a severe pain in the rectum, about the large prostatic plexuses of man and about the cervico-uterine ganglia of woman. I know one patient who has had such an affection for over ten years. The pain rises to a maximum and remains intense, gnawing and grinding for from ten minutes to nearly an hour, when it will suddenly pass away. No cause can be assigned in this case, for the patient lives in apparently perfect health.

The symptom, par excellence, of visceral neuroses, is pain. The patients describe the pain in manifold ways as boring, dragging, burning, stabbing, pressing, lancinating, grinding and tearing. Usually the pain is paroxysmal, ceasing in the intervals. The pain on lessening may be very irregular, slight or intense.

Upon one point concerning neuralgia (visceral or otherwise) I am doubtful, and that is that the nerves have distinct local points of tenderness:—Dr. Valleix's announcement, for example, of the three tender points on the intercostal nerves. But by careful examination and an opportunity to compress the nerves, we would likely elicit pain in any or all points of a neuralgic nerve. The patient can scarcely give distinct localities of tenderness, for mechanical pressure elicits distinct pain. The irregularity of the various localities of pain in visceral neuralgia shows that it is not a mere local disorder but some germinal malnutrition of the sensory apparatus. Visceral neuralgia not only occurs in the trunks but along the branches of nerves, as some patients will complain of pain in various regions of the hypogastric trunks, but of irregular pain in the spermatic branches or in the testicle. During the attacks of visceral neuralgia various accompanying secondary affections arise, as vasomotor disturbances, muscular disturbances. The vessels contract, lessening the amount of blood passing through them, and muscular action brings contractions (colic) in local and remote regions of the abdomen; shifting, colicky cramping pains characterize the visceral neuralgias. In one patient on whom we operated the second time, complaining of varying pains in the right side, we found the liver and stomach prolapsed considerably. Since the operations she complains of irregular pains still in the right side where we made no interference. We do not operate for pain in the right side, but for other reasons, yet we noted much visceral ptosis of the stomach and liver in the region of these neuralgic pains. In many cases I have noted the evil effects of peritoneal adhesions previous and subsequent to abdominal section, and Dr. Lucy Waite and I have operated on many patients a second time for the pain caused by peritoneal adhesions, fixing movable viscera and interfering with their function, rhythm and peristalsis. Peritoneal adhesions produce as symptoms a kind of visceral neurosis, however; the pain of peritoneal adhesions is certainly more constant, in the language of the patient, as dragging sensation repeating itself on prolonged efforts.

Peritoneal adhesions, will, no doubt, explain many cases of visceral neuralgia. In numerous abdominal autopsies I found practically the following percentage of peritoneal adhesions in the following locations, viz.—(1) At the proximal ends of the oviducts, 80 per cent in adults; (2) in the mesosigmoid over the left psoas, 80 per cent in adults; (3) in the ileo-coeco-appendicular apparatus on the right psoas, 70 per cent; (4) in the gall-bladder region 45 per cent; (5) 90 per cent occurs adjacent to the spleen. Also numerous peritoneal adhesions occur at the flexures of the tractus intestinalis, viz.—(a) Flexura coli lienalis; (b) flexura coli hepatica; (c) flexura duodeno-jejunalis. Peritoneal adhesions compromise the circulation (blood

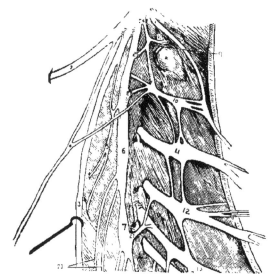

CERVICAL GANGLIA

Fig. 68. 6, superior; 7, middle cervical sympathetic ganglia; 9, 10, 11, 12, 13, cervical nerves (spinal); 24, 25, 26, 27, cervical rami communicantes; 3, vagus; 20, superior cardiac from superior cervical; 2, hypoglossel.

and lymph) peristalsis, absorption and secretion of viscera, as well as traumatises (neuralgia) the visceral nerves.

Another patient complained of a varying pain along the left ovarian plexus, and again for months in the region of the left kidney. Physically, nothing could be discovered except that she was very anemic. I am thoroughly convinced that considerable visceral pain arises from pressure of fecal masses as they pass over the nerve plexuses, also that the hard, irritating fecal masses stir up local bowel contractions (colic) as they move toward the rectum. This accounts for the clinical fact that the visceral neuralgic pains fast disappear when cathartics are so used as to regulate a daily stool. In my practice of gynecology nothing has produced better results in constipation than the drinking of a full glass of water, with one-quarter teaspoonful of epsom salts on retiring, and going to stool promptly after breakfast every morning. The more I practice gynecology and abdominal surgery the more I become acquainted with visceral ptosis and its evil results, and the more I am convinced that visceral neuralgia has a physical basis whose pathology will become more manifest with study.

It is difficult to point out, precisely, the symptoms of visceral neuralgia, for the very simple fact that we do not yet know the definite functions of the visceral nerves. We must compare the visceral neuralgia with the better known neuralgia of the trigeminus. It has been stated that neuralgia is a prayer of the nerve for nourishment or for fresh blood. We often notice that a nerve subject to neuralgia is sensitive to pressure. So in our diagnosis we must follow the track of sensitive nerves in the abdomen. To do this we must know that there are great bundles or trunks of nerves called plexuses which quite generally follow large blood-vessels. Great ganglia exist in different localities of the abdomen, which space forbids even naming. In short, we have to deal with the abdominal brain, the inferior mesenteric ganglion, the cervico-uterine ganglia and the lateral chain of ganglia and hosts of smaller ones, all connected by nerve cords. The sympathetic nervous system which supplies the abdominal viscera is partly independent of the remainder of the nervous system and partly intimately connected with its ganglia by fibers from the brain and cord. The ganglion fibers are the greater part motor and innervate the involuntary muscles of the viscera. We deal with the nervous system of the abdomen as composed of the (a) lateral chain of ganglia, (b) the abdominal and pelvic splanchnics, (c) the rami communicantes, (d) the vagi nerves, and (e) the abdominal brain with all the nerve ganglia. We have but space to mention the special forms of neuralgia which have been attached to different abdominal organs under the general term of visceral neuralgia. Some of the following forms of visceral neuralgia have gained a place in medical literature:

 1. Hepatic neuralgia, or colica hepatica non-calculosa.
 2. Neuralgia of the stomach, or gastralgia.
 3. Enteralgia (colica mucosa Nothnagel; or better, secretion neurosis of the colon).
 4. Ovarian neuralgia.
 5. Neuralgia rectalis.
 6. Neuralgia renalis.
 7. Oviductal colic.
 8. Uterine neuralgia.

Hepatic neuralgia rests on the view that pain of a neuralgic character arises in the liver region when gall-stones do not appear in the stool nor are found in the autopsy. Andral, Budd, Frerichs, Furbinger, Durand, Bardel and Schüppel are names representing belief of hepatic neuralgia with no calculus as a cause. Gastralgia has been so long in medical literature that it need not be supported by any names. Enteralgia in its various indefinite forms is seen by gynecologic practitioners frequently.

With more accurate study the biliary neuralgias will disappear and be replaced by more accurate terms as cholecystitis, choledochitis, etc., in short violent spasm or colic of some segment of the biliary ducts is due to inflammation or calculus. During 700 personal autopsic inspections of the abdominal viscera I demonstrated that some 45 per cent of peritoneal exudates, adhesions existed adjacent to the gall-bladder and other biliary passages. Dr. Robert Morris, of New York, christened these subjects spider gall-bladder adhesions. The peritoneal adhesions adjacent to the gall-bladder, will, no doubt, explain much hepatic neuralgia of the older doctors as well as gastric neuralgia or gastralgia.

Ovarian neuralgia is a disease glibly talked about, but very difficult to diagnose. I have listened perhaps hundreds of times to descriptions of patients' suffering which some would designate ovarian neuralgia. Yet women do have irregular pain, slight and intense, in the ovary. The ovary will be found sensitive and painful on pressure. It is the opinion of the writer that so-called ovarian neuralgia is a secondary process, and yet it doubtless exists, as certain as neuralgia of the upper division of the trigeminus. Neuralgia of the rectum has a definite existence. It comes and goes with great irregularity, arising chiefly at night and appears in persons of apparently robust health.

Neuralgia of the kidney rests on the fact that pain occurs in the region of the kidney; the kidney is sensitive to pressure, and no stone has been found in the kidney at the autopsy. The pain has been so severe that nephrectomy was performed, but the kidney contained no stone. In one patient who had pain and tenderness in the region of the kidney for three years I performed the operation of incising the kidney. No stone was found, but an old scar existed in the kidney pelvis, and also opposite to the scar in the kidney there existed a mass of old cicatricial tissue as large as a plum. The conclusion was that a stone had once ulcerated through the pelvis of the kidney and that she was suffering from the cicatrix in and about the kidney.

Oviductal and uterine colic, or so-called neuralgia, rests on the peculiar structure of the oviducts and uterus. Their involuntary muscular walls, being supplied by sympathetic nerves, are liable to be set in motion by various forms of irritation, and hence from tonic and clonic spasms of their walls are liable to give rise to irregular flying pains or visceral neuralgia.

CHAPTER XXIII.

RELATION BETWEEN VISCERAL (SYMPATHETIC) AND CEREBRO-SPINAL NERVES.

"I have observed matters contained in this book, a large part of which is myself."
"I exist, therefore, I am."—Kant.

THE NERVE MECHANISM OF PELVIC AND ASSOCIATED REGIONS.

The plan of the nerve supply of the pelvis and associated regions is to bring into harmonious action the skin and mucosa and the muscles and viscera. The object of the generative organs is not only gestation and expulsion but also for the varied necessity of copulation, of defecation, and of urination, including muscular and visceral relations.

The nerve mechanism of the external genitals is significant and suggestive of an evolutionary plan. The sympathetic nerves extensively supply the erectile tissues—the corpora cavernosa, glans clitoridis, and bulbi vaginæ. The erectile tissues possess rhythmical action, besides being supplied with nerves from the lumbar plexus (genito-crural) and the sacral plexus (pudendal and internal pudic). The internal pudic nerve (sacral plexus), which chiefly supplies the clitoris with large branches, terminates in the glans clitoridis or adjacent tissue in peculiar tactile or genital corpuscles. The clitoris and considerable of the adjacent region of the distal third of the vagina is exceedingly sensitive to irritation.

The plan of the nervous mechanism of the external genitals is to associate the genitals with certain muscles and overlying skin. The nerves which supply the pelvis and associated viscera are: 1. The sympathetic, the hypogastric plexus and ovarian plexus, both arising from the abdominal brain also branches of the lateral chain of the sympathetic. The pelvic viscera thus involve nerve relations with all the other abdominal viscera. 2. The cerebro-spinal nerve supply, the lumbar plexus furnishes the genito-crural, the ilio-hypogastric, and the ilio-inguinal and inferior pudendal; also the sacral plexus supplying the internal pudic and vesical. The cerebro-spinal nerves supplying the skin and muscle associate them with the genitals. The skin on the pudendum, perineum, and anal region is definitely associated with the skin in the inguinal region, the inner part of the thigh and genital region, because branches from the lumbar and sacral nerve trunks supply the same regions. For example, the genito-crural nerve supplies the skin on the pudendum and the ilio-inguinal supplies the skin over the gluteal muscles. The genito-crural and ilio-inguinal are both branches of the lumbar plexus and what affects the pudendal skin will affect the gluteal skin. Besides the same nerve trunk that sends branches to the skin also sends branches to the underlying muscle. Also the internal pudic, a branch of the sacral plexus, supplies the skin on the pudendum, perineal, and anal region, while the small sciatic, a branch from the same plexus, supplies the skin on the gluteal region. What affects the periphery of one affects that of the other. Both must be physiologic or reflexes will arise. By means of the pudic nerve and the small sciatic (gluteal) the skin and muscles of the pudendum, perineum and anus are brought in harmonious relation with the gluteal muscles (of coition) and skin over them. The genitals, bladder and rectum are supplied by the hypogastric and ovarian plexuses of the sympathetic, and the sympathetic plexuses are joined by the second, third and fourth sacral spinal nerves.

Thus viscera, skin and muscles of the pelvic region are held in close nerve association. The numerous reflexes in the pelvic region of patients will bear close observation in affections of the pudendum, bladder and rectum. Pain may be experienced in the perineum, in the gluteal region or down the thigh. The explanation of this arises from the fact that all these parts, skin of pudendum, anal region, part of the thigh and gluteal region are supplied by the pudic and small sciatic nerves, which come from the same plexus that gives off branches to supply the viscera, pudendum, bladder and rectum. Thus the pelvic viscera and the skin of the gluteal region and thigh, or perineum and external genital region, are held in association by the branches of the same spinal nerves. The pain felt in the urethra by a woman with calculus in the bladder is due to the fact that the trigonal nerve plexus which supplies both trigone and urethra, is prolonged to terminate in the distal end of the urethra. Pain generally is felt at the periphery of nerves, and hence the irritation of calculus in the trigone is experienced in the urethra, that is, at the termination of the trigonal plexus. The sigmoid, two inches above the anus, is provided with very little sensation, while the last two inches in the anus is very sensitive. This is observed by the slight pain in high malignant growth or other swellings of the rectum, by the little pain of large collections of hardened feces. Also by the little pain induced by perforation of the sigmoid during the administration of an enema. Its sensation is limited, like all viscera supplied by the sympathetic. The relation of nerve mechanism between anus and the neck of the bladder is strikingly intimate. Hemorrhoidal operations are accompanied by urine retention and bladder operations by rectal tenesmus.

This intimate nerve relation between rectum and the neck of the bladder is chiefly due to the fourth sacral nerve, which supplies the neck of the bladder and then passes on to supply the anal skin, levator ani, and anal sphincter. The third sacral nerve sends a large branch to terminate in the body of the bladder, but is not related to the levator ani and sphincter ani muscles. The urethral mucosa, the muscles of the pudendum, and the chief part of the skin of the pudendum perineum and anus are supplied by the internal pudic nerve from the sacral plexus. The sacral plexus emits the gluteal nerves which supply the gluteal muscles. It also gives off the interior pudendal (branch of the small sciatic), which supplies directly the perineum. Hence the external genitals and the gluteal muscles are in intimate nerve association.

Hilton struck by the peculiar ending of the inferior pudendal nerve called it the nerve of coition. The genito-crural and ilio-inguinal are from the lumbar plexus and supply the inguinal and vulvar regions. The ilio-hypogastric supplies the hypogastric and groin region.

With diseased condition of the region supplied by the genito-crural and ilio-inguinal nerves, it is explainable how women suffer by reflex action in the region supplied by the ilio-hypogastric and ilio-inguinal nerves—the inguinal region. Many women mistake the inguinal and hypogastric pain for ovarian disease. Irritation in the perineum or rectum may be followed by priapism. Adhesions about the glans clitoridis or accumulated secretions under the prepuce may provoke not only local disturbances in the bladder and rectum but induce genital disturbances. The pain felt through perineal abscess in the gluteal region and in the thigh may be explained by the pressure of the inferior pudendal nerve in the perineum. In neuritis brought on by trauma of the inferior pudendal nerve due to much sitting on hard seats, the pain may be felt in the perineum and the region supplied by that nerve.

Dissection discloses the inferior pudendal nerve crossing the gluteal region toward the perineum, close to the ischial tuberosity, where it is liable to occasional injury with enlarged pudendo vaginal glands. Some patients do not sit down comfortably on account of the irritation of the periphery of the inferior pudendal nerve.

However, the pain may be aroused at the ischial tuberosity, by an inflamed bursa or local traumatic neuritis. Pain in the knee-joint from hip-joint disease is an ever living example of a reflex, pain starting at the periphery of the one branch of a nerve trunk, and experiencing the pain at the periphery of another branch of the same trunk. The branches of nerve trunks (or plexuses) supply groups of muscles and skin in widely distributed regions for the purpose of associating them in function. For example, the lumbar plexus associates the skin of the external genitals with the skin of the gluteal region by means of its branches supplying both regions, as the genito-crural, ilio-inguinal and ilio-hypogastric.

The sacral plexus associates the action of the muscles (and skin) of the external genitals, perineum, and anus with the gluteus maximus, through branches of the same plexus supplying both regions. The pudic, a branch of the second, third and fourth sacral spinal nerve, supplies the external genitals, perineum and anus, while the gluteal (smaller sciatic), a branch of the second, third and fourth sacral, supplies the gluteus maximus muscle (of coition). Finally to perfect a balanced nerve association between muscles and skin of the external genitals and gluteal region, the inferior pudendal nerve actually joins the periphery of the two regions.

A reflex is a disturbance in a distant part from some local peripheral irritation. The pelvic viscera are liable to trauma and infection during the childbearing period from exposed mucosa and serosa, and this traumatic or infection atrium becomes a fruitful source for reflex distribution, through

RELATION OF SPINAL TO SYMPATHETIC

disturbed pelvic mechanism, due to cicatricial contraction and subsequent dislocation. The irritation is transmitted to the abdominal brain, where it is reorganized and emitted to the organs of the abdomen and chest, disturbing their rhythm, secretion, absorption, sensation and nutrition. The visceral rhythm becomes irregular, secretion and absorption become excessive, deficient, or disproportionate and the blood becomes waste laden. The patient is forced slowly or rapidly through definite, though irregular, stages of disease (traumatic or infection atrium), irritation, indigestion, malassimilation, malnutrition, anemia, neurosis and psychosis. The nerve mechanism between ovary, genitals and kidney is very intimate. The ovarian plexus originates from the renal and hypogastric, which connection directly associates the kidney with the internal genitals, and accounts for the disturbed functional relation of kidney and internal genitals during menstruation and pregnancy (pain, albumen, and vomiting). The intimate association of nerve relation between kidney and internal genitals is manifest in diseases of either organ. In menstruation there is a pain in the renal regions. Congestion of one organ produces congestion or anemia in the other (reflex action). Renal calculus or nephritis causes pain and retraction of the testicle, and of course similar disturbances arise in the ovary, though not so easily demonstrated. Ovarian disease may cause pain in the rectum (supplied by the hypogastric). The ovarian and hypogastric plexus have direct communication with the abdominal brain, and hence the severe shock from injury to the ovary, uterus, or rectum, and especially the tendency to vomit. The internal genitals (ovary, oviduct, and uterus) are in just as intimate and profound connection with the great abdominal brain as the enteron, and in trauma or infection of the genitals or enteron, will have like severe manifestations of general disturbances.

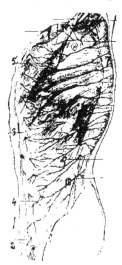

CUTANEOUS NERVES OF THORAX AND ABDOMEN

Fig. 64. The cutaneous nerves of the thorax and abdomen, viewed from the side. (1) Ilio-hypogastric. (2) Ilio-inguinal. (4) Anterior cutaneous of last thoracic. (10) Lateral cutaneous of last thoracic. (9) External oblique muscle. (Henle).

I. PELVIC NERVES (CEREBRO-SPINAL).

The sacral plexus really terminates in two great branches, the sciatic for the lower limb and the pudic, which is a genital nerve, supplying the internal and external genitals.

Patients suffer especially in two regions, viz.: (a) the hypogastric region, (b) the lumbo-sacral region. The explanation is that the uterus by dragging or pressing on the sacral spinal nerves, induces pain in the lumbo-sacral regions and the pain is reflected from the lumbar cord along the ilio-hypogastric, ilio-inguinal, and genito-crural nerves, branches of the lumbar plexus to the hypogastric and inguinal region.

The lumbar nerves supplying the hypogastric and inguinal regions are all branches of the same trunks—the lumbar plexuses.

The irritation of the periphery of any branch liable to be reflected on any other branch of the same trunk. Irritation of the sacral nerves is liable to be reflected from the common lumbar trunk to the branches of the hypogastric and inguinal region. However the complaint of pain in the hypogastric or inguinal region may be only in the skin and purely hyperesthetic (hysteric) in character.

Gynecologic patients complain of a triumvirate of pain, viz.: in the lumbo-sacral region, in the hypogastrium, and in the head. The lumbo-sacral region is the great central depot of gynecologic pain. It is the central telegraphic station where irritated genitals first tell their story. In this case, a sympathetic nerve which supplies the genitals relates the story to the cerebrospinal axis—a nerve of another tongue. It matters little what disease, endometritis, myometritis, endosalpingitis, or peritonitis attacks the pelvis, the lumbo-sacral pain is the characteristic pain. The lumbo-sacral region is the sensorium for pelvic disturbances. The nerves in relation are the lumbar plexus, anterior and posterior, the hypogastric plexus connected to the lumbar plexus by the rami communicantes, and the sacral plexus. In the hypogastric region the ilio-inguinal, ilio-hypogastric and genito-crural play the rôle. The last three have cutaneous branches, and often the skin sensation is mistaken for ovarian or other genital pain. Branches of the intercostal, lumbar, and sacral nerves supply the peritoneum, but conduct chiefly to the sacro-lumbar region.

Extreme precautions are required to discriminate between pain located in the skin over an organ and pain in the organ itself. This may relate to viscera or tumors, but is especially true of the kidney. I have performed nephro-lithotomy for pain in the kidney, with the supposition that a calculus existed. No calculus was found, and the intense hyperesthesia of the skin over the kidney remained long afterward. Grave diagnostic or operative errors may be committed by mistaking intense and persistent cutaneous hyperesthesia for disease underlying viscera and structures. The anesthetic and hyperesthetic zones should be mapped. It is well known among experienced gynecologists that some peritoneal cysts are very painful. The chief painful cysts are located along the oviducts and the two sides of the ligamentum latum. This is in accord with an observation that the chief suffering of gynecologic patients is from pelvic peritonitis, i. e., from dislocated or disturbed pelvic mechanism. The peritoneal cysts, with their contents, are doubtless of an inflammatory character. The pudic nerve is the source of motion to the muscles of the perineum, anus, bladder, urethra and vagina. It is a source of sensation to the integument of the perineum, pudendum labia, mucosa of the clitoris and urethral mucosa. Irritation of the external genitals creates a reflex in the spinal cord which results in turgidity of the genitals and finally a sense of musclar contraction in these parts of the genitals supplied by the musclar branches of the pudic nerve. The integument and immediately underlying muscles are always supplied by branches of the same nerve trunk.

The irritation of the nerves of the genital integument (cutaneous branches of the pudic) induces contractions of the perineal, levator-anal, anal, and vaginal muscles (musclar branches of the pudic) which assist in expulsion of the secretion of the vulval glands, especially the vulvo-vaginal. Occasionally masturbation in the female may be prevented by blistering the mucosa of the clitoris, making it so tender that the subject will cease manipulation.

In certain reported cases of fracture of the vertebral column, irritation of portions of the spinal cord left intact distal to the seat of fracture will induce turgidity of the genitals resembling erections. The expulsion of the last drop of urine is a reflex act due to the irritation of the urine on the sensory pudic nerves in the urethral mucosa, reflecting it to the spinal cord, whence the force returns on the (motor) musclar branches of the pudic, expelling all the urine from the urethra.

The rectum produces sympathetic disease in adjacent viscera, as incontinence of urine, involuntary emission and neuralgic pain. The explanation arises from the distribution of the pudic nerve to the integument about the anus, which permits reflex motor impulses, from rectal irritation transmitted to the spinal cord, to be reflected to the adjacent genito-urinary organs and associated muscles.

The small sciatic nerve supplies the gluteus maximus and sends a branch (the inferior pudendal) to the perineum, pudendal and vagina. This explains the relation in coition, of the genitals and the gluteus maximus muscle. Also it may explain perineal irritation from disease along the trunk of the inferior pudendal, as hardened tissue, which may arise in subjects of sedentary habits.

The periphery of the ilio-inguinal and ilio-hypogastric which in general is the integument of the lower abdomen, may be the seat of neuralgia; or it may be the seat of hyperesthesia or anesthesia. The pain may be paroxys-

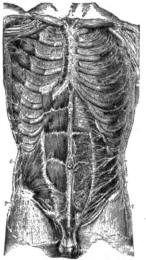

VENTRAL DIVISIONS OF DORSAL NERVES

Fig. 65. A view of the anterior division of the dorsal nerves. The cut shows the nerves distributed to the muscles and skin of the abdomen. It may be easily noted how an irritation on the skin passes to the spinal cord, and thence to the abdominal muscles, putting them on tension to protect underlying viscera. Hirschfield and Leville.)

mal, radiating along the course of the nerves. Painful points may be detected near the spinous processes of the lumbar vertebra (lumbar point), near the middle of the iliac crest (iliac point), near the external inguinal ring (hypogastric point), in the inguinal canal (inguinal point), and finally in the labial points. These are Valleix's puncta dolorosa, or points of tenderness along the course of nerves.

The chief feature for the gynecologist, is the periphery of the iliohypogastric and ilio-inguinal nerves in anesthesia and hyperesthesia of the skin of the hypogastric and inguinal regions. The skin of the abdomen proximal to the umbilicus is supplied in general by the distal intercostal nerves, which may be termed the respiratory region. The skin distal to the umbilicus is supplied by the ilio-hypogastric and ilio-inguinal, which may be called the abdominal region.

The genito-crural and dorsal branches of the lumbar nerves aid in furnishing motor power to the region distal to the umbilicus. The skin, muscles, and peritoneum of the abdomen are supplied by branches of the same trunks, so as to preserve harmony of motion and association of sensation, insuring visceral protection.

For example, if cold water be dashed against the belly, the skin sensation is transmitted to the spinal cord, and reflected to the abdominal muscles, causing an immediate rigidity, for the protection of adjacent and underlying viscera.

The harmony of the skin, muscles and peritoneum (viscera) explains how massage assists in curing constipation For example, skin irritation on the abdomen is transmitted to the cord, whence (a) it is reflected to the abdominal muscles, producing action which aids in fecal expulsion; (b) the reflected force induces visceral peristalsis. This is motor. It appears also that the sensory condition of the skin is in harmony with the sensory condition of the underlying viscera. Diseased underlying abdominal viscera are apparently accompanied with correspondingly disturbed sensory cutaneous areas.

The genito-crural nerve supplies only one muscle, the round ligament, and finally supplies the labia. The periphery of any of the ventral divisions of the lumbar plexus (the ilio-hypogastric, ilio-inguinal, genito-crural and external cutaneous) may show disturbances of motion or sensation by inflammatory products, compressing any part of their trunks. In psoas abscess the genito-crural and the external cutaneous might show a disturbed periphery, as well as other branches of the lumbar plexus. The practical matters for the gynecologist to determine in the complicated nerve mechanism of the pelvis and associated relations, are: 1. Map on the abdomen the areas of anesthesia and hyperesthesia. 2. Hyperesthesia of skin should not be mistaken for a diseased underlying viscus, as the ovary or kidney. 3. Areas of anesthesia and hyperesthesia may change from day to day. 4. Hysteria has certain stigmata, viz.: (a) anesthesia of the conjunctiva bulbi; (b) anesthesia of the mucosa of pharynx; (c) anesthesia or hyperesthesia of skin (especially of abdomen); (d) sudden paresis or exacerbation of muscle (knee, globus, tongue, knotting of belly muscles); (e) occasional mental phenomena, and (f) disturbance of special sense, as sudden blindness or excessive hearing. Some of these six stigmata must be present to diagnose hysteria. 5. Much of the hypogastric pain complained of by s u b j e c t s is located in the skin of the inguinal and hypogastric region. T h i s pain may be caused by sensory disturbances in the skin only, or by reflex disturbances from diseased genitals, through the anterior branches of the lumbar plexus. 6. Gynecologic patients complain of pain: (*a*) in the sacro-lumbar region from diseased genitals irritating the periphery of the sacro-lumbar nerves; (*b*) pain in the hypogastric and inguinal region from irritation of the genitals passing to the lumbar cord, whence it is reorganized and reflected on the anterior branch of the lumbar plexus; and (*c*) pain in the head through reflexes in diseased genitals. Perhaps the occipitalis major and minor constitute part of this nerve route. 7. The stomach is one of the chief organs to suffer reflexly from diseased genitals through the direct route of the hypogastric plexus, extending from the genitals to the abdominal brain, whence it is reorganized and sent to the stomach, over the gastric plexus. The nerves which supply the internal pelvic viscera are located in general between the pelvic fascia and the peritoneum.

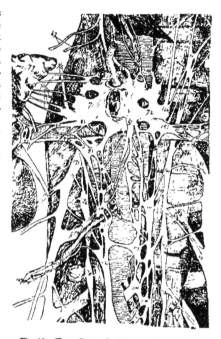

Fig. 66. (From Byron Robinson's life-size chart of the Sympathetic.) Represents the 'abdominal brain and adjacent ganglia. (55) A ganglion of the dorsal lateral chain. (61) Splanchnic. (96 and 97) Rami communicantes. (67) Branches of right vagus to stomach. (69) Trunk of right vagus entering abdominal brain. (70) Phrenic nerve on phrenic artery. (71) Right abdominal brain. (72) Left abdominal brain. (73) Gastric artery. (74) Splenic artery. (75) Hepatic artery. (76) Right great splanchnic. (77) Ad-renal. (79) Suprarenal nerves (6). (82) Inferior renal ganglion. (83) Superior renal ganglion. (84, 85, 86 and 87) Ganglia on renal artery. (88) Renal artery. (89, 90 and 91) Lumbar nerves. (96, 97 and 98) Rami communicantes. (101, 102 and 103) Lumbar lateral chain of ganglia. (106) Superior mesenteric artery surrounded by the abdominal brain. (107, 108 and 109) Genital ganglia. (110 and 111) Genital ganglia (ovarian) as well as (112, 113 and 114) Genito-rectal ganglia. (167) Nerves around the ovarian artery. (171) First lumbar nerve. (172) Second. (173) Third. (176) First. (177) Second, and (178) Third lumbar ganglia. (182) Genital ganglion. (183) Inferior mesenteric artery. (185) Aortic branch of abdominal brain. (186) Ending of left great splanchnic in abdominal brain. (187) Superior, and (188) inferior (left) renal ganglia. (189, 190 and 191) (left) Renal ganglia.

The cervix and vagina are mainly supplied by branches from the third and fourth sacral nerves. The pudendum is supplied by the pudic, which is chiefly composed of the third sacral nerve. The pudic nerve passes from the pelvis from the third sacral by the way of the large sacro-sciatic foramen, winds around the spine of the ischium, and re-enters the pelvis through the lesser sacro-sciatic foramen; it is thus removed from the dangers of the trauma due to labor. The nerve directly traumatized by labor is the obturator. When the child's head engages, the obturator muscles of the thighs act by closing and flexing them. The pudic nerve sends branches to the clitoris, to the pudendum, to the perineum, and to the rectum. Practically the sacral plexus terminates in the two branches, the pudic (genital) and sciatic (limb).

In teaching I have frequently represented the pudic nerve by the hand. For example, the arm represents the nerve itself, the thumb represents the great vesical nerve just before the pudic passes from the pelvis; after the pudic has re-entered the pelvis and passed along the ramus of the pubes, the index finger represents the branch to the clitoris, the middle finger the branch to the pudendum, the ring finger the branch to the perineum, and the little finger the branch to the rectum. Thus the digits of the hand can vividly represent the branches of the pudic nerve.

It can also be remembered that the pudendal nerve, a branch of the small sciatic nerve, sends branches to the anus, perineum, pudendum and clitoris, which unite with similar branches from the pudic to supply the same organs. There is a wonderful design in the union of the periphery of the pudendal and the pudic nerves.

The lesser sciatic nerve supplies but one muscle (gluteus maximus), and then gives off a branch, the pudendal, which directly supplies the external genitals and rectum. This arrangement of the nerve supply brings the gluteus maximus muscle and the skin of the genitals in direct relation. Irritation of the genitals will induce contraction of this muscle. Thus the gluteus maximus muscle must be considered (anatomically and physiologically) the muscle of coition. Observation of copulating animals will confirm this view.

The external genitals are supplied by the plexus pudendus. A small segment is supplied by the fifth sacral nerve through the plexus sacro-coccygeus. The chief nerves concerned in the supply of the external genitals are: 1. The medial hemorrhoidal nerve; (2) the inferior vesical nerve, which sends fibers to the base of the bladder and the urethra, to the vagina and middle portion of the rectum; 3. The internal pudic nerve, which follows the internal pudic artery and divides into (*a*) inferior hemorrhoidal, which supplies the internal and external anal sphincters and the skin of the anus; (*b*) the perineal nerve, which supplies the skin on the perineum, the musculus transversus perinei, sphincter ani externus, sphincter vaginæ and also the labia and the vestibulum vaginæ; (*c*) the dorsal nerve of the clitoris, which passes between the sphincter vaginæ and ischio-cavernosus under the symphysis pubis to the proximal border of the clitoris, whence it sends numerous fine fibers to the skin as well as to the cavernous tissue.

ANATOMY OF THE SYMPATHETIC

II. THE SYMPATHETIC NERVES.

The sympathetic nerve consists of, viz.: (*a*) ganglia (lateral chain); (*b*) conducting cords; (*c*) three ganglionic plexuses located in the chest (thoracic plexus), abdomen (abdominal brain), and pelvis (pelvic brain); and (*d*) automatic visceral ganglia. The conducting cords are not sheathed; they are non-medullated. The ganglia, composed of nerve cells, are little brains. They are reorganizing centers, receiving sensations and sending out motion. The abdominal and pelvic brains and the ganglionic plexuses are simply large brains or aggregations of nerve cells.

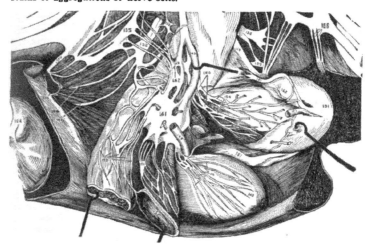

Fig. 67. (Byron Robinson.) From author's life-size chart of the Sympathetic. Represents the cervico-uterine ganglion. (—) The pelvic brain. (127) Second. (128) Third, and (129) Fourth, sacral nerves (left). (131) Second. (132) Third. (133) Fourth, sacral nerves (right). Note the connection of the second, third, and fourth sacral nerves to the pelvic brain. (137 and 138) Second and third sacral ganglia. (139) Branches from the second sacral. (140) Branches from the third and fourth sacral nerves to the pelvic brain (141 and 142). The pelvic brain or cervico-uterine ganglion is marked (141, 142, 143, 144) and (145) branches of it. Third sacral to the levator ani muscle (146). (147) Vesical ganglion. (148) Ureter. (149) Bladder. (150) Vagina. (151) Uterus. (152) Nerves of bladder. (153) Pudic nerve. (158) Right, and (159) left, sacral plexus. (160) Branches of hypogastric plexus which do not enter pelvic brain before distribution. (161) Fallopian tube. (162) Ovary. (163) Round ligament. (164) Acetabulum. (165) Spine of ischium.

A summary of the abdominal brain is: (*a*) It presides over nutrition; (*b*) it controls circulation; (*c*) it controls gland secretion; (*d*) it presides over the organs of generation, and (*e*) it influences in a dominant way the automatic visceral ganglia. With nerve fibers radiating on blood and lymph vessels and to every abdominal viscus, it is no wonder that the abdominal brain has been considered the center of life.

An ideal nervous system should be a neuron and consist of first, a ganglion cell; second, a conducting cord, and, third a periphery. The sympathetic nervous system possesses the neuron or three-nerve elements in an eminent degree. The abdominal brain represents the central ganglion cell. Its thousands of cords, distributing fibers, represent the conducting cord, while the various automatic visceral ganglia represent the periphery.

The sympathetic nerve supplies the uterus, oviducts, and ovaries, as they possess rhythm. Only viscera whose main nerve supply is sympathetic possess rhythm. The cervix is supplied by the spinal nerves, and does not possess rhythm to any marked degree.

The peritoneum is supplied chiefly by the sympathetic nerves. The main spinal nerves which supply the peritoneum are the peritoneal branches of the ilio-inguinal and ilio-hypogastric and distal intercostals. The sense of localization in detail is yet unrecognized in the sympathetic, which preponderates in the peritoneum and tractus intestinalis, while the cerebro-spinal nerves are so much in the minority that they are uncertain in indicating localized areas.

The domain of the sympathetic nerve is beyond the control of the will, as the beating of the heart, uterine and intestinal contraction, erection of cavernous tissue and the systole and diastole of the bladder. Man cannot speculate on his sympathetic system.

The most interesting and delicate structure connected with the genitals is the nervous apparatus. This consists of cerebro-spinal and sympathetic or non-medullated nerves. The uterus (body), oviducts and ovaries are chiefly supplied by the sympathetic nerves, while the pudendum, vagina and cervix are mainly supplied by the cerebro-spinal nerves.

The hypogastric plexus originates in the abdominal brain (solar plexus), and passes along the aorta. It is increased by branches from the lumbar ganglia of the lateral chain of the sympathetic. The combined strands of nerves now pass over the bifurcations of the aorta and sacral promontory, and divide into two large bundles, each of which passes dorsal to the peritoneum to the base of the ligamentum latum where it reaches the side of the uterus and oviducts. Some strands pass to the rectum, but this organ is chiefly supplied by the nerves passing along the inferior mesenteric artery. The ovarian plexus consists of nerve strands derived from the hypogastric plexus and the ganglia in the lumbar lateral sympathetic chain, and the nerves passing along the ovarian artery. The ovarian plexus supplies the ovaries and the ampulla of the oviducts.

At the periphery of the hypogastric and ovarian plexuses are situated small ganglia along the walls of the oviducts and uterus, which I have designated "automatic menstrual ganglia." I have attempted to show that these ganglia rule the rhythm of menstruation. The composite ganglia located at the lateral borders of the cervix and vagina I have denominated the *Pelvic Brain*.

The best method to demonstrate the nerves of the uterus I have found to be the placing of an infant cadaver in pure alcohol for several weeks, when the hypogastric plexus can be traced to its home on the body of the uterus

ANATOMY OF THE SYMPATHETIC

as plainly as though it were composed of white cotton threads. The nerves in the infant are much larger in proportion to its size than in the adult.

Here will be presented a few remarks on the anatomy, physiology, and pathology of the sympathetic nerve, showing the principal points in gynecology relative to the abdominal and pelvic brain. They are the result of my

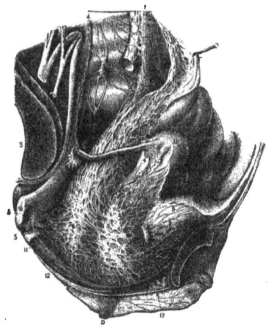

Fig. 68. (Laville and Hirschfield.) Is a cut to illustrate the nerves of the non-pregnant uterus. (1) Hypogastric plexus lying on the bifurcation of the aorta. It divides to pass each side of the rectum. (2) Rectal branches on rectum (R). (3) Lumbar ganglia of the sympathetic. (4) Ovarian plexus. (5) Branch of the third and fourth sacral nerves passing to the pelvic brain (6 and 7) before going to the uterus. (6 and 7) Nerve plexuses on the vagina and rectum. (8) Uterine nerves. (9) Vesical plexus. (10) Trunk of it—great sciatic. (11) Levator ani branch. (12) Trunk of the pudic nerve. (U) Uterus. (B) Bladder. (S) Sacrum. (D) Tranversus perinei muscle cut. This cut is partly diagramatic, as the nerves are not distributed in the form represented in the illustration, but represent more aggregations, as drawn by the author. The nerves in Savage's cut are represented too richly.

investigations of the sympathetic nerve, which I have dissected during the last ten years. The claim is that the ganglia of the sympathetic nerve are little brains; i. e., they receive sensation, emit motion, and control secretion. They are trophic centers, and possess vaso-motor power. They are centers for reflex action, and are endowed with a peculiar quality called rhythm.

The great reorganizing centers in the sympathetic nerves are the abdominal and pelvic brain and the three cervical ganglia. Reorganizing power of a less degree exists in the lateral chain of ganglia situated at the circumference of the elliptical-shaped sympathetic, and in the collateral ganglia in the chest, abdomen and pelvis, and also in the ganglia situated in every viscus which I have designated automatic visceral ganglia.

The sympathetic nerve consists of two lateral chains of ganglia, extending from the base of the skull to the coccyx. Situated anterior to these chains are collateral plexuses known as the cardiac, abdominal and pelvic. Besides these there exist in all the viscera small ganglia, automatic visceral ganglia —for example, the automatic hepatic, cardiac, menstrual ganglia.

The distribution of the sympathetic nerve is (a) to vessels, (b) to glands, and (c) to viscera. It is connected with the cerebro-spinal nerves by the rami communicantes. Its independence of the cerebro-spinal axis is not yet fully settled; but children have been born at term with no cerebro-spinal axis. The part of the sympathetic that appears to be most independent of the cerebro-spinal axis is the cardiac, abdominal and pelvic plexuses (brains). I have kept the intestines of dogs in active peristaltic waves for nearly two hours after death, in a warm room, by tapping them with the scalpel.

The automatic parts of the sympathetic to which I wish to direct attention are, the cervical sympathetic ganglia (superior, middle, and inferior), the abdominal brain (the solar plexus), and the pelvic brain (or cervico-uterine plexus). Due consideration must be given to the three splanchnic groups: (1) the cervical splanchnics, conducted to the stomach, heart, and lungs through the spinal accessory and the vagus; (2) the abdominal splanchnics, originating from the fourth dorsal, running to the second lumbar, and thence to the abdominal brain; (3) the pelvic splanchnics, conducted to the hypogastric plexus by means of the second, third and fourth sacral nerves, to supply the rectum and the genito-urinary organs.

I have observed for some time that the connection of genital and urinary systems with all the great nerve centers is intimate and profound. For example, the organ which has the most intimate connection with the cerebro-spinal axis and the abdominal and pelvic brain is the uterus. The eye, too, is closely connected with both nervous systems, and also with the uterus. This intimate nervous connection of the uterus with the nervous system increases with the ascending scale of animal life.

The physiological function of the sympathetic nerve is rhythm. The sympathetic nerve alone possesses this function. The power to produce rhythm belongs only to a ganglion. The viscera functionate rhythmically. The destruction of this periodical function causes disease. The organs which have the most pronounced rhythm are those intimately connected with the abdominal brain. Chief among these is the uterus and oviducts. So far as I can observe, the uterus is connected with the abdominal brain by twenty or thirty strong nerve strands.

The uterus and oviducts have a monthly rhythm, due to the automatic menstrual ganglia situated in their walls. No doubt the higher physiological orders originate in the great abdominal brain. The breaking of the rhythm of one viscus disturbs the rhythm of all the rest. This is in no organ so significant as in the uterus, because the uterus is more exposed to infection and trauma—disease—than any other viscus. The glandular endometrium, the best germ culture medium, is exposed to the external body service.

The liver has a visceral rhythm, through its automatic hepatic ganglia, similar to that of the uterus. When new food arrives in the liver from the portal vein, the cells of the liver begin to swell, in the performance of their functions of making bile, glycogen and urea. The hepatic capsule (Glisson's) and the peritoneal covering being extremely elastic, the liver can go through its rhythm whenever occasion arises. When the liver arrives at the maximum point of the rhythm, the cells having exhausted themselves in making bile, glycogen and urea, these three products are sent home, (in the lumen of the tractus intestinalis) and the cells begin to contract, Glisson's capsule begins to shrink, and the peritoneum returns to its original state. Then the liver secures rest and repair, in order to be able to accomplish the next rhythm. It is the breaking of the hepatic rhythm by unfavorable food or distant reflexes of diseased viscera that causes disease of the liver. The most prominent organ that induces irregular hepatic rhythm is a diseased uterus. Alcohol, which rushes from stomach to liver

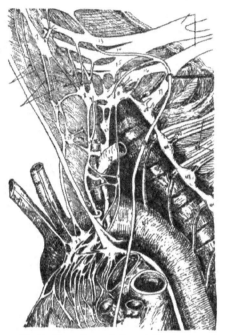

Fig. 69. (From Bryon Robinson's life-size chart of the Sympathetic.) Represents the upper or neck and chest portion. (7) Middle cervical ganglion. (8, 8) Inferior cervical ganglion. (13, 14, 15, 16) Cervical nerves. (17) First dorsal nerves. (18) Phrenic. (19) Branch from inferior cervical to phrenic. (20, 21) Cardiac nerves from middle and superior cervical ganglia. (22, 22, and 22) Cardiac nerves from inferior cervical ganglion. (23) Wrisberg's ganglion (of the heart). (24 to 33) Cervical rami communicantes. (34 and 35) Ganglia on superior, middle and inferior cardiac nerves of the cervical ganglia. (36) Verteral artery. (37) Left subclavian artery. (38) Innominate artery. (39) Right subclavian artery. (40) Carotid artery. (41) Aorta. (43) Intercostal arteries. (45, 46 and 47) Dorsal lateral chain of ganglia. (63) Communicantes.

through the gastric veins, taken without food, destroys the nice balance of the hepatic rhythm by enticing the liver to go through its rhythm without due stimulus or by unnatural stimulus.

It is plain that the heart goes through a rhythm by means of the automatic cardiac ganglia situated in its wall. These ganglia are known as Bidder's, Schmidt's, Remak's, and Ludwig's. The vagi (especially the right) give the heart the slow, steady beat, its sober, regular movements like a pendulum; but the three cervical sympathetic ganglia rule the heart in regard to rapidity and irregularity. It is the breaking of the cardiac rhythm that causes reflex heart trouble. A diseased uterus, from the intimate and profound nerve connection, is preëminently the organ that disturbs the heart and its rhythm (by disturbed circulation in the coronary arteries).

The digestive tract has its own special rhythm through Auerbach's and Billroth-Meissner's plexuses—the one presiding over the peristalsis, and the other over absorption, secretions. The occasion of a digestive rhythm is food. The main rhythm occurs in the enteron and the stomach.

The bladder performs a rhythm by means of automatic visceral ganglia; it has a diastole and a systole. The rhythm of the bladder is broken when its nerves are dragged, as in pregnancy.

The spleen performs its rhythm by its automatic splenic ganglia. The occasion of a splenic rhythm is fresh food. The spleen accomplishes its rhythm by (*a*) the swelling of its tufts and substance, (*b*) by the expansion of its elastic capsule, and (*c*) by the stretching of its peritoneal covering. It rises to a maximum and sinks to a minimum. It is now in action and now in repose.

Thus each viscus performs its peculiar rhythm by means of the automatic ganglia situated in its substance. The higher physiological orders of the abdominal brain must, of course, be obeyed.

III. PATHOLOGY.

We now come to the consideration of diseased viscera. Pathogenesis through the sympathetic, in health and disease, is by reflex action. Of course we have ganglionic sclerosis, recognizable and non-recognizable lesions of the sympathetic, pigmentation and secondary disease, etc., but the great pathology of the sympathetic nerve in gynecology is the transmission of reflexes from diseased viscera.

We will take for illustration a case of uterine cervical laceration occurring five years previous. The patient is now a pale, anemic, neurotic woman, unfitted for the labor of life. A lacerated cervix (an infection atrium) is soon followed by endometritis. Irritation from this is transmitted over the hypogastric plexus to the abdominal brain, where it is reorganized. It should be remembered that any irritation (force, vibration) will travel on the lines of least resistance, and in the direction of least resistance from the abdominal brain toward that organ having the greatest number of nerve strands. The irritation reorganized will flash on all the plexuses. Reaching the liver, it will disturb the hepatic rhythm, causing an over-production, an under-production, or an irregular production, of bile, gylcogen and urea; and finally the functions of the liver suffer impairment. Suppose we follow this same uterine irritation to the digestive tract. At Auerbach's plexus it will cause colic, lethargy, or fitful peristalsis, and at the plexus of Billroth-Meissner it will induce diarrhea, constipation, or development of gases—fermentation. These disturbances, after a painful progress of from six months to two years, culminate in indigestion. Then comes malnutrition, which results from long-continued indigestion. The third stage is anemia from malnutrition. The fourth stage is neurosis: the ganglia have been long bathed in waste-laden blood. Finally psychosis may arise.

Hence endometritis may induce: (*a*) indigestion, (*b*) malnutrition, (*c*) anemia, (*d*) neurosis, and (*e*) psychosis.

Again, consider heart palpitation at the menopause. It can be explained by reflex action. The child-bearing period of a woman is thirty years. During that time regular monthly forces have been transmitted over the hypogastric plexus to induce uterine and oviductal rhythm. Now, at the menopause, the hypogastric plexus degenerates and will not carry the forces, which consequently accumulate. The accumulated forces in the abdominal brain go up the splanchnic to the three cervical ganglia, where they are reorganized and flashed to the heart, causing it to work either too rapidly, or fitfully. This explains palpitation at menopause.

Exactly the same explanation suffices for liver disease during this period.

At the menopause the heat, circulatory, and sweet centers are irritated, and the woman has flashes of heat, flushes of blood and "spells" of sweating.

Pigmentation is also from reflex action: the irritation spending its main force on the liver and the spleen, causes pigmentation.

The genitals are profoundly supplied by the sympathetic. Observe the double lateral supply and also the central hypogastric supply. There are two ovarian ganglia at the origin of the ovarian arteries. There are two giant pelvic brains or cervico-uterine ganglia, and these pelvic brains are connected by some thirty strands to the great abdominal brain. The uterus, the popular center of the genitals, though anatomically the ovary is the real central genital organ, is supplied from the abdominal brain by means of the lateral hypogastric plexus chain, and the second, third, and fourth sacral nerves. The pelvic brain demedullates the nerves, so that, though the three sacral nerves supply the uterus, it is accomplished by first sending the three sacral nerves through the pelvis, where they are demedullated before reaching the uterus. In an anatomic and physiologic sense the pelvic brain is of extreme importance on account of its vascular influence over the uterus and oviducts, on account of its control to some extent of uterine and oviductal rhythm, and on account of its influence on the nourishment of the uterus and oviducts. Also, perhaps, parturition is instigated by pressure or trauma of the cervico-uterine ganglion by the expanding cervix; in other words, trauma to the pelvic brain. There are adjacent ganglia to the pelvic brain which influence the uterus, bladder and vagina, holding these three organs in intimate connection. There is the plexus vesicalis (vesical ganglion), the hypogastric plexus, and the plexus utero-vaginal (pelvic brain), all three closely connected anatomically and also connecting anatomically and physiologically the bladder, cervix and uterus.

It is daily gynecologic observation that the uterus and bladder functionate together through nerve connection—especially the sympathetic. However, the chief function of the pelvic brain is to rule the uterus, as will be observed, by noting that the major branches of this ganglion pass to the body of the uterus. A small part of the uterine nerves originates from the hypogastric plexus, which supplies the side and dorsal surface of the uterus. From the pelvic brain and vesical ganglion, nerves accompany the uterine artery along the lateral borders of the uterus, sending branches to the uterus on the horizontal arteries, and to the oviducts which, by union with the ovarian nerves, form the ovarian ganglion. From the ovarial ganglion, nerves pass to the anterior side of the uterus, to the inner and middle parts of the oviduct and to the broad ligaments.

The ligamentum teres uteri is composed of nonstriped muscle and is supplied by both the uterine and ovarian nerves. The uterus is supplied in its muscularis by an extraordinary, rich network of nerves, which is continued into the muscularis vaginæ. The uterine mucosa has numerous ganglia distributed in its substance. The nerve endings pass to the epithelia of the single organs. The small capillaries are enclosed in a network of nerves.

IV. GENERAL VIEWS OF PAIN IN GYNECOLOGY.

Pain in gynecology is generally described as typical in character. This is observed from the terms which writers employ. Some designate the pain as nongenuine, others as hysteric, and again as illegitimate, ideal or physical. Perhaps with more accuracy one might designate the pain as from the cortex of the cerebro-spinal axis. It should be recognized that a more rational classification of pain in gynecology is demanded.

Hysteria, if the term be employed, must be recognized by definite stigmata. It is true in gynecology we are dealing chiefly with the subjective sensations of the patient. The pain appears to the patient as immeasurably severe and terrible. Frequently the only standard is the patient's tears, fears or moans, and her comparison of dragging, tearing or boring. We can to some extent estimate colic pains of hollow organs as uterine and intestinal conditions. But it is remarkable how gynecologic patients bear the genuine pain of labor and other colicky pains with little complaint and slight fear of its repetition; while the immeasurable and often apparently nongenuine pain of hyperesthesia causes exaggerated and bitter complaints. The intensity of pain can be supposed but never sharply measured. An exudate can be palpated, the amount of blood loss judged, the growth of a tumor estimated, but the determination of pain rests alone on the dogmatic assertion of the patient. It is a physical phenomenon. As Dr. Lomer states in his excellent investigations, pain is an increase of touch sensation, and has a psychical character. Doubtless the sensory periphery apparatus ends first in the skin (hyperesthesia and anesthesia), and second in the mucosa (hyperesthesia and anesthesia).

The chief center of pain for the periphery apparatus of skin or mucosa lies in the dorsal sensory ganglia of the spinal cord.

Disease in either the spinal sensory ganglia or the sensory periphery, unbalances the nervous system. Analysis and clinical observation would indicate that the hyperesthesia and anesthesia are of central (cerebro-spinal) origin. Head, of England, reported some ingenious experiments, in which every visceral disease is announced through the sympathetic nerve by a specific zone of skin tenderness. The center of the sympathetic fiber lies directly in the sensory nerve. If a sympathetic irritation arises it is reflected on the tract of the sensory nerve to its specific skin periphery. The result is a specific tender skin zone. In fact, Head allots a typical sensory skin zone for each individual viscus. For example, there is a specific zone of skin tenderness for a stone in the kidneys, a stone in the gall bladder, or a diseased uterus or ovary. However, this is only another way of saying that visceral irritation passes to the spinal cord, and after reorganization, radiates on the muscular nerves of the abdomen and also on the skin nerves of the abdomen. Irritation of the periphery of visceral, muscular, or skin nerves, affects the other two by reflection. In any case, the process of transmission of pain from periphery to center is a complicated one. The variation of intensity of pain is equally shared by variation of its quality as boring, sticking, burning, cutting, tearing, dull and jumping pain. One can suppose an organ pain, as a toothache, an earache, ovarian pain, uterine and intestinal colic, tenesmus of urethra or rectum. Organ pains require an agent or irritation to start them, and are not a quality of the nerves of the viscus itself.

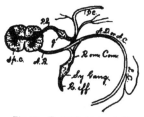

Fig. 70. (Byron Robinson.) Represents a plan of a dorsal nerve. (*Sp. c.*) Spinal cord. (*p. b.*) Posterior branch. (*a. b.*) Anterior branch. (*g.*) Ganglion on posterior root. (*ram. com.*) Ramus communicans. (*sy. gang.*) Sympathetic ganglion. (*p. c.*) Posterior cutaneous. (*a. d. or a. c.*) Anterior division. (*l. c.*) Lateral cutaneous branch.

From practical gynecology, pain may be classified as follows, viz.:

1. Traumatic (wound) pain, the irritation of sensory nerves from external insults. Frequent examples of traumatic pain occur in the urethral, vulval, hymenial, perineal, and anal lacerations. The pain is acute, but quickly subsides. However, it is easily revived by functionating of the organs, or secretions flowing on the wound. Destruction of nerves, as from burns or chemicals, has the most intense and persistent pain. Patients generally describe traumatic (wound) pain as burning or smarting. An ice bag is effectual in alleviating such pain.

2. Contractile (colic) pain, the irritation of the sensory nerves through muscular contraction. It is vascular spasm. The well known examples of contractile pain (colic) are uterine and intestinal colic, the over-filled rectum, oviducts, or urinal or gall bladder. Vaginismus, though of other origin, is a typical example. This pain is rhythmic or peristaltic. It rises to a maximum and sinks to a minimum. It is described as an ache.

3. Inflammatory pain, the irritation caused by trophic changes in sensory nerves. The changes are produced by pressure (exudation) or chemical effects on the sensory nerve endings. It is the degenerative disturbance in the sensory nerve area. Its conditions are calor, rubor, tumor,—dolor. The pain, though complicated, is described as sticky, cutting, and beating, and as a rule is extraordinarily painful.

4. Neuralgic pain; the irritation produced by changes in the sensory nerve itself and perhaps its ganglion. Neuralgic pain is characterized by attacks and intermissions. It is typically observed in herpes zoster and herpes vulvaris. The neuralgic pain is described as lancinating or lightning-like in character. It is characteristic for neuralgic pain to remain limited to a definite nerve territory. It is unilateral. It commonly attacks the ilio-inguinal nerve or external cutaneous, also the pudendal and intercostal.

5. Hysterical pain, the irritation caused by disturbances in the cerebro-spinal system. This pain is limited to no organ or nerve zone. It exists perhaps equally among men, women, and children. Hysteria has no more to do with the uterus than with the liver or testicle. It is not a gynecologic disease. It is true, gynecologic subjects possess it, but often from devitalized power. It exists independent of nerve distribution. It is not influenced by rest, or scarcely, perhaps, through drugs. The fundamental cause of hysteria is heredity, the transmission of defects or a neuropathic condition. The provocative agent of hysteria is some debilitating effect, mental or physical. Dr. Lomer insists that the hyperesthetic and anesthetic zones of the skin are geometrical figures. Hysteria depends on psychical alteration. It is generally described as burning pain. The two chief therapeutic agents for hysteria are (*a*) suggestions and (*b*) limited galvanic electricity. Hyperesthesia may perhaps exist in any viscus, and the typical characteristic of hysteria being hyperesthesia of the abdominal skin, that attribute could be found anywhere on the skin if sought.

Hysteria distinguishes itself from all other diseases by certain stigmata. One or more of these stigmata must be present to diagnose any case of hysteria. The stigmata of hysteria are:

1. Hyperesthesia of the skin, which consists in exaltation of the sensory periphery. These areas, hystero-genetic zones, are especially found on the skin of the abdomen. They are painful or over-sensitive on touch. The patient is often deceived by thinking the pain in the skin of the groin refers to the ovary. Hystero-genetic zones or hyperesthetic areas occur all over the body, but in the sexual region they are apt to be more typical on account of the patient's active attention. The skin over the ovary or the kidney may be so hyperesthetic and tender that grave kidney disease may be suspected. The skin over any abdominal viscus may be so tender that touching it induces the patient to scream, while the viscus itself is quite healthy. Hyperesthesia exists chiefly on the right side. Pinching or pricking the skin enables one to discern the zones of hyperesthesia.

Hyperesthesia of the skin on the abdomen may exist with or without healthy genitals. Of course the hyperesthesia of the skin is more liable to exist with diseased genitals, as the genitals may be the provocative or debilitating agent inducing the hysteria. The patients who are disturbed by crawling sensations on the skin, as of snakes and ants, have hyperesthesia and hence have hysteria. Hyperesthetic spots anywhere on the body constitute one of the stigmata of hysteria. I observed hyperesthetic spots year after year on a woman's back. The hyperesthesia of the skin may change its location. The frequency of skin hyperesthesia in the gynecologic clinic induces me to believe in the wide distribution of hysteria, independent of gynecology.

2. Anesthesia of the skin is also another stigma of hysteria. This is not so frequent in the clinic. The patient complains of the skin being numb and without feeling. It is found, perhaps, most frequently on the skin of the abdomen. Anesthesia exists chiefly on the left side of the body.

3. Anesthesia of the mucosa is one of the stigmata of hysteria seldom absent. The test is easily made by taking a pin with a small glass head and rubbing it over the eyeball. If the conjunctiva bulbi is anesthetic, one can rub the pinhead over the eyeball without a wink or flinch from the patient. Normally the conjunctiva is very sensitive, and to touch it produces reflex actions, tears and pain. Nearly always in the hysteria the rubbing of the pinhead on the eyeball produces no reflexes, no tears, no pain. Of course there are many grades of anesthesia of the conjunctiva bulbi. The corneal anesthesia is the least frequent. The anesthesia of the throat is tested by a lead pencil or sound. On rubbing the mucosa of the throat, no reflex nor pain arises. As Windscheid remarks, however, the diagnosis of hysteria should not be made from anesthesia of the throat alone, as in healthy subjects the mucosa of the throat may show various degrees of anesthesia.

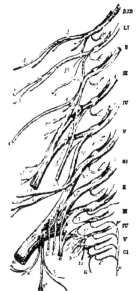

DIAGRAM OF LUMBAR AND PELVIC PLEXUSES (QUAIN)

Fig. 71. (DXII.) Last dorsal. (1S.) First sacral. (8) Pudic. (Sc.) Sciatic. (V.) Lumbo-sacral.

4. Hyperesthesia of the mucosa must be remembered among the stigmata of hysteria, though infrequent. The persistent feeling of animals crawling in the tractus intestinalis (abdomen) is no doubt a symptom of an over-tender mucous membrane. The sudden expulsion of unchanged foods from some stomachs immediately after eating is no doubt due to hyperesthesia (non-toleration) of the gastric mucosa.

Hyperesthesia of the viscera is one of the known stigmata of hysteria. Perhaps visceral hyperesthesia exists the most frequently in the ovary. In such cases the ovary is hypersensitive to touch, yet normal in size and position, perfectly mobile, with no peritoneal adhesions or fever. Castration does not affect the pain unless it exacerbates it. The irritable uterus of the old doctors is undoubtedly of hysteric nature. To show that such cases are hysteric, the uterus, oviducts and ovaries have been removed, but the pain persists just as before the operation. I once operated on a hyperesthetic kidney in which I suspected stone, but no stone existed and the pain persisted as before the operation. Hyperesthesia of the cord and testicle frequently exists. Vaginismus is perhaps as typically hysterical as any example of the viscera. Vaginismus may be called up by the thought of touching the vulva. It is chiefly of psychical origin and occurs in neuropathic individuals. It is common to note hyperesthesia of the orificium vaginæ, and an exacerbation of this leads to various grades of vaginismus.

The hymen has been extirpated in vaginismus, but without good effect. There can be little doubt that hysteric bladders frequently arise in the practice. I once treated a patient two years for a hysteric bladder. Drugs had little or no effect. Rest in bed made no change. Suggestion was the best treatment. Urine was normal. It was so-called irritable bladder, hysteria. The patients with irritable or hysteric uterus are the ones who prepare for the child's advent by making the clothing, and sending for the midwife. They suffer from labor pains, and finally call the obstetrician when labor does not complete itself, only to find that the patient is not even pregnant. She is misled by her irritable, hyperesthetic, hysteric uterus. The abdominal cramps and colic of certain neuropathic patients are doubtless due to visceral hyperesthesia or hysteria.

5. The muscular stigma of hysteria is quite common. It consists in the paresis or paralysis of one or more muscles, or it consists in exacerbation of contractions of one or more muscles. When the tongue suddenly ceases to act, with subsequent normal action, it is quite sure to be hysterical in nature. Globus hystericus is simply exacerbated activity of the esophageal and gastric muscles. Hysteric knee is a spasmodic contraction of the muscles supplying it. The lost voice is frequently of hysteric nature, due to disturbances of laryngeal muscles. The "lumps" or tumors in the abdomen of many patients are simply the contractions of certain abdominal muscles, frequently accompanied by hyperesthesia of the skin over them. The patient complains of a tender tumor, and the diaphragm or groups of muscles become spasmodic.

6. Another stigma of hysteria is psychosis. It is perverted mental action. Hysteria is chiefly manifest to the gynecologist as a psychical disease. It is a part of a neurosis, very changeable, and ever presenting new scenes. It doubtless rests on a psycho-pathic construction. The psychosis rests also no doubt on a defective system. An irritable weakness exists in the nervous system. The central or peripheral nervous system is defective. The hysteric condition is especially susceptible to influence or suggestibility.

7. Exaltation or diminution of the special senses is also a stigma, as blindness or exalted hearing. Heredity or congenital defect is a large factor.

Whatever debilitates the nervous system, local or general, invites hysteria as a provocative agent. It should be remembered that genital disease (infectious) is debilitating, and hence is followed frequently by hysteria. Sexual diseases (in man or woman) no doubt play a vast rôle in hysteria. They are productive agents. Of special interest are the hyperesthetic zones of the abdomen; i. e., the periphery of the sensory nerves of the abdomen.

8. The sensory periphery area of the ilio-inguinal, ilio-hypogastric and that of the eight lower intercostals, become exalted in sensation. Hysteria is a disease of symptoms. There are two theories of hysteria extant at

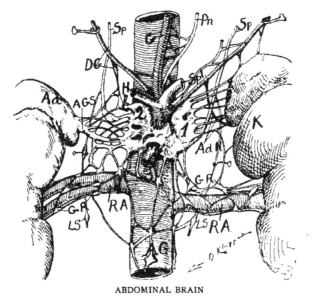

ABDOMINAL BRAIN

Fig. 72. This illustration I dissected under alcohol. It represents fairly accurately the cerebrum abdominale in the general subject.

present, viz.: (*a*) It is a psychosis, a mental disturbance. Its seat is the cerebral cortex. (*b*) It is a neurosis or a psycho-neurosis. It is not limited to the cerebral cortex, but is a disease of the whole nervous system. It is a disease of rapidly changing panorama.

The treatment of hysteria must be rational, systematic, prolonged, and continuously suggestive. Drain the skin by salt rubs, massage; drain the kidneys by ample drinking of fluids; drain the bowels by proper diet, sufficient laxation, and fluid and regular evacuations. Tonics to improve digestion, drugs to act on the senses, especially the olfactory; electricity to act on the cerebral cortex, and continual suggestions with firm discipline. Above all ideas of hysteria or neurasthenia must stand the thought that all operations to cure them are to be abandoned.

In gynecologic patients there is a triumvirate of pain—back, head, and stomach. It represents three groups of painful localities.

1. The lumbo-sacral region is the seat of the most prevalent and persistent. It is the central station which interprets the pain of the pelvic sensory periphery. Almost every gynecologic affection creates lumbo-sacral symptoms, whether it be dislocation, inflammation, contractile pain, sacropubic hernia, mechanical pressure or malignant growths. In short, the lumbo-sacral region is the sensorium of gynecology of the pelvis. The spinal ganglion must act as local substitute for the brain. The explanation of this lies in the kind of nerves: visceral, peritoneal, muscular, and cutaneous, which report to the lumbo-sacral cord.

The visceral nerves are the second, third and fourth sacral and the sympathetic—all transmit reflexes to the lumbo-sacral cord from irritation of the genitals.

The peritoneal nerves are branches of the ilio-inguinal, the ilio-hypogastric, and the seven lower intercostals, which transmit pelvic peripheral irritation to the lumbo-sacral cord.

The muscular nerves of the lumbo-sacral plexus and also those of the muscular seven lower intercostals transmit disturbances to the lumbo-sacral cord.

The cutaneous branches of the lumbo-sacral plexuses, especially the pudic, the pudendal, the ilio-inguinal, ilio-hypogastric and seven lower intercostal cutaneous branches, report irritation to the sacro-lumbar cord.

The irritation of the periphery of any of the three great branches of the lumbo-sacral cord, viz., cutaneous, muscular or viscero-peritoneal, disturbs the balance of the other two. Irritation of the visceral sensory periphery unbalances the sensory periphery of the muscular and cutaneous nerves. The spinal ganglia are reorganizers and transmit all reports to every periphery. This is a cue to therapeutic agents, e. g., cutaneous irritation is carried to the spinal cord and reflected on the muscular and visceral branches, stimulating both.

2. Gynecologic disease refers a group of pain to the stomach.

3. Another group is referred to the head. Laparotomy wounds seldom or never give rise to pain if union is by first intention. The lower angle of the wound is sometimes painful under pressure, but it is undoubtedly due to suppuration from close proximity to the region of the hair. Dorsal muscles are inclined to rheumatism, while those of the abdomen are not; hence, more accurate judgment arises as to painful abdominal incisions. Special attention should be paid to hyperesthesia of the abdominal skin by the gynecologist and surgeon, as it may exist without visceral disease, and hence may be nonsurgical. So-called "irritable" organs with no visible or palpable anatomic change, should be referred to hysteria.

When a rational treatment is systematically carried on against painful local disturbance, without effect, the probability is that it is a hysteric hyperesthesia. The excessive vomiting of pregnancy often has a hysteric base—hyperesthesia of the gastric mucosa. In the same hysteric category must often be numbered, coccygodynia, coxalgia, irritable bladder, breast, and uterus, vaginismus, pruritus, dysmenorrhea, and a sense of lumbo-sacral symptoms. A knowledge of the above factors is particularly valuable to the operator as the sweeping removal of organs for neurosis or hyperesthesia is criminal. Remember that morbid sensibility lies chiefly in the skin, and the patient will complain more of a skin pinch than a deep-seated trauma. What the hysteric coxalgia or hysteric knee is to the surgeon, so is the hyperesthesia of the abdomen to the gynecologist. The puzzle of each solves itself under the analysis for stigmata.

CHAPTER XXIV.

HYPERESTHESIA OF THE SYMPATHETIC.

"Surmises are not facts. Suspicions which may be unjust need not be stated."
—Abraham Lincoln.

"Men are merriest when they are from home."—Shakespeare.

1. Hyperesthesia of the abdominal brain (Neuralgia Celiaca) consists of a sudden violent pain in the region of the stomach. The pain is accompanied by a sense of fainting and impending anxious dread. It manifests itself, objectively, chiefly in the character of the circulation and in the facial appearance. The skin is pale, the extremities cold, the muscles assume vigorous contractions, especially over the abdomen, and the heart beats under tension and may intermit. The abdominal muscles are put on a stretch. Some patients are occasionally relieved by pressure on the stomach. From the intimate and close anatomical connection of the abdominal brain with all the abdominal viscera, and also the thoracic viscera, various other symptoms of a similar character to neuralgia celiaca may and do arise, as disturbance in the action of the heart and of the gastro-intestinal tract. The attacks are irregular, periodical, uncertain in time and intensity. The attack may last a few minutes to half an hour. The attack may disappear slowly or under a crisis of perspiration, emission of gas, vomiting or copious urination, leaving the patient apparently very exhausted. The peculiar characteristics of the attacks in the abdominal brain determine neuralgia celiaca from inflammatory processes of the stomach.

The most typical neuralgia celiaca coming under my notice was (1890) that of a man about 40, a real estate dealer, in whom it had persisted for perhaps ten years. I could discover no gall-bladder, heart or ureteral trouble, and no stomach lesion. He was attacked, irregularly, however, depending on over-exertion, several times a year. When attacked he felt that impending death was at hand. He screamed between paroxysms and would fall on the floor, rolling in agony for a half or three-quarters of an hour. He anticipated the terrific attacks by preparing for them with great care of his health. He would be very quiet for one or two days subsequent to the attacks; otherwise he was quite healthy. I soon lost sight of him.

The second most typical case of neuralgia celiaca in my practice was that of a woman (1888) about 28. She had very severe and frequent attacks which lasted some fifteen minutes; seemed to have terrible dread and anxiety, a wiry, small pulse, rigid abdominal muscles and varying pupils during the attack. She appeared greatly relieved by pressure directly on the stomach during the attack. She recovered with much exhaustion and relaxation; otherwise she appeared well. She died of rectal carcinoma some twelve years later. Neuralgia celiaca may exist in very various degrees of intensity and duration. In some very severe attacks it would seem from appearances and the patient's report that the suffering was more profound than an ordinary death. The chief valuable treatment consists in securing active secretion of the skin and kidneys with free bowel evacuation. General tone is secured by tonics and

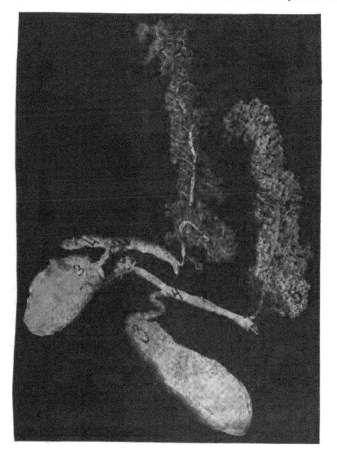

CORROSION ANATOMY

Fig. 73. Corrosion anatomy of the ductus pancreaticus and part of the ductus bilis in two subjects. The illustration suggests the quantity of nerves to control the caliber of the numerous ducts.

wholesome food; even temperature and quiet life tells the rest of the story. The treatment during the attacks is purely expectant—sedative and stimulant. Vigorous baths and wholesome suggestions are valuable. There is often more in the advice given with the medicine than in the medicine itself.

Neuralgia celiaca resembles angina pectoris more than any other neuralgia of the sympathetic ganglia. It requires judgment and skill to diagnose it from some forms of angina pectoris, and its treatment is equally as doubtful. Of course, it is physical lesions which we suspect in neuralgia of the abdominal brain, as the physician cannot consent to the view that a machine (the sympathetic ganglia) may go wrong without its becoming structurally defective somewhere. Electricity, massage and cold packing are quite effective. Some writers consider this subject under the terms gastralgia or gastrodynia. But under whatever term it may be discussed, the peculiar sense of fainting, the anxiety, dread and feeling of impending destruction of the very center of life itself during the attack, and especially its action on the vascular system, sufficiently characterize it as neuralgia of the abdominal brain—neuralgia celiaca. The diseases of the vagus manifest themselves otherwise.

2. Hyperesthesia of the mesenteric plexus (Neuralgia Mesenterica, enteralgia, enterodynia or colic) signifies pain in the region of the bowel supplied by the nerves accompanying the superior mesenteric artery, i. e., the region of the small intestine and the large bowel from the appendix to the splenic flexure. The pain is irregular, dragging, sickening, pinching, boring, accompanied by a sense of tenderness over the abdomen. The pain shifts from one segment of the bowel to another; is generally located below the umbilicus; alternates with intervals of cessation and does not generally begin suddenly, but gradually ascends to a maximum. It may be so severe as to induce a sense of faintness. Some patients assume positions to ease the pain, as pressing the hands on the abdomen, bending the thighs on the abdomen; some are very restless under the attacks. The abdomen may be distended with gas or retracted. The attack may pass off with crisis of the passage of gas, vomiting, sweating, profuse urination. The attacks last from a few minutes to several hours. Some patients are subject to these attacks for some months in succession. The patient may have intervals of entire freedom from the attacks. Yet the general observation is that constipation characterizes patients with mesenteric neuralgia. It is understood here that the pain does not arise from a recognizable, demonstrable organic lesion, as ulceration of the mucosa, lesion of the bowel wall or serosa, but from a nervous base. The pain may be merely short, sharp twinges, which some neurotic women describe year in and year out. The clinical picture of the disease offers manifold variations. Some patients have meteorism, pain about the navel, rumbling (borborygmus) in the bowels. Some have gurgling in the intestines, which appears to be due to a sudden irregular contraction of the bowel which rapidly forces the contents onward. In fact, patients with neuralgia mesenterica often possess a catalogue of other neurotic manifestations. Nausea, dysuria and tenesmus may be present. The chief accompaniment of this disease is perhaps constipation. However, the pains of mesenteric neuralgia should not be confounded with those of intestinal colic.

The first author of celebrity who wrote with clear views on the distinction between neuralgia mesenterica and intestinal colic was Thomas Willis (1622-1675), an English physician well remembered by anatomists in the "Circle of Willis," in numbering the cranial nerves and in the nerve of Willis (the spinal accessory). Willis observed over 230 years ago that mesenteric neuralgia was not a disease, but merely a symptom. He said it should be distinguished from the vulgar term, "the gripes" (intestinal colic). Willis also noted what others see today, that the more violent attacks of mesenteric neuralgia generally have regular periods and follow the changes of the weather and the season; when once excited they yield with difficulty to remedies, do not pass off quickly, and may persist for weeks with great violence. In regard to the seat of pain, it may be noted that in the same individual it generally repeats itself in the same region. The nerve tract sufficiently defective to harbor a neuralgia tends to retain the defect throughout life. It may be remembered that the superior mesenteric nerve supplies over twenty feet of small and nearly three feet of large intestine—a vast area—and besides, the small intestine shifts very much daily; hence, the pains of mesenteric neuralgia may be in the lumbar, umbilical and hypogastric regions. If the pain occurs at the pit of the stomach, it is likely located in the transverse colon.

The clinical picture of mesenteric neuralgia is so manifold in its aspect that it requires the best heads and the finest skill to unravel the complicated symptoms. The differential diagnosis is difficult. In certain cases where the symptoms lessen after the evacuation of peculiarly formed rolls of mucus there is a mixed neorosis.

Again, the mesenteric neuralgia, while it exists, may be complicated by attacks of asthma, nausea, dysuria, hysteria or other nervous affections, to which subjects afflicted with mesenteric neuralgia are prone. In cases of mesenteric neuralgia, certain regions of the abdominal skin may show hyperesthesia from the connection shown to exist between the viscera and the abdominal skin. Mr. Head, of London, in "Brain," 1894, demonstrated the close relation existing between the nerves of the abdominal viscera and the nerves of certain skin areas. Hence, in cases of mesenteric neuralgia hyperesthetic skin areas on the abdomen may be expected. In the incipiency it may be difficult to differentiate a beginning peritonitis from mesenteric neuralgia. But of worth in such a diagnosis as peritonitis are temperature, pain on pressure on the abdomen, general pain and increase of pain by deep pressure on the abdomen. With time the meteorism, singultus and exudate become more evident in peritonitis. In gallstone colic tenderness on pressure arises and is localized. Icterus may follow to aid. Renal colic is differentiated from mesenteric neuralgia by its being localized in the region of the kidney, by its continual radiation along the ureters toward the bladder and testicles, by the severe, dragging character of the pain, and by the occasional expulsion of a calculus; yet renal colic in some cases may so simulate mesenteric neuralgia that differential diagnosis is very difficult, if not impossible. This might occur when the renal irritation flashes to the abdominal brain, becomes reorganized and radiates along the vast area of the superior mesenteric nerve. An ulcer in the bowel shows constant localized pain on pressure. The patient's history, the omission of the characteristic periodic attacks, the formation of the stools, aid in diagnosing ulcer of the intestines. It may be impossible to make a differential diagnosis in the incipient stage of the disease.

The most typical species of mesenteric neuralgia known to the writer is lead colic, colica saturnina. Lead colic is preceded by a stage of constipation accompanied by oppressive pains in the abdomen, chiefly about the umbilicus. Nausea, eructations, destroy the appetite. Pinching, twisting and drawing pains occur with different duration and intensity. The pains are often persistently localized, do not frequently shift, occur in paroxysms. The pains of lead colic, mesenteric neuralgia, are apt to arise to the highest pitch at night and when they lessen are apt to leave annoying sensations, allowing little rest during the intervals of paroxysms. The diagnosis is aided by the patient's occupation, history association, condition and state of climate. Arthritis, rheumatism and malaria induce neuralgia.

Having established the diagnosis of mesenteric neuralgia, the treatment will refer to a certain extent to the etiology. Older practitioners relied too much on evacuation and opium. Modern practice attempts to correct the malnutrition.

The first symptom of significance in mesenteric neuralgia is pain. The second symptom of importance is constipation. Both symptoms demand vigorous attention. The treatment will first consist in attempting to establish the etiology of the mesenteric neuralgia. Is it due to dietetic defects, spirituous liquors, narcotics, intestinal contents, coprostasis, colica flatulenta, animal parasites, metallic poisoning, or catching cold? Or again, is the neuralgia due to general nervous affections, as neurasthenia, to an exalted irritability of the bowel, nerves and ganglia? Is it caused by hysteria or locomotor ataxia? Or is the mesenteric neuralgia induced by some diseased abdominal viscus reflecting its irritation to the abdominal brain, whence reorganized it is flashed over the vast area of the superior mesenteric nerve, rippling the bowel in whole or in segments. An investigation of the above considerations will influence the treatment.

First, the pain, real or pretended, will demand attention. Opium should be avoided if possible. Valerian, asafetida, i. e., drugs with effect on the sense of smell, influence favorably, but perhaps there is more in the suggestion or advice which accompanies the drug than in the drug itself. I have observed better results from hot, moist poultices (corn meal), making the poultice a foot square and three to six inches thick and applying it over the abdomen. Cold packing of the abdomen in heavy, wet towels often does well. Electricity has good moral and physical effects. A hypodermic of morphine, 1-16 of a grain, is effective. However, we must admit that a good dose of opium, e. g., ½ to 1 grain, works wonders for a time in mesenteric neuralgia. The bromides are slow but effective· however, they generally disturb digestion. Potassium bromide should be avoided, as it irritates mucosa and skin, frequently calling up rashes; 20 to 30 grains of sodium

NEURALGIA OF THE NERVUS VASOMOTORIUS

bromide will produce a quiet nervous system, especially inducing restful nights and quiet sleep.

The pain of mesenteric neuralgia being disposed of, the more important subject of the curative treatment should be carefully considered. The most important symptom after the pain is that of constipation. The bowels are indolent and are affected but slowly, even by active purgatives. The evacuations are scanty and difficult to perform. The feces are dry, globular in shape and brittle. The patients are distressed by fruitless strainings. It is useless

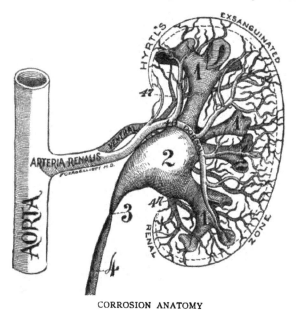

CORROSION ANATOMY

Fig. 74. Corrosion anatomy of the kidney, presenting ureteral pelvis, calyces and arteria renalis, suggesting the quantity of nerves required to control these canals.

to attempt to cure such patients without a strict and rigid regimen. In the first place, such patients will not drink sufficiently; and, secondly, they lack a regular hour for evacuation. I have treated scores of patients successfully for the constipated habit by directing that a large tumblerful of water, with magnesium sulphate, half of a dram to a dram dissolved in it, be drank every night. Also, that the patient be directed to go to stool every morning after breakfast, i. e., after the hot coffee is drank, which aids peristalsis. Direction should be given to eat food which leaves a large bulk of residue, as oatmeal, cornmeal, and graham bread. This residual bulk stimulates the intestines to active peristalsis by contact in every successive segment. Daily passages of the bowel and electricity aid to rouse the indolent digestive tract to normal activity. The constant use of a very small pill of aloin, belladonna and strychnine is very effective. Colonic flushings two to four times weekly, salt water and friction baths, aid nature in restoring lost tone. Change of environment, climate, a sea voyage, but, perhaps better, long daily walks, are beneficial. Horseback and bicycle riding are helpful.

The course of mesenteric neuralgia as regards life is favorable; the attacks, which vary very much as regards intensity, endure from one to several hours. Neuralgias arise in the sympathetic. Collins demonstrated that the arteries of the abdominal viscera were possessed of great sensibility in which the arteries of other parts were wanting. It is likely that the nerves accompanying the mesenteric artery participate in the reflex irritation, inducing the neuralgia.

Hyperesthesia of the hypogastric plexus consists of irregular, periodic pains radiating from the abdomen to the genitals, bladder and down the thighs (including the inferior mesenteric plexus), and in the rectum. The hypogastric plexus passes from the abdominal brain along the aorta, common iliacs, and from the bifurcation of the aorta two large strands pass on to complete the pelvic brain or cervical uterine ganglia. In the female the hypogastric plexus chiefly supplies the uterus and oviducts; in the male the prostrate and vesiculæ seminales. In both sexes it supplies the bladder, along the three vesical arteries and the root of the iliac and femoral. In the female the two large branches of the hypogastric plexus, composed of twenty to thirty strands of nerves, pass off from the region of the inferior mesenteric ganglion and end distinctly in the pelvic brain situated on each side of the cervix. In the male these same branches, though less in size, pass to the prostate and semen-sacs, but the pelvic brain I have found is vastly smaller in males than in females. Yet a small dog possesses quite a large pelvic brain on the side of the prostate and ending of the vas deferens.

The pain in hypogastric neuralgia must be sought for in the anatomical tracts and periphery of the plexus, which will be (a) in the uterus and oviducts, (b) in the bladder, and (c) on the path of the iliaco-femoral arteries (and with the inferior mesenterium), the rectum. Also, since the origin of the hypogastric plexus is inseparably blended with that of the spermatic and hemorrhoidal plexus, we must expect to find more or less pain occurring in the ovaries, testicles, rectum and sigmoid.

So far as I am aware Romberg was the first to describe the hyperesthesia of the hypogastric in 1840. It is a neuralgic affection manifested by tenderness and pain in the hypogastric region. There is a sense of pain and dragging in the pelvis, i. e., in the uterus, oviducts, bladder and to some extent the rectum. In women the pain is spoken of as dragging, i. e., as if the uterus were prolapsing. The characteristic pain is paroxysmal, periodic, and is not relieved by changes of position. Structural changes cannot be demonstrated. Since it is not practical to separate the inferior mesenteric plexus from the hypogastric on account of their intimate and close anatomic relations, we will consider that the hyperesthesia of the inferior mesenteric or hemorrhoidal plexus is intimately blended with hyperesthesia of the hypogastric plexus, the periodic, and is not relieved by changes of position spoken of as hemorrhoidal neuralgia or neuralgia of the rectum, of which I knew a typical case for ten years. Neuralgia of the rectum in male or female is of an intense character. It is apt to arise at night in an abrupt or sudden manner and continue from a few minutes to an hour or two. It passes away as abruptly as it arises. It creates intense suffering. The best relief is opium suppositories. Venereal excesses appear to aggravate it. Coition momentarily relieves, but it returns quickly with more intense vigor than ever. In venereal excess the neuralgia may extend with painful exacerbations along the urethra, especially worse after coition.

In the range of the sympathetic, neuralgia is frequently followed by secondary effects, as in disturbed circulation, nutrition and secretion.

The treatment of hyperesthesia of the hypogastric and inferior mesenteric depends largely on its supposed etiology. It consists in sedatives and evacuants, hydrotherapy, vaginal and rectal douches, electricity, massage and strict diet.

The neuralgia of the hypogastric and inferior mesenteric plexuses exists almost entirely during sexual life, and especially during its active period, and though no demonstrable structural lesion may be found in the plexus of nerves, yet we must be on the alert to remove all visible physical defects for fear that the neuralgia is the secondary effect of the visible ones. The patient should be treated as well as the disease, for it pertains to the wide moral fields. Some patients, male or female, describe all sorts of pains about the genitals for months, and finally they may suddenly disappear. There is a strange connection, however, anatomically and physiologically, between the nasal mucosa (and the olfactory nerve) and the genitals (and also the rectum). Hence, it may be that valerian and asafetida will be effective remedies. A stimulant such as nux vomica is often very beneficial. The beneficial effects of nux vomica on the hyperesthesia of the hypogastric plexus may be owing to the close relation of the lumbar portion of the spinal cord and the genitals, for nux stimulates the nerves. Some old writers termed the neuralgia of the hypogastric plexus menstrual colic. It must be admitted that many of the neuralgic pains spoken of by patients in the hypogastric regions are obscure and would perhaps fit better in the chapter on visceral neurosis.

In hyperesthesia of the hypogastric plexus we must include, for convenience, the pelvic brain. This is a massive collection of compound ganglia similar to the cervical ganglia and the abdominal brain. It is located on each side of the uterus. It doubtless rules the vaso-motors in the uterus, innervates the uterus to a large extent, and is accountable for innumerable pelvic pains and for the irritable and tender uterus which is better considered in the domain of visceral neurosis.

Hyperesthesia or neuralgia of the spermatic and ovarian plexuses has occupied the attention of physicians for over a century. Astley Cooper pubished a notable work in 1880, and Curling wrote later. Romberg wrote on the subject in 1840.

In the male the spermatic plexuses of nerves extend from the origin of the spermatic artery, in the aorta, to the testicle—a long, quite rich strand of nerves. The pain exists mainly in the testicle and extends to some extent along the plexus, i. e., in the spermatic cord. The testicle is generally slightly tender, occasionally exquisitely sensitive; some subjects feel the necessity of a suspensory, and feel unable to live without it. Sometimes movements cannot be tolerated and the patient lies in bed carefully protecting the testicle from trauma or touching the bed clothing. If the testicular or spermatic neuralgia becomes intense the pains radiate down the thighs into the back, irritability of the stomach and even vomiting arising. Spermatic neuralgia generally has a more profound effect on the mind than other similar neuralgias outside of the sexual field. The subjects become melancholic, lose ambition and become full of hopeless forebodings. Many of the subjects have varicocele in various degrees. Spermatic neuralgia attacks man's sexual domain, the most profound and dominating human instinct, and if it persist, sooner or later the mind becomes deeply troubled. The patient becomes really possessed with a sexual mania.

The etiology of spermatic neuralgia is not fully known, but it prevails during the state of puberty and manhood. It is a disease of active sexual life only. Cooper, against his will, removed three testicles for spermatic neuralgia and found the gland to be perfectly healthy. Romberg had a case of spermatic neuralgia where the patient insisted, against the surgeon's advice, that the testicle be removed; however, eight days later the neuralgia appeared in the other testicle, and since it would be only eight days until his coming marriage, he preferred to retain his last testicle.

I have observed cases of spermatic neuralgia before and after operation, and am opposed to operation unless a palpable lesion exists. In males urethral neuralgia is often closely connected with spermatic neuralgia. Such forms are aggravated by coition, and especially excessive venery. Though urethral neuralgia, like other neuralgias, leaves no demonstrable pathology, yet such cases have frequently had a history of gonorrhea, or excessive venery. The passage of graduated sounds, electricity, washing out the bladder, the prohibition of sexual activity, and local applications, relieve. Some old authors, as Cooper, think that these neuralgias belong to a central irritation, but modern investigations would tend to the view that it is a peripheral irritation.

The subject of ovarian neuralgia is very indefinite. However, it is not intended to deny the existence of such a disease, but the difficulty arises in the diagnosis. It appears to me that the so-called ovarian neuralgia should be brought within the domain of visceral neurosis. For example, every gynecologist of experience has observed an irritable uterus, but it should be designated under the term visceral neurosis and not uterine neuralgia. The pain of so-called ovarian neuralgia passes down on each side of the lumbar vertebræ into the pelvis. The pain is irregular, periodic, exacerbated at the menstrual flow, and generally the ovaries are tender. There are certain women who complain of pains in the region of the ovarian plexuses for years. Physical examination discloses at times very little, if any, physical defects. Yet, by close observation and treatment by heavy douches and boro-glycerin tampons, one will frequently note improvement. The pelvic organs feel more normal than at the beginning, hence we rather favor some form of physical defect, congenital or excessive venery or some pathologic imperfection. With this view, the irritable uterus of Gooch, the most of the ovarian and other visceral neuralgias, will be more beneficially considered under visceral neurosis.

Finally, I wish to state that large numbers of subjects complaining of ovarian neuralgia can be definitely shown to suffer only from pain in the skin of the hypogastric region—it is hyperesthesia of the periphery of the ilio-guinal and ilio-hypogastric nerves.

Hyperesthesia of the gastric plexus, gastric neuralgia, is generally known as gastralgia or gastrodynia. Much that was said in regard to neuralgia of the abdominal brain applies to gastralgia. Also, it may be better to include many of the considerations of gastralgia in the chapter on visceral neuroses. Gastralgia leaves no visible trace of its pathology. But in gastralgia we may

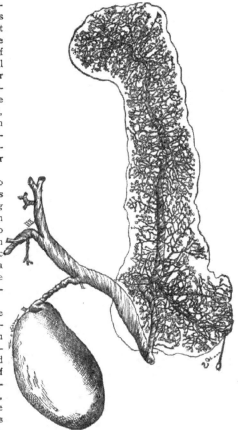

X-RAY OF DUCTUS PANCREATICUS AND PART OF DUCTUS BILIS

Fig. 75. This illustration suggests the quantity of nerves—ensheathed by a nodular, fenestrated, anastomosing plexus—supplying these channels.

look for perverted function of the stomach, as in (a) sensation, (b) secretion and (c) motion. A typical gastralgia is called up in some subjects by taking ice water just following meals; in others, the gastralgia may occur at any time. The chief conditions under which gastralgia is met induces the conviction that it is secondary to some visceral disturbances, and hence the subject is better placed under visceral neuroses.

The Hyperesthesia of the Cervical Ganglia.—Ganglia of such vast size and possessing so much physiologic influence as the cervical must be considered being subject to the same diseases as other similar ganglia. Those who have studied the sympathetic from clinical, experimental and autopsic grounds, chiefly agree that the main pathology is found in the cervical and great abdominal ganglia. The chief influence of the cervical ganglia is manifest on the eye, vessels of the head and neck and the heart.

The Hyperesthesia or Neuralgia of the Cardiac Plexus (Angina Pectoris, Stenocardia, Heberden's Disease, 1768) is a painful affection of the nerves of the heart. It is so far not anatomically definable, but is undoubtedly connected with the sympathetic nerve.

\ Angina pectoris is a disease based on no one factor, but depends on a group of factors, which appear to have origin in the cardiac plexus. It is characterized by its marked tendency to recur in paroxysms occasionally of intense severity. In one case, a man fifty years of age attended by my colleague, Dr. O. W. MacKellar, the patient was attacked with angina pectoris and died in six hours. Hypodermic injection of morphine did not appear to give relief. In conjunction with Dr. MacKellar, I performed a postmortem on the patient's body fifteen hours later. I found the heart large, dilated, slight fatty degeneration and the coats of the coronary arteries a little thickened. The fatty degeneration, the sclerosis of the coronary arteries and the dilatation of the cardiac walls, were distinct enough to be easily observed, but not of a remarkable type.

One of my patients has suffered attacks of angina pectoris for eleven years. Otherwise she has enjoyed fair health. Angina pectoris originates in the circulatory system, which is ruled by the sympathetic.

The lesion of angina pectoris is so variable and uncertain that it is impossible to designate its pathology. The cardiac plexus is so intimately and closely connected with the abdominal brain, both anatomically and physiologically, that each involves the domain of the other. In angina pectoris the cardiac plexus and abdominal brain are in such a state of hyperesthesia or irritability that at any time a terrific attack may arise. The attack comes on suddenly, frequently after some brisk exercise or mental activity. John Hunter died in a paroxysm of angina pectoris, brought on by an altercation with hospital authorities.

The pain begins in the region of the heart, but rapidly radiates in other directions, especially down the left arm even to the fingers, perhaps by means of the nervous tract made by the junction of the intercosto-humeral (second dorsal) and the lesser cutaneous nerve (nerve of Wrisberg). The patient during the attack is profoundly affected. The face shows anxious dread and fear of impending death. The pulse may be small, quick and irregular. Respiration is labored, the face is pale and the patient presents a picture of terrible distress. One of my patients required a couple of days to recover from an attack, fearing a recurrence by any active movement. The attacks of angina pectoris are uncertain in intensity, regularity or even in the organs most severely attacked. Hence, the varying accounts of different observers.

The essential features which we have observed in the attacks are (1) pain in the cardiac region; (2) profoundly anxious feeling of the patient, and (3) disturbed heart action. The disturbed respiration may be due to the terrible pain accompanying the attack. That the paroxysmal pain in angina pectoris arises in the cardiac plexus we do not doubt, but why it arises there and why it is paroxysmal we can only guess, as we are still doing in other neuralgias. If it is due to ossification of the aorta and coronary arteries and consequent pressure on the adjacent cardiac plexuses of nerves, why does it occur so far apart and in such a paroxysmal character? The sympathetic cardiac nerves come from wide areas, hence varied and widely distinct pain. Each of the three cervical ganglia on each side sends a nerve to the cardiac plexus and there repeatedly anastomoses with the vagus.

There is a form of angina pectoris which has its origin or influence in the abdominal viscera. It is a reflex neurosis. The far-famed experiment of Goltz served as the ground of this view. Goltz's "percussion experiment" consists in tapping the intestines when the heart may be arrested (in diastole). This idea serves perhaps to explain deaths from a blow on the pit of the stomach, i. e., on the belly brain. Hence, disturbance, pathologic conditions in the peritoneal viscera, may produce angina pectoris by reflex irritation, through the abdominal brain. Angina pectoris seems to be due to a super-sensativeness or over susceptibility of the nervous system. However, Lancereaux found in a case, which died during an attack of angina pectoris from which he had long suffered, pathologic conditions in the cardiac plexus. So far as I have observed cases of angina pectoris, the chief successful treatment consists in the diligent avoidance of sudden active exercise, physical or mental.

There are some different factors in angina pectoris which may be noted, as (a) spasm of the heart and large blood vessels, (b) a pure neuralgia, and (c) a vaso-motor disturbance produced by reflex irritation. In any or all factors it appears that the sympathetic nerve predominates. The abdominal brain may serve as an irritating factor.

Hyperesthesia of the splenic plexus has not received a description for the reason that it does not produce definite demonstrable symptoms. The plexus of nerves following the large spiral splenic artery from the abdominal brain to the spleen, lying to the left side between the ninth and tenth ribs, must play a significant role in life's action. The section of the large splenic plexus of nerves begun by Jasckhowitz and others demonstrated that the spleen had something to do with the deposit of pigment in various parts of the body. It is evident that the spleen is not a very active viscus in producing pain. Jasckhowitz showed that irritation of the splenic plexus and branch of the celiac axis lessened the size of the spleen, while ligation of the splenic plexus distended the spleen. The vasomotor nerves of the abdominal viscera are included in the sympathetic. In several hundred personal autopsies I found the spleen surrounded by peritoneal adhesions in nearly 90 per cent of adult subjects. Hence, it would be difficult to decide whether the pain was not due to the old perisplenitis. But the spleen is innervated from the same source as the stomach, and there is no reason why the spleen may not suffer from neuralgia as well as the stomach. In regard to the neuralgia of the splenic plexus, it will be required to work it out along the line of experiments, and especially on the vasomotor nerves.

Hyperesthesia of the hepatic plexus or hepatic neuralgia (diabetes mellitus) is still an obscure subject. The hepatic artery is well surrounded by strands of sympathetic nerves, and being innervated from the abdominal brain or the same source as the stomach, we see no reason why the liver will not suffer neuralgia pains similar to the stomach. We of course exclude from hepatic neuralgia all pain produced by hepatic calculus or demonstrable pathologic lesion, wherever located—in the biliary ducts, gall-bladder or common duct. Again, pain in the liver might arise from some vicious condition of the bile inducing a form of colic as it passed through the ducts to the intestine, and, besides, this pain would be of a periodic or neuralgic nature. Hepatic neuralgia signifies pain in the region of the liver possessed of a periodic nature. It may be in hepatalgia the tangible cure is overlooked. Inspissated gall may cause excruciating pain in its passage and be found in the stool in dark flakes. The passage of the dry flakes of gall may be accompanied by severe pain, nausea, exhaustion and vomiting. The right vagus as well as the sympathetic hepatic plexus, attends on the liver, so we must view the nerve supply of the liver as mixed, but since the vagus below the diaphragm is a demedullated or sympathetic nerve the final action is the same. It is found that certain injuries to the solar plexus make more blood circulate in the liver, and consequently an increased flow of bile.

Some writers consider that there is a casual relation between hepatic neuralgia and diabetes mellitus. It is very evident among writers that there exist two forms of hepatic neuralgia, viz., one accompanied with pain only in the hepatic nerves, and one with pain and the excessive secretion of glycogen (diabetes mellitus).

Dr. Powell records a case of profuse and obstinate sweating with congested liver and diabetic urine. Doubtless the hepatic plexus has power to rule the circulation of the liver to produce congestion and decongestion. Hence, the influence of the sympathetic nerve is very great in diabetes mellitus. It includes hyperemia of the liver, congestion in its capillaries, an influence on the formation of glycogen and perhaps on the ferment necessary for its production. But since the production of diabetes mellitus is a very complicated process we cannot enter into its details. The influence of the sympathetic in diabetes mellitus is observed in the menopause; when the hypogastric plexus is passing through a stage of atrophy women frequently have sugar in the urine.

In this sense diabetes mellitus is identical with hepatic neuralgia. By some irritation transmitted over the hepatic plexus the circulation of the liver is increased, and the glycogen may be excessively formed.

The uncertainty and variability of definite lesions in diabetes mellitus seem to prove that glycosuria may be induced by reflex irritation in the sympathetic. Many physiologists believe that glycosuria is due to hyperemia of the liver. Hyperemia of the liver is controlled by the sympathetic nerve. Just as in facial neuralgia, the region of the nerve involved is surrounded by

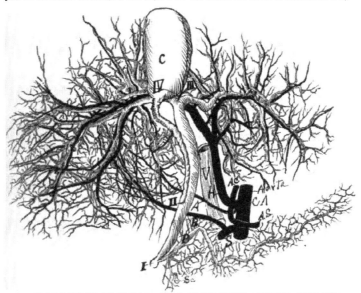

X-RAY OF DUCTUS BILIS ET PANCREATICUS WITH ARTERIA HEPATICA

Fig. 76. This illustration presents the ducts and vessels richly supplying the liver—each channel is well ensheathed with a nerve plexus.

congestion or hyperemic vessels, so in hepatic neuralgia, the vessels of the region of the hepatic nerves are followed by dilation and hyperemia and consequent glycosuria. It is not irritation of the hepatic plexus alone that produces glycosuria; irritation of the sciatic is followed by sugar in the urine.

Hyperesthesia of the Pancreatic Plexus.—Pain in the pancreatic plexus cannot be located or differentiated from hepatic neuralgia. The late researches of Minkowski would indicate that diabetes mellitus is due to disease of the pancreas. Minowski and Mering have done much valuable labor in the field of the pancreas which will aid in solving the problem of the relation of the pancreas to the diabetes mellitus.

Hyperesthesia or neuralgia of the renal plexus, nephralgia (diabetes insipidus) is an affection of the nerves of the kidney unaccompanied by any demonstrable anatomic lesion. The nerves of the kidney are almost entirely non-medullated, i. e., sympathetic. The kidney has the richest nerve supply of any organ in the body except the uterus. The renal artery is abundantly studded with large ganglia, and the nerve strands form a rich network about it. The kidney is closely and intimately connected to the abdominal brain by a large rich plexus of nerves and ganglia. The anatomic and physiologic base for vast influence of the abdominal brain over the kidney is not wanting in abundance of demonstrable sympathetic nerves and ganglia.

Knoll (1871) observed polyuria after division of the splanchnics. He placed canulas in the ureters and then divided one side at a time, so that he could observe the variation. On the side operated, the urine was considerably increased (hyperemia). Some writers claim that neuralgia of the renal plexus is accompanied with excessive flow of urine, polyuria or diabetes insipidus, while others claim that neuralgia of the renal plexus is only accompanied by pain in the nerves of the kidney and no increase of urine. In neuralgia of the renal plexus all renal calculi are excluded.

Neuralgia of the renal plexus is sometimes intense and paroxysmal, while at other times it is more continuous and less severe. The pain does not tend to radiate along the ureter as it does in uretral calculus. It is met with in persons exhausted, anemic, gouty, rheumatic and those poisoned with malaria. Exposure to wet and cold are liable to give rise to renal pain. Sedatives, evacuants, alteratives, electricity and massage are remedies employed against the disease. It is very evident among writers that there exist two forms of renal neuralgia, viz., one with pain only and one with pain and increased flow of urine (diabetes insipidus). With a large sympathetic plexus rich in ganglia, there is no reason, except from experiment, why the kidney should not suffer neuralgia similar to the other viscera, as such a condition is recognized in the nerves of the stomach, intestines, ovaries and liver. It is not presumed to exclude cerebrospinal influences entirely.

However, the renal vessels are ruled by the renal plexus, an almost purely sympathetic apparatus, having its origin in the abdominal brain.

In diabetes insipidus the characteristic feature does not consist in any especial malnutrition of food, but in paralysis of vaso-motor constrictor nerves contained in the renal plexus and consequent dilatation of renal vessels. This allows excessive blood to remain in the kidney (hyperemia). Much of diabetes insipidus depends on the condition of the circulating blood in the kidney brought out by the force of the heart and constriction or dilatation of the renal capillaries. The beneficial influence of ergot in diabetes insipidus demonstrates that the disease has a vaso-motor origin and maintenance.

Some writers speak of an idiopathic form of renal neuralgia, which doubtless means that its origin and persistence is not understood. However, as a matter of clinical knowledge, it is very rare to meet with actual renal pain unless there be some pathologic lesion of the kidney or a renal calculus present. But I have met with persistent pain and tenderness in the kidney, which neither urinary examinations nor renal explorations explained.

It is not probable that patients will persist for several years to complain of pain and tenderness (sensativeness) in the kidney without some real base. I have followed some for long periods with no discoverable pathologic facts. It is like renal neuralgia.

The Hyperesthesia of the Diaphragmatic Plexus.—This form of neuralgia has not been described as far as I am aware. The diaphragm is so thoroughly dominated by phrenic nerves that it is obscured and overlooked. Yet the diaphragm is distinctly influenced by the sympathetic. Very careful dissection will reveal in the human subject a large nerve connecting directly the inferior cervical ganglion, the ganglion stellatum, with the phrenic nerve. Dilatation of the rectum induces the patient to bray like an ass. It induces respiration—the expiratory moan. In peritonitis the experienced abdominal surgeon views with alarm the incipient sighing and irregular respiration. The diaphragmatic plexus supplies and innervates the vessels of the diaphragm. The ganglion diaphragmaticum exists on the right side only, at the point of junction of the sympathetic and phrenic nerves. The diaphragmatic plexus is connected with the adrenal and the hepatic plexuses. Doubtless some of the sharp pains on respiration owe their origin to the sympathetic in the diaphragm.

CHAPTER XXV.

MOTOR NEUROSES.

The rectum is guarded by two sphincters, viz., a larger proximal one supplied by the sympathetic, and a smaller distal one supplied by the cerebrospinal nerves.

"Our greatest danger now in this country is corporation wealth."—Wendell Phillips.

INTESTINAL MOVEMENTS.

In experiments on various animals and by clinical observation on man we may note various kinds of bowel movements. For the purpose of making the subject more intelligible we may note that the bowel wall is composed of an outer longitudinal muscular layer and of an inner circular muscular layer. The bowel is lined by a mucous membrane and covered by a serous or peritoneal membrane. The arterial supply is carried from the celiac axis to supply the stomach (gastric artery); from the superior mesenteric artery to supply the small intestines, the ascending colon and transverse colon; from the inferior mesenteric to supply the descending colon, sigmoid and rectum—in all, three segments supplied by three arteries. The nerve supply to the intestines is from three sources:

1. The cranial nerve (the pneumogastric).
2. The spinal nerves, especially those entering at the distal and proximal bowel segment.
3. The sympathetic system.

The nerve supply of the bowel is a mixed supply of cerebrospinal and sympathetic. In the sympathetic nerve supply of the bowel we must name some four sources, viz.:

(a) The Auerbach plexus (myentericus externus), situated between the circular and longitudinal muscular layers of the bowel wall. It is a nerve plexus supplying muscles.

(b) The Billroth-Meissner plexus (myentericus internus), situated under the mucosa. It is a nerve plexus supplying glandular structure and has to do with secretion.

(c) The abdominal brain (the solar plexus), situated around the origin of the celiac axis, the superior mesenteric and renal artery.

(d) The lateral chain of sympathetic ganglia, located along each side of the vertebral column. From this chain of ganglia arise the great splanchnic nerves (three or four). With a mixed nerve supply we must designate the character of the movement by the nerve which preponderates. The characteristic movements of the bowel are those of a rhythm, rising slowly to a maximum (spasm) and sinking slowly to a minimum (rest).

The ryhthmic, periodic movement belongs to the sympathetic nerve.

So that wherever the initiation or inhibition of motion may reside for the bowel wall, it is dominated by the sympathetic nerve, like all other abdominal viscera With this mixed nerve supply variously localized we may turn to the physiologic movements of the intestinal tract:

1. The peculiar peristaltic movements, which consist of a contraction and dilatation of the bowel lumen.—The motion is towards the anus and the contents move in the same direction. The most typical animal which I have examined to study the bowel peristalsis is the rabbit. In the rabbit the contraction and dilatation of the bowel wall is very rapid, traveling a foot in a few seconds. Of course this rapid traveling cannot force the feces with it. The analward wave is transmitted from one segment of the bowel to the other, in rapid succession. But with the abdomen open and the bowel struck or pinched or irritated, we must think of every successive physiologic action. The peristalsis borders on pathologic conditions. In fact, one can really see that the bowels move in a wild, irregular confusion. By pinching the bowel wall with the finger and thumb or forceps a circular constriction will arise which resembles a pale, white ring, almost closing the bowel lumen, and persisting awhile. This analward alternate contraction and dilatation of the bowel wall is a physiologic process of the bowel, and doubtless is not accompanied by pain unless there be a diseased segment, when pain may arise. The peristalsis of the bowel is perhaps limited to a bowel with contents, i. e., its contents, or, in other words, mechanical irritation that produces physiologic peristalsis. In laparotomy if one will observe, the empty bowel is nearly always still unless irritated by manipulation. If one will watch the bowel waves of peristalsis it will be apparent that the peristaltic waves are limited from three to twenty-four inches. A peristaltic wave will start and stop within a localized space. In the dog the peristaltic wave is neither so rapid in its travel nor does it seem to travel over such a long distance. The intensity of peristaltic waves is most marked toward the proximal end of the jejunum where the muscular fibers, blood and nerve supply are large. The bile and pancreatic duct pour their contents into the proximal end of the bowel, and thus impel the peristaltic waves to force the contents distalward. For secretion or the presence of any bowel contents is what induces peristalsis.

2. Another form of bowel movement may be called the pendulum movement. This is a contraction and elongation of the longitudinal muscular layer which does not propel the contents analward. The lumen of the intestine remains the same. The pendulum movement of the bowel is localized and limited to short stretches of intestine.

3. A third kind of bowel action is described by Professor Nothnagel as a roll motion. Though recognizing Dr. Nothnagel's keen observing powers, I cannot see anything in the roll motion of the bowel except an excessive physiologic, or, better, a pathologic physiology process. It is, in my opinion, only a wild or stormy peristalsis; when, for example, the blood contents, gas or fluid, go onward by spells or jerks. The roll motion doubtless includes those peculiar gurglings which every individual now and then experiences.

And though this form of bowel motion is not accompanied by pain, yet it seems to border on the pathologic lines. Of course almost all bowel motion of any distinct type belongs to the small intestines. Perhaps one can scarcely ever observe the large bowel motion through the abdominal wall, if it be in a physiologic state. Perhaps the roll motion of the bowel described by Nothnagel is due to an irregular action of the nerve supply, the movements of which, as Auerbach's plexus, may become disordered. Formerly I thought that the large bowel did not share but a very small part in the excessive activity of blood motion, but recently I found a two-inch "invagination of death" in the ascending colon of an adult, so that the colon engages in a wild, disordered motion of death when the cerebrospinal system has lost control forever of the bowel motion (sympathetic).

Peristalsis of the small intestines does not consist of waves starting at the duodenum and extending to Bauhin's valve, but the small peristalsis consists of local waves which start and cease within perhaps six inches to two feet. One may recognize peristaltic waves in the same animal two to three or four feet apart, each going through its wave. Now it appears that bowel contents cause the excitants of bowel peristalsis, and even if one observes a full bowel quiet, it does not necessarily overthrow the idea that bowel contents alone excite bowel peristalsis. Empty intestines are still unless excessively stimulated. We must look for the primary anatomical point of motive force of the bowel muscles in Auerbach's plexus. Among the very unsatisfactory experiments are those attempting to find out the location of a nervous center for bowel movement. Pflueger discovered that when the splanchnics are stimulated the bowel motion is prohibited, the bowels become pale and the blood-vessels become narrowed (anemic); but severing the splanchnics induces increased bowel peristalsis, the bowels become more filled with blood and congestion occurs. Some assert one thing and some assert another in regard to the influence of the vagus over the intestinal motion.

Ludwig, Nasse, Kupffer, Mayer and Basch found in the splanchnic prohibitory and vaso-motor nerves, besides nerves which, by stimulation, irritated motion in the bowel. Also Mayer and Basch could, by irritating the vagus, prohibit intestinal movement. Basch and Erhmann believed from experiments that the splanchnics were the motor nerves of the longitudinal muscular layer and the prohibitory to the circular muscular layers, and that the vagus stirred up the circular muscles while it prohibited the longitudinal muscles. Fellner claims that he found the nervi errigentes to be the source of longitudinal muscular action, while the hypogastric nerves were the motor nerves for the circular muscles. Lately Steinach claims that the motor innervation of the intestinal tract is through the posterior sensitive roots of the spinal cord. The portion of the colon supplied by the inferior mesenteric artery, i. e., the descending colon, sigmoid and rectum, have an analogous supply to the upper portion of the digestive tract. The nerves from the spinal cord pass through the rami communicantes, through the lateral chain of sympathetic ganglia into the hypogastric plexus mesentericus inferior, which plexuses supply the sigmoid, rectum and descending colon. The lumbar region was proven by

PERISTALSIS OF TRACTUS INTESTINALIS

Goltz's experiment to have a motor center for the rectum. In this case the spinal nerves course through the hypogastric and mesenteric plexuses to act as motor nerves for the bowel. The sympathetic nerves and ganglia, the unconscious motors of the assimilating laboratory, work steadily while the

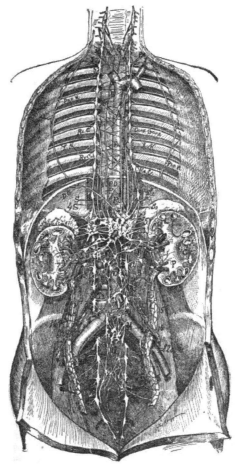

NERVUS VASOMOTORIUS—GENERAL VIEW

Fig 77. The abdominal portion was accurately dissected from specimen under alcohol.

digestive tract has any contents. It is entirely analogous to the uterus. When there exist contents in the uterus its walls pass and repass through constant waves, but if it is empty, it is quiescent, it is still. So it is with the bowels, an empty intestine is still a quiet one; a full one is nearly always in motion.

Anemia of the intestines lessens the peristalsis while hyperemia increases the peristalsis. Chemically indifferent substances will create bowel motion according to their deviation from the normal bodily temperature. It must be remembered that over distention makes contraction impossible, i. e., tympanites is paralysis just exactly according to its degree of distention. Tympanites is accompanied by slight peristalsis but the pain is due to local spasm, especially of the circular muscles. It appears to me that the circular muscles of the bowel can so obliterate the lumen that it practically prevents all passage of contents. Doubtless the muscles would sooner or later tire out and admit of the passages. We may say that it is extremely rare to observe the physiologic bowel peristalsis through the abdominal wall. But it is not at all rare to observe the bowel peristalsis through the abdominal wall in a pathologic state. In the normal state the abdominal wall is so thick, and the change of shape and form of the intestine is so slight that one can seldom definitely mark out bowel peristalsis. In belly walls thinned by wasting disease and muscles thinned and separated by the stretching of the walls one may map out moving bowel coils very easily. Especially is this the case in bowel obstruction.

Peritalsis of a pathologic character may be (a) an increase of normal movement, (b) tonic contraction, or (c) the so-called antiperistalsis. The rolling motion of the bowel described by Prof. Nothnagel, I would call pathologic. If one will open dogs with peritonitis there may be observed irregular bowel movements; sharp contraction of both longitudinal and circular muscles. In fact the peristalsis has become irregular, excessive, wild. The slow, normal, pendulum movements of dilatation and contraction of gut have been displaced by violent movements. The bowel movement or peristalsis is accordingly violent and wild as the bowel wall is inflamed. One may observe increased bowel peristalsis from (a) irritating foods, (b) from strong doses of physic, (c) in sudden mental disturbances, (d) in neurotic patients, (e) from hot or cold fluids, drinks or foods, (f) in enteritis or peritonitis, (g) especially in intestinal stenosis, (h) the absorption of lead into the system, (i) exposure to cold. It did not appear to me that traveling of dogs increased the peristalsis, yet in general, motion aids to increase peristalsis. The important tetanic bowel contraction is significant, for in experiment one can observe by pinching a piece of bowel it will contract into a pale white cord, perhaps entirely closing the lumen for all practical purposes. The tetanic contraction slowly yields its spasm, but doubtless is accompanied with terrific pain. For almost every drop of blood is driven out of the intestinal wall and the nerves are pressed in a traumatic state. If neuralgia is a demand for fresh blood, surely this is a typical example.

Doubtless in the violent pain of lead-colic (colica saturina) the intestine is contracted to a white rod and the condition of persistent pain depends on various segments being successively attacked. Tonic contraction of the intestine is a frequent condition of bowel stenosis. If one will sit down by a patient with sufficient bowel stenosis to produce obstruction of the bowel contents, by placing the hand on the abdomen he can easily perceive the bowel movements, because in such patients the belly wall is usually thin. The bowel movements are almost constantly felt, they gradually increase until the small intestine may feel as hard as a rolling-pin under a sheet, and such a hard bowel will gradually relax, when the same phenomenon will appear elsewhere. It is quite probable that progressive peristalsis is not accompanied by pain, no matter how lively it is. But tonic or spasmodic contraction of the bowel can be and is accompanied by the most sickening pain. The chief pain from the bowels (colic) no doubt arises in disturbed or disordered peristalsis.

Local inflammation in the intestine producing an irritability of the peripheral nerves, induces irregular, disordered and wild bowel contractions with severe pain. Much has been said by writers in regard to antiperistalsis, i. e., peristaltic wave directed toward the pylorus instead of toward the anus. I have studied this subject considerably in an experimental method, but have never been able to see distinctly anything but very irregular antiperistaltic waves. I tried Prof. Nothnagel's claims that sodium salts made antiperistalsis, and that potassium salts induced peristalsis, but after several trials on dogs to test the direction of the intestine I could not consider it of any practical value, neither could I confirm his assertions. After laparotomy we frequently observe considerable pain, and almost always accompanying this pain there is more or less tympanites. The pain is due to irregular contraction of the intestinal wall. Segments of the bowel become over-distended, which is a kind of partial paralysis and it cannot again contract. This distended portion does not give pain. The pain arises from the non-distended or partially distended segments which are in a state of spasm, irregular contraction and with irritable peripheral nerves.

Excessive or irregular bowel peristalsis is observed among hysterical and neurasthenic persons. It is recognized by gurgling, splashing or rumbling noises in the abdomen. It arises in neurotic persons, yet the same person generally suffers no unpleasant sensations, except the mental annoyance. The rumbling noise has no especial connection with mealtimes or drinking. If it occurs in women it is apt to be more active at the menstrual time. Mental influences seem to play a role, for when the subject works or directs the mental energies away from the phenomenon, the gurgling generally ceases. If the abdominal walls be thin, one can observe the intestinal movements, which are confined chiefly to the small intestines. Other subjective symptoms generally fail; however, gas may be belched. The diagnosis of excessive bowel peristalsis is not difficult if one can observe the patient for some time. The trouble may persist for weeks and normal stools continue during the whole time. Excessive bowel peristalsis may be diagnosed from bowel stenosis by its spontaneous appearance and cessation.

324   THE ABDOMINAL AND PELVIC BRAIN

It seems a characteristic of certain persons to have repeated attacks, and I have observed such attacks for many years in certain persons at certain times, when the mental faculties were either on a sudden tension or embarrassed. It is reported that an old and valuable servant felt obliged to give up waiting on account of repeated attacks of loud gurgling when she was serving at mealtimes.

Excessive peristalsis is generally confined to the small intestines. The treatment of excessive bowel peristalsis should be both physical and mental. Hydrotherapy, massage, galvanization of the abdomen and remedies pro-

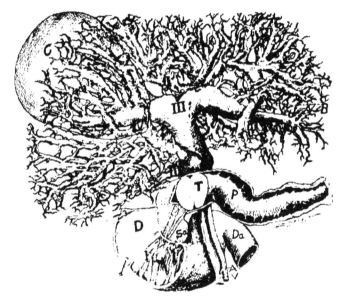

DILATED DUCTUS HEPATICUS

Fig. 78. The dilated hepatic ducts impress with the idea of the quantity of nerves attending the ducts in the form of a nodular, fenestrated, anastomosing plexus ensheathing the channels.

foundly affecting the olfactory nerve, aid to bring about normal bowel peristalsis. As remedies the bromides, arsenic, iron and nux vomica are valuable adjuncts. The regulation of the diet is of first importance.

Enterospasm is a condition of the bowel in which the longitudinal or circular muscular layers are in a state of excessive contraction. To see an actual demonstration of this phenomenon, the most practical method is to open a rabbit's or a dog's abdomen and by pinching the bowel wall with the finger and thumb both the muscular layers will be observed in a state of spasm. The circular muscular layer on being pinched or struck will contract to a small white ring or band. The enterospasm is likely to occur in very limited segments of bowel. If it be primary, it is a motor impulse, but it may be secondary to a sensory neurosis when it is of a reflex nature. In such a case both a motor-neurosis and a sensory-neurosis exists, that is, a mixed neurosis.

Enterospasm is primarily a motor-neurosis, but is frequently combined with reflex sensory factors inducing severe pain. As a result of the spasm irregular constipation arises. The stool is either long retained or forcibly expelled. Enterospasm may owe its origin to misuse of cathartics, the entrance of lead into the system, mental effects, worms or improper use of foods. Meningitis or disease of the cerebrospinal axis may play a role.

The treatment of enterospasm consists of opium and evacuants. It is this form of constipation that the old physicians said, paradoxically, opium cured. It cured the spasm and the bowels naturally become regular. The proper treatment, however, will consist more in diet regulation, colonic flushings, in electrical treatment, in bromides, nux vomica, in massage and hydrotherapeutic measures.

Paralysis of the bowel signifies that the contents are not forced onward, though the lumen is patent; no mechanical obstruction exists. Henrot announces three forms:

We first have direct paralysis of the bowel from affection of its walls, as after reduced hernia; often trauma, as in laparotomy, after peritonitis, enteritis, etc.

Second we have indirect or reflex paralysis, as from injury to the testicle; inflammation of a bowel segment, as inflammation of the appendix, produces paralysis of large bowel segments, the irritation being reflected to the abdominal brain, reorganized and sent out on the various nerve plexuses, laming the said segments. An abscess in the abdominal wall may by reflex action produce paralysis of a bowel segment sufficient to prevent the onward movement of the feces. In many autopsies, experiments on animals or on humans, I have noted where a small perforation had produced paralysis of adjacent segments by spread of peritoneal inflammation. No mechanical obstruction existed. This is what one continually hears of as obstruction of the bowels —it is really peritonitis. The paralysis is due to edema and exudates pressing on the peripheral nerve apparatus of the bowel wall.

Thirdly, by leaving out of consideration the cerebrospinal lesions we have bowel paralysis from hysteria, melancholia, neurasthenia, from atony of the bowel and from persistent coprostasis. It must be remembered that the symptoms of ileusparalyticus are not easy to diagnose from genuine ileus. In genuine ileus the peristalsis of the bowel is increased on the proximal side of the affected locality. The therapeutic application for any form of ileus depends entirely on the original cause. Should the paralysis depend on some neuroses, the treatment will be regulation of diet, electricity and massage of the abdomen, the careful use of evacuants and moral influences. Colonic flushings are excellent in this form of neurosis.

326   THE ABDOMINAL AND PELVIC BRAIN

Deficient peristaltic action observed in old age and anemic persons depends, perhaps, much on exhaustion, and deficient blood of a proper composition. Besides, deficient peristalsis means deficient secretion, and deficient secretion means an empty bowel, and an empty bowel means a quiet one. The parenchymal intestinal ganglia require proper blood to stimulate them to action. The peristaltic movements of the bowels are anatomically excited by the distal visceral ganglia, yet they receive and empty feces from the abdominal brain impulses to accelerate or retard the bowel motion.

McKendrick believes the accelerating nerves of the bowel are from the sympathetic ganglia, while the prohibiting nerves are from the lumbar spinal.

FIG. 2.—PELVIC BRAIN.
NERVES OF THE INTERNAL GENITALS
Fig. 79. Illustration of nerves from my own dissections.

The descending colon and rectum, according to Nasse, receive motor fibers from the plexuses of nerves surrounding the mesenteric artery. The general notions (Fox, McKendrick, Nasse, Bridge, Kolliker) are that the gastrointestinal ganglia send motor fibers to the bowel muscle and that these automatic ganglia are stimulated reflexly by fibers running from them to the mucosa (Henle). Hence, a diarrhea is a reflex matter. Pflueger believed that the splanchnics were inhibitory nerves of bowel action, but Basch showed that the splanchnics were inhibitory nerves only in a secondary manner by changing the circulation in the bowel. The motus peristalticus in lead colic is of much interest, as it should lead to the source of bowel motion, but the special action of lead on tissue is not yet settled. However, it belongs without doubt to the abdominal sympathetic. Is the disturbance due to the action of the lead on the sympathetic ganglia? Does the lead act as an excitant on fibers of the splanchnics? Both views may be retained until more precise data exist. Begbie asserts that irritation of the abdominal brain (or, as he says, plexuses surrounding the aorta) induces active movements of the small intestines and colon. Valentin discovered that irritation of the fifth nerve produces invariably movements of the small intestines. We must remember that the fifth nerve is par excellence the ganglionic cranial nerve, having eight ganglia situated on its branches. It is really a sympathetic cranial nerve. It is not yet clear what is the influence of the cerebrospinal system over the movement of the abdominal viscera, but observers are agreed that fear, fright, emanations, intensely influence the bowel movements, showing the influence of the cerebrospinal axis on the bowel and sphincters. How much is this due to relaxation of sphincters? As Romberg remarked fifty years ago, the field of influence of the cerebrospinal axis over bowel movement is not fully known. From personal experience we know that ordinarily the passing form of colic, bowel spasm, is due to irritating contents. The irritation of the mucosa passes to the automatic ganglia of the bowel wall, which resents the trauma by muscular contraction; the consequence is pain.

The motor bowel, automatic parenchymatous ganglion, is one of the best samples to illustrate the highest degree of independence. The influence of the sympathetic nerve upon the intestines has long been recognized. The long controversy in relation to the influence of the great splanchnic nerve upon the small intestines seems to be more definitely settled. Weber showed some years ago, that the splanchnic exerts an inhibitory action upon the intestines, arresting their movement. Legros and Onimus, however, claimed to show by their experiments that the splanchnic is, on the contrary, the motor nerve of the intestines, and, when stimulated, produces contraction of the intestinal walls.

Recent experiments made by Coutade and Guyon present very clear evidence that the two muscular layers of the intestine are controlled by nerves of a different origin, the circular layer being controlled by branches of the sympathetic, and the longitudinal by the spinal nerves. The conclusions arrived at by these investigators are as follows, to which all experimenters do not agree:

1. The sympathetic causes contraction of the circular muscular layers of the intestine and, at the same time, relaxation of the longitudinal muscular coat.

2. The contraction of the small intestines depends entirely upon the sympathetic, and is wholly independent of the pneumogastric.

Galvanization of the abdominal brain induces active movements of the small intestines and, to a certain degree, of the large. Anatomic and physiologic experiments certainly show that branches of the abdominal brain take part in the innervation of the stomach.

There is a ceratin kind of excessive bowel peristalsis which is disastrous at any age, but especially in infancy. I refer to invagination. One-quarter of all invaginations occur before one year of age, and one-half of invaginations occur under ten years of age. Invagination, telescoping, intussusception, is where one segment of bowel is driven into the adjacent one. Nearly all invaginations are toward the anus distalward, but some report invagination toward the stomach proximalward. Hektoen reports a case of proximalward invagination. Invaginations are especially likely to arise in two classes of subjects, viz.: (a) in children and (b) in persons dying of some cerebrospinal trouble. The invaginations found in autopsies may be called the invagination of death. I have repeatedly found this condition in human and animal autopsies.

The characteristics of the invagination of death are that they are accompanied by no inflammatory process, no exudates, no congestions or peritonitis, and are often multiple. In one dog, dying of peritonitis, I found four points of invagination close to each other. They were invaginations of about an inch distance each. Several times in human autopsies, I have found from one to four points of invagination. The characteristics of ordinary invagination are that it is accompanied by severe and sudden pain and, if continued long enough, by congestion, exudation and inflammation in the bowel tunics. Finally, the apex will begin to bleed and slough, producing bloody stools and finally peritonitis; and its results are found about the point of invagination.

Invagination is due to irregular action of the muscles in the intestinal wall. It is due to irregular peristalsis. In children and persons with diseased cerebrospinal systems it appears that the cerebrospinal axis, the higher nerve center, has lost its normal control over the sympathetic, which rules the bowels, and the result is that the intestines assume wild and disordered movements. Not only the bowel segments but their longitudinal and circular muscles begin to act without harmony, irregular, spasmodic. In infants and children it appears that the cerebrospinal axis has not assumed full control over the sympathetic which rules the bowel muscles. Since invagination constitutes one-third of all forms of intestinal obstruction, regular action of the gut wall assumes an important role. It is curious to note the common localities of invagination. The ileo-colic and ileo-cecal constitute 50 per cent, i. e., 50 per cent of invaginations occurs at the ileo-cecal valve. Thirty per cent occur in the small intestines and 20 per cent occur in the colon. Omitting the region of the ileo-cecal valve as having assumed some mechanical peculiarity tending to invagination, we note that there are more invaginations in the small intestines than in the large, which must be due to a greater possession of muscles.

CHAPTER XXVI.

GASTROINTESTINAL SECRETION.

"Youth's Lexicon has no such word as fail."—Bulwer.
"It is our hearers who inspire us."—Vinet.

1. Gastrointestinal secretion is a significant and important matter in animal life. Gastrointestinal secretions are under the control of the sympathetic ganglia located in the walls of the digestive tract. We designate those ganglia in general as the Billroth-Meissner plexuses (plexus myentericus internus) situated immediately beneath the gastrointestinal mucosa. They rule secretion. We cannot properly separate the submucous nerve plexus from the Auerbach's plexus (plexus myentericus externus) which rules muscular motion and is situated between the circular and longitudinal muscles of the gastrointestinal tract. One nerve plexus is a complement of the other. As secretion without motion is of little avail, and motion without secretion is equally futile, peristaltic motion is necessary to sweep onward the food to be attacked by fresh glandular secretion and to eliminate and drain the system from the debris of food. The remnants of the gastrointestinal feast must be removed by peristaltic movements.

Besides, secretion is doubtless enhanced by the massage muscular contractions. The large degree of independence exercised by the sympathetic ganglia, especially at a long distance from the cerebrospinal center, is quite suggestive that there will be local as well as general gastrointestinal mucous secretion. From the very construction and function of the digestive tract we may expect local labors in it. At several localities new and different secretions are added to the onward moving food, so that local and general digestion and secretion must occur. I repeat that secretion and digestion are both local and general in regard to the digestive tube. Yet the whole nerve apparatus of the digestive tract is a delicately balanced matter both as regards muscular and secretory activity. Let us call up matters that daily occur, but are not always interpreted. For example, a person eats some cucumbers or other indigestible and fermentable substance. At the time that the indigestible substance is eaten the bowels may be as regular as clockwork and the feces of semi-liquid character. Ten hours after eating the indigestible substance, when the regular stool is to be evacuated, it will be observed that: (1) the stool is delayed, the desire for stool is checked; (2) if forced evacuation be exercised, the stool will be hard and relatively dry, for want of secretion is manifest by distinctly formed and shaped feces.

Now what is the cause of this disturbance? The cause is unbalanced secretion due to reflex irritation. The irritation is going on in the business portion of the digestive tract, i. e., in the small intestines. The subject is conscious of this disturbance only by a little pain, colic and excessive peristalsis. He, however, notices that an excess of gases is being formed and passed per rectum. He may not sleep well, but recognizes an indefinable restlessness. This irritation may be active enough to produce seminal emissions during sleep. The irritation in the small intestines has unbalanced the mechanism of secretion, so that it is called away from the large intestine, causing excessive secretion in the small intestine, and hence the dry formed feces in the large. It is very likely that the excessive, deficient or

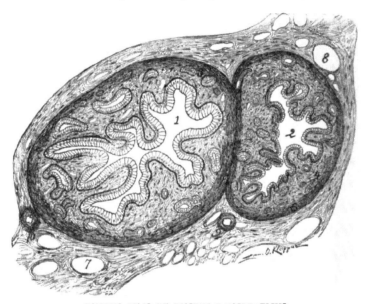

DUCTUS BILIS ET DUCTUS PANCREATICUS

Fig. 80. Drawn from cross section of the pancreatic and biliary duct. The minute glands of Theile may be observed in the walls of the ducts. These are the so-called glands of the hepatic duct. The figure illustrates the vast domain of secretion.

disproportionate secretions may occur in separate localities of the digestive tract, just as peristalsis of the tract may be a local matter. We know from experiment that peristalsis may arise, continue and subside, limited to a short piece of intestine.

The view of local disturbance in both peristalsis and secretion sending out its reflex power and disturbing the whole digestive tract is in accord with pathologic data. For example, a perforation of the appendix may so unbalance the nerve apparatus as to feel it at the umbilicus. It is a reality. The

secretion of the gastrointestinal mucosa is entirely beyond the control of the will. In secretions we are especially dealing with the sympathetic nerve, for secretions have a close relation to the size of the blood vessels.
1. All glands receive vessels.
2. All vessels have nerves to control their caliber.

The gastric secretion may be reviewed in regard to experimental data. The stomach is supplied with nerves for its muscles and for its glands, as motion and secretion are both necessary for normal digestion. The arrangement of the Auerbach and Billroth-Meissner plexuses is similar to the small intestines. The splanchnic nerve is the chief vasomotor nerve, i. e., vasodilator and vasoconstrictor. This is important, for secretion in general depends on the blood supply, as may be observed in location in the season of "rut," in glandular congestion. But the gastric glands are ruled by the sympathetic nerves, whose chief origin exists in the abdominal brain.

It must be claimed, however, that the stomach glands can act independently, from sympathetic influence alone, and also be changed or modified by the cerebrospinal. It is doubtless true that there are not only vasomotor nerves in the spinal cord but that the abdominal brain is a great vasomotor center, in that the abdominal brain regulates the amount of blood to the gastric glands and consequently the amount, and to a certain degree the kind, of secretion of the stomach. Yet there must be secretory nerves in the stomach which belong to the sympathetic. Candor requires the statement that the full knowledge of the nerve supply of the gastric glands is not fully known.

The independence of the sympathetic ganglia of the stomach is signified by the fact that the chief stimulus to the gastric secretion is food in the stomach. It is asserted by some that stimulating any of the nerves going to the stomach does not influence the secretion, for it it found that secretion will go on under the stimulus of food when all the stomachic nerves are severed. It is claimed, therefore, that the sympathetic ganglia in the stomachic walls are sufficient to act as centers for secretion. This delegates large and significant powers to the sympathetic ganglia.

The sympathetic ganglia are especially liable to reflex irritation, and nowhere is it more manifest than in the stomach. The gastric secretion is modified by reflex stimuli from the brain, uterus, kidney, testicle, ovary, heart and spinal cord, etc., etc. Emotions play a role in gastric secretion

The successful treatment of stomachic disease is significant in methods of stimulating the stomach, as irritating its mucous wall, which not only starts secretion, but motion as well. In ordinary stomach diseases there are four factors, viz.: (a) excessive secretion, (b) deficient secretion, (c) disproportionate secretion, and (d) muscular motion. Washing the stomach, irritating its wall with instruments or coarse food, will accomplish much in inducing health. Doubtless this is the action of nux vomica and hot water. The clinging germs should be washed from the dormant stomach wall and the muscular movements must be stirred to excite natural secretions. It has astonished me at the frequent beneficial results of irrigation of the

332   THE ABDOMINAL AND PELVIC BRAIN

stomach. It stirs to more normal rhythm the sympathetic ganglia, both of secretion and motion. Besides, it washes from the stomach wall abnormal matter. The stomach must have rest and repose or it cannot long stand irregular irritation without resentment of the little circulation insults. Hence the distal irritation from a diseased uterus, oviducts and ovaries

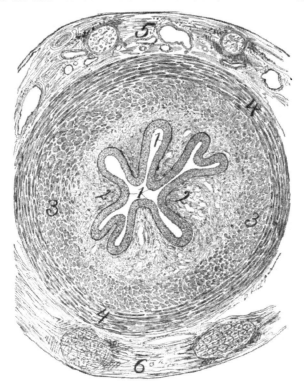

CROSS SECTION OF URETER

Fig. 81. Presents the tunica mucosa, muscularis and serosa of the ureter, with several nerve ganglia located between the tunica serosa and muscularis.

sooner or later unbalances stomach function by its regular passage of the traumatic insults to the abdominal brain where reorganization occurs, perhaps with multiplication of effects. The excitation of the diseased genitals has no season of rest, no day or night repose, but at any or all times it rushes and flashes, now tumultuous or turbulent, now pell mell and explosive. There is nothing like a chronic atrophic myometritic uterus to derange and unbalance the gastric secretion and motion.

The stomach is very highly supplied with blood-vessels and nerves, because it is a vast and complicated laboratory, requiring much energy to hold its delicate but active processes in the balanced order. From experimental data we may view the stomachic glands as under the control of the sympathetic nerves, i. e., the ganglia in them.

CHAPTER XXVII.

SECRETION-NEUROSIS OF THE COLON (MUCOUS COLITIS).

"You can fool some of the people all the time, and all of the people some of the time, but you cannot fool all of the people all of the time."—Abraham Lincoln.

"Thinking is the talking of the soul with itself." —Plato

History notes that Dr. Mason Good gave one of the first communications in regard to the above disease, in 1825, under the name "Diarrhea Tubularis." Woodward collected the literature up to 1879, in the Medical and Surgical History of the War of the Rebellion, Vol. I. Da Costa wrote in regard to the disease, as did also Leyden in 1892. Nothnagel, in 1884, wrote an excellent essay on the disease, naming it colica mucosa. In 1884 Krysinski, of Jena, wrote an inaugural thesis on the disease, detailing six cases, and sought to establish as its cause the presence and effects of microörganisms. Leube thought it a nervous affection. Pick has recently written a short essay on the subject.

Many different names have been applied to this disease on account of the various views as to its causation. If the disease consists of an epithelial inflammation, a catarrh, we may be satisfied with the designation, enteritis membranacea, but should there exist only increased mucous secretion, without inflammation, the terms colica mucosa would be more significant. However, my studies on the subject have induced me to adopt the term, secretion-neurosis. It is possible that there are two ill-defined affections in this field, one being an enteritis and the other a simple increase of the mucous secretion. Autopsies are so rare on subjects dying of secretion-neurosis of the colon that no pathological basis is as yet definitely established. An antemortem diagnosis must be confirmed by a postmortem examination before any pathology can be accepted or established.

All observers agree that secretion-neurosis of the colon is indicated by the peculiar formation and evacuation of the stools. The clinical symptoms are colicky pains and the evacuation of masses of mucus. The mucous masses may consist of flat long bands (even membranes), ribbons, shreds or rolled tubes or scrolls. Some portions assume a spiral form. Some writers assert that the masses are fibrinous, but I have examined quite a number and have never observed fibrin. The mucous masses are white, grayish white, or a color due to the mixing of mucus and feces, yellowish brown. By placing the mucous masses in water they unroll and partially dissolve. However, the peculiar form of the mucous masses may be retained if they are kept in bottles of water for several days, as we have noted in one case. The quantities of these masses evacuated by some patients are enormous. A female attended by Dr. Lucy Waite and myself, would occasionally evacuate nearly half a pint of mucous membranes, masses, bands, tubes or unformed substances. In a male the evacuation showed more string or ribbon-like processes.

All observers agree that women are the chief subjects of secretion-neurosis of the colon. Litten estimates that 80 per cent are women, and according to Kitagawa 90 per cent are female subjects. Dr. W. A. Evans says that of the many samples sent to the Columbus Medical Laboratory 80 per cent are from women.

I had a typical case in a man 36 years of age, who had the disease for nine years. Some report cases in men and children. I never saw a typical case in a child. Almost all writers agree that women who are subjects of secretion-neurosis of the colon are neurotic, nervous, hysterical or hypochondriac. The men possess a similar neurotic or hypochondriac tendency. I have had several mild cases in men.

Patients afflicted with secretion-neurosis of the colon have suffered from constipation for long periods previous to the outbreak of the former disease. This accords with my view that constipation is a neurosis of the colon, or fecal reservoir. The attacks of such patients are irregular, but recur for years. Pain of a colicky nature may suddenly arise in the abdomen and continue until masses of mucus and occasionally feces are expelled. The attacks of pain may be extremely severe, especially when large masses of mucus are evacuated. So far as I can discover, the pain is chiefly located in the transverse and descending colon and the sigmoid flexure; in general, over the left abdominal region. However, when the colicky pain is severe and continuous, the patient may complain of pain in the whole abdominal region. Some of my patients complained of pain running down the legs. Abnormal sensation may arise in the genitourinary organs. After the evacuations of the mucous, slimy masses, especially the larger ones, the patients appear and report themselves to be entirely free from pain. Generally, the larger the mucoid masses evacuated, the longer the patient remains free. However, the colicky pains may be coming on for one or two days before the large masses are expelled. If the evacuation be slight in quantity, the colicky pains are slight, but often continuous. The appetite is generally good, except at the time of attack. An enema will occasionally bring away very large masses of slime. Also, there are patients who pass the mucous masses who do not report nor appear to suffer pain. Hence two classes of patients present themselves, viz.: some pass mucous masses with colicky pains; others pass mucous masses without colicky pains.

Nothnagel, my honored teacher, the ablest of all writers on the subject, shields himself by adopting the term *colica mucosa et enteritis membranacea*. He acknowledges that a variety of pathological processes are here included. Krysinski and Mathieu are both inclined to consider the affection an enteritis and Krysinski endeavors to show that certain low organisms are the primary cause. It does not seem probable that microörganisms would persist for years; and besides, were the disease caused by microörganisms we ought to be able to cure it. Krysinski describes patients who simply gave a desire for stool without colicky pains, i. e., merely "bearing down pains."

Much interest is manifested by writers, in the stools in secretion-neurosis of the colon.

Microscopically, the evacuation consists of membranous or tubular gray masses. They may resemble croupous membrane from the respiratory passages. The mucous masses may be transparent like slime, or opaque like fibrin, of a grayish white, or a dirty color with pigment in it. Sometimes the masses consist of large, wide and thick leathery-like membranes; at other times, long ribbon-like bands or rope-like coils. The mucous masses nearly always come away alone, unmixed with feces. Sometimes they resemble the swollen jackets of baked potatoes. By careful manipulation in water the masses of slime will generally unfold into membranes; hence the term, membranous colitis. They may resemble fascia or tendons, or one may be deceived by milk coagula.

Microscopically, the mass substance represents a hyaline body, which can be preserved only a short time in air, alcohol or water. Degenerating cylindrical epithelia of almost any grade can be noted. The slimy mass represents a glassy, unformed, transparent substance. If acetic acid be added it assumes a wavy, striped or ground glass appearance. Glandular epithelia are almost always found, shrunken, swollen or vacuolated. , Sometimes vast numbers of microbes are present, cholesterin crystals, triple phosphates, fecal masses, pigment and occasionally round cells.

Chemical examination reveals mucin, or mucin-like material, as the chief constituent. This may be considered as definitely established, as it is confirmed by Clark, Thompson, Perrond, Da Costa, Hare, Pick, Nothnagel, Furbringer, Hirsch, Walter, V. Jaksch, Krysinski, Kitagama, Rothmann, Littre, Vanni, Leube and Pariser, a sufficient number of investigators to settle the question. Some authors assert that mucin is the chief constituent with other albuminous bodies. The only author we have found who claims that fibrin exists in the evacuations of secretion-neurosis of the colon is P. Guttmann, who apparently based his support on doubtful microscopical examination.

Pathological records are rare, on account of the scarcity of material on which to establish them. Nothnagel reports a case of secretion-neurosis; Rothmann, one which was examined by C. Ruge. Ruge reported that "in spite of careful examination of the whole intestinal tract, nothing abnormal was discovered." The above patient of Rothmann presented a typical picture of colica mucosa, but died from a duodenal perforation.

Rothmann had another case that died of carcinoma at the base of the skull. The patient was in the hospital from June 14 to Nov. 2, 1892. By taking an enema the patient evacuated large masses of mucus without pain. He made no complaint. The autopsy showed in the transverse colon (where it did not contain feces) and the strongly contracted parts of the descending colon, injected and folded mucosa. Between the folded mucosa lay products, partly membranous, partly strand-formed. The parts of the colon filled with membranes contained no feces. In the ascending colon there were no mucous masses, but feces, with reddened mucosa. In the sigmoid the membranes could be torn from the reddened mucosa without loss of substance. Feces were found in the small intestine, which had reddened mucosa. The chief mucous masses were found in the left half of the transverse colon, descending colon and sigmoid. The microscope demonstrated the mucous masses in the lower colon to consist of mucin, not fibrin. In this case there can be no doubt of the existence of catarrh. Just on this point of catarrh or no catarrh, investigators are divided.

We have, then, three opinions in regard to the nature of secretion-neurosis of the colon, viz.:

1. That it is an enteritis (catarrh).
2. That it is simply excessive secretion of mucus (mucous colic).
3. That it is secretion-neurosis (nervous).

In general visceral neuroses we have, (1) motor neuroses (motus peristalticus); (2) sensory neuroses (hyperesthesia and anesthesia); and (3) secretory neuroses (excessive, deficient and disproportionate secretion). In secretion-neurosis of the colon we have to deal with a patient who has all three secretory disturbances, i. e.: deficient, disproportionate and excessive secretion. These patients have generally been long sufferers from constipation (deficient secretion). Then follows disproportion-secretion, but that is not so evident, as it simply produces fermentation. Finally comes the formation of the habit of excessive secretion of mucus. Now, this excessive secretion of mucus arises from the unfortunate habit which the mucus cell had formed during the early but prolonged state of constipation. The mucus cell had learned a bad, persistent, nervous or irritable habit of excessive secretion. After a long-continued bad habit of secreting excessive mucus, the cells were unable to change their mode of life and assume normal action. Hence, as one of the etiological factors of secretion-neurosis of the colon, we will assume the depraved cell habit from reflex irritation.

A second factor that perhaps plays a chief role is genital disease. Secretion-neurosis of the colon is nearly always manifested in neurotic persons of the female sex. Such subjects nearly always have pelvic disease. Every gynecologist knows from actual experience that pelvic disease produces constipation, a fore-runner of secretion-neurosis. Constipation may be secondary to genital disease, which, through reflex action, produces in the bowel deficient, excessive or disproportionate secretion. Disproportionate secretion induces fermentation, causing gases which distend the bowel, resulting in atony and deranged nerve action in the epithelial cell. Irritation from the diseased genitals induces the development of toxins. The toxins affect the tissues locally, inducing colitis, if not epithelial catarrh. Besides, the absorption of toxins induces neurasthenia. The diseased genitals reflexly lead to a train of conditions which induce defective nutrition and excretion. The evacuation of glassy, viscid mucus, subsequently followed by grayish shreds, extruded with pain, is pathognomonic of secretion-neurosis of the colon. Gynecologists frequently observe these conditions except the grayish shreds and mucomembranous layers. The pain on defecation may be but slight.

The first step in the cure of such patients is to relieve the afflicted genitals, when improvement often supervenes. In one of my patients suffering from chronic pelvic disease and also typical secretion-neurosis of the colon, many complex neurotic symptoms of an intense character would occasionally arise at the time of the evacuations. She presented paroxysms of pain, intense colic, profound hysterical or neurotic symptoms, rapid pulse, disturbed respiration; all of which subsided very slowly after the evacuation of mucus. Reflex neuroses of an intense character were present. In the intervals she was quiet, presented none of the acute egoism of the hysteric, and apparently had no desire for attention or notoriety.

The differentiation of the pathological process in secretion-neurosis of the colon may be aided by (a) the anatomic pathologic findings in autopsies; (b) by analysis of clinical cases; (c) by examination of the evacuations; and (d) by comparison with analogous processes in other mucosa. We have spoken of the findings of the autopsy and in the evacuations; but too much cannot be said in regard to the correct clinical symptoms. The numerous names applied to the disease show that its clinical symptoms are not definitely agreed upon.

Colica flatulenta is a close relative of secretion-neurosis, as is also the motor neurosis (motus peristalticus) of the digestive tract. They consist of invisible derangements of the sympathetic nerve. Secretion-neurosis occurs in subjects who can in almost all cases be demonstrated to be neurotics.

Comparison with similar processes in analogous structures may not clear up the pathology very much. In bronchitis crouposa chronica, a similar disease in a similar structure (mucosa), as in secretion-neurosis of the colon, there is no anatomical change in the bronchial mucosa, as noted by B. Littre, and there is no fibrin present. Klein, Neelson and Beschomer claim that the bronchial membrane and coagula in bronchial croup are thickened mucus or slime. That keen and able observer, Nothnagel, vigorously asserts as a comparison that the membranes of chronic croup speak against the fibrinous product and inflammatory nature of colica mucosa. However, conflicting opinions still exist in regard to the nature of the membranes in bronchial croup.

Do we receive any light in secretion-neurosis of the colon by comparing it with dysmenorrhea, which was first described by Morgagni in 1728, and colpitis membrancea by Farre in 1858? The number of terms applied to membranous dysmenorrhea, as endometritis exfoliativa, endometritis dessicans and decidua mesenteralis, signifies conflicting opinions. There are at least two irreconcilable opinions in regard to membranous dysmenorrhea, the inflammatory and the non-inflammatory conditions. It appears to the writer that a third view should be introduced, viz., that it is a *secretion-neurosis of the endometrium.*

However, it appears quite certain that there are two conditions classed as membranous dysmenorrhea, viz., in one case the membrane consists of fibrin, lymphoid cells and red blood corpuscles—a secretion-neurosis—and in another, the membrane consists of a cellular infiltrated endometrium—an inflammatory process. The second process throws off the endometrium with its blood-vessels, cell infiltration and utricular glands. Hence, under the general term, membranous dysmenorrhea, we are dealing with inflammatory processes (endometritis), and a secretion-neurosis (a fibro-lymphoid membrane enclosing accidentally red blood corpuscles from diapedesis at the monthly congestion). The last process is a perverted nerve-action—a secretion-neurosis of the endometrium.

In an intensely lymphatic organ like the uterus we would expect more lymphoid elements in the membrane than in the colon. This would account for the fibrin and lymph-cells. Also red blood corpuscles are found in the evacuations of colica mucosa; and they are simply more numerous in the membrane of membranous dysmenorrhea, because of the intense endometric congestion, proceeding to rupture (diapedesis). Again, secretion-neurosis of the endometrium, like secretion-neurosis of the colon, evacuates the mucous membranes with or without pain, and at irregular intervals, showing a sustained comparison.

To say that the above diseases of the colon and uterus are forms of malnutrition or deranged innervation means but little.

In secretion-neurosis of the colon an explanation of the string and net-formed stools may be made from the contracted condition of the irritable muscle of the colon, which is thrown into folds, recesses and grooves, which allow the moulded form of the retained secreted mucus to persist. It may be mentioned that some confusion in diagnosis may arise by the so-called colica mucosa and enteritis coexisting. In other words a catarrh and secretion-neurosis of the colon may exist together.

The prognosis of secretion-neurosis of the colon, is, for life, favorable, but for recovery, doubtful. I have known the disease to continue for nine or ten years, with but slight changes. However, it is very variable in its attacks, and very erratic in its occurrence.

The treatment of secretion-neurosis of the colon must be directed to the nervous system, by habit, diet, physical and mental exercise, and general moral influences.

Regular daily bowel movements should be secured by very slight use of cathartics, considerable use of drinking fluids, and diet that leaves a large residue. Baths (medicated) twice weekly are very helpful. I have made some patients happy and helpful to themselves, by urging them to return to their regular business, which have been stopped by other physicians. Clysters, and high rectal and colonic irrigations, aid wonderfully in evacuating the mucus. Intestinal antiseptics ($HgCl_2$), slight massage and long rests at night are beneficial. Much moral influence and helpful courage is given a patient, when he is told he will not die from the trouble; for thought concentrated on the disease makes him much worse—produces pathologic physiology—particularly because he is almost always a neurotic. Electricity aids physically and mentally. Sexual activity should be especially limited. Clothing should be carefully regulated to avoid sudden changes.

CONCLUSIONS.

1. These diseases should be termed secretion-neurosis or enteritis. The first is of neurotic origin and course.
2. Both secretion-neurosis and enteritis may co-exist.
3. Secretion-neurosis of the colon occurs chiefly in neurotic females.
4. It is closely associated with genital disease.
5. It is frequently preceded by constipation.
6. The continuation of the disease is partly due to an irritable, vicious habit of excessive epithelial activity.
7. The disease is characterized by colicky pains with the evacuation of mucous masses.
8. It is non-fatal, variable, capricious and erratic in attacks, with impossible prognosis as to time.
9. Microscopically, the evacuations appear as membranous, yellowish-white masses of mucus.
10. Microscopically, one sees hyaline bodies, cylindrical epithelium, cholesterin crystals, triple phosphates, round cells, various micro-organisms and pigment.
11. Chemically, the evacuations consist of mucin and albuminous substance.
12. Secretion-neurosis of the colon is comparable to the secretion-neurosis of the endomitrium (dysmenorrhea membranacea) or bronchial croup.
13. Secretion-neurosis of the colon appears to be limited chiefly to the part of the colon supplied by the inferior mesenteric ganglion, i. e., to the fecal reservoir.
14. It is a disease of the sympathetic secretory nerves and in analogous to disease of the motor and sensory nerves of the viscera.
15. Its treatment consists of removing the neurosis, which lies in the foreground, and regulating the secretion, which lies in the background.

Regulation of diet—especially limited to cereals, vegetables, milk, eggs—exercise in open air, and systematic "visceral drainage" are the essentials in treatment.

CHAPTER XXVIII.

REFLEX NEUROSIS FROM DISTURBED PELVIC MECHANISM.

"Eternal spirit of the chainless mind."—Byron.
"Uneasy lies the head that wears the crown."—Shakespeare.

The testimony in favor of the production of reflex neurosis from dislocated genitals is ample for the gynecologist. To the physician foreign to gynecology from lack of knowledge and experience, clinical and anatomical facts, comparisons, methods of successful treatment, the domination of the sexual system and instinct and controlling power of genital reflexes over other viscera, in fact, all legitimate arguments of cause and effect, should be presented. Distorted mechanism of the pelvic structures causes genital dislocation. Dislocation of structures compromises circulation by the strangulation of vessels and thus induces malnutrition. Dislocation of structures traumatizes nerve-trunks and nerve periphery, causing pain and reflexes which radiate over nerve-tracks to other viscera and there disturb motion, secretion, absorption and sensation. Tension placed on a woman through dislocated genitals, by compromising circulation and by trauma of nerve periphery, devitalizes her system and exposes her a prey to intercurrent disease and to the great functional neuroses (neurasthenia and hysteria). The gynecologist by removal of the gynecologic dislocation, i. e., the focus of reflexes, can demonstrate that the reflex neuroses will disappear. In view of the prevailing difference of opinion between neurologists and gynecologists as to the consecutive reflex neurosis of genital dislocation a careful weighing of the data is demanded. Careful, comparative examination of gynecologic cases gives a definite series of reflex neuroses. It is admittedly difficult in each individual case to establish genuine genital reflex neurosis. The diagnosis must be made by exclusion. Improvement of the dislocation and lessening of the reflex neurosis under rational treatment is ocular proof. Certain rare cases arise in which no palpable, pathologic anatomic changes are perceptible and still apparently the gynecologic reflex neurosis exists. There are no exceptions to the rule. If an organ becomes diseased secondarily to genital dislocation through reflex neurosis a correction of the dislocation may not always cure the organ. For example, if a round ulcer appear in the stomach secondary to gynecologic dislocation and consequent menorrhagia, the cure of the genital disease would not cure the round ulcer of the stomach, which, if it bleed profusely, could be excised from the stomach wall, i. e., requires a specific treatment. If a general disease, such as a cardiac valvular lesion, create genital dislocation through congestion, the dislocation may produce reflex neurosis, but cure of the genital lesion does not involve the valvular lesion.

The logical force of circumstances impresses the practical gynecologist that genital disease gradually spreads over the other abdominal and thoracic viscera, disturbing visceral rhythm, circulation, absorption, secretion, and sensation by means of arcs of reflex action. Step by step, through compromised circulation, trauma of nerve periphery and infection of the genitals, the woman acquires indigestion due to perverted secretion—excessive, disproportionate, or insufficient. Malnutrition and anemia follow from continued indigestion and finally neurosis, the inevitable consequence of progressive disturbed pelvic mechanism. It requires careful observation to discriminate the onward march of genital disease, since many complications arise to throw one off guard, such as lumbo-sacral pain, tenesmus of sphincters (anus, vagina, and bladder), hyperesthesia of the pudendum, tearing and dragging pain in the thighs (anterior branches of lumbar plexus), pain in coccyx, intercostal neuralgia, especially on the side of the diseased genitals, pains in the breasts and irregular muscular contractions. All these are only incidents in the onward march of a disease of dominating viscera, whose reflexes unbalance life's physiologic laboratory. My observation places 70 per cent of disturbed pelvic mechanism on the left side; however, the neurosis shifts from side to side according to the renewed invasions of the genitals by disease. It is significant that the neurosis falls chiefly on the side of the disturbed pelvic mechanism. It is plain that the genitals have quite an independent nerve-supply and also stand in intimate relation to definite regions; in other words, diseased genitals have a predilection for certain nerves and nerve lesions. This fact is patent in the functional crises, at puberty, during pregnancy, at menstruation, and at the menopause. In pregnancy the irritation from the genitals invades the stomach in a physiologic rather than the pathologic degree. The grade of the genital irritation of pregnancy and menstruation seldom reaches a pathologic condition. During puberty, menstruation, pregnancy, and the menopause certain organs suffer, as the stomach, breasts, larynx and thyroid glands. The cranial nerves deserving mention for a special share during the above periods are the trigeminus and vagus, which may manifest not only excessive physiologic activity but an actual pathologic condition (physiology). The lack of mathematical demonstration of the share of the viscera and nerves in the above-mentioned conditions is because this sympathetic disturbance does not occur in every case. The close relation existing between ovarian disease and breast and iliac pain is often noted by the gynecologist, as well as dragging pelvic pain and stomach disturbance in retrodeviations of the uterus. The significant and dominating influence of the genitals on the life of the individual is manifest by the exacerbation of the nervous conditions at *puberty, menstruation, pregnancy*, and at the *menopause*, i. e., at the sexual crises. If the genitals are healthy, distinct neuroses (functional) at the above phases of sexual exacerbation give a definite clue to the source of the nervousness. No other viscera except the genitals produce through physiologic activity exacerbated phases of neuroses. The sexual is the most denominating instinct in animal life. The physiologic exacerbation of neuroses is the most definite proof of their source, since the pathologic exacerbation of neuroses is so complicated that errors arise in tracing the origin. The coincidence of neurosis and menstruation induced Battey to perform castration in order to anticipate the menopause. However, it is my opinion he began at the wrong end of the genitals, for nothing stops menstruation like removal of the chief part of the organ of menstruation, viz.: the uterus (the oviducts may be left). Menstruation is a vascular periodic wave and belongs to the uterus and oviducts, not to the ovary. Hence, menstrual neuroses are cured by removal of the menstrual organ and not by removal of the ovary. Considerable worth should be placed on certain relations between neuroses and special phases of sexual life. It may be suggested that these sexual phases of exacerbation belong to life during the active existence of the uterus and oviducts, i. e., or the menstrual organs—not during the active life of the ovary, for activity of the latter persists from before birth until the ovarian tissue is worn out at sixty or seventy years. It is an error to perform castration because the menstrual process coincides with the neurosis. In such a case, should an operation be performed, it ought to be hysterectomy and not ovariotomy; the organ which induced the neurosis should be attacked. However, it is simple justice to the patient to be morally sure before performing any operation that the organ to be attacked is the definite etiologic cause, for other etiologic factors may arise to unbalance the visceral nerves of woman; a stitch-abscess, a corn, or domestic irritation may simulate genital neurosis. Extreme precaution is required in diagnosing the neuroses of the sexual organs. This fact is observed from the varied time that a neurosis may arise during menstruation. Menstruation is a complicated process; in other words, what is superficially known as menstruation is perhaps only a part of a comprehensive physiologic mechanism. During menstruation we observe swelling of the mucosa of the uterus and oviducts, supposed maturation and rupture of follicles (?), and various degrees of congestion of the pelvic vessels peculiar to the wave movements or vascular pelvic rhythm, indicating blood-pressure. Almost any of the above factors may induce a menstrual neurosis, as the neurosis may occur in the premenstrual, intramenstrual, and postmenstrual period. Some neurotic factors may be displaced by exacerbation, and neurosis arises. The secretion, blood, may occur at, before, or after the highest *neural* menstrual wave. Menstruation is a change of symptoms in which now one line and now another is put on tension. The tension link manifests the character of the menstrual neurosis. Another factor of menstrual chain, as accentuated by Kirro (1878), is that during menstruation hypertrophy of the thyroid gland occurs, followed by passive congestion of the cerebrum and consequent psychosis. Perhaps hemorrhage from the nasal mucosa during menstruation is from congestion due to the sharing of the thyroid in menstruation and its capacious power of blood storage. With the above noted complication and many others it may be observed how careful the physician must be to establish menstrual neuroses or psychosis. Continual psychosis can, no doubt, be exacerbated by the menstrual periodicity; also, in the periodic diseases there is frequently a neuropathic constitution that results from congenital defects or existing pathology. For example, who can measure the burden of a woman with non-development and atrophy, i. e., before the uterus was fully developed it was attacked by inflammation, producing at first hypertrophy and ending in defective growth and atrophy? Such are among the saddest patients in my practice. They suffer not only from dysmenorrhœa and other painful neuroses, but from a psychosis due to inevitable sterility. Rachel mourns and will not be comforted. The nervous irritation issuing from the sexual organs may be from disease or change of blood-pressure; in other words, from functional or anatomic changes. In neurotic individuals the neurosis exists not only at the menstrual wave but also in the intermenstrual time, when pelvic disease is liable to exist. When a certain congruence exists between the neurosis and the menstrual rhythm it is a strong indication that the neurosis is of sexual origin. Experimentally the congruence of neuroses with phases of the sexual organs is demonstrated by the disappearance of the neuroses after hysterectomy or correlation of the uterus and uterine deviations or the destruction of pelvic peritoneal adhesions or the removal of a pelvic tumor. Gynecologists frequently note that a neurosis will begin with anatomic changes of the sexual organs and the neurosis exacerbates the sexual disease. The extent and the intensity of the pathology of the genitals may not stand in definite relation to the neurosis. One may observe large ovarian tumors without a trace of neurosis. From this clinical fact some have falsely argued that castration does not cure neurosis because disease of the ovaries does not produce it. There are factors in large ovarian tumors which explain partly, at least, why they do not produce a neurosis. First, the tumor has sufficient room to glide out of the way of pressure; second, the style is sufficiently long to avoid trauma from dragging or torsion of the pedicle; and doubtless the sensory nerves which supply the walls of the ovarian cyst have been stretched beyond their integrity and have ceased to transmit sensory disturbances. It is the small genital tumors located in the pelvis which are likely to be accompanied by neurosis. Such small tumors have a short style and are liable to dragging and torsion. They are subject to pressure from their immobility. The filling of the bladder and rectum traumatizes them and frequently a neurosis and a small pelvic tumor exist in casual relations. The life and action of nerves cannot be measured by the yard. Extreme neurosis may arise from the genitals by an irritation of the clitoris, a slight uterine deviation or a small scar, while no neurosis may be detected from extension, of sarcoma or carcinoma of the uterus or large ovarian tumor. Abdominal or pelvic tumors that give rise to a tendency to neurosis are generally from small, fixed growths (especially located in the pelvis) with short pedicles, situated within the range of trauma by muscular activity and by the expansion and contraction of organs.

The excitation or the inhibition of nervous attacks by artificial irritation is known to gynecologists. Mechanical irritation of other viscera seldom or never creates a nervous attack. This experiment indicates that the capacity of the genitals to dominate the nervous system is greater than that of other viscera. I was called in consultation in a typical case—a young woman in whom slight pressure in the ovarian region induced a wild hysteric attack, while vigorous pressure would inhibit it. Such cases, not rare, are a close demonstration of the dominating influence of the genitals over the system and also of the origin of the neurosis. To show how carefully one must discriminate the sources and kind of neurosis, a case from Professor Hegar may be placed in evidence. She was a young, non-neurotic individual who had a fist-sized right ovarian tumor with a long style, which allowed extraordinary mobility; when the tumor glided into the pelvis she suffered from pressure and dragging sensations. She complained daily of dragging on the pedicle, pains in the lumbo-sacral region, shoulder, and iliac region. To be relieved from these tormenting pains she besought Professor Hegar to operate on her. She was without fever or pain for the first nine days—well and happy. On the tenth day she was found with tears and sorrow, claiming that all her former troubles had returned, and all embittered because the operation had not relieved her. The neuralgia, the cramps, the pressure, dragging symptoms, etc., all had returned back. Professor Hegar noted that the patient had fever and, on examining the abdominal incision, discovered a stitch abscess; this was opened and the pains disappeared and returned no more. This was a suggestive case, confirming the rule that when a subject is neurotic for a long time any bodily irritation may be set going the old train of neurotic symptoms. In other words, a primary, complex neurosis, long continued, may be initiated by some distant local irritation. The secondary cause may be slight, such as a fright, an abscess, an injury, a disappointment or an exacerbation of disturbances in a menstruation. Doubtless, in the long continued neurosis a disturbed mechanism arises in the nerves, they lose their fine balance of integrity in motion, absorption, secretion, or sensation, and, being in a state of irritability, they are put to riot by any source of attack. It is in such unfortunate cases that the neurologist has lost sight of the primary cause, which was trauma and infection of the genital system, the dominating neurovascular viscera. For example, those who have much toothache know that any disturbance in health, as colds, getting wet, etc., will finally end in the old disease of toothache. The dental nerves having once become chronically unbalanced by trauma and infection, it is easy to light the old flame again. Observe the man who is suffering the remote effects of an ancient gonorrhea, the stricture fires up with a cold, an extra drink of whiskey or slight excess in coition. The old flame in the disturbed urethral mechanism may be initiated by remote secondary causes. The genitals are defective and do not resist. Demonstrations, by experiment, can be made to show that the neurosis depends on the genital disease. The reposition and retention of a dislocated or incarcerated pregnant uterus is frequently accompanied by a disappearance of the neurosis, while paresis of the lower limbs or uterine cough allows the pathology to recur and the neurosis is again set afoot. Paint the cervix with $AgNO_3$ solution and vicious vomiting follows. No doubt can arise as to the cause of the vomiting. But the terrific vomiting would not occur by painting other viscera not so richly supplied with nerves, such as the rectum or larynx. Professor Hegar had a case where he could repeatedly check a "uterine cough" or irritable cough by introducing a intra-uterine stem which straightened an anteflexed uterus. In the amphibia, in dissecting animals that require a day to die, one can demonstrate ocularly that irritating the rectum, cloaca, will start muscular contractions about the stomach. Doubtless the irritation to the sensory, absorptive and secreting nerves is just as severe but is not so easily seen. But every gynecologist knows that some women with disturbed pelvic mechanism suffer from exacerbated stomach secretion and motion. It is important to demonstrate the causal relations and establish the location at the beginning. This is difficult from the complex, yet somewhat independent, sexual nervous apparatus that gives rise to the neurosis, from the peculiarly highly organized nervous system of women and from the further fact that reflex neuroses are quite indirect and slow in their progressive march. The original cause which may be years old is overlooked in the exciting symptoms. It is not difficult to connect a fresh anal fissure with its accompanying wild disturbance, but when the disturbed pelvic mechanism (the anus and bladder have intimate nerve connection with the genitals) progresses for long periods the cause is buried in the grave of years gone by. Long experience in digital examination is the prerequisite for accurate diagnosis of disturbed pelvic mechanism and for the interpretation of its reflex effect. The disturbed pelvic mechanism, the primary cause of sexual neurosis, begins from simple disturbances in the genitals, such as pressure or dragging of nerves. These two conditions may be combined and we cannot always discriminate one from the other. For example, in the frequent vomiting of early pregnancy it is impossible to say whether it is pressure dragging upon the vesical or uterine distension nerves that induces uterine contractions and is followed by vomiting. After dragging or pressure (trauma) of nerves has become initiated another more distressing trauma of the genital nerves follows from catarrh, erosions, ulcerations, and wounds which expose the periphery of the nerves—all inducing reflexes which radiate to other viscera, unbalancing their rhythm, secretion, absorption and sensation. The compression (trauma) of the nerve periphery arises from dislocation of organs, edema, exudate, or tumor pressure. Such traumatic (compression) neurosis is common in gynecology.

Compression of the periphery of the nerves may be due to cicatricial tissue of both the pelvic peritoneum and subserosium. Rich sources of nerve compression may be found in the inflamed posterior and lateral ligaments of the uterus, as shown by Freund and others. The hyperplastic deposits and subsequent contraction found in the uterus, ovaries, and connective tissue needs but be mentioned to be rocognized. The contracting tissue of the uterus painfully compromises its expansion at the monthly period and the excessive ovarian cicatrices obstruct the expanding ovum and induce painful reflexes. The type of dragging (traumatic) neurosis is observed in sacropubic hernia or uterine prolapse and in retrodeviations of the uterus, the visceral prolapse gradually developing a complex neurosis of the lumbosacral region and thence spreading to unbalance the general abdominal viscera through reflexes of the abdominal brain. Dragging on the style of pelvic tumors is another cause. One may be able to measure, to some extent, the disturbance of dragging on nerves, on over-filled rectum or bladder. I have seen the pelvis, at autopsy, full to the brim with feces. The dragging of free tumors on styles must be considerable, for strangulated axial rotation is not infrequent. The best illustration of suffering from a free tumor on its style is the right kidney. Its dragging and rotation give rise to nausea, vomiting, pain in the back and thigh; excessive, insufficient or disproportionate secretion or absorption in the tractus intestinalis, inducing disturbances of digestion, and to similar disorders in the renal secretion.

Compression neurosis is indelibly associated with dragging neurosis. With inflamed peritoneal and subserous uterine ligaments reflex symptoms occur on standing, walking, and coughing. The reposition of the pelvic organs and their retention by a support relieves the symptoms. The cicatrices of the cervix and vagina may present compression or dragging neurosis, often accompanied, however, by endometritis, with exposed nerve endings, on which play visceral secretions. In acute flexions connective tissue changes cause pinching of the peripheral nerves, which manifest the neurosis chiefly as dysmenorrhea. In endometritis with exposed nerve periphery the irritating secretions induce painful uterine colic, calling up reflexes which reorganize in the abdominal brain and radiate to all abdominal and thoracic viscera, vitiating rhythm, secretion, and sensation. From the swollen endometrium the uterine contractions are futile to expel the secretions. The uterine contractions produce pain by compression of the nerves imbedded in diseased tissue. The gynecologist has a typical case to show the traumatic neurosis of nerves compressed in exudates in the old operations of amputation of the oviduct and ligation with silk, where the silk ligature becomes infected from diseased oviductal mucosa and an exudate arises with monthly exacerbations. It is not uncommon for such cases to last for three years, with terrible complex neurosis and untold misery. Hysterectomy cures such cases by stopping menstruation and relapses. If the uterus and bladder become imbedded in exudates their expansion and also that of the rectum is hindered, and severe reflex pains follow. Collection of secretions in the uterus induces contraction to expel them, and in contracting, the uterus drags on the adjacent fixed exudates. All motion of the uterus, bladder, and rectum is accompanied by compression or dragging pains—neurosis from trauma. In connective tissue hyperplasia of the uterus the uterine contractions are often very painful for compression of the nerves imbedded in the cicatrizing tissue. In myosalpingitis may be observed the recurring monthly exacerbations, the old train of neurosis from the oviductal colic, from congestion, contraction, or compression; lumbosacral neuralgia, however, the associated uterine congestion from adjacent disease, must not be overlooked. In some cases I have noted terrible neurotic symptoms from the amputated end of the oviduct being connected to a loop of a sigmoid by a peritoneal band. In one case in which Dr. Lucy Waite and I operated we found a thin peritoneal band extending from the amputated oviductal extremity to the center of the sigmoid flexure; this woman was bedridden for nearly two years with the most terrible neurosis. The severing of the thin peritoneal band enabled her to recover and gain some thirty pounds six months after the operation, with apparent perfect health. Her neurosis disappeared like magic. Peritoneal adhesions may bind the intestines and genitals together. Irritation of either the genitals or intestines influence peristalsis, and dragging pain and intense neurotic symptoms often follow in the wake. Visceral secretions and sensations are perverted. In such cases disturbances are after mealtimes and evacuations, and are caused by the induced peristalsis traumatizing nerves, imbedded in exudates and congesting vessels. In some young women following castration and in some others following the menopause, the pudendum and vagina atrophy. This doubtless is consequent upon vaginitis and atrophy of bloodvessels. The vessels atrophy irregularly (one can observe red, injected patches among the pale ones on the vaginal wall) and this irregularity causes local congestions. In cases of vaginal atrophy coitus enhances the neurosis on account of the narrow and sensitive vagina, and a kind of vaginismus occurs.

Nervous irritation may be occasioned by exposure of the genital nerve periphery from vaginal catarrh, papillary swellings at the vaginal introitus, or the meatus urinarius externus, or from fissures or erosions about the urethra, pudendum, or anus. Such lesions are often exacerbation by urination, defecation, coitus, or scratching, and may be accompanied by severe neurosis if allowed to persist for a long time. Progressive nervous affections rapidly radiate from the local lesion to the general visceral system. The irritation may remain isolated in the nervous system of the genitals for a longer or shorter period, but if long-continued or severe the neurosis eventually spreads to the general nervous system and is followed by indigestion, constipation, sleeplessness, and a state of more or less high nerve tension; in other words, a peculiar nervous irritability. Entirely isolated neuroses from the genitals are quite rare because the nervous apparatus of the genitals is so intimately and profoundly connected with both the cerebrospinal and the great sympathetic systems that disturbance in the rich nerves of the genitals spreads over the whole nervous system.

Besides, the disturbed pelvic mechanism often sooner or later invades the psychical apparatus and directs the mind to the diseased genitals with additional disadvantage to the individual. The general practitioner is very liable to treat the psychical or mental symptoms, forgetting that the disturbed pelvic mechanism is the rock and base of the neurosis. Not infrequently the psychical symptoms play the chief role in the disease. How often does the gynecologist observe the general practitioner treating the psychical or superficial symptoms—cardialgia, sacrolumbar neuralgia, or sexual disease with little idea of its etiology—though palpable in the pelvis? In short, the psychosis, which has a mental base, and the neurosis, which has a physical base, should be carefully differentiated. However, the psychosis is generally secondary to the neurosis, which latter generally has a palpable pelvic origin. It is what I shall term a vicious sexual circle, viz.: (a) disturbed pelvic mechanism, (b) neurosis, and (c) psychosis. This is accentuated in other ways by Hegar, Freund, Krantz and others to whose excellent labors I am a debtor. More in detail, this vicious sexual circle consists of (a) disturbed pelvic mechanism (trauma and infection); (b) indigestion (from disturbed visceral motion, secretion, absorption, and sensation); (c) malnutrition; (d) anemia; (e) neurosis, and (f) psychosis. From the disturbed pelvic mechanism to the psychosis is a long progressive march, a vicious sexual circle, direct and indirect, due to repeated reflex pelvic storms flashing over the other abdominal visceral plexuses. The viscera (as the stomach, kidney, and liver) possessing the greatest number of connective nerve-cords and hence, the least resistance, will suffer the most in their rhythm, secretion, and sensation. After this vicious sexual circle becomes established there exists a neuropathic condition. Primary and secondary symptoms then become difficult of differentiation. Direct and indirect symptoms become mixed and the clinical picture becomes obscured by its complexity. The causal connection between pelvic disease and neurosis (psychosis) becomes darkened and one cannot tell what is primary and what is secondary, especially when the patient comes to the physician late in the course of the malady. It is difficult to pick up any segment of the vicious sexual circle. Action and reaction are equal. We now have the degenerating influence of the general nervous system on the original disturbed pelvic mechanism. In the vicious sexual circle one should never disregard blood losses, as these often play a significant role. An ordinary monthly period makes women pale and, if slight additional losses occur, the effect is geometrically exacerbated. Excessive, deficient, or disproportionate blood supply to the abdominal brain and its automatic visceral ganglia due to reflexes, deranges visceral motion, secretion, absorption, and sensation. It would create in single viscera local disorderly reflexes. Aside from the vicious sexual circle I know of no experimental method to demonstrate it, except the disease itself, which gynecologists see daily. We must, as Hegar observes, be limited to the indexes of its course in order to diagnose and treat it. We must weigh each indication found in the progressive march of symptoms throughout the vicious sexual circle from genital disease. We must have definite stigmata to diagnose hysteria and not call every nervous woman a hysteric. The exclusion method must be employed for each and every diagnosis, and the treatment must include medical, electrical, surgical, and hydrotherapeutic measures as required. Treatment is experimental but should be rational. The rational diagnosis is to first establish some etiologic pathologic factor, and attempt to improve or remove it. Sometimes a secondary factor, as constipation or gastric disease, requires attention in order to trace our steps to the original pelvic disease. We must attempt to retrace on the links of the causal chain to the swivel where the reflexes began and broke their bounds. Deficient renal secretion may be another secondary symptom which requires improvement before the waste-laden blood will cease traumatizing the innumerable ganglia which it bathes.

In the diagnosis one must observe local diseases in the body which are not of sexual origin. The sexual organs are not the only viscera capable of producing neurosis. Be always on the alert for visceral ptosis, tuberculosis, nephritis, cholecystitis, peritonitis, and appendicitis. Of course, the nonsexual diseases may be coincident with sexual diseases, and both influence the neurosis and general nourishment. Make careful bodily examinations for diseases outside the genitals. Do not overlook heart lesions which allow congestions, hepatic sclerosis which induces some ascites, chlorosis which induces general paleness, with a large glandular system, yet coexists with a well-developed panniculus adiposus, headaches, and breathlessness, anemia, etc., etc. In my experience nothing has been so successful as visceral drainage—draining the skin by salt baths, the kidneys by drinking ample fluids, and the bowels by salines, with set hour for evacuation. Drainage of the bowels, skin, and kidneys is the rock and base of the therapeutics which will benefit the vicious sexual circle. It is rational hydrotherapy. Thus, by treatment, we are often enabled to run over one difficulty after another until the etiologic factor is reached, which is disturbed pelvic mechanism, the beginning of the viscious sexual circle. In other words, the microscope aids to diagnose tuberculosis, or mercury to diagnose syphilis. In diagnosis and treatment the gynecologist must always hold in his mental grasp every abdominal organ.

With the entrance and establishment of the neurosis and psychosis the sexual pathologic circle is completed and persistent rational treatment is required to break it. Now, any segment of the pathologic circle has a degenerating influence on the others. Pathologic processes can arise in other portions of the body, either coincident, independent, or as a result of the pathologic sexual circle. The gynecologist not only should have every abdominal organ in mind but should be able to exclude all other pathologic processes. Among the abdominal organs requiring special care in diagnosis are the stomach and colon. Stomach and colon diseases may lead to reflexes, hypochondria, neurosis, and even psychosis. Note what intense neurosis follows secretion neurosis of the colon (mucous colitis); also, that slackening or paresis of the abdominal wall—splanchnoptosia—accompanied by visceral ptosis and dragging on the mesentery, can lead to lumbosacral symptoms. For example, for years I have noted the hyperplasia of the genitals and hemorrhage therefrom in mitral lesions of the heart. In this case the heart disease is primary and the pelvic disease secondary. The genitals show varicose veins and the pelvic disease and hemorrhage may become so severe that a neurosis results. In this neurosis the diseased genitals were only a link in the chain.

Of course, these conditions—variously known as neurasthenia, neurosis, spinal iritation, or hysteria—may exist without palpable sexual disease, but any gynecologist knows that sexual disease plays an important factor and often enters in combination in their production.

Bibliography: Professor Hegar, Lohmer, Krantz.

CHAPTER XXIX.

CONSTIPATION—ITS PATHOLOGIC PHYSIOLOGY AND TREATMENT BY EXERCISE, HABITAT, DIET AND "VISCERAL DRAINAGE."

"Now is the winter of our discontent made glorious summer by this sun of York"—Shakespeare in Richard III.

"Literature is the immortality of speech."—Schlegel.

Constipation is infrequent or incomplete evacuation of the colon resulting in fecal retention.

ETIOLOGY OF CONSTIPATION.

The etiology of constipation is obscure. One writer alone offers some score of causes. Sluggishness of the bowel, whatever that means, is the most frequently mentioned. The tractus intestinalis is practically under the domain of the sympathetic nerve, nervus vasomotorius. Certain general etiologic conditions may be considered:

I. Physiology of the tractus intestinalis. In the etiology of constipation four physiologic factors are involved, viz., (a) peristalsis, (b) absorption, (c) secretion, (d) sensation. Any one or all of these functions may be impaired.

II. Local Causes.—The *local causes* of constipation may be: (1) splanchnoptosia—inefficient muscular contraction; (2) constriction of some segment of the colon; (3) collections of scybola or intestinal concretions, as in cecum, sigmoid and rectum; (4) enfeebled contraction of the intestinal muscularis; (5) local disease, as appendicitis, cholecystitis, pelvic peritonitis mesosigmoiditis—producing paresis.

III. General Causes.—The *general causes* of constipation are: (1) inefficient function (peristalsis, absorption, secretion, sensation); (2) excessive mental or physical activity; (3) special habits; (4) dietetic errors; (5) diseases of adjacent viscera; (6) factors which induce dryness of feces from inefficient secretion or excessive absorption; (7) impaired peristalsis of the colon.

IV. Anatomy.—The proper function of the tractus intestinalis depends on a normal nerve, blood and lymph apparatus. For perfect physiology, a maximum nerve, blood and lymph supply is required. The muscularis intestinalis, as well as the mucosa intestinalis, must be perfect. From frequent diseases (catarrh) of pueritas and consequent defective digestion, with resulting deficient nourishment, a non-developed and defective tractus intestinalis remains for life.

Atrophic or infantile segments of the digestive tract (especially the enteron or small intestine, which is the essential segment—receiving the secretions from liver and pancreas) burden the adult. For example, I found in the personal measurements of the enteron in six hundred and five adults that the length of the enteron was, maximum, thirty-two feet; minimum, ten and one-half feet, and average, twenty-one feet. The enteron (a single segment and the most essential one), the business portion of the digestive tract, varies more than three times its minimum length. These facts demonstrate that the tractus intestinalis is frequently defective in length, in development, nerve, blood and lymph—in anatomy. Abnormally diminutive digestive apparatus may occur. The following recorded data secured by the personal examination of six hundred and five adults, may be suggestive in regard to the anatomy of the tractus intestinalis:

1. The average length of the enteron in four hundred and fifty-three males was twenty-three feet.

2. The average length of the enteron in one hundred and fifty-two females was nineteen feet.

3. Man's enteron averages four feet longer than that of woman.

4. The enteron increases in length most rapidly a few months subsequent to birth, when it may grow one and one-half feet a month.

5. The enteron assumes its chief length in early childhood.

6. The chief variation in the length of the enteron depends on enteritis, compromising the enteronic peristalsis, absorption, secretion, and sensation, and consequently digestion, during early extrauterine life.

7. Extraordinary lengths of the enteron depend on the favorable conditions of a maximum enteronic nerve and vascular supply, with maximum assimilation continued beyond the usual period of enteronic development.

8. A subject with maximum length of enteron possesses a stronger constitution than a subject with minimum length, as he can digest and economize more food.

9. A maximum enteronic, nerve, vascular, glandular, and muscular apparatus, with similar food, would practically produce a similar length of enteron.

10. The foods which produce the most vigorous enteronic functions (peristalsis, absorption, sensation, and secretion) are those that leave the greatest indigestible fecal residue, which excites the enteronic muscularis into peristalsis, thus attracting more blood and inciting the enteronic mucosa to greater secretion and absorption—increasing digestion and, consequently, enteronic growth.

11. General and local disease influence the length of the enteron, especially during childhood, the period in life of rapid enteronic growth.

12. A child nourished with food which requires vigorous digestion, leaves a fecal indigestible residue, as cereals, would attract more blood to the enteron, enhancing its growth, than one nourished on milk only, which passes through the enteron without inducing vigorous peristalsis, and leaves little indigestible residue.

13. The human enteron presents colossal differences as to length: Males $11\frac{1}{2}$ feet minimum, 32 feet maximum = 20 feet; female $10\frac{1}{2}$ feet minimum

feet, 30 feet maximum=19½ feet. This variation of twenty feet is almost equal to the length of an average enteron. The enteron varies over double, or two and one-half times its length.

14. In adults the relation of the length of the enteron to the body length is as 7.2 is to 1. There is a vast difference between the absolute and relative length of the enteron of man.

15. The enteron measured *in situ* is three to six feet less in length than when extirpated.

16. Different diseases of the enteron may result in elongation or contraction. The above defects are not heredity, but acquired by disease. They will offer a clew to conditions for constipations.

V. Mechanical.—Constipation may arise from stricture, flexions, peritoneal adhesions, neoplasm, splanchnoptosia, obstruction of lumen.

VI. Dietetic.—*Quality* of foods, *quantity* of fluid, *chemical* composition, are important considerations. (a) *Food* must possess sufficient variety (mixed) in quantity, quality, chemical composition, and be ingested at regular intervals. The food should be mixed, however, and possess sufficient indigestible matter to leave ample residue to stimulate peristalsis (and hence absorption, sensation, and secretion). An excessive amount of coarse, indigestible food will result in an excessive fecal residue, which excessively stimulates peristalsis, absorption, secretion and sensation—resulting in muscular fatigue and defective sensibility of the mucosa—consequently reflex action is impaired. (b) Ample *fluids* at regular intervals should be ingested. For a person of one hundred and fifty pounds three pints daily is required to supply the bodily waste (i. e., for tractus intestinalis respiratorius, urinarius, perspiratorius); eight ounces should be drunk every two hours for six times daily.

Fecal matter is about seventy-five per cent fluid and twenty-five per cent solid. The value of fluids for the tractus intestinalis is evident, because in hot weather, with consequent vigorous activity of the tractus respiratorius, constipation results. The chief value of mineral water is the quantity drunk. Excessive fluids deteriorate digestion; (c) foods should possess *chemical* qualities. Carbohydrates produce acidity, nitrogenous foods alkalinity, and mixed foods neutrality of the digestive tract. Evacuation of the tractus intestinalis depends on (a) sufficient volume of feces, (b) sufficient volume of fluid contents, (c) the presence of substances which act as a chemical irritant to peristalsis. Dr. Walter Baumgarten attempted to devise a substance which would not only be difficult to absorb, but would retain its watery contents. He administered eight grains of the dry, shredded agar-agar three times daily, whence he found the stool increased in volume and watery content.

VII. Pathologic.—The pathologic impairment of peristalsis, secretion, absorption, and sensation of the tractus intestinalis, must be studied to account for the constipation.

Chronic peritonitis, an important factor in constipation, is frequently due to chronic peritoneal inflammation. In the major regions of peritonitis tne story of constipation is told. Chronic peritonitis occurs in the oviducts (80 per cent), in the ileo-cœco-appendicular region (70 per cent, over right psoas), in the mesosigmoid (80 per cent, over left psoas), in the cholecyst and right colonic flexure region (45 per cent), between the right kidney and the liver (40 per cent), i. e., muscular trauma on viscera induces the migration of germs or their products through the visceral mucosa, muscularis and finally into the adjacent peritoneum inciting plastic peritonitis.

There may be defective innervation of the muscularis of the digestive tract and abdominal wall (splanchnoptosia). Brain and spinal cord disease (insane and neurotic) and exhausted disease.

Inhibition of reflex action may arise to check defecation, as from fissure, ulcer, hemorrhoid, operation, painful vesical affections, hypertrophy of anal sphincter. Also constipation is associated with lethargy or sluggishness of the bowels from local peritoneal or visceral inflammation, as appendicitis, ovaritis, salpingitis, cholecystitis, pelvic peritonitis. It is in such cases that opium (a sedative to the local irritation) acts as a cathartic.

The state of the contents of the bowels is significant as chronic dyspepsia, irregular eating and evacuation and insufficient fluid accompanying the food.

Anatomic peculiarities may lead to constipation, as elongated cecum, sigmoid, and adherent U-shaped transverse colon, all of which may lie in the pelvis. Much of constipation is a perversion of the sympathetic nerves controlling the tractus intestinalis.

VIII. Sex.—Woman is more liable to constipation than man, because in her the tractus genitalis is violently changed periodically—robbing the tractus intestinalis of its usual quantity of blood (puberty, menstruation, pregnancy, and pelvic disease); (2) woman is less active, more sedentary than man; (3) woman is afflicted with more splanchnoptosia; (4) woman experiences more changes in her visceral circulation (during sexual life) than man (physiology and pathology of genitals).

IX. Age Relations.—In *senescence* constipation may occur from limited food employed, limited exercise, and limited functions, due to the degeneration of senescence. In senility, peristalsis, absorption, secretion and sensation is limited from limited blood supply, due to arterio-sclerosis. In *pueritas* anatomic peculiarities exist. The tractus intestinalis develop irregularly, the nervous system is not in final established control, the mucosa, muscularis, tractus nervosus and tractus vascularis may be defective in development. Catarrh occurs with facility and frequently. The tractus intestinalis is subject to vast vicissitudes of fortune, both in regard to food and attacks of catarrh. Hence its circulatory life—its basic life—is subject to vast, frequent and rapid changes.

Constipation is a neurosis of the fecal reservoir. It belongs essentially among the affections of the sympathetic nerves.

The system of nerves (including Auerbach's and the Billroth-Meissner plexuses) which rule the gastro-intestinal tract is strictly in the domain of the sympathetic. However, the physiological manifestations of the nerves ruling the enteron are quite different from those ruling the colon. The nerves ruling the enteron act with intense vigor and great rapidity. The nerves ruling the colon and rectum act with moderate force and very slowly. The enteron rapidly forces the contents of Bauhin's valve in a few hours. The nerves of the colon and rectum act slowly, evacuating the fecal reservoir usually once every twenty-four hours.

The changes in the physiological action from the vigorous, rapid motion of the enteron, to the moderate, slow movement of the colon and rectum, must be due to the intervention of the inferior mesenteric ganglion, located at the root of the inferior mesenteric artery, which emits its radiating branches along the inferior mesenteric artery, supplying the left end of the transverse colon, the left colon, the sigmoid flexure and rectum. The right colon and the right half of the transverse colon are supplied by the abdominal brain, sending branches along the superior mesenteric artery. Now, it is quite probable that the slow movement of the nerves belongs entirely to the left colon, sigmoid and rectum, which is entirely supplied by branches of the inferior mesenteric ganglia.

Hence, for the regular periodic evacuation of feces, a habit established by ages, we must look to the immediate rhythmic control of the inferior mesenteric ganglion. This is in accord with the idea that the stool, before expulsion, lies in the sigmoid and rectal ampulla. That the portion of the bowel concerned in evacuation is under control of a nervous mechanism, may be inferred from the fact that a person can establish almost any definite hour for regular defecation. A person can sometimes restrain the stool without difficulty for several days. For the cause of constipation we must look to a peculiar nervous disturbance in the peristalsis, absorption, secretion, and sensation of the colon, or of that part of the colon supplied by the branches of the inferior mesenteric ganglion.

In constipation the feces are found in the colon and not in the enteron. This abnormality of the colonic innervation may be congenital, or acquired. Some individuals are constipated from childhood. A boy of fifteen came to my office a short time ago who had never had a stool from babyhood onward without a rectal injection, or some strong physic. By careful examination it appeared that neither the cerebro-spinal nor the sympathetic system was fully or completely developed. However, in a month, from physical procedures, select food, ample fluid at regular intervals, massage, rectal injections, vigorous riding and regular stool hours, we secured a habit of daily evacuation. Here, doubtless, the trouble was congenital—deficient and imperfect development. Depressing mental affections derange the regular bowel action. However, in constipation accompanying melancholia, or mental disturbances, it seems to me that it is impossible, at present, to decide which is the cause and which is the effect. To illustrate the influence of the nervous system over bowel evacuation, observe how a railroad journey, a change of locality, festival and change of labor, affect a constipated condition. Besides, autopsies of persons dead from other diseases teach that in constipation seldom can structural lesions be demonstrated. The chief features of habitual constipation tend to show that the abnormal condition must be sought in a neurosis of the colon (especially to the left colon, the sigmoid and rectum). The exact nature of the colonic affection is unknown. Another factor in constipation is that though the nervous system of the colon be fairly developed, yet the muscularis of the colon is not normally developed. There is atony of the colonic wall, well expressed by old Latin authors as *atonia intestini*. But in this case perhaps the colon muscular atrophy refers to the nerves, as they control the lumen of the blood-vessel, which is the real nourisher and instigator of function.

In regard to the relations of the skeletal muscles to the intestinal muscles, in constipation, we maintain that they are entirely independent of each other, except mechanically.

The subject with the most weakened and miserable condition of the skeletal muscles may be absolutely regular in bowel evacuation, or may suffer severe constipation. Of course, we must not omit the mechanical influence of the abdominal muscles in defecation. The abdominal muscles increase the intra-abdominal pressure, and thus aid evacuation, but it is not likely that they increase peristalsis. Perhaps in general the skeletal or intestinal muscles play but a small role in constipation. The matter lies closer to the nervous system.

Bouveret and Dunin have claimed that habitual constipation was a frequent accompaniment of general nervousness, especially of neurasthenia; that the neurosis was the constipation, not the constipation the cause of neurosis. This idea is apt to prevail with most force among those physicians who, in curing the patient of the general neurosis, neurasthenia, have seen the constipation disappear. Fleiner asserts that stool retardation is due to spasmodic contraction of the colon segments, grasping their contents. This would make the trouble depend on the nervous system.

The mechanical conditions that induce constipation will not be here considered, except so far as their purely nervous mechanism and influence is concerned. Hence, such factors as strangulation by peritonitic bands and through apertures, and the mechanical difficulties of splanchnoptosia and pressure of abdominal tumors, are not here discussed. However, we must not overlook the obstacles placed in the way of the intestinal nerves by inflammation of any one of the bowel coats, or tunics, as peritonitis, or inflammation of the muscularis, or of the mucosa. As abdominal surgeons, we well know that acute peritonitis produces immediate constipation, checking peristalsis by edema, congestion and exudation, into one of the bowel tunics, especially the peritoneum. The peripheral bowel nerve apparatus is deranged by pressure, infection and malnutrition. It may rapidly recover. But, doubtless, a crippled and defective condition frequently remains—nonmechanical. As a result of peritonitis or inflammation of any one of the bowel tunics, producing habitual constipation, we must especially examine the *flexura coli lienalis* and the *flexura sigmoidea*. Not infrequently the action of the distal end of the diaphragmatic muscles produces inflammation of the left colon, by inducing migration of microbes through muscular trauma.

Also the conditions disturbing the rectal nerves must be considered as causing congestion and results. In constipation we only include the colon segment supplied by the branches of the inferior mesenteric ganglion. It must not be supposed for one moment that peritonitis around the evacuating fecal depository is always recognized. Far from it, for in some six hundred recorded adult autopsies I found evidences of peritonitis in the peritoneum of the left colon in fully eighty per cent of subjects. In fact, in the mesosigmoid alone there was about seventy-five per cent of peritonitis.

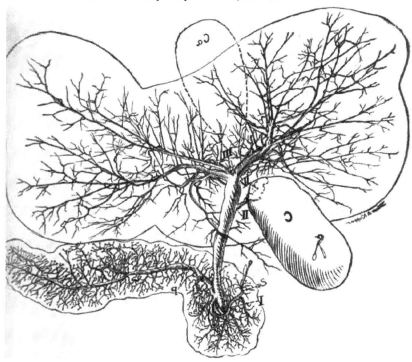

X-RAY OF DUCTUS BILIS ET DUCTUS PANCREATICUS

Fig. 82. This illustration suggests the quantity of nerves required to ensheath the ducts and vessels of the liver and pancreas as fenestrated, nodular plexuses.

Constipation may arise in some persons from deficient or abnormally small abdominal brain, or from premature senility in the abdominal sympathetic, which innervates the gastro-intestinal tract; also from cerebrospinal disease, which inhibits sources of energy. Exhaustion, mental or physical, is a potent factor in constipation. A deficient blood supply to the parenchymal ganglion does not invigorate it sufficiently to induce peristalsis. Exhaustion from over-exertion, excessive sexual action, or extra loss of blood, is a common cause of constipation in young women. Depression from disappointment, from death, from unrequited love, and many other causes, is quite apparent in the youthful, producing constipation—a purely nervous phenomenon.

Constipation in lead colic is a nervous phenomenon, apparent in the intestinal pain, and in the white ring-like contraction of the circular bowel fibers. The etiological factor is the irritation of the parenchymal ganglia of the bowel wall by the lead. Spasm, irregularity of inertia, characterizes the bowel in lead colic, except in the etiology.

Violent and persistent constipation depends on perverted muscular action, peristalsis, absorption, sensation or secretion, due in general to some deficiency of nerve force. Colonic inertia may rest on deficient blood supply to the parenchymal ganglia, but this is directly under the control of the sympathetic, which holds sway over the vessel's caliber.

It must always be borne in mind that the size of the sympathetic differs very much in different individuals. When a small-sized visceral nervous system becomes impaired, as it easily will, its phenomena are not only marked, but difficult to correct. A large dose of digitalis slows the heart, and whether the spinal accessory or vagus, digitalis inhibits its action. Nothnagel suggests that opium works similarly on the splanchnics, i. e., by slowing peristalsis.

The movements of the enteron are largely dependent on the amount of blood in the intestinal wall i. e., the amount of fresh blood which supplies the parenchymal ganglia.

In regard to antiperistalsis, in scores of experiments on dogs, rabbits, guinea-pigs, etc., I saw no such a phenomenon. The vomiting in ileus paralyticus or peritonitis may be due to simple contraction of the stomach on the enclosed contents, when the fluids pass through the esophagus in the direction of the least resistance. The monstrously large, wide cecum of herbivora, a vestigial stomach, as in the cow and horse, is emptied by peristalsis and not by antiperistalsis, as noted by Jreper. It may be that the peristalsis is increased in diarrhea, yet it may be just as active in constipation, but in this the colonic movements are vain and futile, from inability to force the contents into successive new segments, for an empty bowel is a still one, and a full bowel is an active one. Also active peristalsis will invite more blood into the bowel wall, which, in turn, induces active motion in the segments. Doubtless, herein lies the value of abdominal massage. Whatever checks the flow of fresh blood to the bowel wall slows peristalsis, and this explains the constipation of anemia.

The natural secretions, as the bile and the pancreatic fluids, are, perhaps, sufficient alone to excite the parenchymal ganglia to action, with but little or no aid from the splanchnics. Hence, from the inactive hepatic and pancreatic secretion, constipation may result. Consequent swelling of the mucosa from catarrh, in the bile ducts, may exclude the bile from other channels, which would deprive the parenchymal ganglia of their accustomed stimulus.

The relations of adjacent viscera and their condition may influence constipation. If the accustomed secretions, bile, pancreatic and gastro-intestinal, diminish, the bowel will not receive the impulse which the normal amount of secretions impart, and peristalsis partially fails. Diarrhea may be instigated by congestion, then by edema and, instead of infiltrating the bowel wall, the result may be rapid exudation and diarrhea.

Increased peristalsis, however, is not necessarily accompanied by increased secretion and exudation. The irritation which produces the peristalsis may so irritate the parietal intestinal ganglia as to lessen the caliber of the blood vessels and thus check secretion. In administering certain purgatives it is found that they are followed by watery evacuations. But this may be due to exalted peristalsis of the bowel, allowing insufficient time for absorption, e. g., in times of quiet peace in the bowel secretion and absorption balance each other; but if segments of the bowel become irritated by cathartics, the secretions may become very much increased. Yet, owing to the vigorous peristalsis, the fluids are rushed distalward, not allowing sufficient time for absorption.

Constipation is generally a form of neurosis, which may partake of a sensory, motor of secretory nature. It may, however, have a complex course and origin. Constipation is a condition in which the colon is not evacuated daily, except by the aid of evacuants, rectal injections or physical procedures. The great majority of the human family having a daily bowel evacuation establishes the normal frequency at once a day. Exceptions to this rule may be observed in certain individuals who have two stools daily, others one stool in two or three days, while again Pick reports patients who have one stool a week. A doubtful report was made by Dr. Robert Williams, where a woman had four bowel movements a year, three months apart.

This irregularity or deviation from normal defecation, need not necessarily be based on demonstrable pathological conditions. In constipation we have several elements to consider, the mucosa, the muscularis, the blood-vessels, the serosa, and the nerve supply.

Perhaps the greatest etiological factor of constipation is enteritis, catarrh of the colonic mucosa. This would involve the secretory nerves. In fact, catarrhal diseases of the colonic mucosa are the active factors in ever-changing forms of constipation and diarrhea, which, doubtless, involve the secretory nerves more than the motor nerves. Of course, the regularity of stool depends very much on the quality and quantity of food ingested, for if the food leaves no residue it will conduce constipation, for the greatest of all stimuli to colonic motion is food in contact with the intestinal mucosa. The peripheral nerves of the intestinal mucosa receive impetus and sensation from the analward moving fecal remnants.

The chief influence in constipation is the blood and food. The formation of the stool depends mainly on the relation of the solids and fluids introduced into the stomach.

A close relation exists in constipation between the quantity of food ingested, and the resulting fecal residue, which actively counts in treatment.

Water is one of the best adjunct evacuants. An exclusively milk diet may create constipation, because the small residue is insufficient to excite peristalsis through the peripheral nerves. If milk creates diarrhea, it is likely from some sudden development of germs, or fermentation. The utility of graham bread in curing constipation lies in the fact that a large indigestible residue remains, inducing colonic contraction; its contained salts either invite fluids or excite peristalsis, both resulting in a kind of massage, or acting like a foreign body to the mucosa.

The habits of life are closely associated with constipation. Society women and traveling men, with irregular ingestion and habits, are liable to constipation. Sedentary habits, deficient exercise and excessive mental work, tend to produce constipation. The use of narcotics, deficient drinking of water, active perspiration and uncomfortable closets play a role in inducing constipation. Excessive eating or excessive ingestions in the gastro-intestinal canal may lead to atony of the intestinal wall, and consequent constipation. The causal relation of constipation must be sought in the digestive tract itself, in the quality and quantity of food ingested, in the habits, in the relations of other viscera.

In certain cerebro-spinal diseases, the sensory nerves of the intestinal mucosa may be obtunded or blunted, so that the ordinary peristalsis is not excited by the ordinary stimulus of food residue. The peripheral sensory apparatus of the mucosa does not perceive the usual stimulus, and the bowels become torpid. This is common in certains form of hysteria, or better, visceral neurosis. In melancholics and hypochondriacs the barometer of their spirits seems often to tally exactly with the bowel activity. The greater the activity of their bowels the more lively and natural their mentality. But it must not be forgotten that constipation is often occasioned by the mental condition. We know personally that vomiting may be induced by a physical cause, or by a mental one. Some will vomit from seeing a fly in the soup. So it is with a genital neurosis, it may create constipation, or may induce a local neurosis by bathing the innumerable ganglia with waste-laden blood. If secretion be deficient, absorption continues, the feces harden, form an increasing plug, and becomes such an impediment that even vigorous peristalsis will not produce the analward movement required.

Heredity and congenital ailments play a role through the defects in the nerves of the intestines. We deal here chiefly with the purely nervous influence, as the intestinals of the cachectic may be confined, or may act very irregularly. Persons with defective nervous systems, as idiots and the insane, suffer from constipation. The ill-defined hysteric person, or the neurotic subject, is painfully afflicted with constipation, with sluggish bowels, and some of these very subjects are continually complaining of colicky pains, which are to be interpreted as vain attempts of peristalsis to force the bowel contents analward.

In constipation splanchnoptosia plays its role by flexing the intestine, producing conditions which require more vigorous peristalsis to overcome; in short by compromising the bowel caliber. In splanchnoptosia the hepatic and splenic flexures are both made more acute by the consequent dragging of the *ligamentum hepatico-colicum et phrenico-colicum sinistrum.*

Relaxed, pendulous abdominal walls are incapable of exerting normal or sufficient pressure on the tractus intestinalis to control circulation (lymph or blood) or to expel the feces.

The fecal reservoir, as previously stated, is the left half of the transverse colon, the left colon, the sigmoid and rectum, the field ruled by the inferior mesenteric ganglion. It has been asserted by my respected teacher, Nothnagel, that constipation is relatively frequent in comparison with the rarity of peritoneal fixation. I wish respectfully to differ from this excellent and instructive Viennese teacher. In some six hundred personal autopsies I found peritonitis in the fecal reservoir in at least eighty per cent of the subjects. This peritonitis, due to two causes, viz., traumatic muscular action of the psoas magnus on the sigmoid, and of the distal left limb of the diaphragm on the left colon, which induces migration of pathologic microbes to the serosa; and the abrading of the mucosa of the fecal reservoir at the flexures (splenic and sigmoid), allowing the wound to become infected, and the migration of pathogenic germs to the serosa.

Nowhere in the body is infection from the mucal abrasion more definite than at the *ligamentum phrenico-colicum sinistrum.* In six hundred adult autopsies we found that the fecal reservoir was afflicted with peritonitis in more than eighty per cent of the cases. Did eighty per cent of these cases suffer from constipation? We think not. Therefore, according to our six hundred autopsies, peritonitis of the fecal reservoir is far more common than constipation, for eighty per cent of adults do not suffer from constipation. Hence, we are forced to the opinion that peritonitis of the fecal reservoir has undoubtedly an influence in inducing constipation, by traumatizing the nerves presiding over defecation. The nerves may suffer from pressure by exudates or edema, from congestion or malnutrition. The final outcome is derangement of the nerves of the fecal reservoir—exaltation or debasement of sensation and motion. As probability is the rule of life, the results of peritonitis cf the fecal reservoir is here referred to, and not acute peritonitis. I have shown (Peritoneal Adhesions After Laparotomy, *Amer. Gyn. and Obstet. Jour.,* December, 1895) that gross peritoneal adhesions (bands) attached to organs of maximum peristaltic action, as the middle of the sigmoid flexure and the oviducts (or their amputated ends), the mobile bladder, or the active peristaltic loop of enteron, frequently create very much pain, though not necessarily constipation. Yet the finer pathological infiltrations, perhaps, not even microscopic, or at least insufficient to create condition of the fecal reservoir which may be far more effective in causing constipation, than the gross peritoneal bands which simply fix, dislocate viscera, or parts of viscera, are an important factor in inducing constipation in splanchnoptosia. Perhaps splanchnoptosia should be viewed as a constitutional disease, a general neurosis. The viscera supports very gradually elongate in splanchnoptosia, and the nerves as gradually lose their tone. That the visceral nerves are involved in splanchnotosia is very evident from the manifest derangement of the nerves of sensation, motion, absorption, and secretion. Splanchnoptosia is a weakening of the nervous system, a special slackening, or elongation of the visceral supports, which we must acknowledge is not manifest in the digestive tract muscles, but attacks the skeletal muscles (e. g., of the abdominal wall).

Every practitioner has observed that with the induction of habitual constipation a peculiar nervous phenomenon also arises. The popular opinion is that the constipation is the cause of the neurosis, but such an opinion does not always stand the test of analysis. Is the neurosis not the cause of the constipation? The finer beginning of the neurosis was not observed, while the grossness of constipation is discernible from beginning to end. After constipation has once started, a train of symptoms may set in, as long retention of the feces allows them to become dry and hard from absorption of fluids. The feces become pressed into the saccules of the colon, as hard, irregular masses, known as scybala. Such masses, by continued pressure, may produce mucus ulceration. The subject experiences fullness in the abdomen and disagreeable sensations; the appetite disappears, gases are eructed, and a disagreeable taste arises. The skin may assume a muddy color, and the fecal masses may be covered with mucus in various quantities. Some practitioners falsely attribute the slime, or mucus, to colonic catarrh. The excessive mucus is due to irritation of the mucosa by the fecal masses, which irritation may also induce a hyperemia of the mucosa, producing disordered secretion, with fermentation and gases. The fecal accumulation can produce not only a transitory mucal hyperemia, excessive secretion and diarrhea, but anatomic changes, such as colonic catarrh, trauma of the colonic wall and local peritonitis. Considerable colic may arise from the attempts of the colon to expel the large accumulated masses, which palpation may reveal.

But, to speak of the difficulties arising from hardened masses of accumulated feces is only to bring in mechanical difficulties, with all their train of evils, on the three tunics of the colon and their functions, which is not our chief theme. Our contention is that constipation is a neurosis of the fecal reservoir.

To illustrate how intimately the nervous system rules the fecal reservoir in its periodic evacuations, all that is necessary is to recall how many patients relate that, on change of business, residence, or scenery, the evacuations being neglected, cease their regularity. So far as I am aware, constipation always has one of its results, the collection of feces in the colon, from the rectal ampulla to Bauhin's valve, but the chief locality is the middle of the transverse colon to the rectal ampulla. The collection of fecal masses in the right colon is rare, and, perhaps, in the right half of the colon it is also rare, except from mechanical causes, i. e, if half of the colon be full of hardened feces, the right half will be full, from the physical fact of its inability to force them analward.

The train of evils resulting from constipation is almost endless, e. g., the fecal masses produce pressure on the returning veins of the fecal reservoir, causing congestion, especially in the rectal veins, resulting in hemorrhoids. Perier has recently attempted to show that the so-called "fecal fever" is due to absorption from the digestive tract. The proof of this he demonstrates by a cathartic reducing the fever. This view of Perier has some show of truth in it, for in puerperal sepsis, in fever after operation, a cathartic reduces the fever like a charm. The drain by the cathartic directs the poison outward. However, it must be remembered that high temperature subsequent to some pelvic operations, is rather due to absorption of septic matter remaining in the pelvis than absorption from the bowel. For long past and even to-day certain widespread opinions, in regard to certain definite connections between the central nervous system and constipation exist. Constipation and the central nervous system are brought into close relations. All grades of symptoms, from the slightest disturbance to hypochondrical and severe psychical, are included as due to constipation. Certain writers have tried to show that relations exist between dyspepsia and constipation on the one hand, and hypochondria and melancholia on the other. Virchow started such views nearly fifty years ago, and Virchow always wrote with a pencil of light. The celebrated neurologist, Romberg, claimed in 1850, that constipation could induce hypochondria. It is not strange that the opinion of such giants as Virchow and Romberg, both strengthened by observations, should prevail so long. But our belief is that constipation is a neurosis of the fecal reservoir. Hence, constipation, melancholia, and hypochondria are the result of neurosis, and not the cause. We must look to neurasthenia as the forerunner of constipation, as the neurotic invader of the fecal reservoir bringing in its wake constipation. When neurasthenia and melancholia enter, the process becomes retarded. Recently, Dunin has favored the view that constipation is the result of a neurosis and not the cause. True it is that nervous persons do not always suffer from constipation nor are non-nervous persons invariably free from it, but, first, be it remembered that the fecal reservoir is chiefly under the influence of the inferior mesenteric ganglion, and its radiating nerves (sympathetic), and not the cerebro-spinal, though the last-named exercises certain influences over the fecal reservoir; also, that the fecal neurosis is a local affair, i. e., the peripheral nerves supplying the colon in area of the inferior mesenteric artery may be attacked by disease, independently of the remaining sympathetic and cerebro-spinal systems.

The general view here entertained in regard to constipation and neurosis is: That the constipation is the cause of nervous symptoms, e. g., a person suffers for several days from constipation and light cerebral symptoms arise, as headache, dizziness, pressure in the head and inability to think well. There may be feelings of heat in the head and considerable general languor. The urine may be a little scanty and high-colored, with hot and dry skin. There is often slight respiratory disturbance. Physicians generally attempt to prove that all these cerebral symptoms depend on the several days of constipation, from the fact that after a brisk cathartic the cerebral symptoms disappear. This circle may be, and often is, repeated in the same individual.

At first sight this explanation, with its practical demonstration, seems very laudable. But is it satisfactory? Can not the neurosis, the subjective light cerebral symptoms, be the cause of constipation? It is not easy to give a categorical proof of this. The disturbance, or hindrance, in respiration and circulation may find an explanation in the elevation of the diaphragm.

The cerebral circulation may be disturbed by the reflex irritation of the abdominal viscera, transmitting the irritation by way of the lateral chain of the sympathetic and the splanchnics. Leube has recently reported cases where the person became dizzy from pressure in the rectum, either by fecal masses, or by the finger. Here the dizziness arises from irritation of the hemorrhoidal plexus of nerves.

Again, Senator suggests that the absorption of certain gases, as sulphureted hydrogen, might induce poisonous symptoms. Nothnagel suggests that in constipation ptomaines might be absorbed, inducing cerebral symptoms. But Bouchard demonstrated that toxic fecal ptomaines may occur in fluid feces, as is seen in the large amount found in the urine of patients afflicted with diarrhea. Again, the cerebral symptoms depend on the constipation. Is the argument the same with melancholia and hypochondria? Does it depend on constipation? In other words, does constipation cause, in otherwise healthy persons, hypochondria, or other psychoses? We think it does not. The proposition should be made in two forms:

(a) Constipation may occur in otherwise healthy persons. These, we claim, do not suffer the hypochondria and psychoses.

(b) Constipation occurs in patients with a neurotic tendency. These last are the subjects which suffer from melancholic psychoses during constipation. It is undeniable that psychical depression may develop during constipation in certain persons, but they are of the neurotic type, and in these the abdominal disturbance of the bowels would similarly affect (as disturbances in any other functions) the weakest point, i. e., the part of the animal economy which resists the least. Single-handed and alone constipation does not create hypochondria and melancholia, but in a system burdened with neurotic tendencies, with unstable nerves, they may exist, but are, perhaps, the cause of the constipation.

Virchow says the following: "*Das bei einer gewissen erregungs fahigkeit widerstands losigkeit* (predisposition), *des nerven apparatus storhungen mit dem character der exaltation an den sensitiven und dem der depression und den motorichen nerven herrufen.*" Freely translated it is, "That by certain tendencies (non-resistance, predisposition) of the nervous apparatus, disturbances of the abdominal viscera may produce the character of exaltation in the sensitive nerves, and depression in the motor nerves."

It appears to me, however, that the popular professional idea of the effect of constipation on the brain is exaggerated, and much of the belief is untenable.

The celebrated English author and physician, Dr. Barnes, held that constipation was the cause of chlorosis. Perhaps this view arises from the supposed fact that some of the chlorotic girls recovered after cathartic treatment. But, since chlorosis is a disease of a certain age, i. e., from fifteen to twenty-five years, such a fact remains to be proved, for the constipation accompanying chlorosis constitutes but a small portion of the ailments atacked by it. Constipation and neurosis are, nevertheless, close relatives in many subjects with peculiar nervous symptoms.

The relation of the gastro-intestinal canal to other viscera is of prime importance as modifying peristalsis. The emphysematous lungs force the diaphragm distalward, and this destroys the tendency to free peristalsis. Heart, liver and kidney diseases, if they produce congestion in the bowel coats—serosa, muscularis and mucosa—will lessen peristalsis and consequent

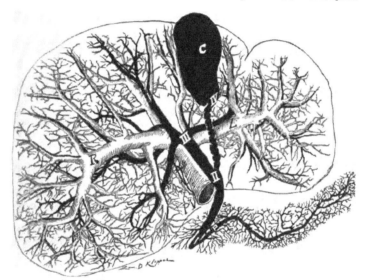

X-RAY OF DUCTUS PANCREATICUS ET DUCTUS BILIS

Fig. 83. The pancreatic and liver ducts, ensheathed by a network of fenestrated, nodular nerve plexuses. Also the portal vein.

fecal motion. Diabetes induces constipation by diverting fluids from the intestinal tract, and the consequent drying of the feces. In the chlorotic and anemic it is difficult to distinguish cause and effect. They are both constipated. But the retardation of fecal movements may be followed by anemia and chlorosis, or auto-intoxication. However, chlorosis belongs to females, in general, from puberty to the age of twenty-five. It is a developmental disease. In fevers deficient peristalsis induces constipation. Excessive sweating, also, renders the feces dry, and the diminution in the amount of food taken leaves less residue to stimulate peristalsis.

Fleischer suggest that in fevers the high temperature of the blood bathing the ganglia in the walls of the bowel tends to inhibit peristalsis, and hence cause constipation.

Under sympathetic nerve influence we are not including constipation from mechanical factors, as volvulus, flexions, obstruction by peritoneal bands and through apertures, pressure from tumors, strictures, or dislocated organs. Experience teaches emphatically that enteritis, or catarrh of the enteron, induces constipation. If catarrh of the colon and enteron exists, diarrhea and constipation will generally alternate. The secretory, as well as the motor nerves, are highly involved in catarrh. Ulcerative processes in the mucosa inducing diarrhea are not included in nerve influence. We, of course, have constipation in atony of the bowel wall, as well as in partial paresis.

Bowel weakness arises in potators, tabetic and tubercular patients, and in those with progressive splanchnoptosia.

It is plain to any one that a neurosis acts in various ways on the tractus intestinalis, influencing constipation or diarrhea. The hysteric and neurasthenic both suffer from irregular constipation. It is a common observation that patients who complain of abdominal neuralgias suffer more or less from constipation. It appears as if the nerves of the bowel do not work in harmony, the bowel is incapable of regularly emptying itself. Besides, neuralgia is, doubtless, a malassimilation of a sensory nerve, and since the sensory and motor nerves are complements of each other, they must work in harmony to accomplish an object—evacuation. The bowel contents irritate the periphery of a sensory nerve in the mucosa, this is carried by the organizing ganglia of the muscular wall, which induces muscular motion. The blood vessels of the bowel wall exert vast influence over peristalsis, and the vessels are ruled by the sympathetic nerves.

With deranged nerves of the intestines there will necessarily be deranged circulation, and either congestion or anemia induces a lowering of peristalsis —constipation. The circulation on the surface of the body is only an index of what is occurring inside. Now, it is common in neurotic persons to observe a dozen marked changes in the superficial circulation in a single day. The changes of circulation affect the bowel wall in a similar way that they do the surface. The effectiveness of circulatory changes is, perhaps, best observed in the serous covering the bowel, as in peritonitis, where constipation exists. In peritonitis the bowel wall becomes edematous, congested, and the peripheral nerve apparatus is compromised by pressure and malnutrition, so that we always expect constipation in peritonitis. The circulation is deranged.

In the territory of the secretory nerves, which belong to the sympathetic, as well as the motor and sensory nerves of the intestines, a vast field lies unopened. At ordinary times secretions progress in definite proportions, but, pathologically, we have excessive, deficient, or disproportionate secretions, e. g., there may be excessive bile, HCl, gastric or pancreatic fluids, or all of these may be deficient. Again, the bile may be secreted in proper amounts, so that we would have disproportionate secretion, which induces fermentation, the development of gases, tympany, and the undue development of certain microbes. If deficient HCl, or bile, be secreted, both of which are antiseptic microbes develop. Also, it must not be forgotten that deficiency of secretion checks peristalsis, whether it be deficiency of bile, pancreatic, or other gastro-intestinal fluids, and slowing of peristalsis invites constipation.

To illustrate the influence of nerves over peristalsis, observe how the irritation of a small fissure will induce constipation, first by abstention from stool and, second, by breaking the regular habit of stool. By forcible dilatation of the rectum the regular stool habit assumes its old course. In the case of anal fissure the irritation is purely reflex on the remaining portion of the gastro-intestinal canal. It would appear that constipation, in certain forms, may be well remedied by daily dilatation of the sphincter. This dilates and flushes its peripheral capillaries. Dr. Bier reports successes in the *Wiener Med. Blaetter*, 1891, No. 25.

The complex symptoms of constipation may be indecisively divided into general and local symptoms. The general and most disastrous symptom is that of auto-intoxication. It represents a series of manifestations in the territory of the nervous system, whether it be chronic or acute, common symptoms or headache, dizziness and neuralgias about the abdomen, as well as sleepiness, melancholia, languor, a feeling of debility and nausea. Pick says the visible expression of the constipation is the richness of excretory principals in the urine, and the increased toxicity of the same.

One of the local symptoms of constipation is the feeling of fullness and pressure in the abdomen, which is generally distended. The passage of gas gives temporary relief. The diaphragm is forced proximalward, compromising the heart, so that it not infrequently palpitates, and the lung manifests difficulty in respiration. In certain cases considerable colic is produced at stool, from irritation of the bowel wall by hard fecal masses. The positions of local colic from expelling hardened feces are the ampulla of the rectum, the cecum, the hepatic and splenic flexures, the middle of the transverse colon, and S-romanum. Large, hard, rough fecal masses not only cause much pain, but they abrade the mucosa and finally produce ulcerations, which heal slowly.

Visceral Circulation in Constipation.—The proverbial advice of the elderly doctor, when he wishes to be social, entertaining and instructive, is to keep the head cool, the feet warm, and the bowels open.

This philosophic advice is frequently theoretical, rather than practical, from an application to the actual living habits of the subject. In the present modes of living among women constipation plays an extensive and damaging role. The evil effects of constipation extend to adjacent visceral tracts, as circulation, respiration, and particularly on the tractus glandularis—secretions. The most important visceral tract of life itself is the tractus vascularis, over which the sympathetic nerve, nervus vasomotorius, maintains direct control. An ample stream of fresh blood can not properly irrigate constipated visceral organs. In constipation one or more of the four great common visceral functions—peristalsis, secretion, sensation or absorption—are disordered. The disturbance of circulation in constipation may be local or general. We observe the profound anemia of girls, frequently following the phase of puberty. The circulatory changes are at first local, later general. The anemic, chlorotic girl (from fifteen to twenty-five years of age) is plump, fat, and beautiful—in fact, it is the anemia of the good-looking girls. It appears concomitant with the disordered local circulation (genital); the later, general, disordered circulation, is accompanied by disordered, hypertrophied glandular system (tractus lymphaticus) and constipation. The chlorotic girl might profitably pose as an alabaster or marble statue. Hence, disordered circulation (pubertas), accompanied by disordered general circulation, disordered tractus lymphaticus, and constipation (disordered peristalsis, or secretion, or absorption).

In the establishment of menstruation numerous local (genital congestion or anemia) or general (chlorosis) circulatory disturbances arise. In pubertas the luxuriant vessels (veins) of the ovary and its compensatory balanced arm, the endometrium, become congested, engorged, which robs the blood from the tractus intestinalis and disturbs not only local, but general circulation, which condition is intensified in gestation.

Until the habit of menstruation is established the local change of circulation may induce constipation. In fact, I have relieved numerous gynecological patients by restoring normal evacuations of the bowels, and *vice versa*, normal genitals may restore normal bowel evacuation.

In short, detailed attention to the circulation—a matter directly under command of the sympathetic—is one of the most important factors in regulating constipation.

It is the detailed study of sanitorium patients, as to life, habits, diet and fluids, that makes the sanitorium financially profitable and suggestive, at least to the so-called surgeon who is so busy with major operations that he walks over gold and silver daily. The neglect of accurate diagnosis and consequent neglect of detailed treatment and defects of common functions, constipation, by the physician, is the reason of the multiplication of sanitoria, and the consequent loss of feces and confidence in the home physician.

It is the duty of the physician in defects of the common visceral functions—peristalsis, absorption, and secretion—to introduce visceral drainage to relieve the patient of waste-laden blood, and restore normal circulation. The physician should decide in detail the quality and quantity of the food and fluids ingested, and determine the methods of sewerage. He should recognize the secretory and motor activity of the tractus intestinalis, and the fascio-elastic muscular apparatus of the abdominal wall, which aids in evacuating the bowels.

Women, especially the young, must be taught the absolute necessity of regular daily evacuations, regardless of environments, time, place, views, or agreeability. The woman should know that exercise, muscular activity, is necessary for the abdominal muscles to force continually the bowel movements, contents, analward. Active bodily movements, fresh air, bicycling, walking, aid very much to maintain visceral circulation.

Artificial checks to respiration, as the corset or tight bands, check circulation, especially visceral, and hence peristalsis, absorption and secretions of the tractus intestinalis is checked. The corset is an enemy to circulation, and a friend to constipation and is unhesitatingly condemned.

Only ocular demonstration will convince a woman against corsets, so firm has become the senseless iron rule of fashion.

To illustrate the important influence of circulation in constipation, the first week of marriage may be noted. The extra irritation of the genitals induces a genital hyperemia, a congestion which robs the blood from the tractus intestinalis, leaving in its wake intestinal paresis—constipation.

Menstrual disturbances, chronic genital inflammation, entice blood from the tractus intestinalis, leaving defective intestinal peristalsis from lack of blood. Removal of chronic congested genitals may restore normal action of the genital tract by returning to them their normal blood stream. Not only does pregnancy induce constipation by enticing a continual blood stream toward the genitals from the intestinal tract, but in the puerperium the abdominal muscular apparatus has lost its original elastic tone, its power of compression. The enforced corporeal rest and non-irritating food administered engenders a constipation by disordered, unbalanced circulation.

In the puerperium, instead of an abdominal binder, the abdominal muscles should be massaged. The patient should practice on the abdominal muscles gymnastic exercises, in order to quickly restore them to normal action, and thus avoid one of the prime factors of splanchnoptosia.

The abdominal binder, the enforced rest, and concentrated food in the puerperium, all tend to lessen the visceral circulation, especially in the intestinal tract, and hence to entice constipation.

The Diagnosis of Constipation.—First and foremost an examination, extending from mouth to anus, is a prerequisite to diagnose constipation.

The mouth, and especially the teeth, unfold an important story.

The state of the abdominal and thoracic walls are significant. Does splanchnoptosia exist with its general consequences?

What is the state of the rectum (fissure, hemorrhoid, ulcer?) is of extreme importance.

The tractus vascularis tells its own story in arterio-sclerosis, which would indicate defective circulation in the splanchnic area.

Careful palpation of the plexuses and connection cords of the abdominal sympathetic should be practiced, as they regulate the caliber of the splanchnic vessels. Tenderness of the abdominal sympathetic plexus indicates an irritable condition of the viscera. If marked sclerosis exists, the abdominal aorta is palpable and tender. It is enlarged, movable, and pulsates vigorously, The tendernesss is to be localized especially along the plexus aorticus distal to the umbilicus, and in the plexus celiacus (abdominal brain) proximal to the umbilicus. This tenderness indicates a neuritis of the sympathetic, or vasomotor plexuses. Colic, due to spasm of vessels (arterio-sclerosis), must be differentiated from colic due to enteritis. In neuritis of the sympathetic plexuses, the pain and tenderness is localized in the celiac and aortic plexuses, and along the route of the ensheathed, which is characterized by spasmodic and periodic exacerbation. Peritonitis announces a more diffuse tenderness, and it is less spasmodic and periodic. Enteritis presents tenderness, localized in the course of the enteron, and is accompanied by other symptoms, as mucus in stools. The diagnosis of constipation is a small factor in practice, but the finest head, with the best skill, is required to diagnose the etiology, for on the cause of this malady rests the successful treatment. It is needless to say that a thorough and complete physical examination is absolutely necessary. For constipation may depend on the kind of food taken, on habits of life, on drugs employed, or on defects in the system. Some affirm that heredity plays a role in constipation; however, this is only a cloak to cover what we do not know. Many persons who have only one stool in two days, and remain healthy, are not constipated, and require no treatment.

Treatment of Constipation—General Remarks.—First and foremost in the treatment of constipation, should be considered the diet. Some physicians have a diet list. In certain cases it is convenient, but generally of little value. Oatmeal and graham bread, with milk as a beverage, leaves ample residue to induce peristalsis, which soon overcomes constipation. In such cases, also, a few daily colonic flushings aid wonderfully, with the establishment of a regular hour for evacuation. Especial stress should be laid on the matter of avoiding cathartics; they are among the chief causes of constipation. The best methods of curing constipation are those which imitate nature the closest, and most perfectly. They are, in order:

1. The regulation of diet (ingesta).
2. Physical procedures.
3. The judicious use of laxatives.

In the regulation of the diet several factors are requisite, viz., food which leaves a large residue, which will impart the necessary constant stimulus to successive bowel segments. Peristalsis requires a physical stimulus, a bolus that will feel its way from stomach to anus. The diet should be a mixed one of cereals, meats and fruits, as well as concentrated foods. It should be eaten at regular, fixed hours. The bowel is an organ wonderfully inclined, in certain persons, to assume sluggish, stubborn habits. Subjects who eat irregularly are apt to become just as irregular in evacuation. To show the effect of the habit, observe how much more women are constipated than men—a result of insufficient physical exercise, or sedentary life. Also, ample fluid should be taken with the foods.

The good effect of graham bread is chiefly due to the large residue, and the contained salts—both acting physically on the bowel, causing peristalsis. The habits of the use of narcotics, drinking, smoking, chewing, and taking of morphine, sexual abuses, over-mental activity, etc., should be modified.

The second method of treatment in constipation is the use of some physical procedure. Of these several are important. Among the first is the establishment of regular habits of evacuation and overcoming irregular ones. The bowels should be evacuated every morning after breakfast, i. e., after drinking hot fluid and eating hot food.

Heat starts peristalsis. The mental state has much influence over the bowels, so that if the mind is set on a distinct hour for an evacuation, it is pretty sure to be secured. Another valuable factor is regular and vigorous daily exercise. The most natural are walking, horseback or bicycle riding. The habit of exercise is nearly always sufficient to overcome constipation. Gymnastics serve a similar object.

When the above exercises are not performed, one of the sovereign cures of constipation is voluntary cultivation of the abdominal muscles, or massage; at first, weak or light rubbing should be employed once or twice daily; subsequently, vigorous massage should be carried on. Stroking, rubbing, tapping, kneading and gripping the abdominal wall should be judiciously performed. The large intestine should be massaged from cecum to rectum, following the line of the colon, and the direction of the fecal current. Rolling a bag of shot or dry sand over the abdomen is effective, if continued many days. Much patience on the part of both physician and patient will be required to continue the massage, for it may need a month to accomplish permanent results by this process. Rolling on the abdomen for ten or fifteen minutes every morning accomplishes goods results in constipation. Another excellent remedy for both its mental and physical effects, is electricity. Either the galvanic or the faradic current is effective. The muscle walls of the abdomen can not only be treated by electricity, but one of the electrodes may be inserted into the rectum. Another physical procedure of great value for a limited employment in constipation is irrigation, or colonic flushings, or rectal injections. However, rectal injections blunt the sensibility of the rectal mucosa. For mild cases a rectal injection of one-half pint of plain or salt water is sufficient to irritate the bowel, and excite an evacuation. In more stubborn cases a quart of water, containing irritants, may be injected, by a fountain syringe, held two feet above the patient, and allowing the fluid to flow into the bowel. Another method is turn a chair upside down, place a quilt over it, and then place the patient over this inclined plane, with the hips well elevated, and shoulders well down. Then allow a quart of water (containing desired ingredients) to gradually pass into the colon.

Besides the water injections, one may employ stimulants, such as epsom salts, olive oil, glycerine and water, at different temperatures. An excellent rectal injection is a half pint each of molasses and milk. It is hygroscopic. The irrigation is accomplished with more safety and efficiency with the fountain syringe at a low level, e. g., about two feet above the patient's hips. Cold fluid injections excite the bowels; however, warm fluids dissolve feces more rapidly.

Olive oil treatment.—Constipation is benefitted by persistent course of administration of olive oil for a period of months. I ordered a tablespoonful after each meal. The chemical action of the olive oil is a result of the separation of the oil by bile and pancreatic ferments. Through the bile and pancreatic fluids the fatty acids and soaps are produced which exert a mild chemical action, inducing evacuation. To soften and dissolve fecal masses olive oil is excellent. The value of the olive oil employed per rectum is dependent not only on its physical properties as softening and dissolving feces, coating and protecting the mucosa, and diminishing the absorption of water, but also on its chemical action.

To produce an immediate stool, a cold-water rectal injection of one-half a pint will be the most effective, as it at once induces active peristalsis. This may be added by rolling a bag of sand or shot over the abdomen. Daily dilatation of the rectum, especially when it is inclined to spasm, or is subject to fissure, ulceration or hemorrhoids, is a usual procedure. However, fissures, ulcers and hemorrhoids are proper cases for operations.

Finally, in the treatment of constipation, we come to use of drugs—at once the most disastrous and inefficient of all methods. Cathartics are to be avoided as much as possible in constipation. Constipation is generally the result of catarrh. Cathartics influence catarrh injuriously by further complicating the circulation, and inducing congestions and depletions. In the treatment of diseases peculiar to women, which I have diligently followed for twenty years, and where constipation is a common matter, I seldom advise a cathartic, pure and simple. The method I have followed successfully for years is what I term visceral drainage, presently to be described. Drastic cathartics are the friends of constipation. The number of cathartics is very great. The choice of one will depend on whether the drug is intended for long or short use. If a cathartic be employed for a short use, to secure an immediate evacuation, one of vigorous nature should be selected. For this purpose none are superior to mild chloride, followed by magnesium sulphate. The mild chloride stimulates the whole gastro-intestinal glandular apparatus, while the magnesium sulphate induces a large flow of fluids into the bowel. I have used these cathartics thousands of times, and have not yet observed superior ones. The violent, drastic cathartics, such as croton oil, podophylin, colocynth and elaterium, are seldom required.

Should a cathartic be required for prolonged use, one of a mild nature should be selected, such as rhubarb, magnesium sulphate, senna, aloes and cascara sagrada. Drugs administered for chronic constipation should be employed at night, so that the quietude of the patient will allow the drug to pass slowly over the whole mucosa. I am of the opinion that the addition of belladonna to cathartic pills is superfluous, and therapeutically only adds injury to insult. The cathartic insults the mucosa, while the belladonna injures it, by attempting to deceive it by anesthesia—both enemies to the normal, peaceful, mucosa life.

The beneficial effects of mineral waters, which generally depend upon the contained glauber and epsom salts, are only secured by long-continued use. Of the two forms of drugs, pills or liquids, given for constipation, the pill form is the superior one, because it works slowly, and thus imitates nature more closely. Nature always resents violent insults, with evil consequences. Nature itself is a bundle of habits, and if we are to be successful, we must imitate her methods. Hence, we must employ for constipation, diet, fluid, exercise, physical procedure, and, lastly, adjuvant cathartics—we must study the sympathetic nervous system.

The treatment of constipation does not consist in searching after and administering drugs, but rather in the avoidance of their use. We may first say that constipation is not curable by any planless method, nor by any planned method imperfectly executed, while there may really be non-removable anatomical conditions causing the difficulty. Planless prescribing of cathartics is worse than useless. The head and front of all therapeutics in constipation is due to an original, abnormal, nervous suspension of the peristalsis of the fecal reservoir. This concerns us and our therapeutics; though we may find difficulty in excluding congenital defects, such as atony of the bowel wall, or constipation due to dislocated viscera. Is the constipation, as

X-RAY OF DUCTUS BILIS ET DUCTUS PANCREATICUS OF HORSE

Fig. 84. Bile and pancreatic ducts of horse which possess no cholecyst or gall bladder.

Dunin suggests, a mere symptom of neurasthenia? If our original proposition be true, viz., that constipation is a neurosis of the fecal reservoir, cathartics are not only useless, but harmful.

In constipation we should attempt to cure the neurosis, the neurasthenia, when the constipation will disappear. The moral part of the patient should receive attention, for often there is far more in the suggestions added to medicine, than the remedies themselves can supply. If constipation depends on suspension of peristalsis, either from muscular atony or deficient innervation, it is plain how malpractice resides in the use of cathartics. Physical procedures must above all be employed in muscular atony, or defective innervation, of the fecal reservoir. In the treatment of constipation it may aid to determine the etiologic cause, as atonic constipation, associated muscular atrophy; neurotic constipation, associated with disorders of the cerebro-spinal axis, or the sympathetic (tabes, lead poisoning); metabolic constipation, associated with disordered metabolism, as excessive obesity, sweating, diabetes, anemia; trophic constipation, associated with subjects ingesting excessive meats, or other dietetic errors.

Suggestion.—I wish here to emphasize the subject of suggestion in the control or cure of constipation. The control of mind over matter has no uncertain sound in the aid to cure constipation. The psychic effect of a well-directed suggestion is often effective in stimulating peristalsis for regular stated times for evacuation. For example, tell a patient, definitely, to go to stool after breakfast, as the hot coffee stimulates the bowel to action. He will not only concentrate his mind on the function, but will cultivate his mind for a definite period for evacuation, which I consider of vast value. Occasionally, particularly in neurotics, this will effect a cure. With the suggestion for a daily evacuation at a stated period should be combined simple convenient remedies, as gymnastic exercise, special diet, in order that the patient may observe cause and effect.

Dietetic Summary—Quality of foods, quantity of fluid, chemical composition, are important considerations. (a) Food must possess sufficient variety (mixed) in quantity, quality, chemical composition, and be ingested at regular intervals. The food should be mixed, however, possess sufficient indigestible matter to leave ample residue to stimulate peristalsis (and hence absorption, sensation and secretion). An excessive amount of coarse, indigestible food will result in an excessive fecal residue, which excessively stimulates peristalsis, absorption, secretion and sensation—resulting in muscular fatigue and defective sensibility of the mucosa—consequently, reflex action is impaired.

(b) Ample fluids, at regular intervals, should be ingested. For a person of one hundred and fifty pounds five pints is required to supply the bodily waste (i. e., tractus intestinalis, respiratorius, urinarius, perspiratorius), eight ounces should be drunk every two hours for six times daily. Fecal matter is about seventy-five per cent fluid and twenty-five per cent solid. The value of fluids for the tractus intestinalis is evident, because in hot weather, with consequent vigorous action of the tractus perspiratorius, constipation results. The chief value of mineral water is the quantity drank. Excessive fluids deteriorate digestion.

(c) Foods should possess chemical qualities. Carbohydrates produce acidity, nitrogenous foods alkalinity, and mixed foods neutrality of the digestive tract. Evacuation of the tractus intestinalis depends on: (a) Sufficient volume of feces, (b) sufficient volume of fluid contents, (c) the presence of substances which act as a chemical irritant to peristalsis. Dr. Walter Baumgarter attempted to devise a substance which would not only be difficult to absorb, but would retain its watery contents (be hygroscopic). He administered eight grains of the dry, shredded agar-agar three times daily, whence he found the stool increased in volume and watery contents.

Visceral Drainage.—I wish here to introduce a method of treatment for constipation which I have employed successfully for a score of years. I have termed it "Visceral Drainage."

One of the most important principles in surgery is ample drainage of (septic) wounds. One of the most important principles in internal medication is ample drainage of the viscera. Fifteen years of the application of what I term "Visceral Drainage," in dispensary and private practice, has afforded me ample time to observe its extensive application and utility. Viscera are drained by several means; however, the two most rational and practical methods of visceral drainage are: (A) by fluids; (B) by appropriate foods. The viscera are the sewers of the body, and their proper drainage and flushing is the key to health and its maintenance. Draining the viscera drains and flushes the internal tissue and tissue spaces.

The muscles are powerful regulators of circulation (as exercise), hence there is stimulation, which increases the tone of vessels, blood currents, and prevents consequent congestion (the arch enemy) in chronic disease. The myometrium, like living ligatures, control the blood supply of the uterus. Visceral drainage initiates and maintains peristalsis, which controls visceral blood supply. A stimulus—whether it be an icicle, red-hot iron, electricity, massage, exercise—is what the flaccid muscles require to maintain peristalsis, which controls secretion and absorption. The endometrium flooded with excessive secretion (leucorrhea) rapidly assumes its normal secretion by stimulating the myometrium (by douche, massage, etc.).

A—*Visceral Drainage by Fluids.*—The best diuretic is water. It is the greatest eliminant. A man of one hundred and fifty pounds should produce daily some forty-five ounces of urine. If we calculate the loss of fluid by the tractus perspiratorius, tractus intestinalis, and tractus respiratorius, it will require about five pints of the ingested fluid to produce daily forty-five ounces of urine. Many subjects do not drink over three pints of fluid daily, and that is performed chiefly at meal time, not only burdening the tractus intestinalis with the meal, but fluid also. Large numbers of people drink insufficiently and suffer consequent oliguria. Such subjects are burdened with waste-laden blood, inflicting irritation and trauma on the nerve periphery. They are in conflict with their own secretions. Many women oppose free drinking, from the idea that it creates fat. Ample quantities of fluid, at regular intervals, is the safety valve of health and capacity for mental or physical labor. Ample fluids not only flush the sewers of the body, but wash the internal tissues and tissue spaces, relieving waste-laden blood. The soluble matter and salts are not only dissolved (preventing trauma and infection) and eliminated, but the insoluble matter and salts are flooded from the system, relieving waste-laden blood by such powerful streams of fluid that calculus is not liable to be formed.

For many years I have diluted the urine, increased its volume (consequently, increased ureteral peristalsis), and clarified it by administering eight ounces of one-half or one-quarter normal salt solution, six times daily. I have made sodium chloride tablets (twelve-grain, each with flavor). The patient places on the tongue a half tablet (NaCl), and drinks a glass of water (better hot) before each meal. This is repeated in the middle of the forenoon (ten A. M.), middle of the afternoon (three P. M.), and at bedtime (nine P. M.). The patient thus drinks three pints of (one-quarter to one-half) normal salt solution daily. This practically renders the urine normal, and acts as ample prophylaxis against the formation of urinary, hepatic, pancreatic, fecal calculus, and sewers the body of waste material. The formation of a calculus can not occur when ample fluid bathes the glandular exit canals. In deficient fluid, crystals form calculus with facility. The maximum concentrated solution of urine, bile, or pancreatic juice, tends to crystalize with vastly more facility than dilute urine, bile, and pancreatic juice. In "Visceral Drainage" single crystals, on first formation, are rapidly floated with facility when ample fluids are present; while in small quantities of fluid, with weak stream, the crystals tend to lodge, accumulate, and form calculus. Oliguria is a splendid base for calculus formation.

If parenchymatous nephritis exists, the NaCl should not be administered, as it excessively stimulates the renal parenchymatous cells. In such cases administer the water only.

For over ten years I have been using sodium chloride tablets, more or less, in my practice. During that time some practical clinical views have been gained, and repeated so frequently that they have become established, I think, beyond the shadow of a doubt. The following propositions have been repeatedly demonstrated so many hundreds of times during the last ten years in our clinics and surgical operations, that I shall consider them established until otherwise disproven:

1. Sodium chloride (in one-half to one-quarter normal physiological salt solution) is a powerful stimulant to the renal epithelium (tractus urinarius).

2. Sodium chloride should not be administered in parenchymatous nephritis (not even in food), as it exacerbates and irritates the diseased, inflamed parenchymatous cells.

3. Sodium chloride (in one-half to one-quarter normal physiologic salt solution) is a vigorous stimulant to the epithelium of the tractus intestinalis, inducing fluid to flow into the lumen, stimulating peristalsis and softening the feces.

4. Sodium chloride increases absorption, secretion and peristalsis of the tractus intestinalis. It is an excellent remedy to quench thirst after peritonotomy, by copious gradual rectal irrigations (allowing a pint in forty-five minutes to flow over the sigmoid and rectal mucosa).

5. The administration of eight ounces of one-half to one-quarter normal physiologic salt solution (better hot), every two hours, for six times daily, will increase the quantity and clarify the urine, eliminate its color, making it appear almost like spring water in three to five days. The feces will be softened, increase, in volume, inciting peristalsis.

6. Sodium chloride is a vigorously active stimulant to glandular epithe-

lium (as that of the tractus urinarius, tractus intestinalis, tractus cutis, salivary, hepatic and pancreatic glands).

7. The effect of the one-half to one-quarter normal physiological salt solution (six times daily) on the tractus urinarius is to increase the quantity and clarify the urine.

B—*Visceral Drainage by Foods.*—To drain the viscera by proper foods may sound paradoxical, but the four grand functions of the tractus intestinalis —peristalsis, absorption, sensation and secretion—are maintained, practically, by food alone. The appropriate food produces the appropriate degree of peristalsis, and the quantity of intestinal secretions, which is absolutely essential for visceral drainage—and to prevent constipation. The food that will induce proper peristalsis, stimulate sensation, absorption and secretion, is that which leaves a large residue to stimulate the distal bowel, enteron and colon, such as cereals, oils, and vegetables. Peristalsis is necessary for secretion, for peristalsis massages the secretory glands in the tractus intestinalis, enhancing secretion, e. g., the rational treatment of excessive uric acid in the urine consists of administering food that contains elements to produce basic combinations with uric acid, forming urates (usually sodium), which are freely soluble. This will diminish the free uric acid in the urine. Excessive uric acid in the urine is an error in metabolism. The question of diet to determine is: (a) What kind of food causes the calculus-producing material in the urine? (b) What kind of food influences the solubility of the calculus-producing material in the urine?

1. The meat-eater is the individual with the maximum quantity of free uric acid in the urine. Flesh is rich in uric acid. Hence, in excess of uric acid in the urine, flesh (meat, fish and fowl, are all about equal in power to produce uric acid) should be practically excluded, because it increases free uric acid in the urine. Flesh eaters have uric acid stone, vegetarians have phosphate, oxalate stone.

Generally, the subject who suffers from uric acid is a generous liver, liberally consuming meat and highly-seasoned foods, indolent and sedentary persons, and alcoholic indulgers. Thirty-three per cent of uric acid is nitrogen. Uric acid is derived from the nuclei that form a constituent of all cell nuclei, and which are taken in the body as a food. Beef bouillon may be cell administered, because the extract matters in it will scarcely increase the uric acid. A general meat diet largely increases the free uric acid in the urine.

2. The food should contain matters rich in sodium, potassium and ammonium, which will combine as bases with uric acid, producing alkaline urates, which are perfectly soluble in the urine. These typic foods are the vegetables, which not only render the necessary alkalies to reduce and transform the free uric acid into resulting soluble urates, but leave an ample residue to cause active intestinal peristalsis, aiding in the evacuation through the digestive tract. Hence, the patient should consume large, ample quantities of cabbage, cauliflower, beans, peas, radishes, turnips, and spinach in order that the sodium, potassium, and ammonium existing in the vegetables may combine, as bases, with free uric acid in the urine, producing soluble urates,

thus diminishing free uric acid. A vegetable diet diminishes the free uric acid in the urine thirty-five per cent less than a meat diet. Again, the administration of eggs and milk (lactoalbumin) limits the production of uric acid. The most rational advice is to order the subject to live on a mixed diet, consuming the most of that kind of food which lessens the uric acid in the urine —vegetables.

If the appropriate food is so valuable in "visceral drainage treatment" of the typical uric acid subject, the appropriate food selected for subjects of biliary and pancreatic calculus will be relatively as useful. The foods that make soluble basic salts with secretions should be selected. Besides, the selection of appropriate food is frequently amply sufficient to drain the intestinal tract to prevent constipation. It is true, foods alone are not a complete substitute for fluids, but vast aid in visceral drainage may be accomplished by administering food containing considerable indigestible matter, so that a large fecal residue, saturated with fluid, will stimulate the intestines, especially the colon, to continuous vigorous activity, maintaining the maximum action of the four grand functions—peristalsis, absorption, sensation and secretion. For many years I have treated subjects with excess of uric acid in the urine by administering an alkaline laxative tablet in fluid. The tablet is composed of: Cascara sagrada, one-fortieth of a grain; $NaHCO_3$ one grain; socotrine aloes, one-third grain; $KHCO_3$, one-third grain; $MgSO_4$, two grains. The tablet is used as follows: One-sixth to one tablet (or more, as required, to move the bowels once daily) is placed on the tongue before meals, and followed by eight ounces of water (better hot). At ten A. M., three P. M., and bedtime, one-sixth to one tablet is placed on the tongue, and followed by a glassful of fluid. In the combined treatment the sodium chloride tablet and alkaline tablet are both placed on the tongue together. This method of treatment furnishes alkaline bases (sodium and potassium and ammonium) to combine with the free uric acid in the urine, producing perfectly soluble alkaline urates, and materially diminishing the free uric acid. Besides, the alkaline laxative tablet increases the peristalsis, absorption, sensation and secretion of the intestinal tract, aiding evacuation. I have termed the sodium chloride and the alkaline laxative method the "visceral drainage treatment." The alkaline and sodium chloride tablets take the place of the so-called mineral waters. Our internes have discovered that on entering the hospital the patient's urine presents numerous crystals under the microscope. However, after following the "visceral drainage treatment" for a few days crystals can not again be found. The hope of removing a formed localized ureteral, or other, calculus, lies in securing vigorous ureteral or other duct peristalsis with a powerful ureteral or other duct stream, aided by systematic massage over the psoas muscle and per vaginam. Subjects afflicted with excess of uric acid in the urine, or other form of calculus, need not make extended sojourns to watering places, nor waste their time at mineral springs, nor tarry to drink the hissing Sprudel, for they can be treated successfully in a cottage, or in a palace. The treatment of a uric acid or other calculus consists, therefore, in the regulation of food and water. It is dietetic. The control, relief and prophylaxis of uric acid diathesis or tendency to other calculus formation, is a lifelong process. When the uric acid or other calculus has passed spontaneously the patient does not end his treatment, but should pursue a constant systematic method of drinking ample fluids at regular intervals, and eat food which contains bases to combine with the free uric acid or other compounds producing soluble urates or other soluble compounds.

I continue this treatment for weeks, months, and the results are remarkably successful. The urine becomes clarified, like spring water, and increased in quantity. The tractus intestinalis becomes freely evacuated regularly daily. The blood is relieved of waste-laden and irritating material. The tractus cutis eliminates freely, and the skin becomes normal. The appetite increases, the sleep becomes improved, the feelings become hopeful. The sewers of the body are well drained and flushed.

Chronic constipation is compensatory, for during this condition a greater portion of the food ingested undergoes digestion and absorption than in the normal individual, and consequently the fecal residue is more limited. By reason of the fecal residue there is less material, and a less favorable medium for the development of bacteria, in consequence of which less irritating products occur, on which the stimulus to the required peristalsis, more or less, depends. The varying pressure of the abdominal walls on the viscera modifies the viscera circulation in quantity and rapidity. The visceral vessels, especially the abdominal, constitute a kind of hemogenous reservoir for surplus of blood, by which general blood pressure may be regulated among viscera. The dilatation of abdominal visceral vessels may be so great that cerebral anemia may advance to a state of syncope, collapse, or shock. We may yet learn to apply Bier's congestion, or blood controlling methods, to cure constipation by practicing on the sphincters. Abdominal visceral circulation must not only be controlled for maximum digestion (which is normal absorption, secretion, sensation and peristalsis of the enteron), but also for maximum colon peristalsis, which is required for normal evacuation. We know that mental or physical excitement at meals modifies digestion (which means modification of circulation). Dilatation of the blood vessels in the splanchnic area lowers the blood pressure, increases rate, rhythm and force of pulse. Maximum circulation in abdominal organs is conducive to maximum absorption, secretion, sensation and peristalsis. Pathologic increase of circulation in the abdominal viscera leads to corresponding activity of unction. This lends a clue to treat constipation. Increased secretion of the glands of the tractus intestinalis, in consequence of nervous influence, is well known (which refers to circulation).

Visceral congestion (chronic) leads to relaxation of visceral supports. Interruption of circulation (anemia) leads to visceral spasm, colic. Spasm of the muscle of the digestive apparatus produces colic. There can be slight doubt, clinically, that spasmodic (anemic) constipation occurs—e. g., lead or (anemic) colic. In the practice of medicine the vascular area governed by the splanchnics will be more utilized in therapeutics. For example, the headaches, dizziness, faintness, syncope, vertigo, which appear and disappear suddenly without sufficient time for autointoxication, infections, are likely to produce circulatory changes in the splanchnic and producing cerebral anemia. So, also, cold hands and feet, aching pains in limbs, neuralgic pains in various bodily regions, may be due to excessive tendency of blood to the splanchnic area. Irritation of the nerves of the splanchnic vessels are transmitted to distant regions, leading to spasms (anemia, ischemia) of vessels, and pain, cramps in muscles. This may explain the frequent colic, cramps, of neurotic subjects.

Circulatory disturbances in the tractus intestinalis should not be mistaken for: (a) Mechanical irritation from coarse food, (b) chemical irritation from ingested irritants (as acids, spices, meats), (c) pathologic physiology, as excessive, deficient or disproportionate secretion and consequent fermentation (microbic). The dilatation of the splanchnic vessels are physiologically opposed to the dilatation of the peripheral vessels, and since the splanchnic vessels are controlled by a nervous mechanism, it may be hoped that a definite therapeutic remedy will appear that will contract, or dilate, these visceral vessels. Since physiologic antagonism exists between the splanchnics and peripheral vessels, agents which dilate the splanchnics contract the peripheral vessels, and *vice versa*. The <u>dilatation of the anal sphincter</u> dilates and flushes the peripheral capillaries with it, contracts the splanchnic vessels. The peripheral vessels may be dilated by mechanical means, as massage, hypertrophy, a hot and cold water chemical irritation, as mustard, turpentine.

Normal evacuations of the tractus intestinalis require an ample stream of fresh blood irrigating the intestinal tract, which is accomplished by administering food with indigestible remnants.

The tendency of the blood stream to any other visceral tract than the intestinal, lessens the peristalsis, absorption, sensation and secretion, favoring constipation.

In pubertas, menstruation, gestation or chronic genital inflammation, the circulation tends toward the genitals, robbing the tractus intestinalis of blood, inducing constipation.

In the puerperium the patient should exercise, employ gymnastics, massage the abdominal muscles, ingest foods which have a residue, and limit the enforced rest to a week, in order to restore muscular action and visceral circulation, especially the intestinal.

Chronic inflammation, tumor, irritation on any one visceral tract, tends to unbalance the normal circulation in all other visceral tracts—inducing constipation—hence to improve constipation, remove the disease or disturbance in other visceral tracts.

Any defective segment of the tractus intestinalis (gastrium, enteron, colon) should be repaired, and any defective function (peristalsis, secretion, sensation and absorption) should be restored.

A subject of one hundred and fifty pounds requires five pints of fluid daily to produce ample visceral circulation (to supply the physiologic demands of the tractus urinarius, tractus cutis, tractus respiratorius, tractus intestinalis).

Vegetables and graham bread (which should contain the flour, shorts and bran) leave ample residue to stimulate the tractus intestinalis, inviting a vigorous circulation.

Rectal injections and colonic irrigation should not be employed frequently, as the rectum may lose its sensitiveness, becoming so blunted in sensibility that it will forget to act when fecal matter is present. Clysters of oil are excellent remedies to soften fecal masses.

Persistent use of galvanic and faradic electricity produces favorable effects on constipation, the electricity energizes the abdominal walls and intestinal muscles. However, I can not report such favorable results as those of C. V. Wild, in his excellent essay, "*Die Verheutung und Behandlung der Chronischen Verstopfung bei Frauen und Madchen.*"

Constipation, if pursued by both patient and physician, with favorable will and energy, is practically a curable disease.

CHAPTER XXX.

SHOCK.

By Lucy Waite, A. B., M. D., Head Surgeon of Mary Thompson Hospital for Women and Children

Shock in its widest significance covers the whole of medicine. From the slightest physical traumatism or the lightest mental depression to the most profound impressions on the vasomotor centers causing instantaneous death, the difference is only one of degree, the phenomena being the same. It would therefore be impossible in one short chapter to follow out the subjects in all its various ramifications in the field of medicine and surgery and it must suffice to treat it in a comprehensive manner as an affection primarily of the nervous system with the secondary involvement of the vascular system as a whole.

HISTORY.

While it is only during the last fifty years that any scientific experiments have been made with a view toward discovering the pathology of shock, as early as 1826, Travers, in his work on Constitutional Irritation, gave an exact description of the phenomena of shock. The first treatise on the subject I have been able to find was published in 1868, by Edwin Morris, F. R. C. S. In this he states that the first mention of shock in medical literature was in 1819, in the works of F. Hennen and Guthrie, writing on military surgery. Morris considered death from shock due to functional disturbance of the brain, the heart being affected only secondarily. He places no emphasis on the part played by the sympathetic system and mentions this only once incidentally as the par vagum and says it connects the spinal cord, brain and heart. He treats of shock under two headings, surgical and shock from mental causes. He gives the classical symptoms and concludes that shock is due to paralysis of the nervous system destroying the normal function of the brain and withdrawing the nervous stimulus from the heart. He confuses shock and concussion of the brain, but warns against confusing this condition with extravasation in injuries to the brain.

I have given a brief synopsis of his brochure because, being written in a comprehensive manner and as late as 1868, we may assume that it contains all that was known on the subject up to that date. Previous to this mention was made of the subject in Cooper's "Medical Dictionary" in 1838 and in Copeland's "Dictionary" in 1858. In Cooper's "Surgical Dictionary," published in 1859, however, there is no mention of shock.

One of the most interesting landmarks in the history of the literature on shock is Davey's work published in 1858. Under the heading of "Syncope" he gives a long dissertation on the phenomena of shock, although this word is used only once, and he foreshadows both the present theory of the pathology and the latest treatment as demonstrated by the experiments of Dr. Geo.

C. Crile and others in his observations on collapse after labor and the too rapid escape of the ascitic fluid in paracentesis abdominis. "I am, however, confident," he says, "that the bona fide explanation of the fact is to be sought for in loss of the long-accustomed adaptation or relationship between the containing and contained parts of the abdomen, whereby the ganglionic nervous system is at its very center more or less paralyzed."

He says he has no doubt that the many cases of sudden death attributed to cerebral hemorrhage, disease of the heart, air embolism, etc., are in reality caused by "syncope," as he terms it, and that the cause is to be found in the fact that "the ganglionic nervous system has been drawn on so largely by the cerebro-spinal and muscular systems that there is nothing remaining for the thoracic and abdominal viscera—no stimulus left for the vital organs." Mr. Paget, writing in 1862, gives the phenomena and treatment. Later Brown-Sequard and Savory (1870) made the valuable discovery of the pathology of shock. Brown-Sequard announced as the result of his work the theory of anæmia of the cerebral centers due to a more or less persistent contraction of the capillaries through the vasomotor center. The experiments of Goltz on frogs was the most important work done in this direction until the last few years. With Brown-Sequard and Savory, he held to the theory of cardiac paralysis. He showed that through the inhibitory influence exerted upon the splanchnics, the abdominal vessels were suddenly dilated. In Quain's "Medical Dictionary" (1884) is a statement of the status of the subject of shock at that date and concludes: "For the present we may thus accept as the most plausible interpretation of the symptoms of shock a sudden dilatation of the abdominal vessels, attributable to an inhibitory influence exerted upon the splanchnics, through the medium of a special reflex center." Not much has been added to this explanation of the real pathology of shock, but valuable experiments have been made in recent years in the line of pathology, and some working toward a more rational treatment by Geo. C. Crile, Robert Dawbarn, Harvey Cushing, Eugene Boise, Guy C. Kennaman, John H. Packard and others of our own profession. In the extensive surgical encyclopedia edited by Dupley and Reclus in 1890, "Traité de Chirurgie," is the statement that it is only during the last twenty years that shock has been studied in France and that the French, in acknowledging the origin of the researches in this subject, often use the English orthography, although having a legitimate word in their own language, "choc." A differential diagnosis is made between shock and syncope and the article concludes by saying that in fact we know nothing of the pathological anatomy of shock or of its pathogenesis. The entire bibliography on shock is so meager that it may be interesting from an historical stand point. In addition to those already maintained, the field is practically covered by the following:

Gross, "System of Survey" (1864).

Erichsen, "The Railway and Other Injuries to the Nervous System" (1866).

Verneuil, "de la mort prompte après certaines blessures ou operations" (1869).

Savory, "Collapse," "Holmes System of Surgery" (1870).
Fisher, "In Volkman Samml, klin. Vortr." (1870).
Demarquay, "In comptes rendus de l'Academie des sciences" (1871).
Renard, "Arch; Gen. de med." (1872).
Blum, "Du choc traumatique Arch. gen de med," (1876).
Le Dentu, "Bull de la Soc. de chir." (1877).
Vincent, "Des causes de la mort prompte après les grands trauma tismes accidentels et chirurgicaux Thesis" (1878).
Piechaud, "Que doit on entendre par l'expression de choc traumatique" (1880).
Jondan Furneaux, on "Shock after Surgical Operations and Injuries," "British Medical Journal" (1880).
Raffer, "La Spermantate" (1882).
Torrier, "choc traumatique Elements de path. chir. generale" (1883).
George Friedländer, "arch. für klin. chirurg." (1903-4).
Dennis, "System of Surgery" (1895).
Mummery, Second Hunterian lecture, "New York Medical Journal" of April 15, 1905.

ÆTIOLOGY.

From clinical observation of the phenomena of shock, a rather arbitrary division of the ætiology has been made, viz.: Predisposing and exciting causes. To establish this as a scientific classification much more must be known regarding susceptibility to shock. Infants are said to be almost immune, while youth is considered the period of the highest susceptibility. Immunity is therefore before the age when the cerebrospinal and sympathetic systems assume their reciprocal positions in the nervous system, susceptibility from the time when the untrained cerebrospinal system assumes more established control over the sympathetic until the element of mental influence comes in as a factor. To counterbalance this extreme susceptibility of youth comes in the fact that at this time the resisting powers are greater and many cases are recorded by different authors of recovering from the most profound shock in the young which must certainly have proved fatal in the old. It would almost seem that the proposition could be laid down that the power to withstand and overcome shock is in inverse ratio to the susceptibility. Dr. Kiernan says that the insane are not susceptible to the influences which produce shock in the sane, and in fact the effects may be directly contrary—a wide field for study and speculation. Certain peoples are said to be practically immune and others to be little affected. Dr. John H. Packard writes interestingly on this subject. He says that Hindoos bear injuries and operations impassively; that Negroes are not easily affected and that Americans are especially susceptible to the influences of shock. It has been observed that injuries inflicted while the subject is under the influence of intoxicating liquors rarely produce severe shock. If all these clinical observations can be substantiated it would point very strongly to a large mental element in every case of shock, either directly or indirectly. When all is said, however, the real factor in each constitution which speaks for or against susceptibility, the vital force, will after all no doubt remain the unknown quantity. As regards the varying degrees of susceptibility in the different organs of the body, the most vascular tissues and those most highly supplied by the sympathetic nerve have been found to be most easily affected.

In the present light of our knowledge we may consider as predisposing causes all conditions which impair the nutrition of the nervous system and consequently the circulation; exhausting diseases, prolonged physical pain or mental strain, insomnia, melancholia, in fact, everything which reduces vital force. Mummery says in his second Hunterian lecture that in elderly patients a very high blood pressure is generally observed, largely accounted for by arteriosclerosis, and that in such patients a relatively slight fall in blood pressure may produce shock. It is as a predisposing cause that hemorrhage plays its proper role through the secondary physiological phenomnea of anæmia which leaves the ganglia to be bathed with impoverished blood and as a surgical condition to be handled surgically should be sharply differentiated from shock proper. The exciting causes of shock may be more satisfactorily considered under the classification of traumatic and mental. Direct traumatism of the tissues may result from accidental injuries or from trauma during the course of surgical procedures. Many writers treat this last condition under a separate classification as surgical shock. It seems true that this subject can be treated scientifically only as a subdivision of the general classification of traumatism, which is either accidental or surgical. The confusion has arisen by considering hemorrhage as an exciting cause of shock instead of giving it its proper classification as a surgical complication and secondly by the involvement of the anæsthesia in the ætiology. All surgical writers agree that the frequency of shock has greatly lessened since the general use of anæsthesia and this fact speaks loudly against operating under partial or local anæsthesia, as a routine practice. I have seen patients profoundly influenced by an excessive quantity of the anæsthetic, either on account of the manner in which it was administered or the length of time the patient has been held under its influence, with no symptoms of shock whatever, and I cannot think the effects of long anæsthesia, serious as they are, can legitimately be considered as factors in the production of shock. The whole story of a depressed nervous system following a prolonged anæsthesia is told in the added traumatism caused by the repeated and unnecessary handling of the tissues and the exposure to atmospheric influences tissues normally protected by the coverings of fascia and skin. During extensive experimentations in intestinal operations on dogs, Dr. Byron Robinson demonstrated that the shock following these procedures was in direct proportion to the amount of manipulation or traction in the abdominal viscera and duration of exposure; that is, the amount of trauma inflicted upon the sympathetic nerve. Sudden blows, especially in the region of the solar plexus, burns and scalds involving large areas, all manner of traumatic injuries, especially those producing extensive crushing of tissues, are the principal exciting causes in shock from accidental traumatism. It has been observed that burns involving a large area, causing extensive nerve periphery trauma, cause more profound symptoms than deeper burns covering a small area. Irritation in one organ may produce nerve storms in a distant one. The introduction of the sound in the uterus or the catheter in the male urethra may produce faintness, nausea or even vomiting. Dr. Nicholas Senn demonstrated a rare case in his clinic which well illustrates the principle of reflex nervous irritation. The patient came into the hospital with a history of anurea for sixty hours. The right kidney was enormously distended, the left apparently normal. A diagnosis was made of right ureteral calculus, which was removed. During the period of convalescence both kidneys secreted an equal amount of urine, proving conclusively that the suppression of urine from the left kidney was caused by the reflex irritation produced by the disturbance in the right. The size and extent of the renal ganglia and their nearness to the solar plexus give to the kidneys an especially strong sympathetic connection. From the first observations made in the subject to the present day, all writers have recognized the mental element in ætiology of the phenomena of shock. Davey, 1858, cites in detail many cases and says the part played by the mind in the production of "syncope" is not sufficiently appreciated. Clinical observation has established the fact that a profound mental impression may cause all the nervous phenomena following a blow over the solar plexus. Sad news, fright, violent emotions may be followed by the same vasomotor paralysis with all its accompanying nervous manifestations; and when this is said, all has been said regarding our knowledge of the influence of the mind in the production of the phenomena of the shock.

PATHOLOGY.

As the result of some experimentation and much speculation two theories regarding the pathology of shock have been evolved, viz.: Vasomotor paresis and cardiac paralysis. Almost all of the modern investigators hold to the theory of vasomotor paresis. The nervous impression is conveyed to the medulla by the afferent nerves, causing vasomotor paralysis and dilatation. There is a more or less rapid fall in blood pressure. The vessels lose their normal tonicity which is necessary to the rapid transition of the blood, the first effect is contraction in the caliber of the capillaries, followed quickly by dilatation, with at first increase in rapidity of the blood current, but in proportion as the dilatation increases the rapidity decreases and may proceed to a complete stasis. The right side of the heart becomes engorged and does not empty at each contraction, accumulating largely in the relaxed veins, leaving the arteries partially emptied; the patient bleeds into his own veins. The blood is normal into the abdominal vessels. Cerebral anæmia results as a natural consequence and a slowing of the activity of all the different viscera dependent for the fulfillment of their physiological functions upon a perfect blood supply. The influence on the heart together with all other viscera is therefore secondary to the paralysis of the vasomotor system through the great reorganizing center, the solar plexus, the abdominal brain. The phenomena of shock are therefore the result of a reflex inhibition affecting all the functions of the nervous system, causing a lowering of the general blood pressure, checking normal metabolism, arresting the exchanges between blood and tissues; the venous blood becomes red, temperature lowers in consequence of the lowered blood pressure, respiration slows and we have a picture of systematic asphyxia. The entire mechanism of life is deranged, the balance of power is destroyed and each organ is in an independent control of its own functions for the time being and consequently only as long and as thoroughly as its limited reserve force will allow. Brown-Sequard, Goltz and Savory advanced the theory of cardiac paralysis. They gave as the conclusion of all their experiments that shock was caused by a violent impression on some portion of the nervous system acting at once through a nerve center upon the heart and destroying its action. No reliable findings have been found at autopsy. Parascandola claims to have found certain changes in the spinal cord after profound shock affecting the cell body, prolongations nucleus and nucleolus, constituting chromatolysis, fragmentation, nuclear and perinuclear.

It must be admitted that the pathology of shock after all remains very indefinite and unsatisfactory, the x, as Dr. Senn has called it in the surgical formula. It is therefore very difficult to give a comprehensive definition of this ignis fatuus in the domain of pathology. Based in reality more on the phenomena than upon the pathology, according to our present light we must consider it as primarily a disturbance of the great sympathetic nervous system afflicting secondarily the entire vascular system, a more or less profound impression on the sympathetic nerve producing a vasomotor paresis with a consequent dilatation of the right side of the heart and the large vessels, especially the abdominal, and in consequence lowering the general blood pressure and deranging through the solar plexus all the automatic visceral ganglia, and consequently destroying their functional activity, rhythm, absorption and secretion.

SYMPTOMS.

The phenomena of shock manifest themselves through the tripod of vital forces, the nervous, circulatory and respiratory systems, and principally in those organs most highly supplied by the sympathetic system. The rhythm of the viscera is disturbed, secretions are diminished, causing an intense thirst, the cry of the tissues for fluids; there is a general trophic disturbance; the heart action and the respirations are increased, the temperature is subnormal, the face is pale, the lips are blue, the pupils dilated; there is nausea, vomiting and restlessness, more or less pronounced according to the degree of shock, until the stage of collapse, when the reflexes are lost. A cold, clammy sweat appears on the entire surface of the body, and the extremities are cold. Shallow respirations, with frequent sighing, yawning, hiccoughs are often added to the clinical picture.

In the most profound shock, where the cerebrospinal system is involved, this picture may be changed by the substitution for the phenomena caused by a hyperirritation of the sympathetic system as nausea, vomiting and restlessness, those manifestations resulting from a secondary depression of the cerebrospinal system causing a loss of reflexes, as involuntary urination and bowel movements; delirium and even stupor may appear. The cold sweat, rapid, irregular pulse, subnormal temperature here persist in a more profound degree, some observers having noted a fall in temperature of 6° F. During the War of the Commune observations were taken in regard to the temperature after injuries. The average temperature varied from 96.5° to 97.5°, the lowest registering at 93.5°. The fall was greater after shell wounds and the curious fact was noted that there was a uniform lower temperature among the insurgents than among the regular troops.

Authenticated cases have been reported where jaundice, deafness and arrest of lacteal and menstrual secretions have followed profound shock. Many efforts have been made to classify the nervous symptoms of shock, but all are unsatisfactory for the reason that one state runs so insensibly into another that it is impossible to measure the degree, except by the rate of recovery, and here again come in the unsolved problems of susceptibility and resistance and we simply travel in a circle and soon find ourselves at the starting place again. The only classification which is any aid in diagnosis and prognosis is a differentiation between the state implicating only the functional activity of the sympathetic system and that in which the cerebrospinal is also involved and even here the symptoms run so imperceptibly into each other that classification is elusive; even in collapse consciousness may be retained until death.

The intensity of physical shock is influenced by four principal considerations: the extent of the injury, that is, the number of nerve peripheries involved; the nearness of the traumatism to the solar plexus; the character of the injury, the more crushing or bruising of the nerves the greater being the nervous impression; and the severity of the pain produced. It is therefore from the standpoint of intensity rather than by means of a scientific classification that we must study the phenomena of shock.

DIAGNOSIS.

The diagnosis of shock is simply the recognition of the clinical phenomena as here we have no pathological findings to aid us. The clinical manifestations of this nerve storm are however so pronounced that practically the only difficulty lies in differentiating this condition from syncope caused by severe hemorrhage, with which there is danger of confounding it. When syncope co-exists with shock it is often extremely difficult to establish the presence of internal hemorrhage as a complication. In one condition the blood leaves the peripheries and congests the abdominal vessels, in the other the large and small vessels are equally deprived of the usual volume of blood. In nervous shock certain tissues only lose their blood supply, while there is no diminution in the quantity of blood. In the one the primary violence is to the nervous system, in the other the circulatory system is attacked directly. Syncope causing always a cerebral anæmia is practically identical with the last manifestations of overwhelming shock, or collapse. As a recognition of the presence of hemorrhage is often of the utmost importance, sometimes meaning even the saving of a life, we should never rest content with a diagnosis of shock until we have excluded the possibility of hemorrhage by every means in our power. If the patient is seen immediately after the injury, or in surgical cases where internal hemorrhage may arise, the most reliable source for establishing a differential diagnosis is by observation of the pulse and temperature. Both conditions, to be sure, produce a rapid pulse with normal or subnormal temperature, but there is a decided difference in the course of the pulse and temperature which with careful observation one can not fail to recognize. In internal hemorrhage there is a *gradually rising pulse*, more or less rapid according to the rapidity of the bleeding, with a *gradual lowering of temperature*, the golden rule in abdominal surgery establishing the presence of internal hemorrhage laid down by Mr. Lawson Tait over twenty years ago. In shock proper, however, we have the maximum rapidity of pulse and depression of temperature at the time of infliction of the trauma and co-existent with all other clinical manifestations, as the rapid shallow breathing, cold sweat, and dilated pupils.

To illustrate: A patient is taken from the operating table with a temperature of 99°-100°, rectal, pulse 90-100. In a half hour the pulse is 110-120, the temperature is found to be 98°; in another fifteen minutes to half an hour the pulse has risen to 130-140 and the temperature is falling towards 97° and the diagnosis of internal hemorrhage is practically established. This rising of the pulse with a corresponding depression of temperature may be extremely gradual and extend over hours and even days in cases of slow bleeding, sometimes a mere oozing, as where an hematoma or an hematocele is forming and before the period of infection or localized peritonitis, and here of course the diagnosis is more obscure, but fortunately less urgent. If, however, the patient is taken from the table with a pulse of 120-140 or upwards, rectal temperatures 98°-97°, respirations 30-40, and even if these conditions persist for several hours, we have no reason to fear internal hemorrhage, and if after the first half hour of the patient's rest in bed the pulse and respiration slow ever so little and the temperature rise even a fraction of a degree we may know that we have to deal with a case of recovering shock. The surgical nurse should be taught to make this differential diagnosis through a clinical study of pulse and temperature and respiration, as it is to her that we must look for the accurate observation and a prompt report of a condition in which minutes count in the saving of a life.

PROGNOSIS.

We have little to guide us in forming a prognosis, as here again the unknown quantity, the vital force of the individual, the power of resistance of the tissues to the nervous impression comes in as the most important factor in the equation. In general the temperature is the best guide here also. A persistence of 96° or below for several hours warrants an unfavorable prognosis while even a slight rise from time to time may be taken as a happy omen.

TREATMENT.

The many and diverse theories regarding the treatment of shock shows conclusively the chaotic state of the professional mind regarding this condition. One writer is so confused in his interpretation of the phenomena that he advised at the same time morphine, strychnia, digitalis, nitroglycerine, whisky and citrate of caffeine. No one has done more to bring order out of this chaos than Dr. Geo. C. Crile, of Cleveland, by his experiments on dogs. He has practically demonstrated not only the uselessness but the harmfulness of strychnia in shock and that the rational treatment lies in raising the blood pressure. He lays down the principle that the treatment must be sedative to the sympathetic system and relaxing to the *arterioles*. To this end he advises compression of the abdomen and extremities to prevent the accumulation of blood in the large veins, with the administration of adrenalin given with salt solution. Dr. Halsted advises morphine also normal salt. It is interesting to note that Morris, as early as 1868, advised opium 1-2 gr. every two hours.

Rest and heat, preferably moist, added to these remedial agents, and we have certainly fulfilled the requirements for treatment in accordance with all that is known of the pathology of shock, to quiet the nervous system and relax the arterioles. The addition of strychnine, digitalis, nitroglycerine and whisky is certainly irrational. The heart is already overworked by nature's effort to repair the damage and strychnine may prove to be what the whip is to the spirited horse at the end of the race, and under its influence the heart may exhaust itself in a last effort. When there has been hemorrhage as a complication the first indication is most assuredly to restore the volume of blood, but it is certainly irrational to increase the quantity of blood suddenly when the normal amount is present in the vascular system and the difficulty lies in reality in properly caring for the usual quantity. It would seem theoretically that increasing the volume of blood rapidly under these conditions would only increase the local congestion in the large blood vessels and make the ultimate restoration of the normal blood pressure more difficult. Small quantities of hot water per mouth or rectum sufficient to allay the thirst, or the slow, continuous rectal irrigation, which introduces the fluid gradually and as the tissues are prepared to appropriate it seems to me to be more rational than intravenous infusion of a large quantity of fluid. Briefly stated, the treatment in hemorrhage is to restore immediately the normal volume of blood, in shock to restore the normal blood pressure. Dr. Robert Dawbarn calls attention to the danger of using plain water in intravenous infusion in hemorrhage and says that experiments on dogs have proven that it will kill almost as quickly as prussic acid. He advises normal salt solution at a temperature of 118°-120° F., one to two quarts, ten minutes to be taken in introducing it. If the kidneys are not functionating normally, the quantity must be lessened.

Some writers make a point on the value of force of gravity and advise lowering of the head. Mummery says that the ideal treatment of shock would be the raising of the external air pressure, and thus substituting an artificial peripheral resistance for the lost peripheral resistance caused by the exhaustion of the vasomotor centers, but that as yet this method is not practical.

The administration of foods and drugs by the stomach is distinctly counterindicated. The same principle holds good here as in the case of the heart. The stomach is exhausted and oversensitive and should not be irritated or stimulated to work until the period of exhaustion has passed. Perhaps the principal factor in the therapeutics of shock is rest, anatomic and physiologic rest. This of course forbids all stimulants, alcoholic as well as stimulating drugs. Light and sound should be excluded that the tired brain may share in the general calm with which we seek to surround our patient.

PREVENTION.

The preventive treatment of shock lies almost entirely in the domain of surgery. Here is indeed the ounce of prevention worth a pound of cure. Paget in 1868 advised hypodermics of morphine after operations before the patient is restored to consciousness to lessen the shock caused by pain. Davey in 1858 recommended waiting in cases of shock injuries not complicated with hemorrhage until some of the "Promethian fire" had returned to the shocked tissues. Dr. Harvey Cushing and Dr. Crile advise the cocainization of main nerve trunks thus "blocking" the nerves proximal to the site of operation, in severe cases where shock may be anticipated. Dr. Crile has invented a pneumatic rubber suit with which he envelops the patient, which he claims assists greatly in preserving the normal blood pressure. There is no doubt that much can be done by the proper preparation of the patient before coming to the operating table to prevent subsequent shock and the practice of some surgeons of rushing nonemergency cases under the knife without any preparatory treatment cannot be too strongly condemned. It is self-evident that the more normal the condition of the system the greater will be the resistance of shock. The indication, then, is to bring all organs as far as possible to their highest function. This is especially important in the case of the kidneys, bowels and skin, the great eliminatory organs; these must actually secrete normally at the time of operation if we are to expect normal conditions to follow. Free drainage by means of nature's own remedy, water used liberally, internally and externally, for several days previous to operation, will in ordinary cases be sufficient to put the kidneys and skin in good condition. A free cathaisis, making sure that the entire intestinal tract is cleared, is of the utmost importance. The liberal use of a normal salt solution as long before the operation as possible not only aids in the systemic drainage but increases the volume of the blood and promotes the rapid metabolism which is so important in preserving the quality of the flood. The stomach should be absolutely empty when the patient is brought to the operating table, as it is one of the first viscera to manifest reflex irritation, and a persistent nausea and vomiting keeps the patient in constant distress and the muscular system in action, preventing the rest and relaxation so necessary to recovery.

Rapid operating, as rapid as is consistent with a proper attention to detail, is unquestionably one of the greatest factors in the prevention of surgical shock. The entire regime of the operating room should be conducive to this end. Every detail, should be attended to as far as possible before the patient is placed under the anæsthetic. Minutes wasted for any reason while the patient is under abnormal conditions is an injustice to all concerned. In abdominal surgery involving the peritoneal cavity there is little doubt that shock is in almost direct proportion to the amount of handling and exposure of the intestines. Mummery says that turning the intestines out of the abdomen is always followed by a sudden and dangerous fall of blood pressure. Methods of operating, therefore, in which these viscera are little or not at all exposed can certainly claim to be a factor in the preventive treatment of shock. I have frequently seen patients put to bed after the removal of large myomata (hysterectomy) per vaginam with no more symptoms of shock than after a normal labor. The choice of anæsthetic in cases where shock is apprehended is considered by some of great importance. Mummery says that ether anæsthesia almost always causes a rise in blood pressure, while chloroform is usually accompanied by a fall in blood pressure, and believes the chloroform-ether mixture to be the best anæsthetic from the point of view of subsequent shock. It would seem, however, that there are more important points to be considered in the choice of an anæsthetic, as the organic condition of the heart, kidneys and lungs, as we have more definite knowledge of the action of ether and chloroform on these organs. The temperature of the operating room is of great importance, and should be kept between $80°$ and $85°F$. Wetting and chilling of the body should be avoided, and heat applied directly by means of a water cushion placed over the operating table assists greatly in preserving the normal body temperature. The mental state in which the patient comes to the operating table is no doubt an important factor. Every effort should be made, therefore, to inspire the patient with confidence in the success of the operation, that the demon of fear may be exorcised from the sick room, that the spirit of hope may hover around the last few conscious breaths and be the first to greet the awakening mind struggling back to consciousness.

CHAPTER XXXI.

SUDDEN ABDOMINAL PAIN—ITS SIGNIFICANCE.

"Give me liberty or give me death."—Patrick Henry, American. (1736-1799.)
Truth should be constantly advocated because the majority constantly advocate error.

Abdominal surgery is no longer a pioneer work. It is the result of the accumulated experience of the past fifty years. Its success is based on well tried practices. It is a jealous field, filled with battles lost and won, marked here and there with sad regrets, chagrin from unavoidable mistakes, however often brightened by the light of success. A master-hand in abdominal surgery is a hard-earned reputation. However, accumulative experience of fifty years has still left obscure points in abdominal surgery which the genius of Lawson Tait has attempted to set at rest by the exploratory and confirmatory incision—a misused and abused field.

During the past fifteen years I have been specially interested in gynecology and abdominal surgery, and during these years has risen the question of abdominal pain and its signification. To interpret abdominal pain requires the best skill of the finest head.

Sudden, severe abdominal pain is the one significant early symptom sounding the hope for relief or the knell of doom. In the interpretation of sudden appearance of abdominal pain lies the physician's chance of success or failure—usefulness or disaster. This cry of sudden pain may come from multiple lesions or sources—it may be the appeal of a strangulated loop of intestine on the verge of gangrene; the demand of an agonizing ureter afflicted with a bristling calculus; the disaster of a perforated appendix in the dangerous peritonitic enteronic area; the horrible, grinding, hopeless pain of a biliary calculus; the calamity of a ruptured gestating oviduct; or from the beginning painful perforative peritonitis of impossible diagnostic origin—accompanied by excruciating pain.

Abdominal pain belongs to the domain of the nervus vasomotorius, the sympathetic nerve, and should be interpreted according to its life and habits, in relation to its anatomy, distribution to viscera and physiology (rhythm) peristalsis. Rhythm is a physical accompaniment of life.

Severe abdominal pain is the appeal for prompt, efficient assistance. In the first place, in my experience, the natural manifestation of sudden abdominal pain is too frequently obtunded, dulled, lulled into a treacherous quietude by the general practitioner's employment of large hypodermic injections of morphia, which obscures diagnosis. Frequently it is the mode of onset, the sudden appearance and localization of the pain that affords the sharpest aid to diagnosis, and if the sharpest, delicate symptoms are obscured by morphia it may jeopardize the patient's life.

Sudden pain in the abdomen is frequently the guiding, suggestive means to a diagnosis. Pain in any location is the conscious expression of nerve trauma, whether it be macroscopic or microscopic.

Pain is an objective as well as a subjective symptom. Its subjective character forces us to depend on the patient's statement for its location, severity, duration. Pain is the most constant beginning feature and frequently the most constant, persistent characteristic. For this reason the practitioner should secure a complete clinical history, mode of onset, location of pain, rhythmic or constant, before he obscures its most delicate and valuable aid to diagnosis by narcotics. Abdominal pain is Nature's warning that mischief is afoot in the abdominal viscera, and its manifestations should not be obscured by opium until sufficient evidence is secured to diagnose the cause. The successful diagnosis depends on the most careful analysis of every available symptom in severe abdominal pain, which is defective in a narcotized patient.

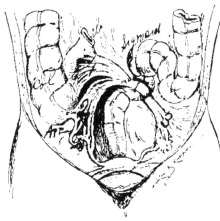

STRANGULATION OF THE SIGMOID BY BAND ORIGINATING FROM BILATERAL PYOSALPINX

Fig. 85. This is an illustration of a peritoneal band obstructing the sigmoid from a woman physician operated by Dr. Lucy Waite. I assisted Dr. Waite and saw the elongated band attenuated in the middle. Its rupture allowed the gas to rush through the sigmoid with recovery. The termination of the band (1) is at 2 and 4 on the right side and at 3 on the left side.

A characteristic of sudden abdominal pain is that at first it is diffuse or mainly in the umbilical region (the abdominal brain, the sensorium of the abdominal viscera). Gradually, with the lapse of time—hours—it becomes more and more localized in the region of the affected organ (beginning local peritonitis).

A suggestive symptom is that almost all patients with sudden abdominal pain especially beginning peritonitis, *vomit*. The failure of the general practitioner in appreciating the significance of sudden severe abdominal pain results in late, and too frequently disastrous, surgery, also in disastrous treatment by administrating cathartics, the enemy of visceral quietude.

In sudden abdominal pain the pulse in general is of more practical value than temperature. In some advanced, grave abdominal diseases the pain is limited or absent. Overwhelming profound sepsis has obtunded sensibility. In sudden abdominal pain the first and foremost matter is its diagnosis—the rock and base of rational treatment. The diagnosis is absolutely required in order to attempt rationally to remove the cause.

Probability is the rule of life and it is just as applicable in diagnosing sudden abdominal pain as in other matters. For example, when a man is attacked by sudden abdominal pain and vomiting with rise of temperature, pulse and respiration, the probability is that it is appendicitis—not perforation of the gastrium, enteron or colon, for that occurs perhaps one hundred times less than perforation of the appendix.

Observation.—I was called to attend a physician who was attacked with sudden abdominal pain while riding in his buggy. The abdominal pain from the beginning was located several inches to the left of the medium line of the abdomen. The diagnosis was ruptured appendicitis from a potential appendix, i. e., one with an elongated meso-cœco-appendicular apparatus capable of extending or moving to locations distant from the usual appendicular site. The improbable diagnosis was intestinal perforation, because the appendix perforates perhaps a hundredfold more than the intestine. In operating on the physician forty hours subsequent to the attack I found the peritonitis localized to the left of the medium line of the abdomen in the enteronic coils located in the left iliac fossa. The potential a p p e n d i x was during operation practically in its usual location, however, surrounded by peritonitis. The explanation was evident. He had a potential appendix, which while wandering amongst the intestinal loops in the left half of the abdomen had become perforated and immediately, before adhesions formed, returned to its usual location in the right iliac fossa. The extensive, varying mobility of the cecum and appendix should be included in the anatomic diagnosis.

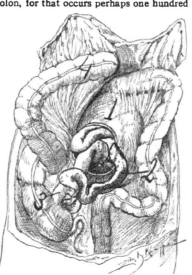

HERNIA OF 8 FEET OF ENTERON IN FOSSA DUODENO-JEJUNALIS

Fig. 86. This occurred in a woman about 35 years of age. The 8 feet of enteronic loops lying in the fossa duodeno-jejunalis were reduced with facility.

Anatomy is the solid ground of nature on which to build a rational diagnosis of sudden abdominal pain.

PATIENT'S HISTORY.

We should study the history of the abdominal pain in each patient for aid in diagnosis.

A clinical study of abdominal pain is of the utmost importance to both general physician and abdominal surgeon. Has the patient experienced similar sudden abdominal pain previously? What was the length of time elapsed between the previous attacks of pain? If the pain is recurrent it is probably from the same original cause, e. g., repeated perforated appendicitis or repeated attacks from calculus Has the pain any regular persistent relation to the ingestion of food or fluid? If so we examine the proximal end of the tractus intestinalis, as for gastritis, ulceration, biliary passages, pancreatic disease and perhaps appendicitis. If the pain persistently precedes or follows defecation, search for rectal disease—hemorrhoids, fissure, ulceration, carcinoma. If the pain recurs with menstruation, one examines the genitals. If the pain be sudden and occurring for the first time, we should scrutinize its history and every visceral function. Pain following extra exertion may be due to hernial strangulation, ruptured pregnant oviduct, breaking of peritoneal adhesions, formation of volvulus, rupture of a cystic tumor, an ovarian cyst, or other tumor or viscus, rotated on its pedicle. Pain following extra trauma may be ruptured bladder, stomach, intestines or other viscera. In gestation an impending miscarriage may cause sudden abdominal pain. Clinical history is the most valuable in acute abdominal pain—not in chronic. Repeated rough rides with repeated abdominal pain is suggestive of calculus. The repeated abdominal pains due to painful peristalsis in inflamed ducts—biliary, ureteral, intestinal, genital—is still difficult to diagnose.

It should be distinctly remembered that sudden recurrent abdominal pain following peritonotomy or peritonitis is mainly due to peritoneal bands checking peristalsis, or painful peristalsis from inflamed viscera. Sudden abdominal pain in a patient who had had hernia is liable to be from constrictions of peritoneal bands. The clinical history is frequently a pencil of light in the diagnosis of sudden abdominal pain.

AGE AND SEX.

Age and sex are of extreme value in diagnosing sudden abdominal pain. In woman, in the maximum sexual phase, the lesions of the tractus genitalis surpass those of the tractus intestinalis. Still a differential diagnosis between appendicitis and right-sided inflamed oviduct, peritoneum and ovary, is frequently difficult.

Sudden pain in anemic young women may be perforating round ulcer of stomach.

In children lesions of the tractus intestinalis preponderate, gasteroenteritis, invagination, enterocolitis, appendicitis.

In senescence malignancy may attack the gastrum, colon, rectum, gall bladder and pancreas, as well as ulceration of the intestinal tract usher in pain.

CHARACTER OF ABDOMINAL PAIN.

Abdominal pain may be acute or chronic, it may be tolerant or excruciating (peritoneal extravasation). It may be due to intra-abdominal or extra-abdominal disease. It may arise from violent peristalsis (colic) in tubular viscera or from inflammation. Abdominal pain may be due to disease or trauma.

If one will closely watch the sudden acute abdominal pain, it will be quite apparent that the character of the pain in most of the acute affections is very similar. We only observe a reality in difference of degree of pain from the bearable to the agonizing. In perforation the character of the pain is the same in all viscera. In invagination it is paroxysmal and periodic, at least at first, due to irregular and violent peristalsis. In internal strang-

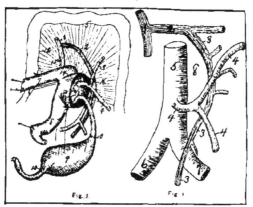

HERNIA IN FOSSA DUODENO-JEJUNALIS

Fig. 87. I secured this specimen from an autopsy. The subject had numerous recurrences as was demonstrated by the marked cicatricial strictures at various points of the enteron. Also saccular dilatations (9) of the enteron demonstrated repeated recurrences.

ulation it is generally intense and periodic, due to violent peristalsis; later continuous and of an aching, dragging character, due to paralysis of the intestinal segments. In appendicitis the pain is nearly always sudden and intense, i. e., the perforative variety. The variety of appendicitis with slowly increasing pain is likely lymphatic in invasion and not dangerous, simply medical, though of course the appendicular mucosa may be perforated. Sudden, acute abdominal pain of a lancinating character, and quite continuous, is very likely to be due to perforation of the appendix or digestive tube, and the continuous, agonizing character of the pain is a heraldic symptom of diffuse peritonitis—the knell of life. It may be remembered that the character of sudden acute abdominal pain will depend on the capacity of any viscus for peristalsis, i. e., its capacity to cause colic by violent, wild, irregular muscular action. In peristalsis periodicity must not be forgotten, and the etiology which gives rise to the initation, inducing the peristalsis. It may be transitory in character, as food irritation, rapidly forming and inducing invagination, or a calculus attempting to enter a duct. Or the pain may be continuously periodic, as a calculus lodged in some canal, appendix, ureter, enteron, colon, or biliary. Head and Sherren claim that the body is endowed with three forms of sensibility conducted by three series of fibers in the efferent nerves, viz.:

1. The nerves which subserve deep sensibility. The fibers of deep sensibility or "deep touch" course chiefly with the motor nerves to the muscles, aiding muscular protection of viscera, and also supply the fibrous structures connected to the muscles—muscular sense.

2. The nerves which respond to painful impressions and to extreme heat and cold responding to light touch—skin sense. This second system of nerves Head and Sherren term "proto phatic."

3. The nerves which enable light touch and the minor degrees of temperature to be appreciated and two points to be discriminated.

To the third system of sensibility the name "epicritic" is applied—temperature and location sense. The sensibility of the abdomen is a significant matter in sudden abdominal pain.

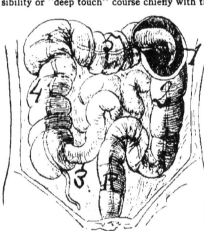

INVAGINATION OF ILEUM

Fig. 88. This was drawn from a child about 10 months old. At the operation, which was on the 4th day, I could not disinvaginate the ileum without inflicting irreparable damage. The child died 12 hours later.

The abdominal cutaneous sensibility must be distinguished from the sensibility of the abdominal musculature and also the condition as to whether the hyperesthenia be unilateral or bilateral, symmetrical or non-symmetrical, e. g., McBurney's point is frequently simply a nervous point. At this point the nerves of the coecum correspond with the nerves of the abdominal wall immediately ventral to it, i. e., the appendicular nerves being irritated transmit sensations to the spinal cord where reorganization occurs and the impulses are emitted over the intercostal nerves to the abdominal wall at McBurney's point. The same condition will occur relative to other viscera, e. g., the kidney.

Pain may be reflex or sensitive, hyperesthesia, neurosthenia, hysteria.

Gastric ulcer is especially liable to manifest pain from cold drink, solid food.

In the diagnosis the pain is the most important element to both patient and physician.

The anatomic and physiologic side must be studied, analytically.

It may be remembered that the dorsal and ventral (parietal) peritoneum is sensitive to trauma according to individuals. The healthy visceral peritoneum is not sensitive to trauma. The healthy viscera may be handled without pain.

Pain on abdominal palpitation may arise from radiation.

Subjects vary as to their susceptibility of pain.

Pain manifests certain characteristics as facial expression, position of body, muscular tension.

Sudden abdominal pain depends on definite cause and it behooves the physician to discover it.

On account of the multiple viscera, complex nerve supply, and numerous functions the abdomen presents the most abundant and varied pain of any body region.

The sudden beginning of severe abdominal pain is frequently significant of serious trouble.

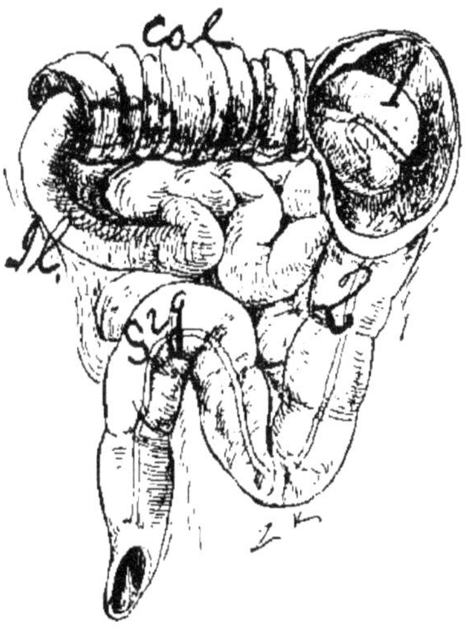

Gastric Crisis. So-called abdominal crises should be studied with care that life may not be placed in jeopardy or disastrous treatment instituted. First and foremost is the gastric crisis of locomotor ataxia in which the patient is attacked with paroxysmal vomiting and severe gastric pain enduring from some hours to several days and may recur after days or weeks. In such cases the symptoms of tabes dorsalis will aid the diagnostician.

ILEO-CŒCAL INVAGINATION

Fig. 89. Drawn from a woman about 38 years old. At the first operation I could easily disinvaginate. The ileo-cœcal invagination recurred some two months later and at the second operation I resected the cœcum and reunited the ileum and colon. The patient died some 10 days later. Autopsy demonstrated that invagination was due to an enormous cœcal ulceration and the colon was beset with perhaps a dozen ulcers from the dimension of a dime to that of a silver dollar. 1, Cœcum and appendix. Il, ileum.

Nephritic Crisis, or the so-called "Dietl's crisis," perhaps should be considered as a trauma on the nerves, vessels and ureter of a dislocated kidney. Torsion of the nephro-neuro-vascular pedicle with flexion of the ureter doubtless accounts for this rare phenomenon. Dietl's crisis is followed by local tenderness in the renal region, hence, infection occurred in the peritoneum.

Gas in the tractus intestinalis is a frequent accompaniment of abdominal pain. However, the presence of the gas does not produce the pain, as that is mainly due to trauma, stretching of the inflamed nerves in the peritoneal sheet.

LOCATION OF ABDOMINAL PAIN.

How far can we diagnose abdominal pain by its locality? Only to a limited degree. Associated circumstances must aid in the diagnosis. There are three common localities of acute abdominal pain or peritonitis, viz., pelvic, appendicular and that of the gall-bladder region; and as probability is the rule of life, it is well to diagnose acute abdominal pain as a disturbance in one of these three localities of the peritoneum until proved otherwise.

Acute abdominal pain in general is referred to the umbilicus—in other words, the region immediately over the solar plexus or abdominal brain, the receiver of the impressions of abdominal viscera. Acute abdominal pain is generally due to a disturbance of the peritoneum, owing to a lesion of an adjacent viscus; but since the peritoneal lesion can arise from many organs and from several points of the same organ, it demands the most experienced diagnostic acumen and the most mature judgment to interpret the significance of the lesion through the abdominal wall. No one can decide what kind of wood lies under a table cloth. I have repeatedly observed in appendicitis that patients say the acute pain, especially in the beginning, is over the whole middle of the abdomen (solar plexus). This may be due to excessive and violent peristalsis of the enteron. As regards locating the pain at any point of the enteron, it cannot be done, first, because the loops of intestines have no distinct order as to locality; second, the patient cannot discriminate a point of pain at any given locality, perhaps from lack of practical experience.

Pain in a particular area does not invariably signify that the cause of the pain is located in that region. The absence of pain in regions is significant.

Though pain in the umbilical region be indeterminate of location, it is frequently the knell of distress in peripheral visceral lesion as appendix, oviduct, invagination, axial relation.

However, a kind of sudden severe abdominal pain may arise from violent irregular peristalsis (rhythm) in non-inflamed (or slightly inflamed) tubular viscera, as foreign bodies (hepatic, pancreatic, ureteral, intestinal calculus) as strictures (intestinal, ureteral, biliary, pancreatic ducts, appendix, oviducts).

In sudden abdominal pain (especially peritonitic extravasation) four factors may be observed, viz.: (a) (Sympathetic), First, diffuse pain in the central abdomen, umbilical region, solar plexus, the three abdominal sensory areas, cutaneous, peritoneal and muscular are affected, shocked. The bed clothing cannot be tolerated (sensory, skin) and the abdominal muscles are rigid—muscular visceral protection.

SUDDEN ABDOMINAL PAIN—ITS SIGNIFICANCE

(b) Later localization of the pain occurs over the affected viscera (peritonitis).

(c) (Spinal nerves) Rigidity of abdominal muscles arise over affected viscus (somatic muscular, protection of viscera).

(d) Hyperesthesia of the skin over the affected viscus (somatic cutaneous, protection of viscera).

It must be noted that cutaneous or sensory manifestations of somatic spinal and visceral nerves may extend over their entire periphery, e. g., in appendicitis, hyperesthesia or supersensitiveness of the skin may be found in the right iliac fossa, over the pubis, pudendum, Poupart's ligament, and the testicle.

In regard to the location of sudden acute abdominal pain we have to

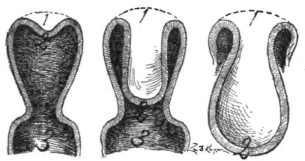

Fig. 90. An illustration to expose the progressive steps of uterine invagination (intussusception or inversion) from the depression at 1, to the completed process at 2. 1, is where the invagination begins. 2, presents the progressive steps of the fundal progress through the os uteri. 3, the vaginal fornices subsequent to the uterine invagination; the cervix presents a vigorous rigid ring, resembling a giant anal sphincter, with steady, continuous, vigorous pressure on the invaginated portion of the uterus; the rigid cervical ring gradually yields, dilates and the uterus disinvaginates like a spring. The uterus becomes reduced like a dislocated joint. Hence, like intestinal invaginations and volvulus, the uterus may tend to reinvaginate.

consider (a) the seat of pain as felt by the patient; (b) the pain elicited by pressure (tenderness); (c) local rigidity of the abdominal muscles; (d) anesthetic or hyperesthetic condition of the skin of the abdomen.

As to local tenderness of pain elicited by pressure, it indicates a pathologic condition of viscus or of the peritoneum (inflammatory). The pain is induced by motion or disturbance communicated to a sensitive inflamed area, peritoneum.

Local rigidity of abdominal muscles indicates adjacent disease of organs supplied by the same nerves as the muscles which exercise a protective agency, to preserve rest for damaged tissue, to assume repair, and to prevent further damage from motion, e. g., distribution of sepsis by peristalsis. Hyperesthesia or sensitiveness of the skin due to transmitted irritation, is often present, but is not very reliable as to locality, for it is dependent on peculiar symptoms and accompanies, more or less, though irregularly, most acute abdominal affections. Of course it would be expected that the severe sudden onset of pain in the renal and biliary ducts, being very near the abdominal brain, would be difficult to separate from the solar plexus. Lead colic may deceive the most elect as to its etiology or seat.

With few exceptions, to locate the seat of lesion in acute abdominal pain, we call to aid the pain elicited by pressure. Pressing the abdominal walls produces a distinct localized tenderness or pain which suggests localized pathology. Again, rigidity or tension of the abdominal wall is suggestive of pathologic locality. The symptom is simply purely reflex, due to irritation passing from the involved viscera to the spinal cord, whence its irritation is transmitted to the periphery of the distal intercostal nerves which control the abdominal muscles over the seat of pain. Dashing cold water on the belly will produce similar protective muscular rigidity. Hence, in general, the location of the disease in the abdomen from the patient's feeling of sudden acute pain, is quite indefinite. But local tenderness and local pain on pressure aid much. Localized rigidity of the abdominal wall is suggestive that such tension is protecting the seat of disease from motion, further bacterial or fecal invasion. In short the rigid muscles are placing the pathologic parts to anatomic and physiologic rest.

Vomiting is a general characteristic of sudden acute abdominal pain. In sudden acute abdominal pain, from visceral lesion, Nature makes profound effort to manifest its distress, however to diagnose the seat of pathology and its nature from localization of the pain requires much reading between the lines from experience and judgment.

Again, a vast difference exists between sudden acute abdominal pain and that which progresses gradually. Much depends on the stage of the disease in which the physician first visits the patient.

The signification of sudden acute abdominal pain may be more actually realized by a short consideration of some of the principal conditions which occasion it.

In some cases the physician is unable to localize the pain in any visceral tract under such conditions, the apt remark is that probability is the rule of life; hence an exploratory operation in the region of the appendix and gallbladder is justifiable in subjects jeopardized by imminent danger. The most frequent point of pain or pressure is the epigastrium, the abdominal brain or plexus coeliacus.

REFLEX OR REFERRED PAIN.

In general, sudden acute abdominal pain is referred by the patient to the umbilical region, to the solar plexus, directly over the abdominal brain. This, in my opinion, is a nervous center, possessing the power of reorganization, of receiving and transmitting forces, controlling visceral circulation and inducing reflex or referred pain. The irritation of peripheral visceral nerves is transmitted to the abdominal pain, when reorganization may localize the pain over the abdominal brain, at the seat of disease, or at a remote abdominal point, due to a supersensitive nervous system. Anal fissure, or ulcer, is one of the most typical examples to produce reflexes in the abdominal viscera, especially in the tractus intestinalis. Short trauma of viscera, as hernia, acute flexion of tubular viscera, induces abdominal pain and especially by reflexes.

OBSCURE SYMPTOMS OF ABDOMINAL PAIN.

Reflex pain from distant areas may simulate severe abdominal pain, multiplying the difficulties in differential diagnosis.

Obscure symptoms of abdominal pain arise from the invasion of the

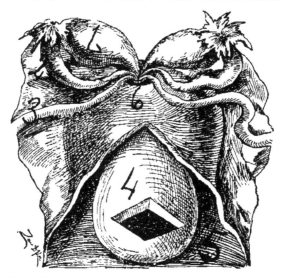

Fig. 91. An illustration presenting complete uterine invagination. The oviducts and ovaries may be entirely included within the invaginated uterus. 1, ovary; 2, oviduct; 3, round ligament; 4, uterine fundus with diamond-shaped aperture resected from its wall; 5, vaginal lumen. Drawn from subject dying from trauma, shock, due to uterine invagination 2½ hours subsequent to labor. I performed the autopsy 4 hours after death.

peritoneum from *pneumonia*. In fact I have seen a half dozen physicians in consultation advise and perform peritonotomy in a case of pneumonia, so deceptive were the abdominal symptoms—pain, tenderness, tympanitis, temperature, muscular rigidity and respiration.

Pleurisy or intercostal neuralgia extending over a large area of intercostal nerves which supply the abdominal wall may simulate sudden abdominal pain—for the trunk of a nerve being irritated manifests its sensation, pain, at its periphery which, in the case of the intercostal, end in the abdominal wall.

Abscess in the abdominal wall may simulate abdominal, peritoneal or visceral pain, from irritation of the intercostal (abdominal wall) nerves. Dr. Lucy Waite had in her charge in the hospital a child with an abscess in the abdominal wall which simulated extremely abdominal visceral (peritoneal) disease.

Amygdalitis mastitis and *hysteria* may simulate abdominal pain.

In *post-operative peritoneal hemorrhage* (peritoneal extravasation) the pain is obscure, as the previously traumatized, and consequently obtunded, sensibility of the peritoneum does not manifest recognition of the bleeding, while peritoneal hemorrhage (peritoneal extravasation) from ruptured pregnant oviduct produces excruciating pain.

Spinal cord lesions may simulate abdominal pain by a diffuse sensitiveness over the affected intercostal nerves, e. g., the girdle, constricting pain in tabes dorsalis or locomotor ataxia.

Uremia may be accompanied by persistent vomiting. Pain in right shoulder may refer to *hepatic disease*.

Spinal caries may produce pain in portions of the abdomen from pressure on dorsal or lumbar nerves, as sensory areas or rigid muscular areas.

Testicular pain may refer to a ureteral calculus. Crushed testicle may induce severe abdominal pain, vomiting and shock, as its route to the abdominal brain is direct and rich in nerves.

Hyperesthesia of the iliac regions are deceptive, because these regions are supplied by the cutaneous branches of the ileo-hypogastric nerve (first lumbar). McBurney's point is practically a skin hyperesthesia, a super-sensitiveness of skin area included in the peripheral region of cutaneous twigs of the last dorsal (twelfth intercostal) nerve and the ileo-hypogastric (first lumbar) nerve.

In short, if any sensory intercostal or lumbar nerve be affected (by somatic diseased viscera) it will manifest sensory skin areas at its corresponding periphery.

Muscular rigidity of the abdominal wall will be manifest in the somatic

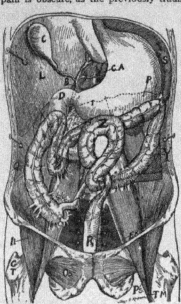

VOLVULUS OF SIGMOID

Fig. 92. Drawn from a subject with physiologic or incomplete sigmoid volvulus. Z, Sigmoid. The volvulus is rotated about 360 degrees.

area of the spinal nerves corresponding to the diseased viscera (simulating the cutaneous area). In short, if any motor intercostal or lumbar nerve be affected (by somatic diseased viscera) it will manifest motor (muscular rigidity) area at its corresponding periphery.

A feature of obscurity in the diagnosis in abdominal muscular rigidity is that when a part of an abdominal muscle becomes irritated, the whole (and not part) of the muscle becomes rigid. Hence the muscular rigidity is the same for perforated appendix or gall-bladder. For general peritonitis the whole abdominal muscular apparatus is rigid.

In the tractus nervosus the *neuroma* of intercostal or lumbar nerves must not be overlooked. I have observed three subjects of neuroma on the ileo-hypogastric or ileo-inguinal nerve. One in Prof. Senn's clinic where a neuroma on a nerve in the abdominal wall in the region of the appendix was exquisitely tender inducing a diagnosis of appendicitis. The analytic, searching diagnostic methods of Prof. Senn soon discovered the tender neuroma, which he removed instead of the appendix. One subject, a female, 24 years of age, was sent to me with a diagnosis of appendicitis. I found a typical neuroma on the lumbar nerve in the region of the appendix. A third case of neuroma of a lumbar nerve in the appendicular region I saw in consultation with Dr. I. Washburn, of Rensselaer, Indiana. Abdominal pain is the surface indication of various pathologic states of the abdominal organs (or

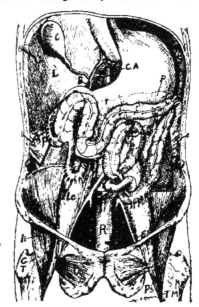

VOLVULUS OF SIGMOID

Fig. 93. Drawn from a subject with physiologic or incomplete sigmoid volvulus which is 360 degrees rotated.

abdominal wall). In abdominal pain the chief skill is in the diagnosis, for the correct treatment depends on the diagnosis. The more correct the diagnosis the less "neurosis" will occur in abdominal pain. The abdominal wall, including the cutaneous and muscular layers, receives its (chief) nerve supply from the spinal cord, which contains sensory and motor nerves. The viscera receive their (chief) nerve supply from the sympathetic, which contain sensory and motor (rhythmic). (The parietal peritoneum has a mixed nerve supply.) The spinal cord emits nerves through the rami communicantes *to* the viscera and receives nerves *from* the viscera. The spinal cord emits nerves to the abdominal wall (muscle and skin). Hence the viscera and abdominal wall are in direct, harmonious, balanced relations and consequently of vast value in diagnosis. Any visceral disorder is reported to the spinal cord which is at once emitted to the abdominal wall for protective purposes (muscular rigidity). The visceral walls are the thoracic and abdominal and cannot be divided —they are supplied by the spinal nerves which overlap, extending from clavicle to pelvic floor.

Man's breathing apparatus consists of the thoracic and abdominal wall. The thoracic visceral rhythm (sympathetic) dominates in the thoracic wall.

All the visceral tracts except the nervous may manifest painful peristalsis from inflamed ducts or canals.

STRANGULATION BY BANDS AND THROUGH APERTURES.

Strangulation by bands and through apertures constitutes one-third of all intestinal obstructions. If the bowel loops glide through an inguinal or femoral aperture, digital examination will detect the cause of sudden, acute abdominal pain. Obturator and sacro sciatic hernia are seldom diagnosed, so that they would practically be included in internal strangulation by peritoneal bands. Sex does not aid in diagnosis, for males and females about balance in peritonitis during life, hence will possess about the same amount of peritonitic bands.

A history of previous peritonitis tells a significant story of strangulation by bands. Vomiting is violent, pain from peristalsis is periodic and general over the abdomen. The pain is not due to checking of the fecal current, but to reflex irritation of the bowel at the seat of obstruction. Temperature is not conspicuous and the pulse is not much changed. Tympanitis arises in exact proportion to the peristalsis of the bowel wall proximal to the seat of obstruction. At first the pain is violent, but it subsides with the progress of the case, becoming more continuous and generally diffused. If the patient be quiet, the pain is so slight that it deceives the most elect. No stool, no gas per rectum, no detectible

VOLVULUS OF ILEO-CŒCAL APPARATUS

Fig. 94. Drawn from subject with physiologic or incomplete volvulus of the ileo-cœcal apparatus. I, presents the state of the volvulus—about 200 degrees.

swelling at any hernial aperture with continuous abdominal pain and vomiting, demand surgical notice. The temperature and pulse are not reliable. Strangulation by bands will generally give no tender location on pressure and no detectible swelling; and, in fact, I have watched cases with the abdomen quite soft and pliable, with no possible physical point of diagnostic value, not even tympanitis, yet with obstruction which proved gangrenous on peritonotomy. In one case the pain was at first severe, general, and almost subsided the day before the operation, yet fifteen feet of intestine was as red

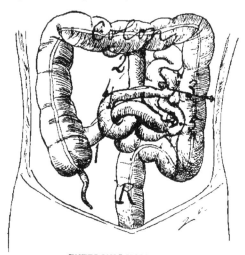

ENTERONIC VOLVULUS

Fig. 95. Drawn from a child 14 months old, referred to me by Dr. Walter Fitch. I operated on the third day and found the pedicle, foot or style, of the volvulus to be located at the cœcum, the constriction being due to the rotation of the distal end of the ileum and proximal end of the jejunum around each other as an axis. On opening the abdomen the colon was collapsed while the enteron was enormously distended. After releasing the volvulitic pedicle the gas rapidly distended the entire colon and large volumes with ample stool passed per rectum. The child died of peritonitis 3 days later. 4, Volvulitic pedicle of enteron.

as sunset. The sudden, acute abdominal pain is not due to the constricting band, but to reflex irritation transmitted to the abdominal brain, where reorganization occurs, whence it is emitted to the whole digestive tract, inducing violent, disordered and wild peristalsis (colic).

Acute, sudden abdominal pain, due to a constricting peritoneal band is one of the most obscure to interpret. To explore the abdomen in the proper time for such a case requires a wise diagnostician and a bold surgeon. The matters to bear in mind by strangulation by bands are, the acute, sudden abdominal pain with a violent onset, vomiting, and the distinct colicky, peristaltic, periodic character of the suffering, not forgetting a previous history of peritonitis. However, the sudden, acute abdominal pain, arising from a strangulation of a loop of bowel by peritonitic bands, is difficult to interpret and seldom diagnosed. It may be asserted, that when a patient is suffering from some grave disease, manifest by sudden acute abdominal pain, the nature of which cannot be interpreted, an early exploratory laparotomy is justifiable and demanded. Such obscure cases require an experienced surgeon, skilled in abdominal work, to meet any emergency, to enter the peritoneum and retire rapidly. I remember very distinctly the case of a man, about 40, who gave consent to my colleague, a general practitioner, who was entirely untrained by experience or observation in abdominal surgery. The doctor told me he opened the a b d o m e n and found a band stretching tightly across the right colon. But he said "the colon was black, and I did not know what to do with it, so I closed the abdomen." It is needless to say that the man made a prompt, fatal exit. But most cases die undiagnosed. The d a n g e r of strangulation by bands is gangrene and perforation.

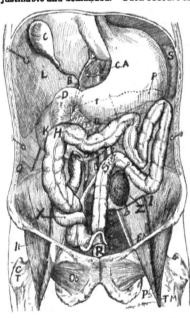

VOLVULUS OF ILEO-CŒCAL APPARATUS

Fig. 96. Drawn from subject with physiologic or incomplete volvulus of ileo-cœcal apparatus. X, shows the state of the volvulus—almost 360 degrees. Z, presents a large pouch in the mesosigmoid.

The starting point of peritoneal bands are—(a) local peritonitis, (b) h e r n i a l apertures (i n g u i n a l, femoral, abturator, f o s s a duodeno-jejunelis, intersigmoid fossa, Winslow's foramen), (c) p e r i t o n i t i s from muscular trauma (psoas, lateral abdominal), (d) infective mesenteric glands, (e) operative sites, (f) fimbriated ends of oviducts, (g) Meckel's diverticulum. A history of typhoid fever, hernia, peritonitis is suggestive.

The intensity of the abdominal pain in intestinal obstruction depends on the completeness of the obstruction. The pain not being inflammatory is paroxysmal, rythmical, due to trauma on the nerve periphery in the intestinal wall.

It should be noted that reduction by taxis of a strangulated intestine in the hernial rings ought to be practiced with care. The danger is reduction in mass (without relief) and the return into the peritoneal cavity of pathological intestinal segments. In strangulation, internal, it is well to inquire whether a patient has suffered from peritonitis or experienced peritonotomy.

In strangulation of an intestinal loop the symptoms will practically simulate perforation or extravasating peritonitis only after the sepsis has begun.

Hernia which may involve several visceral tracts (digestive, genital, urinary) not infrequently presents unsuspected irritation from the natural

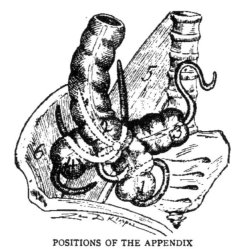

POSITIONS OF THE APPENDIX

Fig. 97. Pelvic position (woman 47 per cent—man 37 per cent). 2, Retro-cœcal position (20 per cent). 3, Potential position (23 per cent). 4, Right of psoas (18 per cent). 4, Resting on the psoas (46 per cent).

hernial rings from the inimical supraumbilical hernia in the linea alba. I have observed much distress and suffering in patients afflicted with hernia which had been overlooked for years.

I assisted Dr. Lucy Waite to operate on a woman some 35 years of age, on whom a previous peritoneal section had been performed. She had suffered from obstruction of the bowels for several days with continuous vomiting. Dr. Waite found an organized peritoneal band of some fifteen inches in length extending tensely across a loop of intestine producing almost complete obstruction. Rupture of the band afforded complete relief with recovery.

Sudden obstruction may arise from intestinal loops gliding to and fro through apertures in the mesentery, omentum.

INVAGINATION.

Invagination constitutes about one-third of all intestinal obstruction, and the sudden, acute abdominal pain arising from this cause is more easily interpreted. Age signifies much in this case, for one-fourth of all invagination occurs before the end of the first year of extrauterine life, and one-half before the end of ten years. Invagination is a disease of childhood. Its mode of onset is sudden and frequently violent. From some twenty-five experiments in invaginating the bowel of the dog, I am sure the pain is periodic at first. The griping, colicky peristalsis is rhythmic, depending on irritation. At stated times the dog suddenly spreads wide his four feet and arches his back, appearing in severe distress, then gradually recovers his natural attitude. In invagination blood occurs in the stool in 80 per cent of cases (especially children), and the vomiting is not violent, nor even always conspicuous, for the bowel is only partially occluded. Seventy per cent occur at the ileocecal apparatus, that land-mark in man's clinical history, 15 per cent in the enteron and 15 in the colon. Invagination manifests abdominal pain similar to an elongated enterolith in the bowel, which in rotating leaves small spaces at its side for the passage of gas and some liquid stool. I have, unfortunately, watched a case of enterolith day after day, with some half dozen physicians, not becoming able to interpret the abdominal pain or to diagnose the case, until gangrene of the bowel occurred at the seat of the enterolith, when nature asserted manifestation to induce us to explore the abdomen, but with a fatal result. The most skilled of abdominal surgeons repeatedly examined this case, but could not interpret the acute abdominal pain, which came on suddenly, though as the days glided it quietly subsided. The patient was a physician, but could not localize any abdominal pain; it was diffuse. Temperature was about 99½ deg. and 100 deg. F., and the pulse was 85 to 95, almost the whole week of illness. The abdomen was generally soft and not tympanitic. Very seldom can abdominal tumor be palpated in bowel invagination. Shock in young children is quite conspicuous, yet I personally know of two autopsies in infants, who were attended in life by three of the most skilled abdominal surgeons, yet the post-mortems revealed invagination as the cause of death. A skilled and experienced physician, such as the late Dr. Jaggard was called to an eight months infant and he stripped the clothing to be more thorough in examination, and yet after all his diagnostic skill, failed to locate disease in the digestive tract from lack of symptoms. The child was very pale, cried a little, and died thirty hours after the attack. The autopsy revealed ileocecal invagination.

Sudden acute abdominal pain in a child may with high probability be interpreted as invagination, especially if one can detect the periodic, peristaltic character, its colicky nature. Blood following in the stool is almost pathognomonic. A tumor will rarely be found, and pressure on it will not generally elicit tenderness, it is not at all likely the patient can locate the seat of the disease from pain. Tympanites and vomiting are not conspicuous, and the temperature and pulse are not reliable. The danger of invagination is sloughing of the apex or neck and consequent perforation and peritonitis.

Invagination presenting at the anus interprets easily the cause of pain.

Tenesmus is a prominent feature. In quite a number of cases of invagination during the last fifteen years I could palpate a tumor but twice, and that was once in an adult, spare woman where the ileocecal invagination had progressed to the flexura coli lienalis. The cause of her invagination was a large ulcer of the cecum, which extensively hypertrophied the cecal wall. I disinvaginated the cecum; however, reinvagination occurred some weeks later when resection of the cecum was practiced with fatal result. Once I could palpate an invaginated tumor in a child.

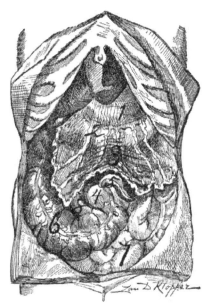

POTENTIAL POSITION OF APPENDIX

Fig. 98. The appendix rests among the enteronic coils; however, on rupture it would be protected by the omentum.

In actual practice we found at the Mary Thompson Hospital for women and children that shock was the chief fatal factor—the children entering the hospital with advanced invagination, when peritonitis had begun and the pulse was uncountable.

From fifteen years of observation on infant invagination, as they enter the hospital in an advanced or late stage of the disease, I am convinced that on the average, more infants will recover from intestinal invagination without an operation than with one. I think actual cases by number will prove this claim—sound unsurgical as it may.

Slowly progressing stricture may suddenly become closed.

VOLVULUS.

Volvulus is so rare that it constitutes about one-fortieth of all intestinal obstructions, and occurs mainly in men, as women and children are practically free from sigmoid volvulus. As in invagination so in volvulus, I was always compelled to suture them in position in a dog. But I never succeeded in establishing a permanent volvulus in the dog. Volvulus is characterized by tympanites, and it is said by periodic pain. Volvulus occurs at the sigmoid in 60 per cent of subjects, at the ileocecal valve in 30 per cent, and in the small intestines in 10 per cent. It is so rare that though I have seen several cases of partial (physiologic) volvulus, however only one case of complete (pathologic) volvulus in man. The subject of enteronic volvulus was in a male child brought to me by Dr. Walter Fitch. He was in the third day of illness. I operated and relieved the volvulus of the enteron but the child died of shock and infection three days later. Nicholas Senn operated successfully on a man, on the eighth day, for sigmoid volvulus. He introduced a tuck plication in the mesosigmoid for prophylaxis. Seven years later another physician operated on the same man for volvulus, recurrence, with fatal result. The man had enormous tympanites; his pain is not described as severe, but no doubt the suffering is severe.

At first the pain is periodic but as time advances it becomes more constant, with now and then exacerbations. Vomiting, though not conspicuous, must arise more or less from trauma to the peritoneum. Perhaps the sudden pain, chronic constipation, and rapid rise of tympanites would aid in interpreting volvulus, but seldom can one diagnose such a disease from its rarity. Pain no doubt would be referred to the abdominal brain. Most clinicians note tympanites as a conspicuous feature of volvulus.

Weller Van Hook treated successfully a case of sigmoid volvulus of eight days' standing.

From observation of the sigmoid and mesosigmoid in hundreds of autopsies I am convinced that the chief etiology of volvulus of the sigmoid is elongated sigmoid located in the proximal abdomen and possessing a narrow foot accompanied by mesosigmoiditis due to vigorous action of the left psoas muscle which traumatizes the sigmoid, inducing migration of germs or their products through mucosa, muscularis into the serosa, inciting plastic peritonitis in 80 per cent of adults.

The plastic peritonitis in general ends in two conditions, viz.: 1. The most frequent, the plastic sigmoiditis binds the left surface of the mesosigmoid to the ventral surface of the psoas muscle. Such subjects cannot have sigmoid volvulus from mechanical condition. 2. The second state of the mesosigmoid arising from the mesosigmoiditis is a progressive shortening, a contraction of the base of the mesosigmoid, that is, the base or pedicle of the mesosigmoid becomes a very narrow pedicle from the progressing, contracting mesosigmoiditis, so that peristalsis of the sigmoid induces a rotation or torsion of its base. In autopsies I have found partial (physiologic) rotation of the mesosigmoid, especially during the existence of mesosigmoiditis—as far as 180 to 860 degrees.

Sigmoid volvulus is due to the torsion, rotation, of the narrow pedicle of a mesosigmoid contracted at its foot by mesosigmoiditis. When one untwists, detorsionizes, the volvulus and releases it, the sigmoid recedes, rotates, like a spring into its original volvulitic condition. To prevent the volvulus from returning to its original torsion in dogs I sutured it in situ. Resection may be required to overcome the acute torsion. Puncture may

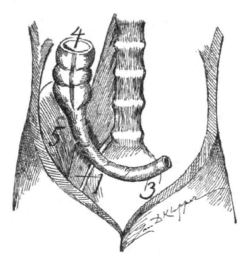

ABSENCE OF APPENDIX (AND CŒCUM)
Fig. 99. Drawn from female, aged 50 years. The diagnosis in this case would be uncertain.

be required to reduce its dimension. Most subjects have ample time to acquire sigmoid volvulus, as they are generally over 40 years of age. There is frequently physiologic sigmoid volvulus in autopsy which is partial torsion of the mesosigmoid; however, obstruction is incomplete. The marked tympanitis or meteorism of sigmoid volvulus is at first localized in the left iliac fossa—a slight diagnostic point. The sigmoid is the most varied of any segment of the colon in location and capacity of its lumen. The tympanitis may be located in the right abdomen while the nontympantic enteronic loops may be forced around the constricted foot of the volvulitic sigmoid. Childhood is not predisposed to sigmoid volvulus, notwithstanding the relatively elongated sigmoid and mesosigmoid, because the angle of mesosigmoid insertion (what I term von Samson's angle) is located well proximalward on the lumbar vertebra. Why woman is practically free from sigmoid volvulus I am, so far, unable to explain. Sigmoid volvulus occurs practically in men possessing what I term the "giant verticle sigmoid" which is located in the proximal abdomen and occurred in perhaps 15 per cent of the autopsies. The foot of this giant verticle sigmoid is narrow and by the contracting mesosigmoiditis results in a narrow style around which may rotate the sigmoid loop. This was the condition I found in physiologic volvulus which occurred in perhaps 2 per cent.

APPENDICITIS.

Appendicitis is the most dangerous and treacherous of abdominal diseases—dangerous because it kills, and treacherous because its capricious course cannot be prognosed. The peritonitis it produces is either enteronic (dangerous—absorptive, non-exudative) or colonic (mild—exudative, non-absorptive).

A concise clinical history should be obtained when sudden pain arises in the right side of the abdomen for it might be due to perforated appendix, gall-bladder or gestating oviduct. The right-sided pain may arise from biliary, pancreatic or ureteral calculus or ureteral flexion.

Pleurisy or intercostal neuralgia (right) may confuse. In the right side, so closely adjacent are eight important viscera, momentous in surgery, that a silver dollar will touch the pylorus, gall-bladder, head of the pancreas, kidney, adrenal, duodenum, ureter and possibly the appendix. Hence differential diagnosis of sudden abdominal pain in the closely adjacent multiple organs of the right side is difficult—frequently impossible.

The conditions that cause the excruciating, agonizing, shocking pain in appendicitis are perforation and extravasation into the peritoneal cavity.

APPENDIX LYING ADJACENT TO MECKEL'S DIVERTICULUM

Fig. 100. This drawing was taken from a subject on whom I operated for a large abscess in the right iliac fossa and at the same time I removed a perforated tube 3 inches in length and of the usual appendicular dimension—supposing it to be the appendix. Three months later the man died from appendicitis, as the postmortem performed by Dr. Arthur MacNeil demonstrated. The first attack and abscess was from the perforation of Meckel's diverticulum, located in the right iliac fossa. The second attack and abscess was from perforation of the appendix, located (retro-coecal) in the right iliac fossa.

SUDDEN ABDOMINAL PAIN—ITS SIGNIFICANCE 415

Right-sided muscular rigidity means that the motor (intercostal) nerves supplying the abdominal muscles are irritated. It may be any kind of peritoneal infection (extravasation from any viscus, hepatic, intestinal, ureteral or genital). Right-sided cutaneous hyperesthesia means that the sensory (intercostal) nerves supplying the abdominal skin are affected. It may depend on any kind of peritoneal infection. Sudden cessation of severe symptoms, as rapid diminishing of high temperature and pulse and abdominal rigidity, is an evil omen—gangrene of the appendix has probably occurred. Immediate operation should occur.

For years I have made it a rule to recommend appendectomy to patients having experienced two attacks. Fifty per cent of subjects who have had one attack experienced no recurrence.

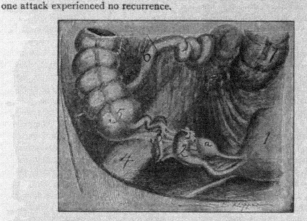

RELATION OF APPENDIX TO THE GENITAL TRACT

Fig. 101. Appendicitis and salpingitis are separate diseases, each arising from its own mucosa. However, infection emanating from either may compromise the anatomy and physiology of the other by peritoneal adhesions.

In perforation it is very difficult to interpret the sudden abdominal pain. Associated circumstances would aid. In typhoid fever one would naturally suspect perforation if sudden acute abdominal pain arose, and my colleague, Dr. Weller Van Hook, successfully operated on a typhoid perforation diagnosed by his medical friend. One might think if he was called to a young woman with sudden acute abdominal pain that it was a round, perforating ulcer of the stomach, after excluding pelvic and appendicular disease, but the sudden acute abdominal pain of perforation is so vague and indefinite that only an exploratory incision would interpret it.

The sudden acute abdominal pain from appendicitis (perforation) is more apt to be diagnosed from probability. Now probability is the rule of life, and when one is called to a boy or man with sudden acute abdominal pain, it is likely appendicitis. The pain of appendicitis is at first sudden and generally diffuse, and in appendicitis this is, in my experience, a characteristic and conspicuous feature. The sudden acute pain in appendicitis is doubtless due to violent appendicular peristalsis (colic) of an inflamed appendix, or to the rupture allowing the bowel contents to come in contact with the peritoneum, and also inducing violent irregular peristalsis of the adjacent bowel loops. It is the agonizing, excruciating pain of peritoneal extravasation. Rigidity of the abdominal muscles over the seat of pathology in appendicitis is a great aid to interpreting the pain. The muscular rigidity is protective and due to the transmission of the visceral irritation to the spinal cord, which is reflected to the abdominal skin (sensory) and to abdominal muscles (motor). There is a nice balance between the peripheral visceral and the peripheral cutaneous nerves in the abdominal muscles through the spinal cord. Local tenderness and local rigidity of the abdominal muscles is a great aid in signification of the sudden acute pain in appendicitis. It might be well to suggest that the position of the appendix is located at any point from the liver to the floor of the pelvis, and also many times where there is more or less of a mesenterium commune, the cecum may approach the vertebral column, and the appendix is then liable to lie among the enteronic coils—the dangerous ground of peritonitis. It is likely the pain in appendicitis depends on the seat of the disease, i. e., the mucous membrane has become ulcerated, inducing painful appendicular colic (peristalsis), while the sudden exacerbation of violent diffuse abdominal pain is due to the involving of the peritoneum itself from the fecal extravasation and from violent peristalsis. I see nothing especially worthy of attention in the so-called McBurney point. It is skin sensitiveness. Pain over the seat of disease is certainly a natural feature, and generally so over the appendix, which lies under a point midway between the umbilicus and anterior superior spine of the ileum. But it is not always so by any means, for I examined with great and anxious care, a short time ago, a young physician with severe pain over the so-called McBurney point, when on operation the long appendix was in the pelvis and perforated. McBurney's point is practically a cutaneous hyperesthesia. Then again pain on pressure may be reflex, appearing in remote regions of the abdomen. The sudden, acute, diffuse abdominal pain arising in appendicitis, generally subsides in the right iliac fossa after thirty-six hours, and one can nearly always elicit pain on pressure there. This pain on pressure is doubtless the motion radiation, transmitted to a sensitive, inflamed peritoneum, and not the dragging of an adhesion, as some assert, for adhesion so newly formed can have no nerves formed in them. But man is subject to appendicitis four times as frequently as woman, due, perhaps to Gerlach's valve being small in man, and thus not allowing the foreign body to escape after entrance, and due also to the greater activity of the psoas muscle in man, inducing more peritoneal adhesions to compromise the anatomy and physiology of the appendix. Contracting adhesions compromises appendicular drainage. The appendix lies on the psoas muscle in man more frequently than in woman, and on its longest range of activity, hence when the appendix contains virulent and pathogenic germs, the long range of action of the psoas so traumatizes the appendix that it induces the escape or migration of the accidental virulent pathogenic microbes through the appendicular walls into the peritoneal cavity. Common sense and experience would dictate that the pain on pressure would occur in any point of the abdomen possessing inflamed structures. Since probability is the **rule** of life it is well to search for pain in the three great regions of dangerous peritonitis, viz., the pelvic, appendicular and gall-bladder regions. In appendicitis the pain on pressure is in the ileo-coecal plexus, i. e., in the

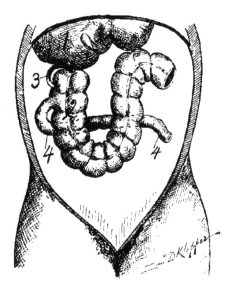

NONDESCENDED APPENDIX

Fig. 102. The appendix is associated with the liver. The appendix (cœcum) is nondescended in males 9 per cent and in females 5 per cent. In this case there is an ileo-cœcal volvulus.

ileo-coecal angle, not at the so-called McBurney's point, which is a nerve skin neurosis—a skin hyperesthesia.

The ileo-colic plexus may be found tender on bi-manual vaginal examination, especially on the right side. However, these hyperesthetic (tender) points are insufficient to establish a diagnosis of appendicitis. Palpable anatomic findings are the only reliable data for the diagnosis of appendicitis.

BILIARY CHANNELS.

The digestive tract has still another common seat for sudden acute abdominal pain, and that is the gall-bladder region. The sudden acute abdominal pain in hepatic colic is not generally so violent as many others accompanying acute diseases of the digestive tract. Patients relate that the pain is aching, dragging, and in the active stage of cutting or tearing. Some relate a feeling of tightness or fullness. But it depends on whether the calculus is attempting to enter constricted portions of the duct, or whether it has already entered. I have had typical cases where operation proved that the calculi only attempted to enter the constricted portion of the duct. No doubt these are the cases which say so often that they have severe pains at any time, but especially after taking hot meals or hot stimulating drinks, or vigorous exercise; whence arises excessive peristalsis, inducing short, temporary hepatic colic. Now, when the gall-bladder has many calculi in it, and when one more or less often attempts to engage in the neck of the gall-bladder, the pain is rhythmical. It begins slowly and rises to a maximum. At the maximum the pain is intense. We have observed such cases and afterwards operated on them, removing many small calculi. Gall-stone exists perhaps four times as frequently in women as in men; why, we do not know. In my experience patients can generally locate the pain in hepatic calculi more accurately and definitely than almost any other sudden acute abdominal pain. They refer the pain to its proper locality; however, I must admit that this reference is before rupture. After rupture of the cholecyst or duct the pain is indefinite, like other perforation in the peritoneum. The sudden acute abdominal pain in biliary duct disease is characterized by more slowness, less acuteness, intensity and distinct periodicity, than in invagination, appendicitis or perforation of the digestive tract. Jaundice is not necessary. Jaundice or icterus is determined by the color of the eye-ball, and not of the skin. A feature in gall-bladder pain is that it extends well towards the dorsum. Age aids in diagnosing calculus in the biliary passages to some extent.

The patient, frequently middle aged women, is suddenly seized with agonizing pain in the epigastrium, vomiting and occasional collapse. The pulse rapid and small, the epigastrium tender (cutaneous hyperesthesia) and the right abdominal muscles rigid (intercostal motor nerves irritated, corresponding to its sensory roots of the spinal cord). With progress of the case the pain localizes in the right hypochondrium and peritonitis begins. I have had cases of rupture of the gall-bladder with no known premonitory symptoms.

It must be borne in mind that gall-bladder perforation presents a different picture than merely violent peristalsis (colic) due to gall-stone in the biliary passages.

The pain of non-perforated biliary colic arises suddenly, is agonizing, and especially intense in the gall-bladder region. It is generally limited in duration, and frequently associated with jaundice. Biliary calculus may exist without pain (autopsies are rich in this testimony).

SUDDEN ABDOMINAL PAIN—ITS SIGNIFICANCE 419

ACUTE HEMORRHAGIC PANCREATITIS.

The pain in acute hemorrhagic peritonitis is characterized by being sudden, terrible, agonizing and remains persistent in the region of the pancreas. The patient is attacked so violently that he faints, collapses. The vomitus is a greenish fluid contained in bile and blood. The patient suffers intensely in the epigastric region. It presents the symptoms of peritoneal extravasation (hence excruciating pain), small, rapid pulse, rigid abdomen with sensitive, tender skin, skin cool and bedecked with a clammy perspiration. Temperature ranges high. Profound sepsis gradually deepens and death supervenes in a few days. Acute hemorrhagic pancreatitis is a rare disease; I saw no case in some 700 autopsies. It is seldom diagnosed, as we still possess no standard differentiating symptoms. Diabetes is suggestive of hemorrhagic pancreatitis or fat necrosis.

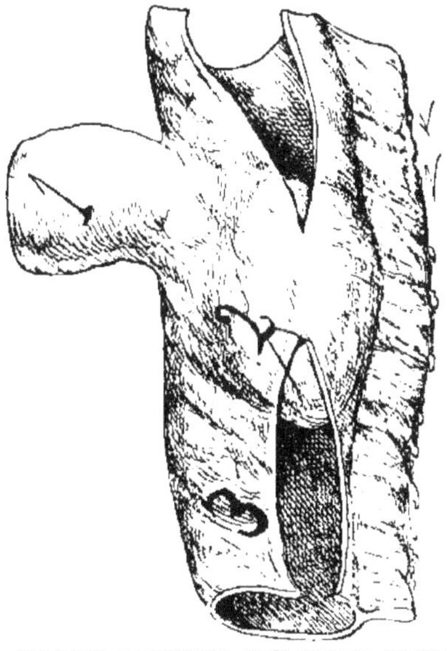

EMBOLUS WITH MESENTERIC VESSELS.

Embolus of the mesenteric vessels, a rare disease, produces sudden severe abdominal pain. It is difficult to diagnose and is likely to be equally difficult to treat by any means at our command. The difficulty will be in estimating the amount of intestinal resection required on account of the indefinite demarcation of the line of gangrene due to the embolus.

BILIARY CALCULUS DISLODGED FROM MECKEL'S DIVERTICULUM

Fig. 103. This illustration is from a woman physician, death from peritonitis following enteronic obstruction by a biliary calculus, which had become dislodged from Meckel's diverticulum.

URINARY TRACT.

In ureteral colic it must be said that the pain resembles that of hepatic colic in many ways, the rhythm being paroxysmal. It intermits and is often agonizingly spasmodic. It requires much careful study to differentiate the sudden acute abdominal pain in hepatic and ureteral colic. This is important, for the plan of action is very different. The pain in appendicitis, ureteral and hepatic colic are in close relation and resemble each other.

Sudden pain in the lumbar region, with progressive radiation toward the inguinal region, and especially testicular retractions, is suggestive of ureteral calculus. The kidney is frequently tender on pressure. Ureteral calculus permits time to complete the diagnosis, as it is non-inflammatory, hence we examine the urine for albumen, blood and pus and with the X-ray for shadows.

The perforation of the ureter will result in extra-peritoneal extravasation which does not induce such excruciating pain as intra-peritoneal extravasation.

1. Pain is a cardinal symptom of ureteral calculus.
2. Pain is not a sign of ureteral calculus.
3. Pain as a single standard is liable to lead to erroneous conclusions and to an incorrect diagnosis.
4. In eighty operations with pain as the guiding symptom for ureteral calculus 70 per cent failed to demonstrate calculus.
5. The vast dimensions of the plexus nervosus ureteris in number of ganglia and number of strands permit irritation from the ureter to pass with facility and rapidity to the abdominal brain, whence it becomes reorganized and emitted: (1) over the sympathetic nerves of the abdominal visceral plexuses, inducing pain, aching, reflexes in the adjacent viscera; (2) the reorganized irritation in the abdominal brain is emitted over the spinal nerves; (a) the intercostals (pain in abdominal walls); (b) over the lumbar plexus (pain in inguinal, hypogastric and external genital regions); (c) over the sacral plexus (pain in the nates, genitals, rectum, thigh, leg and foot). (3) The irritation of the plexus of nerves passes to the abdominal brain where it is reorganized and emitted over the cranial nerves (vagus which aids in inducing nausea and vomiting). These reflex pains in ureteral calculus confuse by involving the sympathetic, spinal and cranial nerves of distant regions, and also because other conditions of the ureters than ureteral calculus may duplicate or simulate the reflex pain.
6. Pain simulating that of ureteral calculus is a common symptom of many diseases of the abdominal viscera.
7. Ureteral calculus may exist without pain (post-mortems are rich in this testimony).
8. Calculus may exist with the manifestation of pain in some adjacent visceral tract only, for example, pain in testicle, or ovary (genitals).
9. Other diseases of the urinary tract than ureteral calculus may simulate or duplicate a pain (ureteritis, malignancy, hematuria tuberculosis, vesical calculus, growth, cystitis).
10. Reno-ovarian reflex, reno-testicular reflex, or reno-uterine reflex pains are not signs of ureteral calculus, but are simply intensified localizations of pain along the ureter, which may exist from numerous conditions.
11. Unilateral pain, stabbing pain, muscular trauma pain (Jordan Lloyd), stamping muscular pain (Clement Lucas), pain from corporeal trauma (muscular), pain from the sensitive ureteral proximal isthmus or pelvis, may arise from various conditions other than ureteral calculus.
12. The characteristic of pain in ureteral calculus is inconstancy, variation or radiation and reflexion. It has a tendency to produce sympathetic aching in other abdominal viscera.

SUDDEN ABDOMINAL PAIN—ITS SIGNIFICANCE

13. The pain in ureteral calculus depends chiefly on its position (ureteral pelvis and proximal isthmus, sensitiveness) and also on the mobility of the calculus.

14. Pain (colic) can arise in the ureter from increased ureteral pressure (calculus, stricture, flexion—obstructing the urinal stream), or from inflamed ureteral wall—ureteritis.

15. Ureteral-lithiasis, cholelithiasis, appendicitis, ureteritis, cystitis, nephritis, may produce practically identical symptoms.

Intoxications.—Uremia may be accompanied by abdominal pain, lead colic, blue gum line and occupation. Food of concentrated nature as meats may produce such concentrated urine that urination is accompanied by pain.

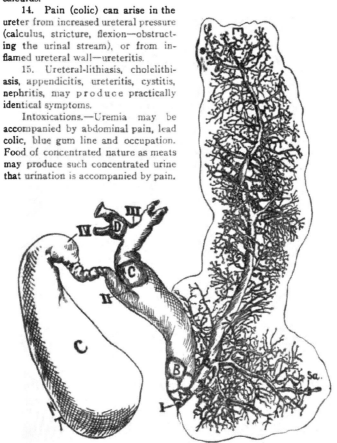

Fig. 104. Roentgen ray of the ductus pancreaticus and part of ductus bilis (it contains six hepatic calculi). From post-mortem specimens. I to II, ductus communis choledochus, dilated to ¼ inch in diameter and containing four hepatic calculi (A, B) in its distal end; II to IV, ductus cysticus, dilated to ⅓ inch in diameter, yet preserving in form six valvulæ Heisterii; II to III, ductus hepaticus, dilated to ½ inch, containing a hepatic calculus; C, cholecyst, normal dimension, containing no calculus; P, ductus pancreaticus (ductus Hofmanii-Wirsungii), ductus pancreaticus accessorius (ductus Santorini). Hepatic calculi, C, D and B.

TRACTUS GENITALIS.

The sudden acute abdominal pain arising from the genitals is more easily interpreted and managed. The pain can be more definitely located by the patient; and sudden disorganization of viscera, being accessible in the pelvis, is much more within control of the gynecologist. The sudden acute abdominal pain from the genitals is generally due to a ruptured ectopic pregnancy, or the very rare matter of the rupture of a pyosalpinx into the peritoneal cavity. Most of the pains are of slower origin and almost diagnosable. Sex and the reproductive age aid in the interpretation of the case.

With a ruptured pregnant oviduct the patient complains of sudden excruciating, terrible pain which at first is generally diffuse, but rapidly localizes in the pelvic region. The sudden pain is persistent, muscular rigidity is intense, the abdomen is tender and the patient's face is anxious; with the impending crisis, vomiting is not conspicuous. If the hemorrhagic peritoneal extravasation is ample the pain is excruciating, and faintness, syncope, shock with extreme anemia occurs. Death frequently occurs from hemorrhage.

Lawson Tait used to advocate that the oviduct would rupture not later than the fourteenth week. However, it may rupture or abort at any time previous to that. To the experienced gynecologist a bimanual vaginal and rectal examination reveals in most cases ample evidence for an operation. In sudden abdominal pain, rapid rise of pulse with lowering of temperature indicates (hemorrhage) gravity and demands surgical intervention. It may be stated that during a decade of attendance in the Mary Thompson Hospital for women and children Dr. Lucy Waite and myself have operated on considerable numbers of ruptured gestating oviducts in which the patient could not furnish a clinical history of very much pain or exact date of rupture.

PYOSALPINX.

In pyosalpinx the pain may be sudden and excruciating (involving the peritoneum).

The patient enforces upon herself extreme physical quietness, breathing with the proximal end of the abdomen only. The thighs are flexed, the face flushed, the abdomen tender, sensitive and rigid, the expression that of an impending crisis. Bimanual vaginal examination reveals a large uneven mass, which is excruciatingly painful.

The mass should be palpated gently for fear of rupture. One of my patients with a very large pyosalpinx strained at stool, causing rupture and death from peritonitis. At the autopsy I found perhaps a quart of pus, free in the peritoneal cavity. She died from excruciating pain and shock in some ten hours.

In regard to the character of sudden abdominal pain arising from the genitalis is more easily interpreted and managed. The pain can be more definitely located by the patient; and similar to other sudden acute abdominal pain, it varies as to its mode of attack, and as to viscera affected.

The pain of pyosalpinx is generally that of a local peritonitis; however, it is limited in its reflexion to other peritoneal areas.

AXIAL TORSION OF PEDICLES OR VISCERA.

Torsion of style or rotation of pedicle of a viscus is characterized by sudden severe abdominal pain. The intensity of the pain depends on the completeness of the constriction in the pedicle.

The tumor rotated on its axis gradually enlarges because the venous blood cannot return, while the arterial blood continues to pass into the tumor. Ovarian tumors rotate on their axes or pedicles perhaps the most frequently subsequent to parturition. The initial pain is generally severe but not excruciating like extravasation in the peritoneal cavity. As usual

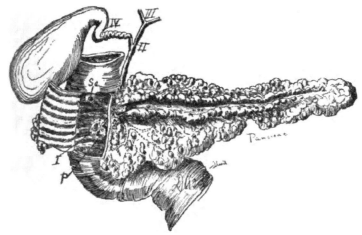

Fig. 105. Specimen containing pancreatic calculus. From a post-mortem; man about 40 years. I to II, ductus choledochus; II to III, ductus hepaticus; III to IV, ductus cysticus; Sa, ductus pancreaticus accessorius; P, separate exit of ductus pancreaticus in duodenum. A calculus ¼ inch in length and ⅙ inch in diameter is incarcerated in the duct of the caput pancreaticum. The calculus of the pancreatic duct projects into the lumen of the duodenum. Also six calculi existed in the ductus pancreaticus, as noted in sketch. The pancreas was in an advanced stage of suppuration and fatty degeneration. This specimen was kindly presented to me by Dr. A. M. Stober. B. J. Beuker sketched it from the pathologic laboratory of Cook County Hospital.

the pain is first diffuse, and later becomes localized in the region of the increasing tumor from accumulating venous blood and nerve trauma.

Hyper-rigidity of abdominal muscles and hyperesthesia of abdominal skin accompanies, exists (on account of reflex irritation in the spinal cord).

One of the most important aids to diagnosis is that the women possess a tumor, and that with accompanying abdominal pain the tumor gradually enlarges because the rotating pedicle easily constricts the thin walled veins, while the rigid walled artery persists in injecting its continuous stream into the tumor.

I have witnessed torsion of pedicles in ovarian tumors, oviduct sigmoid, ileocecal apparatus, myoma, enteron, omentum and kidney. Torsion of pedicles may apply to tubular viscera (ureter, intestine, oviduct) as well as to vessels.

I have operated on subjects with myomata rotated to such an extent that the entire original blood supply was completely obliterated, the tumor being nourished by newly formed blood vessels from adjacent viscera, especially from the omentum majus. Rokitansky of Vienna, first called attention to the axial rotation of tumors some forty years ago.

The facility of pedicular torsion depends on the elongation and limited dimension of the pedicles. Volvulus is but axial torsion facilitated in the sigmoid by a narrow foot or base (due mainly to mesosigmoiditis).

Axial torsion of the digestive tract constitutes about one-fortieth of intestinal obstruction. Perhaps 6 per cent of ovarian and parovarian tumors experience axial torsion. Mr. Lawson Tait saw some 70 cases, and as his pupil I witnessed with admiration his amazing acumen in diagnosing and successfully operating on axial rotated tumors. My assistant, Dr. A. Zetlitz, operated on a patient with almost complete torsion of the uterus, and examining the specimen evidence demonstrated itself that it was a slow chronic process and closely associated with peristalsis.

Axial torsion of viscera may be acute or chronic, complete (pathologic) or incomplete (physiologic), hence the manifestations of pain will vary.

Axial torsion of abdominal viscera (tumors) are no doubt rotated by the peristalsis of the viscus itself or that of adjacent viscera, especially the colon (sigmoid), which by its rhythmic movements rotates the ovarian tumor, the omentum and the ilium about the cecum. Tumors with axial torsions should be at once removed, while vital viscera with axial torsion should be reduced, untwisted, detorsioned, and sutured in situ, for axial torsion tends to recur. It may be due to the constriction, to the blood vessels, to the peristalsis or adjacent peritonitis.

CHIEF FACTORS INVOLVED IN SUDDEN ABDOMINAL PAIN.

The accompanying table presents a bird's-eye view of some of the practical factors involved in sudden abdominal pain. Indelible opinions must be entertained in the diagnosis as to the signification of the abdominal pain, whether it be from peritonitis (septic lesion from adjacent viscera), or pain from violent peristalsis (colic), or tubular viscera (due to mechanical irritation, calculus, stricture, flexion or from inflamed parietes). For practical purposes I will present a skeletal table of sudden pain of the six visceral tracts, intestinal, urinary, vascular, lymphatic, nervous, and genital. It is evident that abdominal pain rests on common factors, as (a) flexion; (b) stricture; (c) calculus (violent peristalsis, colic) of tubular viscera, in which the danger and pain are limited. Perforation (extravasation into the peritoneum) of tubular viscera in which danger and pain are unbounded. A decade ago it was thought sufficient to remember the three dangerous peritonitis regions, viz., pelvic, appendicular, and gall-bladder. With the present accumulated knowledge of the abdominal viscera the field presents problems of increasing complexity as presented in the following bird's-eye view of numerous causes of abdominal pain in the several visceral tracts:

I. Tractus Intestinalis
- 1. Gastrium, enteron, appendix, colon
- 2. Biliary ducts
- 3. Pancreatic duct
  - flexion
  - stricture
  - calculus
  - inflammation
  - perforation
  - neoplasm
  - colic
- 4. Volvulus
  - sigmoid 60 per cent
  - ileocecal apparatus 30 per cent
  - enteron 10 per cent
- 5. Strangulation
  - bands
  - apertures
- 6. Invagination
  - ileocecal apparatus 70 per cent
  - enteron 15 per cent
  - colon 15 per cent
- 7. Ulceration (gastrium, enteron, colon)
- 8. Splanchnoptosia

(Appendages)
- (a) Liver
  - (a) ducts—calculus, inflammation, neoplasm
  - (b) parenchyma, hepatitis, neoplasm
- (b) Pancreas
  - (c) ducts—calculus, inflammation, neoplasm, pancreatitis
  - (d) parenchyma—necrosis, neoplasm
- (c) Spleen—splenitis, neoplasm

II. Tractus Urinarius
- 1. Ureter — flexure, stricture, calculus, inflammation, perforation, colic
- 2. Bladder — calculus, inflammation, perforation, colic
- 3. Prostatitis—vesiculitis seminales.

III. Tractus Genitalis
- 1. Oviduct — perforation, abortion, colic, inflammation, torsion, neoplasm
- 2. Ovary — perforation, inflammation, torsion, neoplasm
- 3. Uterus — perforation, abortion, inflammation, colic, torsion, neoplasm

IV. Tractus Vascularis
- Veins—phlebitis, thrombosis
- Artery—embolus
- Artery—aneurism

V. Tractus Lymphaticus
- peritoneum—peritonitis
- glands—adenitis
- ducts—lymphangitis

VI. Tractus Nervosus
- pain—constant, periodic
- pain—on pressure
- neuritis
- neuroma
- neuralgia
- hyperesthesia

CONCLUSIONS AS REGARDS SUDDEN ABDOMINAL PAIN.

I. There are three kinds of sudden abdominal pain, viz.: (a) that of peritonitis, perforation, inflammatory, septic lesions from adjacent visceral peritoneal extravasation, continuous excruciating pain (pain continuous, unlimited and life in jeopardy), as 1, perforation of the tractus intestinalis (gastrium, enteron, colon, appendix—its appendages, biliary or pancreatic channels).

2. Perforation of the tractus genitalis (oviductal gestation, pyosalpinx, hydrosalpinx, uterus, ovary).

3. Perforation of the tractus urinarius (kidney, ureter, bladder).

4. Perforation of the tractus lymphaticus (chyle duct, chyle cysts, chyle channels).

5. Perforation of the tractus vascularis (aneurism, hemorrhage, embolus, oviductal gestation, is hemorrhage). (The tractus intestinalis, urinarius, genitalis, vascularis, lymphaticus may perforate, intraperitoneal or extraperitoneal. In extraperitoneal perforation, the pain is similar to

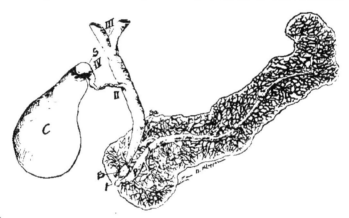

HEPATIC CALCULUS IN HARTMAN'S POUCH (S) AND VATER'S PAPILLA

Fig. 106. Presents hepatic calculus in the usual locations, Hartman's pouch and Vater's diverticulum. A calculus in Vater's pouch aids to obstruct and infect the ductus pancreaticus.

intraperitoneal perforation except in degree, however, the danger of the extraperitoneal visceral perforation is limited); (b) that of violent peristalsis (colic, non-inflammatory) of tubular viscera, as in mechanical irritation, calculus, stricture, obstruction, volvulus, flexion, oviductal gestation, parturition, constipation, aneurism, invagination, hernia, strangulation by band (inflammatory), (pain limited, periodic, life not in jeopardy); (c) that from painful peristalsis (colic inflammatory) from inflamed parietes of tubular viscera, as ureteritis, choledochitis, salpingitis, cholecystitis, cystitis, myometritis, myocorditis, enteritis, colitis, appendicitis (pain, periodic, inflammatory, life not in jeopardy). First and foremost for practical purposes it will be instructive to consider sudden abdominal pain from perforation of the three excretory mucous visceral tracts, viz.: intestinal, genital and urinary (as they not only perforate but develop immediate sepsis and jeopardize life). Second, sudden abdominal pain should be considered from perforation of the two non-excretory, non-mucous visceral tracts, viz., vascular and lymphatic (as they perforate, but do not develop immediate sepsis nor place life in immediate danger).

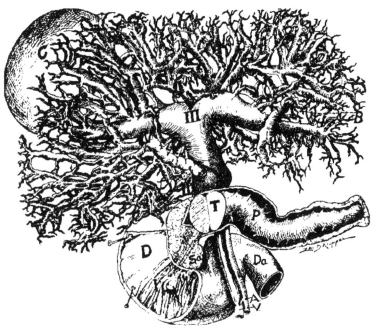

Fig. 107. Carcinoma completely obstructing the biliary and pancreatic ducts. Illustrates an x-ray of enormously dilated biliary passages. The biliary ducts (excepting the gallbladder, which was three to four times its normal dimension) had a capacity of 32 ounces, about six or seven times the natural capacity. The ductus communis choledochus was over 1¼ inches in diameter. The pancreatic duct admitted the index finger. The man, 69 years old, a giant in stature, weighing some 250 pounds with ordinary limited fat, lost 115 pounds in weight during three months' illness. The ductus cysticus, extending from II to IV, had seven Heister's valves, and its lumen would admit a lead-pencil only. At B the biliary ducts were deficient within the liver substance, but were really dilated on the surface. T, the carcinoma (divided with the scalpel), completely severing the lumen of the biliary and pancreatic ducts. There was enormous gastroduodenal dilatation from the compression of the transverse duodenum by the superior mesenteric artery (A) and vein (V). D, foldless, granular, proximal 2½ inches of the duodenal mucosa; I, entrance of ductus communis choledochus in the duodenum; Sa, ductus Santorini; P, ductus pancreaticus. The ductus communis choledochus and ductus pancreaticus, located between the carcinoma and Vater's diverticulum, were normal. Da, is the normal sized duodenum located distal to the compressing superior mesenteric vein (V) and artery (A). Observe the vast dilatation of the duodenum proximal to the superior mesenteric artery (A) and vein (V). I secured this rare specimen at an autopsy through the courtesy of Dr. Charles O'Byrne.

II. In making a diagnosis of sudden abdominal (constant) pain probability is the rule of life, e. g., (a) sudden abdominal (constant) pain accompanied with vomiting, abdominal rigidity, rise of pulse and temperature, tympanitis, is peritonitis (perforative), as appendicular, genital, biliary, gastro-intestinal, hemorrhagic pancreatitis, (b) sudden (inconstant) abdominal pain with practically negative pulse temperature, abdominal rigidity, tympanitis and perhaps vomiting, is violent peristalsis (colic), as flexion, stricture, calculus, inflammation, strangulation, invagination, volvulus, axial torsion.

III. Extravasation in the peritoneal cavity is accompanied by agonizing, excruciating pain.

IV. The leading symptoms should not be obscured by opiates until its complete clinical history as nearly as possible is obtained.

V. The clinical history is frequently a pencil of light in the diagnosis of sudden abdominal pain.

VI. Examine the patient completely from head to foot (especially per rectum and per vaginum).

VII. Exploratory peritonotomy is chiefly justified only in ascertaining the extent of visceral diseases and rarely justified to determine a diagnosis.

VIII. Delay in deciding the diagnosis of sudden severe abdominal pain should be avoided. Prompt diagnosis is the sheet anchor for immediate successful medical or surgical treatment.

IX. It must be remembered that sudden severe abdominal pain is a matter of gravity, and prompt investigation with prompt decisions should occur so that the patient's life may not be placed in jeopardy by delay, or disastrous treatment be instituted.

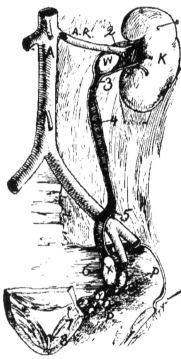

URETERAL CALCULI

Fig. 108. This illustrates uretera. calculus in its usual location, viz., (a) in the ureteral pelvis at the proximal isthmus (w), (b) in the pelvic ureter at P.

X. (a) Determine, if possible, the location of the initial pain; (b) inquire if the pain was at first diffuse in the central abdomen for awhile; (c) later and final observe whether the pain localizes itself in the region of the affected organ (peritonitis).

XI. The location of the pain may be superficial (hyperesthesia of the skin) or deep in the muscularis (rigidity). McBurney's point is a skin hyperesthesia (from the cutaneous branches of the twelfth dorsal and first lumbar nerve—ileo-hypogastric).

XII. The location of sudden abdominal pain is indicated by the segment (somatic) of the spinal nerves in adjacent abdominal muscles (rigidity), skin (hyperesthesia). The diseased abdominal viscus is protected, fixed by muscular and nerve mechanism similar to the muscular protection fixation of an inflamed joint.

XIII. The topographic anatomy of the abdominal viscera should be mastered, for, it is the solid ground of nature on which rests rational diagnosis. This can be accomplished by study in the cadaver and at autopsy.

XIV. Remember the major regions of peritonitis—appendicular, pelvic and that of the gall-bladder.

XV. Remember the major regions of violent peristalsis, colic (calculus), biliary, ureteral, oviductal and pancreatic.

XVI. Call the most available and competent abdominal surgeon early in consultation.

XVII. Remember that operations do not kill—it is disease that tolls the funeral bell.

XVIII. Operations on the dying are unsatisfactory.

XIX. As a general idea it may be stated that it is difficult to determine with precision the cause of sudden abdominal pain. One must frequently ask Jupiter to guide them in the greatest field of probability (appendicitis, salpingitis, chole cystitis).

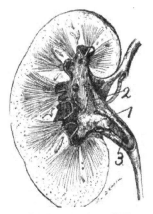

CALCULUS IN URETER

Fig. 109. Calculus at 3 which I removed in 1898 and in 1906 I removed a calculus from the same (left) kidney which was atrophied to one-third of its normal dimensions. Patient is, six months after the second operation, well.

The operator who performs peritonotomy for abdominal pain should be prepared for any emergency for the toxion of pain within the abdomen sounds an alarm, the course of which can not with certainty be determined externally. One can not determine the kind of wood that lies under a table cloth.

XX. Abdominal pain as a single symptom is frequently delusive.

XXI. The more accurate the diagnosis in sudden abdominal pain the less "neuroses," "neuralgia" or "indigestion" will occur.

XXII. A last resort to diagnose sudden abdominal pain is the "exploratory and confirmatory incision" of Lawson Tait.

430   THE ABDOMINAL AND PELVIC BRAIN

GENERAL TREATMENT OF SUDDEN ABDOMINAL PAIN.

First and foremost, should be introduced: (a) anatomic rest, which is maximum quietude of skeletal or voluntary muscles. Retire to bed not to rise for defecation or urination; (b) physiologic rest, which is minimum function of viscera. Food and fluid are prohibited per mouth.

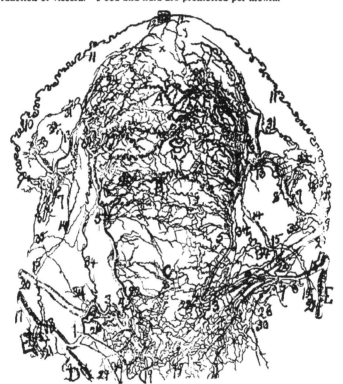

Fig. 110. The arteria uterina ovarica 3 hours subsequent to parturition at term. Every branch of the artery is ensheathed by a fenestrated plexus of nerves.

No anodynes or in minimum repeated doses until clinical history and the diagnosis is completed (maximum doses of anodynes obscure the diagnosis).

[NOTE—The method of treatment for abdominal pain by anatomic and physiologic rest was especially advocated by the distinguished English physician, Wilkes, in 1865 (living at present), continued by the celebrated

American, Alonzo Clark (1807-1887), by the "opium splint," and established forever in 1888 by one of the greatest surgical geniuses of his age—Lawson Tait (1845-1900].

Heat (hot, moist cornmeal poultice, hot water bag, hot bath) aids to relieve pain.

No cathartics—cathartics stimulate peristalsis, increases pain and distribution of sepsis. They induce vomiting. A rectal enema (or two) may be employed—the composition may be equal parts of molasses and milk, soap suds, glycerine, magnesium sulphate. Rectal injections of air.

BIBLIOGRAPHY.

John B. Deaver
J. H. Musser

E. S. Ricketts
E. O. Smith

E. Babler
E. Harlan

CHAPTER XXXII.

GENERAL PATHOLOGIC PHYSIOLOGY.

Hopeful men worship the rising, pessimists the setting, sun.
Bumping one's head against the universe makes brains.

The subject of this paper is pathologic physiology. The theme is the abnormal function of organs, or organs acting under pathologic conditions. The field included lies between normal physiology and pathologic anatomy. It is the zone of pathologic physiology or clinical pathology. In general it is determined with facility whether the visceral functions are pursuing a normal or abnormal course. In certain subjects, however, it is difficult to determine whether the functions are normal or abnormal. Some subjects present unmistakable pathologic symptoms for years, e. g., constipation, dirrahea, renal secretion, sweating; however, such subjects, though not theoretically, they are practically well. Pathologic physiology enables the physician to estimate between theoretical and practical functions. Not infrequently the functions of a subject vary to such a degree that it is difficult to decide whether he is well or ill. I know one subject who, between forty-five and sixty years of age, would periodically (several times annually) urinate some five quarts daily, otherwise he was practically well. He died of an acute attack of diarrhea at seventy.

To understand pathologic physiology one must possess a clear view of physiology. It may be well to remember that the common function of the thoracic and abdominal visceral tracts are sensation, peristalsis, absorption, secretion. Disease is a deviation from one or all these common functions. Disease begins as abnormal function and progresses with its repetition. The study of pathologic physiology constitutes the subject of abnormal function. To the four common functions mentioned of the thoracic and abdominal visceral tracts we must add the three special functions of the tractus genitalis —viz., ovulation, menstruation, and gestation—which offer vast fields of pathologic physiology in daily practice.

Pathologic physiology arises from defects in the living protoplasm (inferior anatomy and physiology) or from environments (bacteria). The subject born with pathologic physiology (heredity, stigma) is unable to withstand the friction of normal life. The subject may occupy such environments that injurious influences affect his protoplasm, such as excessive physical or mental exercise, heat, cold, bacteria. The study of pathologic physiology dignifies the basic study of physiology; it impresses the student with the functions and the structure of viscera. First and foremost, the physiology of an organ must be studied in order that its deviations may be comprehended. The study of physiology of organs will assist in comprehending the factors which influence the functional deviations. The subject of visceral peristalsis, rhythmical movements, the object of which is to propel visceral contents—urine, blood, ingesta, lymph, gestation products, secretions, carbonic acid gas—is of vast practical interest in the daily practice of medicine. Viscera are continually being subject to peristaltic waves. Peristalsis is dependent largely on visceral contents and blood supply. Hence the sluggish bowels (deficient peristalsis) are improved by supplying constant fresh blood. Fresh blood constantly streaming through the tractus intestinalis, urinarius, and genitalis initiates repeated peristaltic waves. The gravid uterus is in constant myometrial waves from extra blood supply. The tractus intestinalis, as the fresh blood streams into its territory, is subject to constantly repeating peristaltic waves. In visceral peristalsis the quantity of blood bathing the automatic visceral ganglia plays a role.

Since pathologic physiology is the zone between physiology and pathologic anatomy it is doubtless the incipient stage of future disease, pathologic anatomy. For example, chlorosis appears to be a precursory stage, a stage of pathologic physiology, to splanchnoptosia; gravidity precedes splanchnoptosia. The study of pathologic physiology cultivates accurate diagnosis in incipient stages of disease, enhancing opportunities for prophylactic measures. Modern investigation has forced us to accentuate functional (incipient) aspect of disease. It stimulates us to discover and recognize abnormality of function. It is returning to physiology as basic study. The discovery of an abnormal function may lead to the diagnosis of a contingent disease. The disordered function in the irritable weakness of the nervous system presents inferior anatomy and physiology.

Pathologic physiology attempts to instruct through disordered functions of the living subject. Pathologic anatomy attempts to instruct through changed structure in the living and dead subject. In practice, recognized disordered functions, or pathologic physiology, are manifest a hundred fold more than recognized pathologic anatomy. The old physicians recognized pathologic physiology under another name, as clinical pathology, functional or sympathetic disease. Among the first to discuss pathologic physiology from a scientific or systematic standpoint was Cohnheim, as found in his celebrated general pathology. However, before me lies the third edition (1904) of Dr. Rudolph Krehl's book, the first edition of which (1898) presented a systematic treatise on pathologic physiology. Practically Dr. Krehl's book is a pioneer work on pathologic physiology, systematizing the labors of Cohnheim and others, as well as making vast additions to the field himself. Pathologic physiology is not a new subject, for physicians recognized its existence in the past. Modern laboratory methods have demonstrated that the normal functions of individual organs vary within an extensive range. The border line between physiology and pathologic physiology is manifest by symptoms of various characteristics. Frequently organs will vary double their usual range, as the quantity of urine may be two or four pints daily, defecation may be once or twice daily, or every second day. Perspiration may be doubled for a period. We may observe the heart beat 120 per minute for weeks with no recognizable pathologic anatomy.

Pathologic physiology is characterized by an abnormal course of the life of an organ or a series of organs. In what does normal course of organs consist? We may designate as normal living processes what is found in the vast majority of individuals, in man and animals, when the individuals are considered healthy. It is granted that the function of an organ has normally an extensive range of healthy action. For example, the quantity of uric acid in the urine of the genera of aves, carnivora, herbivora, and bimana is extremely variable.

Perhaps man would not long survive producing a quantity of uric acid which birds habitually secrete. Each genera and, perhaps, species, have a law for themselves as regards the function of organs, possessing extensive variation of organ functions, without being pathologic. Pathologic physiology should be taught with more exactness in the colleges, so that the graduates may not be compelled to learn it at the expense of their patients. Pathologic physiology should be comprehensively explained to students, as it enables them to secure a general view of organized viscera, as well as the vicarious action of individual viscera. Besides it aids the practitioner to diagnosticate disease when no pathologic anatomy demonstrably exists.

Pathologic physiology is the zone between physiology and pathologic anatomy, an indeterminate, extensive, and frequently rapidly varying zone. It is well to bear in mind that I am discussing pathologic physiology as dominated by the sympathetic nerve (nervus vasomotorius). I will present in this essay some views on pathologic physiology of the viscera which I have taught for years in gynecological and abdominal courses.

No richer field exists in medicine, in inductive research, or for productive scholarship than the establishing of evident cause and effect in pathologic physiology. Pathologic physiology projects physiology into the field and function of philosophy. Physiology is the most noble of medical studies. Science collects facts while philosophy arranges and predicates laws from them. The field and function of philosophy is to deal with all classes and departments of incomplete knowledge for the purpose of utilizing it for man—to prolong life, lessen suffering, and increase happiness. Pathologic physiology will aid in the partial reduction of medical practice to laboratory investigation, e. g., senitlty, local and general, is heralded by observable cellular change—development, differentiation and degeneration of its vital, physiologic, process. The cell is accompanied by a cyclic series of changes from embryoism through differentiation to senescence, termed by Prof. Minot, cytomorphosis. (1) The first stage or embryonic cell is peculiar to itself in its physiology and if prolonged by circumscribed inclusions may become malignantly degenerated in the adult. (2) The second stage of life's cells, that of differentiation, consists of two states: (a) cytostatic differentiation, or the production of a material of definite and stable composition, as connective tissue, intercellular osseous substance—connective tissue framework; (b) cytodynamic differentiation is the production of substance having a metabolic function—parenchyma. (8) The third stage of life's cell is that of degeneration—senescence. Hence the laboratory investigator may yet discern the cause that determines cellular changes—embryonic, differentiation and degeneration (senescence), i. e., the pathologic physiology of life's cyclic cell and also that of disease. The philosophy of physiology at once suggests that the vital processes of cells—embryologic, differentiative, degenerative—cannot be abolished, however, they can be advantageously modified. The destiny of the cell is an aggregative mould into organs—for physiologic function. The composite organs functionating as a unit make man—the animal.

Physiology or function precedes and dominates structure. Man—the animal—is the drama, the play. It calls into being, function, the stage accoutrements, and dramatis personæ which exist and have signification to subserve the drama. The play selects and arranges the scenery, creates and determines the settings, lends coherence and sense to the sentence, furnishes inspiration and purpose to the actors. Now, it may be true in the material presentation of the play that stage furniture is the first structure element manifest, it is however subordinate to the motive of the performance or play. The stage material, furniture, is forgotten, lost in the functions of the play. Man's body is the stage accoutrements and personæ. The drama, the play, is the physiology, the function. Interpreted, this means that function determines structure, not structure function. Progressive motion in animals has traumatized, friction:zed, the proximal end (brain), enticing increasing blood supply (friction) and consequent increase of substance arises, i. e., bumping one's head against the universe develops the brain. Lincoln's body, that is, his anatomy, his stage accoutrements are dead, however, Lincoln, master of men, his play, his physiology, his function progresses unabated. John Brown's body, his physical stage accoutrements, is dead but his function of liberty moves on forever, even to the latest Russian cry for freedom. The staging, the physical accoutrements, of Uncle Tom's Cabin have long disappeared. However, the *motive* of the play, the function of the drama, which was the freeing of the black men, has also ceased as the object of the play had been accomplished. The parallel between the field of music and bilology or physiology is striking. Pipes and strings are the anatomy of music, but music itself, the ultimate object, is not pipes and strings. It consists of a pleasing succession of agreeable sounds—music is the physiology of the pipes and strings. The pipes and strings—the anatomy —are made to functionate as a unit through physiology, which rules anatomy. The several instruments must work in harmony—as a unit—to produce the object, which is the orchestra. Sound is itself an element, unrelated, unclassified, having neither predicate nor attribute and cannot therefore be confused with music—which is the pleasing succession of agreeable sounds to the human sense and purposely designated for that object. The only functional value of sound is to be a pleasant succession.

Physiology harmonizes different structures as music does pipes and strings into a functionating unit. As the instruments in the orchestra must subserve the purpose of the musician—which is music—so the aggregative molds of cells—organs—in the body must subserve the dignified purpose of physiology, i. e., a functionating unit which dominates, determines and precedes structure. We concede to our materialistic friend the physical basis of life and that function is not purely phychic in character. In the final analysis of structure or function we are dealing with the arrangement of matter, and that is structure. To illustrate that function, physiology, dominates structure, anatomy, one need only study large, noninfected, pelvic peritoneal exudates. Not long after pelvic peritoneal exudate arises blood vessels begin to appear in the mass, projecting their course through it, followed by lymph vessels and nerves as well as an endothelial covering, until the jelly-like unorganized mass is a living structural unit, a functionating organism. In this case did not physiology dominate, determine, precede anatomy?—yes, physiology is the central motive power of life. Darwin recognized this principle throughout his investigation of the origin of species. Through physiology he claimed he could modify species by environments that in a few years they could be scarcely recognized. By environmental influences he could modify through physiologic forces the traits or characteristics. Observe how the patent foramen ovale, modifies circulation—i. e., physiology—produces the clubbed fingers. Dr. Thomas G. Atkinson in the editorials of the *Medical Standard* for July and Oct., 1906, writes instructively and strikingly on pathologic physiology. He claims that the influences which determine structure operate from the complex to the simple, e. g., the larger functions of the body peristalsis, circulation, cerebration—are the simplified specific expressions of the multiple, complex, impressions produced on the body in general by circumstances and environment and these consequently are the determining causes of cellular structure. Physiology is the father of anatomy, of form, of characteristics, of hyper-

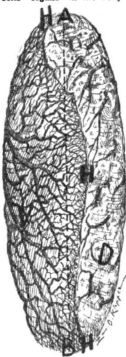

HYRTL'S EXSANGUINATED RENAL ZONE (H, H, H.)
Fig. 111. Corrosion anatomy. Left kidney. H, H, H, is what I term Hyrtl's exsanguinated zone. A, B, equatorial line of lateral longitudinal renal border. D, dorsal vascular renal blade. V, ventral vascular renal blade. H, H, H, indicates the course of Hyrtl's exsanguinated renal zone or the elective line of renal cortical incision with minimum hemorrhage—located ½ inch dorsal to the lateral longitudinal renal border. The quantity of sympathetic nerves required for the kidney may be estimated by the number of arteries in its two vascular blades.

trophy. A myoma in the uterine wall or an ovum on the endometrium are the causes of uterine hypertrophy—increased blood supply has multiplied the cellular elements of the uterus. Physiology or direction of excessive blood to the uterus has determined the multiplication of cellular structure And thus the amphioxis and similar animals that superseded and repeated his structure bumped their heads against the world's physical forces, developing the four skull vertebra and multiplying their cerebral cells by enticing blood, due to the cerebral trauma. The Japanese have long bodies and short legs because they do not use the legs sufficiently to secure blood. Sitting on chairs would entice more blood for larger legs. The lessons to be drawn from these views are that structure has no power to modify itself. It is perverted function that alters structure—pathologic physiology is the father of it. Again Dr. Atkinson claims that perverted function, pathologic physiology, operates from the complex to the simple. Pathologic physiology finally terminates by registering itself as altered adjustment of cellular structure in accordance with the perverted function at issue. Structural changes as a rule are the final responsive reaction of cell arrangement to pathologic physiology, having their origin in the complex relations between organism and environments and operating through the less and less complex physiologic systems of the body. The skillful and scientific physician can discern the origin and course of pathologic physiology and apply the appropriate advice, drug or scalpel, first to correct the function and second to correct the structure.

The Chief Duty of a Physician is to Correct Function.

As nine-tenths of illness is so-called medical and one-tenth so-called surgical, practically the sphere of a physician's influence is limited to the field of *pathologic physiology*, which lies between normal physiology and pathologic anatomy—the zone of pathologic physiology.

The common functions of viscera (sensation, peristalsis, absorption, secretion) do not perform uniformity throughout the same visceral tract and hence demand special attention in physiology, e. g., secretion is more prominent in the proximal end (cerebrum) of the tractus intestinalis while absorption is more pronounced in the distal end (sympathetic). These views should be borne in mind when observing pathologic physiology. In excessive secretion there is not only an expenditure of energy but also a loss of material from the body. Physiology deals with the sources of energy and the transformation of energy. The practically wise physician seeks to trace through the deviating functions the source of erroneous energy.

In the consideration of physiology or pathologic physiology the nervous system must be considered a presiding genius. E. g., food within the duodenum incites both the liver and pancreas to secrete through a nervous mechanism for it appears that if bile and pancreatic juice become mixed in Vater's diverticulum or immediately on arrival within the duodenum, the power of the succus pancreaticus is doubled. It is well to know for practical therapeutics (pathologic physiology) that adrenalin— a product of the adrenal medulla

—circulating in the blood appears necessary for the excitation of any nervus vasomotorius. The thyroid gland manufactures some substance—thyro-iodin—which aids in the proper growth of body tissues and also for the normal discharge of the cerebral functions. The fetus during gestation secretes some substance which aids in enlarging the mammary gland. The ovary secretes a substance which preserves sex and nervous characteristics. Hence with increasing knowledge of physiology we may be able to isolate these substances—adrenalin, thyro-iodin, ovarian secretion, secretions of pregnancy which induce mammary hypertrophy, etc., etc.—and in their isolation place a list of therapeutic messengers at our command which will correct the pathologic physiology of bodily organs. With broader knowledge of physiology present, therapeutic nihilism will be replaced by rational therapeutics which rest on physiology, the solid ground of nature.

The results from the study of the four grand common functions of viscera (sensation, peristalsis, absorption, secretion) must be the rock and base of our authority in pathologic physiology.

Irritable weakness of the nervous system presents inferior anatomy and physiology. The subject of pathologic physiology will force us to study the stigmata of function. It is noteworthy that before the days of legitimate specialism few practical stigmata were recognized. At present every specialty has a chapter of abnormalities, of stigmata. In fact, the study of abnormalities has proceeded to such a degree that a majority of individuals are docketed with telltale stigmata of some sort or kind. The pathologic physiology or stigmata of individuals may with impressive instruction be termed "habitus," by which prefix we may distinctly designate certain classes of subjects. We have the habitus phthisicus, habitus nervosus, and the ensemble of certain symptoms may well be termed habitus splanchnoptoicus. The habitus is an expression of inherited weakness, defect. It presents the idea that inferior anatomy and inferior physiology has been transmitted to or acquired by the individual. The tendency of modern study is to accentuate the functional aspect of disease; hence it is this method of study that has taught that there is an abnormality of function. The mind is a good source of pathologic physiology, as by concentrated thinking one can congest excessively an organ, e. g., genitals, brain. There is frequently more in the physician's suggestions than in his medicine.

Rational Medicine alone will stand the test of science and time. Rational medicine must be the medical amazon of truth, from which will be eliminated the false lateral issues, tangenital fads, distorted views of the unbalanced and the knave. Rational medicine must be founded on the solid ground of Nature to stand forever. Will the teachings and knowledge of pathologic physiology aid the physician to exactuate more rational practice? The comprehension of pathologic physiology will extend the physician's views of physiology, which should resume its original basic position in medicine. The future of clinical medicine lies in the direction of pathologic physiology. Rational medicine consists in the application of scientific laboratory methods to the ambulatory and bedside patient. However, the laboratory seems to advance periodically, beyond clinical application. In the field of science and investigation there is continually clashing of opinions, with statements and counter statements, with evidence and counter evidence, from which established rules of practice evolve. The principles of science require during the progress of discoveries, revision, reconsideration, and recasting.

The perfection of physiological, chemical, and pathologic knowledge, with consequently improved technique, will enable the clinician to advance on the citadel of disease rationally during the premature stage of pathologic physiology with more practical hope of success. Cardiac irregularity, palpatation (which chiefly rests on vigorous muscle or myocardium) is generally pathological physiology, or abnormal disordered function (excessive, deficient or irregular peristalsis) and often a nervous manifestation only. The function or the physiology of the cardiac ganglia (Remak's, Bidder's, Ludwig's, and Schmidt's) have become temporarily disordered, pathological, wild, irregular, yet no pathological anatomy can be detected. It is well enough to attempt to be scientific in explanation to the student, that cause and effect are logical sequence, yet, also, to admit that we cannot detect the cause of cardiac palpitation in any existing pathological anatomy—it is pathological physiology, disordered functions, through nonrecognized channels. Pathological physiology alone will explain the irritable bladder; the cystoscope does not reveal the pathological anatomy. The vesical apparatus is acting unusually, it is assuming an abnormal course. I have noted such bladders for years; they afflict the possessor by frequent evacuations, by loss of sleep, and broken rest. Who will attempt to explain the surface anesthesias by pathological anatomy? They are here to-day and there to-morrow. Many a time and oft have I noted the pharyngeal anesthesia in hysteria; in fact one can apply a uterine sound vigorously to the surface of the pharynx without inducing nausea or reflex muscular action.

We have no more appropriate terms to apply to these phenomena than pathological physiology, disordered function. In practice of medicine the student should be instructed in physiological principles and not that he is always to attempt to remove changed structures by his remedies or scalpel. The practice of medicine is the practice of common sense. We are to use means to an end. For example, if a frog's heart recently removed is placed in a warm physiological salt solution, it will perform its peristalsis for a time and cease; now, I can renew its peristalsis by stimulation; the stimulant may be an icicle, electric current, a hot steel needle, or a current of water or air. The chief duty of the profession is to aid in the resumption of normal functions, not merely attempt to discover some pathological anatomy or changed structure, for it would waste valuable time. We should cultivate pathological physiology rather than surgery, as it will be the vast future therapeutical field for nine-tenths of illness, whereas surgery is of value in about one-tenth of illness.

The mind is frequently the organ that needs the stimulant of which quacks, patent medicines, knaves and pretenders take advantage. Pathological physiology recognizes the influence of mind over matter. The sensible physician realizes that suggestions are a powerful aid to peristalsis, absorption, secretion and sensation, to the restoration of visceral function, and though the honorable physician may not make the bold, false assertions of the quack, he can suggest honest, legitimate aid and comfort to the patient.

The honest physician is secret and reticent. The quack is blatantly false. Secrecy and reticence is better than falsehood. The physician can and should be an honest man. The physician comprehending pathologic physiology becomes master of suggestions for the patient's benefit. The medical profession cannot afford to leave the influence of mind over matter, the field of suggestive therapeutics, to the quack and knave. The world of knowledge is our parish. To alleviate suffering and prolong life from rational demonstrations of science is our duty. To treat the sick by any legitimate means is our privilege.

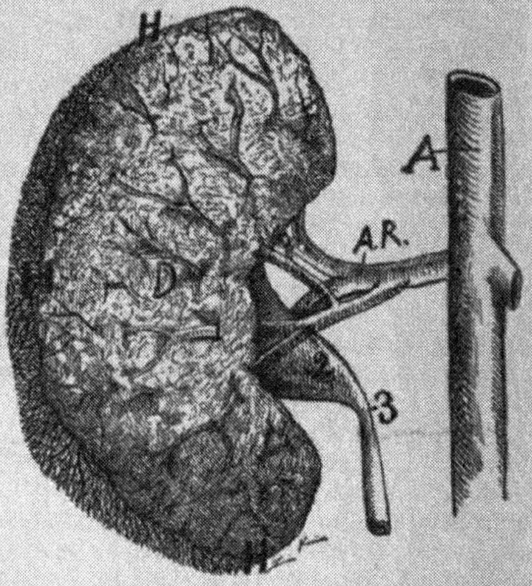

CORROSION ANATOMY

Fig. 112. Left kidney, dorsal surface (D) dorsal vascular blade.—H, H, H, indicates Hyrtl's exsanguinated renal zone, or the elective line of incision, one-half inch dorsal to the lateral longitudinal renal border. Observe that the elective line passes to or invades the ventral renal vascular blade at the proximal and distal poles. Hyrtl's zone is irregular at the renal poles. The dorsal vascular renal blade is the smaller. Observe the quantity of nervus vasomotorius required to ensheath the renal arteries with close fenestrated, network of plexuses.

Diagnosis.—The diagnosis of functional deviation or abnormal visceral action is the rock and base in pathological physiology. This view indicates that the physician understands the physiology. First and foremost is the diagnosis, i. e., what abnormal course are the functions assuming? Disease is abnormal physiology, and the sooner physiological deviation is diagnosticated, the sooner may effective remedial agents be instituted. To be useful to a patient, the incipient stage of diseases, i. e., premature pathologic physiology, must be detected in order to check the progress of the abnormal function before pathologic anatomy establishes itself. We must accomplish the diagnosis by all known aid, medical technique, and laboratory methods.

Pathologic physiology will rest on laboratory methods for rational knowledge and practical application. Laboratory methods are valuable assets to a physician because they will increase his business of rational application and success. The physician's self-confidence, which arises from accurate knowledge, begets confidence in the patient, and this increases his power and clientele. Laboratory methods increase the physician's efficiency, and this contributes to his professional attainments. Laboratory methods are invaluable to the physician himself for his own rational view of any disease. Practically, patients are willing to recompense a physician according to his ability and attainments. The day is not distant when the physician's power to diagnosticate disease will be measured by his laboratory methods, especially in the incipiency or in the stage of pathologic physiology. The judgment of the physician will be heavily taxed as to prognosis. Unfortunately some cases of splanchnoptosia appear with neurasthenia, as an integral part, or splanchnoptosia is imposed on the subject of hysteria. Neurasthenia and hysteria, though not primary in splanchnoptotics, easily thrives among them. It is an indication of defective knowledge and judgment to attribute symptoms of nephroptosia or gastroptosia that belong to general splanchnoptosia.

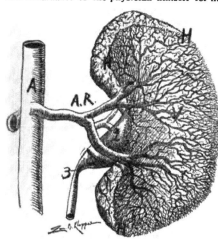

HYRTL'S EXSANGUINATED RENAL ZONE

Fig. 113. Corrosion anatomy, left kidney, ventral view (V) ventral renal vascular blade.—From man about forty-five years of age. The ureter was injected with yellow wax. The ramus dorsalis renalis was injected with celloidin colored with red sulphide of mercury. The trunk of the arteria renalis, including the ramus ventralis renalis was injected with uncolored celloidin. The tissues were corroded in HNO_3 for two weeks. A. R., Arteria renalis sinistra. 2, ureteral pelvis. 3, proximal ureteral isthmus. H, H, H, indicates Hyrtl's exsanguinated renal zone. It may be noted on the ventral renal surface that the renal dorsal vascular blade overlaps or invades the ventral vascular blade at the proximal and distal renal poles. Hyrtl's exsanguinated renal zone is not equatorial at the proximal or distal renal poles nor in the central portion of the kidney. The elective line of renal incision to invade the ureteral pelvis with minimum hemorrhage is located ½ inch dorsal to the lateral longitudinal renal border in the central segment of the kidney and is about two inches in length. The quantity of nervus vasomotorius may be estimated by the number of arteries and ducts present.

Blood Volume.—Pathological physiology combines rational views of living organs, more than that merely based on pathological anatomy. For example, when pathological physiology of the kidney is studied, the instructor must take rational and comprehensive views of the renal viscus. Pathological physiology of the kidney takes into account the condition of the kidney, the constituents of the blood and volume of blood that streams through the organ. The discussion of these three subjects in regard to the kidney lends a comprehensive view to the student in making a diagnosis on the living subject, e. g., the functional capacity of a kidney is the rational test, not albumen and casts. It is common to observe much variation in the quantity of urine, inexplainable, except by pathological physiology, for urinalysis offers none. Pathological physiology teaches that the circulation of an organ is a fundamental factor in comprehending diseased conditions. The teacher who does not comprehend varying phases of circulation of the female genitals in the different stages of pueritas (quiescent), pubertas (development), menstrual (functionating), gestation (functionating), puerperal (involution), climacterium (subsidence), and senescence (quiescent), makes a defective gynecological teacher. No organs except the kidney, offer such an extensively varied base to illustrate pathological physiology of the tractus vascularis as the female genitals.

The circulation of an organ quotes its value in the animal economy; it rates its function. Each organ is supplied by arteries which have automatic visceral ganglia, which regulate, govern, the volume of blood which flows through them. The automatic visceral ganglia tell the story why the volume of blood changes so much in different conditions of the organs when the parenchymatous cells of an organ functionate, as the liver during digestion, the uterus during gestation, the cerebrum during thinking (cerebration), the blood volume is increasingly directed to the organ through the automatic visceral ganglia, dilating the arteries. Hyperæmia indicates the functionating brain, kidney, and genitals, and these organs occupy vast considerations in practice. Pathological physiology indicates that great benefit is secured by controlling circulation, blood volume, by checking peristalsis through withholding food; controlling diet controls the blood constituents to a certain degree. Bier's method of artificial congestion is employing pathological physiology (in the tractus vascularis) for the purpose of curing chronic inflammation.

Treatment of Pathological Physiology.—The treatment of pathological physiology consists: 1. In the detection and removal of causes; 2, the rational regulation of visceral function, *a*, by fluids; *b*, by foods; 3, habitat; 4, avocation; 5, prophylaxis.

1. *The Detection and Removal of Their Causes.*—The detection of the cause in pathological physiology requires the best head and the finest analysis. The detection of a rectal ulcer or fissure as the cause of innumerable reflexes is a credit to the diagnostician. The recognition of damaging effects of præputial adhesions is important. The glans penis or clitoris is like an electric bell button, the pressing or irritation of which rings the whole organism into pathological physiology. A cinder in the eye is a grand master of pathological physiology. I have known the detection and removal of a bleeding, proximally located, rectal polypus to save a child's life and make a physician's reputation. This little rectal polypus had bled and escaped being examined for a whole year by numerous consultants. I know a gynecologist who did five operations on a woman's genitals for pain in the distal abdomen. She became no better, but worse. The cause of all her pain was discovered by a

consultant, who found a marked spinal gibbus or kyphosis of tuberculous nature at the junction of the dorsal and lumbar vertebræ. The reflected pain from kyphosis had dislocated the gynecologist's mind, to make a scapegoat of the genitals. Frequently infected groin glands are associated with an infected corn on a toe. A decayed tooth may cause earache. I knew a woman of twenty-four years, experienced some eight months of crucial suffering from pathological physiology. She was examined by one physician who said her ovaries should be removed, two others said that she must have her appendix extirpated, one physician diagnosticated neurosis, another indigestion, finally a physician was employed who found she had a ureteral calculus and removed it after which she gained thirty pounds in eight weeks. This an excellent example to demonstrate that, though pathological physiology allows ample time for diagnosis and prophylaxis, yet it requires the finest head with the finest skill of analysis to interpret the signification of abnormal visceral function. Hepatic calculus may introduce pathological physiology into the tractus intestinalis and associated visceral tracts, but it requires experience, accumen, and skill to detect the cause of pathological physiology.

2. *Rational Regulation of Visceral Function by Visceral Drainage.*— Pathological physiology teaches the supreme importance of visceral drainage, of maintaining in normal attenuated solution bodily secretions. It teaches the benefit of removing the debris of waste laden blood by means of fluids. When the patient's blood and organs are saturated with waste laden material, he is unprepared to resist the attacks of disease; he is prepared for irritation, for reflexes or neurotic explosions. With scientific views of pathological physiology, the correction of functional deviation with rational ideas of visceral drainage, the physician holds the key of prophylaxis against the formation of pancreatic, hepatic, and renal calculus. With ample visceral drainage, with sufficient fluids taken at regular intervals for visceral functions, the pancreatic, biliary, and renal secretions would seldom precipitate their salts, and colloid material or cohesive ground substance of calculus would be so attenuated that calculus would not form.

Viscera should functionate at a normal maximum for bodily safety and protection. Pathological physiology takes into account of the composition of glandular secretion, as the pancreatic, hepatic, and renal, with the view that pancreatic, hepatic, and urinary salts, especially urates, should be maintained in attenuated solution by ample fluids, that no calculi may form. A study of the remedies recommended as uric acid solvents or eliminators of uric acid reveals the data that are composed of two ingredients, viz.: (a) alkali, (b) water. The plan is to alkalinize the blood current, and thus render the uric acid more soluble and promote its elimination. The administration of an alkali to dissolve uric acid concretions is of limited value. Alkalies and uric acid are solvent *in vitro*, but cannot accomplish the same *in vivo*. The alkalies are ingested with the foods, making soluble urates. After all, the ingestion of alkalies in food and fluid cannot alter materially the uric acid. However, the chief virtue lies in the quantity of water ingested at regular intervals during the day. The water is the chief efficacious ingredient in uric

444   THE ABDOMINAL AND PELVIC BRAIN

acid remedies. The water increases the blood volume which in turn produces a powerful stream irrigating the tractus urinarius and maintaining the uric acid in attenuated mechanical suspension.

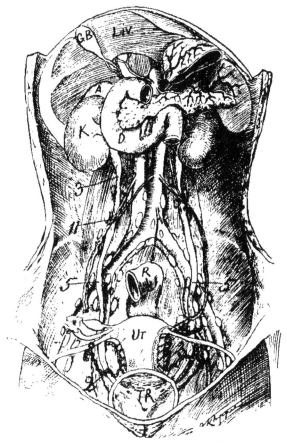

Fig. 114. This illustration represents the lymph glands or nodes located in the course of the blood vessels. The lymph nodes are highly supplied by the nervus vasomotorius.

Pathological physiology indicates that the composition of the blood is essential to health, and that its salts should not be concentrated or abnormal in relation. Pathological physiology accounts for the various reflexes and disordered functions from the irritation of waste laden blood and the damaged functions resulting from nephrolithiasis and cholelithiasis. Pathological physiology dictates that the ample fluids at regular intervals, visceral drainage, is the great safeguard against waste laden blood; it is the prophylaxis against cholelithiasis, pancreatolithiasis, and nephrolithiasis. By the time that pathological anatomy is demonstrable, damaging structural mischief is established, and not infrequently with a lifelong cicatrix. The vast majority of palpitations of the heart cannot be explained on pathological anatomy, which has been the tendency of medical progress for the past decade. The nervous system so intimately and profoundly connects the visceral system, so solidly and compactly anastomosis the viscera, that appropriate stimulation administered to one visceral tract tends to induce adjacent visceral tracts to normal functions and consequent ample visceral drainage, e. g., ample volume of fluid in the tractus vascularis enhances the volume and flow of the tractus lymphaticus, and the general glandular system increases its flow, notably the perspiration, from the tractus cutis. Stimulation of the cutaneous surface by massage or salt rubs not only stimulates the cutaneous nerve periphery, but also the circulation and tractus perspiratorius. Stimulation of the tractus muscularis by exercise stimulates and enhances the function of all visceral tracts.

A. *Visceral Drainage by Fluids.*—About eighty per cent of the body is fluids while about twenty per cent is solids. All viscera functionate by means of a fluid medium. Fluid forms the chief distributing or circulatory agency of the organism. Liquid is essential for assimilation and metabolism. Water forms the bulk of the softer tissue and is an important factor in the composition of the harder. Fluid permeates or flows through all the bodily structures by osmosis or distinct vessels. Water is a more important agency in relating the individual to environments than food or air. It flows universally through the organism. It enters mainly through the tractus intestinalis, and escapes through the mucous membranes, skin and the chief excretory ducts. Water, as related to the skin and lungs in the form of liquid vapor, affords the most important factor in controlling the temperature necessary for organic existence. Diet consists on the average of six parts liquid to one part dry material. These data explain why Dr. Tanner and others could fast such a length of time on drinking water only. I was a watcher of Dr. Tanner's fasting twenty-five years ago, and wondered at the ease and apparent comfort of his abstaining from food so many weeks. Water is more essential for the growth and sustenance of the vital system than food. The most effective diuretic is water. One of the best laxatives is water. One of the best and most natural stimulants to renal epithelium is sodium chloride (one half to one fourth normal salt solution). The blood contains three-fifths of one per cent of sodium chloride. Water is to the organism what oil is to machinery—it prevents friction. For the purpose of stimulating normal visceral action (the great common visceral functions are peristalsis, absorption, sensation, secretion), I administer eight ounces of one-half to one-fourth normal salt solution six times daily, two hours apart. (Note—Sodium chloride is contraindicated in parenchymatous nephritis.) Three pints (of one-half to one-fourth normal salt solution efficiently influences the renal secretion for ample visceral drainage. Renal drainage should be sufficient to maintain in mechanical suspension the free insoluble uric acid to prevent calculus formations. Also it should be sufficient to form soluble urate combinations with sodium, potassium, and ammonium salts.

B. Visceral Drainage by Foods.—To drain the viscera by appropriate foods and fluids may sound paradoxical; however, the common functions of viscera—peristalsis, absorption, sensation, secretion—are initiated and maintained by fluid and food. Rhythm is one of the grand physical manifestations. The tubes of the body under spiral motion assume a spiral direction. Food stimulates the tractus intestinalis through its sensitive mucosa to continual, rhythmical, spiral motion, and consequent absorption and secretion. The sodium chloride is an especial stimulant to the epithelium of the tractus intestinalis. To drain the tractus intestinalis, foods which result in an ample indigestible fecal residue are requisite to maintain the fundamental peristalsis or rhythm necessary for its life of absorption and secretion. If the tractus intestinalis be stimulated to a maximum by sufficient appropriate food and fluid, adjacent visceral tracts from their intimate nervous connection (through the abdominal brain), will share and assume normal function (peristalsis, absorption, secretion, sensation). Rational foods must contain appropriate salts whose basis may form combinations which are soluble, as sodium, potassium, and ammonium, combined with uric acid and urates to form soluble urates.

The proper foods are: *Cereals* (oatmeal, wheat, rice, graham bread); *vegetables* (practically all vegetables, cooked); *albuminoids* (milk, eggs, buttermilk); *meats* (limited, as they produce excessive uric acid formations. A mixed diet is therefore most rational.

In order to stimulate the epithelium (sensation) of the tractus intestinalis, urinarius, and genitalis and the endothelium (sensation) of the tractus vascularis and lymphaticus with consequent increase of peristalsis, sensation, absorption, secretion, in the five visceral tracts I employ a part or multiple of an alkaline tablet of the following composition: 1, Cascara sagrada, one-fortieth grain; aloes, one-third grain; sodium bicarbonate, 1 grain; potassium bicarbonate, one-third grain; and magnesium sulphate, 2 grains. This combination is used as follows: One-sixth one tablet (or more as required to move the bowels freely once daily) is placed on the tongue and followed by eight ounces of water (better hot). Also at 10 A. M., 3 P. M., and at bedtime one-sixth to one tablet is placed on the tongue and followed by a glassful of any fluid. In the combined treatment one third of the sodium chloride tablet (containing eleven grains) and (one-sixth to three) alkaline tablets are placed on the tongue together before each meal and at 10 A M., 3 P M., and bedtime, followed by a glass of fluid. The six glasses of fluid may be water, coffee, tea, milk, buttermilk, cream, eggnog—in short, a nourishment. This method of treatment furnishes alkaline bases (sodium, potassium, and ammonium) to combine with the free uric acid in the urine, producing perfectly soluble alkaline urates, and materially diminishing the insoluble free uric acid in the urine. Also the alkaline laxative and sodium chloride tablet increase the peristalsis, absorption, secretion, sensation of the tractus intestinalis, urinarius, vascularis, lymphaticus, genitalis, which aids secretions and evacuation.

I have termed the sodium chloride and alkaline laxative tablets the *visceral drainage treatment*. The alkaline and sodium chloride tablet inducing maximum visceral function take the place of the so-called mineral waters. I continue this dietetic treatment of fluids and foods for weeks, months, and the results are remarkably successful, especially in pathologic physiology of visceral tracts. The urine becomes clarified like spring water and increased in quantity. The tractus intestinalis becomes freely evacuated, regularly, daily. The tractus vascularis maintains an active peristalsis and full volume. The blood is relieved of waste laden and irritating material. The tractus cutis eliminates freely, and the skin becomes normal. The appetite increases. The sleep improves. The patient becomes hopeful; natural energy returns. The sewers of the body are well drained and flushed to a maximum.

3. *Habitat.*—Habitat has chiefly relations to the environments of air, exercise, heat, cold, moisture. In habitat one of the principle factors is air. The functions of the lungs are sensation, peristalsis, absorption and secretion. It is through the great function of respiration that the internal tissue becomes related to the external world. The medium of exchange between the internal tissue and the external world is the blood. The blood, an universal tissue, a common transporter of oxygen and carbonic acid gas, plays a vast role in the economy of organism. The red blood corpuscles during their passage through the lung (external respiration), automatically appropriate the oxygen, and after their return (from internal respiration) through the tractus vascularis unburden acquired carbon dioxide into the expiring air. The pathological physiology of respiration is a wide zone and especially in an incipient zone to that of pathological anatomy. Its pathological physiology is frequently amenable to treatment. The respiratory apparatus has methods of its own to correct its pathological physiology, as cilia, coughing and sneezing to evacuate harmful material, as mucus and foreign bodies. The grand remedial agent for pathological physiology of the living is continuous, ample, fresh cold air.

4. *Avocation.*—The avocation should suit the individual conditions. In numerous cases the labor is unsuitable for the subject. The hours are too long, the work is excessive or severe for the strength. The condition enhances pathological physiology, rather than cures.

5. *Prophylaxis.*—Prophylaxis of disease is the tendency of modern medicine. Pathological physiology teaches the control of disease by means of diet, fluid, habitat, avocation.

CHAPTER XXXIII.

PATHOLOGIC PHYSIOLOGY OF THE TRACTUS INTESTINALIS.

O, then beware; those wounds heal ill that men do give themselves.—Shakespeare.

The tractus intestinalis possesses three original segments—gastrium, enteron, colon—which differ in form and dimension, anatomy and physiology; however, every segment possesses the four common visceral functions—sensation, peristalsis, absorption, secretion.

The physiology of the tractus intestinalis is peristalsis, absorption, secretion and sensation; its object is to afford general corporeal nourishment. One or all of the functions, the physiology of the tractus intestinalis may present pathologic physiology without demonstrable pathologic anatomy.

A typical example of pathologic physiology in the tractus intestinalis is emesis, e. g., by some, from the observation of a fly in the soup. This is disordered function introduced so rapidly that pathologic anatomy had insufficient time to become established. The so-called reflexes are pathologic physiology not pathologic anatomy. One may observe pathologic physiology where a herd of cattle is placed on a boat and when the boat starts the cattle become excited, nervous, a number having immediate and frequent liquid stools. The peristalsis and secretion of the tractus instestinalis liquifying the feces and expelling them—pathologic physiology but not pathologic anatomy was detectable. A typical example of the utility of pathologic physiology in the tractus intestinalis is the diarrhea of puerperal sepsis—which frequently saves the patient. Certain kinds of food produce pathologic physiology. It is an excessive fermentation—gas. This may be observed the most certainly in the digestion of leguminous substances, e. g., beans. Pathologic physiology may be manifest by excessive, deficient or disproportionate peristalsis, absorption, secretion and sensation. The practitioner observes and treats the following conditions.

(1). PERISTALSIS (EXCESSIVE, DEFICIENT, DISPROPORTIONATE).

The tractus intestinalis possesses peculiar physiologic movements known as peristalsis, vermicular motion passing through periodic activity and repose. Though each segment (gastrium, enteron, colon) possesses peristalsis in common, however, the structure, function and object of each segment is so different that peristalsis in each segment—gastrium, enteron and colon—is best studied separately. The factors which initiate motion in the tractus intestinalis are: (a) blood supply; (b) ingesta; (c) secretion; (e) temperature; (f) sensation.

(a) *Excessive peristalsis* (stomach). Increased gastric movements (pathologic physiology) may arise from excessive secretion of HCl, hence excessively rapid gastric evacuation. Increased gastric movements or contractions may arise from pyloric obstruction. Gastric, enteronic and colonic peristaltic unrest may be prominent without known cause, with perhaps an irritable defective nervous system—a kind of motor neurosis. The splanchnic nerves are perhaps the chief motor nerves of the digestive tract. The peristaltic unrest (pathologic physiology) is eminently manifest in certain individuals as evidenced by the frequent gurgling, splashing sounds heard when standing in close proximity. During fright excessive intestinal peristalsis may occur with sudden evacuation of the colon. Excessive peristalsis may occur during pregnancy or on observation of disgusting matters (as a fly in the soup), intense decomposing odors, certain forms of food create peristaltic unrest. The frequent wild and disordered peristalsis in the digestive tract of the child is based on pathologic physiology—not pathologic anatomy. It rests on disordered peristalsis due to the fact that Auerbach's plexus is not fully developed or established in office. The cramps, and colic and emesis, diarrhea, arise and disappear so quickly that insufficient time exists for pathologic anatomy. Vomiting is pathologic physiology as it forcibly, artificially dilates the cardiac sphincter of the stomach.

(b) *Deficient peristalsis.* The most typical example in the tractus intestinalis of deficient peristalsis is constipation—the so-called sluggish bowels. Evacuation of the digestive tract (especially the stomach and colon) is defective, incomplete. Dilatation of the stomach (generally due to compression of the transverse duodenum by the superior artery vein and nerve) results in series of consequences as decomposion, fermentation, taxemia, inability to force food through the pylorus. The acute gastric dilatation is simply an exacerbation of a previous dilatation. I have shown in numerous cadavers that no pyloric obstruction exists, that it is gastro-duodenal dilatation due to compression of the mesenteric vessels. Gastro-duodenal dilatation is a stage of enteroptosia.

(c) *Disproportionate peristalsis* consists of non-uniform, irregular, disordered muscular movements. It is peristalsis uncontrolled like the irregular invaginations of death and the test of diagnosis is that the invagination is not pathologic anatomy—simply pathologic physiology.

(2). SECRETION (EXCESSIVE, DEFICIENT, DISPROPORTIONATE).

(e) *Excessive secretion*, pathologic physiology is observed in diarrhea. Many kinds of irritating foods induce it. Doubtless excessive secretion is due to the variations in HCl. Chronic supersecretion, is perhaps connected with superacidity. Excessive secretion of the tractus intestinalis is frequently found in neurotic patients, in neurasthenics, in hysteria. Hunger plays a role, e. g., when a hungry subject views food. Abdominal secretion occurs in chronic dyspepsia. Hypersecretion doubtless depends on the blood volume in the stomach, enteron or colon. Hypersecretion frequently accompanies gastroptosia (which is generally gastro-duodenal dilatation) because the gastroptosia is accompanied by stagnation of food material and irritates the gastric wall. The fasting stomach may present supersecretion on reception of food known as alimentary supersecretion. Hyper chloridia from an unknown cause. Infectious processes induce supersecretion as well as ulceration and epithelial desquamation.

In the duodenum, the most important segment of the tractus intestinalis, arrives the extra glandular secretion succus pancreaticus, and succus bilis. These naturally abundant extraglandular secretions, when possessing the pathologic physiology of excess, will present a wide varying zone of effect on nutrition. The excess of biliary secretion, pathologic physiology, is difficult to estimate as the bile is re-absorbed and its excessive flooding stream prevents the formation of biliary concrements. However, we know that in driving cattle several miles previous to slaughter an excess of bile collects in the cholecyst—demonstrating a wide range of variation in the time and quantity of biliary secretion. Excessive biliary secretion may be the cause of glycosuria allowing insufficient time for completion of processes.

The pathologic physiology of excess of pancreatic secretions are equally difficult to estimate with that of biliary. Excessive succus pancreaticus practically prohibits pancreatic calculus. (Enteron and colon) excess of enteronic and colonic secretion is apparent in diarrhea, in fluid evacuations. Abnormal, excessive intestinal secretions are not well understood. The pathologic physiology of excessive intestinal secretion rests chiefly on the kinds of chemistry of food and bacteria within the digestive canal. The multiplication of bacteria incites the intestine to extra secretion. The abnormal bacteria process may continue within the intestinal lumen. The number of bacterial residence usually constitute about one-third of the weight of the dry fecal masses. It is evident from this view that bacteria are a necessary part of the tractus intestinalis of higher organisms. The child's tractus intestinalis possesses a bacterial flora by the fourth day of extrauterine life. Excessive colonic secretion, pathologic physiology, is well known in mucous colitis, or what I considered better termed, secretion neurosis of the colon.

(f) (Stomach) *deficient* secretion of the tractus intestinalis constitutes a frequent condition of pathological physiology. The most evidently marked state of deficient intestinal secretion is constipation. Deficient secretion of HCl, the most significant secretory gastric function in the stomach, may exist, indicating malignancy, chronic gastritis, infectious disease, acute functional disease, presenting a wide zone of pathologic physiology. Deficient HCl is especially noted in gastric carcinoma. (Stomach) deficient secretion HCl changes the bacterial process, as normal gastric secretion is doubtless antiseptic. The most important means to check microbic process in the stomach is continuous movements of food and frequent evacuations. With deficient HCl the bacteria multiply in stagnating stomach contents increasing lactic acid, which favors bacterial growth. Deficient HCl enhances the decomposition of albumen in the enteron and colon. Abundant bacterial decomposition from deficient HCl produces products which irritate the gastric mucosa, inducing pain, colic vomiting, defective appetite, gas.

(Duodenum). The business segment of the digestive tract is the enteron into which flows the succus bilis et succus pancreaticus. Deficient biliary

PHYSIOLOGY OF TRACTUS INTESTINALIS

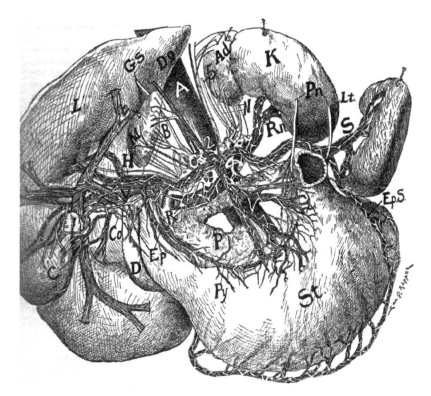

ABDOMINAL BRAIN AND CŒLIAC PLEXUS

Fig. 115. This figure presents the nerves of the proximal part of the tractus intestinalis, that is, the nerve plexuses accompanying the branches of arteria cœliaca. 1 and 2 abdominal brain surrounding the cœliac axis drawn from dissected specimen. H. Hepatic plexus on hepatic artery. S. Splenic plexus on splenic artery. Gt. Gastric plexus on gastric artery. Rn. Renal artery (left). R. Right renal artery in the dissection was rich in ganglia. Dg. diaphragmatic artery with its ganglion. G. S. Great splanchnic nerve. Ad. Adrenal. K. Kidney. Pn. Pneumogastric (Lt. left). Ep. Right and Eps. left epiploica artery. St. Stomach Py. Pyloric artery. C. Cholecyst. Co. Chole-dochus. N. Adrenal nerves (right, 10, left, 10). The arterial branches and loops of the cœliac tripod (as well as that of the renals) with their corresponding nerve plexuses demonstrate how solidly and compactly the viscera of the proximal abdomen are anastomosed, connected into single delicately poised system with the abdominal brain as a center. Hence local reflexes, as hepatic or renal calculus, disturb the accurate physiologic balance in stomach, kidney, spleen, liver and pancreas. Food in the duodenum (or HCl) will induce: (1) the bile to flow; (2) the succus entericus to flow; (3) the duodenal glands (intestinal—especially Brunner's) to flow; (4) secretion to flow—all from the same duodenal stimulant (food or HCl), presenting a delicately poised nervous apparatus.

secretion may manifest itself by clay colored stools, by icterus, by calculus obstructing biliary flow. Pathologic physiology in deficient biliary secretion presents a frequent and an extensive range of action. Deficient biliary secretion occurs with deficient amounts of appropriate food, hence the necessity of rational dietetics. Deficient biliary secretion lays the foundation for the most distressing of hepatic diseases—hepatic calculus. The deficient hepatic secretion induces a limited quantity of bile with a slow stream allowing ample opportunity for crystallization and the formation of biliary concrements. The hepatic calculus consists chiefly of cholesterine and calcium salts of bilirubin. Naunyn has demonstrated that the quantity of cholesterine and calcium salts of bilirubin are independent of the kinds of ingesta, hence to prevent biliary concrements we must employ visceral drainage to maintain such salts in mechanical suspension and irrigate, flood, them onward by powerful, large biliary streams. For dissolving cholesterine the bile possesses powerful agents in cholate, sapo, adeps. Since cholesterine appears in the bile as crystal, or in combination with desquamated epithelial cells, the powerful, large biliary stream from ample visceral drainage will flood, irrigate, the precipitated collected crystals and concrements into the duodenum. Deficient biliary flow is liable to become stagnant, favoring bacterial growth and bile channel infection because the volume of bile stream, being diminished, does not excite the biliary channels to vigorous peristalsis and consequent defective flushing of the bile passages occurs. Deficient biliary secretion is accompanied by the pathologic physiology of diminished bile stream; stagnation of bile from diminished biliary peristalsis; defective irrigation of the biliary passages; the precipitation, formation of cholesterine and calcium and bilirubin crystals or concrements; infection of the biliary passages; insufficient quantity of bile for digestion (clay colored decomposed stools); icterus from obstruction of bile passages and changed direction of bile stream calculus in the biliary channels may produce disease only when infection arises or the calculus becomes clamped (pain, colic). Inflammation (cholecystitis) creates violent peristalsis of the biliary channels and hence projects the calculus in various directions until it is finally impressed, engaged, whence pain and colic.

In icterus the bile with its coloring material becomes transfused through the body, in the blood and lymph—presenting typical pathologic physiology. Icterus depends on complete closure of the ductus choledochus communis but it may depend on hepatitis. For the origin of icterus the kind of disease is less significant than its seat.

Deficient pancreatic secretion is diagnosed by the undigested fat in the stools. In 700 personal autopsic inspections I observed but one complete failure of pancreatic secretions. This subject possessed a carcinomatous invasion of the ductus choledochus and ductus pancreaticus, producing complete obstruction of both ducts. In ten weeks the patient lost 113 pounds. The biliary passages (exclusive of the cholecyst) were dilated seven times their original caliber and the ductus pancreaticus was dilated some 20 times its original caliber. The pancreas possesses two exit ducts, patent perhaps in 60 per cent of subjects. If one becomes obstructed the other acts vicariously for both.

In the above cited case Santorini's duct no doubt conducted succus pancreaticus into the duodenum. Deficient secretion from the pancreas arises from partial and complete obstruction of its ducts by calculus, neoplasm, or by degeneration of the organ.

Deficient secretion in the enteron is not understood. Deficient secretion in the colon results in the well known disease, constipation. The central nervous system, as well as the abdominal sympathetic, is influential in diminishing secretion. In fact, the pure results of constipation are preponderating, psychic and subjective. The assimilation of the individual constipation does not suffer materially; however, defecation is laborious and the care for the evacuation and anxiety as to food selection increases the neurosis; with the evacuation the head becomes free, the voice becomes cheerful, the effect is mainly suggestive.

(g) *Disproportionate secretion* is where the secretions of the segments of the tractus intestinalis are irregular, non-uniform, disordered. When such disordered secretions mingle, fermentation occurs with consequent tympanitis meteorismus. The gastric secretions may be disproportionate, resulting in disordered digestion. Biliary secretion may be excessive, pancreatic secretions deficient, thus making secretions disproportionate, and the same conditions may occur in the enteron and colon.

(3.) ABSORPTION (EXCESSIVE, DEFICIENT, DISPROPORTIONATE).

(h) *Excessive absorption* of the digestive tract is difficult to demonstrate. However, it is conceivable that the absorptive apparatus of the tractus intestinalis might work excessively, absorbing substances which injure the system. Decomposing ingesta, bacterial products, toxines, may be too rapidly absorbed. Excessive absorption induces constipation.

(i) *Deficient absorption* in the tractus intestinalis is not infrequent. We notice this factor when the food passes per rectum undigested. Excessive peristaltic movements may be so rapid that insufficient time is allowed absorption. Deficient pancreatic secretion does not prepare the fats sufficiently for absorption—hence deficient absorption, pathologic physiology, may rest on many factors, neurosis, excessive or deficient peristalsis, unsuitable ingesta, infection.

(j) *Disproportionate absorption* occurs but is difficult to demonstrate the non-uniform, unequal, disordered absorption of the three segments—gastrium, enteron, colon.

4. SENSATION (EXCESSIVE, DEFICIENT, DISPROPORTIONATE).

(k) *Excessive gastric sensation* (hyperesthesia of mucosa) not infrequently arises. The healthy subject notices the digesive organs only when hunger arises or the gastrium becomes excessively occupied with ingesta or gas; one might state that it is a distinct function of the tractus intestinalis to manifest hunger. The physical condition is also of direct influence. Hunger and distension of the stomach are related because subjects afflicted with super activity manifest hunger shortly after ingesting meat, which is rapidly evacuated through the pylorus, leaving an empty stomach with recurring secretions. Hunger and appetites do not always correspond. One may feel hungry but does not eat, as the appetite fails. The Scotch poetry tells much of a story.

> Some have meat but cannot eat,
> Some can eat but have no meat.

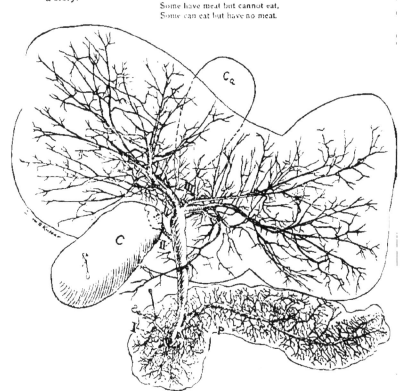

X-RAY OF DUCTUS BILIS AND DUCTUS PANCREATICUS

Fig. 130.—Presents a good view of the biliary and pancreatic ducts. These ducts are sheathed by a minute, anastomosing, fenestrated meshwork of nerves forming a local pathophysiologic unit of animal life by the abdominal brain.

It is possible that a laxity of both motion and secretion induces appetite which has a wide zone of pathologic physiology. In excessive sensation or gastric hyperesthesia the sensation of gastric pressure or fullness in eating arises sooner than it does in the healthy, in fact sooner than the stomach becomes full. Occasionally one meets a patient who on taking ingesta experiences gastric pain—this may be neuralgia, superacidity, ulceration, carcinoma, pergastric peritoneal adhesions. The superacidity, irritable gastric muscularis may experience pain from direct effects on the sensitive nerves, i. e., superacidity induces muscular colic. The fearful "gastric crises" in tabes and the other spinal affections is founded on degeneration and irritation of the vagus. It is well known that certain individuals are supersensitive not only in general but as special organs, e. g., some will vomit on seeing a fly in the soup. From sensitive stomachs appear to arise dizziness, sensory waves, neuralgia, anomalies of cardiac innervation. Also unclear functional disturbances—however I would suggest that such attributes of numerous disturbances rather belong to the abdominal brain. The innumerable "gastric reflexes" are receptions, reorganizations and emissions of the abdominal brain. Vomiting, sooner or later after ingesta, may occur from hyperesthesia of the gastric mucosa. I have had several patients with excessive sensation, or hyperesthesia, of the gastric mucosa. One patient vomited shortly after taking food for fourteen years. Her stomach absorbed sufficient to maintain a fair condition of flesh. Another vomited for two years almost immediately after eating. Excessive sensation in the gastric mucosa presents a wide zone of pathologic physiology in the various degrees of vomiting during gestation. Many subjects possess an extraordinary delicacy and sensitiveness in regard to the stomach. If such subjects exercise care in selection of food and prudence in eating they remain relatively healthy. This pretended and acquired idiosyncrasy is annoyingly manifest in practice when we are continually meeting people who cannot take certain kinds of food, as eggs, milk, graham bread, fruits, etc., etc., such patients cannot live in an ordinary boarding house. Either by heredity or chiefly by habit the employment of certain kinds of food have a wide range of pathologic physiology. The psychical state perhaps plays the preponderating role of idiosyncrasy of foods. The so-called nervous dyspeptic experiences all kinds of sensations in the stomach. There is no structural change in the stomach to correspond to all the functional manifestations—it is pathologic physiology. The crawling of animals within the stomach and tractus intestinalis may be interpreted as ingesta or gas passing over the hyperesthetic or supersensitive mucosa.

(l) *Deficient sensation* in the tractus intestinalis doubtless explains the so-called sluggish bowel, the constipation. The absorption of the food is insufficient. It is not uncommon for patients to tell me that the bowels are dead, no feeling in them.

(m) *Disproportionate sensation* is non-uniform, irregularly located hyperesthesia and anesthesia of the mucosa in the different segments of the digestive tract—gastrium, enteron, colon. In sensation of the tractus intestinalis, excessive, deficient or disproportionate, there is no relation between anomalies of function and anatomic structure. Anomalies of function may present no recognizable anatomic changes—it is simply pathologic physiology. The gastric mucosa rapidly changes at death, hence cautious examinations are required in autopsies. As regards the relations between the kind of anatomic changes and functional disturbances, we are but little informed by any investigations.

456   THE ABDOMINAL AND PELVIC BRAIN

PATHOLOGIC PHYSIOLOGY OF THE TRACTUS NERVOSUS IN REGARD TO THE TRACTUS INTESTINALIS.

The tractus nervosus influences two spheres, viz.: corporeal and mental. The nervous system extends to the deepest and most profound secrets of life —mental and physical, hence, it possesses the highest differentiation of all visceral tracts. The functions of the tractus intestinalis vary within a wide zone of pathologic physiology, e. g., many subjects pass a week without defecation or subjects may practice defecations daily. The tractus intestinalis is preponderatingly controlled by the abdominal sympathetic or nervus vasomotorius. It requires a decade for the nervus vasomotorius to establish

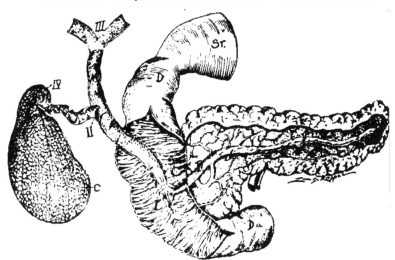

DUODENUM WITH ITS TWO DUCTS—BILIARY AND PANCREATIC

Fig. 117. Illustrates the duodenum, the most important segment of the tractus intestinalis, receiving the ductus bilis and ductus pancreaticus. The nervous system controlling the secretion of the tractus intestinalis must be delicately poised, balanced, as the secretions of one gland (as the liver) is a complement of the secretion of another gland (as the pancreas). The succus pancreaticus multiplies the power and utility of the bile in digestion if the two glandular secretions become mixed immediately on entrance into the duodenum.

its control, its more independent rule. The wild and disordered peristalsis of a child is due to the cerebrum and Auerbach's ganglionic plexus not being completely balanced, in control. A child is frequently subject to peristaltic unrest, intestinal invagination (pathologic physiology). Frequently not long before death in adults the cerebrum and Auerbach's ganglionic plexus lose their complete balance (especially the cerebrum being less influential) and the invagination of death arises. I have observed 4 to 6-inch invaginations in

PHYSIOLOGY OF TRACTUS INTESTINALIS

subjects—absolute pathologic physiology—no pathologic anatomy. Though the function of the nervus vasomotorius is beyond the control of the will, digestion proceeds in spite of us or while we sleep. The five abdominal visceral tracts (tractus genitalis, urinarius, intestinalis, lymphaticus, vascularis) exist in an exquisitively balanced or poised state, hence, the so-called reflexes, from one visceral tract to another, accomplished through the nervus vasomotorius, exert extensive influence in producing pathologic physiology—yes many conditions of pathologic physiology arise in different visceral tracts. The essential conditions of a reflex are: (a) an intact sensory periphery (receiver); (b) an intact ganglion cell—pelvic or abdominal brain—(reorganizer); (c) an intact conducting apparatus (transmitter). A pure reflex consists of a sensation transmitted to a reorganizing center which emits it over a motor apparatus.

A reflex is independent of will. The abdominal viscera are not only intimately connected, associated by means of the tractus vascularis, tractus lymphaticus, tractus nervosus but especially by the peritoneum. Any excessive irritation in any one of the exquisitively poised visceral tracts immediately unbalances the others—at first producing pathologic physiology and perhaps later pathologic anatomy. Hence the sensory apparatus in each visceral tract is significant. The reflex from one visceral tract to the other disorders: (a) the blood circulation; (b) lymph circulation; (c) absorption; (d) secretion; (e) peristalsis; (f) sensation. E. g., when the gestation contents distends the uterus, uneven expansion stimulates, irritates the sensory apparatus of the uterus. The sensation is transmitted over the plexus interiliacus and plexus ovaricus to the abdominal brain where reorganization occurs whence the stimulus is emitted over the plexus gastricus to the gastrium with end results of excessive gastric peristalsis and vomiting. Other abdominal visceral tracts are likewise effected by this uterine reflex, but do not manifest such prominent symptoms as vomiting. Vomiting is pathologic physiology. Ordinary function as gestation will induce pathologic physiology in the tractus intestinalis by: (a) reflexes; (b) robbing it of considerable blood—the extra amount required for the tractus genitalis to gestate the child; (c) instituting indigestion and constipation, from limited blood supply. A calculus in the tractus urinarius (ureter) will produce numerous reflexes with consequent pathologic physiology in the several abdominal visceral tracts—viz.: disordered peristalsis, absorption, secretion, sensation—not pathologic anatomy.

TREATMENT OF PATHOLOGIC PHYSIOLOGY OF THE TRACTUS INTESTINALIS.

Since pathologic physiology is the zone between physiology and pathologic anatomy it should be practically amenable to treatment. First and foremost, the diagnosis should be made and the cause removed, as a ureteral calculus, anal fissure, hepatic calculus or any point of visceral or dietetic irritation. The most essential feature of subjects suffering from pathologic physiology of the tractus intestinalis is deficient *visceral drainage.* The blood is excessively waste-laden from insufficient elimination. The secretions

458 THE ABDOMINAL AND PELVIC BRAIN

are scanty. The urine is concentrated, its crystallized salts are evident to the eye. The skin is dry from insufficient perspiration. Sleep is defective from the bathing of the innumerable ganglia with waste laden blood. Constipation, deficient urine, limited perspiration, capricious appetite and insomnia characterize subjects with pathologic physiology of the tractus intestinalis. For many years I have applied a treatment to such subjects which I term

VISCERAL DRAINAGE.

Visceral drainage signifies that visceral tracti are placed at maximum elimination by dietetics, fluids, appropriate hygiene and habitat, exercise.

X-RAY OF DUCTUS BILIS, DUCTUS PANCREATICUS AND ARTERIA HEPATICA

Fig. 118. Illustrates the vast nerve supply it requires to ensheath the channels of the liver and pancreas with a nodular network, a fenestrated meshwork, of nerve plexuses. The tractus nervosus of the tractus intestinalis is solidly and compactly anastomosed.

The waste products of food and tissue are vigorously sewered before new ones are imposed. The most important principle in internal medication is ample visceral drainage. The residual products of food and tissue should have a maximum drainage in health. I suggest that ample visceral drainage may be executed by means of: (A) *fluids*; (B) *food*.

(A.) *Visceral drainage by fluids.*

The most effective diuretic is water. One of the best laxatives is water. One of the best stimulants of renal epithelium is sodium chloride ($\frac{1}{2}$ to $\frac{3}{4}$

physiologic salt solution). Hence I administer 8 ounces of half normal salt solution to a patient six times daily, 2 hours apart. Note—NaCl is contraindicated in parenchymatous nephritis. 48 ounces of ½ normal salt solution efficiently increases the drain of the kidney, it sustains in mechanical suspension the insoluble uric acid, it stimulates other matters, it aids the sodium, potassium or ammonium salts to form combination with uric acid, producing soluble urates. The ½ normal salt solution effectively stimulates the peristalsis and epithelium of the tractus intestinalis inducing secretions which liquify stool, preventing constipation.

(B.) *Visceral drainage by foods.*

The great functions of the tractus intestinalis—peristalsis, absorption, secretion—are produced and maintained by food. To drain the tractus intestinalis foods which leave an indigestible residue only are appropriate. Rational foods must contain appropriate salts whose bases may form combinations which are soluble as sodium and potassium combined with uric acid and urates to form soluble urates. The proper foods are: cereals, vegetables, albuminates (milk, eggs), mixed foods.

Meats should be limited, as they enhance excessive uric acid formation. In order to stimulate the epithelium of the digestive tract (sensation) with consequent increase of peristalsis, absorption and secretion, I use a part or multiple of an alkaline tablet of the following composition: Cascara sagrada ($\frac{1}{6}$ gr.), aloes ($\frac{1}{4}$ gr.), $NaHCO_3$ (gr. 1), $KHCO_3$ ($\frac{1}{4}$ gr.), $MgSO_4$ (2 gr.). The tablet is used as follows: One-sixth to one tablet (or more, as required to move the bowels once daily) is placed on the tongue before meals and followed by 8 ounces of water (better hot). At 10 A. M., 3 P. M., and bedtime $\frac{1}{4}$ to 1 tablet is placed on the tongue and followed by a glassful of any fluid. In combined treatment $\frac{1}{4}$ of (NaCl) the sodium chloride tablet containing 11 grains and ($\frac{1}{4}$ to 8) alkaline* tablets are placed on the tongue together every 2 hours followed by a glassful of fluid. This method of treatment furnishes alkaline bases (sodium and potassium and ammonium) to combine with the free uric acid in the urine, producing perfectly soluble alkaline urates and materially diminishing the free uric acid in the urine. Besides the alkaline laxative tablet increases the peristalsis, absorption and secretion of the intestinal tract, stimulating the sensation of the mucosa aiding evacuation. I have termed the sodium chloride and alkaline laxative method *the visceral drainage treatment.* The alkaline and sodium chloride tablets take place of the so-called mineral waters. I continue this dietetic treatment of fluid and food for weeks, months, and the results are remarkably successful in pathologic physiology. The urine becomes clarified like spring water, and increased in quantity. The tractus intestinalis becomes freely evacuated, regularly daily. The blood is relieved of waste laden and irritating material. The tractus cutis eliminates freely, and the skin becomes normal. The appetite increases. The sleep becomes improved. The patient becomes hopeful, natural energy returns. The sewers of the body are well drained and flushed.

*The tablets are manufactured by Searle and Hereth Company, Chicago.

CHAPTER XXXIV.

PATHOLOGIC PHYSIOLOGY OF THE TRACTUS GENITALIS.

"The Soul knows only Soul, the web of events is the flowering robe in which she is clothed."—Emerson.

"Furnish the government with neither a kopek nor a soldier."—Final appeal of the Russian Douma, dissolved by the czar, July, 1906.

For over a decade I have been attempting to make prominent in gynecologic teaching, pathologic physiology, disordered function, rather than pathologic anatomy, changed structure. It seems to me that disorder-functions or pathologic physiology of the tractus genitalis impresses itself more indelibly on the student's and practitioner's mind than pathologic anatomy. Besides, in gynecologic practice pathologic physiology occurs tenfold more frequently in the genital tract than pathologic anatomy. For the gynecologist pathologic physiology presents innumerable views of practical interest. Pathologic physiology teaches that the circulation of an organ is a fundamental factor in comprehending its disease and administering rational treatment. It takes an inventory of the volume of blood which streams through the organ as a fundamental factor in comprehending its diseases and administering rational treatment. It takes an inventory of the volume of the blood which streams through the organs at different stages and conditions. We wrote years ago that the arteries of different viscera were supplied with automatic visceral ganglia, and we christened the peculiar nerve nodes found in the walls and adjacent to the uterus, oviducts and ovaries, as "Automatic Menstrual Ganglia." The automatic menstrual ganglia complicate the blood supply of the tractus genitalis by changing its volume during the different sexual phases. In pueritas the blood stream of the tractus genitalis is quiescent as well as its parenchymatous cells; in pubertas it is developing as well as proliferating parenchymatous cells. In menstruation the blood stream is active with active parenchymatous cells. In the puerperium there is retrogression of blood stream and an involution of parenchymatous cells. The climacterium is the opposite of pubertas—subsidence, the decrease of blood volume and parenchymatous cells. Senescence is a repetition of pueritas—the quiescence of the genitals, their long night of rest. The circulation of an organ quotes its value in the animal economy. It rates its function. Observe the enormous volume of blood passing through the kidney or pregnant uterus in a minute.

To study pathologic physiology of any visceral tract we must possess clear views as to its physiology. The physiology of the tractus genitalis is: (1) ovulation; (2) peristalsis; (3) secretion; (4) absorption; (5) menstruation; (6) gestation; (7) sensation.

(1) On account of the numerous theoretic views connected with OVULATION and lack of space we will omit the general discussion on the pathologic physiology of ovulation. It is well known that ovulation has a wide physiologic range. We do not know the life of an ovum or corpus luteum. It was once supposed that a corpus luteum was a sign of pregnancy and the supposition gained legal or judicial position. We know that this is an error. I have found two corpora lutea on one ovary of a lamb which had not been pregnant. The internal secretion of the ovary is important and chiefly manifest by marked symptoms on removal of both ovaries—neurosis, accumulation of panniculus adiposus, extra growth of hair, diminished energy and ambition. These symptoms may occur in women possessing both ovaries, hence, we would conclude that pathologic physiology of ovarian secretion existed. The sensation of the ovary occupies a wide zone of pathologic physiology in the mental and physical being. Forty per cent of women visiting my office remark, "I have pain in my ovaries." On physical examination we find the following conditions: First and foremost in the vast majority of women who complain of pain in the ovaries, palpation of the ovaries elicits no tenderness on pressure. However, the pain of such women is located bilaterally in the area of the cutaneous distribution of the ileohypogastric and ileoinguinal nerves. It is a skin hyperesthesia—a cutaneous neurosis. The bilateral iliac region of cutaneous hyperesthesia corresponds to the segmentation or somatic visceral (ovarian) area, and presents a frequent varying zone of sensory pathologic physiology. In the vast majority of women complaining of ovarian pain no disease of the ovary can be detected—it is cutaneous hyperesthesia of the ileoinguinal and ileohypogastric nerves.

(2) PERISTALSIS (EXCESSIVE, DEFICIENT, DISPROPORTIONATE).

(a) *Excessive* peristalsis of the tractus genitalis (uterus and oviducts) may occur at menstruation, during gestation, parturition by the presence of myomata, during the expulsion of blood coagula, placenta during congestion. The phenomenon of peristalsis in the uterus and oviduct differs from the form and distribution of the muscularis. The myometrium during gestation is in continual peristalsis—uterine unrest. By placing the hand on the abdomen of a four-month gestating woman one can feel the uterine muscular waves. The gestating uterus is always prepared for an abortion, but the cervix, the sentinel on guard, checks the proceeding. Fright will produce such violent, disordered myometrical peristalsis as to break through the guarding cervix. Many women during gestation experience considerable pain (supersensitive uterus) from excessive uterine peristalsis—it is pathologic physiology. Uterine peristalsis may be sufficiently excessive to rupture the myometrical wall. The "after-pains," puerperal pains, is excessive peristalsis in an infected myometrium. Frequently the severe pelvic pain during menstruation is excessive uterine and oviductal peristalsis due to its extramenstrual blood supply. It is chiefly the excessive peristalsis at menstruation that forces many women to assume rest in bed, for, with anatomic rest (maximum quietude of bones and voluntary muscles) and physiologic rest (maximum quietude of visceral muscles) the uterine peristalsis will exist at a minimum. Excessive oviductal peristalsis may produce pain of varying degrees. In excessive peristalsis the automatic menstrual ganglia are stimulated by extra quantities of blood or by other irritation.

PELVIC BRAIN (ADULT)

Fig. 119. Drawn from my own dissection. A, pelvic brain. In this case it is a ganglionated plexus possessing a wide meshwork. Also the pelvic brain is located well on the vagina, and the visceral sacral nerves (pelvic splanchnics) are markedly elongated; V, vagina; B, bladder; O, oviduct; Ut, uterus; Ur, ureter; R, rectum; P L, plexus interiliacus (left); P R, plexus interiliacus (right); N, sacral ganglia; Ur, ureter; 5 L, last lumbar nerve; i, ii, iii, iv, sacral nerves; 5, coccygeal nerve. Observe that the great vesical nerve (P) arises from a loop between the ii and iii sacral nerves. G S, great sciatic nerve.

(b) *Deficient* peristalsis of the tractus genitalis (uterus and oviducts) is not uncommon. Uterine inertia is an example known to every obstetrician. Deficient uterine peristalsis allows hemorrhage in the fourth and fifth decades of woman's life. Deficient peristalsis allows extraglandular secretion (leucorrhea).

(c) *Disproportionate* peristalsis is disordered, wild muscular movements in different segments of the uterus or oviduct.

(3) SECRETION (EXCESSIVE, DEFICIENT, DISPROPORTIONATE).

(d) *Excessive* secretion from the genital tract, pregnant or non-pregnant, has an extensive range and varying quantity. The excessive secretion zone in the tractus genitalis has an important bearing in practice. Typical pathologic physiology may be observed in the pregnant woman from whose uterus may flow several ounces of white mucus daily—no pathologic anatomy is detectable. Excessive uterine secretion is a common gynecologic matter. The glands may not be embraced sufficiently firm by the myometrium. The automatic menstrual ganglia are diseased, insufficiently supplied by blood or the myometrium is degenerated. Flaccid uteri secrete excessively. Excessive secretion and its fluid currents allow insufficient time for localization of the ovum. Excessive uterine secretion is, from apt bacterial media, liable to become infected. During excessive secretion physical examination frequently detects no palpable pathologic anatomy—merely physiology has exceeded its usual bounds.

(e) *Deficient* secretion of the tractus genitalis is not so manifest as its opposite. The mucosa of vagina and uterus present excessive dryness, desiccation, practically as visceral functions are executed by means of fluids, pathologic physiology is in evidence; dryness and abrasion of the mucosa, local irritation, chafing, local bacterial development, dysparunia, dysuria, defective import of spermatozoa and export of ova ending in sterility. Deficient secretion means that waste-laden fluids are bathing and irritating the thousands of lymph channels in the body. Deficient secretion or excessive dryness of the genital mucosa—pathologic physiology with no perceptible pathologic anatomy—is not uncommon in gynecologic practice. Oily applications to subjects with deficient genital secretion may be required for protection of exposed nerve periphery, as abrasion, fissure, ulcers, and also for relief.

(f) *Disproportionate* secretion may occur in the different segments of the genital tract, unequal, excessive, deficient, irregular.

(4) ABSORPTION (EXCESSIVE, DEFICIENT, DISPROPORTIONATE).

(g) *Excessive* absorption presents two views, namely, a dryness of the genital mucosa from excessive absorption of the mucal fluids. This resembles the conditions arising in deficient secretion of the genital tract (see e). Again the mucosa of the genital tract excessively absorbs deleterious substances lying on its mucosa—septic or toxic. Excessive absorption in the genital tract, pathologic physiology, resembles excessive absorption and conditions

464   THE ABDOMINAL AND PELVIC BRAIN

in other localities, as the absorption of poison ivy, lead, arsenic, among art workers. The pathologic physiology possesses a wide range, for some experience no ill-effects while others are severely or even fatally ill from absorption of same substance under similar conditions.

(h) *Deficient* absorption in the tractus genitalis produces an excessive

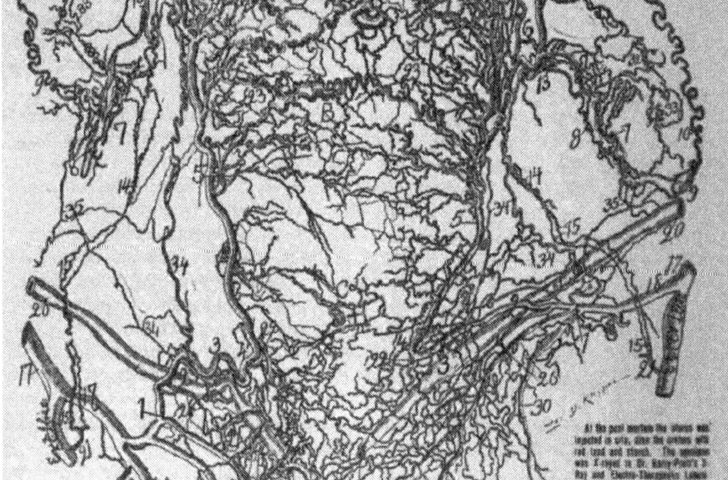

Spiral segment (utero-ovarian artery), 1, 2, 3, 4, 5, 6, 7-7, 8-8, 9, 10, 11, 12, 13, 14, 15.
Straight segment abdominal aorta, 16. Common iliac, 17, and internal iliac, 18

DIVISIONS OF THE SPIRAL SEGMENT.
1. Pelvic floor segment, 1, 2, 3, 4.
2. Uterine segment, 4, 5, 6.
3. Oviducal segment, 6, 7-8, 6-8, 9.
4. Ovarian segment, 9, 10, 11, 12.
5. Round ligament segment, 13, 14, 15. Uterar, 20, 19. Vaginal Arteries, 26.

IMPORTANT LOCATIONS IN THE SPIRAL SEGMENT
Arterio-ureteral loop, 2. Cervical loop, 2, 3, 4. Distal arterio-ureteral crossing, 2. Rami cervicis, 22. Rami corporis, 23. Rami fundi, 24. Rami oviductus, 31, 32, 33.

Arterial Circulation of the Puerperal Uterus.
Four Hours Post Partum. Life Size.
Illustrating the Utero-Ovarian Vascular Circle (the Circle of Byron Robinson).

Fig. 130. This illustration demonstrates the vast amount of nervus vasomotorius it requires to ensheath the arteries of the uterus.

discharge, the decomposition of which lays the foundation of bacterial multiplication and excoriation of mucosa and skin.

(i) *Disproportionate* absorption occurs in the different segments of the tractus genitalis and presents pathologic physiology. However, lack of space makes it impractical to discuss it.

(5) SENSATION (EXCESSIVE, DEFICIENT, DISPROPORTIONATE).

(j) *Excessive* sensation in the tractus genitalis presents a wide zone of pathologic physiology. Vaginismus is the extreme type of genital hyperesthesia. The introitus vaginæ of perhaps fifty per cent of women is supersensitive. When I was a pupil of Mr. Lawson Tait he had a patient, a recently married woman, from whom the husband was suing for divorce as her genital hyperesthesia was so excessive that coition or examination was intolerable. She had to be anesthetized to be examined, which was also suggested for impregnation with the hope that gestation would relieve the condition. Supersensitiveness of the pudendum is not an uncommon matter in gynecologic practice and without demonstrative pathologic anatomy. The pathologic physiology of excessive sensation in the tractus genitalis has a wide range of variation and degree of intensity. Some subjects may be afflicted with excessive sensation in the pudendum for many years. The excessive sensitive genitals may be manifest in the uterus or ovaries. A small number complain of tenderness and soreness in the internal genitals which cannot be detected as pathologic anatomy—simply excessive sensation. The gestating uterus may be so sensitive that it disorders adjacent viscera by reflexes. The treatment of subjects with excessive genital sensation requires unlimited time with continuous patience.

(k) *Deficient* sensation of the tractus genitalis is encountered. With such subjects practically no organism occurs during coition to which they are indifferent. Practically little or no treatment is required.

(l) *Disproportionate* sensation in the genital tract is irregular, indefinite, disordered sensation arising and disappearing in its different segments practically without reason or rhyme.

(6) MENSTRUATION (EXCESSIVE, DEFICIENT, DISPROPORTIONATE).

I will present this subject through a clinical patient. Brief remarks on common examples of pathologic physiology in the tractus genitalis will suffice to illustrate and suggest. As the most apt subject to illustrate pathologic physiology in the tractus genitalis I will choose that of menstruation.

To illustrate the value of pathologic physiology and the methods of teaching it we will place a gynecologic patient before a student to elicit clinical data in reference to menstruation as landmarks for diagnosis. A landmark is a point for consideration physiologic, anatomic, pathologic. To teach gynecology we should instruct by means of disordered function as a base. Menstruation is the first practical function of the genital tract. Hence the student asks in menstruation four questions, namely: (a) How old were you when the monthly flow began? The patient may answer: eleven (premature), fifteen (normal), or nineteen (delayed) years of age. This answer presents a wide range of beginning of the menstrual function. Now, the girl who begins to menstruate at eleven generally represents pathologic physiology, but not pathologic anatomy. For example, the girl who begins at eleven (menstratio precox) will in the majority of cases menstruate profusely and prolonged. She will experience a late climacterium. An early menstruation indicates a late climacterium. Though one can palpate practically no pathologic anatomy, the tractus genitalis is prematurely developed at eleven years of age, premature in dimension (nerves, blood, lymph, parenchyma) and function (menstruation, gestation). The blood stream to the genitals is prematurely excessive, the automatic menstrual ganglia are large and prematurely active. Her menstrual life is accompanied by excessive blood supply and hemorrhage, disordered function, active parenchymatous cells, prolonged reproductiveness. It is pathologic physiology, exaggerated function, but practically not pathologic anatomy. The girl who begins at fifteen is practically normal during her menstrual life. No pathologic anatomy nor pathologic physiology is manifest. The girl who begins to menstruate at nineteen (menstratio retarda) is delayed with her menstrual function; late menstrual appearance means early climacterium; it frequently indicates amenorrhea and dysmenorrhea. It generally means defective genital blood supply and limited parenchymatous cellular activity. It is pathologic physiology, disordered function, limited productiveness, but frequently no palpable pathologic anatomy exists. It is a fact, however, that in some cases atrophy or myometritis is palpable pathologic anatomy and should not be confused with subjects possessing pathologic physiology.

(b) The student asks the patient: Is the monthly flow regular? The answer may be, regular or irregular. The patient with irregular menstruation is afflicted with pathologic physiology but no pathologic anatomy may be detected. It may be stated, however, that the automatic menstrual ganglia require about eighteen months of vigorous blood supply to become sufficiently strong and established to act regularly monthly. The same condition exists in the automatic visceral ganglia (Auerbach's and Billroth-Meissner's) of the tractus intestinalis of a child.

(c) The student, thirdly, asks the patient: Is the monthly flow painful? The answer may be, yes or no. A normal menstruation should be painless. Dysmenorrhea or painful menstruation is pathologic physiology, disordered function, but frequently no pathologic anatomy can be detected. At menstruation the blood volume in the tractus intestinalis rapidly increases, blood pressure is raised, compressing or traumatizing the nerves to a degree; limited hematoma may occur in the endometrium, congestion is intense,

---

TRANSVERSE LONGITUDINAL SECTION OF UTERUS

Fig. 121. This illustration presents the endometrium (secretory and absorptive—glandular—apparatus); the myometrium (peristaltic or rhymic—muscular—apparatus); the perimetrium (secretory, absorptive—lymphatic—gliding apparatus). The uterus is richly supplied by sensory and motor nerves.

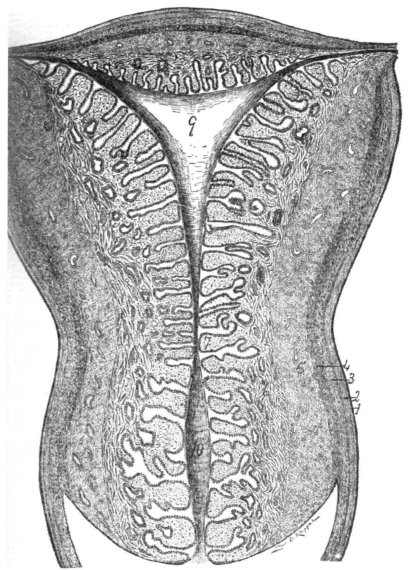

Fig. 121. Transverse Longitudinal Section of Uterus

inciting vigorous and disordered peristalsis of the uterus and oviducts. In short the trauma or shock of menstruation of the genital tract irritates it into a state of pain. It is a state of pathologic physiology, disordered function, but no pathologic anatomy may be palpable. The affliction is functional.

(d) The student finally asks the patient: How many days does the monthly flow continue? The answer may be, two to eight days. Two days is deficient (amenorrhea or oligemia); four days is normal, eight days is excessive (menorrhagia). I have examined scores of gynecologic patients with over a week's flow, menorrhagia, but in many of them no pathologic anatomy or change of structure could be detected. It is typical pathologic physiology, disordered, unusual function. The subject is like a watch with an excessively powerful mainspring. The watch has no detectable pathologic anatomy, no change of structure. The mainspring, the automatic ganglia, is excessively active. The organ is working excessively, the watch is gaining time. The automatic ganglia are prematurely powerful, the watch spring is too strong. Menorrhagia in many subjects is typical pathologic physiology. The pathologic anatomy, if it exists, is too subtle for us to detect. The adult life of the tractus genitalis presents an excellent field for study and teaching in pathologic physiology. Its several periodic functions, its changing volume of circulation, the limited life of its parenchymatous cells and its automatic menstrual ganglia afford a useful field for study and development of pathologic physiology.

(7) GESTATION.

Gestation presents many phases of pathologic physiology. There is the typical pathologic physiology, namely, emesis, albuminuria, hypertrophy of left ventricle, pigmentation, capricious appetite, constipation, increase of panicular adiposus, the peculiar gait, venous engorgement (edema), excessive glandular secretion, osteomalacia. The vomiting of pregnancy may present a vast zone from slight regurgitation of food to profound anemia due to limited nourishment—where pathologic physiology alone tells the tale. The normal physiologic nerve relations between the tractus genitalis (uterus) and tractus intestinalis (stomach) have become disordered. No pathologic anatomy is demonstrable. Constipation (pathologic physiology) is liable to arise during gestation because the normal physiologic blood supply of the tractus intestinalis is robbed to supply the increasing demand of the gestating genital tract. The albuminuria of pregnancy is doubtless partially due to pressure of the expanding uterus on the ureters and veins, obstructing venous and urinal flow. The normal physiologic relations between the tractus urinaria and the gestating tractus genitalis have become projected into the field of pathologic physiology. Pathologic anatomy is not in evidence except as ureteral dilatation—a secondary matter. A comprehensive view of pathologic physiology aids in diagnosis and treatment. It will impress the practitioners with the utility of *visceral drainage*, the administration of ample fluids at regular intervals to relieve the system of waste-laden blood—irritating substances. Pathologic physiology teaches us to restore function and frequently pathologic anatomy will take care of itself.

PHYSIOLOGY OF TRACTUS GENITALIS

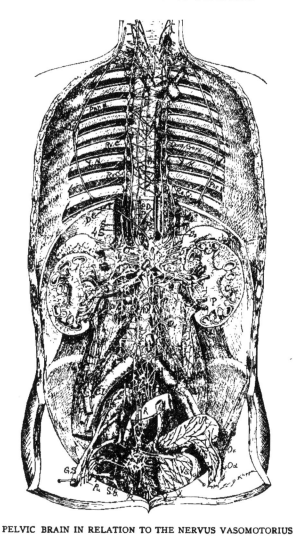

PELVIC BRAIN IN RELATION TO THE NERVUS VASOMOTORIUS

Fig. 122. General view of the nervus vasomotorius (sympathetic). B. Pelvic brain. H. Interilia nerve disc. 1 and 2. Abdominal brain.

TREATMENT OF PATHOLOGIC PHYSIOLOGY OF THE TRACTUS GENITALIS.

Since pathologic physiology is the zone between physiology and pathologic anatomy, it should be amenable to treatment. A diagnosis by exclusion should be made. It must be remembered that in the physiology the entire six abdominal visceral tracts are balanced harmonious, functionating without friction—no reflexes dashing hither and yon disturbing the exquisitively poised visceral physiology. In the treatment of pathologic physiology ot the tractus genitalis it should be remembered that the genitals are not vital for life, but that the richly nerve-supplied genitals dominate the mental and physical existence of woman. In the treatment of pathologic physiology there are the subjects of periodic hyperemia, congestion, hemorrhages, excessive glandular secretions, disturbed sensation (hyperesthesia). First and foremost in the treatment of pathologic physiology of the tractus genitalis, the adjacent visceral tracts must be regulated to normal states as to drainage, but especially as to the physiologic condition of blood. Frequently by producing daily evacuation of the digestive tract and increasing the renal secretion by ample fluids the pathologic physiology of the genital tract improves. The genitals should be examined for adherent prepuce, pudendal fissure, pruritus pudendæ, or other point of irritation. The other five abdominal visceral tracts (urinarius, intestinalis, vascularis, lymphaticus, nervosus) should be examined for points of visceral irritation. The frequent splanchnoptotic condition must be studied and remedied.

I. VISCERAL DRAINAGE.

For many years I have applied a treatment to such subjects which I term *visceral drainage*. Visceral drainage signifies that visceral tracts are placed at maximum elimination. The waste product of food and tissue are vigorously sewered before new ones are imposed. The most important principle in internal medication is ample drainage for every visceral tract. The residual products of food and tissue should have a maximum drainage in health. I suggest that ample visceral drainage may be executed by means of: (A) *Fluids*; (B) *Food*.

(A) *Visceral Drainage by Fluids.*

The most effective diuretic is water. One of the best laxatives is H_2O. One of the best stimulants of renal epithelium is sodium chloride (one-half to one-quarter physiologic salt solution). Hence I administer eight ounces of half normal salt solution to a patient six times a day, two hours apart. (Note.—Sodium chloride is contraindicated in parenchymatous nephritis.) Forty-eight ounces of half normal salt solution daily efficiently increases the drain of the kidney. It maintains in mechanical suspension the insoluble uric acid; it stimulates other matters; it aids the sodium, potassium, or ammonium salts to form combination with the uric acid, producing soluble urates. The half normal salt solution effectively stimulates the peristalsis and epithelium of the tractus intestinalis, inducing secretions which liquefy feces, preventing constipation.

PHYSIOLOGY OF TRACTUS GENITALIS

(B) *Visceral Drainage by Foods.*

The great functions of the visceral tract—peristalsis, absorption, secretion, sensation—are produced and maintained by fluids and foods. To drain the tractus genitalis and adjacent visceral tracts which should be excited to

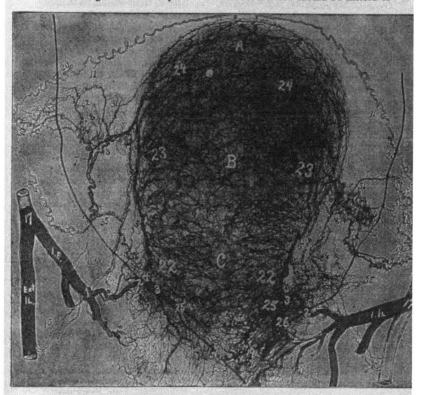

ARTERIES OF PUERPERAL UTERUS

Fig. 123. Illustrates the arteries of a puerperal uterus 5 days post postum. It is a halftone—a so-called bromine photograph. It well illustrates the enormous amount of nerves it would require to ensheath the numerous arteries of the uterus. The uterus was injected with red lead and starch and X-rayed. It represents excellently the author's circle.

peristalsis, foods which leave an indigestible residue only are appropriate. All visceral tracts must be stimulated to maximum peristalsis, secretion and absorption in order to aid that of the tractus genitalis. Rational foods must contain appropriate salts whose bases may form combinations which are soluble, as sodium, potassium and ammonium combined with uric acid and urates to form soluble urates. The proper foods are cereals, vegetables, albuminates (milk, eggs), mixed foods. Meats should be limited as they enhance excessive uric acid formation. In order to stimulate the epithelium (sensation) of the digestive and urinary tracts with consequent increase of peristalsis, absorption and secretion in both I used a part or multiple of an alkaline tablet of the following composition: Cascara sagrada ($\frac{1}{12}$ grain), aloes ($\frac{1}{2}$ grain), sodium carbonate (1 grain), potassium carbonate ($\frac{1}{2}$ grain), magnesium sulphate (2 grains). The tablet is used as follows: One-sixth to one tablet (or more, as required to move the bowels freely, once daily) is placed on the tongue before meals and followed by eight ounces of water (better hot). Also 10 A. M. to 8 P. M., and at bedtime one-sixth to one tablet is placed on the tongue and followed by a glassful of any fluid. In the combined treatment one-third of the sodium chloride tablet (containing eleven grains) and one-sixth to three alkaline tablets are placed on the tongue together every two hours, followed by a glass of fluid. The eight ounces of fluid may be milk, buttermilk, eggnog—nourishing fluid. This method of treatment furnishes alkaline bases (sodium, potassium and ammonium) to combine with the free uric acid in the urine, producing perfectly soluble alkaline urates and materially diminishing the insoluble free uric acid in the urine. Besides, the alkaline laxative tablet increases the peristalsis, absorption and secretion of the intestinal tract, stimulating the sensation of the mucosa—aiding evacuation. I have termed the sodium chloride and alkaline laxative method the *visceral drainage treatment*. The alkaline and sodium chloride tablets take the place of the so-called mineral waters. I continue this dietetic treatment for weeks, months, and the results are remarkably successful, especially in the pathologic physiology of the visceral tracts. The urine becomes clarified like spring water and increases in quantity. The tractus intestinalis becomes freely evacuated, regularly, daily. The caliber of the tractus vascularis becomes a powerful fluid volume to carry oxygen and food to tissue, while the effete matter and waste products are rapidly swept into the sewer channels. The blood is relieved of waste-laden and irritating material. The tractus cutis eliminates freely and the skin becomes normal. The appetite increases. The sleep improves. The patient becomes hopeful, natural energy returns. The sewers of the body are drained and flushed to a maximum.

II. VAGINAL DOUCHE.

(1) The kind of *instrument* to employ is a fountain syringe of fourteen-quart capacity. The simplest and most economic vaginal syringe is a fourteen-quart wooden pail, the kind generally used in transporting candy or tobacco.

(2) The *location* of the syringe should be four feet above the patient.

(3) The *quantity* of fluid administered in the beginning should be two quarts for patients unaccustomed to its use and four quarts to those accus-

PHYSIOLOGY OF TRACTUS GENITALIS

tomed to its use. The quantity should be increased a pint at each administration to fourteen quarts.

(4) The *temperature* of the douche should be 105° in the beginning and increased one degree at each administration until it is as hot as it can be borne (115° to 120°).

(5) The *duration* of the douche should be ten minutes for each gallon.

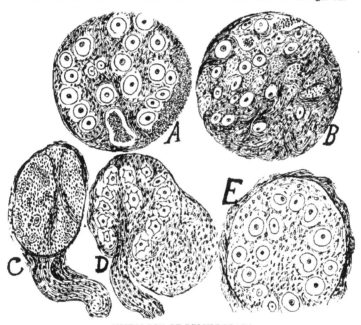

HISTOLOGY OF PELVIC BRAIN

Fig. 124. A, drawn from the pelvic brain of a girl seventeen years of age. The ganglion cells are completely developed. B, drawn from the pelvic brain of a three months' normal gestation. The ganglion cells are completely developed. Observe the enormous mass of connective tissue present. C, child 1½ years old. A nerve process courses within the ganglion. Few and small ganglion cells incompletely developed. D, girl 1½ years old. A nerve process branches and reunites itself with the intercellular substance. E, girl 6 years old. The ganglion cells are presenting development. (Redrawn after Doctor Sabura Hashimoto.)

(6) The *time* to administer the douche is in the evening immediately before retiring and in the morning (after which the patient should lie horizontally for forty-five minutes).

(7) The *position* of the patient should be lying on the back.

(8) As to *method* of administering the douche the patient should lie on a sufficiently inclined plane to allow the returning fluid to drain into a vessel

(pail, pan). The ironing board, wash-tub or board resting on the bath-tub serve convenient purposes. The douche should not be administered in the bed (unless ordered), standing or sitting postures or on the water-closet.

(9) As to *ingredients* a handful of sodium chloride and a teapoonful of alum should be added to each gallon, the sodium chloride to dissolve the mucus and pus, to act as an antiseptic and to prevent reaction, while the alum is to astringe, check waste secretions and harden tissue.

(10) The *vaginal tube* employed in administering the douche should be sterilized, boiled, and every patient should possess her own vaginal tube. The most useful vaginal tube is the largest that can be conveniently introduced or the one that distends the vaginal forces so that the hot fluids will bathe the greatest surface area of the proximal or upper end of the vagina.

(11) The *utility* of a vaginal douche is: (a) It contracts tissue (muscle, elastic and connective); (b) it contracts vessels (lymphatics, veins and arteries); (c) it absorbs exudates; (d) it checks secretion; (e) it stimulates; (f) it relieves pain; (g) it cleanses; (h) it checks hemorrhage; (i) it curtails inflammation; (j) it drains the tractus genitalis. The utility of the vaginal douche depends on the quantity of fluid, the degree of temperature, its composition, the position of the patient during administration, and on systematic methods of use.

(12) *Disinfectants* in a vaginal douche are secondary in value to solvents of mucus, pus, leucocytes.

(13) The *objects* to accomplish by a douche are: (a) The dissolving of the elements in the discharge, as mucus, pus and leucocytes; (b) the mechanical removal of morbid secretions, accumulations and foreign bodies; (c) antisepsis; (d) diagnosis (and it includes number 11).

(14) The *requirements* of a douche; (a) It should be nonirritating; (b) it should be a clear solution; (c) it should possess solvent powers of pus, and especially mucus; (d) it should be continued for months; (e) omit the douche for four days during menstruation.

(15) A vaginal douche, administered according to the above directions, will prove to be of therapeutic value in the treatment of pelvic disease, a prophylactic agent and a comfort to the patient.

(16) The vaginal douche is contraindicated in subjects with oviductal gestation or acute pyosalpinx, as it is liable to induce rupture of the oviductal wall, abortion or leakage of pus through the abdominal oviductal sphincter.

III. VAGINAL TAMPON.

(1) The *composition* of the vaginal tampon consists of a roll of medicated cotton (hen-egg size), tied to a twelve-inch string, placed in a solution of sixteen ounces of glycerine and two ounces of boracic acid.

TRACTUS VASCULARIS AND TRACTUS NERVOSUS OF THE TRACTUS GENITALIS

Fig. 125. Illustrates the tractus nervosus of the genital tract, pregnant 5 months. The utero-ovarian vascular circle (circle of author) is ensheathed by a rich nodular, fenestrated, anastomosing nerve plexus.

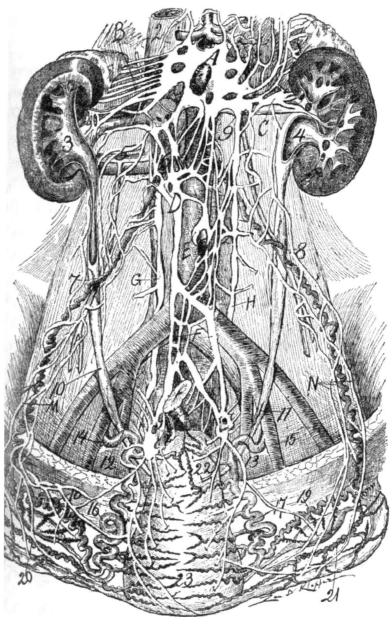

Fig. 125. Tractus Vascularis and Tractus Nervosus of the Tractus Genitalis

(2) The *duration of preparation* of vaginal tampon should be to lie in the boroglyceride solution forty-eight hours before using.

(3) The *utility* of the vaginal tampon is: (a) It is hygroscopic; (b) it serves as a mechanical support; (c) it contracts tissue (muscle, elastic, connective); (d) it contracts vessels, (lymphatics, veins and arteries); (e) it hastens absorption of exudates; (f) it checks secretions; (g) it stimulates; (h) it curtails inflammation; (i) it drains the pelvic organs; (j) it cleanses; (k) it dissolves mucus, pus and leucocytes. The utility of a vaginal tampon depends on its composition, the quantity employed, the duration of its application and on systematic method of use.

(4) The *methods of introduction* consist in placing three to five vaginal tampons (with or, better, without a speculum) in the vaginal fornices in the direction of least resistance.

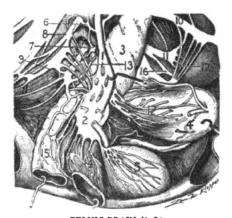

PELVIC BRAIN (1, 2.)
Fig. 126. Dissected from a subject about 37 years old.

(5) *Disinfectants* in a vaginal tampon are secondary to its other qualities, especially that of hygroscopy.

(6) The *object* to accomplish by a vaginal tampon is: Maximum hygroscopy, dissolving the elements in the discharge, as mucus, pus, leucocytes, the mechanical removal of morbid secretions, accumulation and foreign bodies, diagnosis, and mechanical support.

(7) The *diagnosis* is aided by the use of a tampon by collecting and preserving the uterine discharge (as pus, blood, debris).

(8) The *requirements* of a vaginal tampon are: (a) It should be nonirritating; (b) it should possess hygroscopic power; (c) it should be a solvent of discharges (mucus, pus, leucocytes, blood); (d) it should aid in the dissolving of the mechanical removal of morbid secretions, accumulations, and

foreign bodies; (e) it should be aseptic (not necessarily antiseptic); (f) it should not indelibly stain the clothing (this is objection to its use as, for example, ichthyol); (g) it should be reasonably economic.

(9) The *frequency of application* of the boroglyceride vaginal tampons should be in general, twice weekly; more frequent employment may cause irritation.

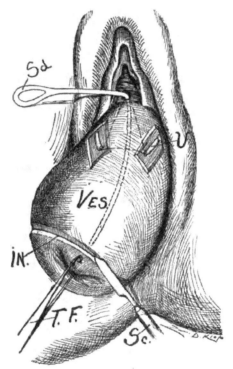

SACRO-PUBIC HERNIA

Fig. 127. This illustration demonstrates how the ureters, bladder and vagina are distorted and consequently how the accompanying sympathetic nerves are traumatized.

(10) The *time* to apply the tampon is at night during maximum anatomic and physiologic rest.

(11) The *duration* the tampon may remain usefully in position is ten to twenty-four hours.

(12) There are no special contraindications to the application of the vaginal tampon (in pelvic disease).

(13) The boroglyceride vaginal tampon may be beneficially applied in: (a) inflammatory pelvic disease (vaginitis, endometritis, myometritis, endosalpingitis, myosalpingitis, pelvic peritonitis, proctitis, cystitis); (b) sacropubic hernia (support for the uterus, cystocele and rectocele); (c) in genital ptosis it depletes the lymphatics and veins.

(14) A vaginal tampon applied according to the above directions will prove to be of therapeutic value in the treatment of pelvic disease, a prophylactic agent and a comfort to the patient.

IV. HABITAT.

The value of fresh air was never realized so much as at present. Fresh cold air cures pulmonary and other tuberculoses. The success of the sanitarium is the continued use of fresh (cold) air. The subject should sleep with fresh cold air passing through an open window space of three by three feet. It appears to be demonstrated that *cold* fresh air is more beneficial than warm fresh air. It is common talk among people that one winter in the mountain is worth two summers for the consumptive. The curative and beneficial effect of cold fresh air continually, day and night, for the family must be preached in season and out of season by physicians. The windows should be open all night. Fresh cold air is one of the best therapeutic agents in pathologic physiology of the tractus genitalis.

Exercise is an essential for health. Muscles exercise a dominating control over circulation (blood and lymph). The abdominal muscles influence the caliber of the splanchnic vessels. They exercise an essential influence over the peristalsis, secretion, absorption of the tractus intestinalis, urinarius, vascularis and genitalis. The muscles massage the viscera, enhancing their function and the rate of circulation. In the uterus, the most typical example, it is prominently marked how the myometrium controls the blood currents like living ligatures. The habitat that furnishes opportunity for abundant fresh air and ample exercise is the one that affords the essential chances for recovery of pathologic physiology in the tractus genitalis.

CHAPTER XXXV.

PATHOLOGIC PHYSIOLOGY OF THE TRACTUS URINARIUS.

I belong to the great church that holds the world within its starlit aisles; that claims the great and good of every race and clime; that finds with joy the grain of gold in every creed, and floods with light and love the germs of good in every soul.—R. Ingersoll

The rising of a great hope is like the rising of the sun.—Charles Kingsley.

The *physiology* or function of the tractus urinarius is: (1) peristalsis; (2) secretion; (3) absorption; (4) sensation. *Pathologic physiology* is a deviation from the usual physiology without, however, invading the field of pathologic anatomy. The tractus urinarius is a fertile field to study pathologic physiology, as it presents a wide zone of varying degrees, especially since recent investigations have enriched our knowledge of renal function. What older physicians considered pathologic anatomy in renal function is now believed to be largely pathologic physiology. The zone of kidney function is a continually increasing one. In the study of pathologic physiology of the tractus urinarius rational and comprehensive views of the renal viscus will be entertained. The study comprises: (a) the condition or state of the kidney; (b) the constituents of the blood; (c) the volume of blood that streams through the organ. The discussion of (a), (b), and (c) in regard to the kidney lends a comprehensive view to the student in making a diagnosis of the living.

We will here consider the pathologic physiology of the urinary tract or some of the common deviations from the usual physiology.

(1) PERISTALSIS (EXCESSIVE, DEFICIENT, DISPROPORTIONATE).

(a) *Excessive* peristalsis may occur in the tractus urinarius from numerous causes. The segment of the urinary tract subject to peristalsis is the ureter and bladder. The ureter is an independent organ resembling the heart, uterus, stomach. It possesses automatic ureteral ganglia as it performs peristalsis and functionates regardless of attitude or force of gravity. Excessive peristalsis is most liable to arise from excessive drinking of fluids, from diabetes or polyuria where excessive volumes of fluid passed through the urinary tract in limited time. The most marked example of pathologic physiology or excessive peristalsis in the urinary tract arises from the presence of an ureteral calculus. The ureter experiences brusk, vigorous, violent, wild and disordered movements accompanied by excruciating pain. A marked example of excessive ureteral peristalsis, based, however, on pathologic anatomy, is ureteritis which may be accompanied by excruciating pain. From experimentation on dogs one observes that the peristalsis of the ureter is brisk, vigorous, resembling that of the heart, uterus.

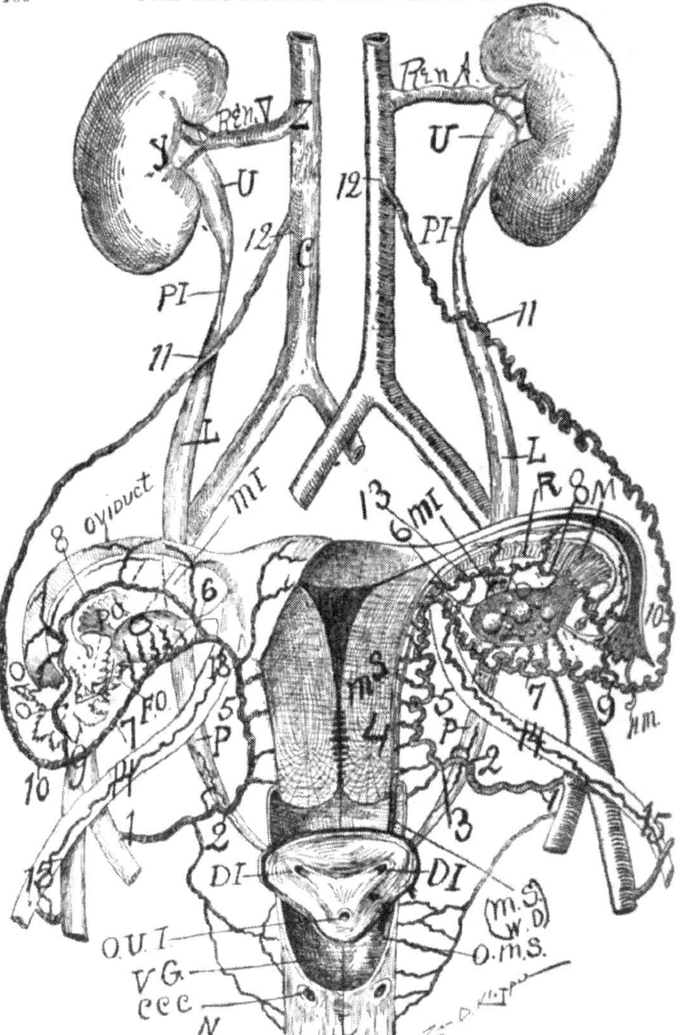

480   THE ABDOMINAL AND PELVIC BRAIN

Fig. 128. INTIMATE RELATION OF THE TRACTUS GENITALIS AND TRACTUS URINARIUS

(b) *Deficient* peristalsis of the urinary tract arises in connection with limited drinking of fluids, limited quantity of urine (the pressure of urine stimulates the ureteral peristalsis); a limited quantity of urine accompanied by a limited peristalsis is liable to be followed by precipitation of crystals and urinary calculus. However, a compensatory action arises from the fact that limited urine is generally concentrated and hence is apt to irritate the ureter, inducing peristalsis. It is probable that the automatic ureteral ganglia, similar to the automatic intestinal ganglia (in constipation) may become sluggish, inducing deficient ureteral peristalsis.

(c) *Disproportionate* peristalsis is irregular, unequal peristalsis in different segments of the tractus urinarius, as bladder or ureter.

(2) SECRETION (EXCESSIVE, DEFICIENT, DISPROPORTIONATE).

(d) *Excessive* secretion from the urinary tract is observed most typically in diabetes mellitus, insipidis or polyuria, frequently fields of simple pathologic physiology where no pathologic anatomy can be detected.

Excessive renal secretion may be marked in change of temperature from warm to cold weather—a difference of a quart of urine may be noted enduring for six or ten days—simple variation of renal function. The function of the perspiratory apparatus has experienced a deficient secretion relatively equal to the pathologic physiology of the excessive renal action. Cold, contracting the cutaneous vessels, forcing the blood into the central large vessels, and increasing heart action, will markedly increase renal secretion. Pathologic physiology, compensatory, no pathologic anatomy; it is a form of vicarious physiology. Sugar may appear in the urine for some time (pathologic physiology) without demonstrable pathologic anatomy—later, however, indigested fats may be found in the stools, which would call attention to the pancreas. However, the pancreas may be suffering from pathologic physiology of secretion only (excessive, deficient, or disproportionate). Pancreatic secretion may be insufficient to dissolve the fats. So that even at the stage of diabetes, pathologic anatomy may not yet be afoot. Paresis (sluggishness) of the renal plexus (ganglia) may allow polyuria. Constipation may impose increased vicarious duties on the kidneys, compelling them to eliminate products usually eliminated by the tractus intestinalis. We know kidney action may be excessive, that is, comprise pathologic physiology only, for we not infrequently observe one kidney successfully accomplishing

---

Fig. 128. This illustration demonstrates how solidly and compactly the tractus urinarius and tractus genitalis are anastomosed, connected. At the proximal arterio-ureteral crossing (11, 11) the ureter and ovarian artery are solidly and firmly anastomosed by the nervus vasomotorius (sympathetic). Again at the distal arterio-ureteral crossing (2, 2) a similar but more extensive anastomosis occurs—hence the balanced relationship between the tractus urinarius and tractus genitalis. Every practitioner realizes the intimate relation of the bladder and the uterus, e. g., in gestation, through the nervus vasomotorius. This intimately solid anastomosis between the two visceral tracts by means of abundant nerve strands aids to explain the vast and interdependent pathologic physiology observed in practice.

duplicate work. We can produce excessive secretion of urine artificially by administering NaCl in ample fluids. Certain foods, as water-melon, produce temporary excessive renal function, with certain subjects, apparently exces-

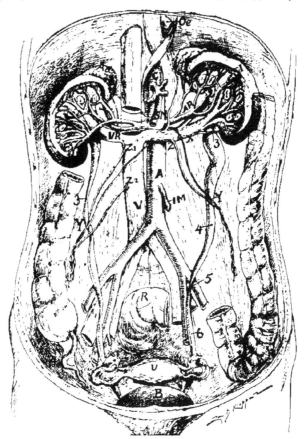

ILLUSTRATION OF THE FEMALE URINARY TRACT

Fig. 129. This specimen was drawn from nature from my own dissection by the aid of distending the ureter's veins and arteries with hardening material. The ureter (calyces, pelvis and ureter proper) is ensheathed with a nodular fenestrated web, an anastomosing network of sympathetic nerves especially at the 3 ureteral isthmuses (of Byron Robinson) 3, 5 and the entrance in the bladder. Z, Y, 3, uretero-venous triangle (of author). The nervus vasomotorius richly supplies the tractus urinarius and manifests itself violently during the presence of a moving calculus or periodic hydro-ureter, or ureteritis.

sive renal secretion (pathologic physiology) exists for years. In excessive renal secretion the urinary salts may be excessive or deficient or vice versa.

(e) *Deficient* renal secretion may be noted in limited drinking of fluids, in restricted diet in diarrhoea (vicarious), in cold weather, in debilitated heart, in fevers, in concentrated foods (flesh-eaters), in sedentary habits and in numerous nameless conditions. Deficient renal secretion is, from my experience, a rather common condition. Deficient renal secretion may present excessive or deficient urinary salts or vice versa.

In certain subjects apparently deficient renal secretions exist for years. In general, deficient renal secretions are saturated with concentrated urinal salts which may irritate the mucosa of the tractus urinarius sufficiently to produce pathologic physiology. Deficient renal secretion may lead to uremia.

(f) *Disproportionate* renal secretion is irregular in different segments of the kidney. The urine may be excessive and the salt deficient or vice versa. The renal glomeruli may secrete deficient or excessive fluids. The uriniferous tubules may secrete deficient or excessive salts.

What influence has the disturbed renal secretion—the pathologic physiology—on the general organism? Manifold injuries may occur. The continual loss in albuminuria is exhausting. The insufficient secretion of urinal constituents from the blood leads finally to bodily disturbance. In other words, pathologic physiology in renal secretion may be the incipient stage of disease—pathologic anatomy. Disturbed renal secretion may be accompanied by disease in different organs—uremia, which represents the accumulated disturbances on various organs.

(3) ABSORPTION (EXCESSIVE, DEFICIENT, DISPROPORTIONATE).

(g) *Excessive* absorption of the tractus renalis would constitute extracting unusual material from the blood. In a certain sense, excessive renal absorption might induce excessive secretion: e. g., on urinalysis albumen may be found which would suggest an inquiry as to the quantity of egg albumen the subject is consuming. Considerable ingesta of albumen may lead to rich albuminuria. Hence, the state or composition of the blood should be investigated to decide the amount of albuminuria. If there be excessive sugar in the blood and sugar being absorbed by the renal apparatus will present excessive secretion of sugar. This suggests inquiry into the quantity of sugar ingested.

(h) *Deficient* absorption would indicate that the renal apparatus does not extract from the blood the proper amount nor the proper material. The pathologic physiology has a wide range in deficient absorption, for some times we may observe an adult person eliminating 8 or 10 ounces of urine daily.

(i) *Disproportionate* absorption constitutes irregular disordered absorption of the different segments of the renal apparatus, as the glomeruli and the uriniferous tubules.

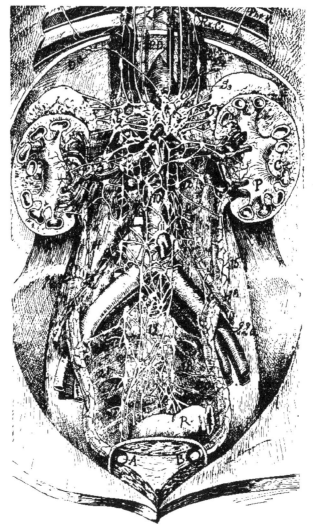

Fig 130. AN ILLUSTRATION OF THE ABDOMINAL SYMPATHETIC NERVE OF THE MALE, ESPECIALLY PRESENTING THE NERVES OF THE TRACTUS URINARIUS

(4) SENSATION (EXCESSIVE, DEFICIENT, DISPROPORTIONATE).

It is evident on watching an exposed ureter of a sleeping dog that the sensation of the mucosa in the urinary apparatus is of vital importance, for each and every time that a certain quantity of urine collects in the dog's ureteral pelvis, the ureter proper executes its brusque, vigorous peristalsis with remarkable rapidity. The automatic ureteral ganglia rule the ureteral peristalsis. We do not realize the exqnisitively poised sensory apparatus of the tractus urinarius until some catastrophy occurs, as ureteral calculus, to appriae us of the wild, disordered peristalsis and excruciating pain. Pathologic physiology of sensation in the tractus urinarius may well comprise excessive, deficient or disproportionate states for sensation much depends on the composition of the urine and the state of the urinary visera. Inordinate meat eaters produce concentrated, irritating urine, exciting excessive ureteral peristalsis with consequent pain—diluting the urine relieves the patient.

In excessive sensation of the tractus urinarius we will include the so-called "irritated bladder," because, though cystoscopy has lessened the actual number of irritable bladders by eliminating pathologic anatomy, it can not exclude the subject—pathologic physiology. Irritable bladder exists without demonstrable pathologic anatomy. The subjective symptoms of an irritable or excessively sensitive bladder are frequent evacuations (peristalsis). The bladder may require evacuations several times an hour. There is an increase in frequency and intensity in the desire to urinate—excessive visceral peristalsis. Irritable bladder may persist day and night. The desire to urinate may be so intense that insufficient time is allowed to prepare the dress and hence "wetting of the clothing" occurs. Excessive vesical peristalsis, irritable bladder may be sufficient to cause vesical colic, which may radiate, reflexly to the tractus intestinalis or genitalis, disordering the function of peristalsis, absorption or secretion. E. g., the patient may evacuate feces and urine simultaneously—so-called nervous diarrhea.

The irritable bladder may produce cold perspiration, emesis, chills, and produce mental depression, hypochondria. The main objective symptom of irritable bladder—pathologic physiology of vesical sensation and peristalsis—is hyperesthesia which manifests itself chiefly in the trigone where nerves congregate. The neck and fundus may present irritability. The hyperesthesia may occur as an increase in normal sensibility to tensions or

---

Fig. 130. An illustration of the nervus vasomotorius (sympathetic) drawn from a specimen which I secured at an autopsy through the courtesy of Professor W. A. Evans. The relation of the nervus vasomotorius to the tractus urinarius is evidently intimate and abundant. The network of nerves on the arteria renalis and ureter are apparent. The enormous supply of nerves to the adrenal is remarkable—7 in number. The solid anastomosis of the plexus ovaricus with the plexus ureteris is noticeable, where the vasa ovarica (spermatica) pass ventral to the ureter. The arteria renalis is ensheathed in a rich, plexiform, gangliated nerve plexus. I dissected this specimen under alcohol, and the nerve relations are practically correct. The artist, Mr. Zan D. Klopper, followed the fresh dissection as a model. The ureter (calyces, pelvis and ureter proper) is dilated bilaterally. Even the 3 ureteral isthmuses (of author) are dilated.

486   THE ABDOMINAL AND PELVIC BRAIN

as abnormal sensibility to pressure. The abnormal sensibility may be manifest on the presence of solid feces in the rectum, digital examination or on cystoscopy. The urine may present nothing abnormal in quantity, in reaction, chemical or physical characteristics; no hyperacidity, no excess of salts, concentration of urine, or glycosuria. What causes the hyperesthesia of

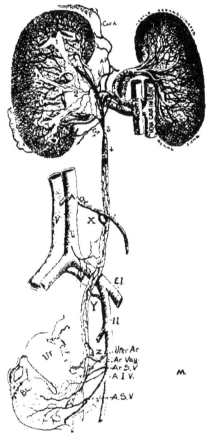

Fig. 131. The nerve supply to the tractus urinarius is best remembered, perhaps, by recalling its arterial blood supply; for the nervus vasomotorius accompanies the arteries. The arteries to the tractus urinarius are: (a) arteria adrenalis; (b) arteria renalis; (c) arteria ovarica (spermatica); (x) arteria media ureteris; (y) arteria ureteris, distal (from iliac); (z) arteria uterina; (w) the three vesical arteries, each of which is accompanied by its own nerve plexus. The upper part of illustration is from corrosion anatomy.

the vesical wall—pathologic physiology, no demonstrable pathologic anatomy —is unknown. Cystoscopic examinations and autopsies and examinations demonstrate that in irritable bladder no pathologic anatomy may exist or that a condition of hyperemia may exist in the bladder wall. The subjects of irritable bladder in which no demonstrable pathologic anatomy exists are simply nervous in character, typical pathologic physiology. The subjects

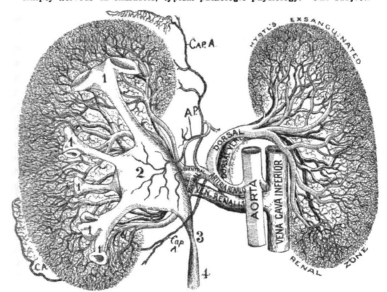

NERVES OF THE TRACTUS URINARIUS—CORROSION ANATOMY

Fig. 132. This specimen presents quite faithfully the circulation, the kidney, calyces and pelvis. The two renal vascular blades I present opened like a book. The corrosion was on the left kidney and the larger vascular blade is the ventral one. The vasomotor nerves accompanying the urinary tract may be estimated by the fact that a rich plexiform network of nerves ensheath the arteries, the calyces, pelvis and ureter proper. When the renal vascular blades are shut like a book their thin edges come in contact, but do not anastomose. The edges of the vascular blades are what I term the *exsanguinated renal zone of Hyrtl*, who discovered it in 1868, and we, at present, employ it for incising the kidney to gain entrance to the enterior of the calyces and pelvis with minimum hemorrhage. This specimen presents excellently the capsular artery—Cap. A. Think of the vast amount of pathologic physiology which could be created by disturbing the rich sympathetic nerve supply to the kidney.

possessing merely hyperemia of the vesical wall are of non-inflammatory type or non-detectable inflammation. The irritable bladder is influenced especially by two factors, viz.: (a) psychic or mental disturbances; (b) tendency of blood to the pelvic organs (bladder). The prognosis of irritable bladder, especially of the severe type, is unfavorable—almost every case I have observed was or has been practically life long. The treatment is hygienic, dietetic—

488 THE ABDOMINAL AND PELVIC BRAIN

visceral drainage, preserving maximum state and contents of visceral tracts. For more extensive views of the subject of irritable bladder see the excellent article by Hirsch, Centralbllatt f. die Grenzgebete Medizin u. Chirurgie, Vol. VIII, Nos. 13 and 14.

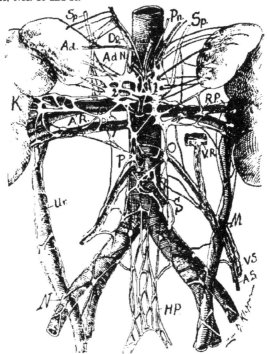

NERVUS VASOMOTORIUS OF THE TRACTUS URINARIUS

Fig. 133. I dissected this specimen under alcohol. It presents excellently the solid and compact anastomosis of urinary nerves to all other abdominal vasomotor nerves. Observe the solid anastomosis at M and N. The reflexes observed in practice may well be interpreted by this illustration. Note the multiple, giant, ganglia accompanying the arteria renalis. The nerves of the tractus urinarius presents a rich field in pathologic physiology.

There are still apparently unsolved problems in the physiology of the tractus urinarius and hence multiple unsolved problems in the pathologic physiology of this important visceral tract. For example, the urine (an acid fluid) is derived from the blood (an alkaline fluid) by a filtration process. What changes the urine into an acid fluid from the blood, an alkaline fluid? The explanation must be that the blood is practically and chemically an acid due to the presence of bicarbonates which are acid salts.

The degree of the acidity of the urine is a measure of the degree of the acidity of the blood. The acidity of both urine and blood is due to acid phosphates or salts of phosphoric acid (H_3PO_4), i. e., salts resembling acid sodium phosphate (NaH_2PO_4), acid calcium phosphate ($CaHPO_4$), and acid magnesium phosphate ($MgHPO_4$), which may assume more atoms in the bone.

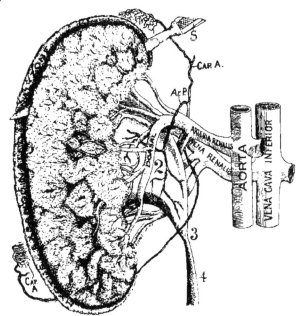

CORROSION ANATOMY (HYRTL'S EXSANGUINATED RENAL ZONE)

Fig. 134. In this specimen of corrosion anatomy the renal vascular blades (ventral and dorsal) are closed like a book. It presents (left kidney) on the margin of the dorsal lateral surface the exsanguinated zone of Hyrtl—the line of minimal hemorrhage for corticle renal incision. A rational method to estimate the quantity of nerves of the tractus urinarius is to expose the number and dimension of the arteries and other tubular ducts which are ensheathed in a plexiform network—a fenestrated, nodular, neural vagina of nerves. The nervus vasomotorius rules the physiology of the renal apparatus. Modern investigation demonstrates an extensive zone of pathologic physiology in the domain of the kidney.

"It is, therefore, obvious that the real urinary acidity is phosphoric acidity." (Editorial, *New York Medical Journal*, May 26, 1906.)

TREATMENT OF PATHOLOGIC PHYSIOLOGY OF THE TRACTUS URINARIUS.

Since pathologic physiology is the zone between physiology and pathologic anatomy it should be practically amenable to treatment. First and

490 THE ABDOMINAL AND PELVIC BRAIN

foremost the diagnosis should be made, and the cause removed, as ureteral calculus, anal fissure, hepatic calculus or any point of general visceral irritation. The most general essential feature of a subject suffering from patho-

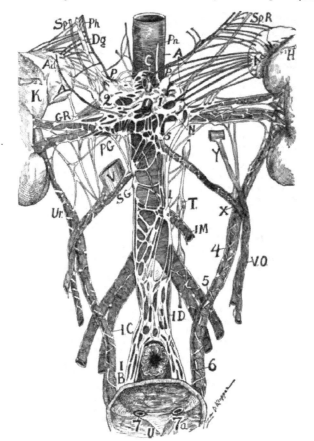

Fig. 135. This specimen I dissected with extreme care under alcohol, and the artist, Mr. Zan D. Klopper, followed the dissection as a model. It well illustrates the nervus vasomotorius in relation with the tractus urinarius.

logic physiology of the tractus urinarius is deficient visceral drainage. The blood is excessively waste laden from inefficient elimination. The secretions are scanty. The urine is concentrated, its crystallized salts are evident to the eye. The skin is dry from insufficient perspiration, sleep is defective from bathing of the innumerable ganglia with waste laden blood. Constipation, deficient urine, limited perspiration, capricious appetite, insomnia and headache characterize subjects with pathologic physiology of the tractus urinarius.

For many years I have applied a treatment to such subjects which I term *visceral drainage*. Visceral drainage signifies that visceral tracts are placed at maximum elimination. The waste product of food and tissue are vigorously sewered before new ones are imposed. The most important principle in internal medication is ample visceral drainage for every visceral tract. The residual products of food and tissue should have a maximum drainage in health. I suggest that ample visceral drainage may be executed by means of: (A) *fluids;* (B) *food*.

(A). VISCERAL DRAINAGE BY FLUIDS.

The most effective diuretic is water. One of the best laxatives is water. One of the best stimulants of renal epithelium is sodium chloride (1-2 to 1-4 physiologic salt solution). Hence I administer eight ounces of half normal salt solution to a patient six times a day, two hours apart. (Note—NaCl is contraindicated in parenchymatous nephritis.) 48 ounces of 1-2 normal salt solution daily efficiently increases the drain of the kidney. It maintains in mechanical suspension the insoluble uric acid, it also stimulates other matters. It aids the sodium, potassium or ammonium salts to form combination with the uric acid producing soluble urates.

The half normal salt solution effectively stimulates the epithelium of the tractus intestinalis, inducing secretions which liquefy feces, preventing constipation.

(B). VISCERAL DRAINAGE BY FOODS.

The great functions of the tractus urinarius—peristalsis, absorption, secretion, sensation—are produced and maintained by fluids and food. To drain the tractus urinarius the adjacent visceral tracts should be excited to peristalsis, hence foods which leave an indigestible residue only are appropriate, all other visceral tracts must be stimulated to maximum peristalsis, secretion, absorption in order to aid that of the tractus urinarius. Rational foods must contain appropriate salts whose bases may form combinations which are soluble, as sodium, potassium, and ammonium combined with uric acid and urates to form soluble urates. The proper foods are cereals, vegetables, albuminates (milk, eggs), mixed foods. Meats should be limited as they enhance excessive uric acid formation.

In order to stimulate the epithelium (sensation) of the digestive and urinary tract with consequent increase of peristalsis, absorption and secretion in both, I use a part or multiple of an alkaline tablet of the following composition: Cascara Sagrada (1-40 grain), Aloes (1-8 grain), $NaHCO_3$ (1 grain), $KHCO_3$ (1-8 grain), $MgSO_4$ (2 grains). Tablet* is used as follows: 1-6 to 1

*The sodium chloride and alkaline tablets are manufactured by Searle and Hereth Co., Chicago.

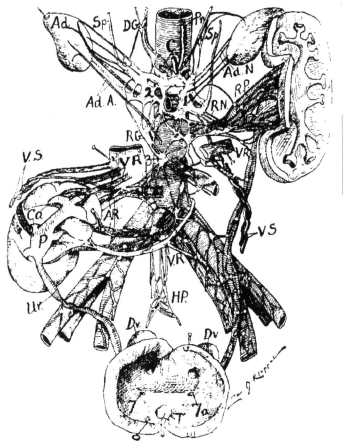

**NERVUS VASOMOTORIUS OF THE TRACTUS URINARIUS
(CONGENITALLY DISLOCATED)**

Fig. 136. This illustration is drawn from a specimen I secured at an autopsy. The right kidney was dislocated, resting on the right common iliac artery, with its pelvis (P) and hilum facing ventralward. The adrenal (Ad.) remained *in situ*. It was a congenital renal dislocation, and was accompanied with congenital malformations in the sympathetic nerve, or nervus vasomotorius. 1 and 2 is the abdominal brain. It sends five branches to the adrenal from the right half (2). Though the sympathetic system is malformed, yet the principal rules as regards the sympathetic ganglia still prevail, viz., ganglia exist at the origin of abdominal visceral vessels, e. g., 3, at the origin of the inferior mesenteric artery; at the root of the renal vessels, HP is no doubt the ganglion originally at the root of the common iliacs (coalesced). In this specimen the right ureter was 5 inches in length, while the left was 11½. This specimen demonstrates that the abdominal brain is located at the origin of the renal, celiac, and superior mesenteric vessels—i. e., it is a vascular brain (*cerebrum vasomotorius*). The solid and compact anastomosis of the nervus vasomotorius of the tractus urinarius with nerve plexuses of all other abdominal visceral tracts is evident.

tablet (or more, as required to move the bowels freely, once daily) is placed on the tongue before meals and followed by 8 ounces of water (better hot). Also at 10 A. M., 3 P. M., and at bedtime 1-6 to 1 tablet is placed on the tongue and followed by a glassful of any fluid. In the combined treatment, 1-3 of the (NaCl) sodium chloride tablet (containing 11 grains) and (1-6 to 3) alkaline tablets are placed on the tongue together every two hours and followed by a glass of fluid. The six glasses of fluid may be milk, butter-

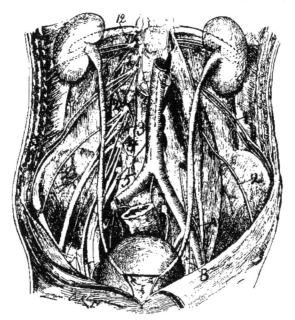

Fig. 137. Illustrates the relation of the spinal nerves to the tractus urinarius, especially to the plexus lumbalis. The ureter is intimately connected with the genito-crural nerve (A); hence the pain reflected in the thigh and scrotum in ureteral colic and other ureteral diseases. (2) Ileo-inguinal nerve.

milk, cream, eggnog—nourishment. This method of treatment furnishes alkaline bases (sodium, potassium, and ammonium) to combine with the free uric acid in the urine, producing perfectly soluble alkaline urates and materially diminishing the insoluble free uric acid in the urine. Besides, the alkaline laxative tablet increases the peristalsis, absorption and secretion of the intestinal tract, stimulating the sensation of the mucosa—aiding evacuation.

I have termed the sodium chloride and alkaline laxative method the *vis-*

ceral drainage treatment. The alkaline and sodium chloride tablets take the place of so-called mineral waters. I continue this dietetic treatment of fluids and food for weeks, months, and the results are remarkably successful, especially in pathologic physiology of visceral tracts. The urine becomes clarified like spring water and increased in quantity. The tractus intestinalis becomes freely evacuated, regularly, daily. The blood is relieved of waste laden and irritating material. The tractus cutis eliminates freely and the skin becomes normal. The appetite increases. The sleep improves. The patient becomes hopeful, natural energy returns. The sewers of the body are drained and flushed to a maximum.

Had space permitted it might have enhanced the clearness of the above subject to first discuss the pathologic physiology of the tractus urinarius, and, second, to discuss the pathologic physiology of the contents of the tractus urinarius.

CHAPTER XXXVI.

PATHOLOGIC PHYSIOLOGY OF THE TRACTUS NERVOSUS (ABDOMINALIS).

The man who builds a home erects a temple—the flame upon the hearth is the sacred fire.—Robert Ingersoll, American (1844-1904).

The peritoneum sheaths and lines.—Dr. P. T. Burns.

The ideal nervous system consists of a ganglion cell, a conducting cord and a periphery, i. e., a receiver, a transmitter and a reorganizer. This simple view of the structure of the nervous system at once suggests its function, viz., that of reception (periphery apparatus—skin, mucosa), transmission (conducting apparatus—nerve cords), reorganization (ganglion cell—brain). The nervous apparatus is the highest and most perfect of known organism. Mental action or nerve force, the most subtle of all forces, depends on it. The nervous system includes the most profound secrets of life—it is the climax of organism. First and foremost, the zone of the physiology of the tractus nervosus is not exactly defined—it is liberally elastic. Secondly, the pathologic physiology of the tractus nervosus possesses an expansive, undefinable zone before established pathologic anatomy can be recognized. The pathologic physiology of the tractus nervosus comprehends the fields of neuralgia, hyperesthesia, anesthesia, sensation, motion, melancholia, hysteria, neurasthenia, with innumerable irritable weaknesses of the nervous system. Absorption, secretion and peristalsis of viscera are the elements or means by which we recognize the pathologic physiology. In the numerous manifestations of symptoms of pathologic physiology of the tractus nervosus of the abdomen a few considerations may be suggestive and helpful in practice. First and foremost, many subjects are not perfect physically or mentally. Such subjects are prone to pathologic physiology. They possess inferior anatomy and physiology. Structure and function are of minimum perfection. Their nervous system is not stable. We should consider these defections or unstable conditions under long-employed or established terms, associated with which has grown a stately literature, as *stigma, habitus, asthenia congenita, heredity, predisposition, degeneracy.*

Nervous persons are afflicted with pathologic physiology. Nervous persons manifest a defective resistence. They are incapacitated for sustained effort. Nervous persons present premature exhaustion on persistent mental or physical effort. The reason of the nervousness is the anatomy and physiology of the tractus nervosus is inferior, its structure and function is deteriorated. Their nervous system is irritable, weak, defective, unstable, functionating much of the time with disorder and friction, like some watches, which maintain incorrect time. Nervous subjects are chiefly congenital unfortunates. They are born with defects, with stigma, a habitus, neuro-pathic predispositions—a condition which tends to degeneracy with facility. Nervousness, though frequently an announcement of an enfeebled nervous system, yet it may be evoked, aggravated, by some irritation external to the nerve apparatus. Neurotic spells appear with as much mysticism as they disappear. The only trace is the memory of the disordered pathologic physiology. There is doubtless more or less foundation, for these inscrutable neurotic conditions, to be established in the state of the tractus vascularis, congestion, anemia. The tone and tension of the abdominal muscles control the abdominal circulation. Diseases of the tractus intestinalis compromise the tractus nervosus by damaging its integrity—in structure and function. One of the best terms to apply to subjects who are persistently afflicted with pathologic physiology is the word *habitus*, e. g., we have the habitus phthisicus, habitus splanchnopticus, habitus nervosus, habitus dyspepticus. The ensemble of symptoms associated with splanchnoptosia may well be termed habitus splanchnopticus. It is heredity in so far that the subject possesses a predisposition and the main defect is inferior anatomy and physiology. In the habitus splanchnopticus there is the gracile skeleton, the elongated flat thorax, extensive intercostal space, acute epigastric angle, the sacculated, pendulous abdomen, limited muscularis and panniculus adiposus, the labored respiration. The costa fluctuans decima of B. Stiller, the peculiar habitus in form—presenting evident pathologic physiology. A marked factor in pathologic physiology of splanchnoptosis is the changed defective circulation, venous congestion. Generally, any subject with a "habitus" possesses an unstable nervous system. The dyspepsia accompanying the habitus splanchnopticus is perhaps more due to the neuropathic disposition than to the splanchnoptosia, hence the terms dyspepsia nervosa, or stigma dyspepticum. The habitus neurasthenicus presents pathologic physiology of the tractus nervosus—a condition of exhaustion or weakness of the nervous system, accompanied by physical and mental efficiency. Habitus neurasthenicus is a fatigue disease of the nervous system. It is characterized by the presence of motor, sensory, psychic and visceral symptoms—all fatigued, tired, exhausted. This habitus is especially characterized by weakness, or inefficiency and irritability of the tractus nervosus. The physician can detect spots of hyperesthesia, spinal irritation, fatigue of the special sense, auditory and retinal hyperesthesia—all pathologic physiology, no pathologic anatomy. However, if pathologic anatomy exists in the body, it is liable to intensify the pathologic physiology, the subject of habitus neurasthenicus, precipitating storms of neurotic spells. The physician can detect the pathologic physiology, but not pathologic anatomy. The subject is afflicted more or less throughout life with pathologic physiology. When such subjects maintain additional strains, as gestation and the care of growing children, pathologic physiology in the tractus nervosus becomes pronounced and frequent, e. g., the habitus neurasthenicus may be in abeyance, quiescent, for a long period of time when the entrance of a pelvic disease, a myometritis, salpingitis, pelvic peritenitis, may initiate, aggravate, an intense neurotic state. It is not due merely to the so-called reflexes, but because the habitus neurasthenicus, the weak, irritable nervous system, has been aggravated, traumatized, become unbalanced, exhausted, fatigued. Its inherent vital power is deficient and readily passes into a state of pathologic physiology.

A lesson right here may be pointed that surgeons should operate for surgical indications only, not for function indications. First and foremost, the gynecologist must learn to decide by an analytic exclusion diagnosis whether the subject has a habitus neurasthenicus, a pelvic disease, or the two combined. The test of a gynecologist is his ability to diagnose the disease—not to do an operation.

The exquisitely, finely balanced nervous system of woman makes it liable to imperfections of development—stigmata. Such a perfect organism as the tractus nervosus is prone to disease. The intimate and profound relation of the tractus nervosus to the tractus genitalis in woman demands that a gynecologist be a physician of comprehension, or knowledge, understanding the vast fields of the tractus nervosus and tractus genitalis, as well as their profound relation.

The indiscreet and general surgeon announces that gynecology is "passing," and has become a segment of general surgery. This assertion presents limited comprehension. Is the oculist and aurist passing? Is the dermatologist, neurologist and laryngologist passing? Among the Germans, the most profoundly learned in medicine, specialists are progressively increasing. The fact is that legitimate gynecology, like all other specialities, is just beginning. Gynecology to-day is practically as broad as the entire medical field of thirty years ago. The gynecologist must comprehend not only the organs in his own special field (tractus genitalis), but also the adjacent organs involved in practice or stimulating gynecological disease, as the tractus intestinalis, tractus nervosus, and tractus urinarius. In the interest of the patient, no specialist can be limited exactly to the organs of his own specialty, for he should study the organs secondarily afflicted or dependent on the affections of the viscera on which he practices. The specialist must understand the anatomic and pathologic relations of specialized organs to adjacent territories, as vomiting (tractus intestinalis) to pregnancy (tractus genitalis), as albumin (tractus urinarius) to pregnancy (tractus genitalis).

The more intimate changing relations of associated organs in structure and function, the more valuable will be the study of the differential diagnosis in disease. The gynecologist should execute all necessary technique which will enable him to diagnose and treat diseases, dependent on or associated with the tractus genitalis—as cystitis, ureteritis, splanchnoptosia, mammary disease, constipation, nephritis, proctitis, thyroid disease. The borders of a specialty cannot be marked by the rim of a circle, but by the diseases dependent on and resulting from the specialized system of viscera. Every special science gradually unfolds its own dependent and associated relations.

Gynecology has been a typical example. It forced a divorce from general surgery, to which it never will return, from sheer magnitude. One mind cannot master more than one visceral tract with its relations. The unfolding of gynecology has increased the interest and usefulness of its domain. It has shown the delicate balance and relations of all abdominal viscera on the abdominal sympathetic brain. Practically all progress, new ideas, must come from specialists. The specialist is a permanent factor in medical progress, from whom will practically emanate discoveries and rational treatment. However, the present and future specialist will not be limited to a single visceral tractus for the diagnosis and therapy of his independent field, but will study adjacent or remote visceral tracts which may lend aid in the differential diagnosis and rational treatment. The gynecologist should diagnose and treat all diseases primarily or secondarily, dependent on the life, function and pathologic conditions of the tractus genitalis, as sacropubic hernia, rectocele, vesicocele, splanchnoptosia; dependent on rapid and frequent gestations (nephroptosia, gastroptosia, coloptosia, hepaptosia—relaxed abdominal walls). The rock and base of medical practice (special or general) is the diagnosis which enables the physician to employ rational treatment, to act for the best interest of the patient. Large numbers of women with marked splanchnoptosia dependent on the work performed by the tractus genitalis, as gestations, come to the gynecologist. The tractus genitalis, though primarily the basic cause of splanchnoptosia, itself is no more ill than the tractus urinarius, tractus intestinalis, or the relaxed abdominal walls. It is the duty of the gynecologist to treat such cases. The general surgeon is no more an expert in special departments than is the general practitioner. The reason for the operation, i. e., the diagnosis, is a thousand fold more expert than the mere technique of surgical procedure. *Predisposing* factors to pathologic physiology in the tractus nervosus are defective nurtrition, variations of metabolism, chlorosis, anemia, hemorrhages, deficient or excessive secretion, premature senescence, strained physical and mental efforts. Heredity transmits defects which are the foundation for aggravated pathologic physiology. When the subject has an established habitus, as habitus splanchnopticus, habitus neurasthenicus, habitus phthisicus, and predisposing factors become imposed to, the subject is burdened with extreme pathologic physiology. An excellent example of artificial habitus is the numerous stigmata arising from the total removal of ovaries in young women, which condition might be termed habitus ovaricae neurasthenicus. The young woman with castrated ovaries experiences an intense, aggravated, premature climacterium—she is suffering from pathologic physiology of the tractus nervosus. The patient is afflicted with flushing (disturbed circulatory centre), flashes (disturbance of caloric centre), perspiration (disturbance of the perspiratory centre). She has depression, melancholia, excessive panniculus adiposus, growths of hair. In some subjects the sensation of the tractus nervosus of the abdomen is awry. Subjects complain of animals crawling within the abdomen. This matter may be explained by supersensitiveness or hyperesthesia of the mucosa of the tractus intestinalis from gas or contents. More than one operation has been performed for such condition. It may be incidentally remarked that it requires much study and discreet judgment to decide neurosis of the tractus nervosus abdominalis and the nervous disturbances produced by the dominating nerve-supplied genital tract—both conditions induce, aggravate, pathologic physiology in the abdominal nerves, e. g., one of the most characteristic lesions accompanying the habitus neurasthenicus—producing pathologic physiology—is defective development of the tractus genitalis. I think among the scores of women I have examined with defective development of the genitals that at least 95 per cent were neurotics manifesting pathologic physiology of the tractus nervosus. Does the neurosis precede (congenital), accompany the defective development of the genitals or is it accidental to it? The most probable view is that it is congenital, and marks an ill development of

Fig. 138. Nerves of the internal genitals.

the organism. The habitus neurasthenicus or habitus hystericus are not diseases of the genitals but of the nervous system with an hereditary burden and perhaps an acquired burden. These conditions required vast study to differentiate in gynecologic practice. The habitus chlorosis is another example of a disease closely associated with the tractus genitalis. It is doubtless hereditary; occurs in girls from fourteen to twenty-four years of age, i. e., at puberty or the developmental stage; is accompanied by increased panniculus adiposus and neurotic symptoms. Chlorosis is associated with defective development of the genitals in 75 per cent of subjects. Genital functions are defective. The nerves governing secretion (ovarian) are perhaps defective. In diagnosing pathologic physiology of the abdominal nervous system it is well to determine the etiology, as acquired factors enhance conditions, e. g., the tractus nervosus of a pregnant woman is more irritable, more liable to pathologic physiology, than the non-pregnant. The nursing woman is frequently in a state of pathologic physiology.

TREATMENT OF PATHOLOGIC PHYSIOLOGY OF THE TRACTUS NERVOSUS.

The treatment of subjects with disturbances—pathologic physiology—in the abdominal nerves is difficult in ordinary practice because the acquired factors are inseparably associated with continuous environments, with habitat. The etiology and consequent habitus or stigma must be diagnosed by careful examination in individual subjects. The reason the sanatorium is so successful in the treatment of the nervous patients is the patient is removed from the environments, from the habitat, in which the disease developed. The provocative or aggravating factors must be generally eliminated. It may be constipation, deficient drinking of fluids, the ingesting of improper concentrated foods, which leave insufficient indigestible residue to provoke intestinal peristalsis. It may be sedentary habits, insufficient exercise or deficient fresh air. It may be excessive work and worry, insomnia. In the subject with the habitus neurasthenicus I am in general opposed to the so-called Mitchell rest cure. The neurasthenic may possess fatigued nerves but not fatigued muscles. I attempt to treat the neurasthenic by maintaining her in the fresh air and muscular activity all day. In the subjects I administer active visceral drainage and coarse foods which leave a large undigestible residue. She is improved by the bicycle, by games requiring muscular activity, rides which massage the viscera, fresh air, appropriate diet, and ample fluid at regular intervals. Some neurasthenics are practically unmanageable. I am now treating a woman twenty-seven years of age who has lain in bed for three years. She says her nerves could not stand walking in the sunshine. Physically I can detect no pathologic anatomy—simply pathologic physiology. By forced feeding she retains ample flesh. During the last six months, by all kinds of persuasion, we succeeded in inducing her to walk one block daily. Maximum visceral drainage and appropriate dietetics maintains apparently a healthy physique. We agree with Dr. John G. Clark that several kinds of neurasthenics exist. The gynecologist meets with three kinds of neurasthenics, viz., (a) a neurasthenic of congenital origin—habitus neurasthenicus congenita—who practice almost continually genital introspection where the physicians can not detect genital pathologic anatomy. She is constantly occupied by views regarding genital and sexual life. The treatment of such neuropathic subjects is lifelong, firm discipline, hygiene, dietetic, fresh air for twenty-four hours a day, ample fluids, physical exercise. (b) A neurasthenic with coincident visceral lesion but each entirely independent of the other, as may occur in the tractus genitalis, tractus intestinalis, tractus urinarius. In the second condition the additional treatment is to remove the lesions of the sole visceral tract; (c) a third kind of neurasthenic is where the neurasthenia is dependent on an organic, visceral lesion. The tractus nervosus of the originally predisposed, neuropathic subject was provoked, aggravated, into a state of pathologic physiology by the organic lesion. The treatment of this third class is repair of the organic lesion and systematic visceral drainage by means of fluids and foods.

1. *Dietetic.* The diet of neurotic patients should be regulated under strict discipline. It should consist of cereals, vegetables, albuminates (egg, milk), and limited meals—mixed diet. The high spices, cakes, puddings, pies, stimulants should be eliminated.

2. *Fluids.* Ample at regular intervals—8 ounces every two hours for at least six times daily. This forty-eight ounces of fluids daily may be nourishing fluid—as, milk, buttermilk, eggnog, cereal gruels.

3. *Salt rubs,* which the patient administers to herself once or twice daily, at stated times for stated duration.

4. *Massage,* which should be administered as much as possible by the patient herself. The patient can be taught massage of the abdominal muscles, which especially benefits the abdominal visceral tracts.

5. *Exercise* is absolutely necessary for health. The neurotic patient continually complains of tiredness and fatigue. The fatigue belongs to the nerves. It is not muscle fatigue, hence the muscular activity should be vigorously maintained in walking, riding, games—all distracting the patient's attention from herself. Muscular exercise influences circulation and hence nourishment.

6. *Fresh air* should be continuous day and night. The sleeping-window should be open all night. The window of the day-room should be continuously open. Cold, fresh air is an invaluable therapeutic agent in neurasthenic disturbances and tuberculoses.

In order to assist the foods and fluids to secure maximum visceral drainage I place on the tongue every two hours a tablet containing 8 grains of sodium chloride (NaCl) and a part or multiple of an alkaline tablet [composed of aloes ($\frac{1}{2}$ gr.), cascara sagrada ($\frac{1}{10}$ gr.), $NaHCO_3$ (1 gr.), $KHCO_3$ ($\frac{1}{2}$ gr.), and $MgSO_4$ (2 gr.),] followed by 8 ounces of fluid. This visceral drainage method I followed systematically for weeks and months, resulting in successful maximum visceral drainage, with increased nourishment, improved sleep. The elimination of waste-laden products benefits the nervous system—the pathologic physiology is reduced to a minimum and the patient recovers.

CHAPTER XXXVII.

PATHOLOGIC PHYSIOLOGY OF THE TRACTUS VASCULARIS.

New ideas are first resented, second tolerated and finally adopted.
Men may come and men may go, but I go on forever.—Tennyson's Brook.

The functions of the tractus vascularis are peristalsis (rhythm), secretion, absorption, sensation. Its object is to transport universal nourishing fluid, the blood, to the general body. In pathologic physiology of the tractus vascularis there are two concomitant factors with which to deal, viz., (A) *the vascular tract*; (B) *its contents*. The pathologic physiology of the tractus vascularis and its contents each possess a wide range.

(A) THE VASCULAR TRACT.

The *tractus vascularis* is a cylindrical tube possessing the form of a complete circle, with localized constrictions (capillaries) and dilatations (heart-arteries, and veins). This vascular canal circulates universal fluid tissue through the body. It has a dual object for tissue, viz., that of import and export service. The tractus vascularis will become of vast therapeutic utility. Dr. Bier, a man of forty-five years of age, Professor of Surgery in Bonn, Germany, has preached for years the value of artificial congestion in the cure of disease. Bier's introduction of artificial congestion is one of the greatest contributions to medicine of the present century. Lister's contribution was but a temporary matter, for now we do not need it, as we have learned asepsis. Bier's method will always be useful while the tractus vascularis remains. Men may come and men may go, but the tractus vascularis goes on forever. Bier suggests to the profession to control the segments of the tractus vascularis and its contents for therapeutic purposes.

In the study of the pathologic physiology of the hemogenous tract the exact functions must be held in view, viz., peristalsis, secretion, absorption and sensation. The condition of the arterial wall and the diameter of the lumen influence the flow of blood. The lumen of the artery is controlled by a plexiform, nodular, fenestrated network of nerves and ganglia which ensheaths the artery. The lumen of the artery is regulated chiefly by reflexes that arise in different regions of the body. Stimulation of peripheral nerve will induce generally reflex arterial constriction and this elevates blood pressure. All nervous impulses from the heart are capable of governing the calibre of arteries; therefore, the degree of arterial contraction depends chiefly on the nervous impulses which they receive. For the theme of our subject—the abdominal vessels—the condition of the numerous abdominal arteries innervated by the splanchnic nerves is of significant importance in regard to maintaining peripheral resistance, as opposed to the splanchnic innervation.

A brief discussion of the four physiologic functions of the tractus vascularis in a condition of pathologic physiology will suffice to present our views.

(1) PERISTALSIS (EXCESSIVE, DEFICIENT, DISPROPORTIONATE).

(a) *Excessive* peristalsis of the vascular tract is a common occurrence in life. The marble paleness of fright and fear present excessive contraction of vessels. The cold hands and feet of certain persons show spasm of vessels. Excessive cardiac activity is frequently noted. The cardiac hypertrophies remain long in the stage of pathologic physiology as compensatory hypertrophies. In certain renal diseases the arterial pressure (arterial peristalsis) increases gradually until the myocardium has attained maximum dimensions for the coronary arteries to nourish. Excessive arterial peristalsis may be an indefinite time in the stage of pathologic physiology, as cardiac hypertrophy, arterial sclerosis, nephritis. It is during the stage of pathologic physiology of the previous immediately noted disease that medical treatment is of practical value by the therapeutic application of appropriate dietetics, fluids and methods of living. Vigorous exercise will produce excessive peristalsis of the tractus vascularis. Not infrequently we observe the abdominal aorta maintaining an extraordinarily vigorous peristalsis for hours—in fact, it performs with such vigor that the inexperienced may diagnose abdominal aneurism. It is the detection of excessive vascular peristalsis (pathologic physiology) in its incipient stage that allows ample time to remove the causes of disease before the destructive pathologic anatomy has appeared in the line that renders utility to medical skill.

Excessive peristalsis does not always result in forcing excessive blood to tissue, because the arterial pulse caused mainly by the variation of pressure within the artery and the results of intermittent expulsion of blood jets from the heart may become so deranged and disordered that blood pressure is low. Arterial blood pressure depends on the amount of blood forced into the arteries by the heart and the peripheral arterial resistance. In other words, blood pressure depends on the blood volume, rigidity of arterial walls and opportunity of escape. Age influences blood pressure. We note pathologic physiology of the tractus vascularis in asphyxia. Lead colic is usually associated with high arterial pressure as well as the early stages of peritonitis. Renal disease may induce high arterial pressure, i. e., an excessive vascular peristalsis.

(b) *Deficient* peristalsis of the vascular system is frequently encountered. The myocardium and arterial muscularis may be diminutive. The vascular lumen may be limited. The nervus vasomotorius may be inactive, sluggish, of minimum power. We frequently meet the small, weak cardiac and pulse action. Deficient arterial peristalsis results in deficient tissue nourishment and cerebral action. We frequently meet persons with deficient vascular peristalsis from dietetic and habitat errors. The subjects consume concentrated foods and insufficient fluids, with a resulting pulse of limited volume and power. This deficient arterial peristalsis and power is pathologic. Physiology, however, sooner or later passes from the incipient stage to that of established pathologic anatomy by continued repetition. The employment of ingesta, which leaves a large indigestible residue, and ample fluids at regular intervals, quickly restores a pulse of full volume, i. e., vigorous arterial peristalsis presenting volume and power. Errors of habitat, inactivity, sedentary, may be accompanied by deficient arterial peristalsis, which are promptly improved by appropriate exercise. Deficient peristalsis of the heart or inability to drive the congested blood through the lungs will, however, act as a prophylaxis against pulmonary tuberculosis (it is a cure by congestion).

Extensive areas of blood vessel dilatation may initiate a marked fall in arterial pressure and slowing of circulation, for the quantity of blood is insufficient to occupy the entire vascular calibre if dilated. General vascular dilatation may result from general loss of vascular elasticity and consequent expansion of the vessel lumen. A general loss of vascular tonus may occur. If the splanchnic vessels lose their tonus they become distended with blood, while the arteries, especially to the periphery, skin, become but partially depleted. In certain autopsies the splanchnic vessels appear so extensively distended with blood that the subject seemed as if he had bled to death in his own abdominal vessel. Deficient peristalsis may be due to paresis of the vaso-motor centre.

(c) *Disproportionate* peristalsis of the tractus vascularis consists in irregularity of action in different segments of the vascular tract, e. g., the blushing of embarrassment, the flushing of the climacterium, is local dilatation of the vascular tracts. The clubbed fingers of the subject with patent foramen ovale is pathologic physiology of the blood channel. The most patent example of disproportionate peristalsis of the vascular tract is the defective cardiac valves —the cardiac insufficiency. The disproportionate arterial peristalsis is due to abnormal volumes of blood in local segments of the tractus vascularis, e. g., in insufficiency of the aortic valves the coronary arteries receive excessive blood and produce cardiac hypertrophy. The volume of blood remains excessive in the heart and dependent portions of the body, while in portions of the body where force is required to propel the blood, it is deficient.

Disproportionate arterial peristalsis may be observed during gestation when the arteria uterina ovarica sports an excessive volume of blood. During constipation the arteria mesenterica inferior is transporting insufficient blood, and hence inducing insufficient colonic peristalsis for regular fecal evacuations. The giant hypertrophic member of the body presents an excellent example of disproportionate vascular peristalsis. The mottled surface is disproportionate circulation. Disproportionate arterial peristalsis may be observed in the maximum functions of the several visceral organs, e. g., food in the gastrium or enteron entices extra blood. Extra fluids increase especially the activity of the arteria renalis. Excessive, deficient, disproportionate vascular peristalsis may long remain in the field of pathologic physiology—functional disease—allowing ample time for diagnosis and therapeutic correction before the field of pathologic anatomy—compromised structure—is reached.

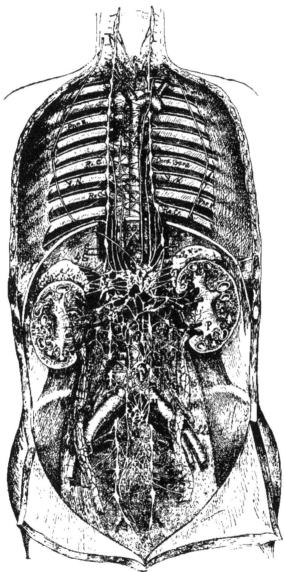

Fig. 139

(2) SECRETION (EXCESSIVE, DEFICIENT, DISPROPORTIONATE).

(d) *Excessive* secretion of the vascular tract may be observed in edema, ascites.

(e) *Deficient* secretion presents few practical examples.

(f) *Disproportionate* secretion is irregular secretion in different segments of the vascular tract.

(3) ABSORPTION (EXCESSIVE, DEFICIENT, DISPROPORTIONATE).

(4) SENSATION (EXCESSIVE, DEFICIENT, DISPROPORTIONATE).

(g) *Excessive* sensation in the tractus vascularis indicates an irritable weakness in the nervus vasomotorius (sympathetic), which rules the visceral tract. It appears that it is the blood in the vascular lumen which incites peristalsis, as may be demonstrated in the urine and the ureter.

The excessive sensation in the vascular tract is synonymous with the state of the nervus vasomotorius. Some vascular tracts with inferior anatomy and physiology execute peristalsis in a wild, irregular, violent, disordered manner on slight provocation; they possess excessive sensation, pathologic physiology, or are afflicted with a habitus nervosus, stigma nervosus. I have observed the heart executing its action irregularly and 120 per minute for weeks with no demonstrable pathologic anatomy. Such a person possesses an excessive sensation in the tractus vascularis. It is an abnormal function. The excessive beating of the abdominal aorta, and beating in various parts of the body, refers to excessive sensation—hyperesthesia—in the tractus vascularis. Blood contents in the tractus vascularis may be waste laden, irritating, and should be sewered by fluids.

(h) *Deficient* sensation in the vascular tract may be observed in the slow, sluggish pulse. In icterus the pulse may be 50; sensation is obtunded, dulled, by morbific elements bathing the innumerable sympathetic ganglia, checking their excitability.

(i) *Disproportionate* sensation is irregular sensation in different segments of the tractus vascularis. Also one may observe in certain persons local congestions or anemia. Cold feet or hands produce disproportionate circulation in the body.

TREATMENT OF PATHOLOGIC PHYSIOLOGY OF THE TRACTUS VASCULARIS.

The treatment of pathologic physiology of the tractus vascularis consists in correcting the deviation of its functions (which are peristalsis, absorption, secretion and sensation).

Since pathologic physiology of the tractus vascularis lies between physiology and pathologic anatomy, it should be amenable to treatment. First and foremost, a diagnosis should be made and cause removed. The treatment is accomplished through: (a) Ample fluids administered at regular intervals; (b) appropriate diet; (c) rational habitat; (d) suitable avocation. Maximum elimination or visceral drainage is the rational treatment.

(a) *Visceral Drainage by Fluids.*—The most general feature of a patient suffering from pathologic physiology of the tractus vascularis is deficient visceral drainage. The sovereign remedy is water. One of the best laxatives is water. The most rational stimulant to the renal (and intestinal) epithelium is sodium chloride—common salt (one-fourth to one-half normal physiologic salt solution). I administer eight ounces of one-fourth to one-half normal salt solution every two hours for six times daily, i. e., three pints daily. (Note.—NaCl is contraindicated in parenchymatous nephritis.) The three pints of normal salt solution fill the lumen of the artery and induce normal reflexes. The pulse becomes a full volume. The powerful arterial stream sewers the body of waste laden blood and irritating material. The arteries functionate best with a maximum volume of blood. Also the fluids induce maximum functions of adjacent visceral tracts—urinary, intestinal, perspiratory. Perfect elimination — maximum visceral drainage—may prevent arterial sclerosis. Maximum visceral drainage maintains in mechanical suspension the insoluble uric acid (preventing the formation of ureteral calculus) and the cholesterine (preventing the formation of hepatic calculus).

It aids the sodium, potassium and ammonium salts to form combinations with uric acid, producing soluble urates. The eight ounces of one-half or one-quarter normal salt solution six times daily stimulates the epithelium of the tractus perspiratorius (inducing sweating) and the epithelium of the tractus intestinalis, inducing secretions which liquefy feces, preventing constipation. It also stimulates the epithelium of the tractus urinarius, inducing increased quantities of urine. The druggist manufactures for me sodium chloride, tablets of twelve grains each, from which I can employ fragments or multiples in the treatment.*

(b) *Visceral Drainage by Foods.*—The great functions of the tractus vascularis—peristalsis, absorption, secretion, sensation—are produced and maintained by fluids and foods. To drain the tractus vascularis, the adjacent visceral tracts (intestinal, urinary, perspiratory) should be excited to peristalsis. Hence, for the intestinal tract foods which leave an indigestible residue only are appropriate; all adjacent visceral tracts must be stimulated to maximum peristalsis, secretion, absorption, in order to aid that of the tractus vascularis. Rational foods must contain appropriate salts whose bases may form combinations which are soluble, as sodium, potassium and ammonium combined with uric acid and urates. The proper foods are cereals, vegetables, albuminates (milk, eggs), mixed foods. Meats should be limited, as they enhance uric acid formation and waste-laden blood.

In order to stimulate the epithelium (sensation) of the digestive, urinary and perspiratory tracts, with consequent increase of peristalsis, absorption and secretion, I use a part or a multiple of an alkaline tablet of the following composition: Cascara sagrada, one-fortieth of a grain; aloes, one-third of a grain; $NaHCO_3$, one grain; $KHCO_3$, one-half grain; $MgSO_4$ two grains. The tablet* is used as follows:

---

*The sodium chloride and alkaline tablets are manufactured by Searle & Hereth Co., Chicago.

One-sixth to one tablet (or more as required to move the bowels freely once daily) is placed on the tongue before meals and followed by eight ounces of water (better hot). Also at 10 A. M., 3 P. M. and at bedtime one-sixth to one tablet is placed on the tongue and followed by a glassful of any fluid (buttermilk is excellent).

The Combined Treatment (Sodium Chloride and Alkaline Tablets).—In the combined treatment one-third of the NaCl, the sodium chloride tablet (containing twelve grains), and one-sixth to two alkaline tablets are placed on the tongue together before each meal, followed by eight ounces of fluid (better hot), and also at 10 A. M., 3 P. M. and at bedtime, followed by eight ounces of fluid (buttermilk is excellent), i. e., every two hours, and followed by a glass of fluid. The six eight-ounce glasses may be fluid food—as milk, buttermilk, cream, beef tea, egg-nog—fluid nourishment. This visceral drainage treatment furnishes alkaline bases (sodium, potassium and ammonium) to combine with the free uric acid in the urine, producing soluble urates. Besides, the alkaline laxative tablet increases the peristalsis, sensation, absorption and secretion of the intestinal tract, stimulating the sensation of the mucosa, aiding evacuation. It ends in correcting the pathologic physiology of the tractus vascularis. The object of the visceral drainage treatment is to improve elimination and digestion.

I have termed the sodium chloride and alkaline laxative method the *visceral drainage treatment.* The alkaline and sodium tablets take the place of the so-called mineral waters. I continue this dietetic treatment of fluids and food for weeks, months, and the results are remarkably successful, especially in pathologic physiology of the tractus vascularis and adjacent visceral tracts. The pulse volume becomes full. The urine becomes clarified like spring-water and increased in quantity. The tractus intestinalis becomes freely evacuated regularly daily. The blood is relieved of waste laden and irritating material. The tractus cutis eliminates freely, and the skin becomes normal. The appetite increases. The sleep improves. The patient becomes hopeful, natural energy returns. The sewers of the body are drained and flushed to a maximum.

The maximum function of viscera by means of fluid diet, activity, induces maximum drainage of viscera, eliminating irritating matters from the body and insures normal peristalsis and normal reflexes for the vascular tract.

(c) The habitat should be suitable. It should allow fresh air day and night. Environments constitute much of the essence of living.

(d) The avocation should suit the physique. In maximum elimination—complete visceral drainage—every visceral tract (urinary, intestinal, perspiratory) must normally functionate. Hence all rational therapeutics (fluid, diet, habitat, avocation) must be applied to secure maximum, universal visceral drainage. No single visceral tract can functionate defectively without damage to adjacent tracts.

(A) PATHOLOGIC PHYSIOLOGY OF THE CONTENTS OF THE TRACTUS VASCULARIS. — THE BLOOD.

The pathologic physiology of the blood cannot be separated from the pathologic physiology of the several visceral organs. The blood represents universal fluid tissue and every organ receives and emits material to it. The blood has an import and export service (transporting oxygen to tissue and carbonic acid gas and waste products from tissue). The significant blood—a medium of exchange between the external world and the tissues—enters every organ through the tractus vascularis, distributing nutritive material to every tissue. It is the source of all secretion. When one concludes the enormous amount of interchange (assimilation and waste) between the blood and tissue, it becomes evident that the pathologic physiology of the blood is a wide zone. It also becomes evident that the zone of pathologic physiology is an incipient zone to that of pathologic anatomy. First, in the foreground of pathologic physiology of the contents of the tractus vascularis should be included those diseases which indicate dominant, recognized changes in the blood, as anemia, chlorosis. Second, single symptoms may represent the changes of an unknown disease, as cachexia ub carcinoma, diseases of the adrenals.

Here projects in the foreground (primary) hemogenous disease or (secondary) visceral disease. The composition of the blood—plasma, red and white corpuscles—depends to a certain extent on the condition of the tissue in the different districts of the body. Though the blood contains an extensive variety of substances, its composition is relatively constant on account of the rapid flow of its current, and the rapid secretion of substances occurring in it in excess. The composition of the blood will change when pathologic physiology arises in any organ. The essential constituents of the blood with which the physician deals are: (a) red corpuscles (130, to 1000 parts); (b) white corpuscles (253, to 1000 reds); (c) plasma (800, to 1000 parts of blood). The great typical fields of pathologic physiology of the contents of the tractus vascularis are 1, anemia—e. g., chlorosis; 2, leukemia—e. g., splenic and glandular diseases; 3, cachexia—e. g., carcinoma and adrenal diseases.

Changes in the blood cells and hemaglobin are recognized with relative facility and hence they are more certainly known than the changes in the plasma. The contents of the tractus vascularis—the blood—presents a rich field for study in pathologic physiology and fortunately for prophylaxis. The blood has an extensive range of pathologic physiology through the variation of hemaglobin, through change in number of white and red corpuscles, through changing composition of plasma. The study of the varying stages of anemia (e. g., chlorosis) and hyperemia (congestion) present far-reaching possibilities in therapeutics. We will first consider the red corpuscles.

I. Red Blood Corpuscles and Hemaglobin (1000 Reds to 8 Whites).

The red blood corpuscles constitute about ⅟ of the blood (130, to 1000 parts of blood). The most striking feature of pathologic physiology of the blood is anemia. In anemia the marked phenomenon is a reduction of the hemaglobin or the red corpuscles or both. Other related changes doubtless occur in the white corpuscles and plasma. Anemia presents many forms, acute and chronic, and grades (from delicate paleness to pernicious anemia) as well as numerous conditions of etiology (acute, or chronic loss of blood). The simplest form of acute anemia results from sudden loss of blood, through vascular wounds, hemorrhages, e. g., during parturition excessive quantities of blood may be lost simply producing anemia. The grades of anemia depend on the relative quantity of blood loss. Should the hemorrhage exceed a certain bound the patient dies from suffocation; there are insufficient red corpuscles to transport oxygen to the tissue for internal respiration. Should the patient lose suddenly 15 per cent to 30 per cent of corporeal blood, it may require weeks and months to recuperate, during which time certain phases of pathologic physiology of the tractus vascularis may be observed. The patient presents a pale appearance.

The simplest form of chronic anemia results from periodic, repeated or continuous loss of blood, as menorrhagia from uterine myoma, repeated loss of blood from hemorrhoids, from renal papillæ. The blood shows a diminishing quantity of hemaglobin. Chronic and acute anemia are not independent diseases, they are clinical symptoms of pathologic physiology. In anemia there is to consider: 1, the quantity of oxygen in the lung; 2, the quantity of hemaglobin in the blood; 3, the rate of transportation by the blood current; 4, the degree of interchange of the oxygen and carbonic acid gas with the tissue. Anemia may arise not only from hemorrhage but from insufficient formation of red blood corpuscles. The red blood corpuscles forming organs are acting abnormally. Starvation as a rule does not cause anemia. If the hemaglobin escape from the red blood corpuscles into the plasma the condition is called hemaglobinemia. The liver forms its bile pigments from hemaglobin, hence in hemaglobinemia the bile, urine and feces will become richer in coloring matter. The pathologic physiology of hemaglobin (albuminous coloring matter of blood) includes a wide zone. It is impossible to assert the minimum quantity of hemaglobin compatible with life. Anemia may progress to the stage of air hunger. I have observed several patients recover with less than 12 per cent of hemaglobin. Operations are dangerous with hemaglobin less than 30 per cent. The above data demonstrate that the normal blood stream transports more oxygen than is absolutely required for tissue repair and waste. Nature employs excessive, abundant supplies.

The blood relates itself differently in the various form of chronic and acute anemia. In the field of chronic anemia, chlorosis is, clinically, a typically well-characterized anemic disease which prevails almost exclusively in females between the ages of 14 and 25 years—the developmental period. The etiology of chlorosis is incompletely known; it is a kind of adolescent pathologic physiology of the blood—perhaps a sexual phase, like a varicocele, as it practically recovers spontaneously. The patient presents various transition grades of color from normal rosy red to pale green. The patient presents a plump paniculus adiposus—chlorosis is the anemia of good looking girls. The formation of the blood volume may be normal, the plasma, white and red corpuscles, however, altered in relations. The composition of the blood may be changed. There may be diminished red corpuscles and hemaglobin. Acute and chronic anemia occupy extensive zone of pathologic physiology allowing time for prophylaxis.

A third class of anemia may be designated *pernicious anemia*, a disease in which the red blood discs may finally assume the highest grade of changes in dimension, form and composition—ultimately evident pathologic anatomy. However, pernicious anemia has a considerable range of pathologic physiology. Anemia renders in general to the diminution of the red blood disc and hemaglobin—with less reference to the white blood corpuscles of plasma.

II. White Blood Corpuscles (Leucocytes).

The normal relation of white to red is 3 in 1000. The pathologic anatomy relation is 50 to 1000. The zone of pathologic physiology of the blood extends through a range of 4 to 40 whites to 1000 reds. In other words, leucocytosis is 1000 reds to 4 whites. From these data the leucocytes of the blood are labile elements markedly influenced by conditions. Leucocytosis is pathologic anatomy where there are 50 whites per 1000 reds. In leucocytosis there exists an abnormal number of white blood corpuscles. There are mononuclear and polynuclear white corpuscles. The origin of the white corpuscle is not definitely settled (spleen, bone marrow, lymphoid tissue). Leucocytes is supposed by some to be the rupture of hypoplastic gland tissue into the circulation. This accounts for the various kinds of cells found in the blood. On account of the variation of the number of leucocytes from different normal conditions of life—digestion, gestation, age, sex—there will be physiologic leucocytosis. The leucocytosis of pathologic physiology is of special interest to us, though its signification is not always understood. For example, is the leucocytosis of infectious disease of utility to the patient? The leucocytes may rise to 30 whites to 1000 reds. Does it furnish a clue for diagnostic and therapeutic purposes? Pathologic physiology as regards leucocytosis is prevalent in middle life. Unfortunately the pathologic physiology of leucocytosis frequently merges into pathologic anatomy before diagnosis has been established and when treatment becomes of little avail in an advanced terminal disease. With established pathologic anatomy in leucocytosis (especially and splenic hypertrophy) the termination of the disease is generally fatal in a couple of years. The hope of treatment benefiting a leucocytotic is while the disease is in the plane of pathologic physiology.

Leucocytosis was first observed by Xavier Bichat (1771-1802) in 1800. Velpeau observed the hypertrophy of the spleen in relation to leucocytosis. Donne (   ) in 1844 thought that leucocytosis was due to imperfect transformation of white into red corpuscles. In 1845 Dr. Hughes Bennett and Dr. Craigie each published a case. To Dr. Hughes Bennett is due the credit of recognizing the salient features of leucocytosis and he proposed the term leucocythemia. In 1845 Rudolph Virchow published, originally and independently, excellent details and comprehensive views of a case. To this date the changes in the blood had been recognized only after death. The changes of the blood during life in leucocytosis was first observed by Dr. H.W. Fuller. The first case of leucocytosis diagnosed during life in Germany was by Dr. Vogel in 1848. At present writing no known remedy is capable of checking the fatal course of leucocytosis.

Cachexia presenting a peculiar white, waxy color of the skin, depends on the deteriorating effect of the disease on individual organs as from malignancy, tuberculosis, arsenic, malaria, alcohol, goiter, etc. Cachexia is associated with a condition of chronic ill health depending on depraved state of blood, from loss of blood elements, malnutrition or the presence of morbific elements (uremia, defective elimination). Pathologic physiology plays a considerable role in the pre-cachectic stage, previous to the establishment of recognizable pathologic anatomy. The term cachexia and constitutional disease are with some synonymous.

III. Plasma (Liquor Sanguinis).

Blood plasma is composed of blood serum and fibrin. Fibrin constitutes about $\frac{1}{2}$ of 1 per cent of blood. If blood contains 1 per cent of fibrin it has merged into pathologic anatomy, which is especially observed in inflammatory states. The range of pathologic physiology as regards fibrin is from $\frac{1}{2}$ of 1 per cent to $\frac{1}{2}$ of 1 per cent in the ascending scale. In the descending scale it may be less than $\frac{1}{10}$ of 1 per cent, as in the anemias and septicaemias. The knowledge of pathologic physiology of blood coagulation is defective, hence our knowledge of the pathologic physiology of blood coagulation is likewise defective. The plasma of the blood is of significance on account of the contained fibrin which is the base of thrombosis and ultimate embolism. The blood serum is able to destroy varieties of foreign cells and bacteria. The blood plasma contains numerous ferments, which act as an enzyme, alexin or complement. Some suppose that the leucocytes produce the alexins. The signification of the blood plasma may be noted in the ideal administration of certain so-called anti-toxins to cure disease, as, diphtheria, tetanus. If foreign cells, as bacteria, be injected into an animal the blood serum of the animal acquires the property of causing the cells to agglutinate. The blood serum contains a variety of substances with a variety of function. It is well for the practitioner to remember for practical purposes, that the chief salts of the serum are *sodium chloride* (NaCl), sodium carbonate (NaHCO$_3$) with phosphates and alkalies. If the blood plasma becomes diluted, attenuated, it is said to be in a state of hydraemia, as in kidney and heart disease. The blood may become thick, excessively condensed, as in Asiatic Cholera or in extensive watery diarrhea.

Treatment of Pathologic Physiology of the Blood.

The treatment of pathologic physiology of the blood demands a knowledge of etiology. When the red corpuscle, white corpuscle or plasma manifests abnormal function (pathologic physiology), first and foremost must we begin the search for the diagnosis with vigor, as the diagnostic data are still few and somewhat uncertain. If it be anemia from loss of blood (uterine sarcoma, myoma, hemorrhoids, the condition may be palliated or cured. If it be anemia from chlorosis, a sexual phase, the health can be improved by treatment, and also it is a self limited disease (15 to 24 years). The associated conditions of glandular hypertrophy may aid as a general hyperplasia, splenic or hepatic hypertrophy. The pathologic physiology of the blood should allot the physician ample time to diagnose and institute appropriate treatment before the destructive fatal pathologic anatomy dominates the field. When the fatalistic cachexia presents its specter, pathologic physiology of the blood has generally merged into hopeless pathologic anatomy.

PATHOLOGIC ANATOMY.

The detection of the terminal disease (pathologic anatomy) from the pathologic physiology of the blood requires the best heads and the finest of skill. If the terminal carcinoma could be detected in the stage of pathologic physiology, i. e., in the precarcinomatous stage, it could be practically cured, as it is in the incipient stage—a local disease. The diagnosis of the pathologic physiology of the blood cannot be separated from the pathologic physiology of individual viscera. For example, carcinoma of any viscus produces pathologic physiology of the blood (cachexia). Again, pathologic physiology of the blood may arise with no palpable course until hypertrophy of the glands, spleen, or liver appears.

Leukemia, a disease of middle life, though in the incipient stage is that of pathologic physiology, yet leads later to pathologic anatomy and generally to a fatal issue, however, through a chronic course. Leukemic changes arise through rupture of the hyperplastic tissue in the vascular tract. This explains the variety of cells found in the blood. The etiology of leukemia is unknown. Some consider it an infectious disease. Leukemia was, originally, chiefly referred to the spleen but other sources, as the bone marrow, account for a share. The various forms of leucocytosis may exist as long as pathologic physiology endures—ultimately pathologic anatomy appears. Whether the origin of the leucocytes be the spleen or glands one cannot decide until physical symptoms arise. The study of pathologic physiology of the blood will progress when physicians practically examine all patients, and the subject of hematology is constantly taught as a required curriculum in the colleges. It is by cultivation of the study of pathologic physiology of the blood that we may hope for early diagnosis of impending disease, the application of effective remedies as well as rational prophylaxis. When pathologic physiology of the blood can only be discovered, the aim of the clinician must be to correct the abnormal deviation, the abnormal function, of plasma, red or white corpuscle. These consist in the application of therapeutics, as diet (food and fluid), induction of maximum visceral function (visceral drainage), recognized remedies, (habitat, avocation), prophylaxis.

CHAPTER XXXVIII.

THE PATHOLOGIC PHYSIOLOGY OF (I.) TRACTUS LYMPHATICUS, (II.) LYMPH.

An original and enterprising man is opposed—opposition develops strength, and criticism accuracy.

A fever in your blood! Why, then, incision would let her out in saucers.—Shakespeare, in Love's Labor Lost.

I. TRACTUS LYMPHATICUS.

The tractus lymphaticus begins and ends in the veins. It is a venous appendage. It was a late developmental addition, differentiation of the blood vascular system—an additional circulatory apparatus.

The tractus lymphaticus resembles the tractus venosus, (a) in possessing afferent or converging vessels which course from periphery to center; (b) in being divided into two sets—*superficial* and *deep*; (c) in contour, the possession of valves—constrictions and dilatations.

The tractus lymphaticus differs from the tractus venosus, (d) in traversing glands; (e) in its reverse arrangement—i. e., the lymphatic vessel does not increase in dimension from periphery to center like the vein; (f) the progressive movements of the lymph depend exclusively on the parietes of the lymphatic vessel—that of the venous blood chiefly on the cardiac action; (g) the lymphatics communicate with intercellular spaces and serous sacs.

The tractus lymphaticus consists of: (A), (*VASA LYMPHATICA*), *Peripheral Anastomosing Plexuses of Lymph Vessels,* which originate in the meshes of the connective tissue. These lymph channels, converging and uniting, pass to the lymph glands, or nodes. In the pathologic physiology of the lymph vessels redness (hyperaemia) along the line of vessels and oedema are conspicuous features.

Vasa lymphatic or lymph vessels arising from all parts of the body were discovered almost simultaneously by George Joylife (1637-1658), an English physician, in 1652; Olaf Rudbeck (1630-1702), a Swede of Upsala in 1651; Thomas Bartholin (1616-1680), a Danish anatomist of Copenhagen from 1650 to 1667. Bartholin proposed the name vasa lymphatica. The chief location of lymphatic vessels is the connective tissue especially associated with blood vessels. The valves of lymphatic vessels are absent at their origin and in the capillaries. The valves are paired and numerous but irregularly located in the collecting vessels, however, rare in the final collecting trunks—thoracic ducts. The arrangement of the vasa lymphatica consist of: (a) *superficial* or epifascial set and (b) *deep* or subfascial set—communicating with each other. The general organs or regions of the body are drained by converging, collecting lymphatic vessels—intermediate collecting trunks. The lymph *capillaries* consist of valveless endothelial tubes. The common collecting trunks consist of three coats, viz., (a) the internal endothelial layer; (b) the middle muscular layer; (c) the external connective tissue layer.

Chyle Vessels (Lacteals).

Vasa chylifera or the lacteals were first observed in the mesentery of man by Herophilus (310 B. C.), a Greek physician living in Egypt, while he was dissecting living criminals.

Erasistratus (340-280 B. C.), a Greek physician, observed the chyle vessels or lacteals while dissecting kids but named them arteries. However, Gasparo Aselli (1581-1626) professor of anatomy and surgery at Pavia, Italy, a prince among anatomists, discovered the lacteals while performing vivisection in a dog. July 28, 1622, Aselli's work (lacteals) was published posthumous by his friends.

(B), (*GLANDULÆ LYMPHATICÆ*), *Lymph Glands or Nodes*, which are structures that receive (afferent vessels) and emit (efferent vessels) lymph vessels. The glands produce leucocytes and modify traversing material. It is estimated that man has some 500 lymph glands or nodes and that the lymph traverses one or more glands before terminating in (subclavian) veins. Glands alter lymph owing to slow circulation. The glands modify the traversing inert or living particles and imprison them, as the carbon infiltration glands of the bronchia. In pathologic physiology of the tractus lymphaticus hypertrophy or tenderness of the glands is a conspicuous characteristic.

(C), (*TRUNCI LYMPHATICI*), *Lymph Trunks*, are large lymph vessels which conduct or transport the lymph from the lymph glands or nodes to the (subclavian) veins. The chief ones are the left and right thoracic ducts.

The lymph trunks are the thoracic duct (left) and the thoracic duct (right). Formerly it was thought the wounds of the thoracic duct were fatal, however, recent observation (H. Cushing, P. Allen, and others) demonstrates that the thoracic duct wounds are frequently not fatal, recovery resulting from: (a) spontaneous closure (coagulation contraction of the duct wall); (b) free

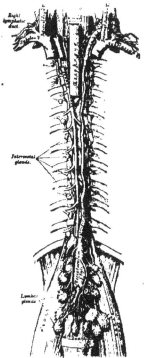

Fig. 140 — The thoracic and right lymphatic ducts.

DUCTUS THORACICUS DEXTER ET SINISTER

Fig. 140. The left thoracic duct with the chief (a) *isthmus* constriction in its central portion, the dilated (b) *cisterna lymphatica* at its distal end and the (c) *cervical dilatation* at its proximal end (which terminates in the vena subclavia sinistra), the right thoracic duct terminating in the vena subclavia dextra. Is the caliber of the thoracic duct (left) sufficient to transport ⅔ of the lymph of the organism? (Gray).

516   THE ABDOMINAL AND PELVIC BRAIN

collateral circulation; (c) ligation (suture) of the wound. If the duct leaks lymph it should be ligated proximal and distal to the perforation, allowing resumption by collateral circulation. (The lymphatic system includes the terms canalicular system, perivascular lymph spaces, lymph capillaries, chiliferous vessels—pleural, peritoneal, pericardial and synovial (serous) cavities, stomata, lacteals.)

The number of lymph channels and glands are unequally or non-uniformly distributed in the organism, occurring most frequently in vascular parts. The number and caliber depend on the density of tissue. Lymph channels (closed, e. g., peritoneum, pleura), in general are lined by endothelium in contradistinction to (unclosed) channels, (e. g., digestive and genital tracts), which are lined by epithelium. The valves of lymph channels are folds of endothelium. The tractus lymphaticus possesses more variation than any other visceral tract. The form of the whole branching lymphatic vascular system is that of a cone. The cone base or periphery is the vast connective tissue spaces of the whole body. The cone apex or center is the termination of the lymphatic trunk (thoracic ducts) in the veins (s u b c l a v i a n). Lymphatic vessels arise from intercellular s p a c e s, however, especially from immediately beneath free surfaces as skin serosa, mucosa. The lymphatic vessels are solidly and compactly anastomosed. Hence the l y m p h plasma may flow in all directions (like the blood in the utero-ovarian artery) direct or reverse to insure complete cell nourishment under complicated conditions. The object of the tractus lymphaticus is universal cell nourishment and universal cell drainage. The functions of the tractus lymphaticus (sensation, peristalsis, absorption, secretion) is controlled by the nervus vasomotorius (sympathetic). The tractus lymphaticus is richly supplied by a plexiform, nodular network, a fenestrated anastomosed meshwork of the nervus vasomotorius which controls its physiology. The lymphatic

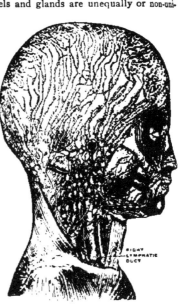

Fig. 141.—The lymphatics of the head and neck. (Sappey.)
LYMPHATICS OF HEAD AND NECK

Fig. 141. This figure presents the source (vasa lymphatica), glands (glandular lymphaticæ) and termination of the right thoracic duct (in the right subclavian vein). The direction of the lymph channels demonstrated why the lymph glands in the neck enlarge toward the clavicle. (Sappey.)

vessels accompany the veins. The lymphatic vessels ensheath the veins as a plexiform anastomosing net or fenestrated meshwork—resembling the plexiform, nodular net or fenestrated anastomosing meshwork of the nervus vasomotorius ensheathing the arteries, i. e., the nervus vasomotorius ensheath the arteries as the tractus lymphaticus ensheath the veins.

Thoracic Duct (Unpaired).

Ductus thoracicus sinistra, ductus pecquetianus, was discovered by Jean Pecquet (of Paris, France, 1622-1674) in 1649, in a dog. It was discovered by Olaus Rudbeck (of Upsala, Sweden, 1630-1702) in man, in 1650.

Also Thomas Bartholin (1616-1680) is credited with discovery of the thoracic duct in man. John Wesling in 1634 saw the thoracic duct. The thoracic duct is in general $\frac{1}{4}$ of an inch in diameter and 18 inches in length with non-uniform caliber and sinuous course with minimum caliber at its middle portion. It is especially dilated at the distal end (receptaculum lymphatica) and at the proximal end is an elongated ampulla (which I shall term its *cervical dilatation*).

The thoracic duct may bifurcate, forming two or several branches, a network, and reunite in its course. Its valves are the most limited in number and dimensions of any portion of the tractus lymphaticus. Its two

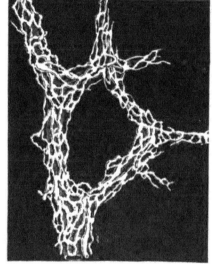

LYMPHATICUS ENSHEATHING A VEIN

Fig. 142. The lymphatic vessels ensheathing the portal vein as a plexiform, anastomosing nodular (valves) fenestrated meshwork. The tabular lymph apparatus richly ensheathing the vein transports abundant fluid for nourishment. (Teichman.)

most remarkable valves are located at its ("cervical dilatation") termination in the subclavian vein where the free borders of the valves are directed toward the venous lumen in order to oppose influx of venous blood into the thoracic duct. The two ductus thoracici—ductus thoracicus major (sinister) et minor (dexter)—flow in the direction of least resistance, i. e., they flow into the subclavian veins at the most distant point from the intra-thoracic and intraabdominal pressure. Has a duct of two lines or $\frac{1}{6}$ of an inch in diameter ample lumen to allow $\frac{1}{5}$ of the lymphatic fluid (constituting about $\frac{1}{5}$ of the body weight) to traverse it?

518   THE ABDOMINAL AND PELVIC BRAIN

Ductus Thoracicus dextra is located at the right side and base of the neck. Its dimensions are: length an inch, diameter 1–8 of an inch. It terminates in right subclavian vein. It is the common collecting lymph trunk for the right side of the head and neck, right proximal extremity, right lung, right heart. The thoracic duct is nonuniform in caliber, possessing dilatations (reservoirs) and constrictions (isthmuses).

(1) *Receptaculum Lymphatica (Distal Dilatation).*

Receptaculum chyli, cisterna chili, cisterna lymphatica or chyle reservoir was discovered by Jéan Pecquet (1622-1674) of Paris, France, in 1649. The cisterna lymphatica was independently discovered by Olaf Rudbeck (1630-1702), president of the University of Upsala, Sweden. In general the dimensions of the receptaculum lymphatica is ⅓ of an inch in diameter and 2½ inches in length. It is an oblong formed sac or dilatation at the distal end of the thoracic duct, located opposite to the I and II lumbar vertebræ.

(2) *Cisterna Lymphatica Cervicis (Proximal Dilatation).*

The thoracic duct in the region of the neck possesses a dilatation which may be termed the "cervical dilatation" or *cisterna lymphatica cervicis*. It is a spindle or oblong formed swelling of the duct located at its terminal end. It, as well as other dilations, has been termed an ampulla.

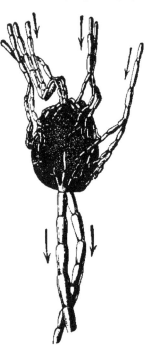

A LYMPHATIC GLAND WITH ITS AFFERENT AND EFFERENT VESSELS

Fig. 143. The valved afferent vessels are more numerous than the valved efferent (Testut).

(3) *Isthmus Medius (Middle Isthmus).*

The thoracic duct possesses a minimum caliber at its medial portion, hence I shall term this the middle isthmus. It is the chief constriction or isthmus of the thoracic duct.

II. THE LYMPH (LYMPH PLASMA).

The contents of the tractus lymphaticus consists of: (A) the lymph or lymph plasma—a fluid tissue; (B) the leucocyte—a guest of lymph plasma.

(A). Lymph—Lymph Plasma.

Lymph plasma *originates* from blood plasma. The lymph or lymph plasma originates as a capillary infiltration from the blood serum. Lymph is doubtless also a product of cell secretion. In *composition* lymph plasma appears to be a mechanical and secretive product from the blood. Perhaps lymph should be viewed chiefly as a secretion of the endothelial (blood capillary) cell. Lymph is different from blood—it is more acid (is less in glucose), as urine is more acid than blood. Lymph plasma is fluid that has escaped from the blood plasma in the capillaries and its composition varies according to source and organ activity. It is a peculiarity that though the lymph should be viewed chiefly as the product of cell secretion, instead of being eliminated externally, it is returned to the venous blood, to retravel

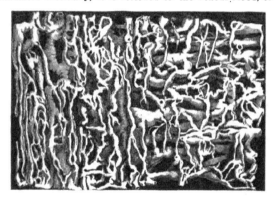

LYMPH VESSELS OF THE TRACHEAL MUCOSA

Fig. 144. Observe anastomosing superficial and deep lymphatics as well as valves. The number and caliber of the lymph channels demonstrate its functional transporting capacity. (Teichman.)

the arteries. However, the lymph is modified by the lymph glands and pulmonary endothelium (oxygen). It is a process which resembles the elaboration of the ductless glands (spleen, thyroid, ovary, thymus, adrenal).

Physically the lymph is in general an odorless, colorless, viscid fluid. Digestion produces a milky color in lymph plasma. The quantity of lymph is estimated from $\frac{1}{4}$ to $\frac{1}{3}$ the weight of the body. The quantity varies extensively according to corporeal activity. Its specific gravity is 1.017. Practically the lymph is a transparent alkaline fluid, perchance, of reddish yellow color. It is soluble in water, becoming turpid in alcohol. Lymph coagulates with more facility than blood and becomes a scarlet red in contact with oxygen and purple red in contact with carbonic acid. The lymph plasma performs an export and an import service. It conducts nourishment (fluid) to the cell and floats waste material (fluid) from the cell. It performs its

520   THE ABDOMINAL AND PELVIC BRAIN

labor through a fluid medium, saturating the cell (nourishment) and irrigating the cell (drainage). Lymph plasma coagulation renders less fibrin than that of blood plasma. This is significant, for fibrin is liable to obstruct vessels and produce thrombosis—eventually embolism. The chief *chemical* constituents of lymph consists of albuminoids (less than that of blood) fats, various metalic salts (NaCl phosphates, sulphates, alkaline carbonates).

(B). *Leucocyte—White Blood Corpuscle.*

The origin of the leucocyte is: (a) medulla (bone marrow); (b) mesoblast (blood vascular endothelium); (c) connective tissue; (d) lymph glands or nodes.

The *location* of the leucocyte is in order of frequency: (a) in the lymph plasma; (b) in the blood plasma; (c) in the connective tissue.

The *structure* of a leucocyte consists of a nucleus and a surrounding protoplasm.

The *number* of leucocytes in man to the cubic millimeter are about 8,000 (R a n v i e r). The number of leucocytes are increased a f t e r passing t h r o u g h glands. The number of leucocytes is greater in the center than in the periphery of the body organism.

The *neucleus* of the leucocyte varies in number, dimension, f o r m, location. The nucleus is s u r r o u n d e d by protoplasm, an almost imperceptible z o n e of non-homogenous   m a t t e r.

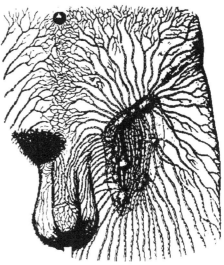

INGUINAL GLANDS OF LYMPHATICS

Fig. 145. This figure represents the course of the lymphatics from the *genitals and rectum* to the abundant inguinal glands—barriers of infection which imprison, sterilize or digest (destroy) infectious or inert material. The inguinal glands are affected by carcinoma and infectious material from genitals and rectum. (Sappey.)

The polymorphism of the leucocyte nucleus has vigorously engaged numerous cytologists with consequent multiple views as to its cause.

The *protoplasm* varies in form, dimension, structure. The contents of the protoplasm varies from environments as iron granules, redblood corpuscles, debris, microbes or their products, particles of air and so forth.

Physically the leucocyte is practically a colorless, soft, extensible non-

TRACTUS LYMPHATICUS AND LYMPH

homogenous mass of protoplasm, noncapsulated (without covering). It is viscous and adheres to the most smooth surface. Thus when circulation slows it lodges against vessel wall.

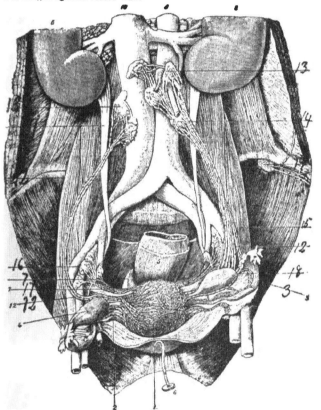

LYMPHATICS OF THE INTERNAL GENITALS

Fig. 146. This illustration of the lymphatics after Dr. Wm. Nagel and Porier demonstrates that the lymphatics accompany the vessels—in this figure they follow the utero-ovarian vascular circle (circle of Byron Robinson). The lymphatics of the genitals are of practical importance on account of the frequent location of carcinoma in the genitals and their distribution of the carcinoma through the lymphatics.

The chief *chemical* constituents of a leucocyte are, albuminoids, nuclein, insoluble matter, fat cholestrin. These substances are important in metabolism, e. g., the nuclein will produce uric acid.

522   THE ABDOMINAL AND PELVIC BRAIN

Biologically the leucocyte or white corpuscle possesses the primary properties of living matter, viz.: sensibility, mobility (rhythm), peristalsis, absorption, secretion, reproduction. One of the most significant characteristics of the leucocyte is that of *mobility* endowing it with the quality of a pro-

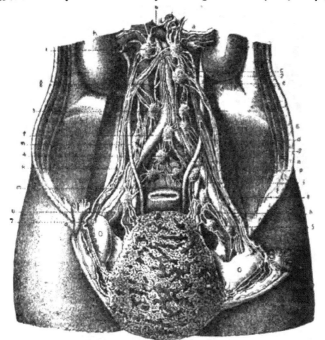

LYMPH CHANNELS AND GLANDS DRAINING THE TRACTUS GENITALIS
(SAVAGE)

Fig. 147. The tractus genitalis is abundantly supplied by lymphatics and consequently possesses a rich lymphatic drainage. The tractus genitalis is peculiarly liable to be attacked by bacterial infection and carcinoma—both manifest in the annexed tractus lymphaticus. Infectious or carcinomatous material, on account of the luxuriant anastomoses of the genital lymph channels may appear to avoid certain of the adjacent genital glands and to attack glands more distant from the genitals. In other words the infectious or carcinomatous material may not attack the genital lymphatic glands in the direct order of the course of their arrangements. This illustration demonstrates the futility of attempting to extirpate all the lymphatic glands attending a carcinomatous infected genital tract—microscopically one is incapable of deciding whether a lymph gland be hypertrophied from bacterial infection or carcinomatous infection.

tector, a body guard—a mobile sentinel. It is a migratory cell (the wandering cell of Recklinghausen). It is a mobile tissue inspector, a heraldic warner for bodily protection. The leucocyte is a guardian against foreign invaders. it is a tester of ingesta, it is a filtering barrier, a retention prison.

The leucocyte absorbs, imprisons, sterilizes matter. It digests some material (food, bacteria), it imprisons some (indigestible, coloring matter), it sterilizes some (bacteria, ferments). These properties enable the leucocyte to protect or supervise against excessive invasion of bacteria, poisonous matter, ferments.

The leucocyte *reproduces* itself by amitosis (direct division) and karyokinesis (indirect division). The leucocyte is a primordial factor of life and its perpetuation.

The leucocyte is a vital, primordial, protoplasmic element which retains its primary property of free and independent life—sensation, motion, absorption, secretion, reproduction—adopting itself to differentiation, environment. It is a functionator preceding a constructor.

The *vital resistance* or constitutional power of a leucocyte is remarkable against destructive agencies. Verworn demonstrated that 24 hours after bodily death of the organism the majority of the leucocytes are living. They may retain their properties external to the general organism for 3 weeks (Recklinhausen, Ranvier).

The chief classification of different leucocytes are: (a) *microcytes*; (b) *macrocyses*; (c) cells with neutrophile granules; (d) cells with acidophile granules; (e) cells with metachromatic basophile granules. This classification

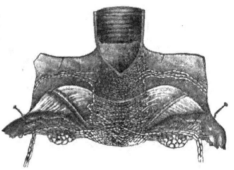

LYMPHATIC CHANNELS DRAINING CERVIX AND VAGINA (POIRIER)

Fig. 148. This excellent illustration demonstrates the facility with which cervical and vaginal carcinoma (the most prevalent forms) may become distributed through the tractus lymphaticus annexed to the tractus genitalis.

demonstrates the extensive range of physiology (and consequent extensive field of pathologic physiology) included within the range of the leucocytes. As disease is deviating or abnormal physiology the key to its etiology, therapuesis and prophylaxis accurate knowledge of organ functions. The functions of the tractus lymphaticus are: I, sensation; II, peristalsis; III, absorption; IV, secretion. Disease in the lymphatic tract consists in deviation, abnormal repetition, of one or all the above four functions. The four functions manifesting pathologic physiology in the disease of the tractus lymphaticus will be recognized by being *excessive, deficient, disproportionate*.

I. SENSATION (EXCESSIVE, DEFICIENT, DISPROPORTIONATE).

1. *Excessive* sensation in the tractus lymphaticus may be associated with irritability of the peripheral nerve ending in the endothelium. Also the lymph plasma may contain irritating matter.

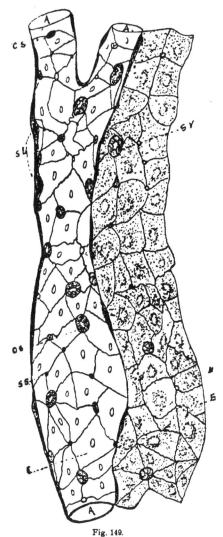

Fig. 149.
LYMPH CHANNEL (A. A.) OF PYLORIC END OF RABBIT'S OMENTERON

2. *Deficient* sensation in the lymphatic tract may be due to excessive or overwhelming poisonous substances in the lymph plasma or paresis (blunted sensibility) of the peripheral nerve ending in the endothelium (traumatic p a r e s i s from compression œdema). Deficient bodily activity may cause deficient lymph flow a n d consequent deficient sensation.

8. *Disproportionate* sensation in the tractus lymphaticus may arise from anæsthesia, hyperæsthesia in its different segments and also from different composition of lymph plasma from different organs. Also disproportional bodily muscular activity may share producing disproportional sensation.

II. PERISTALSIS (EXCESSIVE, DEFICIENT, DISPROPORTIONATE).

4. *Excessive peristalsis* may arise from irritating lymph plasma or irritation of the walls of the lymph tract from supersensitiveness of the endothelium. The

Fig. 149. A, A, is a lymph channel from which I penciled the p e r i t o n e a l endothelium and stained with AgNO₃. One can observe a dozen stomata vera on this lymph channel, directly communicating with the peritoneum. Note the sinuous outline of the endothelium c o m p o s i n g the lymph channel. Parallel to this lymph channel is a zone of peritoneal endothelium stained with AgNO₃, presenting stomata vera (S. V.) and endothelium without sinuous borders.

lymph vessels contract from their own parietes—no apparatus like the heart propel their contents. Peristalsis in the lymph channel is obvious chiefly in the ductus thoracicus. The rate and volume of lymph flow depends on the rate and volume of blood flow, on tissue pressure and muscular activity. In certain localities the lymph flow must depend on the difference of blood pressure and that of the lymph in the tissue. Obstruction of the thoracic duct would induce excessive, vain peristalsis in the lymph channels. Extra distention of the left subclavian vein might induce excessive peristalsis in the thoracic duct. Extraordinary muscular activity may induce excessive peristalsis.

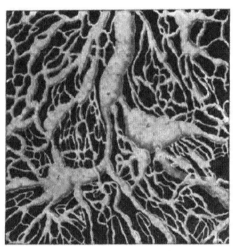

TRANSITION OF LYMPH CAPILLARIES INTO LYMPH TRUNKS WITH VALVES —SACCULATIONS

Fig. 150. a, beginning of lymph trunk; b, b, lymph reservoirs: magnified 15 times. (Teichman.)

5. *Deficient Peristalsis* or stasis of lymph occurs in tissue with limited elastic tension. The same condition favors venous stasis. Also force of gravity favors lymph stasis. Hence general lymph œdema occurs in the ankle region or lumbao-sacral region. The obstruction of a single lymph channel (or vein) does not necessarily produce œdema because the lymph (or venous channel) may assume a collateral circulation from rich anastomosis. Transudation of lymph may not produce œdema as the lymph may be transported by the lymphatics.

If general venous stasis exists the blood pressure in the left subclavian is raised and lymph œdema may be general and peristalsis of the lymphatics is vain. Lymphatic peristalsis may be deficient when the tissues adjacent to the capillaries have been distended with consequent loss of elasticity and power of contraction. Diminished elastic pressure of the adjacent tissue on the lymph spaces diminishes the rate of flow of lymph plasma. Deficient peristalsis (lymph flow) occurs subsequent to tissue inflammation, for the elastic tissue pressure is diminished, paretic.

6. *Disproportionate Peristalsis* (flow) may be observed subsequent to different degrees and different localities of tissue distention following œdema from varying elastic tissue pressure. Subsequent to inflammatory tissue processes the adjacent elastic tissue pressure is unequal, nonuniform, inducing lymphatic peristalsis or flow disproportionate.

III. SECRETION (EXCESSIVE, DEFICIENT, DISPROPORTIONATE).

7. *Excessive* secretion of lymph plasma may be manifest by œdema, tissue fluid accumulation, nephritic œdema. Excessive secretion of lymph plasma is difficult to discriminate from insufficient drainage or transportation of lymph. Excessive secretion of lymph may be found in tissue œdema and especially in the serous cavities. In nephritic œdema (not accompanied by cardiac deficiency) the excessive lymph collected in the tissue is doubtless due to simple stasis, however, for our view, the lymph is excessive. The nephritic œdema occurs first in the subcutaneous tissue and particularly in the tissue possessing limited elastic pressure, e. g., about the ankles and dorsal surface of the lumbar and sacral regions. The lymph œdema may be excessive, lymph formation or accumulation being from obstruction to its escape. The quantity of lymph which escapes from the blood capillaries depends on the difference in pressure between the lymph

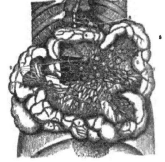

LYMPH CHANNELS AND GLANDS OF THE MESENTERON (HORNER)

Fig. 151. Subject dead from ascites. 1, thoracic duct. 2, section of aorta. 3, adjacent aortic glands. 4, superficial lymphatics of intestines. 5, 6, 7, lymphatic channels and glands of enteron and mesenteron.

spaces and the blood capillaries. Whether there be excessive lymph secretion or lymph stasis—lymph œdema—it is similiar in effect. The stasis of blood in veins results in lymph stasis—lymph œdema. The organs or tissue become most œdematous or swollen which possess the most limited elastic pressure—in fact exactly where venous stasis is at a maximum. The lymph stasis may be local as when a vein is accluded by a thrombosis, or general as when a lung or heart is debilitated. However, mere obstruction of a vein may not produce lymph or venous stasis as circulation in the vein and lymph channels is rich on anastomatic collateral routes. An increased lymph transudation may produce no lymph œdema as the lymph channel anastomoses may transport the excess of lymph sufficiently rapid to equalize the lymph circulation. If there be general venous stasis general lymph œdema may arise from rise of blood pressure in the left subclavian vein obstructing the flow of lymph from the thoracic duct. Local lymph œdema may arise from previous extradistention of tissue which consequently is deficient in elastic pressure. It is evident that the elasticity of tissue and muscular activity exercises a powerful influence over the rate of lymph flow and local accumulation of lymph plasma.

In regard to the nephritic œdema it may be noted that œdema occurs in parenchymatous nephritis—not in interstitial nephritis—and is no doubt due to retention within the body of the watery portion of the urine. A test of this matter may be made by the administration of sodium chloride (which stimulates, irritates, excites renal epithelium). In the nephritic œdema from lymph stasis less than normal urine is evacuated and the œdema increases as the urine diminishes and vice versa. Now, administer 8 ounces of normal salt solution every two hours 8 times daily and the urine will rapidly increase in quantity and clarification, resembling spring water, while the œdema will diminish. It must be well borne in mind that sodium chloride irritates, damages inflamed renal epithelium, hence should not be administered in parenchymatous nephritis. Hammerschlag has shown that patients with parenchymatous nephritis possess diluted blood—an hydræmia or hydræmic plethora. No doubt some damage, lesion, exists in the capillary wall in nephritic œdema, because the heart shares in the process by presenting hypertrophy. Dr. A. W.

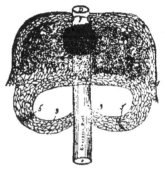

LYMPHATIC DRAINAGE OF DIAPHRAGM

Fig. 152. The centrum tendineum of the diaphragm is drained by lymph trunks—two anterior and two posterior (3, 3,)—which terminate in the thoracic duct 5, 5, valves of lymphatic trunks. D, D, thoracic duct. 6, 7, 8, dilated lymph spaces in the diaphragm. The dark circular disc represents the point of the central tendineum where the heart rests, in which disc there are no lymph spaces.

Howlett asserts that nephritic œdema apparently depends in some subjects on excess of sodium chloride within the body, i. e., the subject secretes deficient quantities of sodium chloride on account of kidney defects (parenchymatous nephritis) which in turn necessitates an accumulation of fluids (lymph within the tissues). Whatever the exact factors be I am distinctly convinced during the past decade as regard the action of sodium chloride on renal epithelium (irritation, excessive, or deficient secretion), that profound effects are exercised on the kidneys by the amount of sodium chloride ingested. So-called *Indurated lymph œdema* occurs subsequent to extirpation of the lymph gland in a territory of considerable dimension.

8. *Deficient* secretion of lymph plasma is difficult to demonstrate, although

it undoubtedly occurs especially where tissue is dense and hence where little lymph will escape, however, in atrophic tissue doubtless deficient lymph is secreted.

9. *Disproportionate* secretion of lymph is evident in different regions of the body. The resistence offered by the different degrees of tissue elasticity and pressure accounts for its share. Also the lymphatics are unequally distributed. The erect attitude presents disproportionate lymph secretion from force of gravity. In the erect attitude the force of gravity exposes extra tissue pressure in certain localities, as the ankle and foot region.

IV. ABSORPTION (EXCESSIVE, DEFICIENT, DISPROPORTIONATE).

10. *Excessive*; 11, *deficient*; 12, *disproportionate*, absorption of lymph plasma is difficult to demonstrate and time and space here forbids.

PROFILE VIEW OF THE DUCTUS THORACICUS

Fig. 153. 1, the *cervical dilatation* of the thoracic duct terminating in the left subclavian vein. 2, the *isthmus* of the thoracic duct in the dorsal region. 3, *receptaculum lymphatica*.

THE DIAGNOSIS OF PATHOLOGIC PHYSIOLOGY IN THE TRACTUS LYMPHATICUS.

For rational views and practical purposes definite ideas should be entertained of the functions of an organ. It is evident that to the tractus lymphaticus the four common visceral functions (sensation, peristalsis, absorption, secretion) belong. When these four functions of the tractus lymphaticus pursue a normal course there is no pathologic physiology—no disease exists—and no correction of function or therapeusis is demanded. As water basins are the great centers of civilization, so the lymph channel is the great center of nourishment. In both instances it is the facility of a transporting fluid medium which accomplishes the object. The signification of the tractus lymphaticus is evident when it is realized that it is the highway of cell nourishment and cell drainage. Along the borders of the great lymph stream every cell is a harbor for import and export service. The object of the tractus lymphaticus is universal cell nourishment and universal cell drainage. Pathologic physiology of the tractus lymphaticus is the zone between nor-

LYMPH CHANNELS IN THE PERITONEUM

Fig. 154. The lymph vessels present elongated endothelium, valves, dilatation and construction.

mal physiology and pathologic anatomy and should be amenable to therapeutics. Pathologic physiology will constitute a useful field for the cultivation of physiology, diagnosis, therapeutics, rational practice and prophylaxis. As the tractus lymphaticus is of vast utility in the animal economy, having an import service (transportation of cell nourishment) and an export service (transportation of cell drainage), its pathologic physiology comprises a correspondingly extensive zone. Pathologic physiology in the tractus lymphaticus is disordered or abnormal function, the beginning of disease. Pathologic anatomy is a disordered or abnormal structure, the establishment of disease. Disease begins as abnormal function and its progress consists in a repetition of the abnormal or deviating physiology. Modern radical surgery in tubercu-

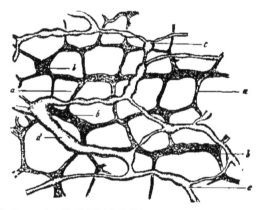

LYMPHATICS FROM ENTERON OF GUINEA PIG WITH PLEXUS MYENTERICUS OF AUERBACH (FREY)

Fig. 155. a, b, a, b, Auerbach's Plexus (Plexus myentericus); c, narrow and d, larger lymph channels. This excellent illustration demonstrates the intimate relation of the rich plexuses of the nervus vasomotorius and rich plexuses of the vasa lymphatica.

losis and carcinoma depends for its sucess on a knowledge of the anatomic distribution of the lymph channels and glands. The pathologic physiology in the lymphatic glands and channels may suggest a diagnosis by leading the physician to a local lesion along their route as enlarging inguinal glands may indicate a genital or rectal lesion, they may lead to the discovery of septic foci or solutions of continuity in distant regions, e. g., an infected foot, a corn, a bunion. A rising pathologic physiology in the axillary glands may enable the physician to diagnose advancing carcinoma. The location of the lymphatic glands and the route of the lymphatic channels are the essentials in the diagnosis. This is strikingly manifest in the phenomena that extensive removal of lymph glands may result in induration of lymph œdema. The anatomy is the solid ground to determine the direction of lymph channels and location of lymph glands. Lymph glands enlarge generally from bacterial disease, carcinoma or sarcoma. Enlarging lymph glands herald the advance of disease. The tractus lymphaticus stands as a sentinel on guard over normal bodily nourishment. It filters and checks the deleterious and poisonous substance from gaining access to the parenchymatous cell. The lymph glands imprison inert substance and the carcinomatous cell, retarding the progress of carcinoma. The detectable route of the most implacable and deadly enemy of man—carcinoma—is through the tractus lymphaticus. The early detection and treatment of the precarcinomatous stage must be accomplished by the recognition of pathologic physiology of the tractus lymphaticus. The lymph system presides as a tissue inspector and protector. It digests, imprisons, sterilizes in the interest of the general organism. The lymph plasma possesses a body guard in its guest—the army of leucocytes.

RELATIONS OF THE TRACTUS LYMPHATICUS TO PRACTICAL MEDICINE.

Clinicians are recognizing the numerous relations of the lymphatic system to practical medicine and surgery. Metastatic manifestations, both bacteriologic and neoplastic, extend through definite routes of lymph channels and their associated glands, and the object of pathologic physiology is to detect the process in ample time to save the organism from destruction by establishing irreparable pathologic anatomy. Armed with a knowledge of the physiology of the tractus lymphaticus and its topographic anatomy the physician is forewarned as to its course of incipient pathologic physiology and considerations of rational treatment should engage his attention.

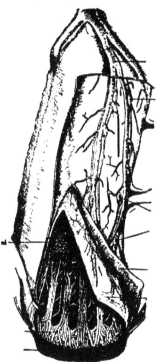

RECTAL GLANDS AND LYMPHATICS

Fig. 156. This figure illustrates the route of carcinomatous or other infectious material through the numerous rectal lymphatics and glands (Gerota).

First and foremost the luxuriant anastomoses of the lymph channels appear to allow bacterial or carcinomatous material to avoid attacking certain lymph glands in the route of the lymph channels. In other words the bacterial or carcinomatous material may not attack lymphatic glands in the direct order of their channels and topographic course. The lymph channels are so richly anastomosed that the course of the lymph current may be direct or reverse. Dr. Emil Ries has demonstrated this view as regards carcinoma in the route of the tractus lymphaticus draining the tractus genitalis. Again the physician is unable to decide macroscopically whether a lymph gland is hypertrophied from bacterial or carcinomatous infection. Hence from abundant anastomoses of lymph channels, thrombotic or other obstruction may induce metastatic manifestations in lymph tracts not primarily involved. The extensive removal of lymph channels and glands, as those of the axilla for carcinoma of the mamma, seldom produces lymph œdema or stasis because the luxuriant anastomoses of lymph channels allow the lymph to flow in multiple directions. The tractus muscularis through its activity, its massage, exercises a wonderful influence over the flow of the lymph. In states of bodily repose the respiratory muscles pursue continuous rhythmical motion maintaining continuous lymph flow. A comprehensive view of drainage may be secured by a study of the tractus lymphaticus, as cells are nourished and drained by the lymph fluid. A lymphagogue is an agent which increases the flow of lymph. Lymph increases its rate of flow under the influence of pilocarpin, ergotine.

The rate of flow of any fluid depends on its consistency. The consistency of the lymph depends on the quantity of fluid injected. Drainage and nourishment of cells depends on the rate of lymph flow as well as on its quantity

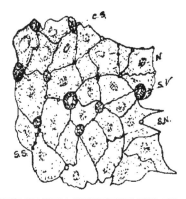

STOMATA VERA CONNECTING THE PERITONEUM WITH THE SUBPERITONEAL LYMPH CHANNELS

Fig. 157. From rabbit's omentum. The endothelium was brushed away and the base stained with ½ per cent of AgNO₃ and haematoxylin. The stomata vera (s. v., 9 of them) are patent channels, communicating tubes, connecting the peritoneum with the sub-peritoneal lymph spaces and vessels.

and quality. The degree of muscular activity or massage determines relatively the rate of lymph flow. Muscular activity or massage increases the cardiovascular action and consequently the blood pressure is elevated. We frequently observe lymph œdema in the abdominal wall in subjects with large abdominal tumor. Here the lymph accumulates in dependent tissue with deficient elasticity, and pressure or mechanical obstruction occurs. The blood pressure within the artery is tenfold greater than the blood pressure within the vein and complete circulation of the blood requires less than a minute. Hence the venous pressure is vastly greater than that of the lymphatics, however, experiments demonstrate that the lymphatic circulation is vigorous and rapid, e. g. salt solution injected in the connective tissue (as beneath the mammæ) rapidly enters the blood circulation.

TREATMENT OF PATHOLOGIC PHYSIOLOGY OF THE TRACTUS LYMPHATICUS AND THE LYMPH.

In general $\frac{9}{10}$ of illness or complaints is pathologic physiology—disordered function—and $\frac{1}{10}$ is surgery—pathologic anatomy—disordered structure. Modern r e s e a r c h is re-instating rational therapeutics, i. e., the correction of disordered f u n c t i o n. Practically the field of influence and utility of a physician is limited to the zone of *pathologic physiology* (which lies between physiology and pathologic anatomy). *The chief duty of the physician is to restore function.* The deviating functions to restore in pathologic physiology of the tractus lymphaticus are sensation, peristalsis, absorption, secretion. Pathologic physiology of the tractus lymphaticus is best corrected and normal function maintained by natural methods or rational therapeutics. The r a t i o n a l agent of therapeutics for the treatment of pathologic physiology of the tractus lymphaticus are: I, Fluids; II, Food; III, Habitat; IV, Avocation; V, Drugs; VI, Surgery; VII, Miscellaneous.

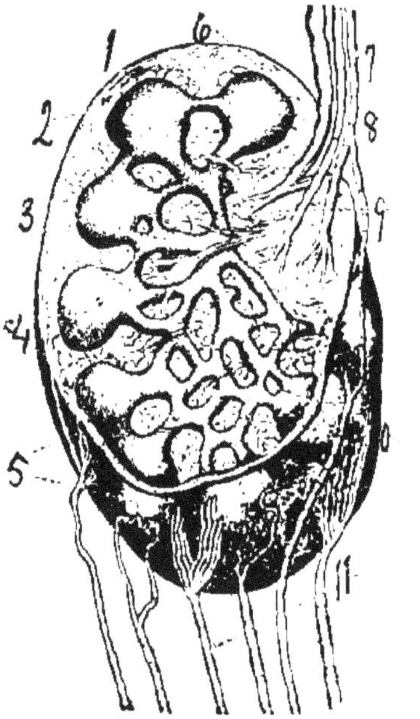

Since pathologic physiology of the tractus lymphaticus is the zone between physiology and pathologic anatomy it should be amenable to treatment. In the treatment of pathologic physiology of any abdominal visceral tract it must be remembered that the half dozen visceral tracts normally functionate in perfect harmony—no friction—and if any one tract be disordered the exquisite physiologic balance of all is

LYMPH GLAND WITH VASA EFFERENTIA ET AFFERENTIA (TOLDT)

Fig. 158. **A schematic illustration of a lymphatic gland with the entering vessels (vasa efferentia, 7) and departing vessels (vasa afferentia, 11). 9 points to the stroma in the hilum. 4, substantia corticalis. 1 and 5, connective tissue capsule. 6, surface of lymph tract. Observe that in the region of 9 and 10 are afferent and efferent vessels anastomoses without first entering the gland.**

disturbed. The pathologic physiology of the tractus lymphaticus is treated mainly indirectly, i. e., through the influence of other visceral tracts, e. g., (1) the tractus vascularis must be restored to normal as to *composition* (blood, plasma, oxygen) and *pressure* (cardio-vascular function must be normal; venous flow depends on arterial blood pressure); e. g., (2) the tractus muscularis must functionate normally (lymph largely depends on muscular activity, on respiration, condition of veins). The pathologic physiology of any viscus is frequently restored by stimulating the four common functions of other viscera (sensation, peristalsis, absorption, secretion).

I. VISCERAL DRAINAGE BY FLUID.

The most useful and safe diuretic is water. It is the natural functionating medium for the kidney. One of the best laxatives is water. Thirst is nature's demand for fluid. Water is the most important constituent of protoplasm, comprising some 70 per cent of it. I was a watcher of Dr. Tanner 25 years ago when he lived 40 days on water alone—without food. However, a few days without water is imminently fatal. The quantity of water required by the organism varies with the quantity eliminated. The quantity of water eliminated, approximately, by a subject of 150 lbs. at rest, is for the tractus urinarius 45 ounces, for the tractus respiratorius 12 ounces, for the tractus perspiratorius 8, for the tractus intestinalis 5 ounces—a total elimination of 70 ounces, almost 5 pints of fluid. It will therefore require two quarts for the demands of elimination or to satisfy living functionation. Many subjects do not drink over three pints daily and that is administered chiefly at meal time, not only burdening the tractus intestinalis with solid food, but fluid also. Many subjects drink insufficiently and suffer consequent oliguria, deficient drainage. Such subjects are burdened with waste laden blood, inflicting irritation and trauma on the nerve periphery. They are in conflict with their own secretions. Many women oppose free drinking from the idea it creates fat.

Ample quantities of fluid at regular intervals is the safety valve of health

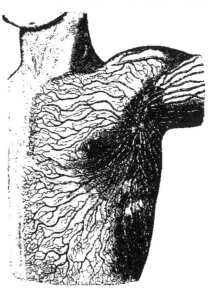

LYMPHATICS OF AXILLA AND MAMMA

Fig. 159. This illustration demonstrates the course of infectious material or carcinoma from mamma to axillary glands. The tractus lymphaticus possesses numerous channels with ample lumen. (Sappey.)

and capacity for mental or physical labor. Ample fluids not only flush the sewers of the body, but wash the internal tissues and tissue spaces, relieving waste laden blood. The soluble matter and salts are not only dissolved (preventing calculus, trauma and infection) and eliminated, but the insoluble matter and salts are floated from the system, relieving waste laden blood by such powerful streams of fluid that calculus is not liable to be formed. One of the most effective and natural stimulants to the renal epithelium is sodium chloride. (Note—Sodium chloride should not be employed in parenchymatous nephritis.) For ten years I have diluted the urine, increased its volume (consequently increased ureteral peristalsis) and clarified it by administering 8 ounces of ½ or ¼ normal salt solution six times daily. I have manufactured sodium chloride tablets (12 gr. each with flavor). The patient places on the tongue a half tablet (NaCl) and drinks a glassful of water (better hot) before each meal. This is also repeated in the middle of the forenoon (10 A. M.), middle of the afternoon (3 P. M.), and at bedtime (9 P. M.). The patient thus drinks 3 pints of (¼ to ½) normal salt solution daily. This practically renders the urine normal, and acts as ample prophylaxis against the formation of urinary, hepatic, pancreatic, fæcal calculus, and drains the body of waste material. The formation of calculus cannot occur when ample fluid in vigorous streams bathe, flood the glandular exit canals. With a deficient fluid stream, crystals form a calculus with facility. The maximum concentrated solu-

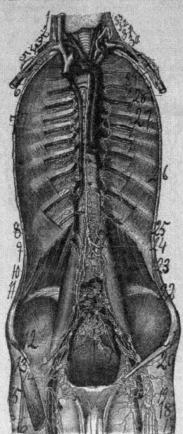

DUCTUS THORACICUS, SINISTER ET DEXTER (TOLDT)

Fig. 100. This illustrates well the terminating lymph trunks as an anastomosing network on the dorsal wall. Note: (a) the *isthmus* of the thoracic duct (at its middle portion, 27); (b) the *receptaculum lymphatica* (25) at its distal end; (c) the *thoracic dilatation* or ampulla at its proximal end.

tion of urine, bile or pancreatic juice tends to crystallize with vastly more facility than dilute urine, bile and pancreatic juice. In "visceral drainage" single crystals on first formation are rapidly floated with facility by the ample fluids present, while by diminutive quantities of fluid, and consequently aggregation, the crystals tend to precipitate, lodge, accumulate and form calculus. Oliguria is a splendid base for calculus formation in the ureter. For over ten years I have been using sodium chloride, normal salt solution, more or less in my practice. During that time some practical clinical views have been demonstrated and repeated so frequently that they have become established, I think, beyond the shadow of doubt. The following propositions have been repeatedly demonstrated hundreds of times—during the last ten years—in the clinics of Dr. Lucy Waite and mine and in our surgical operations that I shall consider them established until otherwise disproven:

1. Sodium chloride ($\frac{1}{2}$ to $\frac{1}{4}$ normal physiologic salt solution) is a powerful stimulant to the renal epithelium (tractus urinarius).

2. The administration of 8 ounces of $\frac{1}{2}$ to $\frac{1}{4}$ normal physiologic salt solution (better hot) every two hours for six times daily will increase the quantity and clarify the urine, by diluting its color and salts making it appear almost like spring water in 3 to 5 days. (Note—Sodium chloride should not be administered in parenchymatous nephritis—not in fluid or food—as it exacerbates, irritates, the diseased, inflamed parenchymatous cell.)

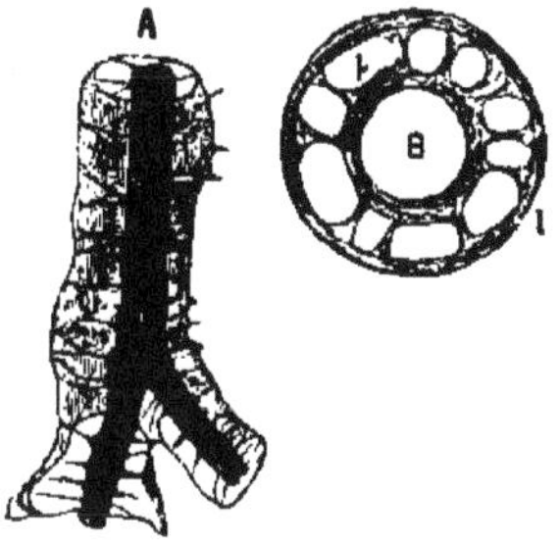

PERIVASCULAR LYMPHATIC (GEGENBAUER)

Fig. 161. A, perivascular lymphatic of the turtle's aorta. B, cross section of an artery from the cerebrum presenting perivascular lymph spaces divided by partitions. It is known as the perivascular lymph space of His. The Virchow-Robin space is the lymph space in the adventitia of blood vessel wall.

3. Sodium chloride (in $\frac{1}{2}$ to $\frac{1}{4}$ normal physiologic solution) is a vigorous stimulant to the epithelium of the tractus intestinalis and its appendages. Normal salt solution is an excellent remedy to quench thirst subsequent to peritonotomy by rectal lavage—a pint every hour.

4. Sodium chloride is vigorously active stimulant to (glandular) epithelium as that of the tractus urinarius, intestinalis, genitalis, cutis respiratorius, salivary, hepatic and pancreatic glands. It stimulates the four common visceral functions—sensation peristalsis, absorption, secretion. It is a natural stimulant (to epithelium and endothelium) as it constitutes over $\frac{1}{2}$ of 1 per cent of the blood. The lymph plasma arises from the blood plasma. Whatever dilutes the blood plasma will therefore dilute the lymph plasma. Eight ounces of partial normal salt solution 6 times daily will increase the blood volume and consequently increase the lymph volume which will irrigate, flush the lymph spaces and wash the cells. Also increased blood volume increases the pressure or rate of lymph flow, perfecting visceral drainage. Since the

lymph plasma contains not only the nourishment for the cells but also the waste product of the cell the drainage of the tractus lymphaticus should be rather excessive than deficient as the abundant fresh nourishment vitalizes, energizes the cell. Cell function is performed through a fluid medium, hence water, which is a fluid transporter, a solvent, an eliminator and regulator of temperature, is first and foremost essential in the pathologic physiology of the tractus lymphaticus. We live in a fluid medium and elimination demands a compensatory supply so that the cells may continue their submerged aquatic life. Living cells, which is life, will persist in a fluid medium only. Ample water drinking affords a bath for the cells. Absorption of fluids from the tractus intestinalis is especially stimulated by NaCl and CO_2, i. e., normal salt solution surcharged with carbonic acid gas passes into the tractus vascularis and consequently in the tractus lymphaticus the most rapidly of any fluid.

Sodium chloride is the most important inorganic salt in the body, e. g., blood plasma contains 0.7 per cent; lymph plasma contains 0.6 per cent; saliva contains 0.8 per cent; gastric secretions 0.2 per cent; pancreatic secretions 0.3 per cent; bile contains 0.7 per cent; muscle contains 0.7 per cent; cerebro-spinal fluid contains 0.5 per cent; milk contains 0.23 per cent; œdematous contains 0.8 per cent. Sodium chloride, being universally distributed in the body, plays some role of maximum importance in the animal economy.

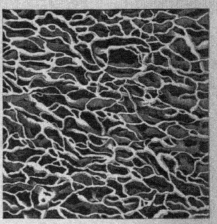

SUPERFICIAL (SMALLER) AND DEEP (LARGER) ANASTOMOSING LYMPHATICS

Fig. 162. From the skin of a child's scrotum. This cut demonstrates the magnitude and importance of the lymphatic apparatus. (Teichman.)

Sodium chloride maintains the body solutions at a fixed density, therefore maintaining the body tissue at a proper percentage of water. It maintains blood plasma density in order to suspend red corpuscles, and lymph plasma density in order to maintain in suspension the guests—white blood corpuscles. Cattle breeders know that a herbivora will not thrive well without a certain quantity of NaCl. Deer will travel miles to frequent the "lick." Carnivora secure sufficient NaCl from their food.

NaCl is required for a stimulus to muscular contraction. NaCl is of special value to digest vegetables (vegetarians). NaCl plays a maximum role in the physiology of the animal economy. Its elimination from diet produces pathologic conditions. In parenchymatous nephritis it should be administered in a minimum quantity as it excessively stimulates the inflamed renal cell. For further details regarding NaCl see Dr. Herbert Richardson, *American Medicine*, July, 1906.

The power of rapidly absorbing water in the tractus intestinalis is in the following order, viz.: (a) absorption is rapid and vigorous in the enteron; (b) absorption is moderately rapid and vigorous in the colon—(however I have observed a pint an hour absorbed per rectum and sigmoid); (c) absorption occurs slowly and moderately in the stomach. Ample water inhibited at regular intervals serves as a medium for prompt conveyance of nourishment to the cells. It accelerates the current of the blood and lymph plasma—at once promptly nourishing and draining the cells. Ample fluids at regular intervals increase the volume and rate of blood flow, hence circulation is more rapid and thus the blood absorbs more oxygen in a definite time to be transported in life to the tissue. Visceral drainage furnishes a maximum nourishment and drainage to cells and hence furnishes a maximum vitality to the organism. In pathologic physiology of the tractus lymphaticus—as in tissue œdema or "dropsies"—ample fluids (carbonated normal salt solution) at regular intervals are beneficial, producing rapid relief, from extrarenal, cutaneous and intestinal elimination. Insufficient fluid ingesta makes the body resemble a stagnant pool, while ample fluid ingesta invigorates it to a mountain stream. Water is a vital stimulant for cell function.

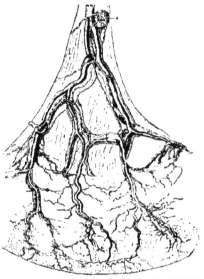

LYMPHATICS AND GLANDS OF THE MESENTERON

Fig. 163. This figure represents excellently the relation of the mesenteronic lymphatics and glands to the vasa mesenterica. The several tiers, rows of mesenteronic lymphatic glands, present characteristic hypertrophy in pathologic physiology of tractus lymphaticus associated with the enteron. (Henle.)

(B) VISCERAL DRAINAGE BY FOOD.

To drain viscera by appropriate food may sound paradoxical, but 75% of food is fluid and both solid and fluid ingesta excite the four grand common visceral functions of the tractus lymphaticus, viz., sensation, peristalsis, absorption, secretion, which are initiated, maintained and subside by fluid and food. The appropriate food produces the appropriate degree of sensation, peristalsis, absorption, secretion in the tractus intestinalis for functionation. The food that will induce proper sensation, peristalsis, absorption and secretion is that which leaves a maximum indigestible residue to stimulate the enteron and colon, such as cereals and vegetables. Peristalsis is necessary for secretion, for peristalsis massages the secretory glands in the tractus intestinalis, enhancing secretory activity. The question of diet to determine is: (a) what kind of food causes calculus-producing material in the urine, pancreatic secretion or bile? (b) what kind of food influences the solubility

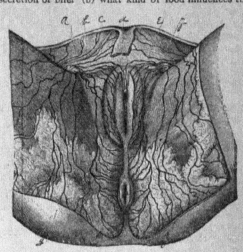

THE INGUINAL GLANDS RECEIVING THE RECTAL AND GENITAL LYMPH CHANNELS (TOLDT)

Fig. 164. This figure demonstrates that rectal or genital infectious or carcinomatous material will be transported to the inguinal glands—hence the hypertrophy and tenderness of the inguinal glands are indicators of pathologic physiology in the genitals and rectum.

of the calculus-producing material in the urine, pancreatic secretion or bile? (1) The meat eater is the individual with the maximum quantity of free uric acid in the urine. Flesh is rich in uric acid. Hence, in excess of uric acid in the urine, flesh (meat, fish, and fowl are all about equal in power to produce uric acid) should be practically excluded, because it increases free uric acid in the urine, *e. g.*, the rational treatment of excessive uric acid in the urine consists of administering food that contains elements to produce basic combinations with uric acid, forming urates (usually sodium) which are free soluble, this will diminish the free uric acid in the urine. Excessive uric acid in the urine is an error in metabolism. Flesh eaters have uric acid and stone. Vegetarians have phosphate, oxalate stone. Generally the subject who suffers from uric acid is a generous liver, liberally consuming meat and highly seasoned foods, indolent and sedentary persons, and alcoholic indulgers. 33% of uric acid is nitrogen. Uric acid is derived

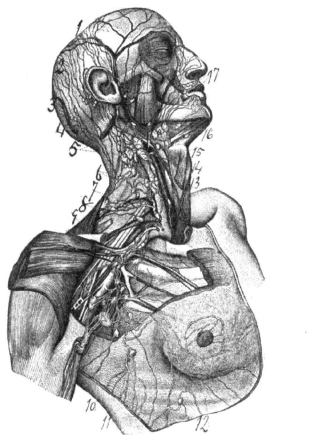

LYMPH GLANDS AND CHANNELS RELATING TO MAMMA AND NECK
(TOLDT)

Fig. 165. This illustration demonstrates the relation of the mamma to the axillary glands and subclavicular glands. This is especially important in pathologic physiology of the route of infectious and carcinomatous material. It is evident that the only hope in controlling carcinoma is by observing its pathologic physiology in the precarcinomatous stage.

from the nuclei that form a constituent of all cell nuclei and which are taken in the body as food. Beef bouillon may be administered because the extract matters in it will scarcely increase the uric acid. A general meat diet largely increases the free uric acid in the urine. (2) The food should contain matters rich in sodium, potassium and ammonium, which will combine as bases with uric acid, producing alkaline urates that are perfectly soluble in the urine.

These typic foods are the vegetables which not only render the necessary alkalies to reduce and transform the free uric acid into resulting soluble urates, but leave an ample indigestible fæcal residue to cause active intestinal peristalsis, aiding in the evacuation through the digestive tract. Hence, the patient should consume large, ample quantities of cabbage, cauliflower, beans, peas, radishes, turnips, spinach in order that sodium, potassium and ammonium existing in the vegetable may combine as bases with free uric acid in the urine-producing soluble urates, thus diminishing free uric acid. A vegetable diet diminishes the free uric acid in the urine 35% less than a meat diet. Again the administration of eggs and milk (lactoalbumen) limits the production of uric acid. The most rational advice is to order the subject to live on mixed diet, consuming the most of that kind of food which lessens the uric acid in the urine—vegetables. Physiologic observations demonstrate that the character and quantity of the ingesta determine the character and quantity of the elimination. If the appropriate food is so valuable in "visceral drainage" in the treatment of the typical uric acid subject the

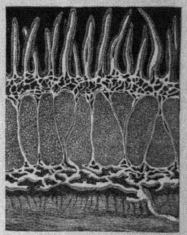

LYMPHATICS OF WALL OF ENTERON OF CALF (INJECTED)

Fig. 166. 1, First upper lymphatics within the intestinal villi. 2, next lower layer internal (sub mucous) lymphatic network. 3, next lower layer langlobate glands (10). 4, external layer of lymphatic network (observe the valves in this layer). 5, circular muscular layer. 6, peritoneal layer. (Teichman.)

appropriate food selected for the subjects of biliary and pancreatic, fæcal calculus, will be relatively as useful. The foods that make soluble basic salts with secretions should be selected. Besides, the selection of appropriate food is frequently amply sufficient to drain the intestinal tract to prevent constipation. It is true, foods alone are not a complete substitute for fluids, but vast aid in visceral drainage may be accomplished by administering food containing considerable coarse residual indigestible matter so that a maximum fæcal residue will stimulate the intestines, especially the colon, to continuous vigorous activity, stimulating to a maximum action of the four grand functions—sensation, peristalsis, absorption and secretion. For twenty years I have treated subjects with excess of uric acid in the urine by administering an alkaline laxative in fluid. The alkaline tablet is composed of cascara sagrada ($\frac{1}{20}$ gr.), aloes ($\frac{1}{2}$ gr.), NaHCO$_3$ (1 gr.), KHCO$_3$ ($\frac{1}{2}$ gr.), MgSO$_4$ (2 grs.). The tablet is used as follows: $\frac{1}{2}$ to 1 tablet (or more, as required to move the bowels once daily) is placed on the tongue before meals and followed by 8 ounces of water (better hot). At 10 A. M., 8 P. M., and bedtime the administration is repeated and followed by a glassful of fluid.

In the combined treatment the appropriate dose of the sodium chloride and alkaline tablet are both placed on the tongue together immediately followed by the 8 ounces of fluid six times daily. This method of treatment furnishes alkaline bases (sodium and potassium and ammonium) to combine

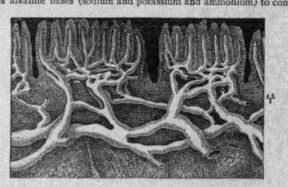

INJECTED LYMPHATIC VESSELS OF THE TONGUE

Fig. 167. The ample transporting lymph apparatus is demonstrated by numerous channels with ample lumen. (Teichman.)

with the free uric acid in the urine, producing perfectly soluble alkaline urates and materially diminishing free uric acid in the urine. Besides, the sodium chloride and alkaline laxative tablets stimulate the sensation, peristalsis, absorption and secretion of the intestinal tract (and all other visceral tracts)—aiding evacuation. I have termed the sodium chloride and alkaline laxative method *the visceral drainage treatment*. The alkaline and sodium chloride tablets take the place of the so-called mineral waters. Our internes have discovered that on entering the hospital the patient's urine presents numerous crystals under the microscope. However, after following the "visceral drainage treatment" for a few days, crystals can scarcely be found again. The hope of removing a formed, localized ureteral or other calculus lies in securing vigorous ureteral or other duct peristalsis with a powerful ureteral or other duct stream. Transportation of ureteral calculus is aided by systematic massage over the psoas muscle and per vaginam. Subjects afflicted with excess of the uric acid (and consequent ureteral calculus) in the urine or other form of calculus need not make extended sojourns to watering places, nor waste their time at mineral springs nor tarry to drink the hissing Sprudel or odorous sulphur, for they can be treated sucessfully in a cottage or palace by *"visceral drainage."* The treatment of a uric acid or other calculus consists, therefore, in the regulation of food and water. It is *dietetic*. The control, relief and prophylaxis of uric acid diathesis or tendency to other calculus formation is a lifelong process. When the uric acid or other calculus has passed spontaneously the patient does not end his treatment, but should pursue a constant systematic method of drinking ample fluids at regular intervals and consume food which contains bases to combine with free uric acid or other compounds producing soluble urates or other soluble compounds.

LYMPHATICS OF THE VERMIFORM APPENDIX

Fig. 168. The lymphatics are injected and present valves. There are two conglobate glands. This lymph apparatus can transport infection with facility on account of its numerous channels of large dimensions. (Teichman.)

I continue this treatment for weeks, months, and the results are remarkably successful. The urine becomes clarified like spring water, and increased in quantity. The volume and rate of blood flow is increased, transporting increased oxygen to tissue. The volume and rate of lymph flow is increased, transporting increased nourishment to the cell and increasing cell drainage, energizing and vitalizing the organism.

The tractus intestinalis becomes freely evacuated, regularly daily. The blood is relieved of waste laden and irritating material. The tractus cutis eliminates freely, and the skin becomes normal. The appetite increases. The four grand common visceral functions—sensation, peristalsis, absorption and secretion—are acting normally. The sewers of the body are well drained and flushed. The sleep becomes improved. The feelings become hopeful.

(C) HABITAT IN VISCERAL DRAINAGE.

Habitat includes all methods of living from the sedentary to the athletic, from the paralytic to the traveler. In general the habitat will refer chiefly to the tractus muscularis and tractus respiratorius. Muscular activity, vigorous exercise, enhances two grand functions, viz., tractus vascularis and tractus glandularis.

The muscles are powerful regulators of circulation (blood and lymph) hence their stimulation (exercise) increases the tone of vessels, magnifies blood currents to viscera which consequently multiplies common visceral function (sensation, peristalsis, absorption and secretion), ending in free visceral drainage. Muscular activity increases blood volume, universally improving nutrition. Maximum blood volume is the primary base of visceral peristalsis. The most typical popular example of the muscles controlling the blood circulation is that of the uterus. The myometrium like elastic living ligatures controls the uterine blood supply (and consequently its functions), (sensation, peristalsis, absorption, secretion, menstruation and gestation), hence drainage with flaccid muscles drain glandular secretion, as in the uterus, may be excessive (leucorrhea).

Exercise is an essential for health. Muscles exercise a dominating control over circulation (blood and lymph). The abdominal muscles influence the caliber of the splanchnic vessels. They exercise an essential influence over peristalsis, secretion, absorption, of the tractus intestinalis, urinarius, vascularis and genitalis. The muscles massage the viscera, enhancing their function and the rate of circulation with consequent free drainage. In the uterus, the most typical example (especially marked during parturition), is prominently demonstrated how the myometrium controls the blood currents like elastic living ligatures. The myometrial bundles by continual contraction decreases the dimension and blood volume of the uterus at a moment's notice subsequent to parturition. The muscular system is equally and continually influential, at all other time as it is parturition, over circulation and visceral function. Regular vigorous habits enhance visceral drainage.

The value of fresh air was never realized so effectively and practically as

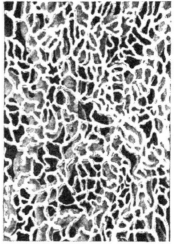

LYMPH VESSELS OF DOG'S STOMACH

Fig. 169. a, a, superficial layer; b, b, deep layer, anastomosing lymphatics. It shows a rich transporting tubular apparatus. (Teichman.)

at present. Fresh cold air cures pulmonary and other tuberculoses. The success of the sanitorium is the continued use of fresh (cold) air. The subject should sleep with fresh continuous cold air passing through an open window space of 8x8 feet. Every physician should advocate the continuous *open window*, day and night for living and sleeping room. It appears to be demonstrated that *cold* fresh air is more beneficial than warm fresh air. It is common talk among people that one winter in the mountains is worth two summers for the consumptive. Much of man's disease is *house disease*. It is lack of oxygen and exercise. The curative and beneficial effect of cold fresh air continually, day and night, for the family must be preached in season and out of season by the physician. The windows should be open all night. Fresh cold air is one of the best therapeutic agents in pathologic physiology of viscera. It stimulates viscera to active function and consequent visceral drainage. Observe the wonderful results of systematic deep breathing,—chest expansion. It utilizes ample oxygen which is rapidly transported to the tissue by the tractus vascularis. If one observes the naked body in rapid deep breathing it will be observed that man's respiratory apparatus extends from his nostrils to his pelvic floor, i. e., it extends to the territory of the spinal (intercostal and lumbar) nerves. Hence, by stimulating to a maximum the functions of the tractus respiratorius (sensation, peristalsis, absorption, secretion)—e. g., by systematic deep respiration—vast benefits result to the organism. The habitat that furnishes opportunity for abundant fresh air, like an open tent on the plains and ample muscular exercise, is the one that affords the essential chances for recovery of pathologic physiology viscera. It enhances visceral drainage. Fresh air is required to transport a continuous, ample supply of oxygen to the muscular apparatus to maintain its normal tone, its contractions and relaxations.

(D) AVOCATION IN VISCERAL DRAINAGE.

The suitability of avocation to health is a daily observation. The prisoners confined in a cell, the clerk confined in a store, stand in contrast to the subjects living in the field, and the traveler continually exposed to sun and wind. The sedentary occupation confining the laborer affords insufficient muscular exercise or fresh air to maintain ample visceral drainage. Visceral drainage is required for health as nourishment. Fresh air aids visceral drainage by transporting well oxygenized blood to the viscera which stimulates the four common visceral functions. The avocation should suit the laborer's physique that the four common visceral functions may be normally maintained.

CONCLUSIONS REGARDING VISCERAL DRAINAGE.

Normal visceral drainage is the key to health. It is maintained by appropriate fluid, food, habitat, avocation. Visceral drainage depends on the normal activity of the four common visceral functions (sensation, peristalsis, absorption, secretion). The chief factor in appropriate visceral drainage is ample fluid administered at regular intervals. It requires five pints of fluid daily to compensate for the visceral elimination. The function of water in the organism is:—1, elimination; 2, solvent; 8, transporter; 4, regulator of the temperature. The cells of the body (parenchymatous and connective tissue) functionate in a fluid medium. Life can persist in a fluid medium only. Visceral drainage is a vast factor in correcting the pathologic physiology of viscera and especially the tractus lymphaticus. Therapeutics must be rational, for nature alone can cure. Therapeutics must imitate and aid nature in restoring function by natural agents. Practically the influence of a physician is limited to pathologic physiology, i. e., the zone between normal physiology and pathologic anatomy. The physician's chief duty is to correct function. Visceral drainage produces maximum cell nourishment and maximum cell drainage, hence creates maximum energy and vitalizes the organism. Practically ample fluids at regular intervals is recommended in pathologic physiology of the viscera, e. g., in obesity, in diabetes, in rheumatism, in fevers, cholelithiasis, nephrolithioses, constipation. Water is a vital stimulant to the life of a cell.

CHAPTER XXXIX.

SPLANCHNOPTOSIA (ATONIA GASTRICA).

Factors. 1. Deranged respiration (due to thoracic splanchnoptosia). 2. Relaxed Abdominal wall. 3. Altered form of Abdominal cavity (Pendulous). 4. Elongation of visceral supports (mesenteries). 5. Gastro-duodenal Dilation (due to compression of the transverse duodenal segment by the superior mesenteric artery, vein and nerve). Splanchnoptosia signifies abnormal distalward movement (sinking prolapse) of viscera. Atonia gastrica signifies abdominal relaxation which is preceded by thoracic relaxation. Splanchnoptosia is included in the diseases of the vasomotor nerve (sympathetic) because the chief and final effect lies in its domain. It is true that the thoracic (diaphragm) and abdominal wall (supplied by spinal nerves) are the primary factors in maintaining and fixing the thoracic and abdominal organs in their normal physiologic position, that relaxation of the thoracic (diaphragm) and abdominal walls are the primary factors in splanchnoptosia, and that in treatment the thoracic (diaphragm) and abdominal walls (areas of respiration) are the primary factors for consideration. However, the damaging effects on the life of the patient rests on the seven visceral tracts (supplied mainly by the sympathetic nerve) viz:—(1) Tractus Respiratorius, (2) Tractus nervosus, (3) Tractus vascularis, (4) Tractus lymphaticus, (5) Tractus intestinalis, (6) Tractus urinarius, (7) Tractus Genitalis (in the order enumerated).

Pathological Relations.

The object of this essay is to demonstrate the relations of splanchnoptosia (atonia gastrica)—to pathologic conditions, as deranged innervation, circulation, respiration, secretion, absorption, muscularis. Relaxation of tissue—muscle, elastic, connective—means elongation of the same. A triumvirate of conditions in splanchnoptosia demand skilled consideration viz.: Anatomy, Physiology and Pathology of the thoracic and abdominal viscera.

In the first place we wish to employ scientific nomenclature only. Splanchnoptosia indicates the ptosis (falling) of the thoracic and abdominal viscera and is the general term we will adopt. It is constantly accompanied by relaxation of the thoracic (diaphragm) and abdominal walls. Gastroptosia signifies abdominal ptosis (not merely of the stomach). Atonia Gastrica signifies abdominal relaxation (and should for accuracy) displace gastroptosia. However, since in stomachoptosia (ptosis of the stomach only) there are other associated visceral ptoses, the terms gastroptosia and atonia gastric are equivalent terms for they both include visceral ptoses and relaxation of the abdominal walls. Enteroptosia is ptosis of the abdominal viscera in general and may include those of the thoracic cavity. I shall reserve for the term enteroptosia the signification of ptosis of the enteron (duodenum, jejunum, and ileum). Coloptosia means ptosis of the colon, and its anatomic segments can be designated by an adjective as coloptosia transversa.

Dr. Achilles Rose of New York and Dr. Kossman of Berlin should be credited for an attempt to introduce scientific nomenclature in this subject.

Splanchnoptosia though a single unit is a general disease of the thoracic and abdominal viscera accompanied by relaxation of the thoracic and abdominal muscular walls. In short splanchnoptosia prevails wherever the nerves of respiration innervate. In splanchnoptosia not only several viscera are simultaneously affected but also the thoracic and abdominal walls are relaxed. From an erroneous and limited view of the founder of splanchnoptosia (Glenard) and the acceptation of the error by numerous followers the idea has prevailed that ptosis of single viscera occur and to them numerous pathologic symptoms have been attributed. Hence a stately literature has arisen from nephroptosia, stomachoptosia, coloptosia (transversa), enteroptosia, etc., etc. On this error of single visceral ptosis has been founded the irrational surgery of so-called visceral pexies. One viscus may be afflicted with greater degree of ptosis than another, however, splanchnoptosia is a general process affecting the thoracic and abdominal walls, the visceral mesenteries and visceral shelves.

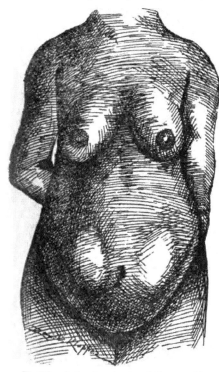

Fig. 170. A female splanchnoptotic, a multipara, ventral view of relaxed abdominal walls. Observe that the relaxed abdominal walls pass sufficiently distalward to conceal the genitals from view. Note the marked distalward position of the umbilicus. There is a depression at the epigastrium. The abdomen is flattened (changed in form), pendulous.

The following table will explain itself:

TABLE OF NOMENCLATURE IN SPLANCHNOPTOSIA WITH RESULTS.

I. Tractus Respiratorius	Ptosis Pulmonalis	Result	excessive respiration / deficient respiration / disordered respiration / distalward movement of the diaphragm
II. Tractus Nervosus	Neuro-Ptosia	Result	trauma (elongation, pain) / altered function {motion, secretion, sensory} / neurosis
III. Tractus Lymphaticus	Ptosis Lymphaticus	Result	flexion / stenosis / elongation / dilatation / neurosis
IV. Tractus Vascularis	Ptosis Vascularis	Result	cardioptosia / flexion / stenosis / elongation / dilatation / neurosis
V. Tractus Intestinalis	1. Gastroptosia / 2. Enteroptosia / 3. Coloptosia / 4. Hepato-Ptosia / 5. Pancrea-Ptosia / 6. Lienoptosia	Result	flexion / stenosis / elongation / dilatation / neurosis / Altered {secretion, absorption, peristalsis, sensation}
VI. Tractus Urinarius	1. Adrenoptosia / 2. Nephroptosia / 3. Uretero-Ptosia / 4. Vesico-Ptosia	Result	flexion / stenosis / dilatation / neurosis / Altered {secretion, absorption, peristalsis, sensation}
VII. Tractus Genitalis	1. Ovario-Ptosia / 2. Oviducto-Ptosia / 3. Metro-Ptosia / 4. Elytro-Ptosia	Result	flexion / stenosis / neurosis / Altered {secretion, absorption, peristalsis, sensation}

Historical.

Though Aberle, Rollet, Rayer, and Oppoltzer presented views of splanchnoptosia, it is probable that J. B. Morgangni (Italian, 1682-1771) was among the first to describe splanchnoptosia anatomically. However, it is my opinion that Rudolph Virchow (1821-1902), my honored teacher, deserves the credit of calling the attention of physicians to splanchnoptosia. He did this practically in 1858 in the fifth volume of his archives by an article entitled "An Historical Critical and Exact Consideration of the Affections of the Abdominal Cavity." The great genius of Virchow is displayed in this extensive autopsic investigation, thirty-two years before Glenard stamped his views on the profession. He called especial attention to dislocation of viscera by peritonitis and advocated that they were the starting points of various symptoms of dyspepsia and indigestion. To Kussmaul we owe the first definite views of gastropsia. The French following Glenard view splanchnoptosia as a congenital affection. The Germans are opposed to this view and maintain that splanchnoptosia is an acquired disease as through pregnancy, peritonitis, method of dress, avocation, living and so forth. Others view splanchnoptosia as a combined effect, congenital predisposition and post natal acquisition. Among some authors, chiefly German, the view is entertained that splanchnoptosia is a reversion to embryonic condition i. e., the viscera gradually reverse their embryonic growth and developmental process.

The year 1885 was an eventful one in the pathology and treatment of relaxed abdominal walls, and consequent splanchnoptosia. This was the period in which Glenard's labors became known. But Glenard was not the only one working on the subject of splanchnoptosis. Czerney and Keher, of Heidelberg, were presenting cases of visceral ptosis in their clinics in 1884 and as a pupil I gained some views on the subject. However, during a whole year's study in Berlin in 1885, with distinguished surgeons, the subject was not once discussed. Subsequently, in a year's course of study with noted German specialists, Professor Schröder showed many subjects of splanchnoptosis. Dr. Landau, who wrote "Wander Niere" (wandering kidney) and "Wander Leber" (wandering liver), gave extensive courses and

Fig. 171. A lateral view of a female splanchnoptotic, a multipara, showing relaxed abdominal walls and umbilicus in a distalward location. The abdomen is pendulous. An attitude of lordosis is assumed for balancing support.

550   THE ABDOMINAL AND PELVIC BRAIN

discussed relaxed abdominal walls and consequent splanchnoptosia, in an interesting manner. In fact, among Germans the term "Hängebauch" (hanging belly) has been common for twenty-five years. Dr. August Martin presented instructive views on the subject in his excellent gynecologic course to physicians. During the past twenty years I have pursued the

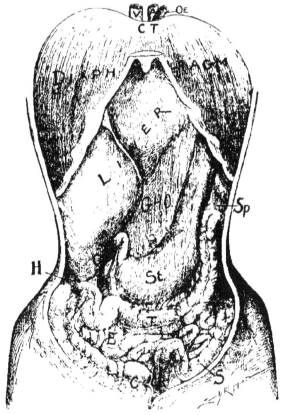

Fig. 172. A female splanchnoptotic with the ventral abdominal walls removed, presenting the viscera in an advanced state of splanchnoptosia. The diaphragm is exposed showing the vena cava (v), the aorta (a) and the œsophagus (œ) projecting through it. A typical splanchnoptotic relation appears with the liver and the stomach (st). In this subject the stomach is practically vertical. The right and transverse colon are forced in the greater pelvis with the main enteronic loop. The flexura coli sinistra (sp) is dragged distalward. The notable phenomenon in this subject is the hypertrophy and distalward movement of the right hepatic lobe—it is at its present stage a typical Riedel lobe.

study of splanchnology among hundreds of gynecologic patients, both medical and surgical, and in the personal abdominal inspection of six hundred adult autopsies. In this paper I will present essentials of the knowledge gained in that experience.

General Views of Splanchnoptosia from Embryology.

The abdominal viscera are maintained in their normal physiologic position by: (a) nerves and vessels; (b) peritoneum; (c) ligaments; (d) visceral pressure; (e) ligaments; (f) visceral shelves; (g) abdominal walls (muscular and osseous). The first idea of importance is that no organ is absolutely or immovably fixed but that each viscus is endowed with a certain degree of movement, hence, the irrational surgical fixation (pexies) of organs is obvious. The mobility of organs is due to various factors as: (a), attitude (prone or erect); (b), respiration; (c), material within the tractus intestinalis (ingesta, gas); (d), material within the tractus urinarius (urine); (e), muscular movement of viscera (rhythm) and abdominal wall; (f), gestation (material within the tractus genitalis). Hence the abdomen should be viewed as occupied with viscera capable of more or less mobility—that fixation of abdominal viscera is abnormal, as e. g., peritoneal bands and visceral pexies.

The embryology of the abdominal viscera is an unending source of interest. It is not a surprise that after noting the development and axial rotation of the tractus intestinalis the view should be entertained that splanchnoptosia is a reversion of development and axial rotation of the digestive tube, i. e., that the tractus intestinalis (and its appendages) has retraced its lines of development. In the early embryo the tractus intestinalis is a straight tube extending from mouth to anus in the middle line of the body (with the liver, spleen and pancreas). Gradually with the progress of months the coecum passes from left to right across the ventral surface of the enteron (duodenum) and ends at birth in the region of the right kidney.

The liver gradually passes from the middle line to the right proximal quadrant of the abdomen ending in the adult in the right concavity of the diaphragm. This process of hepatic development is not complete at birth for the large (pot) belly of the child is due to a large liver. In typical splanchnoptosia the position of the abdominal organs stimulate those of the embryo and infant. Seeking a clue for treatment from embryologic phenomena it would be that splanchnoptosia is a general visceral disease and that rational treatment should be applied to the abdominal walls—not to single viscera as visceral pexies.

Clinical Aspects.

From a clinical view certain organs may appear of more significance in splanchnoptosia than others. For example the general surgeon who does not investigate the subject of splanchnoptosia centers his observations in idol worship on the liver, kidney, uterus or stomach and with his cranium completely occupied with visceral pexies (heathen gods in physiology) initiates his campaign of pexies or visceral fixation by suturing one of those organs to the abdominal wall. What has he accomplished? He has produced one lesion (visceral fixation) in attempting to improve another (supposed excessive visceral mobility). Generally the worst is visceral fixation because the fixation is unphysiologic, irrational and affects but a detached part, a segment of the general splanchnoptosia. The therapeusis should be applied to the abdominal wall.

The embryologic view demonstrates that the seven visceral tracts (respiratorius, intestinalis, circularis, lymphaticus, nervosus, urinarius and genitalis) are practically alike affected—splanchnoptosia is a unit though a general disease. However, the symptoms of splanchnoptosia of some visceral tracts are not so manifest as that of others e. g., the tractus nervosus is practically manifest as that of the urinarious and intestinalis. Embryology suggests that viscera of late development and distant fixation from the radix mesenterica (coeliac and superior mesenteric arteries) are prominent in splanchnoptosia as the liver, stomach, colon, genitals, kidney. They are distantly removed from the solid anchorage of the radix mesenterica and their solid fixation is hence more limited by peritoneal bands to the abdominal wall.

For example the liver is practically fixed to the diaphragm only. Its fixation to the radix mesenterica is limited by the anchorage it may obtain from the arteria hepatica ensheathed with its fibrous tissue from the aorta and its encasement of plexiform nerve network from the abdominal brain. It must be admitted, however, that the late mesenterial development or expanding of the base of mesenteries, the increased areas of peritoneal adhesions (non-pathologic) to the dorsal wall as occurs in the liver, colon, stomach enteron serves as valuable fixation for the viscera. These acquired basal mesenterial expansions produce compact solidarity of organs re-enforcing the supporting strength of the radix mesenterica (vascular).

GENERAL PATHOGENESIS OF SPLANCHNOPTOSIA.

The method of origin (ætiology) and development of splanchnoptosia is explained by different authors through different views. The divergent views entertained depend on the assumed beginning base—whether splanchnoptosia be due to (a) congenital predisposition; (b) acquired defects from life's opposing forces; (c) reversion to embryologic conditions or (d) a combination of the three preceding factors.

First, a congenital predisposition suggests a characteristic body form or congenital weakness or fragility of tissue which predisposes the individual in the conflict of life's resisting forces to splanchnoptosia.

Second, acquired defects producing splanchnoptosia, attempts to explain rationally the varied factors as rapidly repeated gestations, sudden loss of fatty tissues, pathologic conditions of the abdominal wall, body form, the influence of visceral motion in respiration, the evil effect of living and dressing (constricting bands), as well as various industries and traumata.

Third, reversion to embryonic conditions would practically be a constitutional predisposition and hence belong to congenital predisposition.

Fourth, the view which includes the combined factors of each theory (congenital or acquired defects) of splanchnoptosia is the more rational, because the disease is generally prevalent among all nations.

Anatomy and Physiology.

In the pathogenesis of splanchnoptosia two factors must be carefully investigated, viz.: Anatomy and physiology. The anatomy must not only include the elements—connective tissue, muscle, elastic fiber and bone—but bodily form, attitude, avocation, modes of life. The physiology must include all the consideration of visceral functions—respiration, gestation, circulation, absorption, secretion and rhythm.

Glenard a physician at Lyons, France, who practiced at Vichy observed that splanchnoptosia was closely related to neurasthenia and nervous dyspepsia. Glenard observed three groups of symptoms viz: (1) (*atonia gastrica*) abdominal relaxation or lack of tone in the abdominal wall which presented: (a) deformity of the abdominal wall; (b) flabbiness, relaxation of the abdominal wall; (c) ease with which the hypochondrium may be compressed. (2) *Splanchnoptosia* presented: (a) (gastroptosia) splashing sounds in the stomach; (b) epigastric pulsation; (c) nephroptosia; (d) coloptosia transversum. (3) *Enteroptosia* presented three signs: (a) a palpable contracted band of the transverse colon; (Glenard's corde transverse colique) (b) the coecum; (c) the sigmoid.

Glenard found at Vichy resort 148 cases of splanchnoptosia in 1,310 subjects—11%. He practiced among a neurotic class of subjects. Glenard believed that the starting point of splanchnoptosia is the sinking of the flexura coli hepatica due to relaxation of the ligamentum flexura hepatica. He considered that ptosis of single viscera could occur in four conditions, viz.: (a) neurosis; (b) hepatic disease; (c) dyspepsia; (d) general or conditional illness. The three main symptoms of splanchnoptosia according to Glenard are colic, stenosis, nephroptosia and hepatic deformity. Glenard studied 40 splanchnoptotic autopsies and concluded that when the suspensory ligaments of the stomach and intestines are relaxed accompanied by the distalward movements of these viscera, stenosis will occur, and the coecum alone will maintain its normal form as it has no suspensory ligament. Glenard's belt test of splanchnoptosia consists in the physician standing behind the patient, elevating the abdomen with the hands, and if it affords relief the diagnosis is confirmed. The characteristic symptoms are: sensations of weakness, abdominal discomfort, constipation.

Space forbids further views from Dr. Frantz Glenard, the founder of splanchnoptosia whose excellent book of 875 pages lies before me. It was published in 1899 and entitled the author to the pathologic eponym "Glenard's disease." The title of the book is "Des Ptoses viscerales Diagnostic et nosographie (enteroptosie—Hepatisme)." It is a monument of industry which will be admired for all time.

Through all the pathogenesis of splanchnoptosia neurosis is a constant accompaniment, inseparably connected. In 1896 Stiller published an article in which he claims that there is a neurasthenic stigma (stigma neurasthenicum), the floating tenth rib (costa decima fluctuens). Stiller believes that splanchnoptosia rests on embryologic defect (vitium primæ formationis). This should be known by the pathologic eponym "Stiller's costal stigma." This view is supported by finding nephroptosia in children. Splanchnoptosia subsequent to parturition (puerperium) should be designated by the pathologic eponym "Landau's splanchnoptosia."

Splanchnoptosia accompanying chlorosis should be designated by the pathologic eponym "Meinert's splanchnoptosia." Dr. Einhorn believes that constricting bands (corset) play a large role in the pathogenesis of splanchnoptosis.

Keith's Theory.

In the pathogenic theories of splanchnoptosia the latest most elaborate and comprehensive is that of Arthur Keith, in the Hunterian lectures of 1903, published in the London Lancet, March 7, and 14, 1903. Mr. Keith claims in these most excellent and well studied lectures that splanchnoptosia is the result of a vitiated method of respiration. Keith's investigations of splanchnoptosia were conducted on an anatomic base rather than a clinical one and include vast labors based on the solid ground of nature. I wish here to acknowledge my indebtedness to Mr. Arthur Keith.

Fig. 173. Represents the abdominal and thoracic organs separated by the diaphragm. The pillars or crura of the diaphragm (AC and A C) are marked, demonstrating that inspiration drags (forces) the thoracic organs distalward. Observe that the pericardium is solidly and firmly fixed to the diaphragm, hence in inspiration, when the diaphragm moves distalward, the heart, lungs, and great thoracic vessels must accompany it.

Additional Factors in Etiology.

1. Intra abdominal pressure.

Factors which increase intra-abdominal pressure: 1, Gestation. 2, Food. 3, Fluid. 4, Meteorism. 5, Adispose deposits. 6, Ascites. 7, Tumors. 8, Pleurisy. 9, Feces. 10, Urine. 11, Gastro-duodenal dilatation. 12, Coughing. 13, Contracted pelvis. 14, Blood and lymph volume.

2. Relaxed abdominal walls.

This consists in elongation and separation of fascial and muscular fibres of the anterior abdominal walls, the thoracic and pelvic diaphragm.

3. Compression of the transverse segment of the duodenum by the superior mesenteric artery, vein and nerve.

4. Congenital defects in the nervous, muscular and visceral systems.

5. Defective food and excessive labor.

6. Lordosis or anterior curvature of the vertebral column enhances splanchnoptosia.

7. With the progress of relaxed abdominal walls there is a disproportionate or abnormal relation established between the nervous and muscular systems, and coördination is defective and hence nourishment and function are also defective. The trauma to the sympathetic nervous system produces excessive, deficient or disproportionate secretions and peristalsis in the viscera, hence nourishment is again defective. With the advance of splanchnoptosia the blood and lymph vessels become stenosed, their mechanism disturbed, producing irregular circulation and hence nourishment is again defective.

Splanchnoptosia is a kind of neurosis. It is devitalizing of the sympathetic system in which vitality of the neuro-vascular visceral pedicle is impaired, it becoming elongated, stretched. Perhaps the elastic tissue is degenerated.

Notwithstanding the manifold theories and dreams of respected authors and the easily recognized original work of industrious investigators in splanchnoptosia I am still convinced that one of the great factors of splanchnoptosis is the waist or constricting band, not merely the corset, for a corset may be worn so loose that it practically does no damage. During the past 15 years Dr. Lucy Waite and the author have dissected over 35 female bodies for practical topographical and applied anatomy of the abdominal and pelvic viscera. We opened the cadaver and then with the two hands as a corset band or any form of waist band the body was compressed and the result on the abdominal viscera noted. What will happen in tightening the waist band? The answer is clearly evident in watching the progress of constricting the band. First the right more mobile kidney moves medianward and ventralward, compressing the junction of the descending and transverse duodenal segments, ending in a position almost in the middle of the abdomen. The kidney suffers the most movement dislocation of any abdominal organ. The liver is compressed as is shown in autopsies in the corset liver, the gallbladder projects ventralward, allowing stagnation of bile and subsequent formation of hepatic calculi. The daily effect of the waist or constricting band is diminutive, but continued from week to week, month to month, and year to year, its end results are enormous in changing and damaging structure and function. It constricts the right colon, compromising cecal evacuation, the canalization of the ureter, renal and ovarian veins and inferior vena cava. The nephroptosia elongates the renal vessels especially, the artery which is sheathed in a network of ganglia not only traumatizing them, but, by tugging and dragging on the abdominal brain, the trauma produces the stigmata of hysteria and other neuroses.

Peritoneal and Omental Adhesions.

I wish here to direct the attention of the practitioner to a fertile field in the etiology of splanchnoptosia which in short is peritoneal and omental adhesions. I have published numerous articles during the past decade advocating the evil influence of peritoneal adhesions on the abdominal viscera. I am gratified to observe that several physicians as Robert T. Morris and several others are realizing the value of these views. In hundreds of autopsies I have noted the structures of the genitals, appendix, gall-bladder and sigmoid apparently ruined by contracting peritoneal adhesions distorting the viscera into a shapeless mass.

I have explained for years how these peritoneal adhesions induced by muscular trauma, created distorted physiology, ending in appendicitis, cholecystitis, sigmoiditis and salpingitis. Peritoneal adhesions fix the viscera in a single mass so that the several viscera cannot glide on each other. The solid visceral mass acts like a solid piston in the abdomen forcing the viscera distalward. The omentum is frequently found extensively adherent to the pelvic viscera which drags the viscera in the proximal abdomen distalward at every respiration. Peritoneal adhesions are extensively vicious factors in compromising visceral anatomy and physiology and abetting remarkably splanchnoptosia and other diseases.

General Views.

If single viscera become markedly splanchnoptotic, prolapsed by accident, trauma, the general painful neurotic symptoms of splanchnoptosia are markedly absent. The existence and results of splanchnoptosia are not fully explained. The difficulty has its seat: (a), in the determining of the exact or normal position of viscera; (b), the exact forces which establish an organ in its position; (c), the views of the cause or origins of splanchnoptosia are so various as to obscure the picture; (d), the symptoms are so complex that splanchnoptosia appears like a conglomerate disease. The confusion is due to the multiple points from which the disease has been established. The history of splanchnoptosia is that of displacement of single organs.

Glenard, though comprehending a limited field, combined them into a single disease, a unit which should now be termed splanchnoptosia because it involves the thoracic and abdominal viscera (as well as their respective enclosing walls). Splanchnoptosia is a disproportion, a disturbed relation between cavity lumen (chest, abdomen) and contents (viscera) not only anatomically but physiologically, that is the functionating organs are working in a distorted, dislocated position hence experiencing a change of form and function.

The thoracic and abdominal cavities should be viewed as one general lumen, simply divided by the diaphragm. The vertebral column may be viewed as a mast maintaining its erectness by means of the erector spinæ muscles. The ribs, sail arms, receive support from the fixed mastoid process through the sterno-cleido mastoid muscle. The viscera are anchored, fixed to the dorsal wall—the great mast. The solid, visceral contents are confined, maintained to the mast by the circular, fibro-elastic muscular band—the thoracico-abdominal walls.

The physiology of viscera must be credited with the greatest role in splanchnoptosia for during their maximum functions the weakest and most defective anatomy begins to yield—especially in the diaphragm (in inspiration), in the abdominal walls (in gestation, ingesta, gas, defecation); in the circulation, variation of the volume of arterial, venous and lymphatic fluids. Intra-abdominal pressure is the contraction of the circular fibro-elastic muscular abdominal wall plus atmospheric pressure.

Mechanism of Splanchnoptosia.

We know that the extra-abdominal pressure is greater than the intra-abdominal pressure, for, on peritoneal section the atmosphere rushes in with an audible sound. This view would oblige the visceral supports (mesenteries and ligaments) to assume the office of not only anchorage but that of fixation (and support). Viscera are essentially supported by underlying ones (visceral shelves) like bricks in a wall. Schwerdt estimates that the viscera mesenteries or ligaments support about one-eighth of the organ weight. The fixation of the viscera to the (dorsal) abdominal wall and their share in the visceral support might be compared to a boat at anchorage. The boat rests on the water, which represents the compact supporting visceral shelves (like bricks in a wall). The anchor cable (mesenteries, ligaments) merely decides the limit or space range of the boat (in fact seldom becoming tensionized). The banks of the water represent the abdominal wall.

The principal support of the viscera are: (a), the compact underlying visceral shelves; (b), the abdominal wall; (c), the visceral supports (mesenteries, ligaments) perhaps suspending one-eighth of the weight of the viscera. By placing a body erect and removing the ventral wall the viscera pass distalward, prolapse, sink, placing the visceral mesenteries and ligaments on tension. The visceral mesenteries or ligaments might be compared to a string attaching a specimen in a fluid filled jar, to the cork. The string support is limited, but without it the specimen would sink or rest on the floor of the jar.

The abdominal viscera are located more distalward while in the erect attitude (1 inch) than the prone position. The more solid organs as liver, kidneys, uterus and foreign material occupied segments of the tractus intestinalis pass distalward with more facility while organs containing gas pass

558   THE ABDOMINAL AND PELVIC BRAIN

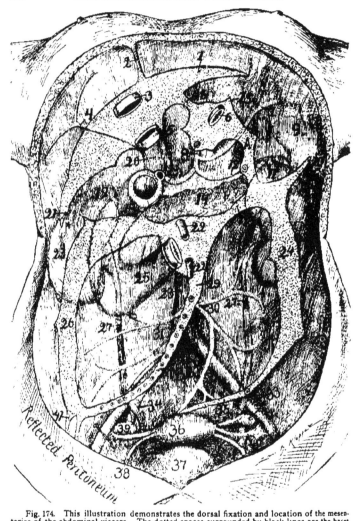

Fig. 174. This illustration demonstrates the dorsal fixation and location of the mesenteries of the abdominal viscera. The dotted spaces surrounded by black lines are the bases or areas of mesenteric insertion. 1, Ligamentum triangulum sinistrum; 2, ligamentum suspensorium (teres) hepatis; 3 and 5, vena cava (distal); 4, arteria phrenica dextra; 16, omentum gastro-hepaticum; 15, ligamentum gastro-phreneum; 8, arteria coeliaca; 7, arteria gastrica; 12, arteria linealis; 13, arteria hepatica; 14, spleen; 17, mesocolon transversum;

proximalward with more facility. Abdominal organs are limited in motion through the mesenteries, ligaments and adjacent organs. The abdominal wall exercises an opposition to the static pressure of viscera. With increased contents (ingesta, fluids, gestation) the ventral abdominal wall yields. If a body be hung by the head and the abdomen incised the viscera will prolapse. In the resting upright attitude the abdominal wall offers but passive pressure opposition to the viscera.

The reason for the slow progress in the knowledge of splanchnoptosia among medical men is: (a), the autopsic reports, for the past years, have been of limited practical value as regards splanchnoptosia. The reason of this fact is that when the subject is in the prone but especially the dorsal position the organs assume chiefly their normal physiologic location. The pathologist does not appear to have anything to report; (b), the clinician seldom witnesses an autopsy on a previously diagnosed splanchnoptotic. Hence the autopsist and clinician have practically opposed each other—possessed no views in common—did not agree and also seldom met at an autopsy. The pathologist in the morgue returned no evidence to aid the clinician on the living. In the symptomatology heretofore a tendency has existed to attribute excessive symptoms to single splanchnoptotic organs, especially the genitals, kidneys, stomach and liver, and deficient symptoms to other organs as the colon, enteron, vascular system and nervous system. Splanchnoptosia is a unit—a general disease. Also excessive symptoms have been attributed to single organs in order to prepare the road for the irrational pexy.

ANATOMY AND PHYSIOLOGY OF SPLANCHNOPTOSIA. ABDOMINAL WALLS.

The abdominal walls consist of oblique, perpendicular and transverse muscular layers woven in a powerful fascial band.

All abdominal muscles are fixed on bony parts, as the costal, iliac and pubic crests, as well as the vertebral column, while the diaphragm is inserted into the ribs and vertebral column with its vault fixed by the pericardium. The abdominal wall is covered externally by skin and internally by peritoneum—both powerful and elastic membranes. Certain weak, yielding muscular and fascial lines exist in the abdominal walls, viz.:

1. Musculi recti abdominales arise from the pubic crest and become inserted into the ribs and os sternum. The two recti muscles which lie parallel to each other are the ones which preserve the delicate visceral poise. Slight extra intra-abdominal pressure produces diastasis of the muscles. In splanchnoptosis, the recti show (a) diastasis, (b) elongation, and (c) separation of the fibres, (d) extensive thinning and flattening, and (e) atrophy.

10, ligamentum casto-coelicum; 11, kidney; a, omentum gastro-splenicum; 18, shows dot between blades of omentum majus; 19, adrenal bodies; 20, foramen winslowi; 22, arteria mesenterica superior; 23, arteria renalis dextra; 24, mesocolon sinistrum. (Insertion line of its two blades.) 25, duodenum transversum (covered by peritoneum); 26, mesocolon dextrum. (Insertion line of its right and left blade.) 27, ureter (shimmering through the peritoneum); 28, aorta; 29, mesenteron; 30, arteria mesenterica inferior; 31, arteria colica dextra; 32, arteria iliaca communis; 33, arteria iliaca externa; 34, arteria iliaca interna; 35, mesosigmoid. (Double blades.) 36, uterus; 37, urinaria vescicae; 38, ligamentum rotundum uteri; 39, ovarium; 40, oviductum (sinistrum).

2. The fascial lines which yield in splanchnoptosia are (a) the linea alba, which I have noted three inches wide, the fascial fibres are elongated and separated, making the abdominal wall very thin and lax in the median line, (b) the lineae semilunaries which also become quite thin and lax, the fascial fibres elongate and separate, (c) the fibres of the linea transversæ, inscriptiones tendinæ or the abdominal ribs, which elongate and separate.

The physiologic action of the abdominal wall is a combined one, as the varied direction of its muscular fibres indicate. We may indicate its physiologic action in certain directions. 1. The abdominal wall acts as a circular band, to fix and support the abdominal viscera as the neuro-vascular visceral pedicles are not intended for primary mechanical visceral support. 2. The abdominal wall is a highly elastic apparatus. It distends and contracts fitting the abdominal contents. The skin and peritoneum are exceedingly elastic. Observe how the skin and peritoneum will return without a fold to the normal state after distention from gestation, ascites or tumors, etc. 3. The physical function of the abdominal wall is aided by its capacity of contraction and of extension in respiration, defecation, urination, expulsion of uterine contents; in laughing and coughing. In short it is the function of the abdominal wall to contract and dilate during the volume changes of the abdominal contents, as well as the volume changes in the thorax. 4. The physiological function of the abdominal wall is to maintain a vigilant guard, a vigorous but delicate elastic regulation of abdominal visceral contents. The elastic spanning of the abdominal walls maintains a delicate visceral poise.

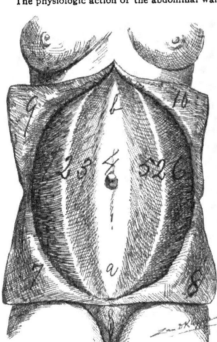

Fig. 175. Represents the separation and elongation of the recti abdominales in splanchnoptosia.

Etiology of Relaxation.

Relaxed abdominal walls arise in various forms in different subjects. Not all thin abdominal walls are relaxed, neither are all relaxed abdominal walls thin. The elements, the fascial, elastic and muscular fibres must be separated and elongated to constitute relaxed abdominal walls, which are best observed in the erect attitude. The causes of relaxed abdominal walls

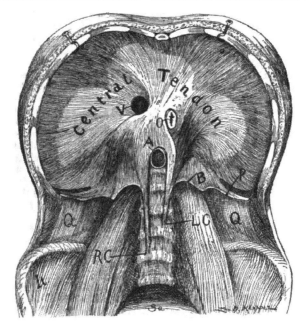

Fig. 176. The diaphragm. (Ventro-distal view.) This illustration presents the central tendon of the diaphragm with its important long right (RC) and short left (LC) crus. The right diaphragmatic crus extends to the (IV) lumbar vertebra. The crura of the diaphragm have a fixed immobile spinal insertion and forcible drag the central tendon of the diaphragm with its attached percardium distalward at every inspiration. In the physiology of the stronger inspiration and weaker expiration begins splanchnoptosia. The inspiratory muscles from sheer force—and to the crura must be attributed the chief factor.

lie in the elements of the wall itself, viz.: fascia, muscle, peritoneum, skin and elastic fibres. The fine tonus of the wall, its delicate elasticity may be lost. Its fascia and muscular fibres are separated and elongated. It is flaccid and hangs excessively distalward and the unsupported viscera follow it. There seems to be a limited life for the abdominal walls, as there is for the utero-ovarian vascular circle of the genitals. For the abdominal walls begin, as a widely applicable rule, to relax at about 35, and continue to relax or atrophy to the end of life. There can be no doubt that the elastic fibres elongate and separate, perhaps also atrophy, for the abdominal wall is not only relaxed but is thinned, attenuated. It may be that at a time of malnutrition the abdominal walls become relaxed, never subsequently recovering their normal state. Relaxed abdominal walls frequently follow continuous fevers, gestation, ascites or any factor which increases intra-abdominal pressure. The most frequent supposed cause of relaxed abdominal wall is rapidly repeated gestation. In every gestation physiologic dastasis of the musculi recti abdominales occur. It is not infrequent to find the recti muscles three inches apart at the end of gestation. But relaxed abdominal walls are not confined to women, as the testimony of the 450 recorded autopsies of men proved, there being frequent splanchnoptosia in these subjects.

The pelvic, thoracic and abdominal viscera are liable to frequent dislocation. In visceral inspection of 600 adult autopsies I found local peritoneal adhesions in over 80 per cent. In other words, more adult subjects have dislocated viscera from peritoneal adhesions than normally situated ones. The neuro-vascular visceral pedicle, the mesentery, becomes elongated and its root glides distalward on the dorsal abdominal wall. The distalward dislocation of the dorsal attachments of the mesentery allows (a) elongation of the mesentery, (b) an excessive range of visceral motion, (c) the abdominal and the pelvic organs pass distalward and become impacted in the pelvis, (d) Splanchnoptosia compromises circulation and deranges absorption secretion, (e) disorders peristalsis, (f) traumatizes nerve periphery, (g) it impairs nourishment, (h) it produces especially indigestion, (i) it invites constipation. Splanchnoptosia accompanies a defective nervous system of perhaps congenital origin. As it increases every decade, after 35 years of age it is liable to cause stenosis or partial obstruction of the canals, tractus intestinalis from traction of one part and elongation of other parts of the mesenteries. It compromises canalization. The effects of splanchnoptosia (Glenard's disease, 1884), on individual abdominal organs, are varied and numerous.

Intestinal Tract.

The tractus intestinalis is affected chiefly by: (a), compromising of circulation, blood and lymph supply, i. e., congestion and decongestion, (b) trauma of nerve centers, strands and nerve periphery, (c) complication from loss of peristalsis and atony of bowel muscle, (d) gastro-intestinal catarrh and indigestion from excessive, deficient and disproportionate secretions, absorptions. Also dragging on the abdominal brain, an independent nerve center producing nausea, neurosis, headache, reflexes, and deranges secretion and motion on other viscera. (e) Dilatation of the stomach and duodenum, caused by the superior mesenteric artery, vein and nerve, obstructing the duodenum at this point where they cross the transverse segment. The stomach is especially liable to dilatation from the above causes, where the prolapse of the enteron (enteroptosia) is sufficiently advanced to allow the

SPLANCHNOPTOSIA

enteronic loops to pass distalward into the lesser pelvis and particularly when the subject lies on the back, for then the superior mesenteric artery, vein and nerve are put on a stretch and they constrict vigorously the trans-

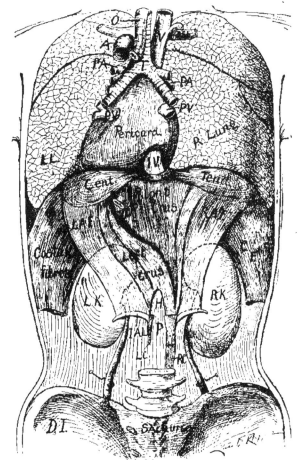

Fig. 177. The diaphragm. (Dorsal view.) This illustration presents the central tendon and the attached pericardium with the powerful right and left crura. During inspiration the diaphragmatic crura, immovably fixed by insertion in the spinal column contract, drawing the tendon of the diaphragm, to which the pericardium is attached, distalward. Splanchnoptosia begin the respiratory organs, i. e., in the conquering of the inspiratory muscles R. A. F., right acute fibres.

verse portion of the duodenum. (f) The enteronic loops being dislocated (enteroptosia) into the pelvis, peristalsis, absorption secretion, circulation and nerve periphery are compromised, followed by catarrh, constipation and indigestion. (g) The colon, especially the colon transversum, may lie in the lesser pelvis, producing similar compromising circumstances as in the enteron. (h) The appendages (liver, pancreas, and spleen) of the tractus intestinalis, in ptosis are compromised in circulation, secretion, absorption, peristalsis and nerve periphery.

Genital Tract.

In splanchnoptosia the genital tract suffers, especially in circulation and nerve periphery as well as secretion and absorption. Uteroptosia may arise to such an excessive degree of mobility that the uterus may be forced proximal to the umbilicus and in any portion of the great pelvis.

Urinary Tract.

The urinary tract suffers in splanchnoptosia, chiefly from dislocation of the kidney (right) nephroptosia. From several hundred autopsic inspections and living abdominal sections, I can say that in many subjects the kidney (right) has extensive motion and is significant in gynecology, as its symptoms mimic or simulate genital disturbances. In

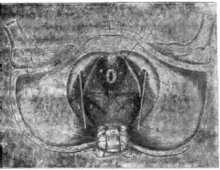

Fig. 178. Proximal view of the pelvic floor. This illustration is drawn from my own dissection (by Dr. Sholer) to present the diaphragma pelvis.

my practice 60 per cent of subjects possess a kidney range of 4 inches, 2 inches proximalward and 2 inches distalward. Large numbers of subjects have a right kidney range of 8 inches, 1 1-2 inches proximalward and 1 1-2 inches distalward. The mobility of the right kidney is of extreme importance in multipara have a movable kidney nephroptosia—proved by examination in the horizontal and erect positions. The mobility of the right kidney is due to (a) the longer right renal artery, (b) the liver through the diaphragm forces the right kidney distalward, (c) muscular trauma of the diaphragm, quadratus lumborum and constricting waist bands, (d) absorption of pararenal fat, (e) the abdominal cavity of woman is funnel-shaped, with the large end of the funnel distalward and hence the kidney receives less support distally than it does in man, (f) subinvolution attacks the "Wolfian body." (g) The erect attitude. By continual relaxation of the abdominal walls its physiological and anatomic functions are impaired.

SPLANCHNOPTOSIA

The physiological regulation and chief anatomic support of the viscera are unbalanced, and the delicate visceral poise is lost. The abdominal viscera move distalward, become prolapsed following the relaxed abdominal walls. The condition of relaxed abdominal walls is followed by splanchnoptosia. Of the three great systems of the abdominal viscera, the tractus genitalis, tractus urinarius and the tractus intestinalis, the last suffers the most severely. Relaxed abdominal walls are followed by dislocated viscera. A viscus is dislocated when it is permanently out of position. In general a dislocated viscus suffers from trauma of its nerve periphery and its blood, and lymph vascular system is compromised. Splanchnoptotic organs become hypertrophied. Also the nourishment of a dislocated viscus is defective, irregular. Dislocated or prolapsed viscera are the segments of vicious circles. Relaxed abdominal walls are followed by partial hernia, especially in the pouches of the most yielding parts, as the linea alba, supraumbilical and the lineae semilunares or the various defective rings.

In the following scheme are noted not only the great factors in splanchnoptosia, but other detailed factors:

The diaphragm.

The diaphragm is a muscular barrier anchored like a buoy between the thoracic and abdominal viscera. It rises and falls with the ebb and flow of respiration.

Fig. 179. Distal view of the pelvic floor. This cut is drawn by Dr. Sholer from my own dissection. The proximal and distal fascia of the levator ani is removed as in previous fig.

There is a visceral tide—a stronger inspiratory ebb and a weaker expiratory flow.

It is a muscular dome for the abdominal viscera and a muscular floor for the thoracic viscera. The viscera move to and fro with the diaphragm. The average height of the diaphragm is on a level with the fifth costal cartilage and its general fluctuating range level is two inches.

The variation in the level of the diaphragm represents the phases of a respiratory rhythm. The distalward displacement of the diaphragm is an essential feature in splanchnoptosia. For the liver, spleen, stomach and kidneys are firmly bound to its abdominal surface. The diaphragm is supported in its position first: by the abdominal muscles forcing the abdominal viscera proximalward against its distal concavity; second, it is supported by the thoracic viscera; by fusion of the pericardium to its proximal surface, the heart, great thoracic blood-vessels, trachea and lungs which attach the proximal surface of the diaphragm to the dorsal thoracic wall; third, the costal support is from the 6 lower ribs and spinal support from the I, II and III lumbar vertebræ. Hence the abdominal, thoracic, costal and spinal supports are required for a normal position of the diaphragm. A defect in any support (contraction or relaxation) of the diaphragm prepares the road for splanchnoptosia.

The crura of the diaphragm send strong fibers to the pericardium, (through the central tendon) roots of the lung (reflected pleuræ), vena cava, the great thoracic vessels, connective tissues of the œsophagus and trachea —all diaphragm and thoracic viscera, being solidly and compactly bound together. With each inspiration the crura of the diaphragm contract on their immobile spinal origin and draw the thoracic viscera (and force the abdominal) distalward. The vigorous contraction of the diaphragmatic crura (in inspiration) is the most important factor in producing incipient splanchnoptosia. For reasons, not fully known, the (inspiratory) diaphragmatic supports of certain individuals yield and splanchnoptosia begins. The yielding of the diaphragm supports occur first in the muscles of inspiration. The diaphragm (especially the crura) during contraction (inspiration) forces the mediastinal contents—heart (pericardium), trachea and œsophagus— distalwards, which elongates the mediastinal mesentery, composed of pleural reflections. By viewing a patient laterally with the fluoroscope the heart may be observed to move proximalward and distalward during respiration. The range of proximalward and distalward action of the heart (and consequently the diaphragm which is fixed to the pericardium) is considerable especially in subjects with abdominal type of respiration and in such the distalward movements of the heart is the greater.

Influence of Diaphragm in Splanchnoptosia.

When the diaphragmatic supports begin to yield the inspiratory distalward movements (displacements) of the thoracic viscera are a cause of incipient splanchnoptosia. Since the pericardium is not only solidly attached to the diaphragm but is also solidly attached to the roots of the lung, thoracic vessels, œsophagus and trachea a movement of the diaphragm (induced chiefly by crural contractions) must be accompanied by movements of the thoracic viscera. In short, the diaphragm is connected to the mediastinum, pericardium root of lung, thoracic vessels, œsophagus trachea, vagi and the respiratory expansion is gained chiefly by a distalward movement of the diaphragm accompanied by the thoracic viscera—lungs and heart. It is when this distalward movement of the diaphragm (inspiration) becomes excessive (from relaxation of diaphragmatic supports) that splanchnoptosia begins. (We will at present not dispute that atonia gastrica abdominal relaxation develops concomitant as respiration includes the abdominal muscles.) The diaphragm is a digastric muscle with two origins viz.: (a) spinal origin (vertebral column—crura—and arcuate fibers; (b) ventral origin (from the 6 lower ribs) and by the contractions of its two bellies enhances thoracic space for inspiration, therefore its share in incipient splanchnoptosia is evident.

From the above evidence it is obvious that the distalward movements of the diaphragm (in respiration) will depend on the opposition offered by the abdominal viscera through the strength of the abdominal wall, as well as the mobility of the 6 lower ribs. If the muscles of the abdominal wall offer normal resistance to the distalward movements of the abdominal viscera the diaphragm will be supported by the abdominal viscera (liver, spleen, pancreas, stomach, kidneys) and cannot descend. However, if atonia gastrica (abdominal relaxation) exist the diaphragm shares in the thoracic and abdominal splanchnoptosia with consequent abdominal type of respiration. If, however, the contraction of the diaphragm (crura) cannot force the abdominal viscera distalward the thoracic viscera must expand (in respiration) within the thorax with consequent thoracic type of respiration. Splanchnoptotics experience abdominal types of respiration.

Spinal Segment.

The spinal segment of the diaphragm has a constant function, i. e., its contraction (inspiration) forces both thoracic and abdominal viscera distalward. The ventral segment of the diaphragm is otherwise for its action on the lower 6 ribs depends on the position of the ribs. If the lower 6 ribs become misplaced the action of the diaphragmatic muscles become altered. The abdominal type of respiration signifies that the pulmonary space is gained chiefly by the expansion of the distal end of the thorax. The thoracic type of respiration signifies that the pulmonary space is gained mainly by the expansion of the proximal end of the thorax. 1. It may be noted therefore that the fixation of the thoracic viscera is through: (a) the thoracic, diaphragmatic and abdominal muscles; (b) thoracic vessels; (c) the œsophagus; (d) the trachea; (e) the pericardium; (f) dorsal thoracic mesentery (reflected pluræ); (g) the thoracic fascia; (h) vagi and phrenic nerves. 2. The motion of the thoracic viscera is noted through: (a) the expansion (inspiration) of the chest; (b) the movements of the diaphragm; (c) the motion of the abdominal wall. The thoracic diaphragm is one of the most important respiratory muscles. It is innervated by a single nerve (Phrenic) therefore it contracts, functionates, as a single muscle. Diaphragma thoracis serves as a floor,

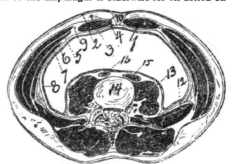

Fig. 180 represents a normal transverse segment of the abdominal wall. About the umbilicus. 1, rectus; 2, skin; 3, fascia; 4, fascia; 5, external oblique; 7, transversalis; 8, peritoneum; 9, linea semilunaris; 10, linea alba; 11, spinal muscles; 12, quadratus lumbarium; 13, psoas muscle; 15, vena cava, and 16, aorta.

THE ABDOMINAL AND PELVIC BRAIN

a support for the thoracic viscera. Its peripheral origin is from the sterum, ribs (lower 6), and lumbar vertebræ (I to III). Its fibers are inserted in the central tendon. Its special fixum punctum is the vertebral column. Its punctum mobile is the centrum tendineum with the two apertures (vena cava and œsophagus. The aortic aperture is practically immobile). Diaphragma thoracis resembles diaphragma pelvis in physiology and anatomy. Both have (a) a similar fixum punctum, (circular bony origin); (b) similar punctum mobile (central tendon); (c) both support superimposed viscera; (d) both have 8 apertures for visceral transmission; (e) both diaphragms are respiratory; (f) both muscles by constriction limit the apertures of visceral transmission; (g) both contract as a single muscle; (h) both share in splanchnoptosia. They differ in that contraction of the pelvic diaphragm draws the 8 visceral apertures proximalward, and ventralward, while contraction of the thoracic diaphragm draws the visceral apertures distalward and dorsalward. Distalward movement of the thoracic diaphragm in splanchnoptosia traumatizes, injures, stretches the phrenic and vagi nerves hence will derange respiration (inducing neurosis).

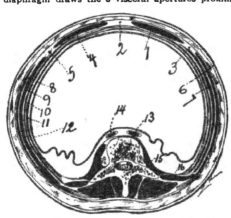

Fig. 181 illustrates a transverse section of the abdomen, about the umbilicus of a splanchnoptotic. The fascial and muscular fibres of the abdominal wall are elongated and separated, the primary factor in the splanchnoptosis, 1, rectus; 2, linea alba; 3, 5, linea semilunaris; 6, skin; 7, fascia; 8, external oblique; 9, internal oblique; 10, transversalis; 11, transversalis fascia; 12, the peritoneum; 13, vena cava; 14, aorta; 16, quadratus lumborum; 15, psoas; 17, vertebra; 18, spinal nucleus.

Derangement of respiration is clinically evident among splanchnoptostics.

Fixation and Motion of the Thoracic Viscera.

Splanchnoptosia begins in the deranged anatomy and physiology of the tractus respiratorius. At every inspiration the crura of the diaphragm contracts on the pericardium (which is fixed to the diaphragm) which in turn drags on the great thoracic vessels which finally tugs on the mediastinal structures (œsophagus, trachea and pulmonic mesentery) carrying the thoracic viscera and forcing the abdominal viscera distalward. The viscera are poised between the two great systems of inspiratory and expiratory muscles which are arrayed in rhythmic opposition during life.

The victory of the inspiratory muscles over their opponent, the expiratory muscles, is the beginning of splanchnoptosia.

Students should be taught that not only the muscles of the thoracic wall belong to respiration but also the abdominal muscles are an integral part. The thoracic and abdominal muscles are a breathing apparatus. Man's respiratory muscles extend from face to pelvic floor.

The XII intercostals with the I and II lumbar nerves practically supply the muscles of respiration which extend from manubrium to symphysis pubis.

A knowledge of the movements of the viscera during respiration indicates the method and location of their fixation within the thoracic and abdominal cavities.

Any prominent deviation of the respiratory muscles is accompanied by deranged visceral movements resulting in splanchnoptosia, disordered anatomy and physiology. We will devote a few remarks to the diaphragm in splanchnoptosia.

The Respiration in Splanchnoptosia (irregular).

The prominent symptoms of the respiration in splanchnoptosia are shortness of breath, irregular long respiration, difficult breathing and asthmatic breathing with cardiac palpitation. The relaxed abdominal muscles, the respiration muscles, have lost their power and perfect muscular relaxation is not possible. Complete respiration is muscular relaxation and contraction. In the erect attitude the dislocated liver drags on the diaphragm through its coronary ligaments, and through the vena cava. Besides, the liver is in turn dragged on by the tractus intestinalis through its two ligaments attached to the liver, viz., ligamentum hepato-colicum and ligamentum hepato-cavoduodenale, resulting in disturbance of a respiratory organ—the diaphragm. The irregular respiration—a frequent symptom of relaxed abdominal walls and consequent splanchnoptosia—is another link in the viscious circle, because it imperfectly and irregularly oxidizes the blood, disturbing nutrition.

CONSIDERATION OF VISCERAL FIXATION IN SPLANCHNOPTOSIA.

Fixation and Movement of Abdominal Viscera.

(a) *Abdominal viscera fixed immovably in position (to radix mesenterica) not sharing in respiratory movements (duodeno-jejunal flexure and body of pancreas).* I examined the viscera of numerous quadrupeds, some 20 monkeys, apes, baboons (i. e., animals which sit or stand practically erect in life) and several hundred humans. The testimony from the investigations is that the more the animal lives in the erect attitude the more firmly and extensively are the viscera fixed to the abdominal walls. The extensive and firm fixation of abdominal viscera to the abdominal walls found in man (and erect apes) marks the final process developing in erect animals. However firm and extensive the fixation of viscera to the abdominal wall, it plays a minor role in the prevention or cure of splanchnoptosia, in comparison with diaphragm and muscular abdominal walls. I found marked relaxed abdominal walls and advanced splanchnoptosia in erect apes. The method of abdominal visceral fixation may now be considered.

Through the courtesy of Prof. W. A. Evans I was sufficiently fortunate to secure an autopsy on the orang recently dying in the Lincoln Park Zoologic department. This human-like orang, a native of Borneo, was a female some 10 years of age and weighed 80 pounds. The thoracic and abdominal viscera resembled those of man in relation (to peritoneum), form, fixation and motion. The appendix was precisely typical of man, six inches in length, and was located in the pelvis (woman's appendix lies in the pelvis in 48 per cent of subjects). The coecum rested on the psoas muscle, however, since the orang does not walk (but sits) the psoas had not produced sufficient trauma to cause pericoecal peritoneal adhesions. The colon in all its segments resembles that of man in relation, form, fixation and motion. The transverse colon measured 12 inches while the sigmoid flexure measured 13 inches in length.

In one matter of degree (not of difference) the colon presented more numerous appendicae epiploicae than that of man. The fixation of the viscera on the dorsal abdominal wall, the location of the mesenteries, and the radix mesenterica, the relation of pancreas, liver, duodenum, stomach and spleen were duplicates of homo. The omentum majus resembling man's (except its blades had not completely coalesced) ceased at the flexura hepatica. The tractus genitalis in relation (to peritoneum), form, fixation and location precisely resemble that of man. In the orang the relation (to peritoneum and viscera) of the diaphragm, the most important respiratory apparatus, precisely resembles that of man in location, relation, fixation and motion. The psoas muscle was relatively not so large as that of man because the orang does not walk (practically lives sitting). In the orang especially, but also in the human-like apes, baboon, monkeys I found that their viscera were similarly developed and point for point was fixed in detail similar to those of man. The method of visceral fixation in man is due to respiration and attitude.

Radix Mesenterica.

The radix mesenterica or root of the mesentery consists of the coeliac axis and superior mesenteric artery encased by its fibro-muscular sheath (prolonged from the sheath of the aorta and diaphragmatic crura). The root of the mesentery (major visceral arteries) arise from the aorta as it enters the abdominal cavity between the crura diaphragmatica and at the junction of the intercrural arch through which the aorta encased in its fibrous sheath enters the abdominal cavity may be termed the hilum of the peritoneum. In a limited area located at the root of the mesentery only is the abdominal viscera immovably fixed in position. The root of the mesentery is the solid immovable center around which the abdominal viscera play in the ebb and flow of respiration.

From the root of the mesentery (coeliac and superior mesenteric arteries) radiate strong fibrous bands from the sheath of the aorta and fibro-muscular bands from the diaphragmatic crura, on the peripheral arterial trunks toward the viscera (stomach, spleen, liver, pancreas and enteron) At the root of the

SPLANCHNOPTOSIA

mesentery is located the solar plexus, ganglion coeliacum (abdominal brain) which emits rich plexiform network of nerves along the fibrous sheaths of the arterial trunks to the viscera. Numerous lymphatic vessels pass along the vascular sheath. A considerable fibro-muscular band, muscle of Treitz (musculus suspensorius duodeni), (Wenzel Treitz, Bohemian, 1819-1874, Prof.

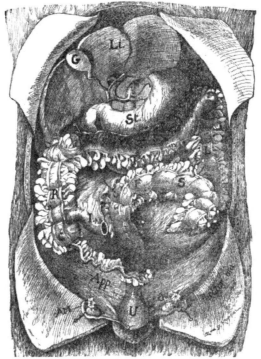

Fig. 182. This figure illustrates the viscera of a female orang from Borneo. Its age was about ten years. App., appendix, six inches long, lying on the pelvic floor; U., uterus; C., coecum; F.S., signoid flexure; Am., oviductal ampulla; Ov., ovary; St., stomach; G., gall bladder; L, liver; hook drawing the severed omentum majus proximalward.

Pathology in Prague) is emitted from the diaphragmatic crura (right or left) to terminate in the duodeno-jejunal flexure binding it solidly to the root of the mesentery.

The dorsal surface of the corpus pancreaticus is solidly and firmly bound by strong fibrous tissue in the fork between the coeliac and superior mesenteric arteries. Hence whatever form of splanchnoptosia may afflict other abdominal viscera the duodeno-jejunal flexure and the middle of the body of the pancreas remain fixed, immovably, in position. The radix mesenterica, root of the mesentery, is immovably fixed in position and hence does not move in respiration. The duodenal-jejunal flexure and body of the pancreas are firmly fixed to the root of the mesentery and hence do not share in respiratory movements of the viscera.

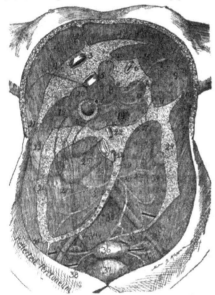

Fig. 183. The areas of peritoneum shown at 25 and 27, as well as at 34 and 11, also at 5, 8, 12, 14, are additional aids to support the viscera. They are practical extensions of the mesenterial bases. The granular areas are the mesenterial bores, while the intervening areas are where the peritoneum is fixed to the abdominal wall.

All abdominal viscera (except those fixed to the root of the mesentery as the duodeno-jejunal flexure and body of the pancreas) are fixed to the abdominal wall and therefore share in respiratory movements. (Remark: — From the above anatomic facts reports of extensive hernia do not record the pancreas or duodenum as having passed through the hernia ring into the hernial sac.)

(*b*) *Abdominal viscera fixed to the abdominal wall and sharing in respiration.* (The only exception are the duodeno-jejunal flexure and pancreas.) A brief reference to the fixation of individual viscera to the abdominal wall and their share in respiratory movements will now be made in order to comprehend the nature and anatomy of the vast domain of splanchnoptosia.

Fixation of Tractus Intestinalis.

The degree of firmness and extent of fixation of the tractus intestinalis increases with the erect attitude. The erect apes and man form the culmination of extensive fixation of abdominal viscera. The erect attitude is responsible for splanchnoptosia. From careful examination of the viscera of mammals, monkey and erect apes, it is evident to me that all these animals progress through precisely the same stages of visceral development and that visceral fixation is exactly the same, analogous in all—the chief change in all the visceral fixation is due to attitude (erect) and respiration.

In the fixation of abdominal viscera there must be held in view (a) the abdominal wall; (b) respiration and erect attitude; (c) the mesenteries—their basal organ and method of insertion on the abdominal wall. The mesenteries are not for mechanic support but for the conduction of nerves, vessels and prevention of visceral entanglement. The mesenteries separate the viscera into compartments which enables them to be supported with greater facility by means of visceral shelves. I. The primary visceral support except the abdominal wall is vascular: (a) coeliac axis; (b) the superior mesenteric artery; (c) the inferior mesenteric artery. II. The secondary visceral support to the abdominal wall is peritoneal adhesions (cellular-non-pathologic). In splanchnoptosia the base or insertion of the mesentery on the dorsal abdominal wall may glide distalward. The basal fixation of the foetal mesentery is unlike that of the adult. The base of the foetal mesentery contains the cells, which later multiply, spreading into the broad base of the adult mesentery that lends to erect man his extensive width of mesenteric adhesions.

A few remarks should be made as regards the acquired mesenteric adhesions of erect man.

1. Mesogastric Adhesions.

In quadrupeds like the cat the origin or root of the mesogastrium is at the coeliac artery, the radix mesenterica. With the erect attitude the root of the mesogastrium becomes increasingly adherent to the dorsal abdominal wall in an oblique line. From the coeliac axis, the mesogastric root, the adhesions spread leftward over the adrenal and kidney to the spleen which is attached to the mesogastrium. In embryos and infants one can trace the development of the mesogastric adhesions from the single point, the radix mesenterica to the extensive adhesions of adult man. The mesogastric adhesions or insertion on the dorsal wall aids in the fixation of the stomach.

2. Mesoduodenal Adhesions.

The duodenal loop is early in the human embryo entirely free, non-adherent, and is still free in adult lower mammals. Gradually in man the rightward movement of the liver draws the duodenal loop with it and the right side of the mesoduodenum loses its endothelium and its mesenterii membrana propria becomes adherent to 'he right dorsal wall and especially to the renal hilum. In dissection and operations in the biliary passages the mesoduodenal adhesions are released with facility. However, the mesoduodenal adhesions afford a strong support to the duodenum itself and also make of the duodenum a solid visceral shelf for the liver and stomach. The mesoduodenal adhesions are especially solid dorsal to the line crossed by the colon (coecum) in its journey to the right iliac fossa.

The duodenum is the most fixed segment of the tractus intestinalis due to: (a) the muscles of Treitz; (b) the extensive fixation of the mesoduodenum; (c) ligamentum hepato-duodenale; (d) biliary passages; (e) pancreas (the body of which is solidly fixed to the coeliac axis). Observe the absence of the duodenum (and the pancreas) in hernial reports on account of their solid fixation to the immobile radix mesenterica.

3. Mesenteronic Adhesions.

The mesenteronic adhesions (of man) extend some six inches in an oblique line from the duodeno-jejunal flexure to the coecum. Originally in features the mesenteron and mesocolon were in one line, and fan-shaped, being attached by its apex to the coeliac axis or radix mesenteria. With development of the tractus intestinalis a rotation occurred on the radix mesenterica and the coceum journeyed to the right, crossing ventrally to the duodenum, forming extensive acquired fixations for the testinal tract. The extent of the mesenteronic adhesions (which are on the right side) depends on the degree of distalward movement acquired by the coecum. Frequently (9 per cent in man and 5 per cent in woman according to my 700 autopsies) the journey of the coecum to the right iliac fossa becomes interrupted (nondescent of coecum) at any point distal to the liver. In such a case the mesenteron (except the duodenum) and a corresponding pact of the transversum and right colon are suspended practically (without adhesions) by the radix mesenteria, i. e., the superior mesenteric artery (as it originates from the aorta about one-half inch from the coeliac axis).

Not long before birth (man) the mesenteronic adhesions beginning at the transverse (or right) colic margin radiate distalward toward the right ilias fossa. From dissection it will be observed that with normal mesenteronic adhesions, the chief enteronic support is practically the radix mesenteria, i. e., the arteria mesenterica superior. This can be demonstrated with facility in the dead. However, the mesenteronic adhesions lend solid support to the enteron aiding to a high degree to prevent enteroptosia.

4. Mesocolic Adhesions.

Acquired mesocolic adhesions in the erect attitude assume two directions, viz.: (a) those of the left colon; (b) those of the right colon. Originally the mesocolon was located in the medium line. With development of the foetus the left mesocolic blade becomes adherent to the lumbar wall especially the splenic flexure becomes fixed to the ventral surface of the left kidney and the left colon becomes fixed to the lumbar wall as far as the intersigmoid fossa. This extensive peritoneal adhesion in the lumbar region added to the vascular support (inferior mesenteric artery) reinforces to a high degree the effective fixation of the left colon. It also forms a peritoneal compartment for enteronic loops.

(b) Adhesions of the Right Colon.

By peritoneal adhesions of the transverse colon, the hepatic flexure and right colon are fixed in position. The coecum and appendix being projections from the original digestive tube possess no peritoneal adhesions to the abdominal wall. In all erect apes examined as to the right colon I found the same exact condition of peritoneal adhesions as man except that in man the anal rotation of the tractus intestinalis was more advanced or complete ending with coecum in the right iliac fossa or in the lesser pelvis. In man the peritoneal adhesions of the right colon are more extensive than that of the left colon (which seldom possesses a mesocolon). The adhesions fixing the duodenum to the abdominal wall and the adhesions fixing the right colon to the abdominal wall are practically developed at the same time. The adhesions of the right colon spreads over the mesoduodenum, duodenum, distal ventral face of the right kidney and right lumbar region. The mesocolon being fixed to the immobile mesoduodenum lends strong support to the flexura colihepatica. The transverse colon and hepatic flexure of the colon secure additional peritoneal fixation apparatus from the fact that as soon as the rotating coecum comes in contact with the ballooned mesogastrium a fusion of the mesogastrium and mesocolon from base to viscera occur. Finally the mesogastrium (or rather gastro-colic omentum) envelopes the entire proximal segment of the colon.

On the left colon there is an important fixation apparatus known as the ligamentum costo-colicum (sinistrum) located on the ventral surface of the left kidney. On the right colon there is a similar fixation apparatus ligamentum costo-colicum (dextrum) located at the distal pole of the right kidney. This band prevents frequently the coecum from further distalward movements and also from falling into the lesser pelvis. The ligamentum costo-colicum dextrum is an important fixation apparatus for the coecum (and appendix) and prevents frequently the coecum from being a resident in the lesser pelvis. Not infrequently the ligamentum costo-colicum dextrum, together with the right colon, offers more or less support to the right kidney especially at its distal pole. At birth, so far as I am able to report on some 60 infant autopsies, the coecum lies in general at the junction of the duodenum and kidney.

The peritoneal adhesions of the right colon are formed while the child is learning to walk, i. e., by the end of 18 months. The peritoneal adhesions of the tractus intestinalis (secondary visceral supports) to the dorsal wall of the abdomen reinforce to remarkable degree the strength of the primary visceral supports (arteria coeliaca, mesenterica superior et inferior). The secondary visceral supports (acquired peritoneal adhesions form visceral shelves), the contact of the viscera, like bricks in a wall, form solid barriers for visceral support. The mesenterial partitions among the viscera, producing peritoneal compartments aid in visceral support by distributing their force separately against the abdominal wall.

Respiration Movements of the Tractus Intestinalis.

The transverse colon moves freely with respiration as it is a shelf for the sub-diaphragmatic viscera (stomach, liver and spleen). The flexura coli dextra (lying ventral to the right kidney) and the flexura coli sinistra (lying ventral to the left kidney) move with the kidneys in respiration. Since the transverse mesocolon acts as a visceral shelf it is markedly forced distalward during splanchnoptosia, especially in enteroptosia. I have seen it lying on the pelvic floor and once 9 inches in an inguinal hernia, where as its average location is immediately proximal to the umbilicus. The two colonic flexures in coloptosia produce vigorous traction in the kidneys.

In the usual autopsy the enteron is found in a compartment formed by the mesocolonic square and closed ventrally by the omentum majus. The transverse mesocolic shelf prevents the subdiaphragmatic viscera from exercising vigorous respiratory movements on the enteron. Defective respiratory movements of the diaphragm will aid in forcing the enteron distalward, from the right and left lumbar regions, into the lesser pelvis. In final advance states of enteroptosia, the transverse segment of the duodenum becomes obstructed by the traction, compression of the superior mesenteric artery, vein and nerve—a distant stage in splanchnoptosia.

The tractus intestinalis is affected chiefly in splanchnoptosia by: (a) compromising of circulation, blood and lymph supply, i. e., congestion and decongestion, (b) trauma of nerve centers (ganglia), strands and nerve periphery, (c) complication from loss of peristalsis and atony of bowel muscle, (d) gastro-intestinal catarrah and indigestion from excessive, deficient and disproportionate secretions. Also dragging on the abdominal brain, an independent nerve center producing nausea, neurosis, headache, reflexes, and deranged sensation, secretion and motion on other viscrea. (e) Dilatation of the stomach and duodenum, caused by the superior mesenteric vessels at the point where they cross the transverse segment. The stomach is especially liable to dilatation from the above causes, where the prolapse of the enteron, enteroptosia, is sufficiently advanced to allow the enteronic loops to pass distalward into the lesser pelvis and particularly when the subject lies on the back, for then the superior mesenteric artery, vein and nerve are put on a stretch and they constrict vigorously the transverse portion of the duodenum. (f) the enteronic loops being dislocated (enteroptosia) into the plevis, peristalsis, secretion, circulation, sensation and nerve periphery are compromised, followed by catarrh, constipation and indigestion. (g) the colon, especially the colon transversum may lie in the lesser plevis producing similar compromising circumstances as in the enteron. (h) The appendages (liver, pancreas, and spleen) of the tractus intestinalis, in ptosis are compromised in circulation, secretion, absorption, sensation and nerve periphery.

CONSIDERATIONS OF GASTROPTOSIA AS PART OF SPLANCHNOPTOSIA.

The stomach is fixed to the diaphragm by the œsophagus and part of the gastro-hepatic omentum (peritoneum). It is fixed to the liver by the gastro-hepatic omentum (peritoneum), hepatic artery, biliary duct and ligamentum hepato-duodenale and peritoneum (all important bands). The stomach is fixed to the radix mesenterica by the gastric artery. The root of the mesentery is not only an important gastric support, but a solid anchor, around which occur all visceral movements. Besides the stomach rests on visceral shelves composed of the transverse colon and its mesentery, pancreas, duodenum and left kidney. It is maintained on the visceral shelves by the abdominal muscles. The distal end of the stomach is bound to the diaphragm through the liver (gastro-hepatic and meshepaticon) and in a similar manner the proximal end of the stomach is bound to the diaphragm, through the spleen (gastro-splenic, lienorenal and suspensory ligament) which is, however, a band of limited strength.

The Respiratory Movements of the Stomach.

The diaphragm rests on the liver, stomach and spleen like a muscular dome, hence with each respiration the above three organs (if the stomach be

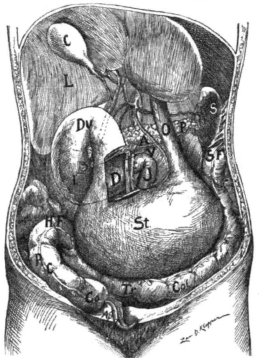

Fig. 184. Gastro-duodenal dilatation—gastroptosia. This illustration is drawn from e subject. This subject was 67 years old, dying of carcinoma of the ductus bilis et ductus ncreaticus. It is a so-called transverse stomach, and as the stomach dilates it extends ore distalward until in this case it extended to the pelvis. Du and D presents the enormously dilated duodenum, obstructed by the superior mesenteric artery A and vein V. bserve the difference in dimension between the duodenum immediately to the right of the esenteric vessels and that immediately to the left of them. The jejunum, J., is normal in mension, while the duodenum is as large as a man's arm. A segment of the stomach d duodenum is resected at D to show the dimension of the distal duodenum. I, a sected segment of the ventral surface of the duodenum in order to expose Vater's pilla. O, elongated œsophagus. In this subject the pylorus was dilated in proportion the duodenum and gastrium. This figure is from the same subject as Fig. 185. I secured is specimen at an autopsy by the professional courtesy of Dr. Charles O'Byrne.

distended) will act similarly—pass distalward according to the resistance offered by the muscles of the abdominal wall. The distended stomach will move ventralward at each inspiration. The stomach exists in the shape of a wedge with its base to the left. The liver also exists in the shape of a wedge with its base to the right. The apex of the liver wedge proximally overlaps the apex of the stomach wedge distally. At every inspiration the apex of these wedges glide on each other, shortening the gastro-hepatic omentum, while at each expiration the gastro-hepatic omentum is placed on tension. The radix mesenterica or root of the mesentery having sent one of its branches to the liver—the hepatic artery—and the other branch to the stomach—the gastric artery—it remains the central axis around which the stomach and liver rotate. A third branch of the radix mesenterica—the splenic artery—passes to the spleen, hence, the root of the mesentery is the central axis of the visceral rotation (in respiration) of the liver, stomach and spleen. Strong fibrous sheaths of connective tissue and nerves radiate on the hepatic, gastric and splenic arteries to their respective viscera constituting an important band between the viscera and the immobile mesentery root. The ventral elevation of the epigastrium at each inspiration is mainly due to: (a) The contraction of the diaphragmatic viscera (liver, stomach and spleen) distalward; (b) the apices of the liver and stomach wedges glide on each other toward their bases increasing their dorso-ventral diameters. The degree of elevation of the epigastrium at each inspiration depends on the resistance of the abdominal wall and the splanchnoptotic state of the diaphragm and of the subdiaphragmatic viscera.

Clinicians may observe that hepatic calculus is more frequent in splanchnoptosia but this is rationally explained by the facility in splanchnoptosia of infectious processes invading the biliary passages from lack of visceral drainage and stasis of tissue fluids—blood and lymph. In splanchonptotics the ducts are flexed, especially the biliary ducts, obstructing the normal flow of visceral products. Gastroptosia is practically constantly accompanied by gastric dilatation. Gastric dilatation must be viewed as a result of displacements and not a cause. In gastroptosia the vessels and nerve plexuses are traumatized, elongated, which impairs gastric innervation, circulation (lymph and blood), nourishment and a muscularis ending in dilatation.

In general it may be noted that the coeliac axis (the immobile root of the mesentery vessels with strong fibrous and neural sheaths) is a secure support to the liver, stomach and spleen. However, the visceral shelves of the subdiaphragmatic organs must not be overlooked. The pancreas (with its corpus securely bound to the immobile coelac axis with strong fibrous tissue) is the strongest visceral shelf support. The next strongest visceral shelf is the duodenum which in the adult is devoid of dorsal epithelial peritoneum but the strong fibrous subperitoneal tissue binds the whole proximal duodenum to the dorsal wall while the distal duodenum is solidly bound to the cruva of the diaphragm by the muscle of Treitz, (musculus suspensorius duodeni) and to the coliac axis by strong fibrous tissue. Hence the duodenum and pancreas (both fixed to the root of the mesentery) are excellent visceral shelves for liver, stomach and spleen. (Duodenum and pancreas are the rara avis in hernia.) When the splanchnoptosia has advanced sufficiently to involve the proximmal duodenum and head of the pancreas the duodenum is liable to present a diverticulum at the location of entrance of the ducts choledochus communis, while the pancreas being fixed in its middle (corpus) will locate its head near sacral promotory.

Hepatoptosia and gastroptosia rest chiefly on two causes, viz: (a) relaxation of the abdominal walls; (b) constriction of the trunk by clothing. In both (a) and (b) the normal respiration has become deranged.

Gastroptosia.

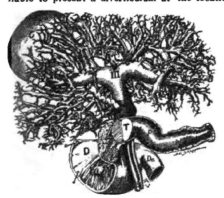

Fig. 185. Carcinoma completely obstructing the biliary and pancreatic ducts. From same subject as Fig. 184. Illustrates an X-ray of enormously dilated biliary passages. The biliary ducts (excepting the gallbladder, which was three to four times its normal dimension) had a capacity of 32 ounces, about six or seven times the natural capacity. The ductus communis choledochus was over 1¼ inches in diameter. The pancreatic duct admitted the index-finger. The man, 69 years old, a giant in stature, weighing some 250 pounds with ordinary limited fat, lost 115 pounds in weight during three months' illness. The ductus cysticus, extending from II to IV, had seven Heister's valves, and its lumen would admit a lead-pencil only. At B the biliary ducts were deficient within the liver substance, but were really dilated on the surface. T, the carcinoma (divided with the scalpel), completely severing the lumen of the biliary and pancreatic ducts. There was enormous gastroduodenal dilation from the compression of the transverse duodenum by the superior mesenteric artery (A) and vein (V). D, foldless, granular, proximal 2½ inches of the duodenal mucosa; 1, entrance of ductus communis choledochus in the duodenum; Sa, ductus Santorini; P, ductus pancreaticus. The ductus communis choledochus and ductus pancreaticus, located between the carcinoma and Vater's diverticulum, were normal. Da is the normal sized duodenum located distal to the compressing superior mesenteric vein (V) and artery (A). Observe the vast dilatation of the duodenum proximal to the superior mesenteric artery (A) and vein (V). I secured this rare specimen at an autopsy through the courtesy of Dr. Charles O'Byrne.

Gastroptosia or atonia gastrica signifies abdominal relaxation. It includes distalward movement of the stomach and relaxation of the abdominal wall. It is a part and parcel of splanchnoptosia. Gastroptosia (or its equivalent atonia gastrica) practically includes the terms dilatation of stomach, ectasis ventriculi, insufficiency of the stomach, gastric insufficiency, motor insufficiency, ischochymia (retention of chyme), myasthenia, extasis gastrica, because it signifies abdominal relaxation and relaxation includes dilatation and motor insufficiency. Therefore gastroptosia is a proper, comprehensive, scientific term which signifies ptossi, dilatation and motor insufficiency of the stomach. Gastroptosia is of paramount importance to physicians as its existence is frequent in every day practice.

In early embryonic life the stomach is absolutely vertical and the child is practically born with a vertical stomach and besides I have observed scores of permanently vertical stomachs in adult autopsies (perhaps from arrest of development). With the growth of the child the stomach rotates following the atrophying liver. In the adult the rotated stomach is supplied on its ventral surface (left) by the left vagus and on the dorsal surface (right) by the right vagus. Food aids by its weight and distention to force the stomach distalward. In gastroptosia the lesser curvature and pylorus moves distalward.

Etiology.

Gastroptosia arises from a variety of causes. Disordered respiration with consequent descensus of the diaphragm and distorted distal thorax (ribs) is among the first disturbances. In short gastroptosia coexists with splanchnoptosia. Gastroptosia may be due to an abnormally distalward location of the diaphragm. In hepatoptosia the liver forces the pylorus distalward and to the left. Relaxed abdominal walls, rapidly repeated pregnancies, infected puerperium (i. e., practically subinvolution of the abdominal wall), compression from waist bands, liver or spleen tumors, pleuritic effusions or adhesions, pericarditis are fruitful causes of gastroptosia. I have observed in autopsies that peritoneal and especially omental adhesions play an extensive role in gastroptosia.

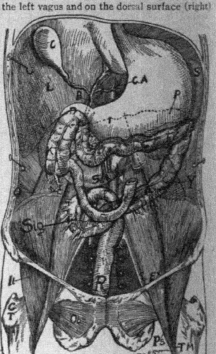

Fig. 186. This illustration presents the horizontal stomach, which in gastroptosia dilates from pylorus to cardiac extremity, and passes distalward as in Fig. 184—a gastro-duodenal dilatation. Sig. represents the sigmoid flexure in a 180 deg. condition of physiologic volvulus.

Gastroptosia is congenital or acquired. The acquired gastroptosia is discernible in the change in normal relations of the space in the proximal abdomen and distal thorax especially in the manifestation of respiration. In general we observe at post mortems two forms of gastroptosia, viz.: (a) the whole stomach appears (with the lesser curvature and pylorus with a transverse position) moving caudal, (b) the distalward moving stomach assumes more or less a distinctly vertical position.

I wish to state, that, from personal autopsic observation in the abdominal viscera in over 700 subjects, the stomach varies extensively: (a) in position, (b) in dimension, (c) in form.

Gastroptosia may be due to constitutional defects or anomalies in both sexes. The peculiar formed chest, as funnel shaped, chicken breast, may be observed in subjects with gastroptosia which is part and parcel of splanchnoptosia. Gastroptosia occurs in subjects with tubercular habitus—constitutional defects.

Gastroptosia (or splanchnoptosia) does not as a rule occur in strong robust subjects. Obvious stigmata of degeneracy accompanying splanchnoptosia subjects with elongated narrow thorax are liable to gastroptosia because the diaphragm occupies an abnormally distalward location. Pulmonary emphysemia or pleural effusions force the diaphragm distalward favoring gastroptosia (and concomitant splanchnoptosia). Mechanical conditions may enhance stomachoptosia as supraumbilical hernia, inguinal or femoral hernia, peritoneal adhesions. Rapidly repeated gestations present a large field of gastroptosia so fully discussed by Landau as well as rapid loss of large quantities of fat. In multipara and subjects with loss of quantities of flesh the abdominal muscles become relaxed and lose their delicate active poise in maintaining the viscera in their normal physiologic position.

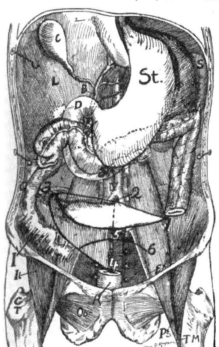

Fig. 187. This represents a vertical stomach. During gastro-duodenal gastroptosia the chief gastric dilatation occurs at the distal end of the stomach. The superior mesenteric, S, compressing the transverse duodenum, causes the gastro-duodenal dilatation. This figure presents a non-descended cecum, and an ileum, I, adherent to the ileopsoas muscle. 1, 2, 4 representing the dorsal insertion line of the meso-sigmoid.

Gastric Dilatation in Splanchnoptosia.

Many times I have observed in autopsy extensively dilated stomach, the existence of which in life had not been suspected, first, because the physical condition of the patient was favorable and second compensatory action between stomach and pylorus was still favorable. A relation exists between the dimensions of the pylorus and that of the stomach—a compensatory action. I performed an operation on a woman who had vomited for years with a dilated stomach. In this case the pylorus had dilated slightly and its flexion increasing by ptosis obstructed the free evacuations of the stomach contents.

Again we note autopsies in which a subject possesses a markedly dilated stomach with slight difficulty in evacuation of stomach contents through the pylorus because the pyloric ring had dilated proportionately with the stomach dilatation allowing free evacuation, free passage of food from stomach to duodenum, free drainage—here is compensatory dilatation of stomach and pylorus, resembling that of the cardiac valves, however, suddenly the stomach and pyloric compensatory action may fail and the patient passes swiftly onward and swiftly downward —exactly as in valvular heart lesions.

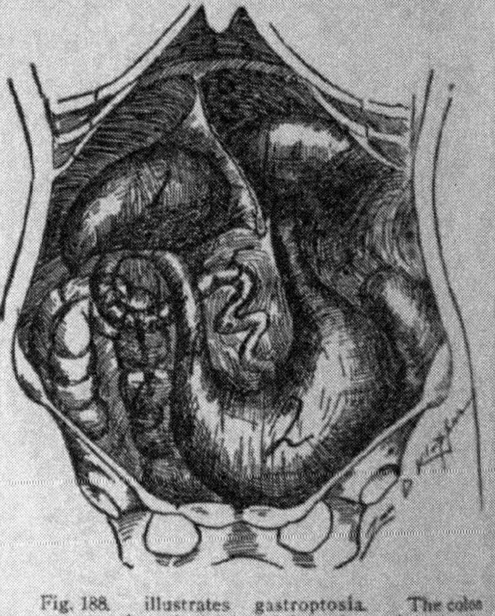

The etiology of gastroptosia may be sought chiefly in constitutional defects. However, mechanical derangement is sufficiently obvious in gastroptosia. Gastro-duodenal dilatation which plays such an extensive role in splanchnoptosia will be discussed and illustrated in a future chapter. Combined gastro-duodenal dilatation due to the compression of the transverse duodenal segment by the superior mesenteric artery vein and nerve is a frequent condition and though I have published articles on it for a decade it is still but limitedly recognized.

The symtomatology may be practically negative or of the most aggra-

Fig. 188. illustrates gastroptosia. The colon transversum forced distalward into the pelvis by the stomach. 1, liver with hepatoptosis; 2, stomach in the lesser pelvis; 3, 4, duodenum dilated; 5, the jejunum, normal caliber; 6, transverse colon. This cut represents gastro-duodenal dilation—the second stage of splanchnoptosis.
The artist neglected to present the duodenum dilated.

vated kind. It may be stated, in general, that gastroptosia is without symptoms so long as the stomach functionates normally which mainly prevails while the subject is in favorable physical condition. Gastroptosia presents symptoms when detention and composition food occurs and general infection results. Indirect symptoms may arise as in splanchnoptosia, e. g., fatigue, debility, constipation, insomnia. Meinert insist that gastroptosia is a common cause of chlorosis.

The symptoms of gastroptosia are generally proportionate to the degree of stomachic dilatation. Kussmaul originally observed that gastroptosia is frequently accompanied by a disturbance of the motor nerves of the stomach. This may be due to the trauma traction on the vagi from change of gastric position. Gastroptosia frequently coexists with multiple nervous symptoms, but the nervous symptoms may be due to splanchnoptosia. However, gastroptosia is a disease and is liable to be accompanied by disturbed motion, absorption, secretion and sensibility of the stomach. Change of form and position of the stomach may not lead to any more nervous symptoms than change of form and position of the uterus, however dislocation of the uterus, i. e., permanent fixation, is the result of some disease.

Malposition of the stomach does not produce neurasthenia any more than malposition of the uterus. The position of a mobile viscus is not responsible for neurosis, for mulitple positions or multiple deviations must not be considered abnormalities. It is disease that produces neurosis, not position of viscera. Original disease which produced the malposition of the viscus should be held responsible for the nervous disturbance. Again there can be no doubt that the symptoms of gastroptosia and nephroptosia are constantly mistaken for each other especially by the careless examining surgeon with a tendency to nephropexy. There is no characteristic stomach contents peculiar to gastroptosia. In gastroptosia pain is generally prevalent in the proximal abdomen and lumbar regions. It is true that subjects with gastroptosia (a part and parcel of splanchnoptosia) present multiple neurotic symptoms simulating disturbed mobility, secretion, absorption and sensibility of the stomach. However, this may belong in the congenital debility or predisposition of the patient—due to the disturbance created by anatomically dislocated viscera and consequently pathologic physiology. Gastroptosia increases the weight of the stomach.

Diagnosis.

Gastroptosia is less recognized than nephroptosia which is diagnosed with more facility and besides the pexyites are more vigorously in search of nephroptotic victims.

Percussion and auscultation with various quantities of fluid in the stomach may suggest the position and dimension of the stomach.

Palpable epigastric pulsation, absence of projecting abdominal wall in the epigastrium and projecting abdominal walls in the hypogastrium aid in the diagnosing gastroptosia.

The most exact method to determine the position and dimension of the stomach is by inflation, viz.: (a) by generation of gas within the stomach. The most frequent method of gastric inflation practiced is by directing the patient to drink a glass of water containing some sodium bicarbonate and immediately to drink another glass of water containing tartaric acid whence carbonic acid gas is formed distending the stomach by air. (b) Another method to inflate the stomach is by introducing into the stomach a tube whence air is forced through it for distention, whence its form, position and dimension may be observed through the abdominal wall. (c) A third method of diagnosing the form, position and dimension of the stomach is by distending the stomach by fluid.

When the major curvature is at or below the umbilicus and the pylorus and lesser curvature have moved distalward the diagnosis of gastroptosia is confirmed. A healthy stomach maintains the position of its borders regardless of the subject's attitude. In gastroptosia the borders of the stomach change according to the patient's position. In gastroptosia with the patient in the erect posture the major stomach curvature and pylorus will be more caudal, while if the patient's posture is recumbent the pylorus and major curvature cephalad. Succussion (splashing sound) is a method to diagnose gastroptosia by agitating air and water in the stomach through shaking the body. The splashing sound may also be obtained by palpating the stomach while the patient is in the recumbent position. A splashing sound elicited from the stomach means practically gastroptosia—relaxation, atony. Some persons by practicing pressure of the abdominal muscles of the stomach can produce various sounds in the stomach. Such persons perhaps possess abnormally a large stomach and powerful abdominal muscles, however, like a fakir have exaggerated an anomaly. Gastroptosia may be diagnosed by transillumination, i. e., introducing an electric light in the stomach whence its contour may be observed. This method was advocated in 1845 by Casenave, later in 1867 Milliot improved it by experimentation, however, Dr. Max Einhorn of New York practically first made successful use of (the gastro-diaphane) transillumination of the stomach in man and demonstrated the utility of gastro-diaphanes copy.

Inspection may present a depression in the epigastrium and a projection in the umbilical region. This method of diagnosis may be sufficient in spare persons to announce gastroptosia. The X-ray may be used to note the position of the stomach by administering substances which will cast a shadow, as subnitrate of bismuth or metallic salts administered in capsules. Treatment is medical, mechanical, surgical.

Treatment.

1. The medical treatment consists in regulation of diet and function. The dietetic management consists in administering limited quantities of prescribed food at regular three-hour intervals. The diet should be cereals, vegetables, milk and eggs. All high seasoned food, pastry, pie, cake, spices, meat should be excluded to avoid fermentation.

The most essential medical treatment consists in "visceral drainage" as

SPLANCHNOPTOSIA

ample sewerage the evacuating channels should be flushed. Gastroptotics may live healthy with ample visceral drainage. The tissues and tissue spaces in gastroptosia (splanchnoptosia) require flooding, washing, so that the subject may be free from waste laden blood and residual debris. Every evacuating visceral tract (tractus intestinalis, perspiratorius, urinarius respiratorious) should perform maximum duty. The sheet anchor treatment for gastroptosia is regulation of food and fluid, and maximum sewerage of visceral tracts. Dietetics, hygiene, anatomic and physiologic rest, properly supervised, tend extensively to the welfare in the life of a splanchnoptotic.

2. Mechanical treatment in gastroptosia judiciously applied affords wonderful relief. Stomachic irrigation occasionally renders much comfort. The treatment consists in the application of abdominal wall to support the viscera. This is accomplished by various kinds of abdominal binders —elastic and non-elastic. I use sometimes an abdominal binder within which is placed a pneumatic rubber pad which is distended with air to suit the patient's comfort. Dr. E. A. Gallant employs a suitable fitting corset. The adhesive strapping method of Achilles Rose is practical, rational and economical and affords excellent relief. The recumbent position aids the patient. The mechanical method attempts the forcible reposition of the stomach to its normal physiologic position and there to maintain it by aids applied to the abdominal wall—a rational method. Pregnancy practically relieves the gastroptosia for a season. Splanchnoptotics experience more comfort from rational adhesive strapping (mechanical supports) than from surgical procedures.

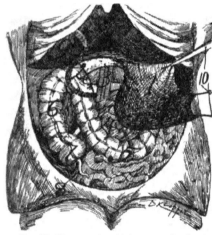

Fig. 189 illustrates the third stage of splanchnoptosia, viz.: gastro-duodenal dilatation. It shows the transverse colon (5) in the lesser pelvis. The widely dilated stomach (1) is drawn leftward by hooks (10) from its bed to show the duodenum (2) dilated by the superior mesenteric artery, vein and nerve, (3) 4, the normal calibered loops of enteron; 6, right colon; 7, cecum; 8, the appendix. Note the enteron loops crowded into the lesser pelvis.

3. Surgical treatment in gastroptosia is a very limited field. It espouses two methods, viz.: (a) The surgery is applied to the stomach itself as gastro-enterostomy, the Heinicke-Mickulicz operation (both tend to cure by visceral drainage) the replication of the stomach parietes or the attempt to shelve the stomach by omentum or mesentery (both unphysiologic, irrational).

(b) The abdominal wall is employed to support the stomach as by incision and over-lapping like a double breasted coat, or by enclosing, uniting the two musculi recti abdominales in one sheath. Both methods attempt to relieve by lessening the abdominal cavity and forcing the stomach into its normal physiologic position (both rational). A third method is to perform gastropexy, i. e., suture the stomach to the abdominal wall (limited, irrational in general).

HEPATO-PTOSIA, COLOPTOSIA AND ENTEROPTOSIA IN SPLANCHNOPTOSIA.

Fixation of the Liver.

The liver is firmly fixed to the diaphragm only. It has the most extensive fixation to the diaphragm of any abdominal viscus, hence the action of the diaphragm in respiration will be the most comprehensive. The structures which maintain the liver in contact with the concavity of the diaphragm are: (a) peritoneal folds; (b) connective tissue; (c) vessels; (d) abdominal muscles (most important). The liver rests on a visceral shelf, composed of the stomach, duodenum, right kidney, pancreas and transverse colon. The vena cava and hepatic veins by their intimate fusion with both liver substance and the diaphragm constitute a strong bond of union. The dorsal mesentery of the liver—the mesepaticon meso-hepor—is constituted by the extensive connective tissue which binds the right lobe of the liver to the distal concave surface of the diaphragm together with the reflexion of peritoneum which surrounds the connective tissue area.

The mesepaticon forms the most important passive band of the liver and diaphragm. The right and left lateral ligaments are mere extensions of the mesepaticon. The suspensory ligament, the remnant of the ventral hepatic mesentery, is long and loose to allow respiratory movements. An excellent example of what the respiratory movements of viscera may accomplish is observed in the bursa of Spiegel. Spiegel's lobe moves proximalward and distalward with each respiration and by this continual action has formed a diverticulum in the lesser sac of the peritoneum—Bursa spigelii. The proximalward and distalward movements of Spiegel's lobe produced by the diaphragm in respiration is responsible for Spiegel's diverticulum in the peritoneum.

Respiratory Movements of the Liver.

If one studies the diaphragm it will be observed that its muscular contractions tend toward the radix mesenterica. When the diaphragm contracts (inspiration) on the broad dorso-proximal dome-like hepatic surface it will force the liver distalward, ventralward and medianward. At every inspiration the liver pounds on the abdminal viscera distal to it like a hammer, especially in thoracic splanchnoptosia. The degree of distalward movements of the liver in inspiration depends on the resistance offered by the muscles of the abdominal wall. These movements of the liver in inspiration imposed on it by the diaphragm do not disturb its function, on the contrary doubtless aid in massaging the liver into vigorous function.

The normal respiratory movements of the liver may become disturbed by relaxation of the diaphragm or abdominal walls which rob it of normal support. Tight lacing may force the liver from its visceral niche and shelf whence the normal respiratory muscular action becomes ungeared. Perihepatic peritoneal or pleuritic adhesions particularly distort respiratory muscular actions on the liver and consequent normal function. Hepato-Ptosia is not a rare condition, especially when the liver has lost its visceral shelf and the abdominal walls become relaxed.

Etiology of Hepato-Ptosia.

Hepato-Ptosia is a part and parcel of splanchnoptosia and depends on the same causes—as deranged respirations, relaxed abdominal walls, yielding of the diaphragm, hepatic ligaments and visceral shelves (kidney, duodenum transverse colon, pancreas, stomach) peritoneal and omental adhesions, plueritic effusions and exudates asthma, rapidly repeated pregnancies, hereditary or congenital debilities, persistent vomiting and coughing, hernia, tight waist band, corsets, trauma, congenital predisposition.

The elongation of the hepatic ligaments are secondary to the relaxation of the abdominal wall. Further etiologic factors in hepato-ptosia are the weight of the liver, cholelithiasis, weight of the gall-bladder, laxity or elongation of the hepatic ligaments (which are probably secondary to the relaxation of the abdominal wall), trauma as during parturition, disappearance of the visceral shelves. The chief immediate course of hepato-ptosia is relaxation of the ventral abdominal wall. The liver like the uterus rests on a floor or visceral shelf.

Frequency.

Hepato-Ptosia occurs the most frequently in women. During the past 15 years I have observed about one typical advanced clinical case a year; however, numerous subjects may be observed with a moderate degree of hepato-ptosia, especially those having a tendency to develop Riedel's lobe. The frequency of hepato-ptosia is concomitant with splanchnoptosia, which is a common ailment. Perhaps seven women suffer from hepato-ptosia to one man. I have examined subjects of extreme hepato-ptosia in whom I could palpate the liver per vaginum. The history of hepato-ptosia is recent, as Portal was among the first to call attention to it in autopsy (1804) and the first case described in the living was by Cantani in 1866. Autopsies revealed its condition previous to that, but its interpretation remained unsolved.

The liver lies in an excavation in the concavity of the diaphragm resting on a visceral shelf. Its primary maintainers are the power of the abdominal wall. Its secondary maintainers are the suspensory, coronary, triangular, ligaments and mes-hepaticon, mesohepar. The elongation of these five supports allows distalward movements of the liver. Floating liver is intimately associated with splanchnoptosia—is part and parcel of it—for in autopsy it is common to note the kidney, hepatic flexure, enteron passing distalward before the liver. I have personally examined in the living and dead about a dozen typical, advanced, so called Riedel's lobes. In every subject of marked Riedel's lobe splanchnoptosia was marked. The vast majority of the subjects were women.

First, when the right liver lobe becomes forced excessively distalward the costal margin tends to separate the proximal form the distal part of the lobe by compressing a crease in the liver. The distal part of the right lobe which is extended distal to the costal margin becomes an increasing Riedel's lobe. Second, the space between the distal costal margin and the proximal crest of the ilium allows Riedel's lobe to develop, as here the abdominal walls offer the direction of least resistance.

Symptomatology.

The symptoms of hepato-ptosia are acute or chronic, partial or complete. In general the clinical symptoms are dragging pain in the abdomen, nausea, vomiting, dizziness, constipation alternating with diarrhœa, ascites, a peculiar rhythmic distressing "hepatic" cough with numerous neurotic disturbances and malassimilation. Curiously enough one not infrequently meets a subject with hepato-ptosia presenting no objective symptoms.

Diagnosis.

The diagnosis rests on bimanual palpation, percussion, a mobile mass in right side, change in location of tumor by change of attitude. Liver dullness changes with different positions and the liver may be felt in each different position. The liver in hepato-ptosia may assume any position in the abdominal cavity. If the kidney is not enlarged nephroptosia can be differentiated from hepato-ptosia; however, with enlarged kidney it may be impossible. I have examined subjects with the best of experts in urology, where it was impossible to decide until peritonotomy was executed.

An excellent factor in diagnosis is to attempt to replace the liver with the patient recumbent, which if successful is confirmatory of hepato-ptosia; examine the liver in the erect and prone position. As the liver passes distalward it is liable to rotate to the right on the ligamentum umbilicale as an axis. A warning is offered that Riedel's lobe should be differentiated from hepato-ptosia. Riedel's lobe is a direct extension distalward of the distal portion of the right hepatic lobe. Its etiology, though obscure, appears to be associated with diseases of the gall-bladder, cholelithiasis or tight waist bands.

The development of Riedel's lobe appears to be intimately connected with cholelithiasis; however, I have seen Riedel's lobe sufficiently frequent in both the living and the dead with no cholelithiasis present, to know it is not the only cause.

Occasionally we can diagnose floating liver of considerable degree accompanied apparently by no symptoms. I have observed subjects of hepato-ptosia when a distinct bulging presented in the distal right quadrant of the abdomen with no symptoms.

In hepato-ptosia the liver rotates on its pedicle (transverseaxis), the

SPLANCHNOPTOSIA

torsion of which compromises its anatomy and physiology (biliary ducts, Portal vein, hepatic artery, lymphatics and nerves). With change of position (hepato-ptosia) the liver experiences change of form. Hepato-ptosia does not occur without dislocation and change of adjacent organs. In hepatoptosia the change in form and position of the liver is not due merely to pressure of the abdominal wall (muscle or bony) but to the necessity of physiologic movement as liver rhythm and application of adjacent viscera against the liver by respiratory movements. The liver is dislocated through disease, i. e., by pathologic physiology or pathologic anatomy of adjacent viscera or body walls.

Treatment.

The treatment is: 1, Medical, such as diet, "visceral drainage," stimulation of the functions of the visceral tracts to a maximum degree of elimination by injesting liberal quantities of fluids at regular intervals, ample horizontal rests. Forced nutrition aids in restoring the fat cushions. The patient must avoid excessive or traumatic exertions. 2, Mechanical treatment consists in forcible reposition and maintaining the liver in its normal physiologic position. Apply abdominal binders, adhesive strapping or an applicable, suitable corset (Gallanet). The mechanical methods afford wonderful relief, especially Achilles Rose's method of adhesive strapping. 3, Surgical. Hepatopexy should be performed only as a last resort. It has an extremely limited field of usefulness. It has been performed over 50 times since its introduction in 1877 with doubtful results. Overlapping the abdominal walls like a double breasted coat is more rational and secures more successful results, as such a procedure would diminish the abdominal cavity and force the liver in its normal dome-like excavation in the diaphragmatic concavity and on its normal visceral shelf.

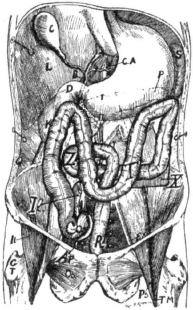

Fig. 190. Coloptosia. The transverse colon extends into the lesser pelvis. Coloptosia increases the flexion of the flexura hepatica coli and the flexura linealis coli, increasing the difficulty and friction of fecal circulation. Z The cupola of the sigmoid, presenting a physiological sigmoid volvulus. CO Coecum located in the lesser pelvis, with the appendix Ap. Il. Ileum, coursing proximalward and parallel with the right colon, assuming conditions favorable to an ileocecal volvulus. X illustrates that during volvulus of the sigmoid it appropriates peritoneum, and formulates it into an additional elongated mesosigmoid.

Coloptosia.

The colon has received some attention in splanchnoptosia from its relation to nephroptosia and hepato-ptosia gastroptosia: (a) Coloptosia transversa.

The dislocation of the middle of the transverse colon producing more or less of a curve with its concavity proximalward, is one of the most frequent factors in splanchnoptosia. Dislocation of the colon is placed in relation with the relaxed abdominal wall with elongation of the mesocolon with constipation, with tight waist bands, with gastroptosia, nephroptosia, hepatoptosia; however, no one theory is satisfactory.

It is true that by circular constriction of the abdomen one can force some viscera proximalward and many distalward. However, at autopsy I found even in youth, in nullipara in absence of corset, that the colon transversum may be located well distalward from the umbilicus. We can observe that not only the mesocolon transversum was elongated but also the ligamentum gastro-colicum, i. e., the visceral mesenteries were elongated. With the elongated mesocolon transversum the transverse colon can assume various positions.

In autopsy it is common to observe the middle of the transverse colon projecting into the pelvis and not frequently the colon may lie in the lesser pelvis and on its floor. The middle loop of the transverse colon can be moved with facility to any portion of the peritoneal cavity. The enteronic loops may glide proximalward ventral to the transverse colon. The right portion of the transverse colon is frequently prevented from distalward movements by reason of pathologic peritoneal adhesions binding it to the liver. The mesocolon transversum measures generally 4½ inches; however, in subjects of coloptosia, I have observed it nine inches in length and frequently six inches. The membrana mesenterii propria, i. e., the submesocolic tissue, vessels and nerves, are elongated, attenuated. Coloptosia transversum plays a prominent role in autopsic observations.

Hepato-ptosia and nephroptosia may be advanced sufficiently to force the colonic hepatic flexure so far distalward that it becomes reversed. In such cases the colon extends from the coecum obliquely across the abdomen to the spleen. The clinical hisotory of such patients was mostly unknown. However, I am not convinced that these marked dislocations of the right and transverse colon manifested grave symptoms. For the transverse colon in general will measure about 22 inches, and since the abdominal cavity between the points of the splenic and hepatic flexures is some 14 inches the transverse colon must assume a sinuous or looped course of more or less deviation from an extended line.

Coloptosia Dextra.

The right colon becomes of significant interest in coloptosia on account of its relation to nephroptosia and hepato-ptosia, the appendix and tractus genitalis as well as to the fact that the colon dextrum not infrequently possesses a mesocolon. The resistance to coloptosia dextra is chiefly offered by the ligamentum costo-colicum dextrum, which vigorously fixes the cecum, in many subjects, checks its distalward movements, preventing it from becoming a resident in the lesser pelvis (woman 20%, man 10%).

The base or root of the right mesocolon is fixed to the ventral surface of the distal renal pole, hence maintains intimate relations to nephroptosia dextrum. The right colon is about eight inches plus two inches for the cecum, assumes a sinuous or looped course in most bodies and the additional loops of moderate coloptosia dextra perhaps produce few symptoms.

Coloptosia Sinistra.

The left colon is so infrequently dislocated from the fact that it is rarely possessing a mesocolon that I omit its discussion in coloptosia.

Coloptosia Sigmoidea.

It is difficult to define splanchnoptosia of the sigmoid, as it has an extensive normal range of mobility. In general it is 17 inches in length in woman and 19 in man. Its mesosigmoid will average 2½ inches. The base of the mesosigmoid insertion—its foot—is but a few inches in length and hence the sigmoid will move about freely in the peritoneal cavity. In autopsies the sigmoid may be found the most frequently in the lesser pelvis (65% to75%), in the right iliac fossa (15%), in the proximal abdomen (15%). It may be in contact with the spleen, stomach, liver or cecum. The most distinct reason for the nonsplanchnoptotic state of the sigmoid is that the trauma of the psoas produces more or less plastic peritonitis in the mesosigmoid (mesosigmoiditis) in 80% of subjects and the mesosigmoiditis contracts the mesosigmoid, fixing it to the Psoas muscle, preventing coloptosia sigmoidea. It is claimed that in coloptosia of the sigmoid that it forms dangerous obstructing angulation which is yet to prove.

Symptomatology.

The symptoms of coloptosia include many due to general splanchnoptosia. Some of the symptoms are (a) constipation; (b) diarrhœa—(a) and (b) alternating—(c) colonic catarrh, mucous colitis or which I prefer to term secretion neurosis of the colon. The colonic secretion, absorption, sensations, and peristalsis may be excessive, deficient or disproportionate. Fermentation, and borbyrigmus arise. Dragging sensations, fatigue, debility, multiple nervous symptoms. In general the symptoms of coloptosia are stenosis compromised and irregular caliber, dilatation, retention, obstruction, constipation, disturbed circulation and ennervation, relaxed abdominal wall, pendulous abdomen, practical relief of symptoms on assuming the prone position.

The dislocation of the colon favors constipation because the defective abdominal wall has lost its effective power to force the fæces distalward. Since in dyspepsia, nervopathies of the tractus intestinalis, no local subjective pain is experienced by the patient, we do not palpate the abdomen sufficiently frequently. First and foremost we should palpate the abdomen to determine whether the pathologic physiology of the tractus intestinalis be secondary or primary. Many diseases have an intestinal origin. Dyspepsia refers to the stomach only.

Splanchnoptosia is a disease of malnutrition. Palpation of the tractus intestinalis attempts to explore systematically the various segments and susceptibility to pain caliber, contents, tension, and mode of fixation. Simon's method of rectal exploration with the hand we discard as unsuitable. In palpation of the abdomen we must devote sufficient time to understand the occasional variation in the aortic rhythm. As to Glenard's colic cord we must consider the small contracted stomach, the pancreas and colon transversum, as any one may be mistaken for the "colic cord." Whatever this cord can be, found in perhaps 10% of splanchnoptotics, we should attempt to note its accessibility, position, length, form, volume, consistence, mobility, sensation. In palpation the idea of gliding the intestinal segments under the hand or gliding the hand over them must be practiced. The colic cord is located in the relation with the umbilicus. In the diagnosis of coloptosia search should be made for colonicptosia, dilation, constriction, stenosis, atony, decalibration, obstruction, retention.

Diagnosis of coloptosia may be confirmed by colonic inflation per rectum whence one can by inspection and percussion trace the course of the colon fairly accurately. By palpation one may manipulate the colon. Glenard mentions a diagnostic clue to coloptosia transverse which he calls "corde colique transverse"—the cord of the transverse colon. I have practiced on this subject in the dead splanchnoptotic and it is my opinion that Glenard's cord of the transverse colon is simply the pancreas in general. It may be possible from the direction, dimension, location, consistence, mobility, sensibility, inflation, of the "colic cord" to detect the transverse colon in splanchnoptosia. The cecum and right colon will be best located by inflation whence inspection and percussion are further aids. We must attempt to note the location, dimension, consistence, mobility of the cecum and right colon.

In the diagnosis of coloptosia the means at hand are (a) inspection; (b) palpation; (c) distension, inflation; (d) consistence; (e) mobility; (f) sensibility; (g) colonic peristalsis.

Treatment.

The treatment of coloptosia is medical, mechanical, surgical.

1. *Medical* treatment is comprised in diet, regulation of function, ample anatomic and physiologic rest and appropriate hygiene. First and foremost is what we term "visceral drainage." By appropriate food which results in ample fæcal residue, copious fluids at regular intervals with established hours for evacuation. It may be practically claimed that every case can be controlled. If colonic secretion, absorption and peristalsis be appropriately stimulated by proper food and ample fluid the colonic circulation and innervation will practically remain normal and the coloptotic though necessarily afflicted with a certain amount of pathologic physiologic physiology will remain practically with a few symptoms.

2. *Mechanical* treatment comprises abdominal bands, corsets, adhesive strapping, prone attitude. Adhesive strapping (of Achilles Rose), which is economical, practical and rational, has in my practice rendered much comfort to patients.

3. *Surgical* treatment in coloptosia is absolutely limited. It comprises two methods, viz.: (a) operations on the colon itself, fixing it to the abdominal wall or other viscus—colopexy. As coloptosia is but a part and parcel of splanchnoptosia, colopexy is limited in its range and rational application. (b) The surgical treatment of diminishing the space of the peritoneal cavity by incising the abdominal and reuniting by superposition, overlapping its fascial and muscular walls like a double breasted coat, though limited in application, is the more rational. This treatment attempts forcible retroposition of the colon to its normal location and maintenance in its normal visceral shelf by the abdominal wall.

Enteroptosia.

In enteroptosia the enteron passes distalward and ventralward. In advanced cases the enteron passes almost entirely into the lesser pelvis. In this condition the transverse duodenum is compressed against the vertebral column by the superior artery, vein and nerve—the axial cord of the mesenteron producing gastro-duodenal dilation. If the abdominal wall becomes relaxed the mesenteron becomes elongated from the viscera following the walls, the enteronic loops pass distalward into the pelvis and ventralward in contact with the relaxed abdominal wall. Besides the basal mesenteronic insertion on the dorsal wall passes distalward.

In advanced enteroptosia, the enteron experiences mulitple flexions, stenoses, dilation, dislocation, compromising circulation (fæcal, blood and lymph), peristalsis, decalibration and traumatizing nerve periphery. In enteroptosia the enteron not only changes its location but also its form, hence pathologic physiology must be expected as altered secretion, absorption, peristalsis, and sensation. The blood and lymph circulation is compromised by flexion, elongation, contraction or dilation of the vascular channels ending in malassimilation.

The splanchnoptotic is continually in the condition of pathologic physiology. In splanchnoptosia absorption, secretion and sensation are disturbed, the blood and lymph occupy the greater and lesser pelvis, hence the nerves and vessels are placed on tension, in which the soft walled veins and lymphatus suffer. In the examination of the abdomen for enteroptosia, inspection, palpation, percussion, attitude, location the gliding movement, auscultation the belt test, gurgling, should be employed. The consistence, limited dimension and multiple enteronic coils increase the difficulty in diagnosis. The enteronic coils are confined in the colonic square, greater and lesser pelvis. Attenuated abdominal walls aid in diagnosis.

NEPHROPTOSIA IN SPLANCHNOPTOSIA.

Fixation of the Kidney (tractus urinarius).

The two most important factors maintaining the kidney in position are the muscular action of the diaphragm and abdominal wall. The action of the diaphragm is direct, that of the abdominal muscles indirect through the adjacent viscera. Ventral to the right kidney are the liver, duodenum, colon and enteron. Ventral to the left kidney are the stomach, spleen, colon and enteron. Next to the muscles in importance is the perirenal tissue—the fatty capsule in which the kidney lies imbedded.

The perirenal areolar tissue binds the kidney to the diaphragm and at the proximal renal pole it fuses with the meshepaticon on the right side while on the left side the perirenal tissue fuses with suspensory ligament of the spleen and coronary ligament. A strong renal support is the renal pedicle composed of the renal artery, vein, nerve plexus, lymphatics and fibrous sheath which emanates from the radix mesenterica. The renal pedicle limits the extent of renal motion because the renal artery arises so near the radix mesenterica—the coeliac artery—that its origin is practically immobile. The kidney possesses no visceral shelf, simply a shallow renal fossa or niche. It lies proximalward and distalward on the dorsal abdominal wall in a shallow renal groove. Hence the structures or bands which maintain the kidney in position are: (a) the diaphragm and abdominal wall; (b) perineal capsule; (c) renal pedicle; (d) viscera (indirect).

Respiratory Movements of the Kidney.

The respiratory motion of the kidney is due to the contraction of the diaphragm on its proximal dorsal surface. The kidney experiences respiration movements which include all splanchnoptotic viscera. The proximal dorsal surface of the kidney lies on the diaphragm (hence diaphragmatic area) while the distal dorsal surface lies on the lumbar structures (Psoas, quadratus and transversal muscles, hence lumbar area). Inspiration forces the kidney distalward and ventralward (rotation) by means of the diaphragm while expiration allows the return of the kidney to its physiologic location (to its renal niche in the abdominal wall). No doubt the ratatory motion of the kidney if extensive produces pain from renal pedicle torsion. (Dietl's Crisis).

The kidney becomes nephroptotic by decreasing its subdiaphragmatic space. On the right side the liver and kidney completely occupy the right subdiaphragmatic dome and one or both must yield in splanchnoptosia when the subdiaphragmatic space is diminished, hence Riedel's lobe or nephroptosia or both results. From clinical observation it may be observed that the right kidney is manifestly nephroptotic 10 fold more than the left and that woman have 10 fold more nephroptosia than man. However, this is more apparent than real and refers rather to palpable degrees than to actualities.

If one examines a series of embryos, no difference can be observed between the right and left kidneys in males and females, hence the difference in position and degree of nephroptosia is a post natal acquirement. One special variable element arises and progresses after birth and that is the relation of the coecum to the kidney. The difference in position of the kidney begins in male and female at pubertas. At pubertas in females the diameter of the interiliac space begins to increase more rapid than the diameter of the intercostal space producing a distalward expanding funnel in the body trunk and this truncated funnel is irregularly compressed by the construction of clothing aiding to force the viscera distal to the corset line of constriction. In long trunked, waisted women the constriction of the corset may force the kidney proximalward dorsal to the liver surface. In short waisted women the corset is the more liable to force the kidney distalward extending it from the costo-diaphragmatic space where it is palpated with facility.

The Relation of Nephroptosia to the Liver or Bile Ducts.

The nephroptotic kidney maintains two relations with the liver, viz.: (a) The kidney may be extended distal to the liver when its peritoneal and subperitoneal tissue connections may produce traction on the biliary passages, flexing and obstructing them a distalward nephroptosia. I published such a case with illustration in the Medical Critic, May, 1908. In this subject a peritoneal band extended from the kidney to the ductus choledochus communis. (b) The nephroptotic kidney may pass proximalward on the dorsal surface of the liver. This is proximalward nephroptosia—a symptomless dislocation. The influence of the nephroptotic kidney on the colon (hepatic flexure) or coecum is marked, however, limited in clinical influence.

Nephrotosia ends in compromising of the subdiaphragmatic space, as: (1) contraction of the diaphragm on a relaxed abdominal wall (as in respiration). (2) by collapse of chest walls (consequent to disease); (3) constriction of the trunk (by clothing). The left kidney is limited in motion in nephroptosia because it is maintained in position by the splenic flexure of the colon.

The production of appendicitis by nephroptosia, as reported by Edebohls. I have been unable to confirm clinically or by autopsy.

Nephroptosia has no special influence on disease of the tractus genitalis. In nephroptosia the essential element to observe is the ventralward displacement produced by axial rotation on the renal pedicle induced by the diaphragm and which constitutes the mobile kidney that rotates on its pedicle occasioning a "crisis." It is not the distalward nor proximalward dislocation of the kidney that produces the so-called crisis.

Nephroptosia, Ren Mobilis.

Floating or movable kidney, Nephroptosia, has received the major attention in splanchnoptosia and has unfortuately been the scapegoat for the numerous symptoms belonging to general splanchnoptosia. It is admitted that nephroptosia may be the most striking feature in the examination of the splanchnoptotic patient, however, in the vast majority of subjects it is but a part and parcel of splanchnoptosia. What is nephropotsia? It is understood to be excessive renal mobility. The kidney is a mobile organ, not absolutely fixed. It moves with respiration, perhaps ½ an inch of range. It is difficult to draw the line between a normally mobile kidney and a pathologic one except through complex clinical symptoms.

Perhaps 10% of subjects only possessing palpably mobile kidney suffer from nephroptosia. In my practice among women I have palpated and perceived mobile right kidney in 60% of subjects. However, 60% of patients were not afflicted with nephroptosia—floating kidney—as no symptoms existed. In some 700 personal autopsic abdominal inspections I found that the general movement of the right kidney in its fossal bed was one inch

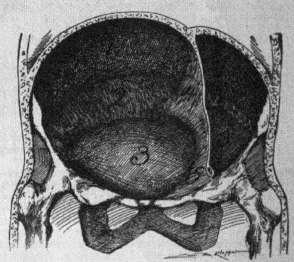

Fig. 191. This figure presents established hepatic dislocation. 1, diaphragm; 2, meshepaticon; 3, lobus dexter hepatis; 4, ligamentum suspensorium hepatis; 5, colon transversum; 6, enteron.

proximalward and one inch distalward. The left kidney moved about one-quarter of an inch less in its proximalward and distalward translations.

In the bodies of large men the right kidney would not infrequently move over 1½ inches proximalward—a range of renal movements of over 2 inches (proximo-distalward). (However, it is my opinion that the dorso-ventral renal motion—the axial rotation of the kidney on its neuro-vascular visceral pedicle that inflicts damage and pain.) These subjects during life had not complained of mobile kidney nor had it been diagnosed. From the induration of the perirenal areola, fatty capsule, the kidney has a greater range of motion in the living than the dead.

Etiology of Nephroptosia.

The main causes are: (a) a predisposing body form; (b) rapid loss of perineal fat; (c) rapidly repeated gestations; (d) heredity—degeneration, inferior anatomy and physiology; (e) yielding of diaphragmatic supports; (f) debilitating disease, form and dimension of the renal fossa. The renal fossa varies in form and dimensions within certain limits in different individuals. The narrower the distal end of the renal fossa the more immobile the kidney. The renal fossa is broader and shallower in woman than man, hence more ren mobilis in woman than man. The broad, shallow fossa renalis connected with a funnel-shaped trunk accounts for increased renal mobility.

Frequency of Nephroptosia.

I think that 10% of female adults are afflicted with symptomatic nephroptosia. In 60% of adult women visiting my office I can palpate mobile kidney.

Age Relations of Nephroptosia.

Nephroptosia is at its maximum frequency and extent at 40 years of age.

Diagnosis of Nephroptosia.

Nephroptosia is diagnosed by bimanual palpation in the lumbar region while the patient assumes the dorsal, prone, semi-prone and erect attitude. Mobile kidney should not be mistaken for neurosis.

If, in nephroptosia, one can find distinct renal pain, renal tenderness, renal hypertrophy, and that the ureteral pelvis of the same side will contain a greater quantity of fluid than the other, periodic hydro-ureter has probably begun. If in a kidney of extensive mobility irregular pain presents it is probably due to rotation of the kidney on its uretero-neuro-vascular pedicle (Dietl's crisis) and ureteral dilatation (periodic hydro-ureter) has probably begun.

Position of the Kidney.

In about 15% of subjects the kidneys are of the same level. Doubtless the combination of longer right renal artery, the erect attitude (force of gravity) and the liver explains the variation in position between the right and left calyces and pelvis (kidney).

In mammals the right kidney lies more proximal than the left because the right renal artery is longer, the attitude or force of gravity tends proximalward and the liver does not wedge itself between the kidney and diaphragm so vigorously as in that of man. Also the left liver half is much more developed in quadrupeds than man and hence the gastrium and spleen is more distalward than in man. Hence taking into account the larger size of the right hepatic lobe and the larger volume of the embryonic liver which checks the growth of the Wolffian body proximalward (Strube) it would appear that the liver has considerable influence in the more distal position of the right than the left kidney. There is an age and functional relation of the position of the kidney, especially in children and women. A child's kidney is more distal than that of an adult on account of its relative small volume and large volume of the liver. Also during reproduction when the elements of the abdominal wall (elastic, muscular and connective tissue) elongate and separate, allowing the kidney to move distalward. Besides the splanchnoptosia that increase after 30 years of age lends data to an age and functional relation of the renal position.

The statment is common among general surgeons who are prone to perform nephropexy, that the right kidney, which is most frequently operated, extends distalward to crista iliaca. However, if one will carefully examine 100 male and female cadavers in regard to the position of the kidney and iliac crestit it will be found that the distal pole of the male kidney will be chiefly ¾ of an inch proximal to the iliac crest and that the distal pole of the female kidney will average over ½ inch proximal to the iliac crest. Perhaps in man 10% of right distal kidney poles touch the iliac crest and perhaps 20% in woman touch the iliac crest.

The left kidney is more proximally located. When the distal renal pole projects distal to the crest of the ilium pathologic conditions (splanchnoptosia) will probably exist. The kidneys are located in an excavation (what I shall term renal fossa) on the dorsal wall of the abdominal cavity on each side of the vertebral column fixed to the diaphragm and lumbar muscle by the capsula adiposa renalis or perirenal tissue, anchored medially by the neuro-vascular renal pedicle and maintained ventrally by the intraabdominal pressure (adjacent viscera and abdominal wall). A most excellent and practical standard, notwithstanding individual variations for kidney measurements and for the purpose of noting the position of the kidney is the crista iliaca. I used it as the chief standard in all measurements in some 700 autopsies. In general the distal pole of the kidney extends to the IV lumbar vertebra. In the examination of over 620 cadavers (man 465, woman 155), the general average was that the right kidney was one finger (¾ inch) proximal to the iliac crest while the left kidney was 2 fingers (1½ inches).

The kidneys of woman were about ½ inch more distal than those of man. In about 15% of the females the right distal kidney pole was on a level with the crista iliac. These data have no relation with the artificial range of motion that one can impose on the kidney during life and in the cadaver. The kidneys of males had not such a high per cent of distalward position nor such free motion as those of females. However, individual variation is prominent for in some male cadavers I found the highest form of free mobility, e. g., in one large male cadaver the right kidney presented a proximaward range of 2 inches and a distalward range of 2 inches—a total vertical range of 4 inches. Conclusions in regard to the factors affecting the position of the kidney: 1. The chief factors in retaining the kidney in position is the length of the neuro-vascular renal pedicle, in short the arteria-renalis. 2. Pressure and counter-pressure of adjacent viscera. 8. Intra-abdominal pressure (pelvic and thoracic diaphragm and ventral abdominal walls). 4 Bodily attitude and force of gravity. In man the right kidney is locat distalward to the left. In quadrupeds, the right kidney is located proximal to the left. In man and quadrupeds the right arteria renalis is the longer. 5. The shape of the trunk, especially of woman, is that of a funnel with the larger end distalward. 6. In woman age and functional relations aid in inducing nephroptosia. 7. The diminished amount of panniculus adiposus renalis, through absorption tends to nephroptosia. 8. Elongation and separation of the elements (fascia, muscle and elastic fiber) of the abdominal wall, relaxation are among the most potent factor as regards the position of the kidney. 9. The peritoneum aids in maintaining the kidney in position.

10. The liver, in foetal and adult life, the long right renal artery, the absence of the colon on the ventral right renal surface, the shallow right renal bed or niche and the less strong perineal fascia in the right kidney makes the right kidney more mobile than the left.

Symptoms of Nephroptosia.

Among the chief disturbing symptoms of nephroptosia I think is renal anteversion, torsion of the renal pedicle with ureteral flexion. Torsion of the renal pedicle can be observed in life only in the erect attitude as the recumbent position, immediately corrects renal dislocation. When the subject of nephroptosia sits or stands the proximal pole of the kidney moves ventralward producing torsion or rotating of the renal pedicle (artery, vein, nerves, lymphatics) and flexion of the ureter. Torsion of the renal pedicle, renal anteversion, compromises the renal lymph, venous and arterial vessels as well as traumatizes the nerves in the renal pedicle. Doubtless the essential benefit of mechanical abdominal supports in nephroptosia is the correction of the renal anteversion and consequent correction of torsioned renal pedicle. Doubtless Dietl's crisis is torsion of the renal pedicle. Kidneys with extensive range of motion (3 to 4 inches) in the living may be accompanied with no symptoms. We frequently observe this phenomena. If the proximal pole of the kidney becomes detached from the diaphragm, as it does in nephroptosia renal anteversion begins its slow march which is con-

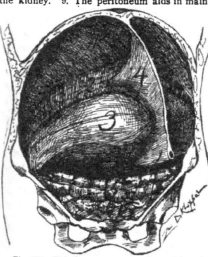

Fig. 192. This figure represents advanced hepatic dislocation. 1, diaphragm; 1, hepaticon; 3, dexter et sinister lobus hepatis; 5, ligamentum rotundum hepatis. The liver is advanced sufficiently distalward to conceal colon, enteron, and kidneys.

tinually accelerated by the distalward movements of the liver and spleen through the contracting diaphragm. Renal anteversion and consequently torsion of renal pedicle may be observed in the large, spare splanchnoptotic multipara by palpating especially the right kidney. During the last 15 years in some 700 autopsies I have tested the renal range of motion in large numbers. The verticle or proximo-distal translation of renal motion is but a factor in nephroptosia. I have found both in the living and dead that the dorso-ventral renal translation motion and the torsion or twisting of the renal pedicle are potent factors in the symptom-complex of nephroptosia.

The dorsal-ventral movements of the kidney consists of ventralward motion only in a zone of perhaps 2 inches.

Nephroptosia comprehends the view of clinical symptoms complex in which the role of dragging sensations, pain in the anterior crural and genito-crural nerves, gastric crisis, constipation, dyspepsia and various degrees of neuroses, violent palpitation in the epigastrium. Pains in the sacral and lumbar region. Dietl's crisis—paroxysmal attacks of severe and intense pain, nausea and vomiting. Dietl's crisis may be due to torsion of the renal pedicle or to periodic hydro-ureter. We may note improvement during pregnancy and discomfort during menstruation. Increased symptoms during walking occur and relief of symptoms on assuming the prone position. The above symptoms simulate those of splanchnoptosia. Nephroptotic symptoms are generally an incident only in splanchnoptosia. A warning is here offered not to attribute symptoms to nephroptosia that belong to splanchnoptosia. For practically nephroptosia and splanchnoptosia are coexistent.

Treatment of Nephroptosia.

I. Medical.

(a) Visceral drainage. The most important treatment in nephroptosia (which practically coexists with splanchnoptosia) is what I shall term visceral drainage, i. e., maximum sewerage or flushing by ample fluids of the tractus intestinalis, urinarius and perspirations with liberal supply of coarse foods which leave an indigestible foecal residue to stimulate peristalsis in the colon. (b) Position. Nephroptotics should assume the recumbent position as much as convenient for they possess inferior anatomy and physiology. It relieves symptoms—acts as a prophylaxis and aids in curing by inducing the kidneys to persist in their normal prevertebral fossae. (c) Nutrition. Improve nutrition in order to redeposit the perirenal areolar capsule. (d) Pregnancy. Gestation improves nutrition (and acts as a temporary mechanical support). (e) Massage. (f) Gymnastics. (g) Electricity.

II. Mechanical.

Mechanical treatment signifies forcible reposition and retention of the kidney in its normal physiologic location. This is excuted by: (1) Attitude. The horizontal position relieves symptoms and aids in curing the disease. (2) Abdominal binders. (a) These may be elastic or nonelastic and are applied during the day (or erect attitude). (b) An elastic binder which contains between the binder and abdomen a pneumatic rubber pad (Byron Robinson). This binder is applied while recumbent and the pneumatic pad distended to suit the comfort of the patient. (3) The corset. This method has been successfully conducted by Dr. E. A. Gallant of New York. The corset is made under individual measurements, applied while in the prone position and removed for the recumbent attitude. (4) Adhesive strapping. This is executed by means of adhesive straps applied to the abdomen and is known as Achilles Rose's method (also independently introduced by Dr. N. Rosewater of Cleveland, Ohio, and Dr. B. Schmitz of Germany). Straps of adhesive plaster of various width are passed entirely around the body, elevating and maintaining the abdominal viscera in the normal physiologic position. Rose's method of adhesive strapping is simple, economical, rational and of vast practical utility. (5) Pregnancy. Gestation temporarily relieves the symptoms of nephroptosia.

The Effect of Relaxed Abdominal Wall and consequent splanchnoptosia in Nephroptosia.

Women with relaxed abdominal walls frequently suffer with nephroptosia. In regard to the nephroptosia, the renal secretion is deficient, excessive, or disproportionate. The exact relations of factors of the nephroptosia and relaxed abdominal walls to the disturbed renal secretion are not easy to be determined.

The disturbed renal secretion would appear to be mainly due to disturbed renal mechanism. The renal artery, vein and ureter become compromised in relation to the nephroptosia. The passing distalward of the kidney from relaxed abdominal walls stenoses the ureter and renal vein. The blood pressure in the renal vein is low, and hence light disturbed renal mechanism will easily compromise its blood flow.

In nephroptosia the distal pole of the kidney approaches the vertebral column disproportionately, and hence compromises the lumen of the ureter, damming the urine. Outside of disturbed urine flow from changed renal mechanism, equally disturbing factors in nephroptosia arise from trauma to the renal plexus. The renal plexus is a large collection of nerve plexuses and ganglia, and besides it is directly connected with the ganglia coeliacum, the abdominal brain, the largest ganglia in the body, which, being a reflex center outside of the spinal cord, reorganizes the reflexes and sends them to all other abdominal viscera. Thus the patient with nephroptosia complains of nausea and vomiting and dragging pains. She gradually becomes neurotic from reflexes due to trauma on the renal plexus. The damage in nephroptosia is, perhaps, in order:

1. Trauma of the renal plexus (and abdominal brain), producing a vicious circle by continuous reflexes on the abdominal viscera.
2. Traumatic stenosis of the vena cava, ovarian and renal veins.
3. Stenosis of the ureter with dislocation of the kidney, preventing drainage.
4. Trauma of renal artery.

5. A combined dislocation of the renal mechanism is changing the relation of the renal vein, artery and ureter, a disturbed mechanism of the uretro-ureteral triangle.

6. The producing of deficient, excessive or disproportionate renal secretion.

7. The subject with right nephroptosis suffers nausea, headache, foul breath, gastric disturbances and constipation, accompanied by the stigmata of hysteria and other neuroses. As nephroptosia is only a part and parcel of general splanchnoptosis, nephropexy, which should be done by placing the kidney in the abdominal wall without sutures, must be limited in its local and general utility, practically to periodic hydroureter.

The Uretero-Venous Triangles.
(*Byron Robinson.*)

In dissecting, one finds on the left side of the body a triangle formed by the ureter on the left side, the ovarian vein on the right side, and the renal vein on the proximal end or base. The sides of the triangle are about 2 to 3 inches and the base (the renal vein) is about 1 inch. The apex of the triangle is at the proximal arterio-ureteral crossing of the utero-ovarian artery, located proximal or distal to the iliac crest.

This is what I term the left uretero-venous triangle. Its outlines are distorted in left nephroptosis.

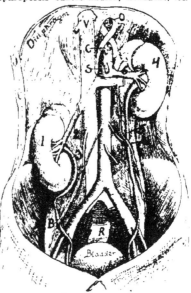

Fig. 198. presents a common condition found especially in the multipara. The left kidney is presented as normal to compare the contrast. 1, right kidney with its distal pole projecting distal to the iliac crest; 2, the elongated right arteria renalis 3, the ureter in a sinuous course. B, point where vasa ovarica crosses ventral to the ureter (apex of uterovenous triangles of author). A presents the apex of the utero-venous triangle of the left side. 4, left kidney. 5, left ureter. 6, left arteria renalis. O, oesophagus. C, arteria coeliaca. S, arteria mesenterica superior. V, vena cava.

On the right side of the body what I term the right uretero-venous triangle is formed by the ureter on the right side, the vena cava and ovarian vein on the left side, and the renal vein on the proximal end or base. The right uretero-venous triangle is about an inch at its base (the renal vein) and 2 inches on its sides. Its apex is at the proximal arterio-ureteral crossing of the utero-ovarian artery, and is located 1½ to 2 inches distal to the iliac crest. The significant factor in the right uretero-venous triangle is that in nephroptosia it becomes markedly distorted, compromising the lumen of the ureter, ovarian and the renal veins. The uretero-venous triangles, bilateral distinct, constant structures, are significant landmarks in topographical anatomy. I have not observed them named or described. They vary considerably in size from the varying location of the apex at the crossing of the ureter by the ovarian vein and artery. The apex of the uretero-venous triangle I have designated as the proximal arterio-ureteral crossing (of the utero-ovarian artery). In nephroptosia the uretero-venous triangle is distorted and the lumen of the vein and ureter is compromised.

III. Surgical.

Nephropexy in general is irrational and unjustifiable (except in periodic hydroureter), because: (a), it is unphysiologic to fix mobile viscera; (b), the kidney does not remain fixed; (c), the nephroptosia is but an incident, a fragment of splanchnoptosia; (d), the remaining or adjacent viscera are deranged, splanchnoptotic; (e), the surgeon attempts to relieve one lesion or disease (excessive mobility) by producing another lesion or disease (fixtion)—which is the more irrational; (f), the multiple methods of nephropexy condemn it; (g), nephropexy does not remove the splanchnoptotic symptoms which coexist; (h), surgeons do not agree as to the idications for nephropexy, as the symptoms of nephroptosia are not proportionate to the degree of mobility; (i), the mortality of nephropexy is at least 1 per cent; (j), nephropexy should be systematically refused, discarded, condemned, for more rational methods (unless periodic hydroureter exist). The therapeusis should be executed through the abdomial wall (medical, mechanical, surgical). The incised abdominal walls should be superimposed, overlapped like a double-breasted coat. It is doubtfully justifiable to perform nephropexy on a replaceable kidney unless periodic hydroureter can be demonstrated.

Nephropexy should be performed only after all palliative measures have been tried.

By observing the final results of nephropexy extending over a decade and including numerous subjects, it is not flattering. Professor John A. Robison, of Chicago, relates to me personally that during the past ten years that a considerable number of his patients had visited different surgeons and had undergone the operation of nephropexy. Dr. J. A. Robison asserts that he not only observed that the patients received no benefits from the nephropexy but that the results were damaging in almost every subject.

GASTRO-DUODENAL DILATATION IN SPLANCHNOPTOSIA.

A Phase or Complication in Splanchnoptosia.

The dilatation of the stomach and duodenum (gastro-duodenal dilation) is due to pressure of the superior mesenteric artery, vein and nerve on the tranvserse segment of the duodenum.

In 1893, the time of the Chicago World's Fair while giving courses to physicians on abdominal visceral anatomy and its applied surgery, I became interested in the manner in which the transverse segment of the duodenum was compressed by the superior mesenteric artery, vein and nerve. I well remember the discussions of the physicians in the classes at that time, who concluded that the superior mesenteric vessels and nerves would not obstruct the duodenum, because the duodenal contents were almost entirely fluid and gas. However, we all observed that in a spare, though normal subject, the superior mesenteric vessels and nerves very suspiciously compressed the transverse duodenal segment. We selected spare, fatless, subjects for visceral demonstration, and the distinct mechanical apparatus of mesenteric

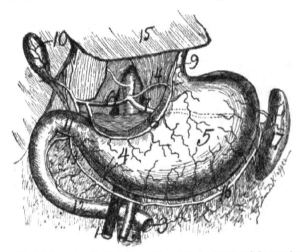

Fig. 194. is a cut to illustrate the position of the duodenum and the superior mesenteric artery, vein and nerve. 1, the superior mesenteric vein; 2, superior mesenteric artery, the nerve not represented in the cut; 3, distal end of duodenum; 4 and 5, stomach; 6, hepatic artery; 7, splenic artery; 8, gastric artery, the hepatic and gastric arteries making what I shall term the gastro-hepatic circle; 9, the œsophagus; 10, the gall-bladder; 11, the pylorus; 12, the duodenum; 13 and 16, gastro-epiploca sinistra et dextra; 17, spleen; 15, part of liver. This cut shows that the duodenum in the acute mesenterico-aortic angle is the acute mesenterico-vertebral—however, the real angle of strangulation.

vessels and nerve clamping the transverse duodenum against the vertebral column as a base made an indelible impression.

I have persued the matter during the past thirteen years in subjects possessing visceral ptosis, and found that when the coils of enteron lie in the pelvis the superior mesenteric artery vein and nerve compress the transverse segment of the duodenum in such a manner that gastro-duodenal dialatation begins in the transverse segment of the duodeum immediately on the right side of the superior mesenteric vessels and nerve. I have observed this so frequently in hundreds of autopsies thatI know it to be an important factor in gastro-duodenal dilatation in persons suffering from visceral ptosis, splanchnoptosia.

Previous to 1893 I had performed a considerable number of autopsies, but without detailed records of abdominal inspection. Since 1893 I have detailed records of personal autopsic inspection of the abdomen in 165 adult

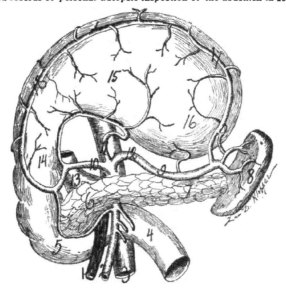

Fig. 195. shows the relation of the duodenum transversum, pancreas, celiac axis, superior mesenteric artery, vein and nerve with the stomach drawn proximally. 1 and 2, superior mesenteric artery and vein; 3, aorta; 4 and 5, transverse segment of duodenum passing posterior to vessels; 6 and 7, pancreas; 8, spleen; 9, splenic artery; 10, hepatic, and 11, gastric arteries forming the gastro-hepatic circle; 13, portal vein; 14, duodenum; 15 and 16, stomach; 17 and 18, epiploic arteries. This cut shows how naturally the vessels could compromise the distalward-moving fecal current in the duodenum. The fixation of the transverse segment of the duodenum by the muscularis suspensorius and the fibrous band from the left crus of the diaphragm is not drawn in the cut.

females, and 480 adult males and some 50 children. Besides, I have also pursued the study of visceral ptosis, and relaxed abdominal walls—splanchnoptosia in the living patients and abdominal sections. In clinics and autopsy it is realized with facility that splanchnoptosia is a frequent, common disease. I systematically examined in the 700 detailed autopsies the tractus intestinalis, tractus genitalis, the tractus urinarius and also the peritoneum.

Since Glenard's celebrated labors on splanchnoptosia (1884) considerable study has been devoted to the position of the abdominal viscera. The study of the position of the abdominal viscera has progressed, however, in an irregular method. When Dr. Eugene Hahn, the brilliant Berlin surgeon, first introduced and performed nephropexy, superficial surgeons made a rush for a so-called new operation, with little idea that nephroptosia is only a part and parcel of general splanchnoptosia. Visceral ptosis may begin in early years of age, and increases every subsequent decade of life. My knowledge of splanchnoptosia or visceral ptosis was gained during the past twenty years by the personal autopsic inspection of 700 adult abdomens, 50 children, quite a number of fetuses with hundreds of peritonotomies.

I have been for years attempting to prove, by post-mortem examination and peritonotomies and celiotomies, that in a considerable number of cases dilatation of the stomach is caused through pressure of the superior mesenteric artery, nerve and vein on the transverse segment of the duodenum. In these subjects the stomach does not begin to dilate at the pylorus, but in the duodenum at the right side of the superior mesenteric artery, vein and nerve. The stomach alone is not dilated. The compression of the duodenum by the superior mesenteric artery and vein and nerve is typically manifest in a subject with splanchnoptosia or visceral ptosis, and especially while lying on the back. Practically it is not gastric dilatation—it is gastro-duodenal dilatation.

In 700 autopsies I have noted perhaps 50 advanced typical subjects presenting some distinct and some extensive gastro-duodenal dilatation, which began in the duodenum on the right side of the superior mesenteric artery, vein and nerve.

The careful dissector wonders why the superior mesenteric artery, vein and nerve, all bound in a strong fibrous bundle and tightly compressing the transverse segment of the duodenum, do not produce obstruction in the duodenal segment of the tractus intestinalis. At first thought it is because the bowel contents in the duodenum is liquid or gas. This may be always, or nearly always true in absolutely normal subjects, but in the numerous subjects with splanchnoptosia or visceral ptosis it is not true. It must be remenbered that gastro-duodenal dilatation is a phase or stage or a complication in progressive splanchnoptosia. The more splanchnoptosia exists the more the loops of the enteron pass distalward into the lesser pelvis, dragging and tugging on the superior mesenteric artery, vein and nerve, which more and more tightly constricts the duodenum transversum, because the latter scarcely at all moves distalward. If the subject possesses considerable splanchnoptosia, and for any reason lies considerable time on back, the gastro-duodenal dilatation may progress quite readily.

The most typical case in the living I have witnessed was one to whom Dr. Coons, of Chicago, called me in 1898. The patient, a man, about 45 years of age, had been in bed perhaps 5 months with hip-joint disease. He had some lordosis. The abdomen was enormously distended, and he vomited continually. I thought of some form of obstruction in the tractus intestinalis, and proposed that abdominal section gave the only faint hope of relief. The patient quickly and cheerfully gave his consent. I made an incision in the median abdominal line and found the abdomen absolutely filled from pelvic to thoracic diaphragm with a white, shiny distended cyst, which proved to be the enormously dilated stomach and duodenum. If the subject had been a woman the tumor would be immediately taken for an ovarian cyst. In the patient's debilitated condition I could do nothing with such an enormous dilated stomach, and finding no apparent intestinal obstruction closed the abdominal incision. The patient subsequently died and an autopsy was allowed. We found the enormously dilated stomach and duodenum—gastroduodenal dilatation—caused by constriction of the superior mesenteric artery vein and nerve on the transverse segment of the duodenum. The subject possessing considerable degree of splanchnoptosia and lordosis, with several months lying on his back in bed made the progress of the gastro-duodenal dilatation rapid in its course. Gastro-duodenal dilatation—a slow, gradual, chronic process—doubtless accounts for numerous so-called idiopathic gastric dilations subsequent to laparotomies. The explanation of acute gastric dilatation (it is gastric-duodenal dilation) is an exacerbation of chronic gastro-duodenal dilatation. In every fifty autopsies I have noted typical cases where it was gastro-duodenal dilatation, not merely gastric dilatation. In many cases one observes a slight dilatation which does not present itself as typical, but by careful examination and test by forcing the gaseous contents of the stomach through the duodenum distinct gastro-duodenal dilatation can be seen to begin at the right side of the band formed by the combination of the superior mesenteric artery, vein and nerve.

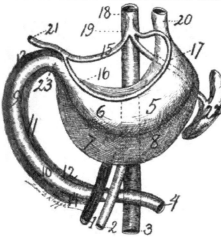

Fig. 196. is a cut to illustrate the final growing gastro-duodenal dilatation due to obstructing the duodenum by the superior mesenteric artery, vein and nerve. The white portion of the stomach and duodenum represent the normal size, the adjacent dark portion is the dilated part. 1 and 2, the superior mesenteric vein and artery; 3, aorta; 4, the non-dilated portions of the duodenum, distal to the constricting vessels; 5 and 6, original normal stomach; 9 and 10, the non-dilated duodenum; 11, 12, 13 and 14, the dilated portions of the duodenum; 15, the hepatic, and 16 and 17, the gastric arteries forming the gastro-hepatic circle; 18, aorta; 19, celiac artery; 20, esophagus; 21, hepatic artery; 22, spleen; 23, pylorus. In this cut the acute mesenterico-vertebral angle shows plainly how it strangles or obstructs the transverse duodenal segment in visceral ptosis.

One can easily experiment on the cadaver to prove that the obstruction lies at the point of the duodenum where it is crossed by the superior mesenteric artery, veins and nerve. By placing the superior mesenteric artery, vein and nerve on a tension, i. e., by dragging the enteronic loops distalward and compressing the gas in the stomach, the obstruction is plainly visible by a distension of the duodenum at the right side of the structure (vessels and nerve) which constrict the duodenum transversum. The dilatation is caused first by gas and second by fluids. I have studied the subject of gastro-duodenal dilatation from 1893 and since I have found no records of it in literature, except that of Albrecht, in 1899, six years after I began, it seems to be original. The subject of gastro-duodenal dilatation as caused by the constriction of the superior mesenteric artery, vein and nerve is original with me. I published my first formal article in 1900.

Dr. John M. T. Finney, associate professor of surgery in Johns Hopkins medical school, wrote the following in the Annals of Surgery: "It is a fact worthy of note in passing that Dr. Byron Robinson of Chicago in 1900 appears to have been the first one in this country to bring this condition to the attention of the profession in a publication."

In 1896 I made an abdominal autopsy on a case for Dr. Holman. We found extensive gastro-duodenal dilatation with marked distalward dislocation of the stomach (gastroptosia).

The woman vomited, I was informed, for a couple of years before her death, which appeared during life as a kind of marasmus. Death was undoubtedly due to malassimilation, due to disturbances in the system caused by extensive gastro-duodenal dilatation.

Fig. 197. a profile view of the acute mesenterico-aortic (mesenterico-vertebral) angle presenting the method of duodenal obstruction by the mesenteric vessels. This obstruction is especially increased when in visceral ptosis. The loops of enteron drag on the superior mesenteric artery (3) and pass in the direction of the arrow toward the pelvis. The mesenterico-aortic angle (eventually the mesenterico-vertebral angle) has already advanced to a partial obstruction of the duodenum. 1, duodenum; 2, aorta; 3, superior mesenteric artery; 4, superior mesenteric artery passing to coils of enteron; 5, superior mesenteric angle passing to colon; 6, transverse colon; 7, blades of omentum majus passing proximalward to gastrium; 8, blades of omentum majus passing distalward; 10, inferior mesenteric artery; 11, abdominal aorta lying between the origin of the superior and inferior mesenteric arteries. The arrow points to the pelvis and indicates how the superior mesenteric artery clamps tighter and tighter the duodenum with advancing visceral ptosis.

In 1895 Drs. Fruth and Henry, of Ohio, referred to me a patient who had scarcely kept fluid or food long in the stomach for twenty months or more. She was emancipated, and I could detect only a distended or dilated stomach. The gastroptosia is easily detected, for, after the stomach is irrigated, it is pumped full of air and this method easily demonstrates its outline. I thought this patient had a stricture of the pylorus, and perhaps a carcinoma, but she did not lose flesh nor had she paled sufficiently for malignancy. On opening the abdomen all we found was an enormous gastro-duodenal dilatation which extended distal to the pelvic brim, yes, into the lesser pelvis. I performed gastro-jejunostomy with my segmented rubber plates. She made a favorable recovery, and wrote to me seven years after the operation that she was perfectly well. Dr. Henry, of Fostoria, Ohio, her physician, reported in 1905, ten years subsequent to the operation, that she is well. In hundreds of personal autopsic abdominal inspections I have noted the state of the duodenum and stomach since 1893, and gastro-duodenal dilatation is a common disease in subjects over 30 years of age, especially in multiparae, in whom I have palpated the liver partly resting in the lesser pelvis. After fifteen years of observation of visceral ptosis I am convinced that gastroduodenal dilatation is the indirect cause of ill health and of many deaths in persons above thirty years of age.

Gastro-duodenal dilatation is not found in normal subjects. It would appear that the main disturbance in gastro-duodenal dilatation begins when the enteronic loop passes distalward over the pelvic brim or promontory. It might appear strange that the mechanical arrangements of animal structure would tend to destroy its own existence. A little study of this region will explain why the duodenal obstruction arises. The gist of the explanation lies in the anatomic fact that (a) the transverse duodenal segment in the splanchnoptosia does not travel distalward as rapidly as does the enteron. (b) In adults the duodenum possesses a mesenterii membrana propria only (no peritoneal mesentery). It does not possess a peritoneal mesentery. This fact alone explains why the duodenum does not move distalward as rapidly as the remaining enteron, which possesses a 6-inch mesenteron. (c) Again, the musculus suspensorius duodeni of Treitz arises adjacent to the coeliac axis and inserts itself into the duodenum, circumscribing limited motion to it—duodenum—practically imposing localized fixation on the doudenum. This second important anatomic factor serves as a second explanation why the transverse segment of the duodenum does not pass as rapidly distalward as the enteron, which is maintained by an elongated mesentery. (d) A third explanation why the transverse duodenal segment does not pass distalward as rapidly as the enteron is that, the transverse duodenal segment maintained by the mesenterii membrana propria, does not yield and follow the relaxed abdominal walls as does the mobile enteron. Hence, since the transverse segment of the duodenum does not travel distalward as rapidly as the enteron in visceral ptosis, it becomes clamped tighter and tighter in the diminishing acute angle between the vertebral column and the mesenteric cord (formed by the mesenteric vein, artery and nerve). The chief clamping of the duodenum begins when the enteronic coils pass distalward into the lesser pelvis. The expanding and proximalward moving uterus during pregnancy forces the enteronic coils proximalward, increasing the angle between the vertebral column and the mesenteric cord (superior mesenteric artery, vein and nerve), and this relieves the gastro-duodenal obstruction similar to an abdominal binder.

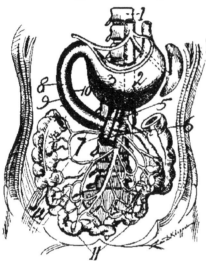

Fig. 198 shows diagrammatically how the superior mesenteric artery, vein and nerve obstructs the transverse segment of the duodenum as it crosses the vertebral column. Increasing enteroptosis (i. e., the passing of the enteron more and more into the lesser pelvis) makes more and more acute the mesenterico-vertebral angle, and, as the duodenum does not pass distalward as rapidly as the enteron, obstructs rapid progress. 1, vertebral column; 2 and 3, normal stomach; 4, the dark outline represents the dilated portion; 5, superior mesenteric artery; 6, superior mesenteric vein; 5, 6, and 7 are bound by a strong sheath of connective tissue into a bundle as large as the little and ring finger. Occasionally in visceral ptosis one must lift several pounds in order to elevate this superior mesenteric band from the duodenum. 8, the white, is normal duodenum; 9 and 11, dark, is the dilated portion of the duodenum due to the obstructing mesenteric vessels and nerve, hence the end result is gastro-duodenal dilatation; 11, the enteronic loops in the pelvis dragging the mesenteric vessels over the sacral promontory like a rope over a log. The colon transversum is resected and removed P. S. In the abdomen of such a case of visceral ptosis as Fig. 184 the stomach would extend to the sacral promontory and the transverse duodenum would be relatively slightly moved distalward on account of its fixation apparatus (i. e., the musculus suspensorius duodeni and the fibrous band connecting the duodenum to the right crus of the diaphragm). In enteroptosia the superior mesenteric artery, vein and nerve must elongate and attenuate, unlike the uterine artery in pregnancy, which not only elongates, but thickens.

One scarcely sees the duodenum in a hernia. The text-books on hernia note that every organ of the abdomen has been found in hernia except the duodenum, pancreas and liver. Dr. Lucy Waite and myself have made autopsies in which the stomach rested on the pelvic floor. This extends tubular viscera and dislocates the parts so that partial obstruction arises from mesenterial vessels.

In 1794, when Sir Astley Cooper and Mr. Cline performed an autopsy on Mr. Gibbon, one of the greatest of English writers and philosophers, they found the whole tractus intestinalis except the duodenum (and cecum) in the hernial sac. The distinguished patient had suffered and died from a left inguinal hernia, and the fact of the long continued hernia and visceral ptosis shows that the transverse duodenum is the last segment of the tractus intestinalis to yield to the dragging hernial sac, the lax abdominal wall and intra-abdominal pressure. For thirty years, in the case of Mr. Gibbon, the duodenum transversum had resisted traction of the hernial sac and intra-abdominal pressure and still practically retained its relative position. The scrotal hernial swelling extended to his knees, placing all neuro-vascular visceral pedicles on high tension, as well as extending pathologically tubular viscera and visceral ligaments.

I have observed no record of the duodenum or pancreas in a hernia. My dissections appear to demonstrate the musculus suspensorius duodeni chiefly originates in the tissues about the coeliac axis, and is then inserted into the duodenum transversum as a broad, ribbon-like muscular band. Besides a powerful fixation apparatus is given to the duodenum by a strong fibrous (and perhaps muscular) band, which, by traction, shows that it arises from the left crus of the diaphragm. Hence, the coeliac axis and the crus of the diaphragm being the fixation apparatus of the transverse duodenum by means of the musculus suspensorius duodeni and the fibro-muscular band from the crus of the diaphragm, the duodenum transversum becomes the most fixed organ of the abdomen.

Diagnosis of Gastro-Duodenal Dilatation.

To be useful to subjects afflicted with gastro-duodenal dilatation (a phase of splanchnoptosia) we must first and foremost establish the diagnosis. The first postulate to entertain is that in established splanchnoptosia gastroduodenal dilatation—a phase, a step in the progress of splanchnoptosia—in all probability exists. The gastric dilatation can be established with facility by aid of the sodium bicarbonate and tartaric acid test of the forcing of air in the stomach demonstrating the contour of the stomach. If gastric dilatation exists in splanchnoptosia the probability is that duodenal dilatation also exists, i. e., gastro-duodenal dilatation is the probable diagnosis. To my mind this explains the so-called acute idiopathic dilatation of the stomach subsequent to laparotomies. A factor that increases gastro-duodenal dilatation is the dorsal position of the patient which is assumed almost immediately after the operation. The trauma and infection resulting from manipulation of the viscera becomes suddenly manifest after the operation by paresis of the stomach and consequent rapid dilatation. Splanchnoptotics do not resist infection vigorously. The gastric fluids and gases accumulate and not being expelled distalward or proximalward distend the stomach. There is nothing idiopathic in this condition. The factors are evident, viz: (a) a preexisting gastro-duodenal dilatation (splanchnoptosia); (b) gastric (visceral) paresis from traumatic manipulation; (c) gastric (viscera) paresis from infection. The stomach contents of patients suffering from so-called acute (idiopathic) gastric dilatation subsequent to peritonotomy seems to flow out of the mouth like a river—it resembles the facile flow from the verticle stomach of an infant. The treatment for such patients is immediate and repeated gastric lavage furnishing immediate and wonderful relief. All fluids and foods for such a patient should be by gradual slow rectal irrigation—say a pint of normal salt solution should be introduced in the rectum every two hours and require thirty minutes to flow from the fountain syringe into the rectum.

The Treatment of Gastro-Duodenal Dilatation Due to Compression of the Superior Mesenteric Artery, Vein and Nerve.

(1) Medical; (2) mechanical; (3) surgical.

I. Medical.

The medical treatment has regard to maintaining normal functions of the stomach (and other viscera), viz.: (a) sensation; (b) peristalsis; (c) secretion; (d) absorption. The functions of the stomach are maintained by appropriate foods and fluids.

(A) Fluids.

The splanchnoptotic requires ample drainage of the tractus intestinalis (and urinarius). The patient should drink eight ounces of fluid (the most useful is ½ to ¼ normal salt solution) every two hours for six times daily. The fluids stimulate sensation, peristalsis, absorption, secretion in the stomach enabling the gastrium to wash itself, to irrigate its surface and by stimulation of its muscularis to evacuate itself. The sodium chloride stimulates the gastric epithelium. The fluid increases the blood volume (which especially stimulates gastric peristalsis), eliminates waste laden material especially through the kidney and bowel. In order to stimulate the tractus intestinalis to maximum function or activity I add to the eight ounces of one-half normal salt solution every two hours a part or multiple of an alkaline tablet (composed of cascara sagrada (1-40 gr.), $NaHCO_3$ (gr. 1), $KHCO_3$ (1-3 gr.), $MgSO_4$ (2 gr.), Aloes (gr. 1-3). The tablet is used as follows: One-sixth to one tablet (or more as required to move the bowels, once daily) is placed on the tongue before meals and followed by 8 ounces of water (better hot). At 10 a. m., 3 p. m., and bedtime one-sixth to one tablet is placed on the tongue and followed by a glassful of fluid. In the combined treatment the fragment or multiples of sodium chloride tablet and alkaline tablet are

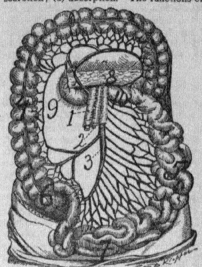

Fig. 199. (author) illustrates the superior mesenteric artery, vein and nerve bound in a large strong bundle and clamping the transverse segment of the duodenum, producing gastro-duodenal dilatation. 1, superior mesenteric vein; 2, nerve and third artery; 3, the duodenum on the right side of the vessels and nerve. The artery, vein and nerve forms the mesenterico-aortic angle, but the actual compression angle is the mesenterico-vertebral angle. The loops of enteron are drawn to the left in order to expose the vessels and nerve.

both placed on the tongue together. I employ for the sodium chloride solution or NaCl tablets of 12 grains each and use fragments of it.

(B) *Foods.*

Appropriate foods are a necessity in gastroduodenal dilatation. Food must be wholesome as cereals, vegetables, albuminoids. All fermentative foods should be avoided, as pies, cakes, pastries, puddings, concentrated spices and condiments. The appropriate food excites the functions of the stomach which promptly evacuates itself. If food remains in the stomach for over 8½ hours indigestion, fermentation will result. In gastro-duodenal dilatation the essential necessity is rapid and complete gastric evacuation, i. e., maximum stomach drainage. In gastro-duodenal dilatation two conditions exist, viz.: (a) one is where the pyloric ring dilates in proportion to the gastro-duodenal dilatation. This condition permits favorable gastric evacuation; (b) the second condition is where the pyloric ring does not dilate in proportion to the gastro-duodenal dilatation. This condition is unfavorable for proper gastric evacuation and is a serious menace to the splanchnoptotic. It is a condition requiring surgical interference—gastro-jejunostomy.

Maximum nourishment produces and maintains a normal panniculus adiposus which aids to maintain, support, viscera in their normal physiologic position.

Fig. 200. An illustration of the clamping of the duodenum, in splanchnoptosia, by the mesenteric vessels. D, duodenum, the enteronic coils are well distalward in the lesser pelvis.

Numerous subjects exist with advanced gastro-duodenal dilatation, but do not suffer marked symptoms because physical conditions are favorable and the pyloric ring is ample in dimensions to allow complete gastric evacuation. In 1894 Dr. Lucy Waite and I performed an autopsy on a man 70 years of age. We found gastro-duodenal dilatation advanced to the degree that the stomach rested on the pelvic floor. No record of any symptoms existed during life because the pyloric ring was proportionately dilated with the gastrium and duodenum offering limited obstruction to the evacuation of the stomach contents. Whereas in another autopsy in 1895 on a woman who vomited for two years with gastro-duodenal dilatation the data was reversed. In this female subject I found enormous gastro-duodenal dilatation and the stomach projected practically to the lesser pelvic floor—however, the pyloric ring was remarkably limited in dimension and gastric contents were forced through with difficulty. Residual food and fermentation occurred. The continued combined treatment of the 8 pints of ¼ sodium chloride solution and alkaline tablets 1-6 to 8, as required to move the bowels once daily, are the necessary visceral drainage treatment in gastro-duodenal dilatation (splanchnoptosia). The alkaline and sodium chloride tablets take place of the so-called mineral waters. I continue this dietetic treatment of fluids and foods for weeks, months (the splanchnoptotic requires lifelong treatment) and the results are remarkably successful especially in pathologic physiology of visceral tracts. The urine becomes clarified like spring water and increased in quantity. The tractus intestinalis becomes freely evacuated, regularly, daily. The tractus vascularis increases in volume and power. The blood is relieved of waste laden and irritating material. The tractus cutus eliminates freely, and the skin becomes normal. The appetite increases. The sleep improves. The patient becomes hopeful, natural energy returns. The sewers of the body are drained and flushed to a maximum. Subjects with gastro-duodenal dilatation should take a limited quantity of food every three hours for four times daily so that the stomach may not be extensively distended or taxed.

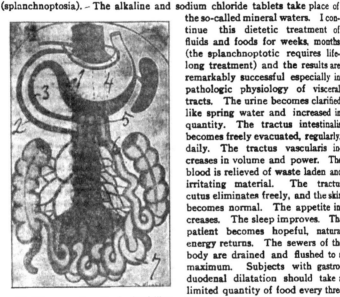

Fig. 201 represents gastro-duodenal dilatation ending when the mesenteric vessels cross the transverse duodenum.

II. Mechanical.

(1) *Abdominal binders* generally afford comfort and relief in gastro-duodenal dilatation (if the pyloris is proportionately dilated). The kinds employed are: (a) the author's pneumatic rubber pad placed within an abdominal binder and distended to suit the comfort of the patient (it should be removed at night). (b) E. Gallant's corset. (c) Achilles Rose's adhesive strapping. The above mechanical contrivances afford vast comfort and relief in gastro-duodenal dilatation by: (1) forcing the viscera proximal-

ward in their normal physiologic position. It aids the stomach in evacuation. (2) They force the viscera (especially the enteron) proximalward and increase the dimension of the mesenterico-vertebral angle relieving the transverse duodenum of pressure and permitting free evacuation of stomach and duodenum. Achilles Rose's rubber adhesive strapping is particularly useful—rational, practical, economical.

(*2*) *Position.* I found that by experimenting with the dead body that position had much to do with the pressure of the mesenteric vessels on the duodenum. The pressure of the mesenteric artery, vein and nerve on the transverse segment of the duodenum is the greatest when (a) the patient lies on the back and the enteronic coils lie in the pelvis; (b) when lying on the abdomen the pressure is mainly relieved; (c) when the patient is turned on the side the pressure is relatively light. Hence the best position of the patient in gastro-duodenal dilatations is lying on the abdomen; and second, lying on either side. Lying on the back or standing increases compressions of the duodenum by the mesenteric vessels.

III. Surgical.

Surgical intervention should be applied to gastro-duodenal dilatation when all other therapeutic measures have been tested and failed.

(*1*) *Visceral anastomosis or Gastro-jejunostomy.* I consider one of the most useful surgical methods to overcome extreme gastro-duodenal dilatation is gastro-jejunostomy. It limits the food journey and time for fermentation, and facilitates gastro-duodenal drainage. I proved in gastro-jejunostomy in dogs, ten years ago, that it will enable the stomach to completely evacuate itself, to contract because the food does not tarry in the stomach but passes immediately into the jejunum and ileum, the business portion of the tractus intestinalis. Any segment of the tractus intestinalis containing no contents or over which no food travels will remain contracted. Anyone can prove this by excluding a segment of the bowel from faecal circulation; it soon contracts and remains in that condition.

Gastro-enterostomy is the most certain and useful of all operations for gastro-duodenal dilatation. It affords the one necessity, gastric evacuation —complete visceral drainage. I have reports of gastro-enterostomy for gastro-duodenal dilatation of 12 years' duration and perfectly well.

(*2*) *Superposition of the abdominal wall.* Longitudinal overlapping of the abdominal wall resembling a double breasted coat is an excellent operation for some subjects afflicted with gastro-duodenal dilatation. I perform it with permanently burned silver wire sutures, three to the inch. In the Mary Thompson Hospital during the past five years its application has been remarkably successful. The Mayos have advocated the proximo-distal superposition of the abdominal walls (especially in umbilical hernia).

(*3*) *Resection of the duodenum.* The duodenum could be resected at a point to the right of the constricting mesenteric vessels and its divided ends reunited ventral to that of the constricting mesenteric vessels. Perhaps it would be practically better to perform gastro-jejunostomy.

(*4*) *Enclosing the musculi recti-abdominales in a single sheath.* My attention was called to the subject of lax abdominal walls by Prof. Karl Schroeder, whose pupil I was for a year.

In that year (1884-1885) Prof. Schroeder, the greatest gynecologic teacher of his age, was at the zenith of his fame, and his clinic was vast; in fact, he tapped the whole of Europe for his material. He discussed in his clear style the misfortune of lax abdominal walls, and he resected large oval segments of the abdominal wall lying between the diastatic recti-abdominales. He then united the sheaths of the recti in the median line. But Prof. Schroeder said then to his pupils that he was not fully satisfied; however, it was the best surgery that he knew at that time. Later German surgeons improved on Schroeder's idea by splitting the sheath of the recti and enclosing both the recti-abdominales in one sheath by uniting the recti sheaths ventral and dorsal to the recti muscles.

In 1894, Prof. N. Senn, in his clinic, began splitting the sheaths of the recti-abdominales and uniting the sheaths anterior and posterior, enclosing both musculi recti-abdominales in a single sheath.

In 1895, Dr. Orville W. MacKellar and I operated on a woman pregnant for five months for an ovarian tumor where the diastasis, of the recti-abdominales was very marked, and the uterus, on coughing or extra intra-abdominal pressure, would project between the recti-abdominales. We united the split sheaths of the recti ventrally and dorsally, enclosing the two musculi recti-abdominales in one sheath. Dr. MacKellar reports to me that his case is perfectly well and the operation was a success. Dr. MacKellar was at the delivery and the recti sheaths remain perfectly intact. For a large post-operative hernia for the past four years at the Mary Thompson Hospital I have split the recti and enclosed them in a single sheath for every one with sufficient experience knows that the post-operative hernia of any considerable size in women over 35 is in nearly every case accompanied by visceral ptosis. Dr. MacKellar and I have records to show that ten years after the enclosing of the two recti-abdominales in a single sheath for visceral ptosis (utero-ptosis) the operation is a success. The mesenteron is not to suspend the enteron but to act as a neurovascular visceral pedicle and to prevent the enteron from entanglement with either viscera. It is the abdominal wall that holds the viscera in position. Besides, I showed in 600 detailed records of personal autopsic abdominal inspections that in 96 per cent of subjects the enteron had a mesenteron sufficiently long to herniate through the inguinal femoral or umbilical ring. Hence, the mesenteries must be viewed as neurovascular visceral pedicles, and not as suspensory organs, while the abdominal walls are the great supporters and retainers of the viscera. And as every anatomist knows the recti-abdominales are among the chief regulators or governors of visceral poise, at least they retain the viscera in their first delicate normal balance. Besides, enclosing the recti abdominales in a single sheath my plan of operating in very extreme cases is to sever the recti-abdominales and invaginate one rectus sheath into the other and fix them with sutures. This is similar to the "stove pipe" operation on the intestines that I presented to the profession in 1891 (Annals of Surgery, 1891 and "Practical Intestinal Surgery," 1891).

TRACTUS GENITALIS IN SPLANCHNOPTOSIA.

Fixation of the Tractus Genitalis.

A. Pelvic diaphragm (primary support).

Diaphragm pelvis consist of muculus levator ani plus its superior and inferior fascia. What maintains the genital organs in their normal positions?

(a) The form and function of the pelvic floor (levator ani with its proximal and distal fascia). (b) The position of the genitals and the adjacent viscera. The mesenteries of the tractus genitalis (ligamenta lata) are not for mechanical support. They are to conduct vessels, nerves, and to maintain structures in order for function. It is true that the ligamenta saco-uterina acts as vigorous supports if placed on tension but in their present normal state of existence they simply direct the cervix dorsalward. The vagina extends from the pubus to the cervix and the sacro-uterine and the ligaments extend from the sacrum (rectum) to the cervix. Hence the vagina and sacro-uterine ligaments act as a supporting beam on which the cervix and uterus is supported. The same story, that the thoracic and abdominal viscera are chiefly maintained in position by their respective walls, is true as regards the position of the pelvic viscera, and its walls. The so-called uterine ligament (mesenteries of the genitals act only in pathologic relations as in sacropubic hernia). As an anatomic demonstration that the pelvic floor supports the uterus one can observe (with evacuated bladder and rectum and uterus in physiologic position) that the transverse vaginal slit in the pelvic floor lies 2 inches ventral to the cervix (i. e., the corpus uteri lies doro-ventral across the transverse vaginal slit). If pressure be exercised on the corpus uteri, exactly as intra-abdominal pressure is applied the previous position of the uterus will not be endangered, i.e., it will not enter the vaginal slit but simply force the pelvic floor distalward. In other words the pelvic floor, the distal wall of the pelvic or levator ani maintains the tractus genitalis (uterus) in the normal physiologic position. If one wishes (in the cadaver) to force the uterus through the vagina, vaginal slit in the pelvic floor the hand seize the fundus and corpus while the cervix is pushed vigorously distalward in the vaginal slit where the cervix may be observed in the entroitus vaginae.

If the pressure is removed from the uterus it returns to its normal position. One cannot force the corpus and fundus through the vaginal slit with any ordinary hand power. During energetic forcing of the cervix through the vaginal slit the ligamenta rotunda, ligamenta lata and ligamenta sacro-uterina are scarcely put on tension (they are entirely secondary supports). If all the uterine ligaments are severed and the experiment repeated the cervix can be forced through the vagina to the entroitus only. The impossibility of forcing the corpus and fundus through the vaginal slit and entroitus vaginae is due to the increasing volume of the corpus and fundus on account of the addition of the oviducts, vessels, nerves, and ligamenta lata. The sacro-pubic hernia of senescence is due to atrophic conditions of the genitals which glide through the vaginal slit from diminutive volume. Ziegenspeck claims that sacro-pubic hernia (uterine prolapse) is due to the difference between intra-abdominal pressure and atmospheric pressure. Hence the primary support of the pelvic viscera (genitals) is the pelvic floor—levator ani with its proximal and distal fascia. By relaxation it includes the tractus genitalis in splanchnoptosia.

Diaphragma thoracis resembles diaphragma pelvis in physiology and anatomy. Both have (a) a similar fixum punctum (circulatory bony origin), (b) similar punctum mobile (central tendon), (c) both support superimposed viscera, (d) both have three apertures for visceral transmission, (e) both diaphragms are respiratory, (f) both muscles by contsriction limit the apertures of visceral transmission, (g) both contract as a single muscle (h) both share in splanchnoptosia. They differ in that contraction of the pelvic diaphragm draws the 8 visceral apertures proximalward and ventralward, while contraction of the thoracic diaphragm draws the visceral apertures distalward and dorsalward.

(B) Ligmenta Uterina (secondary supports).

All uterine ligaments arise from the pelvic wall and become inserted in the lateral borders of the uterus. They act as guy ropes, to maintain the uterus in a physiologic position in order to functionate. The ligamenta lata, the real neuro-vascular visceral pedicle is a physiologic support only not a mechanical serving as a conducting bed for vessels, nerves and tubular viscera. These secondary uterine supports in splanchnoptosia become primary which is a pathologic condition.

Movements of the Tractus Genitalis During Respiration.

To demonstrate that the diaphragm pelvis is a muscle sharing in respiration one need only to witness a single perineorrhaphy. Whence the proximalward and distalward movements of the levator ani are evident. To prove that the genitals share in respiration one need only to observe the regular motion of 6 month gestating uterus or the motion of the vagina and uterus in a coughing anaesthetized patient, whence not only the blue vagina everts through the vaginal slit, but the uterus may also be present at the pudendum. The genitals and pelvic floor move with respiration. The respiratory movements of the genitals are the chief factors in genital ptosis. To illustrate if in a case of uterine prolapse or better sacro-pubic hernia the uterus may be returned to the pelvis and the patient told to force it distalward. She immediately inspires deeply whence she retains the inspired air, fixes the thoracic diaphragm, and forces the uterus rapidly distalward through the vagina external to the pudendum. She accomplishes this act by respiratory motion. With relaxation of the pelvic the uterine fundus passes dorsalward and the cervix by this mechanism gains entrance to the vaginal slit in the pelvic floor whence intra-abdominal pressure forces the uterus distalward.

If the uterus loses its volume becomes atrophic, respiratory movements may force it distalward through the vaginal slit without loss of integrity of the pelvic floor.

The continual respiratory trauma, when visceral supports are deranged, produce progressive sacro-pubic hernia. From a study of the anatomic supports of the genitals it is evident how irrational are the surgical attempts to fix the uterus in some preconceived position by means of hysteropexy or the shortening of some secondary uterine support. It appears that the function of respiration is not confined to a single location in the spinal cord, but extends to wide areas on its egress nerves so that man's trunk is a respiratory apparatus closed at the proximal and distal end by a diaphragm—both actively involved in respiratory movement. The relaxation of the pelvic floor and consequent genital ptosis is simply a demonstration of the pathologic anatomy, and physiology of respiration. The genitals present various grades of splanchnoptosia. In the first place the portio vaginalis is found moved distalward in the pelvic axis, the corpus may be in normal anteflexion, but more frequent in a beginning of retroflexion—the whole uterus is excessively mobile. In the second place the entire uterus lies parallel and against the sacrum (rectum). The cervix is not infrequently fixed through parametritis posterior. According to the degree of genital splanchnoptosia arise pain in the back and sacrum, radiating pain in the extremities, menstrual disturbances, venous congestion and constipation. Later the cervix projects through the pudendum. Advanced splanchnoptosia of the genitals presents prominent features of relaxation of the pelvic floor and venous congestion.

Etiology of Genital Ptosia.

The chief etiology of genital ptosia is:

(I) Results of parturition, i. e., elongation, separation or laceration of the pelvic floor tissue (the levator ani muscle and its proximal and distal fascia).

(II) Atrophy of the genitals.

(III) Respiratory movements forcing the genitals distalward (constantly forcing the deranged genitals in the direction of least resistance).

(IV) Relaxation of the thoracic and abdominal walls.

(V) Superimposed splanchnoptotic viscera.

(VI) Genital sub-involution (infection).

The Treatment of Genital Splanchnoptosia.

The treatment should be medical, mechanical, surgical.

I. Medical.

One of the essential remedies is visceral drainage. Hot vaginal douche (with salt and alum as ingredients) increased to 12 quarts which contracts tissue (elastic, muscle, connective), massage, electricity, ample and horizontal rest are valuable means. The boroglyceride tampon serves as an excellent remedy. It is hygroscopic and may be prepared so that it can be worn one to several days.

II. Mechanical.

The horizontal position should be used as much and frequent as possible. Abdominal binders (in which may be placed a pneumatic rubber pad) Achilles Rose's adhesive strapping, Galant's corset furnish much comfort. Various kinds of pessaries may be worn.

III. Surgical.

Since the uterus is supported by the pelvic floor rational surgical proceedures should be applied to it in splanchnoptosia. Relaxed pelvic floor means relaxed, elongated, fibrous separation of the levator ani with its superior and inferior fascia. Hence perineorrhaphy should include the careful repair of the levator ani with its superior and inferior fascia. It is fascia that supports, not muscle. Ventral colporraphy aids in forcing the bladder proximalward and narrowing the vaginal exit. The most effective and enduring operation for splanchnoptotic genitals is: (a) amputation of the cervix (if required), (b) ventral colporrhaphy (c) and extensive colpo-perineorraphy, i. e., an extended Tait flap splitting operation with reunion of the torn muscle and fascia of the levator ani. In cases of uterine atrophy extensive vaginal narrowing is required. For splanchnoptosia of the genitals hysterectomy should not be performed (as it renders supports less efficient). The uterus is the key to the support of the genital viscera. I have seen subjects of splanchnoptotic genitals where the uterus had been removed and subsequently the everted, distended vagina extended to the middle of the thigh with almost hopeless views of repair. As to suspending or fixing the genitals to the abdominal wall proximal to the pelvis it is an irrational operation, unphysiologic and harmful. The anatomy and physiology of the genitals belong to the pelvis.

Ventral abdominal hysteropexy should not be performed in a reproductive subject. Also patients do not present symptoms indicative of malposition of the uterus. The position of the uterus has no special relation to disease. As the symptoms do not emanate from the position of the uterus fixing it will have no relation to the symptoms (except to exacerbate them). The symptoms of patients with retroversions for example emanate from other causes than the uterus.

RESULTS OF RELAXED ABDOMINAL WALLS ON THE TRACTUS INTESTINALIS.

In splanchnoptosia one of the most damaging influences rests on the tractus intestinalis—sensation, peristalsis, absorption and secretion are deranged. The normal position of the tractus intestinalis with its appendages (liver, pancreas, and spleen), is changed disordered. The circular band apparatus of the abdominal wall is relaxed. The elongated neuro-vascular visceral pedicle allows the segments of the tractus intestinalis and its appendages to follow the relaxed abdominal wall, and hence move out of their normal physiologic range, compromising blood and lymph circulation and traumatizing nerve periphery. There is at once a disproportionate action between traumatized nerve periphery and separated, elongated fascial and muscular fibres of the abdominal wall. Muscular tone and nerve energy become deranged. Since the abdominal wall becomes relaxed, the segments of the tractus intestinalis become dislocated permanently from a normal position. Since the neuro-vascular visceral pedicles are not elastic, and not for the purpose of mechanical support, the viscera will pass distalward, i. e., in the direction of least resistance. There is pathologic physiology and pathologic anatomy. The spacious abdominal cavity allows the viscera to shift and

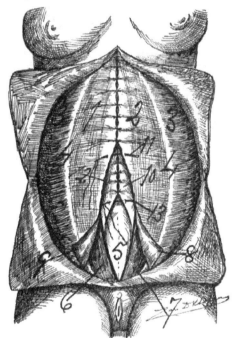

Fig. 202. Represents the surgical procedure which encloses the musculi recti abdominales in a single sheath. 1 and 2 represent the anterior sheaths of the recti partially united in the middle lines. 10 and 12 represent the posterior sheaths of the recti partially united in the middle line. 5, the linea alba. 8 and 9 the recti sheaths lifted up to show the recti muscles. This operation I have employed for 5 years.

glide from weight according to the position of the patient. The mesenteries of course elongate when their essential support, the abdominal wall, yields. The visceral supports or visceral fixation apparatus are (a) the abdominal wall, (b) the pelvic diaphragm, (c) the thoracic diaphragm (d) what I shall term "visceral shelves." Any yielding of any one of these segments a, b, c, or *d* increases the abdominal space and creates a disordered relation between viscera and supports with consequent pathologic physiology. It may be a neurosis malassimilation from disordered circulation (lymph and blood), or it may be disordered visceral motion (peristalsis) from the trauma and infection of the ganglia mysenterica (Auerbach's ganglia) or disordered secretion from disordered action of the Billroth-Meissner plexuses from trauma and infection. Constipation may occur. The form of the abdomen pendulous shows that the tractus intestinalis is dislocated distalward. In aged and spare persons the actual form of the bowel segments and the peristaltic movements may be observed through the thin abdominal wall. The tractus intestinalis in splanchnoptosia is manifoldly dislocated. On account of the fact that while the subject of relaxed abdominal walls does not manifest the disease while lying on the back because the abdomen is flat, the autopsist does not observe the splanchnoptosia. It is the clinician who is impressed with the splanchnoptosia, when the subject is in the erect attitude manifesting the "hanging belly," but the clinician loses his usefulness because he scarcely witnesses the autopsy. It is the clinical and autopsic observation that demonstrates vividly the required data. The great segments of the tractus intestinalis, gastrium, enteron, and colon, become disordered, deranged in relation, changed in situation. The flexures of the tractus intestinalis become more flexed, rigid supports become elongated, secondary supports are put on tension and the lumen of the tractus intestinalis is stenosed, compromised in numerous places. Canalization is compromised. The rigid ligaments as the ligamentum hepato-duodenale, ligamentum costo-colicum, will not yield as much as the adjacent slacker and weaker ligaments, hence the hepatic and splenic flexures become more and more flexed, stenosed. Food passes them with difficulty. For example, there are 5 points to consider in regard to the fixation apparatus of the duodenum, viz.:

1. The duodenum is as a whole fixed. It has lost its peritoneal mesentery on both surfaces of the mesoduodenum and its middle mesenteric layer (membrana mesenterii propria) is fixed or coalesced to the dorsal wall. It is also fixed by the musculus suspensorius duodeni, and the strong ligamentous band from the left crus of the diaphragm. Also the head and body of the pancreas aid in fixing the duodenum.

2. The pylorus or proximal end of the duodenum is fixed to the vertebral column, to the liver, kidney and stomach.

3. The flexura duodenalis jejunalis or distal end of the duodenum is especially fixed by musculus suspensorius duodeni and the strong fibrous and ligamentous band from the left crus of the diaphragm.

4. The duodenum being fixed, it can not move distalward, while all the other abdominal organs glide distalward during splanchnoptosis. Hence since the transverse segment of the duodenum becomes fixed it becomes compressed by the superior mesenteric artery, vein and nerve, inducing gastro-duodenal dilatation. The compression of the duodenum is due to the mesenterico-aortic (vertebral) angle becoming more and more acute as

the splanchnoptosia progresses, and finally, when the enteron lies mainly in the pelvis, the mesenterico-vertebral angle is very acute, allowing only a small space for the duodenum. The passing distalward of the stomach stenoses the fixed pylorus, and the passing distalward of the enteron makes more and more acute the flexura duodeno-jejunalis, because the distal end of the duodenum especially is quite rigidly fixed. The simple anatomic fact in splanchnoptosia is that the proximal end of the duodenum is dilated (with the stomach). The ileo-cecal sphincter and angle are not so much stenosed, as both colon and distal ileum move distalward together, retaining the normal angle or relations. The duodenum may be deranged by the mobile right kidney through the ligamentum duodeno-renale. The dragging

Fig. 203. Byron Robinson's rubber air pad for splanchnoptosia half distended. It is to be placed inside an abdominal supporter. 1, side of rubber pad; 2, the rubber tube through which the rubber pad can be distended with air. (This rubber air pad is manufactured by John Drake & Co., of Chicago.)

of the dislocated kidney aids to flex or stenose the duodenum, the retention of foods in the stomach, and thus enhances gastric fermentation, catarrh and dilatation.

The Flexura Coli Hepatica.

The flexura coli hepatica suffers in splanchnoptosia, because as the stomach passes distalward it forces the colon transversum before it and hence makes more and more acute the hepatic flexure. I have seen the transverse colon in the pelvis and 9 inches of it as an inguinal hernia. It would at first appear impossible for the food to pass such acute colonic angles, but it should be remembered the peristalsis is continued by means of the activity of local segments. However, since the hepatic flexure is generally an obtuse or right angle, its flexure is seldom drawn so acutely by the ligamentum hepatocolicum as to produce very vigorous stenosis. Besides, in splanchnoptosis the liver yields through its mesohepar and follows to some extent the distalward movements of the hepatic flexure, relieving its angle from acute flexing.

The Flexura Coli Lienalis.

The flexura coli lienalis forms normally an acute angle. It is the remnant of the ligamentum recto-lienalis of the lower mammals and quadrumana. It is a distinct, direct apparatus fixing the colon to the costal wall and kidney. In splanchnoptosia the splenic flexure is forced distalward and its angle made more acute. The spleen also participates in the general splanchnoptosis passing distalward, gliding ventral to the colon, as shown in the autopsies, as far as the pelvic floor. This increases the acuteness of the colonic flexure, obstructing the fecal current. The stomach also forces the middle of the transverse colon distalward, which stenoses the hepatic and splenic colonic flexures in direct degree to the extent of the gastroptosia (splanchnoptosia).

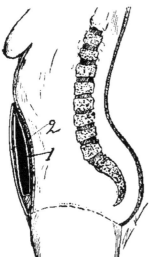

Fig. 204. (Byron Robinson) profile view to illustrate the pressure of the rubber air pad on the abdomen. 1, distended pneumatic rubber pad; 2, wall of abdominal supporter over pneumatic rubber pad.

Also the colon transversum in extensive distalward movements is often forced into a V-shaped condition, with acute adjacent panetel flexions becoming adherent by plastic peritoneal adhesions, due to bacteria or their products passing through the colonic mucosa, myocolon to the serosa, resulting in peritoneal exudates and organized peritoneal adhesions. All dislocation of the viscera compromises them in physiology and anatomy especially if it be by a progressively contracting peritoneal adhesion. All dislocation of viscera compromises function, peristalsis, sensation, absorption, secretion—fecal blood and lymph circulation and traumatizes nerve periphery. Besides, splanchnoptosia is a general term. The tractus intestinalis and its appendages, the tractus urinarius, the tractus genitalis, lymphaticus, vascularis and nervosus, all share in the distalward movement due to relaxed walls, so that splanchnoptosia of the tractus intestinalis is made worse by the nephroptosia (especially on the right side), hepatoptosia, splenoptosia and genital ptosis. The enteroptosia is especially responsible for the gastroduodenal dilatation, because the duodenum cannot pass distalward from a definite fixation apparatus, and the superior mesenteric artery, vein and nerve—the constricting arm—compresses the transverse duodenum the more acutely the more the enteronic loops pass distalward into the pelvis. Again, the distalward dislocation of the colon favors fecal accumulation, which favors migration of germs or their products through mucosa, muscularis into the peritoneum, inducing plastic peritoneal exudates and organized peritoneal adhesions. The peritoneal adhesions compromise anatomy and physiology of the segments of the tractus intestinalis. Again, a tractus intestinalis made defective by dislocation and fecal accumulation becomes an easy prey to *muscular trauma*. Muscular trauma of the psoas, for example, makes over 70 per cent. of the peritoneal adhesions on the right side (adjacent to the appendix, cecum, and distal ilium), and over 80 per cent. on the left side (in the mesosigmoid). Other abdominal muscles produce equal damage in proportion to their power of traumatism by trauma of their segments of the tractus intestinalis. In minimum and maximum defect the more damage arises in the tractus intestinalis from muscular trauma than other visceral tracts.

The fecal accumulations produce maximum damage when collected in the most dependent colonic segments, as the cecum, middle or transverse colon and sigmoid; besides it favors hernia, invagination and volvulus. Doubtless it is the stenosed and superior flexed splenic flexures of the colon which produce the dull pain and fecal accumulation with dulness on percussion. The multiple stenosing of various segments of the tractus intestinalis (and perhaps the ductus hepaticus) in splanchnoptosia is of a temporary character, because on change of the erect to the horizontal position the stenosis of the tractus intestinalis is damaging from the point of circulation, nourishment and assimilation.

Splanchnoptosia induces trauma on secretory, sensory and motor nerves, it produces irregular congestion and decongestion, muscularis is impaired by irregular local contraction and dislocation. Dislocation of the tractus intestinalis favors absorption of deleterious products. The relaxed abdominal walls having lost their power of contraction, the fecal current is defectively driven distalward. From loss of tone in the diaphragm, abdominal wall and pelvic floor, through excessive distention, defecation is difficult and hence fecal and gas accumulations are distressing. Discomfort almost always attends the patient with any considerable degree of splanchnoptosia from traumatized nerves, or from distension with gas or food, from incapacity of the abdominal walls to maintain the viscera in the normal physiologic position. If a subject with distinct relaxed abdominal walls be examined per vaginum or per rectum, stagnated fecal accumulation may be found in the sigmoid and if the cecum assume the pelvic position (female 20 per cent., males 10 per cent.), it may also be found occupied with feces. The abdominal wall (thoracic and pelvic diaphragm) having lost its tone, defecation is not only difficult but defective. Besides, long retained feces in the colon induce catarrh of the colon resulting in the absorption of toxic substances. *Meteorism* arises in splanchnoptosia from excessive, deficient or disproportionate secretion and consequent fermentation, from stenosing of the tractus intestinalis, from loss of power in the abdominal walls, from catarrh due to constipation, from expansion of gas due to rise of the temperature after toxic absorption. Such subjects have a foul-smelling breath from the gases being absorbed by the veins in the tractus intestinalis and becoming exhaled through the lungs. Meteorism induces pain and discomfort from nerve pressure, and dislocated viscera and obstruction to circulation. The results of splanchnoptosia are constipation, catarrh of the different segments of the tractus intestinalis, icterus through pressure, and stenosing of the ductus hepaticus. Also the nephroptosia induces stenosing of the duodenum and ureter by flexing and rotation.

Patients subject to splanchnoptosia suffer frequently from discolored skin and irregular kidney secretion, also from nausea, vomiting, irregular and obscure pains, with continual weakness, debility. From these anatomic and physiologic considerations it is amply evident that in order to support the viscera in splanchnoptosia the thoracic and abdominal walls (with pelvic and thoracic diaphragm) must be forced into rational application.

In splanchnoptosia it must be remembered that the anatomy thoracic and abdominal viscera (tractus respiratorius, intestinalis, vasculoris, genitalis, lymphaticus, urinarius nervosus) is dislocated and that the physiology of these seven visceral tracts is deranged.

The chief aim of therapeutics in splanchnoptosia is to restore function, physiology. We may live comfortable with pathologic anatomy, however, in general we live in discomfort with pathologic physiology.

CIRCULATION IN SPLANCHNOPTOSIA.

In operating on the deep glands of the neck, where the large veins are isolated, it is very plain that respiration governs to a certain extent the venous circulation. Now, the diaphragm, pelvic and thoracic, as well as the ventral abdominal walls are relaxed, it becomes evident in difficult defecation and in the same manner the venous circulation of the abdomen suffers from lack of pressure. With relaxed abdominal walls, the abdominal veins (and the entire system) are congested and stenosis results. As a sample of the evil effects of relaxed abdominal walls and consequent splanchnoptosis, in rapidly repeated pregnancy there is heart weakness, because the veins of the abdomen are too constantly, excessively occupied with excessive blood, robbing the heart of its required amount. Since receiving instruction of Prof. Schröder, some twenty years ago, I continued the study and investigation of splanchnoptosia. In relaxed abdominal walls one sees the distended veins of the extremities, and extensive and prominent veins of the pudenum, as well as the large hemorrhoidal nodes. Besides frequent and free uterine hemorrhages occur. Splanchnoptosia has deleterious effect on the pelvic organs by pressure and especially by obstructing the venous return flow. In post mortems I have carefully noted that subjects with splanchnoptosia possess a plexus pampiniformis extended with straight, irregularly dilated veins. Spiral and uniform calibered veins are normal. In advanced splanchnoptosia the pelvic veins, especially the genitals and those of the rectum, are widely and irregularly dilated, containing enormous quantities of blood. This causes hyperaemia, congestion and stasis of the pelvic organs, resulting in hemorrhage, malnutrition, and pathologic changes in the genitals as hypertrophy. The liver suffers likewise from congestion, hyperaemia and blood stasis, for it drains the tractus intestinalis (spleen and pancreas) and the liver, by its dislocated position, compromises the blood current, especially in the portal and hepatic veins, besides, the dislocated liver drags or compresses the inferior vena cava, stenosing it. Stagnation, stasis, congestion, hyperaemia are the characteristics of the circulation in the splanchnoptotic.

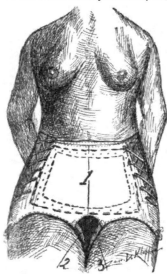

Fig. 205. Byron Robinson's pneumatic rubber air pad is fitted to the abdomen inside the abdominal supporter. 2, 3 are rubber tubes passing between the limbs to fix the abdominal supporter. It requires several days, a week for patients to become adjusted to the pad. Patience on the part of the patient and encouragement on part of the physician will soon adjust the use of the pad.

If the liver be dislocated to any considerable extent, which is frequent in gynecologic patients, the definite relations of the portal vein are disturbed, the liver veins and the inferior cava are dislocated or compromised, as the vena cava lies on the rigid dorsal wall. Venous circulation is more physiologic and of complex delicate nature than arterial, which is more mechanical, and is easily compromised as is noted by the enlargement, conspicuously observed in the inferior and superior epigastric veins. Continuous hyperaemia, congestion and stenosis in the dislocated viscera produces pathologic changes in the organs themselves, impairing sensation, motion, secretion, absorption, and nutrition. We have thus a vicious circle which might be called the visceral disease. Relaxed abdominal walls and consequent splanchnoptosia disturb a wide area of complicated functions. They distort an extensive and delicate mechanism, resulting in impaired respiration, circulation, sensation, motion, absorption, and secretion and in the end result in malnutrition and neurosis.

Tension of the visceral vessels in splanchnoptosia limits their lumen and consequently more vigorous heart action is required to force the blood to the viscera—taxing the heart's power, ending in anaemia, congestion, throbbings, headaches, dizziness. With loss of the controlling influence of the abdominal wall on the visceral circulation a fullness of feeling or weight in the abdomen may occur from visceral congestion and continuous congestion may lead to relaxation of visceral supports occurring in splanchnoptosia.

In splanchnoptosia the visceral circulation is impeded by flexion, dilatation, constriction, decalibration, elongation, of vessels (and the accompanying plexiform nerve sheath is consequently traumatized). In splanchnoptosia the veins from thin, flaccid walls, deficient muscularis and slow pressure current suffer more than the arteries which possess rigid walls, powerful muscularis and vigorous high pressure current. Atonia gastrica is responsible for two important phenomena of visceral vessels, viz.: (a) flexion or angulation; (b) elongation and consequent decrease in lumen, decalibration. Conspicuous examples of flexion or angulation of vessels may be observed in extensively distalward movements of the kidney which is frequently located in the middle of the abdomen on the pelvic brim and the spleen which is not infrequently found located at any point from the kidney to the pelvic floor. The distalward dragging of the viscera at different points on the visceral ligaments fixed to the abdominal wall flexes or angulates the vessels in extra-extended ligaments producing hyperaemia or anaemia, engorgement or ischaemia. If one explores by dissection the abdominal visceral vessels in a normal subject and again in a splanchnoptotic subject by comparison it will be observed that the visceral vessels of the splanchnoptotic may be several inches longer than those of the normal subject, e. g., when the kidney lies in the iliac fossa or lesser pelvis, when the spleen lies on the pelvic floor, when the enteron lies almost completely on the pelvic floor.

The visceral vessels become elongated in splanchnoptosia and elongation compromises the canals and lumen of the vessels, limiting vascular supply, inviting defective viscera, resulting in innervation, constipation, deficient secretion, limited and disordered peristalsis. In enteroptosia the superior mesenteric artery and vein is the one set of vessels which suffers from dragging, trauma, from marked elongation of parietes and constriction of lumen. The elongated superior mesenteric artery, vein and nerve constricts, stenoses the transverse segment of the duodenum by compression. Thus in splanchnoptosia one distorted viscus compromises another. It may be observed that the visceral vessels are compelled to elongate in splanchnoptosia as their base or origin, the aorta, is immobile. In gestation the utero-ovarian artery elongates, experiences parietal hypertrophy, increases its spirality and diameter of its lumen. However, gestation practically cures, symptomatically relieves splanchnoptosia for some six months. In splanchnoptosia practically the opposite condition to that of the arteria uterina ovarica in gestation occurs in the visceral arteries, viz.: the visceral arteries elongate, decrease in diameter, diminish in spirality, experience parietal atrophy. Finally during the elongation of visceral vessels vast sympathetic nerve trauma is inflicted on the plexiform, nodular network of nerves which ensheath the visceral vessels, damaging vascular function (especially rhythm) for the tractus vascularis and tractus nervosus is an automaton. Hence, from the dragging of the viscera on their elongated tensioned vessels, from vessel extension, flexion and trauma on associated ganglia, excessive, deficient, or disproportionate circulation arises. In splanchnoptosia palpatation, vigorous beating in the abdominal aorta which may be palpated from partial uncovering or exposure of the aorta by dislocated viscera and atrophy of the abdominal wall. The arterial pulse beat is disordered—irregular, deficient, excessive. Splanchnoptotics are afflicted frequently with debility, impending weakness, faint with facility and present rapid, variegated changes in circulation in different parts of the body. The patient is flushed (congestion), pale (anaemic), mottled (disproportionate circulation). They have headaches from irregular cerebral circulation and extensive abdominal venous stasis. In autopsies on some advanced splanchnoptotics the numerous vastly distended blue veins presenting among the abdominal viscera suggest the idea that the patient had bled to death in his own abdominal veins. The veins of the viscera and ganglia are engorged, flooded with stagnant venous blood surcharged with carbonic acid gas—while the arterial blood invigorated with life's messenger, oxygen, is excluded.

The similar conditions as regards haemogenous circulation in splanchnoptosia may be practically applied to the lymphatic circulation in splanchnoptosia.

The abdominal walls aid to regulate the circulation in the viscera (especially in the veins). The abdominal vessels (veins) are a kind of reservoir for surplus blood by which blood pressure and other visceral supply is regulated. If the abdominal muscles become deficient the blood will accumulate in the abdominal veins to the detriment of other viscera, e. g., the cerbro-spinal axis—manifesting many nervous phenomena. The extensive venous stasis in the abdomen from atonia gastrica deranges visceral function (peristalsis, absorption, secretion, sensation) ending in malassimilation (indigestion, fermentation, meteorism, constipation). The meteorism so frequent an accompaniment of the splanchnoptotic is a marked factor in disturbing circulation and digestion. In the splanchnoptotic the dilatation of the blood vessels in the splanchnic area may lead to a decrease in general blood pressure and consequent increase of cardiac action. The symptoms due to the pathologic physiology of circulation in the abdominal vessels are varied and numerous as rate, nature, force of peristalsis in the heart, and consequent effect on the abdominal viscera. The extent of distention of the abdominal vessels would no doubt produce pathologic manifestations as dragging, feeling of fulness, weight. Long continued congestion due to vaso-motor paralysis (from lack of abdominal pressure) may account for relaxation of visceral supports. The manipulation of the plexiform nodular network ensheathing the arteries may be followed by palpation and be found tender, sensitive—indicating an irritable condition of the blood vessels, arteritis, arterio-sclerosis, or a neuritis of the ensheathing nerve plexus (which is the more probable).

Dilatation of the splanchnic vessels appear to be physiologically opposed to a similar condition of the peripheral vessels and the exquisite balance is due to a nerve mechanism. Our remedies should be applied with 2 views, viz.: (a), to deplete the visceral congestion. This can be especially accomplished by visceral drainage and aided by mechanical supports, the abdominal wall which regulates venous circulation (as by binders, Rose's strapping);

(b), stimulate the peripheral or cutaneous vessels (by friction heat, chemicals) in order to entice the blood to the surface (as massage, salt rubs, hydrotherapy, wet cold pack).

TRACTUS NERVOSUS IN SPLANCHNOPTOSIA.

The ideal nervous system consists of: (a) a ganglion cell (a central receiver and reorganizer), (b) a conducting cord (a transmitter), (c) a periphery (a sensory apparatus, a collector). In splanchnoptosia the ideal nervous apparatus is deranged. I am convinced from years of observation—in the living and dead—that the tractus nervosus in splanchnoptosia indicates inferior anatomy and physiology with more facility than other visceral tracts. Splanchnoptotics are prone to be afflicted with stigmata, degeneracy, a habitus. They possess a weak, irritable nervous system. They are not perfect physically or mentally. Their anatomy and physiology are inferior structure and function of minimum perfection. The nervous system is unstable. Splanchnoptotics manifest defective resistance, and are incapacitated for sustained effort, presenting premature exhaustion on persistence mentally or physically. Their tractus nervosus functionates under friction most of the time like some watches which maintain incorrect time. Splanchnoptotics are chiefly congenital, physical unfortunates. They are born with defects, stigmata, a habitus, a neuropathic predisposition—a condition or state which tends to degeneracy with facility. One of the best terms to apply to subjects with excessive distalward movement of viscera, relaxed muscles, defective circulation, and defective nourishment is the word habitus, e. g., we meet the subjects with habitus splanchnopticus, habitus nervosus, habitus phthisicus, habitus dyspepticus. The ensemble of symptoms associated with splanchnoptosia may well be termed habitus splanchnopticus. It is heredity in so far that the subject possesses a predisposition and the main defect is inferior anatomy and physiology. In the habitus splanchnopticus there is the gracile skeleton, the elongated, flat thorax, extensive intercostal space, acute epigastric angle, the sacculated pendulous abdomen, limited muscularis and panniculus adiposus, the labored respiration. The costa fluctuans decima of B. Stiller, the peculiar habitus in form—presenting evident pathologic physiology. A marked factor in pathologic physiology of splanchnoptosia is the changed defective circulation, venous congestion. Generally any subject with a "habitus" possesses an unstable nervous system. The habitus splanchnopticus is perhaps more due to neuropathic disposition than to the splanchnoptosia, hence the term dyspepsia nervosa, or stigma dyspepticus. The habitus neurasthenicus presents pathologic physiology of the tractus nervosus—a condition of exhaustion or weakness of the nervous system accompanied by physical and mental inefficiency. Habitus neurasthenicus is a fatigue disease of the nervous system. It is characterized by the presence of motor, sensory, psychic and visceral symptoms—all fatigued, tired, exhausted. This habitus is especially characterized by weakness, or inefficiency and irritability of the tractus nervosus. The physician can detect spots, of hyperaesthesia, spinal irritation, fatigue of the special sense, auditory and retinal hyperaesthesia. When the subject predisposed to the habitus splanchnopticus is afflicted with strain, as gestation, the care of growing children, extra mental or physical effort, the tractus nervosus—habitus neurasthenicus—manifests itself deranged with rapidity and facility. Also the instability of the tractus nervosus in splanchnoptosia is aggravated, irritated with facility in the habitus neurasthenicus by disease, as salpingitis, myometritus, pelvic peritonitis. The weak, irritable tractus nervosus with its inherent defective vital power—its deteriorated anatomy and physiology—readily passes into a state of manifest pathologic physiology.

In splanchnoptosia the nervous system is involved in manifold conditions. In fact, in splanchnoptosia the nervous system is the central reference of investigators. Hence, writers note that splanchnoptotics are afflicted with melancholia neurasthenia, nervous dyspepsia, neurosis, irritability, weakness and debility. The splanchnoptotic experiences pain of various kinds in any portion of the abdomen. They are afflicted with heavy feelings in the abdomen. Pain radiates to the scapulae, especially in the region of the V to the VII dorsal vertebrae. The pain is increased in the erect and decreased in the prone attitude (indicating nerve trauma). Continuous standing, long labor or severe efforts increase the pain. The multiple pain of the splanchnoptotic is described as dull, sticking, dragging, boring, cramps, faintness, lumbar and sacral pains. Some have pain in many parts of the body. The sensible visceral nerves and ganglia become traumatized, dragged by the dislocated viscera. The visceral arteries are ensheathed by a ganglionated, plexiform network of nerves. In splanchnoptotics the visceral arteries become elongated (sometimes several inches, in extra length) and their ensheathing nerves stretched, damaged, traumatized, altering their functions. The pain is protean. Hegar called it Lendenmarks symptome, i. e., lumbar cord symptoms. The dislocated viscera drag on the great plexuses, resulting in irritability. Hyperaesthesia and anaesthesia of the abdomen exist over the site of viscera—which suggests caution in pronouncing the stigmata of hysteria. The plexus aorticus is frequently so stimulated that the vigorous, violent aortic pulsations may be mistaken for an aneurysm. When no anatomic or histologic changes in the nerves can be demonstrated we are compelled to resort to such terms as neurosis, molecular disturbances in the nerve substance or peripheral. Is splanchnoptosia due to a relaxation of the entire nervous system? Splanchnoptosia attacks the *motor* nerves as it is shown by muscular fatigue, energy. Evident incapacity for bodily labors present. The *sensory* nerves may suffer in splanchnoptosia as in anaesthesia and paraaesthesia. The patient is sensitive to heat and cold. Exaltation and depression occur. The sympathetic nerve or nervus vasomotorius receives the brunt of the disease as is manifest in disturbed secretion, absorption, sensation and rhythm (peristalsis) of viscera. Violent aortic palpation of the aorta exists. Secretion, absorption and peristalsis may be excessive, deficient or disproportionate.

Frequency of Splanchnoptosia.

In the vast majority of splanchnoptotics in general the viscera are displaced, prolapsed, and the visceral walls relaxed. Splanchnoptosia is perhaps six times more prevalent in females than in males (some say ten). I have no method to estimate the frequency of splanchnoptosia in my own practice except from the frequency of mobile kidney and in the personal autopsic abdominal inspection of over 650 adults and 75 children, infants, fetuses, 60% of the female patients in my practice present palpably mobile kidney, not splanchnoptosia, as no pathologic symptoms accompany many. The difficulty of estimating the frequency of splanchnoptosia is due—and also the conditions of splanchnoptosia which present symptoms—to the different views of different authors. I should estimate that 20% of the women with mobile kidney, in my private practice, have demonstrable splanchnoptosia—with attributable symptoms (i. e., 20% of 60%=12%). Part of this 20%, say 12%, do not suffer markedly, for in many the physical condition remains favorable. Practically twenty years includes the clinical and autopsic study of splanchnoptosia, hence, older statistics are almost worthless. Twenty years ago Mr. Lawson Tait, one of the greatest surgical geniuses of his age, and my own well-remembered teacher, denied movable kidneys. The difficulty with statistics in splanchnoptosia is that it presents a wide range from the minimum scarcely perceptible to the maximum grade—an unsightly, sad appearance. Hence we still lack a recognized standard to estimate the frequency of splanchnoptosia.

Symptomatology of Splanchnoptosia.

Splanchnoptosia presents complex symptoms. It may exist without recognizable symptoms or be accompanied by the most aggravated kind. The general subjective symptoms of splanchnoptosia are (debility) a general sense of weakness; an impending irritable nervousness (neurosis), frequent relief in the prone position (attitude). Practically, splanchnoptosia should be viewed as pathologic physiology, as a disease of symptoms and the object of the physician is to restore function. Fatigue and pain are marked. The general objective symptoms are: (abdomen) flattened pendulous abdomen especially in the epigastric region (Stellar's costalstigma), sensitiveness to pressure in the region of the tenth rib, palpation reveals excessive, multiple, visceral mobility. A cord-like transverse colon (which is probably the pancreas) may be established by gliding it on the aorta. A marked pulsation of the aorta, constipation. A peculiar phenomenon may exist in splanchnoptosia which is in short that the intensity of the symptoms may not correspond to the degree of splanchnoptosia. This doubtless depends on favorable or unfavorable physical conditions. Marked splanchnoptosia may exist with practically no symptoms while a slight degree of splanchnoptosia may exist accompanied with striking symptoms. Frequently the visceral ptosis is so slight that it is overlooked and consequently the treatment is misapplied. An important matter in atonia gastrica, splanchnoptosia, is that symptoms are pronounced while the patient is in the erect attitude. With the patient lying prone the symptoms diminish and may disappear. This phenomenon deludes many physicians who consider merely that the patient requires physical rest. Frequently I have noted immediate relief by supporting the abdomen with the hands from behind the patient (Glenard's belt test). Besides the ordinary symptoms of fatigue, dragging, there is backache and side ache The backache in splanchnoptosia may be due to fatigue of the sacro-spinalis muscle simulating that observed in corpulent persons with fatty abdomen where the muscle becomes overworked in maintaining the center of gravity which is projected excessively ventralward. In respiration in splanchnoptotics the expiratory power is not only lessened by loss of tone in the abdominal muscles but the floor of the thorax, the diaphragm, is dragged distalward by the distalward moving viscera. The epigastrium may show a marked depression. The relation of the diaphragm and ribs is disturbed, inducing shortness of breath on exertion. To observe the splanchnoptotic one must examine in the prone and erect attitude with trunk clothing removed. The patients frequently complain of weakness, dizziness, fatigue which may be enhanced by the distalward moving viscera dragging, traumatizing the splanchnic (sympathetic) nerves. Most cases of splanchnoptosia are accompanied by pendulous abdomen, changed in form, however, with normal abdominal walls a single viscus may glide excessively distalward while mechanical pendulous abdomen may be caused by fat deposit. Splanchnoptosia may exist without symptoms so long as the physical condition is favorable. Atonia gastrica springs into prominence in association with neurosis and so-called nervous dyspepsia. The symptoms of the splanchnoptotic are chiefly those of neurasthenia, neurosis. Pain may be felt and is mainly referred to the lateral and dorsal region. Splanchnoptosia is practically a unit though a general disease, seldom do single viscera suffer ptosis. Exception may arise from sudden trauma, for example, instrumental parturition, sudden physical strain. However, the ordinary case of recognizable splanchnoptosia, atonia gastrica, is general visceral ptosis with relaxed enclosing walls. Splanchnoptosia must not be judged by the extent of dislocated viscera but by the degree of distress—the intensity of symptoms, the pathologic physiology. The distalward dislocation of the diaphragm is an essential feature of splanchnoptosia. Hence in marked subjects of splanchnoptosia the chest is deformed, the thoracic viscera occupy abnormal positions and the abdominal viscera are splanchnoptotic—the subject generally presents stigmata, physical defects, tubercular habitus, deformed distal thoracic borders. A study of the subject of splanchnoptosia has exposed many previous puzzles. A faint feeling after the morning rising, fatigue after exercise sense of weight in distal and dorsal abdomen, dragging in epigastrium, flatulence, constipation, frequent micturition, lends clues to widespread splanchnoptosia. Neurasthenia, flaccid and pendulous abdomen, loss of flesh, diastasis of the recti muscles shed light. The aorta frequently strongly pulsates, and with spare subjects one feels what Glenard calls the "transverse colon cord," however, I am fully satisfied at present after investigating these symptoms frequently in autopsies that this transverse band or "colon cord" is the pancreas mainly.

result in ample, indigestible faecal residue in order to stimulate the functions of the tractus intestinalis (peristalsis, absorption, secretion, sensation). The kinds of foods for the splanchnoptotic should be (a) cereals (oatmeal, prepared wheat, rice, graham bread—i. e., the entire wheat as bran, shorts, and flour), (b) vegetables (cooked), (c) albuminoids (milk, eggs), (d) meats (limited in quantity). Diet should be strictly regulated. Food should be administered every three hours in limited quantities. All fermentative substances should be avoided. Fruits unless strictly regulated do more harm than good (from fermentative processes). Pies, puddings, cakes, sugars, sauces, and condiments should be prohibited. Diet should be wholesome and nutritive to produce fat for visceral padding whence the visceral shelves and fossae are increased and the abdominal wall thickened enabling it to diminish the abdominal cavity to aid in visceral reposition and maintenance in the normal physiologic position. One of the essential pathologic conditions in splanchnoptosia is malnutrition, inanition. Splanchnoptosia is best cured by rebuilding the organism which signifies normal blood and panniculus adiposus. The practical therapeutics in splanchnoptosia is to improve the pathologic physiology, for splanchnoptotics live continually under pathologic physiology. The visceral drainage treatment improves health. It places visceral function and elimination at a maximum. Hence, the subject is better prepared to institute local repair which means resisting and checking infection, absorbing exudates. The visceral drainage treatment can be conducted at the patient's home, be it a cottage or a palace, without cessation of his occupation. There is no necessity of making long sojourns to distant watering places to drink hissing sprudel or odorous mineral waters.

(4). Habitat.

Habitat or the environments of life are significant in the general treatment of the splanchnoptotic. First and foremost, the splanchnoptotic should have ample fresh air night and day. The window should be open all night summer and winter. Clothing should be suspended from the shoulder avoiding all tight waist bands. Physical exercise should be regular and practiced daily.

(5). Avocation.

The business or association of a splanchnoptotic is a matter of importance as he is unable mentally or physically to withstand persistent continued effort. Mental and physical rest is necessary for the subject afflicted with inferior anatomy and inferior physiology. Heavy labor he cannot endure. Constant standing on the feet for hours exhausts the splanchnoptotic. He should assume a horizontal position frequently in order to change the circulation and rest the fatigued muscles. Assuming frequent physical rests the splanchnoptotic's inferior physiologic functions and inferior anatomic structures may maintain fair health and accomplish a reasonable degree of labor.

(6). *Electricity.*

Electricity is of considerable value in relaxed abdominal walls, especially faradization of the muscles.

(7). *The Cold Douche or Spray.*

The cold douche or spray is of limited value. It can be applied to the abdomen, per vaginam or per rectum.

II. MECHANICAL TREATMENT.

The essentials of mechanical treatment is forcible reposition and maintenance of the viscera, on the visceral shelves and in the visceral fossae—i. e., viscera are restored and maintained within the normal physiologic position.

The object of mechanical treatment is forcible visceral reposition and retention of the organs (on their shelves in their fossae), i. e., in their normal physiologic position by means of the abdominal wall. In the treatment the unfavorable standing posture, the excessive physical labor, the imperfect respiration in the distal zone of the chest and the absence of tone in the abdominal wall should be considered. The dislocated viscera, in splanchnoptosia, are easily replaced, reduced to their physiologic range of action and maintained with facility through rational therapy applied to the abdominal wall. The reposition of dislocated groups of viscera in splanchnoptosia to their normal physiologic range improves related visceral functions and structure. Splanchnoptotics are mainly neurotics, mechanical reposition of the visceral on their visceral shelves and in their visceral fossa, ameliorates the neurosis, affords ample relief and comfort. Splanchnoptotics are neurotics, consequently unable to judge; therefore, should not be informed as to the excessive mobility of individual organs.

(1). *Abdominal Supporters.*

Much utility, relief and comfort arises from the use of properly fitting abdominal supporters. The kinds we have used are: (1), non-elastic, (2), elastic, and (3) the author's pneumatic ax shafted rubber pad which can be placed within an elastic or non-elastic abdominal binder and distended with air to suit the comfort of the patient. The objection urged against the use of an abdominal binder in splanchnoptosia that it does not teach the muscles self-strength, is worthless as the objection against the use of a splint in fractures. The fact to remember is that the abdominal muscles are extended, stretched beyond self or independent help. Abdominal supporters do not cure, but properly fitting ones help the patient to relief, comfort and usefulness. It is not sufficient to recommend an abdominal binder. The physician should examine it to be sure that it fits properly, both for the grade of splanchnoptosia and for the avocation of the patient. The difficulty of fitting a proper support is due to the varying position of the patient—walking, sitting or lying. I have invented a rubber air pad which is the shape of an axe. This is placed within a binder and subsequently distended with air through an attached rubber tube to the desired dimension. The rubber pneumatic pad insures a uniform fitting of the abdomen like a water bed, whether spare or fleshy, and also the dimensions may be adjusted to the comfort, relief of the patient. The binders are useful in moderate nephroptosia, which is the easiest of all portions of splanchnoptosia to aid, but when it has become advanced, binders are not only of little value but frequently harmful. In severe or distinctly diagnosable hepatoptosia (with liver projected into the lesser pelvis, I have seen none or little utility in binders. All tight waist bands should be removed, and the clothing should be suspended from the shoulders or from hooks on a corset waist. If one experiments on a dead body with a tight-fitting corset, the organ which will suffer the most extensive displacement will be the right kidney. All commercial tight corsets should be abandoned but a so-called waist corset is useful to adjust and from which to suspend clothing.

Since a binder is to reposit the viscera by restoring elongated and separated fascial and muscular fibres of the abdominal walls it must fit snugly, especially in distal abdomen. Unfortunately binders glide and slide and do not continually maintain a force on the distal surface (of the visceral shelf) of the viscera. The viscera may glide distal to the binder. Two rubber tubes must be employed passing between the limbs to fix the binder so that it will not slip proximalward. The binder generally only forces dorsalward and proximalward the abdominal wall, but the addition of the author's rubber pad adds to this the forcing of the viscera proximalward by acting like a pregnant uterus which elevates the viscera toward the thoracic diaphragm. If the splanchnoptosia is not excessively advanced, the rubber visceral air pad being adjusted and distended with air while the patient lies on the back (Trendelenburg's posture) will prevent the viscera gaining the lesser pelvis—the dangerous ground for stenosis of ducts, vessels and viscera, and traumatizing nerve periphery. The binder should be removed or loosened for the night's rest.

(2). *Horizontal Position.*

A dominant factor in splanchnoptosia is venous congestion during erect attitude, hence the splanchnoptotic should assume especially the horizontal position. When a patient with established splanchnoptosia assumes the erect attitude, the viscera in general pass distalward with the extra-expanded abdominal walls, the veins immediately enlarge, the abdominal wall is put on a tension, and it projects or bulges distal to the symphysis pubis sufficiently to conceal the genitals from the patient's view. The patient in the erect attitude assumes a position of lordosis as in advanced pregnancy, in order to secure a compensatory weight balance.

In the horizontal position the patient with splanchnoptosia should lie on the side and not on the back. All patients with established splanchnoptosia suffer from gastro-duodenal dilatation (a phase in the progress of splanchnoptosia) due to pressure of the superior mesenteric artery, vein and nerve on the transverse segment of the duodenum. I experimented with dead subjects who had been afflicted with splanchnoptosia, and when such subjects were placed on the back, the viscera, especially the enteronic loops, passed distinctly more and more into the lesser pelvis, dragging and tugging on the superior mesenteric artery, vein and nerve, which compressed more and more the transverse segment of the duodenum. When the subject of splanchnoptosia lies on the back, the enteronic loops glide into the lesser pelvis, which makes the superior mesenteric artery, vein and nerve approach closer and closer to the vertebral column and thus diminishing the superior mesenterico-vertebral angle, vigorously compressing the transverse duodenum.

I have observed personally splanchnoptosia and gastro-duodenal dilatation progress until the stomach completely occupied the abdomen like an ovarian cyst. (The more acute the mesenterico-vertebral angle becomes, the more the transverse duodenum segment is compressed.) Pregnancy increases the (superior) mesenterico-vertebral angle, forcing proximalward the enteronic loops and thus releasing the transverse duodenum from pressure. A great benefit in the wearing of an abdominal binder or Rose's strapping is to increase the (superior) mesenterico-vertebral angle, releasing the duodenum from compression and preventing increased gastro-duodenal dilatation. Lying on the abdominal surface of the body, with a pillow under the thorax and the symphysis pubis would be the ideal position to insure the maximum (superior) mesenterico-vertebral angle (as it exists in quadrupeds) Hence the splanchnoptotic should lie in the horizontal lateral position as much as is convenient to increase the (superior) mesenterico-vertebral angle, to avoid venous congestion and to prevent the viscera from passing distalward, producing stenosis and flexion of the lumen of the vessels, ducts and viscera. Lying on the back, or standing, diminishes the mesenterico-vertebral angle and increases the compression of the duodenum by the mesenteric vessels and nerves.

(3). Massage.

The massage of the abdominal wall as well as that of the tractus intestinalis aids materially in the treatment. However, it is of limited value.

(4). Achilles Rose's Adhesive Strapping.

I wish to recommend strongly the strapping of the splanchnoptotic abdomen by rubber adhesive plaster introduced first by Dr. Achilles Rose of New York and independently later by Dr. N. Rosewater of Cleveland, Ohio, Dr. Walther Nicholas Clemm of Darmstadt, Germany, and Dr. B. Schmitz of Wildungen, Germany.

Dr. Achilles Rose's strapping method is rational, economical and practical and affords prompt comfort and effective relief. Abdominal binders slip and glide but adhesive straps will remain permanently in place and not slip.

Method of Applying the Adhesive Strap.

Previous to applying the abdominal adhesive straps the abdominal skin should be thoroughly cleaned with soap and water and later alcohol to dissolve oily substances applied in the line of adhesive straps. The patient should be strapped either in the standing position by elevating the abdominal wall (Glenard's belt test) by the hands before the straps are applied or strapped in the Trendelenburg's position.

Place an adhesive strap 2 inches in width around the trunk immediately proximal and parallel to the crest of the pubis, Poupart's ligament and crests of the ilia, superimposing or overlapping the adhesive straps on the medial dorsal line. The dorsal position of the adhesive straps is located considerable proximal to the ventral position which endows the straps with its useful, visceral supporting properties.

Secondly, apply a pyramid formed adhesive strap 8 inches wide ventrally and 2 inches wide dorsally immediately proximal and parallel to the first adhesive strap. These two lateral adhesive straps overlap ventrally and dorsally. This method of adhesive strapping forces the abdominal wall and viscera proximalward so that the relaxed portion of the abdominal wall is in the region of the umbilicus and stomach. In other words the adhesive strapping reverses the position of the abdominal splanchnoptosia (atonia gastrica), i. e., the excessive mobile viscera and relaxed abdominal wall are transferred to the proximal end of the abdomen (instead of the distal end). I allow the adhesive straps to remain in position for 10 days to a month. Local bathing can be practiced with the adhesive straps in position (avoiding the moistening of the immediate region of the straps). Beginners are apt to apply the strap too tightly. Dr. E. Gallant of New York reports excellent results from his corset method of treatment. Patients experience prompt and ample relief from mechanic supports, avoiding the danger of a fragmentary operation, its recurrence and the inevitable unfavorable cellular and peritoneal adhesions accompanying viscero-pexy.

(III). SURGICAL.

Surgery is not advised excepting for obvious pathologic lesions. Splanchnoptosia cannot be cured by surgery though every abdominal viscus has imposed on it a "Pexy." Some surgeons encourage splanchnoptosia by allowing and advising the patient to leave the bed in an incredible limited time subsequent to an abdominal section or peritonotomy. The treatment of splanchnoptosia is, in general, not by the scalpel, needle and suture. The surgical therapeutics employed to relieve in splanchnoptosia are: (a) application to the abdominal wall, (b) viscero-pexy, (c) visceral anastomosis.

(A) *Abdominal Walls.*

(1) Resection of portions of abdominal wall. (2) Union of musculi recti abdominalis in a simple sheath. (3) Superposition of abdominal wall.

(*1*). *Resection of Portions of the Abdominal Wall.* The early attempts to diminish the abdominal cavity in splanchnoptosia originated from the gynecologists, particularly from Prof. Karl Schroeder and Dr. Landau of Berlin, Germany. I was a pupil of Dr. Theodore Landau in 1885 and his books, "Wander Niere" and "Wander Leber," have been for teachers and authors an unbounded source of credited and uncredited data.

(2). *Union of the Musculi Recti Abdominales in a Single Sheath.* My attention was first called to the subject of relaxed abdominal walls by Prof. Karl Schroeder whose pupil I was for a year. In that year (1884-1885) Prof. Schroeder of Berlin, Germany, the greatest gynecologic teacher of his age, was at his zenith of fame, and his clinic was vast. In fact, he tapped the whole of Europe for his material. He discussed in his clear style the misfortune of lax abdominal wall lying between the diastatic recti abdominales.

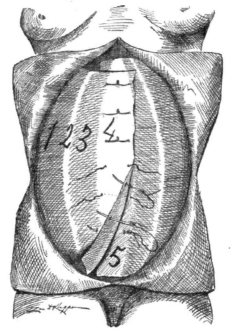

ABDOMINAL WALLS

Fig. 206. Presenting the fascia and muscles of the abdominal wall with the introduction of sutures.

He then united the sheaths of the recti in the median line. But Prof. Schroeder said then to his pupils that he was not fully satisfied, however, it was the best surgery that he knew at that time. Later German surgeons improved Schroeder's ideas by splitting the sheaths of the two recti muscles and enclosing both muscles in one sheath by uniting the recti muscle sheaths dorsally and ventrally and dorsally to the recti muscles.

In 1895, Dr. Orville W. MacKellar and I operated on a woman pregnant four or five months, where the diastasis, the musculi recti abdominales was very marked, and the uterus, on coughing or extra intra-abdominal pressure, would project between the recti abdominales. We united the split sheaths of the recti muscles ventral and dorsal, enclosing the two musculi recti abdominales in one sheath. Dr. MacKellar reports to me at present (1908) that his patient is perfectly well, and the operation was a success. Dr. MacKellar was at the delivery and the recti sheaths remained perfectly intact. For the post-operative hernia, for years past at the Mary Thompson Hospital, I have split the recti and enclosed them in a single sheath. Every one with sufficient experience knows that post-operative hernia of any considerable size, in women over 40, is in every case accompanied by splanchnoptosia. Dr. MacKellar and I have records to show that 11 years after enclosing the two recti abdominales in a single sheath, for splanchnoptosia, the operation is a success. The mesenteries are not for mechanical support to suspend the viscera, but to act as a neuro-vascular visceral pedicle, and to prevent the entanglement with other viscera. It is the abdominal wall that maintains the viscera in position.

Besides, I showed in over 600 detailed records of personal autopsic abdominal inspection, that in 96% of subjects the enteron had a mesenteron sufficient in length to herniate through the inguinal, femoral and umbilical rings. Hence the mesenteries must be viewed as neuro-vascular visceral pedicles, and not as suspensory organs, while the abdominal walls are the essential supporters and retainers of the viscera. And as every anatomist knows, the recti abdominales are among the chief regulators or governors of visceral poise, at least they retain the viscera in their first delicate normal balance.

In uniting the two recti abdominales into a single sheath the operation may be performed without entering the peritoneal cavity or after laparotomy. During the past 4 years I have practically abandoned the union of the muscli recti abdominales in a single sheath for the operation of superposition, overlapping of the abdominal walls, taught me by Mr. Jordan Lloyd, of Birmingham, England, in 1891.

(3). *Superposition of the Abdominal Walls.* In 1891 in a visit to Mr. Jordan Lloyd of Birmingham, England, he demonstrated to me the operation of superposition (overlapping) of the abdominal walls in abdominal section to strengthen the line of union. He used a matras form of suture. Since that time I have employed the superposition (overlapping, like a doublebreasted coat) of the abdominal wall. Contrary to Mr. Jordan Lloyd, I employ the buried silver wire suture—some 8 to an inch. The superposition or overlapping of the abdominal walls in splanchnoptosia is the most rational, effective, durable and successful of all parietal surgical procedures. It diminishes, to the desired extent, the abdominal cavity, forcibly repositing organs on their visceral shelves and in their visceral fossae and retaining them in their normal physiologic position. I have superposed, or overlapped, some abdominal walls as much as 8 inches on each side, diminishing the abdominal cavity by six inches of the ventral wall. I observed that some patients with extensive superposition of the abdominal wall, and consequent diminution of the abdominal cavity, complained for a few months of compression feelings, as if the abdomen were too tight or constricted.

(B) *Viscero-pexy (fixation of organs)*.

All abdominal viscera are physiologically mobile, hence, to perform viscero-pexy, or visceral immobilization, fixation of any organ, is unphysiological or in other words viscero-pexy produces a physiologic and anatomic lesion. Excessive visceral mobility is exchanged for visceral fixation. That is, to cure one disease (excessive visceral mobility), another lesion (visceral fixation) is substituted. Therefore viscero-pexy is in general an irrational, harmful, surgical procedure. However, in surgery as in other matters the lesser evil should be chosen, i. e., one should choose which is the greater evil, excessive visceral mobility or visceral fixation—viscero-pexy. The lesion of viscero-pexy or visceral fixation is compromisation of physiology and anatomy, viz.: the lymph and blood circulation as well as peristalsis, absorption, secretion, sensation, are compromised. Nerve periphery is traumatized. The viscero-pexy in order of frequency have been the following: hystero-pexy, nephro-pexy, gastro-pexy, hepato-pexy, spleno-pexy and colo-pexy. In general viscero-pexy is irrational surgery and will be limited in application, as:

(a) It attempts to cure one lesion (excessive visceral mobility) by producing another lesion (visceral fixation). Which is the worse? It is unjustifiable surgery that substitutes one pathologic visceral position for another (for a mobile, pathologic visceral position is no doubt less damaging than a fixed pathologic position).

(b) It attempts to cure a general defect or disease (splanchnoptosia—excessive visceral mobility) by fixation (a physiologic and anatomic lesion) of a single part (e. g., nephroptosia) fragment of the dislocated viscera. Also, when, accidentally, by trauma ptosis of single viscera occur the distinct, marked symptoms and suffering are not indicated. Instead of irrational, individual viscero-pexy, the diminution of the abdominal cavity is more rationally secured by Rose's abdominal strapping (or a binder) or by the superposition, overlapping of the abdominal walls (mechanical), as this does not produce the unfortunate peritoneal fixation lesions of viscero-pexy yet forcibly reposits the viscera on their normal anatomic shelves and within physiologic range. If splanchnoptosia is to be cured by viscero-pexy it will require multiple visceral and parietal operations on one and the same patient as nephro-pexy, gastro-pexy, spleno-pexy, hepato-pexy, entero-pexy and in females (the usual subjects) utero-pexy. Observe what extreme compromisation of visceral anatomy and physiology this would entail. Besides, the thoracic and abdominal walls will require effective repair (diminution). Hence a dangerous number of surgical repetitions would confront the patient.

(c) The viscero-pexy (a lesion of visceral fixation) is generally temporary as the viscus becomes practically eleased sooner or later from absorption of the adjacent artificial parieto-visceral exudate, from absorption or the yielding of suture, from the trauma of the visceral peristalsis, from adjacent muscular trauma, from the trauma of respiration (especially the diaphragm), from lack of support of the abdominal wall.

(d) The viscero-pexy compromises visceral function and structure, of which the most striking example is that of dystocia due to hystero-pexy I have performed autopsy, the death being directly due to dystocia resulting from hystero-pexy. Fixation damages other viscera similarly, perhaps according to the degree of solidarity of fixation.

(e) The peritonotomy or the invasion of the peritoneum alone, regardless of the viscero-pexy, may produce considerable damaging peritoneal adhesions, compromising not only the structure and function of the fixed viscus, but also of adjacent viscera. Peritoneal adhesions are ample reasons in many subjects for primary or secondary peritonotomy. I have shown in hundreds of autopsies that peritoneal adhesions damage viscera by compromising anatomy and physiology, e. g., especially in the caeco-appendicular, gall-bladder, sigmoid and pelvic regions—that a peritonotomy is required.

(f) The patient is not suffering nor are the symptoms due to dislocation of single organs (in splanchnoptosia)—the suffering and symptoms are the result of general dislocation of viscera (splanchnoptosia—neurosis) and extra-expansion of the abdominal and thoracic walls, i. e., splanchnoptosia.

(g) Viscero-pexy is irrational because it compromises visceral function (peristalsis, absorption, secretion sensation) and structure (the connective tissue and the parenchyma of the organs is damaged).

(h) Viscero-pexy compromises circulation (blood and lymph). It traumatizes nerve periphery. It deranges nourishment, resulting in malassimilation, neurosis.

(i) Viscero-pexy is a pathologic surgical substitute for hygienic measures with a high cost and risk. The anatomic rest (maximum quietude of voluntary muscles) and physiologic rest (minimum function of viscera) in bed, with mental hope of cure, tells the favorable story rather than the viscero-pexy.

(j) The patient recovers after the viscero-pexy from symptoms which did not practically belong to the organ attacked. It was a mistake in diagnosis and an unnecessary operation. E. g., to fix a retroverted state of the uterus is to substitute one pathologic condition for another, and also the subject is not suffering from the retroversion but either from complications or disease, as neurosis.

(k) Three views may be held on the favorable reports in viscero-pexy or visceral fixation, viz.: (1) the patient secures a period of favorite anatomic and physiologic rest in bed after the viscero-pexy—with mental hope of cure. In other words the viscero-pexy is a hygienic measure— with high price and risk. (2) The patient recovers after the viscero-pexy from symptoms which did not belong to the attacked organ. The symptoms presented by the patient were due to other causes—especially neurosis (neurasthenia, hysteria). It was a mistaken diagnosis. Hence for individual viscero-pexy should be substituted rational hygienic measures and correct diagnosis. Neurosis should not be mistaken for splanchnoptosia or enteroptosia. (3) A third view in the favorable reports of viscero-pexy is that they are prematurely published. The operation from the anatomic and physiologic rest in bed, as well as diminution of the accompanying neurosis, has afforded temporary relief. Individual viscero-pexy in the majority of subjects does not secure permanent relief.

INDIVIDUAL VISCERO-PEXY.

Viscero-pexy on two organs—kidney and uterus—has become unfortunately prevalent during the past decade.

NEPHRO-PEXY.

Nephro-pexy should be performed for periodic hydro-ureter only.

If in nephroptosia one detects distinct renal pain, renal tenderness, renal hypertrophy and that the ureteral pelvis of the same side contains a greater quantity of urine than the pelvis of other side, periodic hydro-ureter has probably begun. If in a kidney of extensive mobility, and irregular pain presents it is probably due to rotation of the kidney on its uretero-neurovascular-vascular-visceral pedicle (Dietl's crisis) and ureteral dilatation (periodic hydro-ureter) has probably begun.

As regards nephro-pexy there is practically one condition which indicates nephro-pexy and that is periodic hydro-ureter. In this case the damage of periodic hydro-ureter is greater than—unphysiologic renal fixation—that of nephro-pexy. Besides, nephro-pexy is generally not permanent; the kidney again appears in the field of nephroptosia. The patient has assumed the risk of operation, with its consequent anatomic and physiologic damage, peritoneal and connective tissue adhesions, for temporary relief. The multiple methods of executing nephro-pexy condemn it. Practically every advocate of the irrational nephro-pexy pretends to possess his own method. Also nephroptosia is but a fragment of splanchnoptosia, and to produce a single, pathologic, unphysiologic, harmful viscero-pexy to cure a general spanchnoptosia adds further damage to the patient. Nephro-pexy has perhaps a mortality of 2% (the dead are not reported—the living are reported). In nephroptosia the most rational treatment is mechanical reposition and retention of the kidney by means of mechanical supports (for 60% of adult women possess mobile kidney), it avoids operation with consequent connective tissue and peritoneal adhesions. It is a doubtful justifiable surgical procedure to perform nephro-pexy on a replacable kidney, when the organ can be retained by mechanical means, i. e., by utilizing the abdominal wall through a binder—strapping—if no periodic hydro-ureter exists (because mechanical aids will reposit and maintain the kidney in its normal position a 1000 times more physiologic than fixation—nephro-pexy). If nephro-pexy be performed (for periodic hydro-ureter) it should be executed according to the Senn method—i. e., the distal pole of the kidney should be placed in the wound in the abdominal wall and maintained there by a loop of gauze without sutures.

Later the kidney is fixed in this position by granulations and the skin is drawn over its longitudinal border by means of adhesive straps.

Hystero-pexy.

As regards fixation of the genital organs we offer the following consideration: *Hystero-pexy should not be performed on a reproductive subject.* (Alexander operation is a pathologic surgical substitute for hygienic measures at a high cost and risk. It demands repetition as frequent as man requires his hair cut.) Since the primary support of the genitals is the pelvic floor, rational surgery suggests pelvic floor repair for general support in visceral ptosis. Anatomically and physiologically the genitals belong permanently in the pelvis. The genital organs are permanent pelvic organs, hence it is irrational to remove them from the pelvis into the abdomen in order to fix them permanently to the abdominal wall—the genital nerve, lymph and blood apparatus are located in the pelvis in the resting state.

To create new external supports external to the pelvis for the genitals (ventral hystero-pexy) is unphysiologic, pathologic, as it dislocates the organs and compromises structure and function—especially mobility and peristalsis—beside disturbing adjacent organs. The utility of ventral (abdominal) hystero-pexy has not been established; however, its damaging effects have been recognized many hundreds of times: (a) in pain following the operation, (b) from dystocia, (c) in abortions, due to it, (d) in the necessity of surgical procedures in parturitions (as instrumental delivery symphysiotomy, Caesarian section, Porro operation), (e) in the necessity of producing abortions, (f) from postoperative hernia (Theilhaber repor's 30% of hernia subsequent to ventral hystero-pexy—and these were p..ctically originally aseptic subjects), (g) in the mortality of some, 2%.

To forcibly substitute or transform secondary genital supports into primary ones or to create artificial ones is rarely applicable and of doubtful utility. However, secondary supports are more rational than to create artificial new supports external to the pelvis. The Alexander operation, of shortening the round ligaments, is imposing on a secondary uterine support (the round ligaments) the duty of a primary uterine support.

(B) Visceral Anastomosis.

The anastomosis of viscera employed to relieve in splanchnoptosia are the stomach and enteron. The reason for this is that gastro-duodenal dilatation is simply a phase in splanchnoptosia due to the compression of the duodenum by the superior mesenteric vessels. Gastro-enterostomy allows the food to escape from the stomach into the enteron without first passing through the obstructed portion of the duodenum from the compression of the superior mesenteric artery vein and nerve. With rapid stomach evacuation and no food in the duodenum the gastro-duodenal dilatation is quickly changed to gastro-duodenal contraction. (See discussion of gastro-duodenal dilatation.)

RESUME AS REGARDS SPLANCHNOPTOSIA.

1. Splanchnoptosia presents two grand divisions, viz.: I. *Thoracic splanchnoptosia* which includes the factors of: (a) relaxation of the thoracic wall (with diaphragm), (b) thoracic splanchnoptosia (heart and lungs), (c) consequent deranged function of the thoracic viscera and wall (respiration and circulation). II. *Abdominal splanchnoptosia* which includes the factors of: (d) relaxed abdominal walls (atonia gastrica), (e) splanchnoptosia of abdominal viscera (the six visceral tracks), (f) elongation of mesenteries (neuro-vascular visceral pedicle), (g) gastro-duodenal dilatation (due to compression of transverse portion of the duodenum by the superior mesenteric artery vein and nerve), (h) altered form of the abdomen (erect—pendulous, prone—projecting laterally).

In general, in splanchnoptosia, canalization is compromised, nerve periphery traumatized, common visceral function (peristalsis, secretion, absorption, sensation) deranged; circulation (blood, and lymph) disordered; respiration disturbed—ending in malnutrition and neurosis.

Splanchnoptosia compromises the lumen of ducts, vessels and viscera—tubular canals—through flexion, stenosis, decalibration, elongation, constriction.

2. The numerous and complex groups of symptoms produced by splanchnoptosia must be considered independent of inflammatory processes.

The symptoms of the splanchnoptotic are complex and numerous. Each cause in splanchnoptosia produces a vicious circle of—pathologic physiology—pathologic effects on the visceral tracts—digestive, genital, urinary, lymphatic, vascular, nervous, respiratory—impairing nourishment. Splanchnoptosia is often mistaken and wrongly diagnosed as neurasthenia, nervous exhaustion, hysteria, spinal anaemia, menopause, nervous dyspepsia, and neurosis.

Splanchnoptosia appears to be chiefly of congenital disposition as its subjects are generally feeble, slender, atonic, neurotic, marked with a habitus, ill-nourished, deficient in vital force with marked inferior physiologic function and inferior anatomic structure, with apparently a hard struggle to battle for life and against its forces. It seems sufficiently difficult for the splanchnoptotic to live merely—without attempting productive labors or to rear children. Splanchnoptotics are inferior physically and incapable of sustained effort mentally. They are easily fatigued and present a neurotic life. Splanchnoptosia rests on evident inferior anatomy and inferior physiology—on stigma, on habitus, on heredity. The heredity of the splanchnoptotic is habitus splanchnopticus.

In splanchnoptosia the visceral tracts are deranged in function (manifesting pathologic physiology) and their anatomy is distorted (the elastic, muscular and connective tissue fibres are elongated and separated). Splanchnoptotic organs are liable to become hypertrophic—e.g., spleen, liver, uterus—from hyperaemia (especially venous congestion).

3. In splanchnoptosia in common, the tractus intestinalis, urinarius, vascularis, respiratorius, lymphaticus, genitalis, experience excessive,

deficient disproportionate function peristalsis, absorption, secretion, sensation); excessive mobility (distalward dislocation), obstruction (from flexion), pain.

In splanchnoptosia the chief manifestation of distinctive characteristic features are:

(a) *From the tractus intestinalis*, viz.: indigestion, fermentation, meteorism, constipation, malassimilation.

(b) From the *tractus urinarius*, hydro-ureter (periodic), axial rotation of renal pedicle (Dietl's crisis).

(c) From the *tractus genitalis*, hyperaemia, hypertrophy, abortion.

(d) From the *tractus vascularis*, hyperaemia, anaemia, cardiac and aortic palpitation.

(e) From the *tractus lymphaticus*, congestion, decongestion, hypertrophy.

(f) From the *tractus nervosus*, irritability (from trauma), instability, debility, neurosis.

(g) From the *tractus respiratorius*, excessive, deficient, disproportionate respiration.

The splanchnoptotic is the typical subject of manifest pathology physiology (i. e., he lives in the zone between normal physiology and pathologic anatomy).

Splanchnoptosia consists of a distalward dislocation of thoracic and abdominal viscera resulting from extra extended walls. A viscus is dislocated when it is permanently fixed. More adults have dislocated viscera (e. g., splanchnoptosia and from peritoneal adhesions) than normal ones.

B. Stillar's costal stigma or floating tenth rib—costa decima fluctuens— I have studied insufficiently to make authoritative statements.

The objective appearance of the splanchnoptotic is neurotic, slender with gracile skeleton, flattened thorax, increased intercostal spaces, delicate and poorly nourished, pale, non-energetic; a sad, helpless picture. Splanchnoptotics form a distinct class with peculiar characteristics resembling the class of tubercular subjects to which they are related.

Splanchnoptosia is a general disease of the abdominal and thoracic viscera; the tractus respiratorius, intestinalis, vascularis, nervosus, urinarius, lymphaticus, genitalis are equally affected, but from anatomic mechanism and manifestations the tractus nervosus (neurosis) and tractus intestinalis (indigestion), appear to suffer the most.

Since my clinic and private practice has consisted of 85% of women I can not estimate the percentage of splanchnoptosia as regards sex; however, in over 650 personal autopsic abdominal inspections (475 men, 160 women) splanchnoptosia was amply evident in men.

Rapidly repeated gestations play an influential role in progressive splanchnoptosia, as when the fascial, elastic and muscular fibre of some abdominal walls are once well elongated and separated (expanded) they do not return to normal.

The second, third, fourth, fifth decades of life are the chief ages of suffering in splanchnoptosia.

The symptoms which chiefly predominate in splanchnoptosia are from the side of the *nervous*, digestive, and circulatory systems. From the nervous sphere one observes mental depression, melancholy, excitability, irritability, and the nervous stigmata, as e. g., neurosis, hysteria, neurasthenia. From the side of the *circulatory* system one observes hyperaemia, anaemia, cardiac, and aortic palpitations—excessive peristalsis. The aorta may appear as a beating tumor which may be mistaken for aortic aneurysm, because the aorta (while in the prone attitude) is so extensively uncovered, exposed by separated viscera, presenting a protection of thin abdominal wall only.

From the side of the *digestive* system one observes indigestion, fermentation, meteorism, constipation. These three groups of symptoms are marked in every advanced case of splanchnoptosia.

I can not agree with Meinert in attempting to establish an evident etiologic relation between chlorosis and splanchnoptosia. I could observe no distinct relation in series of observation.

The large number of women who have not borne children, who have not laced tight, who have not suffered from ascites, nor wasting disease, however being afflicted with splanchnoptosia, indicates a predisposing or congenital factor.

In splanchnoptosia there are two factors to study, viz.: (a) congenital and predisposing cause, (b) exciting cause. The secondary or exciting causes are any forces which tend to debilitate (elongate and separate the fibres of the abdominal parietes), the abdominal wall, as rapidly repeated gestation, abdominal tumors, ascites, septic disease, constipation, and wasting disease, especially the disappearance of panniculus adiposus and adjacent to the viscera. A congenitally defective system may persist in maintaining fair health; however, exciting or aggravating causes may precipitate invalidism with facility.

Splanchnoptosia may exist with no recognizable symptoms, however, while the subject is in fair physical condition. The rule is that splanchnoptosia may be accompanied by pathologic physiology (and pathologic anatomy) in part or all of the visceral tracts (thoracic or abdominal).

Splanchnoptosia is a general disease—not a local one. It belongs to the area of respiration, which is the trunk. This is well to remember when the pexyite is attempting to impose fixation on some single viscus (which should remain physiologically mobile).

The physician should learn to discriminate the effects in splanchnoptosia from the different visceral tracts, e. g., nephroptosia and genital ptosis manifest almost identical symptoms. The immediate relief by mechanical treatment of forcible reposition by adhesive strapping would decide in favor of nephroptosia as support from the abdominal walls is inefficient in genital ptosis.

Observe how nephroptosia from trauma of the plexus renalis produces reflex symptoms on the proximal end of the tractus intestinalis, ending in nausea, pain, malassimilation, constipation, neurosis. Ureteral calculus induces vomiting, and sooner or later renal and gastric disease coexists. Genital disease occasions more gastric disturbances than the reverse because the gastric functions (secretion, absorption, peristalsis, sensation) are deranged more effectually than those of the genitals. Trauma or infection of the nerve periphery of any abdominal visceral system deranges the peristalsis, absorption, secretion, sensation of the other abdominal systems. The connection between diseases of the tractus genitalsis (uterus) and tractus intestinalis (stomach) is profound and intimate. Disease of the uterus and stomach frequently coexist. A differential diagnosis of the symptoms arising from nephroptosia, from genital ptosis or from gastroptosia is often difficult, as similar symptoms may be referable to any one of these visceral tracts. This may be due first to the nerve tract, the center of which is not in the brain or spinal cord but in the sympathetic nervous system—(e. g., cerebrum abdominale or cerebrum pelvicum). From reflex action symptoms arise which relate to kidney, stomach or uterus. The reflex tracts being anastomosis ovarica, anastomosis pudendo-haemorrhoidalis, anastomosis genito-gastrica, anastomosis cutaneo-cavernosa, anastomosis collateralis and the nervi splanchnici. Also the anastomosis utero-coeliaca, anastomosis utero-cerebro-spinalis, anastomosis reno-coeliaca. The immediate routes of the reflex are direct connections of the vagus (excluding the ganglion abdominales) with the sympathetic nervous system. The second manner in which the mistakes may occur are due to dislocation of the respective organs. As splanchnoptosia is a general disease, local operation—viscero-pexy—as nephro-pexy, hystero-pexy, hepato-pexy, gastro-pexy, colo-pexy, will evidently be of limited value.

In diagnosis the patient's trunk should be divested of clothing. Respiration should be observed in both the erect and prone attitude. Every abdominal organ should be palpated in the erect and prone attitude. Glenard's belt test may be employed. Inspection, palpation, percussion, gastric distension and colonic inflation are decisive aids to diagnosis.

Splanchnoptosia is congenital disease attacking the abdominal and thoracic viscera. Observers associate with splanchnoptosia other stigmata as exopthalmic goiter, myxoedema, neurosis, defective physical form, Stiller's floating rib. It begins in disordered function—pathologic physiology—and structure of the tractus respiratorius. Man must be considered to possess respiratory muscles in whatever location the spinal nerves supply the thoracic and abdominal wall. The intercostal (thoracic) and lumbar (abdominal) nerves are not sharply separated in function. Man's muscular trunk is a respiratory apparatus. The diaphragm is the most important organ in splanchnoptosia. The splanchnoptotic is mainly a neurotic (and hysteria if not present thrives well). Mechanical reposition of organs through therapy applied to the abdominal wall rapidly ameliorates the symptoms and that is the general rational treatment. The symptoms of the splanchnoptotic are chiefly those of neurasthenia with or without local distress or pain. Pain may be experienced anywhere; however, it is chiefly referred to the small of the back. The first impression one receives in studying splanchnoptosia is a picture of multiplicity, kaleidoscope, dissimilars. However, with continued investigation the dislocated organs present themselves in groups and types. In splanchnoptosia the viscera of the thorax, abdomen and pelvis share proportionally in the disease.

GENERAL CONCLUSION AS REGARDS SPLANCHNOPTOSIA.

Splanchnoptotic (dislocated) organs are accompanied by more or less change of form and consequently function. No dislocation in the form of an organ occurs without dislocation and change of form and relaxation of neighboring organs. In splanchnoptosia the change of form of organs is not due merely to the pressure of opposing adjacent organs or the abdominal wall (muscle or skeleton) but the change of organ form is due to function or to physiology it is due to the physiologic necessity of visceral motion rhythm. Practically no organ becomes dislocated without co-existing relaxation of the abdominal wall. The dislocation of single organs does not occur without changing the relations of adjacent organs.

Pathologic Physiology.

In the rise and progress of splanchnoptosia two matters should be held in view, viz.: (a) pathologic physiology, and (b) mechanical pathology. Pathologic physiology is disordered function which is abnormal innumerable times before the pathologic anatomy is perceptible. It is true organs have a wide range of normal physiology but in splanchnoptosia the organs have progressed beyond the normal physiologic range and have entered the range of pathologic physiology. In splanchnoptosia the pathologic anatomy is difficult to detect, judge and estimate. However, it is plainly evident that the physiology of the organs and enclosing walls is pathologic because the functions are going wrong and it is the office of rational treatment to correct the erroneous physiology. A large field of the pathologic physiology in splanchnoptosia is mainly mechanic—it is visceral and parietal dislocation—hence mechanical pathology will demand the chief consideration in the subject. First, in splanchnoptosia by appropriate stimulation (*visceral drainage*) of the organs affected with the sluggish, pathologic physiology to normal maximum action, tolerant, normal physiology is restored. Second by the mechanic measure applied to the abdominal and thoracic walls the mechanical pathology is rationally removed.

In splanchnoptosia the linea alba may be elongated and expanded, stretched to a thin blade.

In splanchnoptosia the organs should be first palpated in the horizontal or prone position and the outline marked with colored chalk, later in the erect position whence the difference in location of the viscera is plainly evident during the horizontal and erect attitude. The percussion should be executed both in the standing and lying position and in each case the organs outlined with colored chalk.

Umbilicus. A test of splanchnoptosia is the change of position of the umbilicus on coughing while standing and while lying. With pendulus abdomen the umbilicus moves proximalward while standing and coughing but not while reclining. The amount of proximalward movement of the umbilicus is an index to the degree of splanchnoptosia. If the proximal half of the rectus abdominalis be relaxed the umbilicus moves distalward. In coughing while in the most erect attitude, the proximal half of the rectus is contracted and hence the umbilicus moves proximalward. To make a diagnosis of splanchnoptosia the patient's clothing should be removed from the trunk.

The symptoms of splanchnoptosia may be grouped into three phases, viz.: (a) the prodromal phase in which arises neurasthenia, hysteria hypochondria. They are subjective symptoms. Visceral dislocation and relaxed parietes may be insufficiently advanced to diagnose. However, in this first stage the viscera becomes dislocated and the parietes become relaxed, the intra-abdominal pressure becomes reduced. In this phase the circulation (lymph and blood) begins to be compromised, as well as visceral channels; secretions are diminished and toxic absorption becomes evident.

(b) The second stage of splanchnoptosia is characterized by dyspepsia, constipation, colic, headache, dizziness, insomnia, weakness, loss of flesh, marked visceral dislocation and relaxation of muscular parietes. Anaemia, tympany and foecal stagnation exist. Lack of intra-abdominal pressure is marked. The visceral ligaments are elongated.

(c) The third stage of splanchnoptotic symptoms are characterized by multiple, many sided subjective symptoms. The clinical picture is pronounced, body weight diminishes, capacity for nourishment is at a minimum, muscular weakness is at a maximum with scarcely sufficient capacity of forcing stool through the rectum. Functional anuna and psychical changes may exist. Sensation is blunted. Glandular secretions, absorptions and visceral peristalsis are extremely deranged. Symptoms become manifold, and the patient is a pathologic picture.

The treatment of splanchnoptosia is:

I. Medical (hygienic regulation of visceral function, diet, habitat, avocation).

The medical treatment for splanchnoptosia is by means of ample *visceral drainage* of the tractus intestinalis and tractus urinarius which increases the volume of fluid in the lumen of the tractus vascularis and tractus lymphaticus, effectually sewering, draining the body of waste laden material. It is visceral drainage, appropriate food, ample rest.

II. Mechanical (forcible reposition and maintenance of viscera in their normal physiologic position—i. e., on their visceral shelves and in their visceral fossae).

The mechanical treatment consists in the employment of abdominal binders, especially Achilles Rose adhesive strapping (being rational, economical and practical). The straps do not slip. Also the author's abdominal binder within which is placed a pneumatic rubber pad which can be distended with air to suit the patient's comfort. The splanchnoptotic must make the best of his hereditary burden and assume as much (horizontal) rest as possible.

III. Surgical (superposition of the abdominal wall, viscero-pexy anastomosis.)

The surgical treatment consists of: (a) viscero-pexy, i.e., fixation of mobile viscus to the abdominal wall (extremely limited, as it attempts to cure one alleged visceral lesion—excessive mobility—by producing another—visceral fixation). (b) Diminishing the abdominal cavity and forcing the mobile organs on their visceral shelves and visceral fossae by superposition (overlapping) the elastic, fascio-muscular apparatus of the abdominal wall like a double breasted coat (rational, practical). (c), Anastomosis as gastroenterostomy.

Some of the photographs in this chapter were executed by Dr. William E. Holland, from my wall charts.

A PARTIAL BIBLIOGRAPHY OF SPLANCHNOPTOSIA

Rudolph Virchow—Virchow's Archiv., vol. V, 1853. An historical, critical and exact consideration of the affections of the abdominal cavity.
Aberle, Rallet, Rayer, J. B. Morgazni, Kusmaul, Bayer, Hertzka, Lindner.
Fischer-Benyon, Becker and Lenhoff, Frickhinger, Kuttner, Strauss, Chvostek, Memert, Kelling, Huber, Flemer, Hufschmidt, Ewald, Bruggemann, B. Stiller, Bial, Obvortzow, Boaz, Ostertag.
Frantz Glenard—Articles from 1885 to 1906. Book on splanchnoptosia (875 pages) published in 1899.
Theodore Landau—Wander Nieve, 1881.
Theodore Landau—Wander Leber, 1887.
C. Schwerdt—Beitrag (splanchnoptosia), 1897.
J. G. Sheldon—Is Nephroptosis Hereditary? 1903.
Byron Robinson—Gastro-duodenal Dilatation, Cincin-Lancet-Clinic, Dec. 8, 1900.
A. W. Lea—Enteroptosis, Medical Chronicle, 1902.
Saunby—British Med. Jr., Nov. 29, 1902.
Beyea—Pennsyl. Med. Jr., Nov., 1902.
Charles Adron—Splanchnoptosia in Pregnancy, Am. Jr. Surg. and Gynecol., July, 1902.
A. P. Francine—Gastroptosis, Philadel. Med. Jr., Jan. 3, 1903.
J. D. Steele—Analyses of 70 cases of gastroptosis, Am. Jr. Med. Assn., Nov. 8, 1902, also Jan. 25, 1902.
R. C. Coffey—A method of suspending the stomach, Philadel. Med. Jr., Oct. 11, 1902.
Earnest Gellant—The Rational Treatment of movable kidney and associated ptosis, Am. Jr. Surg. and Gynecol., Dec., 1902, N. Y. Med. Jr., April 29, 1905.
Robert J. Reed—Movable Kidney, Philadel. Med. Jr., Nov. 8, 1902.
L. Schoeler—Movable Kidney, Virg. Semi-Med. Monthly, April 14, 1899.
J. E. Moore—Splanchnoptosis from a surgical standpoint, Jr. Am. Med. Assn., July 29, 1905.
O. Kraus—Emfluss des Korsetts, 1904.
H. Quincke—Enteroptose, Therapic de Gegenwart, XLIV, page 538.
H. A. McCullum—British Med. Jr., Feb. 18, 1905.
Thomas R. Brown—Enteroptosis, American Medicine, July and August, 1903. Three articles.
C. A. Meltzurg—Enteroptose und Intra-abdominales, Druck, 1898.
Byron Robinson—Splanchnoptosia, Philadel. Med. Jr., Nov. 30, Dec. 7, 1901.
J. M. Taylor—The Rational Treatment of visceral ptosis, N. Y. Med. Jr., Aug. 4, 1906.
J. N. Le Conte—Gastroptosis, N. Y. Med. Jr., July 25, 1903.
Arthur Keith—Hunterian Lectures, Lancet, March 7, 1903.
L. Krez—Frage der Enteroptose, 1892.
H. Goelet—Annals of Gynecology and Pediatry, vol. XV, 1903.
M. L. Harris—Movable Kidney, Jr. Am. Med. Assn., June 1, 1901, Feb. 13, 1904.
C. A. Meltzurg—Gastroptose, Wiener Med. Presse, July 28, Aug. 4, Aug. 11, Aug. 18, Aug. 25, 1895.
J. Chalmers Da Costa—Nephroptosia, N. Y. Med. Jr., Aug. 4, 1906.
Agness C. Vietor—Splanchnoptosia, Boston Med. and Surg. Jr., Aug. 9, Sept. 9, 1906.
Achilles Rose and R. C. Kemp—Atonia Gastrica (Book), 1906.
R. Weissmann—Ueber Enteroptose, Monograph.

CHAPTER XL.

SYMPATHETIC RELATION OF THE GENITALIA TO THE OLFACTORY ORGANS.

One's rainbow of desires changes color with the passing years.
It is when you come close to a man in conversation that you discover what his real abilities are.—Samuel Johnson.

It is a curious fact that even laymen have for ages noted that the organ of smell is closely related to the generative organs, but it is very recently that specialists (gynecologists and rhinologists) are putting together the connected story. The relation of the olfactory organ and nasal mucous membrane with the genitals are by way of the sympathetic. The anatomic path of travel from the nasal mucous membrane to the genitals is through the fifth cranial nerve, or trigeminus, which is supremely the ganglionic cranial nerve. It is the type of mixed nerves. It has eight ganglia situated on its branches. It also sends a large branch to the mucous membrane of the nose—the nasal nerve. This will at once explain its wide influence in reflection or disease, because of its extensive influence over the caliber of adjacent blood and lymph vessels, and the extensive periphery in the nasal mucosa, allowing opportunity for numerous reflexes.

Let us examine for a moment the ganglia of the trigeminus (trifacial or fifth cranial nerve—the ganglionic nerve of the brain). A significant statement may precede the short description, by saying that one of the chief offices of a ganglion is to demedullate nerves. 1, We may note the Gasserian ganglion of the fifth cranial nerve, situated in a depression in the apex of the petrous portion of the temporal bone. The ganglion is as large as the end of the little finger. The ganglionic nature of this swelling was perceived by Raimund Balthasar Hirsch, a Vienna anatomist, in 1765, who christened it the "Ganglion Gasserii" in honor of his teacher, Gasserius, who in 1779 was "Privat Docent" in anatomy under Prof. Joseph Jans, in Vienna. Since Du Bois-Remond announced from personal experience that he thought facial neuralgia was due to spasmodic contraction of the blood vessels controlled by the sympathetic, surgeons have attempted to cure facial neuralgia by destruction of Gasser's ganglion. This is at least a recognition of the sympathetic nature of the Gasserian ganglion, and its consequent influence over the caliber of the blood vessels.

The Gasserian ganglion has close and intimate connection with the sympathetic nerves. The blood vessels alone which are necessary to supply the Gasserian ganglion would produce a close and intimate relation between the sympathetic and trifacial. The trigeminus shows a very intimate and extensive connection with the tonsils, the sebaceous glands of the face and genitals. This is seen at puberty of both boys and girls (facial acne), and in the menopause. The changes in voice of boys at puberty, and the changes of voice of women at the monthly, may be easily worked out anatomically, by dissecting out the connection between the superior cervical ganglion and the pneumogastric and glosso-pharyngeal. Also the spheno-palatine sends branches to the tonsils in the descending palatine nerves. One may find from three to five branches of nerves passing from the superior cervical ganglion to the glosso-pharyngeal and pneumogastric nerves. During menstruation the vocal cords are congested and hence the hoarse, husky voice; and a similar but permanent physiological process of congestion and growth occurs in the boy at puberty. Hence the close and intimate relations of the vocal cords (voice) and nasal mucosa (smell) and reflex action with the genitals, have a distinct, concrete, anatomical explanation. Besides, the larynx is supplied by the sympathetic branches which accompany the superior and inferior recurrent laryngeal nerves.

2. The ophthalmic, lenticular or ciliary ganglion is a pinhead sized ganglion situated in the orbit. It is closely connected by roots with the nasal branch of the fifth nerve, i. e., has relations with the nasal mucosa, by a sympathetic branch from the cavernous plexus. It is also connected with the third cranial. This second ganglion has intimate connections with the nasal mucosa. Joseph Guiscard Duverny (1648-1730), a French anatomist, discovered this ganglion.

3. The spheno-palatine, or Meckel's ganglion, situated in the spheno-palatine fossa and on the superior maxillary branch of the trifacial, is a large mass of nerve cells. It is intimately connected with the nasal mucosa by the descending palatine nerves. The spheno-palatine ganglion was discovered and described by Johann Friedrich Meckel (1717-1774), a celebrated German anatomist. Like all the other ganglia of the fifth cranial nerve, it possesses motor, sensory and sympathetic roots. It sends a considerable nerve supply to the tonsils. Hence we again observe that this ganglion shares in distributing nerves to the nasal mucosa and the region of the tonsils. But the premise of our argument is that the fifth nerve, being studded by eight sympathetic ganglia, is intimately and closely connected, anatomically and functionally, with the genitals. Therefore what affects the fifth nerve will affect the genitals, and vice versa.

4. The optic or Arnold's ganglion is located just below the foramen ovale, on the inferior maxillary branch of the trifacial. Its sympathetic branches are derived from the sympathetic plexuses which surround the adjacent middle meningeal artery. It is connected with the facial and glosso-pharyngeal nerves and sends branches to the tensor palati. In our library may be seen Friedrich Arnold's "Anatomie des Menschen," 3 vols. On page 909, Vol. II, Arnold says, "Der Ohrknoten wurde von mir im Winter 1825-26 endeckt." In English, "The optic ganglion was discovered by me in the winter of 1825-26." Professor Arnold noted 75 years ago that many tried in vain to show that others than himself discovered the ganglion. This ganglion shows connection with the larynx by way of the glosso-pharyngeal and tensor palati; and, through the Vidian nerve and Meckel's ganglion, with the nasal mucosa.

5. The submaxillary ganglion is situated on the lingual branch of the inferior branch of the trifacial nerve. Its sympathetic branch is derived from the plexus which surrounds the adjacent facial artery. This ganglion was discovered by Meckel in 1748. It has been named after him—Ganglion Meckelii Minus. The ganglion communicates with the facial or the seventh nerve.

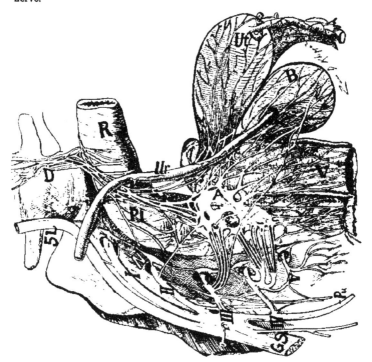

Fig. 207. Nerves of internal genitals, pelvic brain, dissected under alcohol.

6. The sublingual or Blandin's ganglion is situated on the branch of nerves going to the sublingual gland. This collection of nerves may be only a plexus or a ganglion. It should have a similar connection with the submaxillary ganglion. Phillippe Frederic Blandin (1798-1849), a French surgeon, first described this ganglion in 1849.

7. The ganglion of Bockdalek is located at the junction of the middle superior dental nerve with the anterior superior dental nerve. It is not constant, and besides, the swelling may not always be a ganglion, i. e., may not

contain nerve-cells. It lies above the upper canine tooth. Its discovery is due to Victor Alexander Bockdalek, Professor of Anatomy in Prague until 1869 (papers published in 1866), and Victor Bockdalek, his son, also an anatomist in Prague. However, it appears to be the father who discovered this ganglion, previous to 1851.

8. The ganglion of Valentine is situated at the junction of the middle superior dental nerve and posterior superior dental nerve. It is located above the second bicuspid tooth. The ganglion was discovered by Gabriel Gustave Valentine (1810-1883), a German anatomist. All the ganglia of the fifth cranial or trifacial have systematic connections.

We should have known that the trigeminus is supremely the ganglionic cranial nerve; that it is closely and intimately connected, especially with the genitals by way of the sympathetic tracts; also that the trigeminus is closely and intimately connected, especially with the nasal mucosa, and to a considerable extent with the larynx and vocal cords. There are found to be numerous and intimate connections between the fifth cranial nerve (the trigeminus) and the seventh cranial nerve (the facial). Observation shows the intimate relation is accomplished by means of the sympathetic nerves, especially the ganglia on the trifacial. This physiologic relation of the genitals to the trifacial and facial nerves may be plainly observed in the sexual relations and cohabitations of animals.

Irritation of the nasal mucosa will cause congestion and erection. Occasionally irritation of the genitals will cause congestion of the face or the region of the trigeminus. Urethral irritation will induce "gritting" of the teeth, i. e., action of the masseter muscles, supplied by the inferior branch of the fifth.

Dr. A. G. Hobbs describes two cases of severe priapism, accompanying acute rhinitis (Jour. Am. Med. Assn., 1897). On spraying the nasal mucosa with cocaine the priapism immediately subsided. Opium affected the priapism in each case, but only to slight degree.

A reflex sneeze is not infrequent previous to erection. In preparations for coition the involvement of the nasal mucosa is quite apparent in animals, as the horse, dog, bull, etc. In monkeys the nasal mucosa is not only involved in coition, but it is evident that the larynx is highly involved, from the active and vigorous chattering, emitted previous to and during coition. The mare neighs at the approaching of the stallion or cow bellows at the approach of the bull, the growling of dogs, noise of cats and cackling of hens, are doubtless not accidental at times of coition, but due to irritation of nerve tracts.

The tissue covering the turbinated bones is quite erectile. A nasal reflex will induce an erectile action in the corpora cavernosa. We know that the genitals are intimately and profoundly supplied by the sympathetic nerves. We know that the fifth nerve is supremely the ganglionic (sympathetic) nerve of the brain. The fifth nerve sends a rich supply to the nasal mucosa and to the larynx through the vagus and glosso-pharyngeal.

Clinically and anatomically we note a close and intimate relation between the genitals and the nasal mucosa, the larynx and the sebaceous glands of the face. The whole manifestation is due to reflex action carried through the sympathetic nerves. The frequent hemorrhages from the nose during and subsequent to puberty in both sexes, demonstrate the intimate relation of the nasal mucosa. Again, why is it that so many women we note with chronic uterine disease also have rhinitis in different forms? A typical example came to my office a few days ago. She was 24 years old and single. At 20 she began to be irregular in menstrual function, and to have menorrhagia. Digital examination revealed quite a large, hypertrophic, metritic uterus, fixed by old adhesions, with distinct retroflexion. She said she bled frequently at the nose. The tissues covering the turbinated bones were thickened, inflamed and congested. Chronic rhinitis and metritis co-existed.

Many diseased generative organs co-exist with diseased nasal mucosa. The eight ganglia on the fifth cranial nerve—(1) Ganglion Gasser; (2) Ophthalmic; (3) Spheno-palatine; (4) Optic; (5) Submaxillary; (6) Sublingual; (7) Bockdalek; (8) Valentine—not only show the sympathetic nature of the fifth cranial nerve, but also intimate relation with the nasal mucosa, larynx, abdominal brain, and especially with the genitals.

NASAL DYSMENORRHEA.

The relationship between the nasal mucous membrane and the sexual apparatus is often forgotten. One should always remember that there is always a woman behind the uterus. In cases of persistent dysmenorrhea relief may sometimes be afforded by painting the genital spots in the nose with 1 per cent solution of cocaine, as demonstrated by Schiff, Emil Ries, Fliess and others. During menstruation there is congestion of the Schneiderian membrane not present during the rest of the month; a congestion which may also be produced by violent sexual excitement—the popular expression "bride's cold" being a laity recognition of the relation between the nose and the sexual sphere. In most people there is a temporary swelling of the nasal mucous membrane just preceding and during the sexual act, disappearing with detumescence.

INDEX

Subject	Page
Anesthesia	297
Angina Pectoris	313
Appendicitis	414
Brain, Abdominal	62, 112, 195, 225, 287, 300, 318
Anatomy	112, 123
Afferent	112
Efferent	114
Holotopy	54, 131
Idiotopy	54, 115, 133
Position	114
Skelotopy	54, 114, 131
Syntopy	54, 114, 131
Ganglia	118
Diaphragmatic	118
Splanchnica	118
Renalia	118
Borders	116
Dimensions	115
Form	115
Surfaces	116
Relations	122
Genitalis	123
Intestinalis	123
Urinarius	123
Physiology	123, 129, 163, 287
Circulation	163
Nutrition	163
Reproduction	163
Secretion	163
Visceral Automatic Ganglia	163
Brain, Cranial	63, 159, 121
Brain, Pelvic	131–152
Anatomy and Topography	131, 152
Arrangement	135
Borders	134
Dimensions	133
Fenestra	136
Form	134
Ganglia	138
Ganglionic Cells	138
Holotopy	131
Idiotopy	133
Position	131
Skelotopy	131
Syntopy	131
Physiology	144–156
Age Relation	150
Climacterium	150, 154
Digestive Disturbances	175, 186
Gestation	150, 155
Menstruation	150, 155
Pathological Remarks	151
Pubertas	150, 155
Pueritas	150, 155

Subject	Page
Brain, Pelvic—	
Physiology—	
Senescence	150–155
General Considerations	159, 186
Rhythm	169
Bowel Atomy	325
Calculus Hepatic	314
Cholecystitis	452
Colonic Appendicitis	414
Colic Lead	306
Constipation	351–377
Age Relation	354
Anatomy	351
Causes	351
Diagnosis	369
Dietetic	353
Etiology	351
Fluids	375
Foods	377
Mechanical	353
Physiology	351
Pathology	353
Treatment	370
Sex	354
Visceral Circulation	367
Visceral Drainage	375
Fluids	375
Foods	375
Digestive Tract Disturbances	175
Diabetes Mellitus	314, 315
Diabetes Insipidus	316
Enteralgia	304
Entorodynia	304
Enteromic Appendicitis	414
Enteroptosia	268, 270
Exopthalmic Goiter	19, 20
Gastralgia	304, 311
Gastrodinia	304, 311
Glycouria	315
Ganglia	79
Aortic Visceral	108
Automatic Visceral	239, 277
Arteriæ Phrenic	120
Automatic Menstrual	240, 252
Cervical	312
Diaphragmatic	118
Lumbalis	79
Oviductal	246
Renalis	118
Sacralis	80
Semilunar, Left	118
Right	120
Sympathetic	289, 318
Physiology	289
Visceral, Abdominal and Pelvic Brain, Physiology	204

659

INDEX

Subject	Page
Ganglia—	
Visceral, Automatic, Abdominal and Pelvic Brain, Reference to Sexual Organs	227
Genitalis, Tractus, Pathologic Physiology	432–437
Avocation	447
Blood Volume	441
Diagnosis	440
Prophylaxis	447
Visceral Drainage.	
Habitat	447
Fluids	445
Foods	446, 459
Douches	472
Fluids	472
Gestation	468
Habitat	477
Menstruation	465
Ovulation	461
Peristalsis	461
Secretion	463
Sensation	465
Tampon	474
Treatment	47, 480
Gentalia, Female	304, 341, 346, 347
Traumatic	346
Ovarian Tumor Weight	346
Pressure Neurosis	347
Olfactory Organs	654–658
Nasal Dysmenorrhœa	658
Neurosis	341–350
Puberty	253, 259, 342
Menstruation	343
Pregnancy	342
Menopause	200, 253
Tumors	208, 221, 356, 396, 423
Infection	208
Cicatrices	208
Sexual Crisis	227, 342
Abdominal and Pelvic Brain with Automatic Visceral Ganglia	227, 239
Genitals, Tractus	87
Anatomy	87
Interiliacus Plexus	92
Ovaricus Plexus	90
Pelvic	94
Rectalis	96
Sacralis Spinalis	92
Uterinus, Plexus	94
Vaginalis, Plexus	96
Vesicalis, Plexus	96
Physiology	98
Peristalsis	100
Rhythm	100
Gynecological	294
Hyperesthesia	296, 317
Abdominal Brain	302
Cardiac Plexus	312
Cervical Ganglia	312
Diaphragmatic Plexus	317
Gastric Plexus	311
Hepatic Plexus	314
Hypogastric Plexus	308
Inferior Mesentric	309
Mucosa	297
Mesenteric	304
Ovarian	310

Subject	Page
Hyperesthesia—	
Pancreatic Plexus	316
Pelvic Brain	309
Renal	316
Splenic Plexus	313
Spermatic	310, 319
Sympathetic	302
Skin	296
Secretions	329, 333
Auerbach's Plexus	329
Billroth-Meissner	329
Excessive	329
Deficient	331
Disproportionate	331
Gastric	331
Glands	331
Muscular Motion	331
Nose	331
Treatment	331
Hysteria Stigmata	284, 296, 325
Cutaneous	300
Head	300
Lumbosacral	300
Muscular	300
Muscular Stigma	298
Neurosis	343
Pain	300
Peritoneal	300
Pyschosis	298, 343, 344
Special Senses	298
Stomach	300
Treatment	300
Stigma	284, 296
Heberden's Disease	312
Hyperesthesia	296
Hysteria	325
Icterus	452
Invagination	410
Intestinalis, Tractus, Physiological	
Pathological	448
Nervosis	456
Pathologic	448
Peristalsis	448
Intestinalis	62
Anatomy	62
Arteria Hepatical	65
Cœliacus	62
Ductus Bilus	65
Gastricus	62, 64
Hemorrhoidal Plexus.	
Medius	70
Inferior	70
Hepaticus	64, 65
Mesenterica Superior Plexus	67
Physiology.	
Distal End Supply	74
Middle	73
Proximal	72
Lymphatic Tract	514, 545
Absorption	516
Genital	123
Intestinal	123
Peristalsis	516
Secretion	516
Sensation	516
Treatment	533
Urinarius	123
Melancholia	325

INDEX

SUBJECT	PAGE
Menopause	253, 259, 280, 314, 342
Flushes	256
Flashes	256
Malnutrition	259
Reflex Irritation	259
Sweat Centers	256
Uterine Disturbances	312
Menstruation	343
Automatic Menstrual Ganglia	240
Neurosis	343
Psychosis	343, 344
Premenstrual Pain	248
Nerves	342
Anatomy	290
Cerebral	278–302
Cerebrospinal Relation	278
Genital External	286
Pelvic	278
Peritoneum	288
Spinal	278–302
Splanchnic	42, 43
Sympathetic, Independence of	187
Sympathetic	187, 287, 292, 294, 304
Trigeminus	342
Vagus	342
Vasomotor	205
Visceral Sympathetic	278, 302
Pathological	281
Neuralgia	307–317
Cardiac	312
Celica	302
Diaphragmatic	317
Gastric	311
Hypogastric	302
Hemorrhoidal	309
Mesenteric	304, 309
Ovarian	310
Renal	316
Splenic	314
Urethral	310
Nerves Vascularis	103–110
Anatomy	103–106
Aortic Visceral Ganglia	108–110
Physiology	106–110
Nerves.	
Genital	286
Pelvic	278
Peritoneum	288
Cerebral	298, 302
Neurasthenia	325
(Neurosis Abdominalis)	495–501
Absorption	495
Asthenia	496
Congenita	497
Degeneracy Habitus	497
Heredity	497
Predisposition	498
Secretion	498
Sensation	498
Stigma	499
Treatment	500
Neurosis	267–277
Enteralgia	304
Gastralgia	304
Hepatis	276
Hysteria	284
Melancholia	325
Neurasthenia	325

SUBJECT	PAGE
Neurosis—	
Oviductal	277
Peristalsis	277
Rectalis	277
Renalis	277
Uterine	277
Visceral	267
Neuroses, Colon Secretion	334
Age	335
Catarrh	337
Chemical	336
Colicky Pains	334
Microscopical Examinations	336
Motor Neuroses	337
Mucous Colic	337
Mucous Stools	334
Menstrual	343
Nervous	337
Pathology	336
Treatment	339
Neuroses, Motor	318
Anemia	322
Abdominal Brain	318
Atomy of Bowels	325
Auerbach's Plexus	318
Bilbroth-Meissner's Plexus	318
Cranial Nerves	318
Colon	334
Enterospasm	324
Intestinal Movements	318
Invagination	328
Hysteria	284, 296, 325
Melancholia	325
Paralysis	325
Sympathetic Ganglia	318
Spinal Nerves	318
Sympathetic System	318
Nervosus, Tractus	495–501
Physiological Pathological.	
Abdominalis	495
Absorption	496
Secretion	498
Sensation	499
Treatment	500
Neuroma	405
Nephralgia	316
Neurasthenia	325
Obstructions	406, 414
Apertures	406
Appendicitis	414
Bands	406
Colonic	414
Enteronic	414
Invagination	410
Pancreatic Secretions	452
Strangulation	406
Volvulus	412
Pains	393
Abdominal	393
Abdominal, Sudden	393, 441
Age	396
Appendicular	400
Character	397
Gastric	399
Nephritic	399
Pelvic	400
Sex	396
Reflex	402

SUBJECT	PAGE
Pains—	
Reflex—	
Abscess in Abdominal Wall	404
Amygdalitis Mastitis	404
Appenditis	414
Axial Torsion of Viscera	424
Complete	424
Incomplete	424
Biliary Channels	418
Embolism with Mesenteric Vessels	419
Genitals	422
Hyperesthesia	404
Intoxication	421
Invagination	410
Mesenteric Vessels Embolus	419
Muscular Rigidity	410
Neurasthenia	325
Pancreatic Hemorrhage, Acute	418
Pyosalpinx	422
Pleurisy	402
Spinal Caries	404
Spinal Cord and Hysteria	404
Strangulation by Bands through Apertures	419
Strangulation	406
Testicular	404
Paralysis	325
Direct	325
Indirect	325
Pathologic	322
Peristalsis	322, 326
Normal	322
Deficient	324
Increased	326
Pendulum	319
Rhythmic	318
Roll Motion	319
Spinal	318
Sympathetic System	318
Sympathetic Lateral Chain	318
Tonic Contractions	322
Plexus Aorticus Abdominalis	46, 51
Anatomy	46, 49, 76, 78, 98
Ganglia	46, 48
Nerve Trunks and Cords	48, 49
Physiology	49, 51, 71, 76
Age Relation	59
Interiliac Vasomotor	52
Interiliacus Truncus Plexus	56
Interiliacus, Distal End	58, 92
Utility in Practice	60
Arteria Uterinæ	80
Cœliacus	62, 64
Communis Arterie	80
Gastricus	63, 64
Genital	87
Ganglia Lumbales	79
Hemorrhoidal	70
Medium	70
Inferior	70
Hypaticus	62, 64, 65
Hypogastricus	80, 308
Iliacus Communis Arteriæ	82, 92
Lienalis	62, 68
Mysentericus	69
Inferior	69, 80
Superior	67
Ovaricus	78, 90, 310

SUBJECT	PAGE
Plexus Aorticus Abdominalis—	
Physiology—	
Pelvic Brain	94
Rectalis	96
Renalis	76
Sacralis Spinalis	92
Sacralis	81
Supra Renalis	76
Ureteris	78
Urethralis	81
Uterinus	94
Vaginal	96
Vesicalis	96
Pathological	546-549
Pathogenesis	552
Polyuria	316
Pregnancy	342
Psycosis	342, 344
Puberty	253, 259, 342
Respiratorious	548, 569, 648
Sexual Crisis	342
Shock	382-392
Diagnosis	388
Etiology	384
History	382
Pathology	386
Prevention	391
Prognosis	389
Symptoms	387
Treatment	390
Spinal Segment	567
Strangulation	406
Splanchnoptosia (Atonia Gastrica)	546-653
Adhesions	556-574
Mesocolic	574
Mesoduodenal	573
Mesogastric	573
Mesenteronic	574
Omental	556
Peritoneal	556
Bibliography	653
Physiology and Anatomy	553, 559
Circulation	626
Colon, Right	574
Diaphragm	565, 566
Factors	555
Etiological	555
Fixation and Motion of Thoracic Viscera	568, 569
Fixation of Intestinal Tract	572
Mechanism	557
Radix Mesenterica	570
Relaxation	561
Segment, Spinal	567
Theory, Keith's	554
Pathological Relations	546
Clinical	551
Embryology	511
Genitals	564, 617, 648
Historical	548
Intestinalis	562, 575, 648
Lymphaticus	648
Nervosus	630, 631, 648
Pathogenesis	552
Respiratorius	548, 569, 648
Urinarius	564, 594, 648
Vascularis	648
Coloptosia	590, 591

INDEX

Subject	Page
Splanchnoptosia (Atonia Gastrica)—	
Coloptosia—	
Symptoms	591
Treatment	592
Enteroptosia	593
Fixation	617
Flexure Coli Hepatica	623
Flexure Coli Lienalis	624
Gastroptosia	576
Dilitation	582
Diagnosis	583
Etiology	580
Respiration	577
Treatment	584
Gastro-Duodenal Dilatation	604
Diagnosis	611
Treatment	612, 617
Genitals	564, 617, 619, 648
Fixation	617
Respiration	618
Hepatoptosia	268, 274, 586
Diagnosis	588
Etiology	587
Frequency	587
Fixation of Liver	586
Movements, Respiratory	586
Treatment	589
Nephroptosia	594, 603
Age	597
Diagnosis	597
Etiology	597
Fixation	594
Frequency	597
Relation	595
Respiration	594
Robinson, Byron, Triangle	602
Symptoms	
Treatment	603
Neuroses	630, 631, 648
Frequency	632
Symptoms	632
Treatment	634
Sympathetic Nerve	39, 187, 287, 292, 294, 304
Absorption	187, 188
Anatomy and Physiologic Anatomy	33, 38, 192, 203, 290
Automatic Menstrual Ganglia	240, 252
Cervical	40
Circulation	187
Classification of Diseases	28, 32
Considerations for Removal of Tumors	206, 226
Dorsal	42
Growth	187
Gynecology	175, 292
Historical Sketch	11, 27
Independence of Sympathetic	187, 192
Macroscopic	21, 26
Microscopic	26, 27
Nutrition	187
Pathology in Gynecology	292
Pelvic	44
Peristalsis	188

Subject	Page
Splanchnoptosia (Atonia Gastrica)—	
Sympathetic Nerve—	
Anatomy—	
Physiology of Abdominal and Pelvic Brain with Automatic Visceral Ganglia	204, 207
Relation to Cerebrospinal	278
Sacral	44, 45
Secretion	187
Sensation	188
Thoracic	42, 43
Trunks of	39, 45
Uterine Changes	175
Vasomoter Nerves	205
Pathology	187, 287, 292, 294, 304
Tumors	221
Axial Rotation	221, 324, 356, 396, 425
Reflex Action on Sympathetic	208, 226
Kidney	347
Urinarius	76, 86, 98, 123
Anatomy	76
Arteria Uterina	80
Arteria Communis	80
Ganglia Sacrales	80
Ganglia Lumbales	79
Hypogastricus	80
Mesentericus Inf	80
Mesentericus Sup	80
Ovaricus (Spermaticus)	78
Renalis	16, 78
Renalis Superior	76
Sacralis	81
Ureters	78
Urethralis	81
Vesicales	80
Urinarius, Tractus, Physiological Pathological	479-494
Absorption	483
Peristalsis	479
Secretion	481
Sensation	485
Treatment	489
Uremia	404
Urinary Colic	419
Vascularis, Tractus	502
Pathologic Physiology of	502, 513
Combined Treatment	508
Excessive Secretion	506
Deficient	506
Disproportionate	506
Peristalsis	503
Excessive	503
Deficient	503
Disproportionate	503
Vascular Tract	502
Visceral Drainage by Fluids	507
Visceral Drainage by Foods	507
Pathologic Physiology of the Blood	509
Red Blood Corpuscles and Hemaglobin	509
Plasma (Liquor Sanguinis)	512
Pathologic Anatomy	513
Treatment	512
White Blood Corpuscles	511
Vascularis	648
Volvulus	412

LIST OF ILLUSTRATIONS

No.		Page
1	An Illustration of the Sympathetic Nerve	13
2	An Illustration of the Abdominal Sympathetic Nerve of the Male	29
3	A Diagram of Sympathetic from Proximal to Distal End	34
4	Abdominal Brain, Lumbar Lateral Chain	35
5	Lumbar and Sacral Portions of the Sympathetic	37
6	Trunk of the Vasomotor	41
7	Plexus Aorticus Abdominalis	47
8	Plexus Aorticus Abdominalis	50
9	Plexus Interiliacus	53
10	Plexus Interiliacus of Adult	55
11	The Vasomotor Interiliacus Plexus	57
12	Plexus Interiliacus of Adult	59
13	The Nerves of the Tractus Intestinalis	63
14	Anastomosing Arteries of the Tractus Intestinalis	67
15	Nerves of the Hepatic Artery and Biliary Duct	69
16	Arteries of Cœcum and Appendix	71
17	X-ray of Ductus Pancreaticus and Part of Ductus Bilis	73
18	Arterial Supply of Tractus Urinarius	77
19	Nerves of Tractus Urinarius, Corrosion Anatomy	79
20	Corrosion Anatomy (Hyrtl's Exsanguinated Renal Zone)	81
21	Nerves of Tractus Urinarius	83
22	Corrosion Anatomy	84
23	Relation of Spinal Nerves at Tractus Urinarius	85
24	Nerves of Tractus Genitalis	89
25	Nerves of Tractus Genitalis, Pregnant about Three Months	91
26	Genital Nerves of Infant	93
27	Genital Nerves of Adult	95
28	The Nerves of the Tractus Genitalis	97
29	The Arterial Circulation of the Puerperal Uterus	99
30	Circles, Arcs and Arcades of the Abdominal Arteries	105
31	Nerves Accompany the Arteries	107
32	Nerves of the Blood-vessels	109
33	Abdominal Brain	113
34	Abdominal Brain	117
35	Abdominal Brain	119
36	Abdominal Brain	121
37	Abdominal Brain	125
38	Ganglion Cells in the Abdominal Brain	127
39	Abdominal Brain of an Infant	133
40	Pelvic Brain	137
41	Pelvic Brain of an Adult	143
42	Pelvic Brain	149
43	Pelvic Brain	153
44	Pelvic Brain of an Adult	157
45	Cardiac Nerves	163
46	Abdominal Brain and Cœliac Axis	166
47	Pelvic Brain	170
48	Ductus Bilis and Ductus Pancreaticus	174
49	Corrosion Anatomy of the Kidney	178
50	Ductus Pancreaticus with Part of Ductus Bilis	182
51	Corrosion Anatomy, Uterus, Oviducts and Ovary of New-born Infant	185
52	Abdominal Brain and Plexus Aorticus	194
53	Ductus Bilis and Ductus Pancreaticus et Aorta Hepatica	196
54	Nerves of the Heart	198
55	Renal Vascular Supply	200

LIST OF ILLUSTRATIONS

No.		Page
56	Nerves of the Tractus Genitalis	202
57	Schemic Drawing of the Sympathetic Nerve	209
58	Pelvic Brain	243
59	A Schematic Drawing of the Sympathetic Nerve	254
60	Lumbar and Sacral Portions of the Sympathetic (Sappey)	260
61	Sympathetic Nerve in Lumbar Region	263
62	Sacral Sympathetic and Sacro-spinal Nerves	273
63	Cervical Ganglia	275
64	Cutaneous Nerves of Thorax and Abdomen	281
65	Ventral Division of Dorsal Nerves	283
66	Sympathetic, from Life-size Chart Sympathetic	285
67	Sympathetic, from Life-size Chart Sympathetic	287
68	Nerves of Non-pregnant Uterus	287
69	Life-size Chart of Sympathetic	291
70	Plan of Dorsal Nerve	295
71	Diagram of Lumbar and Pelvic Plexus	297
72	Abdominal Brain	299
73	Corrosion Anatomy of Ductus Bilis	303
74	Corrosion Anatomy of Kidney	307
75	X-ray of Ductus Pancreaticus and Part of Ductus Bilis	311
76	X-ray of Ductus Bilis et Pancreaticus with Arteria Hepatica	315
77	Nervus Vasomotorius	321
78	Dilated Ductus Hepaticus	324
79	Nerves of the Internal Genitals	326
80	Ductus Bilis et Ductus Pancreaticus	330
81	Cross-section of Ureter	332
82	X-ray of Ductus Bilis et Ductus Pancreaticus	357
83	X-ray of Ductus Pancreaticus et Ductus Bilis	365
84	X-ray of Ductus Pancreaticus et Ductus Bilis of Horse	373
85	Strangulation of the Sigmoid by Band Originating from Bilateral Pyosalpinx	394
86	Hernia of Eight Feet of Enteron in Fossa Duodeno-Jejunalis	395
87	Hernia in Fossa Duodeno-Jejunalis	397
88	Invagination of Ileum	398
89	Ileo-Cœcal Invagination	399
90	Progressive Steps of Uterine-invagination	401
91	Complete Uterine Invagination	403
92	Volvulus of Sigmoid	404
93	Volvulus of Sigmoid	405
94	Volvulus of Ileo-Cœcal Apparatus	406
95	Enteronic Volvulus	407
96	Volvulus of Ileo-cœcal Apparatus	408
97	Position of the Appendix	409
98	Potential Position of Appendix	411
99	Absence of Appendix (and Cœcum)	413
100	Appendix Lying Adjacent to Meckel's Diverticulum	414
101	Relation of Appendix to the Genital Tract	415
102	Nondescended Appendix	417
103	Biliary Calculus Dislodged from Meckel's Diverticulum	419
104	X-ray of the Ductus Pancreaticus and Part of Ductus Bilis	421
105	Specimen Containing Pancreaticus Calculus	423
106	Hepatic Calculus in Hartman's Pouch (S) and Vater's Papilla	426
107	Carcinoma Completely Obstructing the Biliary and Pancreatic Ducts	427
108	Ureteral Calculi	428
109	Calculus in Ureter	429
110	The Arteria Uterina Overica Three Hours after Parturition at Term	430
111	Hyrtl's Exsanguinated Renal Zone	436
112	Corrosion Anatomy Kidney	440
113	Hyrtl's Exsanguinated Renal Zone	441
114	Lymph Glands in Course of Blood Vessels	444
115	Abdominal Brain and Cœliac Plexus	451
116	X-ray of Ductus Bilis and Ductus Pancreaticus	454
117	Duodenum with Its Two Ducts—Biliary and Pancreatic	456
118	X-ray of Ductus Bilis, Ductus Pancreaticus and Arteria Hepatica	458
119	Pelvic Brain (adult)	462
120	Arterial Circulation of the Puerperal Uterus	464
121	Transverse Longitudinal Section of Uterus	467
122	Pelvic Brain in Relation to the Nervus Vasomotorius	469
123	Arteries of Puerperal Uterus	471
124	Histology of Pelvic Brain	473

LIST OF ILLUSTRATIONS

No.		Page
125	Tractus Vascularis and Tractus Nervosus of the Tractus Genitalis	475
126	Pelvic Brain	476
127	Sacro-pubic Hernia	477
128	Intimate Relation of the Tractus Genitalis and Tractus Urinarius	480
129	Illustration of the Female Urinary Tract	482
130	An Illustration of the Abdominal Sympathetic Nerve of the Male, Especially Representing the Nerves of the Tractus Urinarius	484
131	Nerve Supply Tractus Urinarius	486
132	Nerves of the Tractus Urinarius, Corrosion Anatomy	487
133	Nervus Vasomotorius of the Tractus Urinarius	488
134	Corrosion Anatomy (Hyrtl's Exsanguinated Renal Zone)	489
135	Nervus Vasomotorius in Relation with the Tractus Urinarius	490
136	Nervus Vasomotorius of the Tractus Urinarius (Congenitally Dislocated)	492
137	Relation of Plexus Lumbalis to Tractus Urinarius	493
138	Nerves of the Internal Genitals	499
139	Lymphatics	505
140	Ductus Thoracicus Dexter et Sinister	515
141	Lymphatics of Head and Neck	516
142	Lymphatics Ensheathing a Vein	517
143	A Lymphatic Gland with Its Afferent and Efferent Vessels	518
144	Lymph Vessels of the Tracheal Mucosa	519
145	Inguinal Glands of Lymphatics	520
146	Lymphatics of the Internal Genitals	521
147	Lymph Channels and Glands Draining the Tractus Genitalis (Savage)	522
148	Lymph Channels Draining Cervix and Vagina (Poirier)	523
149	Lymph Channel (A. A.) of Pyloric End of Rabbits	524
150	Transition of Lymph Capillaries into Lymph Trunks with Valves—Sacculations	525
151	Lymph Channels and Glands of the Mesenteron (Hoenir)	526
152	Lymphatic Drainage of Diaphragm	527
153	Profile View of the Ductus Thoracicus	528
154	Lymph Channels in the Peritoneum	528
155	Lymphatics from Enteron of Guinea Pig with Plexus Myentericus of Auerbach (Frey)	526
156	Rectal Glands and Lymphatics	530
157	Stomata Vera Connecting the Peritoneum with the Subperitoneal Lymph Channels	531
158	Lymph Glands with Vasa Efferentia et Afferentia (Toldt)	532
159	Lymphatics of Axilla and Mamma	533
160	Ductus Thoracicus Sinister et Dexter (Toldt)	534
161	Perivascular Lymphatic (Gegenbauer)	535
162	Superficial (Smaller) and Deep (Larger) Anastomosing Lymphatics	536
163	Lymphatics and Glands of the Mesenteron	537
164	The Inguinal Glands Receiving the Rectal and Genital Lymph Channels (Toldt)	538
165	Lymph Glands and Channels Relating to Mamma and Neck (Toldt)	539
166	Lymphatics of Wall of Enteron of Calf (Injected)	540
167	Injected Lymphatic Vessels of the Tongue	541
168	Lymphatics of the Vermiform Appendix	542
169	Lymph Vessels of Dog's Stomach	543
170	Splanchnoptotic, a Ventral View	547
171	Splanchnoptotic, Lateral View	549
172	Splanchnoptotic, Abdominal Walls Removed	550
173	Abdominal and Thoracic Organs Separated by the Diaphragm	554
174	Dorsal Fixation and Location of the Mesenteries	558
175	Separation and Elongation of the Recti Abdominalis in Splanchnoptosia	560
176	The Diaphragm (Ventro-distal View)	561
177	The Diaphragm (Dorsal View)	563
178	Proximal View of the Pelvic Floor (Sholer)	564
179	Distal View of the Pelvic Floor	565
180	A Normal Transverse Segment of the Abdominal Wall	567
181	A Transverse Section of the Abdomen, about the Umbilicus of a Splanchnoptotic	568
182	Viscera of a Female Orang from Borneo	571
183	Areas of Peritoneum	572
184	Gastro-duodenal Dilatation, Gastroptosia	577
185	Carcinoma Completely Obstructing the Biliary and Pancreatic Ducts	579
186	The Horizontal Stomach, Gastroptosia	580
187	The Vertical Stomach, Gastroptosia	581
188	Gastroptosia	582
189	Splanchnoptosia, The Third Stage	585
190	Coloptosia	589
191	Presents Established Hepatic Dislocation	596

LIST OF ILLUSTRATIONS

No.		PAGE
192	Presents Advanced Hepatic Dislocation	599
193	Common Condition Found in Multipara	602
194	Position of Duodenum and the Superior Mesenteric Artery, Vein and Nerve	604
195	Relation with Stomach Drawn Proximally	605
196	Gastro-duodenal Dilatation	607
197	Profile view of Obstruction	608
198	Superior Mesenteric Artery, Vein and Nerve Obstructs the Transverse Segment of Duodenum as it Crosses the Vertebral Column	610
199	Gastro-duodenal Dilatation	612
200	Clamping of Duodenum by the Mesenteric Vessels	613
201	Gastro-duodenal Dilatation Ending when the Mesenteric Vessels Cross the Transverse Duodenum	614
202	Closure of Musculi Recti Abdominales in a Single Sheath	621
203	Byron Robinson's Rubber Air Pad for Splanchnoptosia	623
204	Byron Robinson's Rubber Pad, Profile View	624
205	Byron Robinson's Rubber Pad, Adjusted	627
206	Placing of Sutures in Fascia and Muscles of the Abdomen	641
207	Nerves of Internal Genitals dissected under Alcohol	656

LIST OF NAMES

A

	PAGE
Aberle	548
Addison	19
Akermann	17
Alexander	12
Allen	515
Andersch	16
Andral	276
Arabians	11
Aran	19
Aristotle	11, 12
Arnold	16, 655
Aselli	515
Atkinson	436, 437
Auerbach	62, 168, 169, 241, 242, 243, 244, 250, 260, 292, 298, 329, 354, 466, 526, 622
Axman	16

B

Babler	431
Bachat	14, 15, 16, 17, 262
Baker	17
Ball	17
Bardel	276
Barnes	364
Bartholine	514, 517
Basch	320, 326
Basedows	19, 30
Basel	52
Battey	348
Bauhin	320, 355, 362
Baumgarten	353, 374
Bayly	17
Beck Snow	18, 24, 25, 52, 130, 131, 156, 158
Beclard	14
Begbie	327
Bell	19
Bennett	511
Bernard	19, 38, 130, 187
Bergan	16
Beschomer	338
Beuker	423
Bichat	14, 15, 16, 17, 511
Bidder	18, 19, 104, 168, 241, 242, 292, 439
Bier	367, 379, 442, 502
Bilroth	68, 78, 292, 293
Billroth-Meissners	62, 68, 70, 104, 318, 329, 466, 554, 622
Bishop	169
Blane	16
Blandin	656
Blumenbach	14, 17
Bockdalek V. A.	656, 657, 658
Bockdalek V	657
Boivin	156

C

	PAGE
Bohemian	571
Bouchard	364
Bourgery	130, 156
Bouveret	356
Bowman	17, 112
Brachet	15, 16, 17
Bridge	326
Brown	435
Brown-Sequard	19
Broussais	15, 16, 17
Budd	276
Budge	19, 152
Buffon	16
Burgess	241
Burdachi	33

C

Cabanis	16
Cautani	587
Casenare	584
Chapin	20, 21, 159
Chaussier	14, 33, 34
Clark	336, 431, 500
Clay	18, 25, 156
Clemm	639
Cline	610
Cohnheim	433
Cohnstein	147, 158
Collins	308
Coons	606
Cooper	18, 309, 310, 610
Coutade	327
Craigie	511
Crisis	594
Cruveilhier	19
Curling	310
Czerney	549

D

Dalrymple	25
Dambo	147
Darwin	436
Davy	14, 15, 16, 17, 18
Deaver	431
DeCosta	334, 336
Descartes Reni	12
Dietl	594, 597, 600, 645
Donne	511
Du Boise	19
Dun	356
Durand	276
Duverney	16, 655

E

	PAGE
Edebohls	595
Einhoen	554, 584
Ellinger	147
Erasistratus	12, 515
Erhmann	320
Eulenberg	18, 19, 20, 21, 159, 190
Eustachius	12, 22, 156
Evans	29, 112, 117, 119, 335, 570

F

Farre	338
Fellner	320
Finney	608
Fitch	407, 412
Fleiner	356
Fleischer	365
Fletcher	16, 17
Fliess	658
Flower	34
Fox	21, 159, 189, 190, 326
Frankenhauser	12, 17, 18, 26, 27, 88, 90, 130, 140, 141, 158, 159
Françoise	29
Frey	27, 526
Frerichs	276
Freund	130, 151, 156, 158, 346, 348
Fruth	608
Fuller	512
Furbinger	276, 336

G

Gail	15, 17
Gallant	585, 614
Galen Claudius	11, 27
Gallianet	589, 601, 620, 640
Gaskell	21, 159
Gasser	658
Gasserius	654
Gawvousky	158
Gegenbauer	535
Gerlachs	416
Gerald	16, 268
Gerota	530
Gianozzi	19
Gibbon	615
Glenard	610, 547, 549, 553, 556, 562, 592, 605, 633, 640
Goetz	18
Goltz	146, 158, 313, 321
Gooch	249, 311
Good	15, 234
Graff	22
Grant	16
Gray	515
Graves	19, 30
Griesinger	20
Gubler	21
Gunn	16
Guttman	18, 19, 20, 21, 159, 190, 336
Guyon	327

H

Hall	16, 17, 18
Hahn	606
Haller	16, 22, 67, 156
Hammerschlag	527
Hare	336
Harlan	431
Hartmans	426
Hashimoto Sabura	131, 153, 158, 475
Head	295, 305, 398
Hearst	21
Heberden	19, 30, 312
Hegar	345, 348, 349, 350, 631
Heffer	19, 158
Heister	427
Hekton	328
Heinicke—Mickulicz	585
Henry	608, 609
Henles	19, 35, 52, 71, 281, 326, 537
Henrot	325
Hermann	189
Herophilus	12, 515
Hershfield	26, 158, 283, 289
Hilton	280
Hippocratis	12
Hirsch	336, 488
Hoare	14, 373
Hofman	73
Howlett	527
Huber	16
Hunter, J.	17, 23, 26, 312
Hunter, Wm.	18, 23, 26, 156
Hyrtl	79, 81, 127, 148, 436, 440, 441, 487, 489

J

Jackhowitz	313
Jacquemier	24
Jaksch	336
Jaggard	410
Jans	654
Jactreboff	131, 158
Jastowitz	19, 181
Jaylife	514
Jobert, J. A.	26
Jobert, De Lamella	131
Jreper	358
Jung	131, 141, 158

K

Keher	549
Kehrer	27, 141
Keilmann	146, 158
Keith	554
Kerner	140
Killian	18, 26, 27, 156
Kirro	343
Klein	338
Kitagama	335, 336
Klopper	490
Knoll	19, 316
Koch	27, 140, 158
Kokitansky	264
Kolliker	19, 27, 326
Kossman	547
Krantz	348, 350
Kraus	16
Kressmaul	549
Krehls	433
Knjsinski	334, 335, 336
Kunpffer	130, 158, 320

L

Name	Page
Lancicus	14
Lancereaux	313
Landau	549, 581, 640
Lambell	18, 158
Larastine	152
Larage	289
Lecorche	363
Le Gallois	14, 17
Lee	17, 18, 24, 25, 26, 130, 134, 156, 159
Legros	327
Leube	334, 336, 364
Leville	283
Leyden	334
Lincolns	435
Litten	335
Littre	336, 338
Lloyd	86, 420, 642
Lobstein	16, 18, 24, 156, 159
Lohmer	350
Lomer	29, 42, 96
Longet	158
Lucas	85, 420
Ludwig	19, 104, 168, 241, 242, 292, 320, 339
Luschka	34

M

Mac Kellar	312, 616, 641, 642
Mayo	16, 615
Martin	252, 263, 550
Mayer	20, 158, 255, 320
Manee	16
Mathieu	335
McNeil	414
Meckel	14, 293, 408, 414, 419
McBurneys	398, 404, 416, 417, 427
McKindrick	326
Meinert	634
Meirert	554
Mering	315
Meissner	241, 243, 244, 250, 292
Meissner, Billroth-	242
Mitchell, Weir	500
Miller	245, 252
Minkowski	315
Milliot	584
Minot	334
Morris	277, 556
Morgangui	16, 338, 548
Monro	14
Muller	17
Musser	431

N

Nagel	521
Napier	18
Nasse	19, 320, 326
Naunyn	452
Neelson	338
Nothnagel	319, 320, 322, 323, 334, 335, 336, 338, 358, 364

O

O'Byrne	29, 112, 117, 427, 577, 579
Onimus	327
Oppoltzer	548

Name	Page
Osiander, J. F.	23, 156
Osiander	18, 156

P

Name	Page
Pacquet	517, 518
Patherson	159
Pariser	336
Parry	19, 30
Pavy	30
Perrond	336
Pessimski	131, 150, 158
Petit	16
Philip	15
Perier	363
Pfeulers	19
Pflueger	19, 320, 336
Pick	334, 336, 359, 367
Pickford	19
Pinel	14
Poetal	587
Polle	27
Pouparts	30
Powell	314
Porier	521
Prochaska	14, 17

R

Rachel	334
Radcliff	16
Ralando	17
Ranvier	520, 523
Rauber	21, 159
Rayer	547
Recklinghausen	522, 523
Reid	16
Reil	16
Rein	130, 131, 146, 147
Remak	16, 19, 104, 140, 168, 241, 242, 292, 439
Remond	654
Reyner de Graff	156
Richmond and Gall	15, 17
Richardson	537
Ribes	33, 254
Rickets	131
Riedel	550, 587, 588, 594
Ries	531, 658
Robin	16
Rhorig	158
Robinson Byron	25, 99, 130, 147, 158, 255, 286, 287, 291, 295, 482, 521, 602, 603, 606, 623, 624, 627
Rochefontaine	19
Rokitansky	424
Rollet	548
Romberg	308, 310, 327, 363
Rose	547, 585, 589, 593, 601, 614, 615, 620, 639
Rosewater	601, 639
Rothmann	336
Rudbeck	514, 517, 516
Rudolphi	16
Ruge	336

S

Salvage	26
Samsonvon	414
Santoeine	453

LIST OF NAMES

	Page
Sappey	260, 516, 520, 533
Savage	262, 289, 522
Scarpa	14
Schanzoni	148
Schiff	19, 658
Schroeder	616, 641
Schlem	18
Schmitz	603, 639
Schneiderian	658
Schmidt	104, 168, 241, 242, 292, 439
Schröder	549, 640
Schüppel	276
Schwerdt	268, 557
Senn N.	405, 412, 616
Sedlein	12
Senator	364
Sherren	398
Sholer	564, 565
Smith	31
Solly	17
Sommering	16
Spugel	586
Stiller	496, 553, 554, 630, 634
Steinach	320
Stilling	33
Stober	423
Stube	597

T

Tait, Lawson	251, 263, 422, 424, 429, 431, 465
Tanner	445, 533
Tarchanoff	19
Teichman	517, 519, 525, 536, 540, 541, 542, 543
Testut	518
Theile	330
Thompson	336
Tiedemann	18, 22, 23, 24, 26, 52, 130, 156
Todd	17, 112
Toldt	532, 534, 538, 539
Treitz	571, 573

V

Valentine	52, 327, 657, 658
Valleix's	274, 284

	Page
Van Hook	412, 415
Vanni	336
Vaters	426, 427, 437
Verworn	523
Velpeau	511
Vesalius	22
Vidian	655
Viensseni, R.	12, 14, 22, 42, 156
Virchow	363, 511, 548
Virchow-Robin	535
Vogel	512
Volkmann	19
Vulpian	189

W

Waite, Lucy	268, 271, 274, 334, 347, 394, 404, 409, 422, 533, 555, 610, 613
Wagner	16
Waldeyer	52, 158
Walther	130
Walter	16, 19, 22, 24, 25, 130, 156, 336
Washburn	405
Watzer	15, 17
Weber	16, 327
Wenzel	571
Wesling	517
Wild	381
Wilford	16
Windscheid	297
Williams	359
Wilkes	430
Willis	12, 14, 15, 22, 33, 88, 112, 156, 305
Wirsing	73
Winslow	14, 15, 408
Wrisberg	16, 35, 106, 112, 168, 249, 291, 312
Wolffian	597
Woodward	334
Wutzer	15, 17

Z

Zetlitz	424
Ziegenspeck	618
Zinn	14

CPSIA information can be obtained
at www.ICGtesting.com
Printed in the USA
BVHW090117180920
588932BV00001B/12